# Teacher's Edition

PACEMAKER®

# Basic English Composition

by Bonnie Walker

PEARSON
AGS Globe

Shoreview, MN

# About the Author

**Bonnie L. Walker** taught for 16 years in secondary schools and college. She holds a Ph.D. in curriculum theory and instructional design from the University of Maryland, an M.Ed. in secondary education, and a B.A. in English. She studied psycholinguistics at the University of Illinois Graduate School and was a curriculum developer at the Model Secondary School for the Deaf at Galludet University. She is the author of Pacemaker® *Basic English,* Pacemaker® *Basic English Grammar, Life Skills English,* and numerous curriculum materials in written expression, grammar, and usage. Since 1986, Dr. Walker has been president of a research and development company specializing in the development of training and educational materials for special populations.

## Reading Consultant

**Timothy Shanahan,** Ph.D., Professor of Urban Education, Director of the Center for Literacy, University of Illinois at Chicago; Author, AMP Reading System

## Reviewers

The publisher wishes to thank the following educators for their helpful comments during the review process for Pacemaker® *Basic English Composition.* Their assistance has been invaluable. **Sylvia Berger,** Special Education Resource Teacher, Markham District High School, Markham, ON, Canada; **Racquel Gadsden,** ESE Teacher, Chamberlain High School, Tampa, FL; **Wendy Mason,** Special Education Teacher, Magnolia High School, Anaheim, CA; **John Petitt,** Special Education Resource Teacher, Culver Elementary School, Niles, IL; **Phyllis Romine,** Special Education Teacher, Florence Freshman Center, Florence, AL; **Monica M. Thorpe,** Language Arts Teacher, El Paso, TX; **Sandra Tuck,** Special Education Teacher, Talladega County Central High School, Talladega, AL

**Acknowledgments** appear on page 442, which constitutes an extension of this copyright page.

**Copyright © 2008 by Pearson Education, Inc., publishing as Pearson AGS Globe, Shoreview, Minnesota 55126.**
All rights reserved. Printed in the United States of America. This publication is protected by copyright, and permission should be obtained from the publisher prior to any prohibited reproduction, storage in a retrieval system, or transmission in any form or by any means, electronic, mechanical, photocopying, recording, or likewise. For information regarding permission(s), write to: Rights and Permissions Department, One Lake Street, Upper Saddle River, New Jersey 07458.

Pearson AGS Globe™ and Pacemaker® are trademarks, in the U.S. and/or in other countries, of Pearson Education, Inc. or its affiliate(s).

ISBN-13: 978-0-7854-6331-3
ISBN-10:  0-7854-6331-3

1 2 3 4 5 6 7 8 9 10   11 10 09 08 07

1-800-992-0244
www.agsglobe.com

# Contents

# Contents

**Pacemaker® *Basic English Composition*** is designed to help secondary students and adults develop practical writing skills. Throughout the text, comprehension is enhanced through the use of simple sentence structure and low-level vocabulary. To add motivational interest, the instruction and activities revolve around a group of high school students experiencing a typical school year.

*Basic English Composition* reflects students' needs by first focusing on writing sentences and then paragraphs, followed by reports and other projects. All of these skills have been identified as important for students to have.

A major emphasis of *Basic English Composition* is on writing sentences. Many older students who are in need of basic writing instruction need to develop a sense of good sentence structure. Most writing textbooks focus on writing complete compositions, which intensifies the frustration of many students who struggle to master the basics. By focusing on sentence development, students using this textbook experience success earlier and are motivated to continue.

Short, concise lessons hold students' interest. Clearly stated objectives presented at the beginning of each lesson focus on what students will learn in the lesson. Chapter features include open-ended questions to encourage students to use critical-thinking skills. Full-color photographs add interest and appeal as students learn key writing concepts.

The ability to write clearly and accurately is an important skill for most jobs and in everyday situations. *Basic English Composition* provides instruction in the basic writing skills students need to succeed in school and in the workplace.

***Enhance your language program with Pacemaker® Language Arts textbooks.*** AGS Globe has three language arts Pacemaker titles—*Basic English Composition, Basic English Grammar,* and *Basic English*—that offer an easy, effective way to teach students the practical skills they need. Each Pacemaker textbook builds and reinforces basic language skills. Written at a low reading level, these programs are ideal for students and adults who need help with language concepts, or those who are learning English as a second language. The full-color books use student-friendly text and real-world examples to show students the relevance of language in their daily lives. Each provides comprehensive coverage of skills and concepts. The short, concise lessons will motivate even reluctant students. With readabilities of all the texts below a fourth-grade reading level, students can concentrate on learning the content. AGS Globe is committed to making learning accessible to all students.

***For more information on AGS Globe's textbooks and worktexts:***
call 1-800-992-0244, visit our Web site at www.agsglobe.com,
or e-mail AGS Globe at mail@agsglobe.com

Students who have difficulty reading are not equipped for the challenges of middle school and high school. The *AMP Reading System* uses research-based content combined with best practices in instruction to help striving readers learn.

The *AMP Reading System* focuses on the seven strategies identified by the National Reading Panel that demonstrated the greatest effect on students' reading proficiency. Each strategy is taught explicitly and incorporated into guided reading and independent reading activities. The systematic instruction enables students to internalize the strategies and apply them to cross-curricular school work. Academic vocabulary is reinforced in motivating reading passages that are 85% peer-selected nonfiction.

Materials from the *AMP Reading System* also provide a consistent instructional design that helps teachers. FYI notes and research references are woven throughout the teacher's manual to offer pedagogical background information. In addition, ELL/ESL strategies are included with every lesson. The program also offers a professional development DVD that features program author Dr. Timothy Shanahan and classroom teachers modeling lessons in a secondary classroom. Customized reading strategies for math, science, language arts and literature, and social studies enable content-area teachers to reinforce and apply the reading comprehension strategies taught in the *AMP Reading System* in their own classrooms with content-area texts.

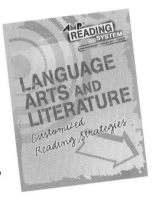

***For more information about the AMP™ Reading System:***
call 1-800-992-0244 or visit our Web site at www.agsglobe.com

# Student Edition Highlights

- Each lesson is clearly labeled to help students focus on the skill or concept to be learned.

- Vocabulary terms are boldfaced and then defined in the margin at the top of the page and in the glossary.

- Many features reinforce and extend student learning beyond the lesson content.

- Goals for Learning at the beginning of each chapter identify learner outcomes.

- Vocabulary Builder focuses on specific words in the English language; designed to broaden students' vocabulary skills.

- Grammar Builder focuses on specific grammar issues; designed to broaden students' grammar skills.

- In each chapter, students can focus on one of seven reading strategies. A Reading Strategy note appears at least once in each lesson to give students practice with applying the strategy.

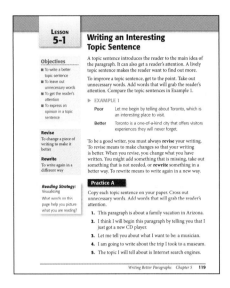

## LESSON 5-1
### Writing an Interesting Topic Sentence

**Objectives**
- To write a better topic sentence
- To leave out unnecessary words
- To get the reader's attention
- To express an opinion in a topic sentence

**Revise**
To change a piece of writing to make it better

**Rewrite**
To write again in a different way

**Reading Strategy:**
Visualizing
What words on this page help you picture what you are reading?

A topic sentence introduces the reader to the main idea of the paragraph. It can also get a reader's attention. A lively topic sentence makes the reader want to find out more.

To improve a topic sentence, get to the point. Take out unnecessary words. Add words that will grab the reader's attention. Compare the topic sentences in Example 1.

▶ EXAMPLE 1

**Poor**    Let me begin by telling about Toronto, which is an interesting place to visit.

**Better**    Toronto is a one-of-a-kind city that offers visitors experiences they will never forget.

To be a good writer, you must always **revise** your writing. To revise means to make changes so that your writing is better. When you revise, you change what you have written. You might add something that is missing, take out something that is not needed, or **rewrite** something in a better way. To rewrite means to write again in a new way.

**Practice A**

Copy each topic sentence on your paper. Cross out unnecessary words. Add words that will grab the reader's attention.

1. This paragraph is about a family vacation in Arizona.
2. I think I will begin this paragraph by telling you that I just got a new CD player.
3. Let me tell you about what I want to be: a musician.
4. I am going to write about the trip I took to a museum.
5. The topic I will tell about is Internet search engines.

*Writing Better Paragraphs*   Chapter 5   **119**

## Revise
To change a piece of writing to make it better

## Rewrite
To write again in a different way

### Brush Up on the Basics
For verbs that end in *-e*, remove the e before adding *-ing* or *-ed*. *Race* becomes *racing* or *raced*. See Spelling 37 in Appendix A.

### NOTE
Conjunctions are used to connect *related* words or groups of words. Do not use conjunctions to connect *unrelated* sentences. In the run-on sentence in Example 2, the conjunction *and* is used incorrectly.

## GOALS FOR LEARNING

- To write interesting topic sentences
- To use sentence variety
- To make smooth transitions between sentences
- To revise paragraphs
- To edit paragraphs for mistakes

## VOCABULARY BUILDER

**Using Root Words**
A root word is a word from which other words are made. Word parts may be added to the beginning or ending of a root word. Add *mis-* to the root word *place*. This makes *misplace*. Add *-ment* to *place* to make *placement*. Look at each pair of words. Write the root word used to make them.

1. opening, reopen
2. mistake, taken
3. trusted, distrust
4. remove, mover

**Reading Strategy:**
Questioning

Read the title of this lesson. What do you think you will learn?

## GRAMMAR BUILDER

**Using *Sit* and *Set* Correctly**
Many people confuse *sit* and *set*.

| Present | Past | Past Participle | Verb Meaning |
|---------|------|-----------------|--------------|
| sit | sat | (has) sat | to rest with legs bent |
| set | set | (has) set | to put or place |

Write each sentence using the correct form of *sit* or *set*.
1. Kay ___ the dishes in the sink.
2. I usually ___ in the last row.
3. The boys have ___ the table for dinner.

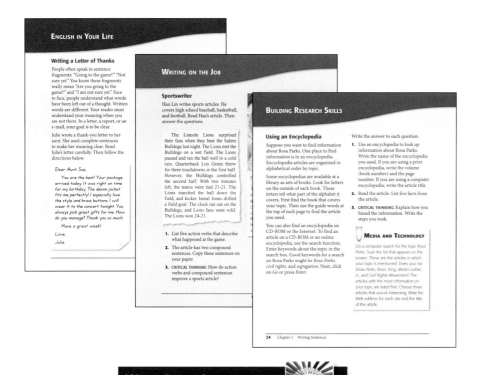

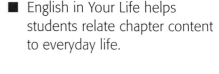

- English in Your Life helps students relate chapter content to everyday life.

- Writing on the Job presents some examples of jobs in which people use writing skills.

- Building Research Skills encourages students to use a variety of research tools and expand their research skills.

- Write About It offers writing assignments that relate to chapter content.

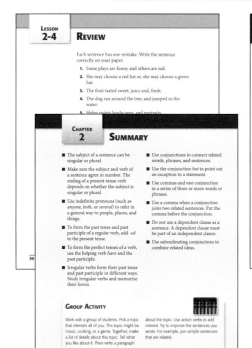

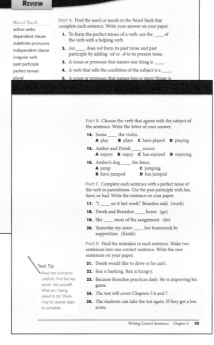

- Students practice applying different writing traits to their writing assignments through the Six Traits of Writing. Page WPH1 of the Writing Process Handbook offers more information about the traits.

- Lesson Review questions allow students to check their understanding of key concepts presented in lessons.

- Chapter Summaries highlight the main ideas for students.

- Chapter Reviews allow students and teachers to check for skill mastery. These reviews cover the objectives in the Goals for Learning at the beginning of each chapter.

- A Test Tip at the end of each Chapter Review helps reduce test anxiety and improve test scores.

The comprehensive, wraparound Teacher's Edition provides instructional strategies at point of use. Everything from preparation guidelines to teaching tips and strategies are included in an easy-to-use format. Activities are featured at point of use for teacher convenience.

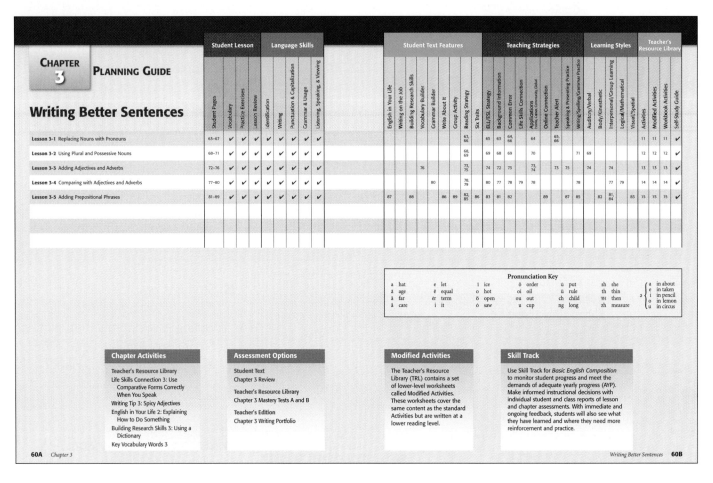

## Chapter Planning Guides

- The Planning Guide saves valuable preparation time by organizing all materials for each chapter.

- A complete listing of lessons allows you to preview each chapter quickly.

- Assessment options are highlighted for easy reference. Options include:

    Lesson Reviews

    Chapter Reviews

    Chapter Mastery Tests, Forms A and B

    Writing Portfolios

    Midterm and Final Mastery Tests

- Page numbers of Student Text and Teacher's Edition features help you customize lesson plans to your students.

- Many teaching strategies and learning styles are listed to support students with diverse needs.

- Activities in the Teacher's Resource Library are listed.

- A Pronunciation Key is provided to help teachers work with students to pronounce difficult words correctly.

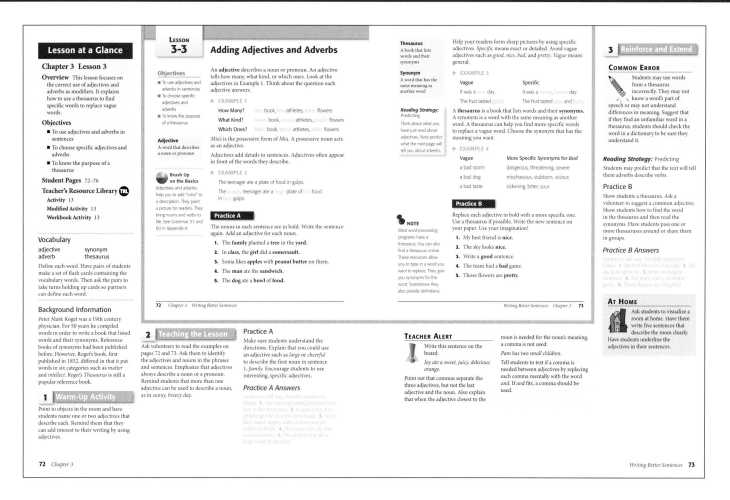

# Lessons

- Quick overviews of chapters and lessons save planning time.

- Lesson objectives are listed for easy reference.

- Page references are provided for convenience.

- Easy-to-follow lesson plans in three steps save time: Warm-Up Activity, Teaching the Lesson, and Reinforce and Extend.

- Teacher Alerts highlight content that may need further explanation.

- Students use language concepts in real-life applications through Life Skills Connection activities.

- Applications: Four areas of application—At Home, Career Connection, Global Connection, and In the Community—help students relate language to the world outside the classroom. Applications motivate students and make learning relevant.

- The Writing Portfolio chapter project addresses chapter goals and can be used as an alternative form of assessment.

- Online Connections list relevant Web sites.

- Learning Styles activities provide teaching strategies to help meet the needs of students with diverse ways of learning. Modalities include Auditory/Verbal, Visual/Spatial, Body/Kinesthetic, Logical/Mathematical, and Interpersonal/Group Learning. Targeted teaching activities are provided for ELL students.

- Answers are provided in the Teacher's Edition for all reviews in the Student Text. Answers to the Teacher's Resource Library and Student Workbook are provided at the back of this Teacher's Edition and on the TRL CD-ROM.

- Several worksheets, including Activities, Workbook Activities, and Chapter Mastery Tests from the Teacher's Resource Library, are shown at point of use in reduced form.

# Support for Students Learning English

Increasing numbers of students learning English are among the students in most schools and classrooms. The purpose of the ELL/ESL Strategy feature in this Teacher's Edition is to incorporate the language and content needs of English Language Learners in a regular and explicit manner.

ELL/ESL Strategy activities promote English language acquisition in the context of content area learning. Students should not be separated or isolated for these activities and interaction with English-speaking peers is always encouraged.

The ELL/ESL Strategy helps the teacher scaffold the content and presentation in relation to students' language and skill proficiency. Each activity suggests to the teacher some ideas about how to adjust the presentation of content to meet the varying needs of diverse learners, including students learning English. *Scaffolding* refers to structuring the introduction of vocabulary, concepts, and skills by providing additional supports or modifications based on students' needs. Ideally, these supports become less necessary as students' language proficiency increases and their knowledge and skill level becomes more developed.

---

### ELL/ESL STRATEGY

**Language Objective:** *To increase vocabulary by learning roots and building word families*

Students who are learning English may share some native vocabulary based on Latin and Greek roots. For example, *viv* means "life" and can be used to build the words *vivid* and *revive*. Encourage students to build word families for *sci* ("know") and *man* ("hand") and to write meanings and example sentences for each word they collect. As they share their word families, ask students to teach classmates about words in their native language that are derived from these same roots.

---

Each activity includes a language objective and strategy related to *listening, speaking, reading,* or *writing.* The language objective and activity relate to one or more content objectives listed in the Teacher's Edition under Lesson at a Glance. Some examples of language objectives include: reading for meaning, understanding different styles or purposes of writing, identifying and practicing common grammar structures, learning vocabulary specific to the content area, preparing and giving a group presentation, speaking in front of a group, or discussing an assigned topic as a small group.

## Strategies That Support English Learners

- Identify and build on prior knowledge or experience; start with what's familiar and elaborate to include new content and new connections, personal associations, cultural context
- Use visuals and graphic organizers—illustrations, photos, charts, posters, graphs, maps, tables, webs, flow charts, timelines, diagrams
- Use hands-on artifacts (realia) or manipulatives
- Provide *comprehensible input*—paraphrase content, give additional examples, elaborate on student background knowledge and responses; be aware of rate of speech, syntax, and language structure and adjust accordingly
- Begin with lower-level, fact recall questions and move to questions that require higher-order critical-thinking skills (application, hypothesis, prediction, analysis, synthesis, evaluation)
- Teach vocabulary—pronunciations, key words or phrases, multiple meanings, idioms/expressions, academic or content language

- Have students create word banks or word walls for content (academic) vocabulary
- Teach and model specific reading and writing strategies—advance organizers, main idea, meaning from context, preview, predict, make inferences, summarize, guided reading
- Support communication with gestures and body language
- Teach and practice functional language skills—negotiate meaning, ask for clarification, confirm information, argue persuasively
- Teach and practice study skills—structured note-taking, outlining, use of reference materials
- Use cooperative learning, peer tutoring, or other small group learning strategies
- Plan opportunities for student interaction—create a skit and act it out, drama, role play, storytelling
- Practice self-monitoring and self-evaluation—students reflect on their own comprehension or activity with self-checks

## How Do AGS Globe Textbooks Support Students Learning English?

AGS Globe is committed to helping all students succeed. For this reason, AGS Globe textbooks and teaching materials incorporate research-based design elements and instructional methodologies configured to allow diverse students greater access to subject area content. Content access is facilitated by controlled reading level, coherent text, and

vocabulary development. Effective instructional design is accomplished by applying research to lesson construction, learning activities, and assessments.

AGS Globe materials feature key elements that support the needs of students learning English in sheltered and immersion settings.

| Key Elements | AGS Globe Features |
|---|---|
| Lesson Preparation | ■ Content- and language-specific objectives |
| Building Background | ■ Warm-Up Activity<br>■ Explicit vocabulary instruction and practice with multiple exposures to new words<br>■ Background information; building on prior knowledge and experience |
| Comprehensible Input | ■ Controlled reading level in student text (Grades 3–4)<br>■ Highlighted vocabulary terms with definitions<br>■ Student glossary with pronunciations<br>■ Clean graphic and visual support<br>■ Content links to examples<br>■ Sidebar notes to highlight and clarify content<br>■ Audio text recordings (selected titles)<br>■ Modified Activity pages (Grade 2 reading level) |
| Lesson Delivery | ■ Teaching the Lesson/3-Step Teaching Plan<br>■ Short, skill- or content-specific lessons<br>■ Orderly presentation of content with structural cues |
| Strategies | ■ ELL/ESL Strategy activities<br>■ Learning Styles activities<br>■ Writing prompts in student text<br>■ Teaching Strategies Transparencies provide additional graphic organizers<br>■ Study skills: Self-Study Guides, Chapter Outlines |
| Interaction | ■ Vocabulary-building activities<br>■ Language-based ELL/ESL Strategy activities<br>■ Learning Styles activities<br>■ Reinforce and Extend activities |
| Practice/Application | ■ Skill practice or concept application in student text<br>■ Reinforce and Extend activities<br>■ Career, home, and community applications<br>■ Student Workbook<br>■ Multiple TRL activity pages |
| Review and Assessment | ■ Lesson reviews, chapter reviews, unit reviews<br>■ Skill Track monitors student progress<br>■ Chapter, Unit, Midterm, and Final Mastery Tests |

For more information on these key elements, see Echevarria, J., Vogt, M., & Short, D. (2004).
*Making content comprehensible for English language learners: The SIOP model* (2nd ed.). Boston, MA: Allyn & Bacon.

# Learning Styles

Differentiated instruction allows teachers to address the needs of diverse learners and the variety of ways students process and learn information. The Learning Styles activities in this Teacher's Edition provide additional teaching strategies to help students understand lesson content by teaching or expanding upon the content in a different way. The activities are designed to help teachers capitalize on students' individual strengths and learning styles.

The Learning Styles activities highlight individual learning styles and are classified based on Howard Gardner's theory of multiple intelligences: Auditory/Verbal, Body/Kinesthetic, Interpersonal/ Group Learning, Logical/Mathematical, and Visual/Spatial. In addition, the various writing activities suggested in the Student Text are appropriate for students who fit Gardner's description of Verbal/Linguistic intelligence.

Following are examples of activities featured in the Pacemaker® *Basic English Composition* Teacher's Edition:

## Logical/Mathematical

Students learn by using logical/mathematical thinking and problem solving in relation to the lesson content.

### LEARNING STYLES

**Logical/Mathematical**
Point out that end punctuation marks in written language work much like mathematical symbols. Ask students to name some mathematical signs, such as $+$, $-$, $\times$, $\div$, $<$, $>$, and $=$. Write them on the board and discuss what they communicate to readers.

## Visual/Spatial

Students learn by viewing or creating illustrations, graphics, patterns, or additional visual demonstrations beyond what is in the text.

### LEARNING STYLES

**Visual/Spatial**
Have each student print a topic in the middle of a sheet of paper, for example, *cars, songs, pets, TV shows*. Have students make a web of related facts, feelings, details, examples, and thoughts about the topic. Ask them to draw lines from the topic to their ideas. Demonstrate on the board how this creates a web of information that students can use to expand a topic sentence into a paragraph or essay.

## Auditory/Verbal

Students learn by listening to text read aloud or from an audiorecording, and from other listening or speaking activities. Musical activities related to the content may help auditory learners.

### LEARNING STYLES

**Auditory/Verbal**
Have students listen to an explanation, directions, or a description that has been recorded on audiotape or videotape. Ask them to write down the transitional words and phrases they hear. Then provide students with a paragraph of story text from which the transitional words and phrases have been removed. Ask a volunteer to read it aloud. Discuss problems listeners have following the text. Finally have students practice reading the same text aloud with the transition words and phrases restored. Encourage them to use expression with transitions to add meaning.

## Interpersonal/Group Learning

Students learn from working with at least one other person or in a cooperative learning group on activities that involve a process and an end product.

### LEARNING STYLES

**Interpersonal/Group Learning**
Have students work in groups of three. Ask each student to write five adjectives that are not in this lesson. One group member should read one of his or her words. Then a second group member should say the comparative form of the adjective. Then the third group member should say the superlative form.

## Body/Kinesthetic

Students learn from activities that include physical movement, manipulatives, or other tactile experiences.

### LEARNING STYLES

**Body/Kinesthetic**
Complete Practices B–D on page 105 as a game. Assign each student a sentence from one of the three paragraphs. Students should copy their sentences on a sheet of paper and get together with others who have sentences from the same paragraph. Then ask them to decide who has the sentence that does not belong. Have each group line up and read its sentences in order but not the one that does not belong. Have them explain why they did not include the sentence.

All of the activities you'll need to reinforce and extend the text are conveniently located on the AGS Globe Pacemaker® Teacher's Resource Library (TRL) CD-ROM. All of the reproducible activities pictured in the Teacher's Edition are ready to select, view, and print. You can also preview other materials by linking directly to the AGS Globe Web site.

## Workbook Activities
Workbook Activities are available to reinforce and extend skills from each lesson of the textbook. A bound workbook format is also available.

## Activities
Activities for each lesson of the textbook give students additional skills practice.

## Modified Activities
These activities cover the same content as the Activities but are written at a lower reading level.

## Life Skills Connections
Relevant activities help students extend their knowledge to the real world and reinforce concepts covered in class.

## Graphic Organizers
Students can use the graphic organizer pages to organize information about important chapter concepts.

## Self-Study Guides
An assignment guide provides teachers with the flexibility for individualized instruction or independent study.

## Mastery Tests
Chapter, Midterm, and Final Mastery Tests are convenient assessment options. Critical-thinking items are included.

## Teacher Management Tools
These resource tools can assist teachers with lesson planning and classroom management.

## Answer Key
All answers to reproducible activities are included in the TRL and in the Teacher's Edition.

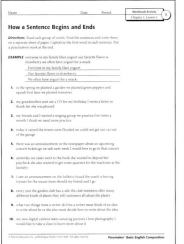

**Workbook Activities**

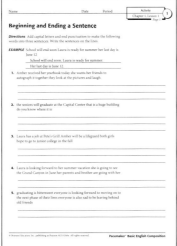

**Activities**

**Life Skills Connections**

**Mastery Tests**

# Synopsis of the Scientific Research Base

| Research-Based Principles | AGS Globe Textbooks | References |
|---|---|---|
| **Standards Alignment** | | |
| Subject area instruction needs to be based on skills, concepts, and processes represented by common standards for that subject area. | ■ Textbook content and skills aligned with national standards and state grade-level or course-specific content standards, where available | Matlock, L., Fielder, K., & Walsh, D. (2001). Building the foundation for standards-based instruction for all students. *Teaching Exceptional Children, 33*(5), 68–72.<br><br>Miller, S. P., & Mercer, C. D. (1997). Educational aspects of mathematics disabilities. *Journal of Learning Disabilities, 30*(1), 47–56.<br><br>Reys, R., Reys, B., Lapan, R., Holliday, G. & Wasman, D. (2003). Assessing the impact of standards-based middle grades mathematics curriculum materials on student achievement. *Journal of Research in Mathematics Education, 34*(1), 74–95. |
| **Readability** | | |
| Many students struggle to learn from core content-area textbooks that are written too high above their reading level. Students need access to textbooks written at a level they can read and understand, where the reading level is within the students' range of comprehension. | ■ Grade 4.0 or lower readability using the Spache formula<br>■ Controlled vocabulary matched to student reading ability and use of synonyms to replace non-essential difficult words above grade 4<br>■ Simple sentence structures<br>■ Limited sentence length | Allington, R. L. (2002). You can't learn much from books you can't read. *Educational Leadership, 60*(3), 16–19.<br><br>Chall, J. S., & Conard, S. S. (1991). *Should textbooks challenge students? The case for easier or harder textbooks.* New York: Teachers College Press.<br><br>*Readability calculations.* (2000). Dallas: Micro Power & Light Company. |
| **Language Complexity and Sequence** | | |
| Students struggling with vocabulary and text comprehension need textbooks with accessible language. | ■ Simple, direct language using an active voice<br>■ Clear organization to facilitate understanding<br>■ Explicit language signals to show sequence of and links between concepts and ideas | Anderson, T. H., & Armbruster, B. B. (1984). Readable texts, or selecting a textbook is not like buying a pair of shoes. In R. C. Anderson, J. Osborne, & R. J. Tierney (Eds.), *Learning to read in American schools* (pp. 151–162). Hillsdale, NJ: Lawrence Erlbaum Associates, Inc.<br><br>Curtis, M. E. (2002, May 20). *Adolescent reading: A synthesis of research.* Paper presented at the Practice Models for Adolescent Literacy Success Conference, U.S. Department of Education. Washington, DC: National Institute of Child Health and Human Development. Retrieved September 15, 2003, from http://216.26.160.105/conf/nichd/synthesis.asp<br><br>McAlpine, L., & Weston, C. (1994). The attributes of instructional materials. *Performance Improvement Quarterly, 7*(1), 19–30.<br><br>Seidenberg, P. L. (1989). Relating text-processing research to reading and writing instruction for learning disabled students. *Learning Disabilities Focus, 5*(1), 4–12. |
| **Vocabulary Use and Development** | | |
| Students need content-related vocabulary instruction in the context of readable and meaningful text. | ■ New vocabulary boldfaced on first occurrence, used in context, and defined in a sidebar<br>■ Glossary with pronunciation, definition, and relevant graphic illustrations for all vocabulary words<br>■ Direct vocabulary instruction introduced in the Teacher's Edition and reinforced in context throughout<br>■ Multiple exposures to new vocabulary in text and practice exercises | Ciborowski, J. (1992). *Textbooks and the students who can't read them: A guide to teaching content.* Cambridge, MA: Brookline.<br><br>Kameenui, E. J., & Simmons, D. C. (1990). *Designing instructional strategies.* Columbus, OH: Merrill Publishing Company.<br><br>Marzano, R. J. (1998). *A theory-based meta-analysis of research on instruction.* Aurora, CO: Mid-Continent Research for Education and Learning. Retrieved October 1, 2003, from http://www.mcrel.org/topics/productDetail/asp?productID=83<br><br>McAlpine, L., & Weston, C. (1994). The attributes of instructional materials. *Performance Improvement Quarterly, 7*(1), 19–30.<br><br>National Reading Panel. (2000). *Teaching children to read: An evidence-based assessment of the scientific research literature on reading and its implications for reading instruction.* Reports of the subgroups. Washington, DC: National Institute of Child Health and Human Development.<br><br>Taylor, S. E., Frackenpohl, H., White, C. E., Nieroroda, B. W., Browning, C. L., & Birsner, E. P. (1989). *EDL core vocabularies in reading, mathematics, science, and social studies.* Austin, TX: Steck-Vaughn. |

| Research-Based Principles | AGS Globe Textbooks | References |
|---|---|---|

## Text Organization: Presentation and Structure

Students need an uncluttered page layout, with easy-to-read print, that clearly directs the reader to main ideas, important information, examples, and comprehensive practice and review.

Reading comprehension is improved by structural features in the text that make it easier for learners to access the content.

*Print characteristics and page layout:*
- Serif font for body copy; sans serif font for boxed features, examples
- Maximum line length of 5" for ease of reading
- Unjustified (ragged) right margins
- Major/minor column page design presents primary instructional information in the major column and support content in the sidebar or in a box

*Presentation characteristics:*
- Lesson introductions, summaries
- Explicit lesson titles, headings, and subheadings label and organize main ideas
- Signals alert readers to important information, content connections, illustrations, graphics
- Cues (e.g., boldface type) highlight important information

*Text structure:*
- Lesson heads in question or statement format guide comprehension
- Text written to explicitly link facts and concepts within and across lessons; text cohesiveness
- Each skill or concept linked to direct practice and review

Armbruster, B. B., & Anderson, T. H. (1988). On selecting "considerate" content area textbooks. *Remedial and Special Education, 9*(1), 47–52.

Beck, I. L., McKeown, M. G., & Grommoll, E. W. (1989). Learning from social studies texts. *Cognition and Instruction, 6*(2), 99–158.

Chambliss, M. J. (1994). Evaluating the quality of textbooks for diverse learners. *Remedial and Special Education, 15*(5), 348–362.

Ciborowski, J. (1992). *Textbooks and the students who can't read them: A guide to teaching content.* Cambridge, MA: Brookline.

Dickson, S. V., Simmons, D. C., & Kameenui, E. J. (1995). *Text organization and its relation to reading comprehension: A synthesis of the research* (Technical Report No. 17) and *Text organization: Curricular and instructional implications for diverse learners* (Technical Report No. 18). National Center to Improve the Tools of Educators. Eugene, OR: University of Oregon. Retrieved January 26, 2000, from http://idea.uoregon.edu/~ncite/documents/techrep/tech17.html and http://idea.uoregon.edu/~ncite/documents/techrep/tech18.html

Dickson, S. V., Simmons, D. C., & Kameenui, E. J. (1998). Text organization: Research bases *and* Text organization: Instructional and curricular basics and implications. In D. C. Simmons & E. J. Kameenui (Eds.), *What reading research tells us about children with diverse learning needs: Bases and basics* (pp. 239–278; 279–294). Mahwah, NJ: Lawrence Erlbaum Associates, Inc.

Mansfield, J. S., Legge, G. E., & Bane, M. C. (1996). Psychophysics of reading. XV: Font effects in normal and low vision. *Investigative Ophthalmology and Vision Science, 37*, 1492–1501.

McAlpine, L., & Weston, C. (1994). The attributes of instructional materials. *Performance Improvement Quarterly, 7*(1), 19–30.

McNamara, D. S., Kintsche, E., Songer, N. B., & Kintsche, W. (1996). Are good texts always better? Interactions of text coherence, background knowledge, and levels of understanding in learning from text. *Cognition and Instruction, 14*(1), 1–43.

Tyree, R. B., Fiore, T. A., & Cook, R. A. (1994). Instructional materials for diverse learners: Features and considerations for textbook design. *Remedial and Special Education, 15*(6), 363–377.

## Differentiated Instruction and Learning Styles

Student learning is more successful when tasks are aligned with academic skill levels and developmental stage, and adjustments are made to allow students multiple means to engage and express their learning strengths and styles at appropriate levels of challenge and support.

Differentiated instruction allows teachers to organize instruction to adjust for diverse learning needs within a classroom.

Learning activities that capitalize on students' learning styles can structure planning for individual differences based on multiple intelligences theory.

- Multiple features, including Learning Styles activities, help teachers match assignments to students' abilities and interests
- Variety of media to select from—print, audio, visual, software
- Step-by-step, part-by-part basic content and skill-level lessons in the Student and Teacher's Editions
- Modified Activities written at a Grade 2 (Spache) readability in the Teacher's Resource Library
- Variety of review materials, activities, sidebars, and alternative readings
- Multiple assessments—lesson or chapter reviews, end-of-chapter tests, cumulative midterm/final mastery tests, alternative assessment items

*Learning Styles activities include:*
- Auditory/Verbal
- Body/Kinesthetic
- Interpersonal/Group Learning
- Logical/Mathematical
- Visual/Spatial

*ELL/ESL Strategies provide support for students who are learning English and lesson content concurrently.*

Allington, R. L. (2002). You can't learn much from books you can't read. *Educational Leadership, 60*(3), 16–19.

Carnine, D. (1994). Introduction to the mini-series: Diverse learners and prevailing, emerging, and research-based educational approaches and their tools. *School Psychology Review, 23*(3), 341–350.

Forsten, C., Grant, J., & Hollas, B. (2003). *Differentiating textbooks: Strategies to improve student comprehension and motivation.* Peterborough, NH: Crystal Springs Books.

Gardner, H. (1983). *Frames of mind: The theory of multiple intelligences.* New York: Harper and Row.

Gersten, R., & Baker, S. (2000). The professional knowledge base on instructional practices that support cognitive growth for English-language learners. In R. Gersten, E. P. Schiller, & S. Vaughn (Eds.), *Contemporary special education research: Syntheses of the knowledge base on critical instructional issues* (pp. 31–80). Mahwah, NJ: Lawrence Erlbaum Associates, Inc.

Hall, T. (2002, June). *Effective classroom practices report: Differentiated instruction.* Wakefield, NJ: National Center on Accessing the General Curriculum. Retrieved September 29, 2003, from http://www.cast.org/cac/index.cfm?i=2876

Lazear, D. (1999). *Eight ways of knowing: Teaching for multiple intelligences* (3rd ed.). Arlington Heights, IL: Skylight Training and Publishing.

Orlich, D. C., Harder, R. J., Callahan, R. C., & Gibson, H. W. (2001). *Teaching strategies: A guide to better instruction* (6th ed.). Boston: Houghton Mifflin Company.

Roderick, M. & Camburn, E. (1999). Risk and recovery from course failure in the early years of high school. *American Educational Research Journal, 36*(2), 303–343.

Tomlinson, C. A. (1999). *The differentiated classroom: Responding to the needs of all learners.* Alexandria, VA: Association for Supervision and Curriculum Development.

# Synopsis of the Scientific Research Base

| Research-Based Principles | AGS Globe Textbooks | References |
|---|---|---|

## Instructional Design: Lesson Structure and Learner Support Strategies

Instruction that includes the components of effective instruction, utilizes effective strategies and interventions to facilitate student learning, and aligns with standards improves learning for all students, especially diverse learners and students who are struggling.

Elements of effective instruction:

*Step 1: Introduce the lesson and prepare students to learn*
*Step 2: Provide instruction and guided practice*
*Step 3: Provide opportunities for applied practice and generalization*

Organizational tools:
*Advance organizers*
*Graphic organizers*

Instructional process techniques:
*Cooperative learning*
*Student self-monitoring and questioning*
*Real-life examples*
*Mnemonics*

---

**Step 1: Introduce the lesson and prepare students to learn**
*In the Student Edition:*
- "How to Use This Book" feature explicitly teaches text organization
- Chapter and lesson previews with graphic and visual organizers
- Goals for Learning
- Sidebar notes review skills and important facts and information

*In the Teacher's Edition:*
- Lesson objectives
- Explicit *3-Step Teaching Plan* begins with "Warm-Up Activity" to inform students of objectives, connect to previous learning and background knowledge, review skills, and motivate students to engage in learning

**Step 2: Provide instruction and guided practice**
*In the Student Edition:*
- Short, manageable lessons break content and skills into smaller, step-by-step, part-by-part pieces
- Systematic presentation of lesson concepts and skills
- Chapter and lesson headings presented as questions or statements
- Graphic organizers arrange content visually—charts, graphs, tables, diagrams, bulleted lists, arrows, graphics, mnemonics, illustrations, and captions
- Models or examples link directly to the explanation of the concept
- Multiple opportunities for direct practice throughout

*In the Teacher's Edition:*
- *3-Step Teaching Plan* for each lesson includes "Teaching the Lesson" with direct instruction, and helps teachers present and clarify lesson skills and concepts through guided practice and modeling of important ideas
- Supplemental strategies and activities, including hands-on modeling, transparencies, graphic organizers, visual aids, learning styles

**Step 3: Provide opportunities for applied practice and generalization**
*In the Student Edition:*
- Each skill or concept lesson is followed by direct practice or review questions
- Multiple exercises throughout
- Generalization and application activities in sidebars and lessons link content to real-life applications
- Chapter reviews and summaries highlight major points

---

Allsopp, D. H. (1990). Using modeling, manipulatives, and mnemonics with eighth-grade math students. *Teaching Exceptional Children, 31*(2), 74–81.

Chambliss, M. J. (1994). Evaluating the quality of textbooks for diverse learners. *Remedial and Special Education, 15*(5), 348–362.

Ciborowski, J. (1992). *Textbooks and the students who can't read them: A guide to teaching content.* Cambridge, MA: Brookline.

Cole, R. W. (Ed.). (1995). *Educating everybody's children: Diverse teaching strategies for diverse learners.* Alexandria, VA: Association for Supervision and Curriculum Development.

Curtis, M. E. (2002, May 20). *Adolescent reading: A synthesis of research.* Paper presented at the Practice Models for Adolescent Literacy Success Conference, U.S. Department of Education. Washington, DC: National Institute of Child Health and Human Development. Retrieved September 15, 2003, from http://216.26.160.105/conf/nichd/synthesis.asp

Dickson, S. V., Simmons, D. C., & Kameenui, E. J. (1995). *Text organization: Curricular and instructional implications for diverse learners* (Technical Report No. 18). National Center to Improve the Tools of Educators. Eugene, OR: University of Oregon. Retrieved January 26, 2000, from http://idea.uoregon.edu/~ncite/documents/techrep/tech18.html

Dixon, R. C., Carnine, D. W., Lee, D., Wallin, J., & Chard, D. (1998). *Review of high quality experimental mathematics research: Report to the California State Board of Education.* Sacramento, CA: California State Board of Education.

Jarrett, D. (1999). *The inclusive classroom: Mathematics and science instruction for students with learning disabilities—It's just good teaching.* Portland, OR: Northwest Regional Educational Laboratory.

Johnson, D. W., Johnson, R. T., & Stanne, M. B. (2000, May). *Cooperative learning methods: A meta-analysis.* Minneapolis: The Cooperative Learning Center, University of Minnesota. Retrieved October 29, 2003, from http://www.cooplearn.org/pages/cl-methods.html

Kameenui, E. J., & Simmons, D. C. (1990). *Designing instructional strategies.* Columbus, OH: Merrill Publishing Company.

Lovitt, T. C., & Horton, S. V. (1994). Strategies for adapting science textbooks for youth with learning disabilities. *Remedial and Special Education, 15*(2), 105–116.

Marzano, R. J. (1998). *A theory-based meta-analysis of research on instruction.* Aurora, CO: Mid-Continent Research for Education and Learning. Retrieved October 1, 2003, from http://www.mcrel.org/topics/productDetail/asp?productID=83

Marzano, R. J., Pickering, D. J., & Pollock, J. E. (2001). *Classroom instruction that works: Research-based strategies for increasing student achievement.* Alexandria, VA: Association for Supervision and Curriculum Development.

Miller, S. P., & Mercer, C. D. (1993). Mnemonics: Enhancing the math performance of students with learning difficulties. *Intervention in School and Clinic, 29*(2), 78–82.

Montague, M. (1997). Cognitive strategy instruction in mathematics for students with learning disabilities. *Journal of Learning Disabilities, 30*(2), 164–177.

Reiser, R. A., & Dick, W. (1996). *Instructional planning: A guide for teachers* (2nd ed.). Boston: Allyn and Bacon.

Roderick, M., & Camburn, E. (1999). Risk and recovery from course failure in the early years of high school. *American Educational Research Journal, 36*(2), 303–343.

Steele, M. (2002). Strategies for helping students who have learning disabilities in mathematics. *Mathematics Teaching in the Middle School, 8*(3), 140–143.

Swanson, H. L. (2000). What instruction works for students with learning disabilities? Summarizing the results from a meta-analysis of intervention studies. In R. Gersten, E. P. Schiller, & S. Vaughn (Eds.), *Contemporary special education research: Syntheses of the knowledge base on critical instructional issues* (pp. 1–30). Mahwah, NJ: Lawrence Erlbaum Associates, Inc.

Tyree, R. B., Fiore, T. A., & Cook, R. A. (1994). Instructional materials for diverse learners: Features and considerations for textbook design. *Remedial and Special Education, 15*(6), 363–377.

Vaughn, S., Gersten, R., & Chard, D. J. (2000). The underlying message in LD intervention research: Findings from research syntheses. *Exceptional Children, 67*(1), 99–114.

## Instructional Design: Lesson Structure and Learner Support Strategies, *continued from previous page*

| | AGS Globe Textbooks | |
| --- | --- | --- |
| | *In the Teacher's Edition:* | |

- 3-Step Teaching Lesson Plan concludes with "Reinforce and Extend" to reinforce, reteach, and extend lesson skills and concepts
- Unit or chapter projects link and apply unit or chapter concepts
- Multiple supplemental/alternative activities for individual and group learning and problem solving
- Career, home, and community application exercises

*In the Teacher's Resource Library:*

- Multiple exercises in Student Workbook and reproducibles offer applications, content extensions, additional practice, and modified activities at a lower (Grade 2 Spache) readability

*Skill Track:*

- Monitors student learning and guides teacher feedback to student

## Ongoing Assessment and Tracking Student Progress

Textbooks can incorporate features to facilitate and support assessment of learning, allowing teachers to monitor student progress and provide information on mastery level and the need for instructional changes.

Assessment should measure student progress on learning goals over the course of a lesson, chapter, or content-area textbook.

Students and teachers need timely and ongoing feedback so instruction can focus on specific skill development.

- Test-taking tips and strategies for students who benefit from explicit strategy instruction
- Lesson and chapter reviews check student understanding of content
- Workbook and reproducible lesson activities (Teacher's Resource Library) offer additional monitoring of student progress
- Discussion questions allow teachers to monitor student progress toward lesson objectives
- Self-Study Guides (Teacher's Resource Library) allow teacher and student to track individual assignments and progress
- Chapter assessment activities and curriculum-based assessment items correlate to chapter Goals for Learning:
  - Chapter reviews
  - End-of-chapter tests
  - Cumulative midterm and final mastery tests
  - Alternative chapter assessments
  - Skill Track assesses and tracks individual student performance by lesson and chapter

Deshler, D. D., Ellis, E. S., & Lenz, B. K. (1996). *Teaching adolescents with learning disabilities: Strategies and methods* (2nd ed.). Denver, CO: Love Publishing Company.

Jarrett, D. (1999). *The inclusive classroom: Mathematics and science instruction for students with learning disabilities—It's just good teaching.* Portland, OR: Northwest Regional Educational Laboratory.

Reiser, R. A., & Dick, W. (1996). *Instructional planning: A guide for teachers* (2nd ed.). Boston: Allyn and Bacon.

Tyree, R. B., Fiore, T. A., & Cook, R. A. (1994). Instructional materials for diverse learners: Features and considerations for textbook design. *Remedial and Special Education, 15*(6), 363–377.

**For more information on the scientific research base for AGS Globe Textbooks, please go to www.agsglobe.com or call Customer Service at 1-800-992-0244 to request a research report.**

# Pacemaker® Basic English Composition Scope and Sequence

## CHAPTER

| Writing Skills | HTUTB | WPH | 1 | 2 | 3 | 4 | 5 | 6 | 7 | 8 | 9 | 10 | 11 | 12 | 13 | 14 | App |
|---|---|---|---|---|---|---|---|---|---|---|---|---|---|---|---|---|---|
| active/passive verbs | | | | | | | | | | | | | | | | | ● |
| addressing envelopes | | | | | | | | | | | | | | ● | | | |
| assignment directions/writing prompts | | ● | | | | ● | ● | ● | ● | ● | ● | ● | | | ● | ● | |
| audience | | ● | | | | ● | ● | | ● | ● | | | | | | ● | |
| bibliographies/citing sources | | ● | | | | | | | | | | | | | ● | ● | |
| choosing and narrowing a topic | | ● | | ● | | ● | | | | | | | | | ● | | |
| conclusions/summaries | | ● | | | | ● | | | ● | ● | ● | | | | ● | ● | ● |
| details/evidence to support main idea | | ● | | | | ● | ● | ● | ● | ● | ● | ● | ● | ● | ● | ● | ● |
| dialogue | | | | | | | | | | | ● | | | | | | ● |
| editing | | ● | | | | | ● | | | | | | | | | | |
| graphics/photos to support main idea | | ● | | | | | | | | ● | | | | | | ● | |
| italics/underlining | | | | | | | | | | | | | | | | | |
| main ideas | | ● | | | | ● | ● | ● | ● | ● | ● | ● | ● | ● | ● | ● | |
| organization | | ● | | | | ● | ● | ● | ● | ● | ● | ● | | ● | ● | ● | |
| paragraph development | | ● | | | | ● | ● | ● | ● | ● | ● | ● | ● | ● | | ● | ● |
| point of view | | | | | | | | | | | ● | | | | | | |
| prewriting/planning to write | | ● | | | | ● | | | | | | ● | | | ● | | |
| process writing | | ● | | | | ● | ● | ● | ● | ● | ● | ● | | | ● | | |
| proofreading | | ● | | | | | | | | | | | | | | | |
| purposes for writing | | ● | ● | | | ● | ● | ● | ● | ● | ● | ● | ● | ● | ● | | |
| revising/rewriting | | ● | | | | | ● | | | | | ● | | | | ● | |
| sentence development and fluency | | ● | ● | ● | ● | ● | ● | ● | ● | ● | ● | ● | ● | | | ● | ● |
| sequencing | | ● | | | | ● | ● | ● | | | ● | | | | ● | | |
| style | | ● | | | | | | | | ● | | | | | | | |
| summarizing/paraphrasing | | | | | | ● | | ● | | | | ● | | | | ● | ● |
| topic sentences/topic paragraphs | | ● | | | | ● | ● | ● | ● | ● | ● | ● | | | | ● | |
| transitions | | ● | | | | | | ● | ● | | ● | | | | | ● | |
| voice | | ● | | | | | ● | | | ● | ● | | ● | ● | | ● | |
| word choice | | ● | | ● | ● | | ● | ● | ● | ● | ● | ● | ● | ● | ● | ● | ● |

| Types of Writing | HTUTB | WPH | 1 | 2 | 3 | 4 | 5 | 6 | 7 | 8 | 9 | 10 | 11 | 12 | 13 | 14 | App |
|---|---|---|---|---|---|---|---|---|---|---|---|---|---|---|---|---|---|
| addresses/envelopes | | | | | | | | | | | | | | ● | | | ● |
| answers to questions | | | | | | | | ● | | | | ● | | ● | ● | | |
| autobiographies/biographies | | | | | | | | | | | ● | | | | ● | | |
| business letters | | | | | | | | | ● | | | | | ● | ● | | |
| cause/effect | | | | | | | | ● | | | | | | | | | |
| comparing/contrasting | | | | | ● | | | ● | | | | | | | | | |
| descriptive | | | | | | | | | | ● | | | | | ● | | |
| dialogue | | | | | | | | | | | ● | | | | | | |
| directions/instructions | | | | | ● | | | ● | | | | | ● | | | | |
| e-mail | | | | | | ● | | | | | | | ● | ● | | | |
| essays | | | | | | | | | | | | ● | | | | | |
| explanatory/informative/expository | | | | | | | | ● | | | | | | | | | |
| memos | | | | | | | | | | | | | | ● | | | |
| messages | | | | | | | ● | | | ● | | | ● | ● | | | |
| narrative | | | | ● | | | ● | | | ● | ● | | | | | | |
| outlines | | ● | | | | | | | | | | | | | ● | | |
| personal letters | | | ● | | | | | | | | | | ● | | | | |
| persuasive | | | | | | | | | ● | | | | | | | ● | |
| problem/solution | | | | | | | ● | ● | | | | | | | | | |
| reports/research reports | | | | | | | | | | | | | | | ● | ● | |
| requests | | | | | | | ● | | | | | | | ● | | | |

**HTUTB**=How to Use This Book    **WPH**=Writing Process Handbook    **App**=Appendixes

| Types of Writing, cont. | HTUTB | WPH | 1 | 2 | 3 | 4 | 5 | 6 | 7 | 8 | 9 | 10 | 11 | 12 | 13 | 14 | App |
|---|---|---|---|---|---|---|---|---|---|---|---|---|---|---|---|---|---|
| resumes/applications | | | | | | | | | ● | | | | | | ● | | |
| reviews/book reports | | | | | | | | | | | | ● | | | | ● | |
| speeches | | | | | | | | | | | | | | | | ● | ● |
| summaries | | | | | | ● | | ● | | | | ● | | | | ● | ● |
| test answers | | | | | | | | | | | | ● | | | | | |

| Grammar Skills | HTUTB | WPH | 1 | 2 | 3 | 4 | 5 | 6 | 7 | 8 | 9 | 10 | 11 | 12 | 13 | 14 | App |
|---|---|---|---|---|---|---|---|---|---|---|---|---|---|---|---|---|---|
| adjectives | | | | | ● | ● | | | | ● | | | | | | | ● |
| adverbs | | | | | ● | | | | | | | | | | | | ● |
| appositives | | | | | | | ● | | | | | | | | | | ● |
| conjunctions | | | | ● | | | | | | | | | | | ● | | ● |
| interjections | | | | | | | | | | | | | | | | | ● |
| nouns/possessive nouns | | ● | | ● | ● | | | | | | | | | | | | ● |
| prepositional phrases | | | | | ● | | | | | | | | | | | | ● |
| pronouns/antecedents | | ● | | | ● | | | | | | | | | | | | ● |
| run-on sentences/fragments | | ● | ● | | | | | | | | | | | | | | ● |
| sentence purposes | | ● | ● | | | | | | | | | | | | | | ● |
| subjects/predicates | | | ● | ● | | | | | | | | | | | | | ● |
| subject-verb agreement | | ● | | ● | | | | | | | | | | | ● | | ● |
| syntax/sentence structure | | ● | ● | ● | ● | | ● | | | ● | ● | | | | ● | | ● |
| verbs/verb phrases/tenses | | ● | ● | ● | | | | | | ● | | | | | ● | | ● |

| Punctuation/Capitalization Skills | HTUTB | WPH | 1 | 2 | 3 | 4 | 5 | 6 | 7 | 8 | 9 | 10 | 11 | 12 | 13 | 14 | App |
|---|---|---|---|---|---|---|---|---|---|---|---|---|---|---|---|---|---|
| apostrophes | | ● | | | ● | | | | | | | | | | | | ● |
| capitalization | | ● | ● | | | | | | | | | | | | | | ● |
| colons | | | | | | | | | | | | | | ● | | | ● |
| commas | | ● | | ● | | | | ● | | | ● | | | ● | | | ● |
| end punctuation marks | | ● | ● | | | | | | | | | | | | | | ● |
| hyphens | | | | | | | | | | | | | ● | | | | ● |
| quotation marks | | ● | | | | | | | | | ● | | | | | | ● |

| Vocabulary Skills | HTUTB | WPH | 1 | 2 | 3 | 4 | 5 | 6 | 7 | 8 | 9 | 10 | 11 | 12 | 13 | 14 | App |
|---|---|---|---|---|---|---|---|---|---|---|---|---|---|---|---|---|---|
| antonyms/synonyms | | | | | ● | ● | | | | | | | | | | | |
| commonly confused words | | | | ● | ● | | | | | | ● | | ● | | | | ● |
| connotations | | | | | | | | | | ● | | | | | | | |
| contractions | | | | | | | | | | | | | | | | | ● |
| dictionary/thesaurus use | | ● | | | ● | | | ● | | ● | | ● | | | | | |
| figurative language | | | | | | | | | | ● | | | | | | | |
| homonyms | | | | | | | | | | | | | | | | | ● |
| multiple meanings | | | | | | | | | | | | | | | | | ● |
| prefixes/suffixes/base words | | | | | | | ● | ● | | ● | | | ● | | ● | | ● |
| pronunciation | | | | | ● | | | | | ● | | | | | | | |
| spelling | | | | | | | ● | | | | | | | | ● | | ● |
| word choice | | ● | | ● | ● | | ● | ● | ● | ● | ● | ● | ● | ● | ● | | ● |
| word meaning | | | ● | ● | ● | | | ● | ● | ● | | | | | | | ● |

| Research/Study Skills | HTUTB | WPH | 1 | 2 | 3 | 4 | 5 | 6 | 7 | 8 | 9 | 10 | 11 | 12 | 13 | 14 | App |
|---|---|---|---|---|---|---|---|---|---|---|---|---|---|---|---|---|---|
| bibliographies | | | | | | | | | | | | | | | ● | ● | |
| choosing and narrowing a topic | | ● | | ● | | ● | | | | | | | | | ● | | |
| documenting information | | ● | | | | ● | | ● | | | | | | | ● | | |
| following instruction/writing prompts | | ● | ● | ● | ● | ● | ● | ● | | | ● | ● | ● | ● | ● | | |
| gathering details/evidence | | ● | | | | ● | ● | ● | ● | | | | | | ● | | |
| graphic organizers | ● | ● | | | | | | | | ● | | | | | | | |
| inquiry/questioning | | ● | | ● | | | | | | | | ● | | ● | ● | | ● |

**HTUTB**=How to Use This Book   **WPH**=Writing Process Handbook   **App**=Appendixes

**CHAPTER**

### Research/Study Skills, cont.

| | HTUTB | WPH | 1 | 2 | 3 | 4 | 5 | 6 | 7 | 8 | 9 | 10 | 11 | 12 | 13 | 14 | App |
|---|---|---|---|---|---|---|---|---|---|---|---|---|---|---|---|---|---|
| Internet/electronic media | | ● | ● | ● | ● | ● | ● | ● | ● | ● | ● | ● | ● | ● | ● | ● | |
| library/library catalog use | | ● | ● | | | | ● | | | | | | | | ● | | |
| managing information | | ● | | | | ● | ● | ● | | ● | | ● | | | ● | | |
| note taking | ● | ● | | | | ● | | ● | | | | | | | ● | | |
| organizing information | | ● | | | | ● | | ● | | | ● | | | | ● | ● | |
| outlining | | ● | | | | | | | | | | | | | | | |
| reading strategies | ● | ● | ● | ● | ● | ● | ● | ● | ● | ● | ● | ● | ● | | ● | | ● |
| reference materials/sources | | ● | ● | | ● | | ● | ● | | | | | | | ● | | |
| summarizing/paraphrasing | | ● | ● | | | ● | | ● | | | | | | | ● | | |
| synthesizing content from many sources | | ● | | | | ● | | ● | | | | | | | ● | ● | |
| test preparation/test taking | ● | | ● | ● | ● | ● | ● | ● | ● | ● | ● | ● | ● | ● | ● | ● | |

### Critical-Thinking Skills

| | HTUTB | WPH | 1 | 2 | 3 | 4 | 5 | 6 | 7 | 8 | 9 | 10 | 11 | 12 | 13 | 14 | App |
|---|---|---|---|---|---|---|---|---|---|---|---|---|---|---|---|---|---|
| applying information | | | ● | ● | ● | ● | ● | ● | ● | ● | ● | ● | ● | ● | ● | ● | ● |
| classifying and categorizing | | | ● | ● | ● | ● | ● | ● | ● | ● | ● | ● | ● | ● | ● | ● | ● |
| distinguishing facts and opinions | | | | | | | | | ● | | | | | | | | |
| drawing conclusions/inferring | | | ● | ● | ● | ● | ● | ● | ● | ● | ● | ● | ● | ● | ● | ● | ● |
| evaluating writing/sources | | ● | ● | ● | ● | ● | ● | ● | ● | ● | ● | ● | ● | ● | ● | ● | ● |
| organizing information | | ● | | | | ● | ● | ● | | ● | | ● | | | ● | ● | |

### Speaking/Presenting Skills

| | HTUTB | WPH | 1 | 2 | 3 | 4 | 5 | 6 | 7 | 8 | 9 | 10 | 11 | 12 | 13 | 14 | App |
|---|---|---|---|---|---|---|---|---|---|---|---|---|---|---|---|---|---|
| debates | | | | | | | | | | | | | | | | | ● |
| descriptive | | | | | | | | | | ● | | | | | | | ● |
| drama/role playing | | | | | | | | | | ● | ● | | ● | ● | ● | | ● |
| entertaining | | | | | | | | | | | ● | | | | | | ● |
| explanatory/informative/expository | | | | | ● | | | ● | | | | ● | | | | | ● |
| group discussions/presentations | | | ● | ● | ● | ● | ● | ● | ● | ● | ● | ● | ● | ● | ● | ● | ● |
| interviews | | | | | | | | | | | | | | | ● | | |
| multimedia presentations | | | | | | ● | | | | | | | | | ● | | ● |
| narrative | | | | | | | | | | | ● | | | | | | ● |
| oral reports/presentations/speeches | | | ● | ● | ● | ● | ● | ● | ● | ● | ● | ● | ● | ● | ● | | ● |
| persuasive | | | | | | | | | ● | | | | | | | | ● |
| reading aloud | | | ● | ● | | | | | ● | | | | | | | | |

### Listening/Viewing Skills

| | HTUTB | WPH | 1 | 2 | 3 | 4 | 5 | 6 | 7 | 8 | 9 | 10 | 11 | 12 | 13 | 14 | App |
|---|---|---|---|---|---|---|---|---|---|---|---|---|---|---|---|---|---|
| listening as part of a discussion | | | | ● | | | ● | | | | | | | | ● | ● | |
| listening to ask questions | | | | | ● | | | | | | ● | | | ● | | ● | |
| listening to comprehend | | | ● | ● | ● | ● | ● | ● | ● | ● | ● | ● | ● | ● | ● | ● | ● |
| listening to evaluate | | | ● | ● | ● | | | | | ● | | | | ● | ● | ● | |
| listening to follow directions | | | | | | | | ● | | | | | | | | | ● |
| listening while taking notes | | | | | | | | | | ● | ● | | ● | ● | | ● | ● |
| skimming/scanning | | | | | | | | | ● | | | ● | | | ● | | ● |
| viewing to evaluate | | | | | | | | | | | | | | | | ● | ● |

### Media and Technology

| | HTUTB | WPH | 1 | 2 | 3 | 4 | 5 | 6 | 7 | 8 | 9 | 10 | 11 | 12 | 13 | 14 | App |
|---|---|---|---|---|---|---|---|---|---|---|---|---|---|---|---|---|---|
| advertisements | | | | | | | | | ● | | | | | | ● | | |
| audio/visual/multimedia presentations | | | | | | | | | | ● | | | | | ● | | ● |
| computer/software use | | | ● | ● | ● | ● | ● | ● | ● | ● | ● | ● | ● | ● | ● | | |
| Internet sources | | | ● | ● | ● | ● | ● | ● | ● | ● | ● | ● | ● | ● | ● | | |
| magazines/journals | | | | ● | | | | | ● | | | | | | ● | | |
| movies/video/television/radio | | | ● | ● | ● | ● | ● | ● | | ● | ● | ● | ● | ● | ● | | ● |
| newspapers | | | | ● | | | | | | | ● | | | ● | | | |
| reviews of literature/film | | | | | | | | | | | | ● | | | | ● | ● |

**HTUTB**=How to Use This Book   **WPH**=Writing Process Handbook   **App**=Appendixes

PACEMAKER®

# Basic English Composition

by Bonnie Walker

PEARSON
AGS Globe

Shoreview, MN

# About the Author

**Bonnie L. Walker** taught for 16 years in secondary schools and college. She holds a Ph.D. in curriculum theory and instructional design from the University of Maryland, an M.Ed. in secondary education, and a B.A. in English. She studied psycholinguistics at the University of Illinois Graduate School and was a curriculum developer at the Model Secondary School for the Deaf at Galludet University. She is the author of Pacemaker® *Basic English,* Pacemaker® *Basic English Grammar, Life Skills English,* and numerous curriculum materials in written expression, grammar, and usage. Since 1986, Dr. Walker has been president of a research and development company specializing in the development of training and educational materials for special populations.

## Reading Consultant

**Timothy Shanahan,** Ph.D., Professor of Urban Education, Director of the Center for Literacy, University of Illinois at Chicago; Author, AMP Reading System

## Reviewers

The publisher wishes to thank the following educators for their helpful comments during the review process for Pacemaker® *Basic English Composition.* Their assistance has been invaluable. **Sylvia Berger,** Special Education Resource Teacher, Markham District High School, Markham, ON, Canada; **Raequel Gadsden,** ESE Teacher, Chamberlain High School, Tampa, FL; **Wendy Mason,** Special Education Teacher, Magnolia High School, Anaheim, CA; **John Petitt,** Special Education Resource Teacher, Culver Elementary School, Niles, IL; **Phyllis Romine,** Special Education Teacher, Florence Freshman Center, Florence, AL; **Monica M. Thorpe,** Language Arts Teacher, El Paso, TX; **Sandra Tuck,** Special Education Teacher, Talladega County Central High School, Talladega, AL

**Acknowledgments** appear on page 442, which constitutes an extension of this copyright page.

1-800-992-0244
www.agsglobe.com

# Table of Contents

### How to Use This Book: A Study Guide

**Overview** This section may be used to introduce the study of English composition, to preview the book's features, and to review effective study skills.

### Objectives

- To introduce the study of composition
- To preview the student textbook
- To review study skills

### Student Pages viii–xv

### Teacher's Resource Library

How to Use This Book 1–4
Preparing for Writing Tests 1–4

### Introduction to the Book

Have volunteers read aloud the three paragraphs of the introduction. Discuss with students why studying English composition and developing writing skills are important.

### How to Study

Read aloud each bulleted statement, pausing to discuss with students these good study habits. Distribute copies of How to Use This Book 1, "Study Habits Survey," to students. Read the directions together and then have students complete the survey. After they have scored their surveys, ask them to make a list of the study habits they plan to improve. After three or four weeks, have students complete the survey again to see if they have improved their study habits. Encourage them to keep and review the survey every month or so.

To help students organize their time and work in an easy-to-read format, have them fill out How to Use This Book 2, "Weekly Schedule." Encourage them to keep the schedule in a notebook or folder where they can refer to it easily. Suggest that they review the schedule periodically and update it as necessary.

Give students an opportunity to become familiar with the textbook features, the chapter and lesson organization, and the structure of *Basic English Composition*.

# How to Use This Book: A Study Guide

**W**elcome to Pacemaker® *Basic English Composition*. This book focuses on practical writing skills that you can use now and later in life. Why study English composition? Think about how often you put ideas in writing. You probably write phone messages or e-mails at home. You express your ideas when you write for school. In this book, you will learn how to write sentences correctly. You will study the steps in the writing process. You will practice writing paragraphs for different purposes. You will learn how to write letters, messages, essays, and reports. You will also learn how to do your best on tests.

As you read this book, notice how each lesson is organized. Information is presented and then followed by Examples and Practices. Read the information. Study the Examples. Then do the Practice activities. If you have trouble with a lesson, try reading it again. If you still do not understand something, ask your teacher for help.

It is important that you understand how to use this book before you start to read it. It is also important to know how to be successful in this class. This study guide can help you to achieve these things.

## *How to Study*

These tips can help you study more effectively:

- Plan a regular time to study.
- Choose a desk or table in a quiet place where you will not be distracted. Find a spot that has good lighting.
- Gather all of the books, pencils, paper, and other materials you will need to complete your assignments.
- Decide on a goal. For example: "I will finish reading and taking notes on Lesson 1-1, by 8:00."
- To stay alert, take a five- to ten-minute break every hour.

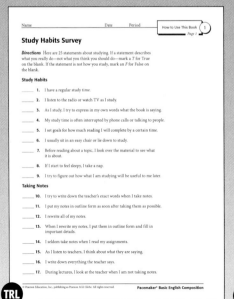

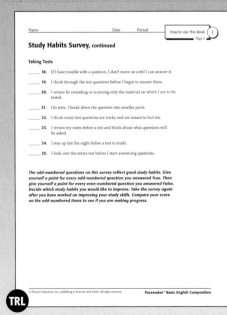

How to Use This Book 1, pages 1-2

## Before Beginning Each Chapter

- Read the chapter title and study the photo.
- Read the opening paragraphs. How is the photo related to the chapter?
- Read the Goals for Learning. These are the main objectives of the chapter. Each goal represents one lesson.
- Read the Reading Strategy feature. There are seven different strategies described in this book. They are also summarized in Appendix E. As you read the chapter, try to use the strategy. It will help you become a better reader.
- Study the Key Vocabulary Words. Say each one aloud. Read its definition. These words will also be defined and explained in the chapter.

List the following text features on the board: Table of Contents, Chapter Opener, Lesson, Lesson Review, English in Your Life, Writing on the Job, Building Research Skills, Chapter Summary, Chapter Review, Appendix A: Handbook on Editing, Appendix B: Speaking Checklist, Appendix C: Listening Checklist, Appendix D: Viewing Checklist, Appendix E: Reading Checklist, Glossary, Index.

Remind students that they can use the Table of Contents to help identify and locate major features in the text. They can also use the Index to identify specific topics and the text pages on which they are discussed.

## Before Beginning Each Chapter

Chapter Openers explain the purpose of each chapter and summarize its content in an easy-to-read format.

The third page of each chapter has a Reading Strategy feature followed by a list of the Key Vocabulary Words in the chapter. Each chapter features one of seven strategies—summarizing, questioning, predicting, text structure, visualizing, inferencing, and metacognition. The Reading Checklist in Appendix E summarizes the strategies. Students will also find Reading Strategy notes in the margins of each lesson. Encourage students to watch for these questions and use them as they read to gain understanding of the text.

When students begin their study of Chapter 1, you may wish to have them read aloud and follow each of the bulleted suggestions under "Before Beginning Each Chapter." Actually trying the suggestions will help students recognize how useful the suggestions are when previewing a chapter.

At the beginning of other chapters, refer students to page ix and encourage them to follow the suggestions. You may wish to do this as a class each time or allow students to work independently.

In addition to these bulleted suggestions, the Teacher's Edition text for each Chapter Opener offers teaching suggestions for introducing the chapter. The text also includes a list of Teacher's Resource Library material for the chapter.

---

| | | Name | Date | Period | How to Use This Book | 2 |

**Weekly Schedule**

*Directions* Fill in your classes and other activities. Fill in a time when you will study each subject.

| Hour | Monday | Tuesday | Wednesday | Thursday | Friday |
|------|--------|---------|-----------|----------|--------|
| 7:00 – 8:00 | | | | | |
| 8:00 – 9:00 | | | | | |
| 9:00 – 10:00 | | | | | |
| 10:00 – 11:00 | | | | | |
| 11:00 – 12:00 | | | | | |
| 12:00 – 1:00 | | | | | |
| 1:00 – 2:00 | | | | | |
| 2:00 – 3:00 | | | | | |
| 3:00 – 4:00 | | | | | |
| 4:00 – 5:00 | | | | | |
| 5:00 – 6:00 | | | | | |
| 6:00 – 7:00 | | | | | |
| 7:00 – 8:00 | | | | | |
| 8:00 – 9:00 | | | | | |
| 9:00 – 10:00 | | | | | |

© Pearson Education, Inc., publishing as Pearson AGS Globe. All rights reserved.        **Pacemaker® Basic English Composition**

**TRL**

## How to Use This Book 2

## Note These Features

Use the information on pages x–xi to identify features included in each chapter. As a class, locate examples of these features in Chapter 1. Read the examples and discuss their purpose.

Examples give students a concrete application of concepts. For instance, Example 1 on page 3 of Chapter 1 shows a sentence with no capital letter or end mark, then presents the corrected sentence with a beginning capital letter and ending period.

Next, have students look at Practice A on page 3 of Chapter 1, which has students correct sentences that lack capital letters and end marks.

Point out that each chapter has a Writing on the Job feature or an English in Your Life feature.

Writing on the Job describes a work setting and a type of writing the job requires. After reading each one, tell students to ask themselves, *What writing skill(s) were needed to compose the writing in this feature?*

Tell students that English in Your Life highlights a practical application of writing. Have a volunteer read the title of the English in Your Life feature on page 23. Ask students: *How does this topic relate to your life?*

Have students read the title of the Building Research Skills feature on page 24. Ask students to tell how the ability to use an encyclopedia well will help them at school and in their personal lives.

Have students locate the Vocabulary Builder (page 5), Grammar Builder (page 14), and Write About It (page 18) features in Chapter 1. Explain that these features expand on and provide practice in using chapter concepts. The Teacher's Edition has answers to questions that appear in these Student Edition features.

Together look at the Group Activity on page 25, which asks a group to write an announcement using five sentences. Point out that these features allow students to work together and to use all the concepts they have learned in the chapter to produce a written product.

---

## Note These Features

▶ **EXAMPLE 1**

**Example**
Example sentences that show a lesson idea

**Practice A**

**Practice**
An activity designed to practice a lesson skill

**Writing on the Job**
Information about a job that requires writing skills

**English in Your Life**
A practical application of writing skills

**Building Research Skills**
Information about a research tool or a research skill

**Vocabulary Builder**
Vocabulary practice

**Grammar Builder**
Grammar practice

**Write About It**
A writing activity that uses skills taught in the chapter

**Group Activity**
A writing activity designed for a small group

---

**Reading Strategy:**
Summarizing

### Reading Strategy

A prompt to help you use the chapter's reading strategy (See Appendix E for a description of these strategies.)

**Six Traits of Writing:**

*Ideas* message, details, and purpose

### Six Traits of Writing

A prompt to remind you about a trait of good writing (See page WPH1 for a description of the six traits.)

**Brush Up on the Basics**

### Brush Up on the Basics

A tip on grammar, spelling, capitalization, or punctuation (Each tip refers to a section in Appendix A.)

Test Tip

### Test Tip

A tip to help you do your best on tests

**NOTE**

### Note

Additional information related to the lesson

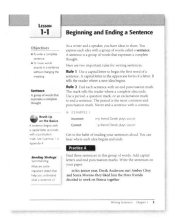

## Before Beginning Each Lesson

Read the lesson title and restate it in the form of a question. For example, write: How do you begin and end a sentence?

Look over the entire lesson, noting the following:

- Objectives
- bold words
- text organization
- notes and features in the margin
- Examples
- Practices
- Lesson Review

*How to Use This Book: A Study Guide*  **xi**

---

Point out the Reading Strategy notes in the margin on pages 3 and 4 in Chapter 1. Explain that each chapter highlights a different strategy for reading comprehension. Encourage students to watch for these notes and use them as they read to gain understanding of the text.

Have students skim page WPH1 to note the six traits of good writing. Explain that a Six Traits of Writing prompt is placed beside each Write About It feature. They can use it to help them focus on a quality that their written product should exhibit.

This Teacher's Edition also includes additional traits that may be used for each step in the writing process. If you use the Six Traits of Writing in your classroom, you may wish to have students make connections with these traits, as well as the featured trait, in their writing.

Explain that Brush Up on the Basics notes offer reminders about grammar, capitalization, punctuation, or spelling rules. References guide students to sections in Appendix A where they can read more about the rules and see examples.

Test Tips and Notes give students information to help them with the chapter or with preparation for tests. Point out that Test Tips are located in the Chapter Review.

## Before Beginning Each Lesson

With students, read through the information in "Before Beginning Each Lesson." Then assign each of the five lessons in Chapter 1 to a small group of students. Have each group restate the lesson title in the form of a question. Then have them make a list of the bold words in their lesson. Explain to students that these words are important to the content of their lesson. Have groups note subheads, Examples, and Practices in their lesson. Then have them study any margin notes.

After they survey the lesson, have each group report to the class on its findings. Then have each group turn to the Lesson Review at the end of their lesson. Explain that the Lesson Review provides an opportunity to determine how well they have understood the lesson content.

*How to Use This Book: A Study Guide*  **xi**

## As You Read the Lesson

Have students read the bulleted list silently. Point out that following these steps will take them through each lesson logically. The lesson title focuses on the main idea. The text explains the main idea. Examples show how to apply it, and Practices give students a chance to apply it for themselves. Then the Lesson Review tests whether students have understood the lesson's important ideas.

## Using the Bold Words

After students have read the section, point out that they have multiple ways to learn important vocabulary terms:

- by reading the text definition when the term is first introduced
- by reading the definition listed in the margin of the lesson where the term is used
- by looking up the vocabulary term in the Glossary

Point out that they should use each of these resources when it is logical. For example, the text definition is useful when they first read the lesson. The margin definition is easy to find when they need to look back within the chapter to refresh their memory. The Glossary definition is helpful if they need to find a term's meaning when they are in another chapter.

## Word Study Tips

As students read Chapter 1, have them return to this section and follow the steps to start their vocabulary file using index cards.

Distribute copies of How to Use This Book 3, "Word Study," to students. Suggest that as they read, students write unfamiliar words, their page numbers, and their definitions in the sheet. Point out that having such a list will be very useful for reviewing vocabulary before taking a test. Point out that students can use words they listed on How to Use This Book 3 to make their vocabulary card file.

You may wish to have students keep their files in a small box in the classroom. Periodically, have students alphabetize and review their flash cards.

## As You Read the Lesson

- Read the lesson title.
- Read the subheadings and paragraphs that follow.
- Study the Examples.
- Do the Practices.
- Complete the Lesson Review.
- Make sure you understand the main ideas in the lesson. If you do not, reread the lesson. If you are still unsure, ask for help.

## Using the Bold Words

Knowing the meaning of the red vocabulary words in the left column will help you understand what you read. These words are in **bold type** the first time they appear in the text. They are defined in the lesson text.

You express each idea with a group of words called a **sentence.** A sentence is a group of words that expresses a complete thought.

All of the boxed vocabulary words are also defined in the **glossary.**

**Sentence** (sen´ təns) A group of words that expresses a complete thought

---

**Bold type**
Words seen for the first time will appear in bold type.

**Glossary**
Words listed in this column are also found in the glossary.

---

Sentence

A group of words that expresses a complete thought

Lesson 1-1

## Word Study Tips

- Start a vocabulary file with index cards to use for review.
- Write one term on the front of each card. Write the definition, chapter number, and lesson number on the back.
- You can use these cards as flash cards by yourself or with a study partner to test your knowledge.

---

Name _____ Date _____ Period _____    How to Use This Book  3

**Word Study** Chapter _____

*Directions* As you read, write words you don't know in the left-hand column. Write the page number the word is on in the next column. Find the meaning of the word and write it in the right-hand column.

**Word**        **Page number**   **Meaning**

© Pearson Education, Inc., publishing as Pearson AGS Globe. All rights reserved.    Pacemaker® Basic English Composition

**How to Use This Book 3**

## Taking Notes

It is helpful to take notes during class and as you read this book.

- Use headings to label the main sections of your notes. This organizes your notes.
- Summarize important information, such as main ideas and supporting details.
- Do not try to write every word your teacher says or every detail in a chapter.
- Do not be concerned about writing in complete sentences. Use short phrases.
- Use your own words to describe, explain, or define things.
- Sometimes the best way to summarize information is with a chart or an example. Use simple word webs, charts, and diagrams in your notes. Write your own example sentences.
- Try taking notes using a three-column format. Draw two lines to divide your notebook page into three columns. Make the middle column the widest. Use the first column to write headings or vocabulary words. Use the middle column to write definitions and examples. Use the last column to draw diagrams, write shortcuts for remembering something, write questions about something you do not understand, record homework assignments, or for other purposes. An example of three-column note-taking is shown on the left.
- After taking notes, review them to fill in possible gaps.
- Study your notes to prepare for a test. Use a highlighter to mark what you need to know.

| Purposes of sentences | | |
|---|---|---|
| Declarative | Amber and I are in the same English class. | ☺ |
| Interrogative | Do we have to cover our new textbook? | ? |
| Imperative | Please make a cover for this book tonight. | ☺ |
| Exclamatory | The school year is off to a great start! | ! |

## Taking Notes

Have students set up a separate notebook for taking notes. You may choose to distribute copies of How to Use This Book 4, "Taking Notes," which provides a blank three-column template for students to use. If students are familiar with outlining, point out that chapters are organized with lesson titles representing the main ideas (Roman numerals I, II, etc.). Some lessons have subheadings that represent supporting points about each main idea (capital letters A, B, etc.).

Emphasize that notes should represent the main ideas in an understandable language. This is why students should attempt to rephrase textbook ideas in their own words.

Point out that the three-column format has a column for students to record questions they have or special ways for remembering a concept.

Explain that notes pay off by giving students a better grasp of important ideas in a chapter and giving them a tool for reviewing that will help them study for tests.

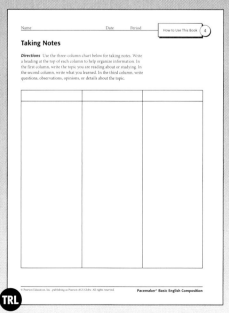

**How to Use This Book 4**

## Using the Chapter Summaries

Have students turn to page 25 and examine the Chapter 1 Summary. Emphasize that Chapter Summaries identify the main ideas of the chapter. Suggest that students use the summary to focus their study of the chapter content. They might check each of these main ideas against their chapter notes to be sure they have understood the ideas and included details that reinforce them.

## Using the Reviews

Have students turn to page 5 and examine the Lesson 1-1 Review. Explain that Lesson Reviews provide opportunities for students to focus on important content and skills developed in the lesson.

Then have students turn to the Chapter Review on pages 26–27. Point out that each two-page Chapter Review is intended to help them focus on and review the key terms, concepts, and skills presented in the chapter before they are tested on the material. Before they complete Part A, have students study the words and definitions and say them aloud. Then have them answer the questions in order to help them remember vocabulary.

## Using the Writing Process Handbook

Ask volunteers to read aloud the paragraph and bulleted list. Then have students turn to the Handbook and page through each section, noting the headings to get a sense of what is involved in each step of the writing process. Point out that the Six Traits of Good Writing on page WPH1 offers a description of each trait.

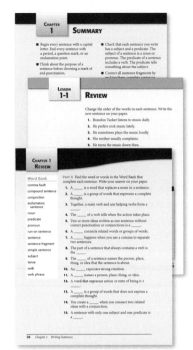

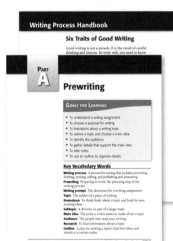

## *Using the Chapter Summaries*

- Read each Chapter Summary to be sure you understand the chapter's main ideas.

## *Using the Reviews*

- Complete each Lesson Review. It covers the most important ideas and skills from the lesson.
- Complete the Chapter Review. Part A covers the chapter vocabulary words. The rest of the review covers the main ideas and skills taught in the chapter.
- Read the Test Tip. Try to remember this tip when you take a test.

## *Using the Writing Process Handbook*

There is a Writing Process Handbook in the front of this book. Its page numbers start with WPH. This handbook explains the five steps to follow when you write. Refer to this handbook when you write paragraphs, essays, and reports.

- Read about the six traits of good writing on the first page of the handbook. Remember these traits during each step of the writing process.
- Read Part A on prewriting. This first step of the writing process is an important planning step.
- Read Part B on drafting, the second step.
- Read Part C on revising, the third step.
- Read Part D on editing and proofreading. This is the fourth step.
- Read Part E on publishing and presenting. This is the final step in the writing process.

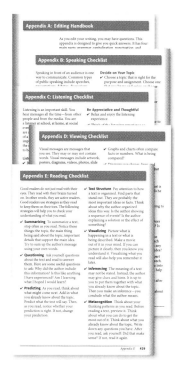

## Using the Appendixes

There are five appendixes in the back of this book. Become familiar with them before starting your study of English composition.

- Appendix A is an Editing Handbook. It has four sections: grammar, capitalization, punctuation, and spelling. Each section contains numbered tips. If you have a question about the correct way to write a sentence, look for the answer here. The Brush Up on the Basics features in the lessons refer to this appendix.
- Appendix B is a Speaking Checklist. Use this list to help you prepare a speech or presentation.
- Appendix C is a Listening Checklist. Use this list to help you become a more careful listener.
- Appendix D is a Viewing Checklist. Use this list to help you evaluate a visual message.
- Appendix E is a Reading Checklist. It summarizes the seven reading strategies that are also described on the chapter opener pages. Use these strategies to become a better reader.

## Preparing for Tests

- Read the Goals for Learning at the beginning of the chapter. A test may ask questions related to these goals.
- Review the Examples in each lesson. Ask yourself: What main idea does each one show?
- Complete the Practices in each lesson. Review your work.
- Study the Key Vocabulary Words at the beginning of the chapter. If you made flash cards, use them to study.

- Complete the Lesson Reviews and the Chapter Review.
- Read the Chapter Summary.
- Use a list, chart, or word web to summarize main ideas.
- Review your notes. Highlight key ideas and examples.
- Review the Writing Process Handbook. It starts on the next page.
- Make up a sample test. You may want to do this with another student and share your test questions.

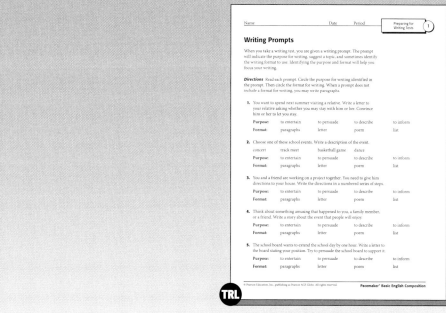

Preparing for Writing Tests 1–4

## Using the Appendixes

Have students turn to Appendix A, which begins on page 456. Have them find each section: grammar, capitalization, punctuation, and spelling. Remind students that this appendix can answer their questions about the technical aspects of using words correctly in sentences. Have students continue paging through Appendixes B through E. Explain that they will use these appendixes to help them learn how to give better oral presentations, be a better audience, and interpret visual messages. Point out that the Reading Checklist offers a handy summary of all the reading strategies explained in the chapter openers.

## Preparing for Tests

Encourage students to offer their opinions about tests and their ideas on test-taking strategies. Ask students: *What do you do to study for a test?* List their comments on the board. Then ask a volunteer to read the set of bulleted statements under "Preparing for Tests." Add these suggestions to the list on the board if they are not already there.

Discuss why each suggestion can help students when they are taking a test. Lead students to recognize that these suggestions, along with the Test Tips in their textbooks, can help them improve their test-taking skills.

Have students find a Test Tip in the Chapter Reviews. Remind them that Chapter Reviews are located at the end of each chapter. Ask several volunteers to read aloud the tips they find. Discuss how using the tips can help students study and take tests more effectively.

## Preparing for Writing Tests

Today many tests are designed to assess students' ability to communicate effectively in writing. Preparing for Writing Tests 1–4 (Writing Prompts, Organizing Your Writing, Proofreading for Errors, and Writing Test Practice) will give students focused practice with organizing and writing for tests.

## Writing Process Handbook
pages WPH1–WPH30

**Overview** This handbook begins by describing six traits of good writing. It then takes students step by step through each of the five steps in the writing process. Explanations and descriptions are presented with examples. Students are asked to complete a practice activity to apply each concept.

## Objectives

- To understand these writing traits: ideas, organization, voice, word choice, sentence fluency, and conventions
- To identify the five steps in the writing process
- To understand the purpose and outcome of each step
- To use the writing process to produce a paragraph

**Teacher's Resource Library** TRL
**Resource Files** 1–3

# Writing Process Handbook

## Six Traits of Good Writing

Good writing is not a miracle. It is the result of careful thinking and choices. To write well, you need to know about six traits that determine the quality of writing.

**Six Traits of Writing:**
*Ideas* message, details, and purpose

**Six Traits of Writing:**
*Organization* order, ideas tied together

**Six Traits of Writing:**
*Voice* the writer's own language

**Six Traits of Writing:**
*Word Choice* vivid words that "show, not tell"

**Six Traits of Writing:**
*Sentence Fluency* smooth rhythm and flow

**Six Traits of Writing:**
*Conventions* correct grammar, spelling, and mechanics

**Ideas** What message do you want to get across? Ideas are the heart of any writing. Begin the writing process by developing strong, clear ideas. Support your ideas with details that stand out and catch attention.

**Organization** A piece of writing has a structure, just like a building. Place your ideas in order. Organize them into a structure that makes sense. Organization holds writing together and gives shape to ideas.

**Voice** Your writing should "sound" like you. It should capture your thoughts and opinions. This is your "voice." In writing, your voice shows that you are interested in your topic. Your voice adds a unique tone to your writing.

**Word Choice** Choose vivid, interesting words. Name things exactly. Use strong action verbs and specific adjectives. Good word choice helps you say exactly what you want to say. It helps the reader create a mental picture.

**Sentence Fluency** Well-made sentences make your writing easy to read. Aim for sentences that flow. Use a variety of sentence types and lengths. Then your sentences will move the reader through your writing with ease.

**Conventions** Ask yourself: Could my writing be published in a newspaper? Make sure your writing is free from mistakes in spelling, grammar, and mechanics. Mechanics includes correct capitalization and punctuation.

The rest of this handbook describes the writing process. As you follow this process, remember to include these six traits of good writing.

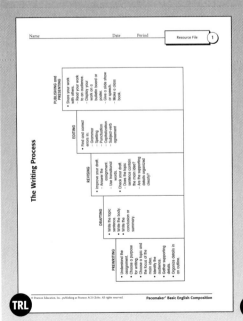

Resource File 1

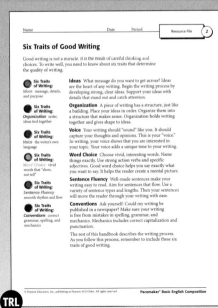

Resource File 2

# Prewriting

## GOALS FOR LEARNING

- To understand a writing assignment
- To choose a purpose for writing
- To brainstorm about a writing topic
- To narrow a topic and choose a main idea
- To identify the audience
- To gather details that support the main idea
- To take notes
- To use an outline to organize details

## Key Vocabulary Words

**Writing process** A process for writing that includes prewriting, drafting, revising, editing, and publishing and presenting

**Prewriting** Preparing to write; the planning step of the writing process

**Writing prompt** The directions for a writing assignment

**Topic** The subject of a piece of writing

**Brainstorm** To think freely about a topic and look for new, exciting ideas

**Subtopic** A division or part of a larger topic

**Main idea** The point a writer wants to make about a topic

**Audience** The people who read your writing

**Research** To find information about a topic

**Outline** A plan for writing a report that lists ideas and details in a certain order

## Introducing the Section

Explain that the writing process has five steps. List *prewriting, drafting, revising, editing and proofreading,* and *publishing and presenting* in a column on the board. Have students scan each part in this handbook and read the headings within each part. Use discussion to guide students to understand the purpose and main activities of each step. Add columns to create a chart such as the following:

| Step | Purpose | Activities |
| --- | --- | --- |
| Prewriting | prepare to write | plan and organize |
| Drafting | write ideas down | write freely |
| Revising | improve writing | add, remove, change, reorder |
| Editing and Proofreading | fix mistakes | correct spelling, grammar, punctuation, capitalization |
| Publishing and Presenting | share with others | present, post, read aloud |

## Writing Process Practice

Have students explain the meaning of the prompt and the key words in the directions. Suggest that they compare the prompt to the example in the text above before completing the practice.

### Writing Process Practice Answer

Answers will vary. A sample answer is given.

<u>Write a paragraph</u> about your <u>favorite kind of movie. Explain why</u> you chose this kind of movie. <u>Give three reasons</u> for your choice. Your paragraph should be <u>at least five sentences</u>.

I can plan my paragraph based on the key words in the prompt. The topic is my favorite kind of movie. The prompt says I have to write a paragraph. The paragraph must give three reasons. My paragraph must be five sentences long.

### Six Traits of Writing Focus

| | | | |
|---|---|---|---|
| ✔ | Ideas | | Word Choice |
| ✔ | Organization | | Sentence Fluency |
| | Voice | | Conventions |

### Ideas

To help them decide which words to underline in the prompt, have students focus on these questions:

- What is the purpose of this writing assignment?
- What message will it contain?
- What details will back up this message?

### Organization

Have students think about the key words in the prompt, then write an organization plan for their paragraph. Suggest that they write this plan as a numbered list. The first thing they will include in their paragraph will be written beside the number 1, the second thing beside 2, and so on.

---

# Understanding Your Assignment

**Writing process**
A process for writing that includes prewriting, drafting, revising, editing, and publishing and presenting

**Prewriting**
Preparing to write; the planning step of the writing process

**Writing prompt**
The directions for a writing assignment

**Topic**
The subject of a piece of writing

How do writers move from simple words to sentences, paragraphs, essays, and reports? They use the **writing process.** Each writer handles the steps in the writing process a little differently. However, every writer must answer questions such as *What do I write about?* and *How do I organize my ideas?* The basic steps in the writing process help you answer these questions.

**Prewriting** is the first step of the writing process. During this step, you are preparing to write. It is a time for thinking and planning. The plans you make will help you write later. Prewriting makes your job as a writer easier.

When you are given a writing assignment, you are asked to complete a certain writing task. Read the assignment directions carefully. Notice the words that tell you what to do. Sometimes, writing directions are called a **writing prompt.** The key words are underlined in this prompt:

Decide what <u>your favorite type of music</u> is. <u>Write a paragraph that explains</u> why you like this type of music. <u>Give three reasons for your choice.</u> Write a paragraph of <u>at least five sentences</u>.

The key words in a prompt help you plan your writing. A prompt may give the **topic,** or the subject of the writing. The topic in this prompt is *your favorite type of music.* The prompt says to write *a paragraph that explains.* The paragraph must *give three reasons.* This prompt also tells the length of the assignment: *at least five sentences.*

 **Six Traits of Writing:**
*Ideas* message, details, and purpose

 **Six Traits of Writing:**
*Organization* order, ideas tied together

### Writing Process Practice

Copy the prompt below. Underline the key words. Then explain how these words can help you to plan your writing.

Write a paragraph about your favorite kind of movie. Explain why you chose this kind of movie. Give three reasons for your choice. Your paragraph should be at least five sentences.

# Choosing Your Purpose for Writing

Before you begin to write, ask yourself: Why am I writing? Your reason, or purpose, for writing will guide the way in which you write. There are four main purposes for writing. These purposes are to explain, to persuade, to tell a story, and to describe.

Key words in a writing assignment may give you your purpose for writing. An assignment may ask you to tell how something works or why something happens. If so, your purpose is to explain. An assignment may ask you to convince someone to believe in something. In this case, your purpose is to persuade.

Another assignment may ask you to tell about an experience you had. Here, your purpose is to tell a story. Yet another assignment may ask you to tell what someone or something is like. In this writing, your purpose is to describe. Knowing your purpose helps you decide what ideas and details are best for your writing.

For the sample prompt about music on page WPH3, the purpose is to explain a choice.

## Writing Process Practice

Think about the paragraph you plan to write about your favorite kind of movie. What is the purpose of your paragraph? Explain why you chose this purpose.

**Six Traits of Writing:**

*Ideas* message, details, and purpose

## Writing Process Practice

Ask students to name the purposes for writing explained on this page. (*to explain, to persuade, to tell a story, to describe*)

## *Writing Process Practice Answer*

Answers will vary. A sample answer is given.

The purpose of my paragraph is to explain. I chose this purpose because the prompt asks me to tell why I like a certain kind of movie.

## Six Traits of Writing Focus

| | | | |
|---|---|---|---|
| ✔ | Ideas | | Word Choice |
| | Organization | | Sentence Fluency |
| | Voice | | Conventions |

## Ideas

Have students search the writing prompt for a key word that explains the purpose. (*Explain*) Have them complete this sentence on their own paper: *My paragraph will explain why _____ are my favorite kind of movie.* Then have students consult the prompt again to complete this sentence: *The details in my paragraph will give _____.*

## Writing Process Practice

Have students make a word web like the one on page WPH5 and write *kinds of movies* in the center. Point out that students should list as many kinds of movies as they can, since they can cross out inappropriate choices. Encourage students to be fairly specific. Categories such as *funny* and *serious* are too broad to be useful.

## Writing Process Practice Answer

Webs will vary but should list at least four distinctly different kinds of movies. See Ideas text below for possible categories.

## Six Traits of Writing Focus

| | | | |
|---|---|---|---|
| ✔ | Ideas | | Word Choice |
| | Organization | | Sentence Fluency |
| | Voice | | Conventions |

## Ideas

In this step, students should choose a clear subcategory within the broad category. If students have difficulty naming categories of movies, have them name specific movies they like and guide a discussion to appropriate category names such as adventure, western, spy thriller, murder mystery, romantic comedy, dramatized novel, animated, documentary, and epic.

---

# Choosing Your Topic

**Brainstorm**
To think freely about a topic and look for new, exciting ideas

**Brainstorming** is one way to find writing topics. When you brainstorm, you think freely about a general subject and list all the ideas you can think of. It is helpful to get these ideas on paper. You can write your ideas as a list or in a word web or chart. You can brainstorm by yourself or in a small group. You may also find writing topics by:

- thinking about people you know, places you have seen, and activities you enjoy
- thinking about past experiences
- reading newspapers, listening to radio, watching TV
- asking questions about a subject

Reread the prompt in the middle of page WPH3. Then look at the word web below. A group of students created this word web as they brainstormed about types of music. They placed each music type in a circle around the main subject.

When a word web is finished, judge the ideas. Cross out ideas that do not relate to the main idea. Cross off topics that do not interest you. Place a star next to the one that interests you most. This is your topic.

**Six Traits of Writing:**
*Ideas*   message, details, and purpose

Brainstorm ideas for the paragraph about your favorite kind of movie. Make a word web. Cross out ideas you do not like. Mark the topic you like most.

**Subtopic**
A division or part of a larger topic

**Main Idea**
The point a writer wants to make about a topic

rap artists

music videos

rap messages/sounds

my own raps

⬤ **Six Traits
of Writing:**

*Ideas* message, details, and purpose

# Narrowing Your Topic and Choosing Your Main Idea

Once you choose a topic, you need to narrow it. Think about a photo that is out of focus. Everything looks fuzzy. To take a photo that is sharp and clear, you need to focus the camera on a specific object. You narrow a writing topic for the same reason. A focused topic is clear and easy to understand.

To narrow your topic, ask yourself: Will this topic work for the assignment? If you first choose a topic that is too narrow, you will have little to say about it. If the topic is too broad, you will have too much information for the length of the assignment. Most often, you need to narrow a topic.

To narrow a topic, make it smaller by focusing on one part of it. List some specific parts of your topic. These are **subtopics**. Choose one subtopic. See the sample list on the left.

Now write some ideas about that subtopic. These ideas should be sentences. They may give an opinion. Choose your favorite idea. Use this as the **main idea** for your paragraph. The main idea is the main point you want to make.

## Writing Process Practice

Think about the topic you chose for your paragraph about movies. List some subtopics. Choose the one you like best. Then write some possible main ideas about that subtopic. Choose one as the main idea of your paragraph.

## Writing Process Practice

Point out to students that each outer circle in the example web on page WPH6 is related directly to the broad topic in the center. These subtopics can and should go in different directions. Make sure students understand they will choose only one of them to develop in their paragraph.

### *Writing Process Practice Answer*

Answers will vary. A sample answer is given.

## Six Traits of Writing Focus

| ✔ | Ideas | | Word Choice |
|---|-------|---|-------------|
| | Organization | | Sentence Fluency |
| | Voice | | Conventions |

## Ideas

Have students make their own graphic organizer to narrow the topic they chose on WPH5. Point out to students that by narrowing their topic they will make it more specific. This focus will make their ideas clear. For example, *special effects in adventure movies* is more focused than *adventure movies*.

## Writing Process Practice

Point out that a writer chooses his or her words and the content of the writing based on who will read it. Have students read the directions and write out the questions to be answered, leaving space between each question. Have students list their limited topics at the top of the page.

### Writing Process Practice Answer

Answers will vary. Sample answers are given.
**1.** My readers will be classmates and my teacher. **2.** They know what adventure movies are like, but they might not know about special effects. **3.** I need to explain how special effects are created.

## Six Traits of Writing Focus

| ✔ | Ideas | | Word Choice |
|---|---|---|---|
| | Organization | | Sentence Fluency |
| ✔ | Voice | | Conventions |

### Ideas

Have students make notes on their word webs from Prewriting 4. Have them:

**1.** name the audience for their paragraph

**2.** tell what this audience knows about the topic

**3.** suggest how they will state their main idea to interest this audience

**4.** list the kind of details that will be suitable for this audience

### Voice

Have students imagine themselves telling a friend about their topic. Then suggest that they write down phrases that occur to them in this context. This technique will help them capture language in their natural voice.

---

# Identifying Your Audience

**Audience**
The people who read your writing

Before you write, you also need to think about who you are writing for. Ask yourself: Who is my audience? Your **audience** is the person or people who will read your writing. Often, your audience will be a teacher or your classmates. You may want others to read your writing, too.

Think about your readers. What are their interests? You want your audience to understand what you say. How much do they know about your topic? If they do not know much about it, you will need to include basic information. You may need to explain some things. Your audience may know something about your topic. In that case, you can skip some of the basic details.

If you write with your audience in mind, you will be a better writer.

 **Six Traits of Writing:**
*Ideas*  message, details, and purpose

**Six Traits of Writing:**
*Voice*  the writer's own language

### Writing Process Practice

Think about the audience for your paragraph. Who are your readers? How much do they know about your topic? What information do they need to understand your ideas? Write the answers to these three questions on your paper.

# Gathering Supporting Details

**Research**
To find information about a topic

You have your topic and your main idea. You know why you are writing and who you are writing for. Now you need to find information to support your main idea. Gather details such as facts, reasons, experiences, examples, and quotations from experts. As you look for information, think about what your audience knows and does not know.

The assignment about your favorite kind of movie asks you to explain your choice. The details in this paragraph should be reasons. Where do you get these details? First, look at the ideas you wrote while looking for a topic. Then, think about your main idea. What details would support it?

For some assignments, you will need to **research** to find details that support your main idea. You can find information at a library or on the Internet. You might interview an expert. For the movie assignment, you can gather details just by brainstorming. Read the supporting details that a student listed below.

Topic: My favorite kind of music
Main idea: I like the sound of rap and the messages in the songs.
Supporting details:
The lyrics tell about real-life situations.
It has a good beat that I can dance to.
The ideas in the songs make me think.

 **Six Traits of Writing:**
*Ideas* message, details, and purpose

 **Six Traits of Writing:**
*Organization* order, ideas tied together

**Writing Process Practice**

Look at your favorite movie topic and your main idea. List at least three details that support your main idea.

*Writing Process Handbook* **WPH8**

## Writing Process Practice

Ask students to read the supporting details in the example on page WPH8 and explain how they relate to the main idea. (*Each detail explains something about the sounds or the messages in rap songs.*)

### Writing Process Practice Answer

Answers will vary. A sample answer is given.

**Topic:** My favorite kind of movie

**Main idea:** I love adventure movies because their special effects are so spectacular.

**Supporting details:** Images are changed digitally by computers so that the impossible appears to happen.

Computer-generated images are created electronically but they look real on the screen.

Mechanical effects can make us believe dinosaurs or dragons live among us.

## Six Traits of Writing Focus

| | | |
|---|---|---|
| ✔ Ideas | | Word Choice |
| ✔ Organization | | Sentence Fluency |
| Voice | | Conventions |

## Ideas

As students gather supporting details, have them list as many as they can. Then select the strongest three to use in their paragraph body. To decide which details are strongest, they will need to ask: How does this idea support my main idea? If students need more facts, have them research their topic further on the Internet.

## Organization

After they choose their supporting details, have students consider the order in which these details should be presented. Is there an order that gives the ideas a natural flow? Should details be ordered by their importance? Have students pencil in the numbers *1, 2, 3* beside their details to show the order they want to use.

## Writing Process Practice

Read the directions and ask students what questions they might use to find information about cold packs. (*What are cold packs? Where are they used? Why are they important? How do they work?*)

### Writing Process Practice Answer

Answers will vary. Notes should include sources of information. Sample details are given.

Cold packs contain freezer gel. They replace ice in a cooler to keep foods cold.

They are placed in a freezer to freeze. In a cooler, they draw heat from food, bringing its temperature to a safe level (below 40 degrees Fahrenheit).

This temperature is important to prevent bacteria from multiplying quickly.

## Six Traits of Writing Focus

| ✔ | Ideas | | Word Choice |
|---|---|---|---|
| | Organization | | Sentence Fluency |
| | Voice | | Conventions |

## Ideas

Discuss with students where they might find the answers to their questions on cold packs. Ask what key words they might use for an Internet search. Tell students that it is important to use reliable Web sites. Sites sponsored by government agencies and educational institutions usually provide trustworthy information.

Then have students list questions they could answer in researching their paragraph topics. For example, for special effects in adventure movies, they might ask:

- Who creates special effects?
- What equipment do they need?
- When are special effects added to the movie?

---

# Taking Notes

When you research to gather supporting details, take notes. Many writers like to use index cards to take notes. Your notes are your record of the information you find. One way to take notes is to answer the *wh-* questions. The *wh-* questions are *who, what, when, where,* and *why.* As you search for information and read it, ask yourself these questions. The answers are usually important details.

Suppose a student is writing about a favorite rap artist. The student may not know many details about this artist. Brainstorming will not help. The student needs to research. Here are some questions and notes that the student wrote:

> - Who was an important early rapper?
>   Kool Herc was an important early rapper.
> - What did he do?
>   He said rhyming words over parts of songs he played as a DJ.
> - When did he perform?
>   He performed in the early 1970s.
> - Where did he work?
>   He worked in the Bronx in New York.
> - Why did he emphasize the beat and bring in his own rhyming words?
>   He wanted to make the music good for dancing.

**Six Traits of Writing:**

*Ideas* message, details, and purpose

### Writing Process Practice

Suppose you are writing a paragraph about how cold packs keep food cold. Use the library or Internet to find information on this topic. Then take notes. Write two or three details that could be used in the paragraph.

# Organizing Details in an Outline

**Outline**
A plan for writing a report that lists ideas and details in a certain order

Once you have enough details, you need to organize them. A good way to do this is to create an **outline.** An outline is a plan for writing. It lists the main ideas and supporting details. A writer uses this outline as a guide for writing.

The ideas and details in an outline are written in an order that makes sense. For example, you could order details according to the time they happen. You could order details by importance, starting with the most or least important one. A good order helps the reader follow your ideas.

Look at the outline below. The main idea is labeled with a Roman numeral I. All the details that support this idea go under it. They are labeled with the letters A, B, and C.

> I. I like the sound of rap and the messages in the songs.
> A. The lyrics tell about real-life situations.
> B. It has a good beat that I can dance to.
> C. The ideas in the songs make me think.

This outline is for one paragraph. For a longer assignment, the outline will have more main ideas (I, II, III, and so on). Each main idea will have details under it. Sometimes, an outline needs a third level for listing details under each letter.

## Writing Process Practice

Organize the details about your favorite kind of movie. Make an outline using your main idea and supporting details. Place the details in an order that makes sense.

**Six Traits of Writing:**
*Organization* order, ideas tied together

*Writing Process Handbook* **WPH10**

## Writing Process Practice

Review the format and labeling for an outline. Point out in the example that an outline for a paragraph will not have a section II, since it focuses on one main idea.

### Writing Process Practice Answer

Outlines will vary. A sample outline is given.

I. I love adventure movies for their spectacular special effects.
   A. Computers change images digitally so that the impossible appears to happen. For example, the world stands still but a character moves normally.
   B. Computer-generated images aren't real, but they look real on the screen.
   C. Mechanical effects can make us believe dinosaurs or dragons live among us.

## Six Traits of Writing Focus

| | | |
|---|---|---|
| | Ideas | Word Choice |
| ✔ | Organization | Sentence Fluency |
| | Voice | Conventions |

## Organization

After they write their outlines, have students check the logic of their organization. Items A, B, and C should all be directly related to the main idea in I. The main idea should be stated in broad enough terms that every detail fits within its boundaries. Have students point out which detail in this outline does not belong:

I. Special effects in adventure movies
   A. Computer software
   B. Movie stars that do their own stunts
   C. Camera techniques

(*B does not belong.*)

# Drafting

## GOALS FOR LEARNING

- To write a topic sentence for a paragraph
- To write a body of supporting details
- To write a conclusion or summary for a paragraph

## Key Vocabulary Words

**Drafting** The writing step of the writing process

**Draft** An early version of writing; not the final version

**Topic sentence** A sentence that states the main idea of a paragraph; usually the first sentence of a paragraph

**Indent** To start a sentence a certain distance from the left margin

**Body** The sentences in a paragraph that explain and support the main idea

**Conclusion** A logical decision or opinion based on facts or evidence; the sentence at the end of a paragraph

**Summary** A sentence at the end of a paragraph that repeats the main idea using different words

# Writing the Topic Sentence

**Drafting**
The writing step of the writing process

**Draft**
An early version of writing; not the final version

**Topic sentence**
A sentence that states the main idea of a paragraph; usually the first sentence of a paragraph

**Six Traits of Writing:**
*Ideas* message, details, and purpose

**Six Traits of Writing:**
*Voice* the writer's own language

**Six Traits of Writing:**
*Sentence Fluency* smooth rhythm and flow

You have completed the prewriting process. The next step is **drafting,** or writing your ideas down on paper. A **draft** is an early version of writing. It is not perfect, so do not worry about writing a finished paragraph. Later, you will make your first draft better.

Paragraphs begin with a **topic sentence.** This sentence states the main idea of the paragraph. All other sentences in the paragraph will explain or support the topic sentence.

The topic sentence is the first sentence to be read. It should be interesting. It should grab the reader's attention. After reading it, the reader will want to read more.

Look at the sample outline on page WPH10. It lists the main idea. Use this to write an interesting topic sentence. Notice how the topic sentence below states the main idea.

> Topic: My favorite kind of music
> Main idea: I like the sound of rap and the messages in the songs.
> Topic sentence: Rap is my favorite kind of music because I like the sound of it and the messages in the songs.

## Writing Process Practice

Look at the outline you created about your favorite kind of movie. Use it to write a draft of your topic sentence.

## Writing Process Practice

Ask a volunteer to explain how the topic and main idea have been combined in the example topic sentence.

### *Writing Process Practice Answer*

Topic sentences will vary. A sample answer is given.

Adventure movies are my favorite because they have it all—danger, thrill after thrill, and (most of all) spectacular special effects.

## Six Traits of Writing Focus

| | | | |
|---|---|---|---|
| ✔ | Ideas | | Word Choice |
| | Organization | ✔ | Sentence Fluency |
| ✔ | Voice | | Conventions |

### Ideas

Students might highlight the key words in statement I of their outline from page WPH10, then combine the words in different sentences that express what they want to say about the topic. Remind students that their topic sentence should attract interest. Have students think about what makes them interested in their topic.

### Voice

Have students read their topic sentence to a partner. The partner should give feedback on what they think the topic is and whether the sentence sounds natural or forced.

### Sentence Fluency

With their partners, have students suggest other wordings for the topic sentence. For example, its rhythm and interest may be varied by adding an introductory phrase or adverb.

## Writing Process Practice

Remind students that a draft does not need to be neat or even well written. It is a way to get down onto paper the ideas a writer needs to include.

### Writing Process Practice Answer

Answers will vary. A sample paragraph is given.

Computers can change images in a movie to make the impossible seem real. For example, a character can move while the rest of the world stands still. Scenes can also be totally computer generated, like a background with a sixteenth century castle on a hill and dragons flying around it. With mechanical effects, moving models can make us believe that dinosaurs live among us.

### Six Traits of Writing Focus

| | | | |
|---|---|---|---|
| ✔ | Ideas | | Word Choice |
| ✔ | Organization | ✔ | Sentence Fluency |
| ✔ | Voice | | Conventions |

### Ideas

As they write the body of their paragraph, have students think about how each detail sentence is related to the topic sentence. This relationship should suggest an appropriate wording for the detail sentence.

### Organization

Remind students that they ordered their details according to a rationale in their outlines on page WPH10. The order should be maintained as they write their drafts. If the order no longer seems appropriate, they may change it to make it more logical.

### Voice

Have students write their detail sentences as though they were speaking to a friend. Remind them that their personal interest in the topic should shine through their words.

---

# Writing the Body

**Indent**
To start a sentence a certain distance from the left margin

**Body**
The sentences in a paragraph that explain and support the main idea

To start your paragraph, write the topic sentence at the top of your paper. Remember to **indent** the first line. Now you are ready to write the **body** of the paragraph. The body explains and supports the main idea. It contains all of the supporting details.

The body of a piece of writing can be several sentences or several paragraphs long. The length depends on the writing assignment. Each paragraph you write should have a topic sentence followed by supporting details.

Use your outline as a guide to help you write the body of your paragraph. Your outline lists your supporting details. Use these details to build the body of your paragraph. Write a sentence about each of these ideas. Write the ideas in the order shown on your outline.

Compare the paragraph below to the outline on page WPH10. Notice how the details from the outline make up the body of the paragraph.

 **Six Traits of Writing:**
*Ideas* message, details, and purpose

 **Six Traits of Writing:**
*Organization* order, ideas tied together

 **Six Traits of Writing:**
*Voice* the writer's own language

 **Six Traits of Writing:**
*Sentence Fluency* smooth rhythm and flow

> Rap is my favorite kind of music because I like the sound of it and the messages in the songs. The lyrics tell about real-life situations. It has a good beat that I can dance to. The ideas in the songs make me think.

### Writing Process Practice

Look at the details in the outline you wrote. The details tell why you like the kind of movie you chose. Use these details to write the body of your paragraph.

---

## Sentence Fluency

Students might read their drafts to a partner. If the draft seems awkward, the partners can decide why. For example, sentences may be too short, ideas may have been left out, or the order of ideas may be confusing.

# Writing the Conclusion or Summary

**Conclusion**
A logical decision or opinion based on facts or evidence; the sentence at the end of a paragraph

**Summary**
A sentence at the end of a paragraph that repeats the main idea using different words

Most paragraphs end with a **conclusion** or a **summary.** This sentence closes the paragraph for the reader. A conclusion is a logical decision or opinion based on the supporting details. A summary is a sentence that sums up the paragraph or repeats the main idea using different words. The last sentence tells the reader what to remember about the paragraph.

Make the conclusion or summary interesting. You want the reader to remember it. If you are writing to persuade, your conclusion should move the reader to agree with your idea. Use this sentence to sum up the paragraph details in a logical and convincing way.

Look at the following conclusion. Do you see how it sums up the paragraph?

 **Six Traits of Writing:**
*Ideas* message, details, and purpose

 **Six Traits of Writing:**
*Voice* the writer's own language

 **Six Traits of Writing:**
*Sentence Fluency* smooth rhythm and flow

> Conclusion: I like rap music the best because I can relate to it.

### Writing Process Practice

Decide how you will end your paragraph about your favorite kind of movie. What do you want your readers to remember? How can you sum up the paragraph in an interesting way? Write your conclusion.

*Writing Process Handbook* **WPH14**

## Writing Process Practice

Have students compare the example conclusion sentence to the example topic sentence in the draft on page WPH13. How are they similar? (*Both state "rap is favorite" or "best" and bring in the writer by stating "I like".*) How are they different? (*The conclusion adds a new element about being able to relate to rap.*)

### *Writing Process Practice Answer*

Answers will vary. A sample answer is given.

Adventure films like *Jurassic Park* and The *Lord of the Rings* are the best because they make the impossible very real to us in a thrilling way.

## Six Traits of Writing Focus

| | | | |
|---|---|---|---|
| ✔ | Ideas | | Word Choice |
| | Organization | ✔ | Sentence Fluency |
| ✔ | Voice | | Conventions |

### Ideas

Point out to students that, while the final sentence in a paragraph must relate to their main idea, it cannot simply restate the topic sentence. To write this sentence, have students look back at their paragraph and ask themselves: What is all this leading up to? Why did I write this paragraph?

### Voice

Encourage students to choose their words to create interest and also to blend in with the rest of their paragraph. If they have written in language that is natural to them, the whole paragraph will then have a consistent voice.

### Sentence Fluency

Part of the interest generated by the final sentence may come from the way it is constructed. If all the detail sentences have a similar syntax (for example, subject—action verb—direct object), then writers may choose to give the final sentence a different structure (for example, subject—linking verb— predicate adjective, or a question).

# Revising

- To revise a draft to match the purpose and audience
- To revise the organization of a draft
- To revise the content of a draft
- To make your writing flow smoothly

## Key Vocabulary Words

**Revise**  To change a piece of writing to make it better

**Content**  The information in a piece of writing

**Transition**  A change from one thing to another; often a change in time, place, situation, or thought

**Revise**
To change a piece of writing to make it better

# Revising to Match the Purpose and Audience

You have written a first draft. After drafting, the next step in the writing process is revising.

When you **revise** your writing, you change it to make it better. First, read your draft aloud. How do the words and ideas sound? If possible, have someone else read your draft and suggest ideas for making it better.

Check the writing prompt or assignment directions. Does your draft match the assignment? Did you follow the directions? Think about the purpose of the assignment. Does your draft match this purpose?

Also think about your audience. Your teacher—and maybe other students—will read your writing. Will it be clear to them? Have you used any words or ideas they do not know? Define words that might be unfamiliar. Add basic explanations so your audience will not be confused.

Look at the paragraph below. Notice that the writer defined *lyrics* and added words to make the ideas clearer.

⬤ **Six Traits of Writing:**
*Voice* the writer's own language

> Rap is my favorite kind of music because I like
> the sound of it and the messages in the songs.
> *or words,* *Rap*
> The lyrics ^ tell about real-life situations. It ^
> *lively rhythm*
> has a good beat. I can dance to it. The ideas in
> *about important issues.*
> the songs make me think^. I like rap music the
> best because I can relate to it.

⬤ **Six Traits of Writing:**
*Word Choice* vivid words that "show, not tell"

## Writing Process Practice

Read your paragraph aloud to another student. Ask him or her to tell you which words and ideas are hard to understand. Revise your paragraph so your audience will understand it. Also, revise it to meet the purpose you want.

## Writing Process Practice

Ask students to identify the revisions in the example and explain why they were made. Have students work with a partner or a small group to get feedback.

## *Writing Process Practice Answer*

Answers will vary. A sample answer is given.

Adventure movies are my favorite because they have spectacular special effects. Computers can change images in a movie to make the impossible seem real. For example, a character can move while the rest of the world stands still. Scenes can also be totally computer generated, like a background wiht a sixteenth century castle on a hill and dragons flying around it. With mechanical effects, moving models can make us believe that dinosaurs live among us. Aventure films like *Jurassic Park* and *The Lord of the Rings* are the best because they make the impossible very real to us in a thrilling way.

## Six Traits of Writing Focus

| | | | |
|---|---|---|---|
| | Ideas | ✔ | Word Choice |
| | Organization | | Sentence Fluency |
| ✔ | Voice | | Conventions |

## Voice

Make it clear to students that "using their own language" does not mean that they should choose vague or inaccurate words. For example, if a student overuses clichéd words such as *cool* or *awesome*, they will need to think of replacements that give a specific picture to readers of the qualities they want to express.

## Word Choice

As they revise their paragraphs, have students think about alternative words and phrases that will create clear images (word pictures) in readers' minds and draw readers in by appealing to their five senses. At the same time, students' sentences should never deviate from the main purpose expressed in the topic sentence.

## Writing Process Practice

Explain to students that in this practice, they will decide whether their details would be more logical if their order were changed.

### Writing Process Practice Answer

Answers will vary but changes in order should improve the flow or logic of the paragraph. A sample answer is given.

Adventure movies are my favorite because they have spectacular special effects. Some adventure movies use mechanical effects. For example, models of dinosaurs can move along with the actors and make us believe that dinosaurs live among us. Computers can change images in a movie to make the impossible seem real, like a character moving as the rest of the world stands still. Scenes can also be totally computer generated, like a whole background with a sixteenth century castle on a hill and dragons flying around it. Adventure films like *Jurassic Park* and *The Lord of the Rings* are the best because they make the impossible very real to us in a thrilling way.

### Six Traits of Writing Focus

|   |   |   |   |
|---|---|---|---|
|   | Ideas |   | Word Choice |
| ✔ | Organization |   | Sentence Fluency |
|   | Voice |   | Conventions |

## Organization

At this point, students must identify the organizing principle behind their writing. Talk with students about basic rationales for organization:

- a cause followed by an effect
- events in time order
- steps in order of completion
- ideas that build in importance

After they identify the best principle for organizing their paragraphs, ask students to check their sentences to see if they follow this order.

---

# Revising the Organization

Each paragraph you write should have three parts. Does the topic sentence state the main idea? Does the body explain and support the main idea? Does the summary or conclusion help the reader remember the paragraph?

The body of your writing contains all of the details. Check the organization of these details. Although you followed an outline, sometimes you can see ways to improve it.

If the body of your writing is several paragraphs, look at the order of paragraphs, too. Should any paragraphs be moved? Would a different order make more sense?

One way to organize details is by importance. Often, writers give the most important detail or reason first. Sometimes, they save the most important one for last. Another way to order details is by time. Events are presented in the order they happened. Steps in a process are presented in the order they should be done.

Look again at the paragraph about rap music. The writer has decided to put the most important reason last.

> Rap is my favorite kind of music because I like
> the sound of it and the messages in the songs.
> The lyrics, or words, tell about real-life situations.
> Rap has a lively rhythm. I can dance to it. The
> ideas in the songs make me think about important
> issues. I like rap music the best because I can
> relate to it.

**Six Traits
of Writing:**

*Organization*  order, ideas tied together

### Writing Process Practice

Revise your paragraph about your favorite kind of movie. Organize the details in a way that will help the reader.

# Revising the Content

**Content**
The information in a piece of writing

Revise the **content** of your writing. The content is the information in your writing. Read your draft, especially the body of details. Ask yourself: Is anything missing? Was an important supporting detail left out? Sometimes, after taking a break, you may reread your draft and notice something you need to add.

Next, remember that each sentence in a paragraph must support the topic sentence. Read your draft again and ask yourself: Does each detail support the main idea? If a detail in a paragraph does not relate to the topic sentence, take it out. Also take out extra words that are not necessary. Make your writing clean.

Notice how the writer added content to this paragraph:

> Rap is my favorite kind of music because I like the sound of it and the messages in the songs. Rap has a lively rhythm. I can dance to it. The lyrics, or words, tell about real-life situations. The ideas in the songs make me think about important issues. I like rap music the best because I can ~~relate to it.~~ it speaks to what I think and how I feel.

Revise your draft by adding new content or taking out content that does not fit.

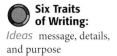

**Six Traits of Writing:**
*Ideas* message, details, and purpose

### Writing Process Practice

Read your draft about your favorite kind of movie. Look for ways to make the content of your draft better. Add any missing details. Take out details that are not needed.

## Writing Process Practice

Remind students that they can change their paragraphs at any stage of the writing process. If they question a detail or its wording, it probably should be changed, worded more clearly, or replaced.

### Writing Process Practice Answer

Answers will vary. A sample answer is given.

Adventure movies are my favorite because they have spectacular special effects. Some adventure movies use mechanical special effects, such as realistic models of dinosaurs that move along with the actors. Computer-generated images can be placed into a live action scene to make a sixteenth century castle appear real. No real person could do what an adventure hero does, but filmmakers reduce images digitally to computer data. They add, remove, or change objects on the film and make the impossible happen. A character can move while the rest of the world stands still. Adventure films such as *Jurassic Park* and *The Lord of the Rings* thrill us by taking us into an impossible world that seems real.

## Six Traits of Writing Focus

| ✔ | Ideas | | Word Choice |
|---|-------|---|-------------|
| | Organization | | Sentence Fluency |
| | Voice | | Conventions |

## Ideas

Students can use these questions to analyze the ideas expressed in their sentences:

- How does this sentence relate to my main idea?
- Is my paragraph more focused on the topic if I remove this sentence?
- What other idea(s) would help my readers better understand my topic?

Have students use the answers to these questions to delete irrelevant details and add missing details.

## Writing Process Practice

Point out that the topic sentence is not just a statement of the main idea. It is also the way writers draw readers into the message. Emphasize the importance of transitions and talk about the relationships they show, like cause and effect (*as a result, so, because, therefore*), time (*after, first, then, when, finally*), and example (*for example, for instance, that is, such as*).

## Writing Process Practice Answer

Answers will vary. A sample answer is given.

What could be more exciting than an adventure movie filled with spectacular special effects? Some adventure movies use mechanical special effects, such as realistic models of dinosaurs that move along with the actors. Computer-generated images can also be placed into a live action scene to make a sixteenth century castle appear real. No real person could do what an adventure hero does, but film makers make the impossible happen by reducing images digitally to computer data so they can add, remove, or change objects on the film. For example, a character can move while the rest of the world stands still. Adventure films such as *Jurassic Park* and *The Lord of the Rings* thrill us by taking us into an impossible world that seems real.

## Six Traits of Writing Focus

| | Ideas | | Word Choice |
|---|---|---|---|
| | Organization | ✔ | Sentence Fluency |
| ✔ | Voice | | Conventions |

## Sentence Fluency

Have students count the words in their sentences to see how they vary in length. Ask them to revise sentences so that some have more than 10 words and some have fewer. Then have them look for transitions and add them to make sentences sound smoother. (There is a partial list in the fourth bulleted point on page WPH19. List other transitions on the board.)

---

# Making Your Writing Flow

**Transition**
A change from one thing to another; often a change in time, place, situation, or thought

You want your writing to be interesting and easy to read. You want it to flow smoothly. This happens when sentences are well built. Here are ways to make your ideas flow:

- Revise your topic sentence to make it more interesting. It should get the reader's attention.
- Use different types and lengths of sentences.
- Use a variety of sentence beginnings. Start some sentences with an adverb phrase or clause.
- Use **transitions** to connect related sentences. These words and phrases help the reader move from one idea to the next. They help the writing flow. Some common transitions are *also, finally, most important, next, in addition, first, for example, therefore,* and *then*.
- Revise your sentences so they sound like you. Use your own words. Help the reader "hear" your voice.
- Revise your conclusion so that your readers will remember it. Make your conclusion a strong one.

The following changes make this paragraph smoother:

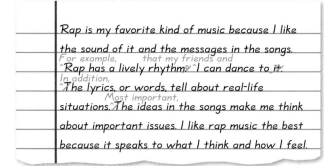

● **Six Traits of Writing:**
*Sentence Fluency* smooth rhythm and flow

● **Six Traits of Writing:**
*Voice* the writer's own language

### Writing Process Practice

Read your paragraph about your favorite kind of movie. Look for ways to make the sentences flow smoothly.

---

## Voice

After revising length and wording of some sentences, have students read their paragraph aloud and pinpoint any language that sounds unnatural for them or their audience.

**PART D**

# Editing
# and Proofreading

## GOALS FOR LEARNING

- To edit for word choice and spelling
- To edit for grammar
- To edit for capitalization and punctuation
- To use proofreading marks

## Key Vocabulary Words

**Edit** To correct mistakes in a piece of writing; to check spelling, punctuation, capitalization, grammar, and word choice

**Thesaurus** A book that lists words that are similar in meaning

**Grammar** A set of rules for writing and speaking a language

**Proofread** To mark editing changes on paper using proofreading marks

*Writing Process Handbook* **WPH20**

## Writing Process Practice

Caution students that thorough editing requires reading their work carefully several times. Point out that this handbook shows them one way to break the editing process down into stages.

## Writing Process Practice Answer

Answers will vary. A sample answer is given.

What could be more exciting than an adventure movie filled with spectacular special effects? Some adventure movies use mechanical special effects, such as lifelike models of dinosaurs that move along with the actors. Computer-generated images can also be placed into a live action scene to make a sixteenth century castle appear actual. No real person could do what an adventure hero does, but filmmakers make the impossible happen by reducing images digitally to computer data so they can add, remove, or change objects on the film. For example, a character can move while the rest of the world stands still. Adventure films such as *Jurassic Park* and *The Lord of the Rings* thrill us by bringing a fantastic world vividly to life.

## Six Traits of Writing Focus

|   | Ideas | ✔ | Word Choice |
|---|---|---|---|
|   | Organization |   | Sentence Fluency |
| ✔ | Voice | ✔ | Conventions |

### Voice

At this point, student writers will benefit by reading their work aloud to a partner to see if their changes have created unnatural or stilted phrasing. Any portions of the paragraph that confuse or distract listeners need more work.

### Word Choice

Suggest to students that they circle words that are repeated and consider replacing some with synonyms. Students should be cautious, however, because some synonyms may only be interchangeable in certain contexts and most synonyms have different degrees of meaning.

**Edit**
To correct mistakes in a piece of writing; to check spelling, punctuation, capitalization, grammar, and word choice

**Thesaurus**
A book that lists words that are similar in meaning

**Six Traits of Writing:**
*Voice* the writer's own language

**Six Traits of Writing:**
*Word Choice* vivid words that "show, not tell"

**Six Traits of Writing:**
*Conventions* correct grammar, spelling, and mechanics

# Editing for Word Choice and Spelling

After you revise your writing, you are ready to edit it. When you **edit**, you check your writing for mistakes in grammar, spelling, capitalization, and punctuation. You also improve your choice of words.

Using just the right words is important. Your words make the message. Choose words that sound like you and express your ideas. Your writing should have your "voice."

In a draft, you may have used some words too often. Other words may be too general. They do not create a sharp picture. Replace common or general words with more specific ones. Choose specific nouns, verbs, adjectives, and adverbs. Add prepositional phrases. A book called a **thesaurus** can help. It lists words with similar meanings.

As you edit, check your spelling. Some words sound the same, such as *their* and *there*. Use a dictionary to check the spellings you are not sure about.

Notice how the writer edited this paragraph:

A kind of Jamaican music had a ~~big~~ *an important* influence on rap music in America. In Jamaica, blues dances were held outdoors or in a big hall. A DJ, or person who played music, set up a ~~big~~ *loud* sound system. It needed to be ~~big~~ *powerful* so many dancers could hear the ~~base~~ *bass* line beat. The DJ would ~~say~~ *chant* words over the music.

### Writing Process Practice

Revise your paragraph. Look for words that are used too often. Replace general words with more specific ones. Check your spelling.

## Conventions

Caution students that the spell check function of a computer cannot correct spelling errors such as using *their* for *there* or dropping a letter (using *our* instead of *hour*). Students may work with a partner to help them look for spelling errors. Be sure to have dictionaries available for student reference.

# Editing for Grammar

**Grammar** is a set of rules for writing and speaking a language. You know a lot of grammar already just from speaking and listening to others. Still, it is easy to make grammar mistakes. Use these guidelines as you edit:

- Make every sentence a complete thought. Fix all sentence fragments and run-on sentences.
- Check that each pronoun has a clear antecedent. The pronoun and antecedent must agree in gender and number.
- If a subject is singular, the verb form must be singular. If the subject is plural, the verb form must be plural.
- Check verb forms. Irregular verbs do not use *-d* or *-ed* to form the past tense. For example, the past tense of *see* is *saw*. Check a dictionary to help you decide which verb form is correct.
- Check the tenses of your verbs. The tense should be the same throughout your writing. Do not go back and forth between present tense and past tense.

Notice how the writer edited this paragraph:

> Today's rapper is a singer, speaker, and poet.
> All rolled into one. He or she chants a kind
> of street poetry. The ideas ~~be~~ *are* rhymed ~~they~~ *, and*
> have a strong rhythm. In early rap, lines were
> ~~speaked~~ *spoken* to the rhythm of a record.

**Six Traits of Writing:**
*Conventions* correct grammar, spelling, and mechanics

### Writing Process Practice

Edit your paragraph for grammar. Fix any sentence fragments or run-on sentences. Check subject-verb agreement. Check verb forms and verb tenses.

## Writing Process Practice

Point out to students that the rules for each bulleted point are taught in this textbook and summarized in Appendix A: Editing Handbook.

### *Writing Process Practice Answer*

Answers will vary. Students' corrections should show understanding of subjects, predicates, pronouns, subject-verb agreement, verb forms, and verb tenses.

### Six Traits of Writing Focus

| | | | |
|---|---|---|---|
| | Ideas | | Word Choice |
| | Organization | | Sentence Fluency |
| | Voice | ✔ | Conventions |

## Conventions

Students may refer to Appendix A for more guidance about the bulleted points on page WPH22. Suggest that they read through their paragraph once for each bulleted item. First, they should check sentences to be sure each has a subject and verb. Then they should identify pronouns and their antecedents and evaluate accuracy, and so on. Have dictionaries available for student reference.

## Writing Process Practice

Review basic rules of capitalization and punctuation with students by having them read aloud the bulleted list. Provide an example sentence on the board for each rule.

### *Writing Process Practice Answer*

Corrections will vary but should reflect an understanding of proper nouns, sentence conventions, and punctuation marks.

## Six Traits of Writing Focus

|  | Ideas |  | Word Choice |
|---|---|---|---|
|  | Organization | ✔ | Sentence Fluency |
|  | Voice | ✔ | Conventions |

### Conventions

Point out to students that punctuation shows when ideas begin and end or are interrupted. By reading their work aloud, they can hear whether they have incorrectly inserted end marks, created sentence fragments, or created run-on sentences. If students are uncertain about rules for capitalization, have them refer to Appendix A in the textbook.

### Sentence Fluency

As they correct sentence errors such as fragments and run-ons, students will find the flow of sentences improves and the logic of their ideas becomes clear.

# Editing for Capitalization and Punctuation

Which words should you capitalize? Every sentence begins with a capital letter. Proper nouns, such as *Springfield High School* or *Jackpine Road,* also use capital letters.

Punctuation marks make the meaning of your writing clear.

- Every sentence should end with a period (.), a question mark (?), or an exclamation point (!).
- Use a comma and a conjunction to join two sentences.
- If you list three or more items in a series, use a comma after each item except the last one.
- Use an apostrophe (') in contractions and in possessive nouns: *That's the dog's bowl.*
- Use quotation marks (" ") around the exact words of a speaker: *Nadia said, "That's the dog's bowl."*
- Use quotation marks around the titles of songs, short stories, and poems: *"Take Me Out to the Ball Game."*

Notice how the writer edited this paragraph:

> Kool Herc made a name for himself as a DJ. He
> worked in the bronx, new york, in the 1970s. with
> a powerful sound system and two turntables, he
> made special music. He would replay sections of a
> record with a heavy beat. Herc would talk over
> the music to people in the crowd he might say,
> "Yo, this is kool herc in the joint-ski saying my
> mellow-ski Marky D is in the house."

**Six Traits of Writing:**
*Conventions* correct grammar, spelling, and mechanics

**Six Traits of Writing:**
*Sentence Fluency* smooth rhythm and flow

### Writing Process Practice

Check the capitalization and punctuation in your paragraph. Fix any mistakes you find.

# Using Proofreading Marks

**Proofread**
To mark editing changes on paper using proofreading marks

Sometimes you may be editing your writing on a computer. At other times, you may be editing a paper copy.

You are **proofreading** when you mark editing changes on a paper copy. When you edit your writing on paper, you can use special marks called proofreading marks. You have seen these marks in this handbook. They are shown in blue in the samples.

Here are some common proofreading marks:

### Proofreading Marks

| | | | |
|---|---|---|---|
| Delete or take out | ℉ | Insert an apostrophe | ⌄ |
| Spell out | ⓈⓅ | Insert quotation marks | ⌄ |
| Insert | ∧ | Change to lowercase | / |
| Insert space | # | Change to capital letter | ≡ |
| Insert a period | ⊙ | Close up; take out space | ◯ |
| Insert a comma | ∧ | Begin a paragraph | ¶ |
| Insert a semicolon | ⋏ | Transpose letter or words | ∿ |

### Writing Process Practice

Copy the following paragraph. Then use proofreading marks to show how to fix the mistakes.

```
    Rap music is part of a culture known
as Hip-Hop. The turm hip-hop was first
used. In the 1979 recording rapper's
delight. Hip-hop also includes other form's
of Expression. Brake dancing and loose
clothing are part of hip-hops culture, to.
```

## Writing Process Practice

Display unedited paragraph of text on an overhead projector (or write it on the board). Demonstrate proper use of the proofreading marks on page WPH24 using a second color.

### Writing Process Practice Answer

```
    Rap music is part of a
culture known as Hip-Hop.
            term
The turm hip-hop was first
used. In the 1979 recording
rapper's delight. Hip-hop
also includes other form's
of Expression. Brake dancing
and loose clothing are part
of hip-hops culture, to.
```

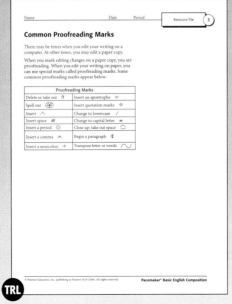

Resource File 3

# PART E

# Publishing and Presenting

## GOALS FOR LEARNING

- To prepare to publish a piece of writing
- To publish or present a piece of writing

### Key Vocabulary Words

**Publish** To share a written or visual message with others

**Word-processing program** A computer program, or software, used to write, revise, edit, and format a document

**Font** A style of type

# Preparing to Publish

**Publish**
To share a written or visual message with others

To **publish** means to share your writing with others. All your hard work has led up to this step. Publishing is the final step in the writing process.

In some ways, publishing is the most important step. It lets you share your ideas with others. When others enjoy your work, you feel good. You want to write more. Publishing is also a way to give something to others. Your writing may teach the reader something. It may help the reader to understand a new idea or opinion.

Finally, publishing prepares you for the future. In other school or work situations, you may have to write reports, letters, notes, or memos. You should feel comfortable sharing your writing with others.

You can publish your writing in many forms. You might give it to your teacher after writing it by hand or on a computer. You might post it on a bulletin board or read it aloud to others. You might create a poster or give a slide show or speech. Your writing could be published in a class book, a school newspaper, or a writing magazine.

As you prepare to publish, take time to think about the writing process you just finished. How did you do? By reviewing your writing process, you will learn how to do even better next time. Ask yourself these questions:

- What would I do the same next time?
- What would I do differently next time?
- What parts of the writing process do I need to work on?

## Writing Process Practice

With a group, brainstorm a list of ways to publish a piece of writing. For each way of publishing, describe the audience that you would reach.

*Writing Process Handbook* **WPH26**

## Writing Process Practice

You may want to have some volunteers explore opportunities for publishing writing in magazines or Web sites. A good reference in the library is *Literary Market Place*.

## *Writing Process Practice Answer*

Answers will vary but should show understanding of who reads or listens to each publication. A list of publishing opportunities not described in the text follows:

newsletters

private blogs

radio programs

poetry slams

## Writing Process Practice

Have students practice reading their paragraphs aloud until they can do so smoothly and with proper expression and pacing.

### *Writing Process Practice Answer*

Speeches will vary but should show familiarity with the material as well as natural and clear expression with appropriate pitch, volume, and gestures.

# Publishing and Presenting

**Word-processing program**
A computer program, or software, used to write, revise, edit, and format a document

**Font**
A style of type

You often publish your writing on paper. Before you hand in your finished work, think about its format.

- Consider adding photos, drawings, or diagrams. They can make your message clearer and stronger.
- Give your writing a title if one is needed.
- Use only one side of the paper.
- Make sure your name and date is on the paper. Your teacher may ask you to list other details.
- If you are handing in a longer report, you may need a title page or cover sheet.

If you are writing on a computer, you are using a **word-processing program.** It allows you to revise, edit, and format your writing easily.

- Use the program's spelling and grammar checker. This feature does not catch every mistake, but it catches many of them.
- Format your writing according to your teacher's directions. You may need to use a certain margin width, **font,** font size, or line spacing. A font is a style of type. If your work is to be part of a poster or bulletin board, choose a font and font size that are easy to read.

Not all writing is published only on paper. You may be asked to give a speech or presentation. This is a talk given to a group of people. When you are preparing a speech, use the checklist in Appendix B at the back of this book. Before you listen to someone else's speech, read the listening checklist in Appendix C.

### Writing Process Practice

Prepare a speech. Present your paragraph to the class. Then listen carefully as others present their paragraphs. After the speeches, say what you liked about each one.

When you create a piece of writing, you move through five steps. This writing process helps you organize your ideas and form them into well-built sentences and paragraphs. The five steps of the writing process are summarized below.

- **Prewriting** Prewriting is the planning step. First, you read your writing assignment carefully and think about your writing purpose. Then you decide what to write about. You gather and organize your ideas and supporting details. You take notes. During all this planning, you keep your audience in mind.

- **Drafting** In the drafting step, you put your ideas into sentences. Then you build your sentences into one or more paragraphs. Each paragraph you write should have a topic sentence, a body of supporting details, and a summary or conclusion. Your first draft will have mistakes that you will fix later.

- **Revising** Revising means making your writing better. When you revise, you check that your writing matches the purpose and audience. You decide whether to put the ideas and details in a different order. You decide whether to add or take away information. You look for ways to make your writing flow smoothly.

- **Editing and Proofreading** Editing means fixing mistakes in your writing. You fix mistakes in spelling, punctuation, and capitalization. You fix grammar mistakes, such as run-on sentences and wrong verb forms or tenses. You also choose better words as you edit. You replace general words with more specific words that will create a mental picture for the reader. If you edit a paper copy of your writing, you can use proofreading marks.

- **Publishing and Presenting** In the last step of the writing process, you prepare your final work to be published. You check the page format of your work. You consider adding photos or pictures. Then you share your writing with others. You may publish your writing by handing in a paper copy. You may also publish it by presenting it to a group.

*Writing Process Handbook*   **WPH28**

## Writing Process Summary

Have volunteers read aloud each Summary item on page WPH28. Then ask volunteers to explain each writing process step in their own words.

## Writing Process Review Answers

### Part A

1. editing and proofreading
2. prewriting 3. drafting 4. publishing and presenting 5. revising

### Part B

6. to describe 7. to explain 8. to persuade 9. to tell a story

### Part C

10. C 11. D 12. C 13. B

---

## WRITING PROCESS REVIEW

### Steps in the Writing Process

prewriting

drafting

revising

editing and
  proofreading

publishing and
  presenting

### Writing Purposes

to tell a story

to explain

to persuade

to describe

**Part A** Use the box at the left. Match each description below with a step in the writing process. Write the step.

1. correcting mistakes and choosing better words

2. preparing and planning what you will write

3. writing a topic sentence, a body, and a conclusion

4. sharing your writing with others

5. changing your writing to make it better

**Part B** Use the box at the left. Match each writing prompt below with a purpose for writing. Write the purpose.

6. Tell about one of your favorite places.

7. Tell how to fix or make something.

8. Should your school have a dress code? Give three reasons for your answer.

9. Share an experience when you had to be brave.

**Part C** Write the letter of your answer.

10. What is a draft?
    **A** a writing outline that puts the details in order
    **B** the part of a paragraph that states the main idea
    **C** an early version of writing that is not final
    **D** a style of type in a word-processing program

11. How can a thesaurus help you when you edit?
    **A** It gives sample topic sentences.
    **B** It gives rules for grammar.
    **C** It lists proper nouns.
    **D** It lists words with similar meanings.

12. Which of the following is *not* a supporting detail?
    **A** a fact   **B** an example   **C** a topic   **D** a reason

**13.** Which of the following is *not* a part of a paragraph?
   **A** topic sentence  **B** outline  **C** conclusion  **D** body

**Part D** Write your answer to each question.

**14.** What is the purpose of brainstorming?

**15.** Give three reasons why prewriting is important.

**16.** Why is it important to narrow a writing topic?

**17.** Why is it wise to make an outline before you write?

**18.** What is the purpose of a topic sentence in a paragraph?

**19.** What do details add to a piece of writing?

**20.** What is the purpose of a conclusion?

**21.** Why is it important to organize the sentences in your paragraph?

**22.** How do you improve your writing when you revise it?

**23.** What kinds of mistakes do you look for when you edit?

**24.** What do you use proofreading marks for?

**25.** List two ways you might publish a piece of writing.

## Writing Process Review Answers
### Part D

Answers will vary. Sample answers are given.

**14.** Brainstorming provides a writer with ideas for writing or with details to use as support. These ideas and details come from prior knowledge. **15.** Prewriting helps writers be sure they understand their purpose, focus on an appropriate topic, and organize their ideas. **16.** If a writing topic is too broad, then the writing will be too general or incomplete because there is too much information to fit into the space allowed. **17.** An outline organizes your ideas in a logical order. The writer refers to it while writing. **18.** The topic sentence states the main idea of the paragraph and grabs the reader's attention. **19.** Details add support to the main idea. They explain or flesh it out by giving facts, examples, reasons, and so on. **20.** A conclusion closes a paragraph by stating a logical decision or opinion based on supporting details. **21.** The organization of sentences allows the reader to follow ideas easily. **22.** When you revise, you delete, add, or move parts to make sure your ideas are clearly stated and your reader will understand them. **23.** When you edit, you correct mistakes in spelling, grammar, punctuation, and capitalization. You also replace overused or vague words with synonyms or vivid words. **24.** Proofreading marks are a shorthand way of showing what needs to be corrected in your paper and how to correct it. **25.** To publish your writing, you could read it aloud or post it on a bulletin board or the Internet.

# PLANNING GUIDE

# Writing Sentences

| | Student Pages | Student Lesson | | | Language Skills | | | | |
|---|---|---|---|---|---|---|---|---|---|
| | | Vocabulary | Practice Exercises | Lesson Review | Identification | Writing | Punctuation & Capitalization | Grammar & Usage | Listening, Speaking, & Viewing |
| **Lesson 1-1** Beginning and Ending a Sentence | 3–5 | ✔ | ✔ | ✔ | ✔ | ✔ | ✔ | ✔ | ✔ |
| **Lesson 1-2** Understanding the Purpose of a Sentence | 6–10 | ✔ | ✔ | ✔ | ✔ | ✔ | ✔ | ✔ | ✔ |
| **Lesson 1-3** Finding the Subject and Predicate | 11–14 | ✔ | ✔ | ✔ | ✔ | ✔ | ✔ | ✔ | ✔ |
| **Lesson 1-4** Correcting Sentence Fragments | 15–18 | ✔ | ✔ | ✔ | ✔ | ✔ | ✔ | ✔ | ✔ |
| **Lesson 1-5** Correcting Run-On Sentences | 19–25 | ✔ | ✔ | ✔ | ✔ | ✔ | ✔ | ✔ | ✔ |

## Chapter Activities

**Teacher's Resource Library**
Life Skills Connection 1: Writing
   Complete Answers to Questions
Writing Tip 1: The Purpose of a
   Sentence
English in Your Life 1: Writing a
   Letter of Thanks
Building Research Skills 1: Using an
   Encyclopedia
Key Vocabulary Words 1

## Assessment Options

**Student Text**
Chapter 1 Review

**Teacher's Resource Library**
Chapter 1 Mastery Tests A and B

**Teacher's Edition**
Chapter 1 Writing Portfolio

| English in Your Life | Writing on the Job | Building Research Skills | Vocabulary Builder | Grammar Builder | Write About It | Group Activity | Reading Strategy | Six Traits | ELL/ESL Strategy | Background Information | Common Error | Life Skills Connection | Applications (Home, Career, Community, Global) | Online Connection | Teacher Alert | Speaking & Presenting Practice | Writing/Spelling/Grammar Practice | Auditory/Verbal | Body/Kinesthetic | Interpersonal/Group Learning | Logical/Mathematical | Visual/Spatial | Activities | Modified Activities | Workbook Activities | Self-Study Guide |
|---|---|---|---|---|---|---|---|---|---|---|---|---|---|---|---|---|---|---|---|---|---|---|---|---|---|---|
| | | | 5 | | | | 3, 4 | | 5 | 3 | 4 | | | | | | 4 | | 5 | 4 | 4 | | 1 | 1 | 1 | ✔ |
| | | | | | | | 7, 9 | | 7 | 6 | | 8 | 6, 9 | | 8, 9 | | 7 | 7 | | | | | 2 | 2 | 2 | ✔ |
| | | 14 | | | | | 12, 13 | | 13 | 11 | 13, 14 | | | | 11, 13 | 12 | 13, 14 | | 12 | | | 12 | 3 | 3 | 3 | ✔ |
| | | | | | 18 | | 15, 17 | 18 | 16 | 15 | | | 16, 17 | | | | | | | 17 | | | 4 | 4 | 4 | ✔ |
| 23 | 24 | | | | | 25 | 19, 21 | | 21 | 19 | | | | 25 | 20 | | 21 | 20 | | | 20 | | 5 | 5 | 5 | ✔ |

## Pronunciation Key

| | | | | | | | | | | | |
|---|---|---|---|---|---|---|---|---|---|---|---|
| a | hat | e | let | ī | ice | ô | order | u̇ | put | sh | she |
| ā | age | ē | equal | o | hot | oi | oil | ü | rule | th | thin |
| ä | far | ėr | term | ō | open | ou | out | ch | child | ℠H | then |
| â | care | i | it | ȯ | saw | u | cup | ng | long | zh | measure |

ə { a in about / e in taken / i in pencil / o in lemon / u in circus }

## Modified Activities

The Teacher's Resource Library (TRL) contains a set of lower-level worksheets called Modified Activities. These worksheets cover the same content as the standard Activities but are written at a lower reading level.

## Skill Track

Use Skill Track for *Basic English Composition* to monitor student progress and meet the demands of adequate yearly progress (AYP). Make informed instructional decisions with individual student and class reports of lesson and chapter assessments. With immediate and ongoing feedback, students will also see what they have learned and where they need more reinforcement and practice.

## Chapter 1:
## Writing Sentences
pages 1–27

## Lessons

## Skill Track for
## Basic English
## Composition

## Teacher's Resource Library TRL

Activities 1–5

Modified Activities 1–5

Workbook Activities 1–5

Life Skills Connection 1

Writing Tip 1

English in Your Life 1

Building Research Skills 1

Key Vocabulary Words 1

## Chapter 1 Self-Study Guide

## Chapter 1 Mastery Tests A and B

(Answer Keys for the Teacher's Resource Library begin on page 446 of the Teacher's Edition.)

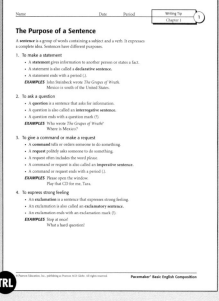

### The Purpose of a Sentence

A **sentence** is a group of words containing a subject and a verb. It expresses a complete idea. Sentences have different purposes.

1. To make a statement
   - A **statement** gives information to another person or states a fact.
   - A statement is also called a **declarative sentence**.
   - A statement ends with a period (.).
   - **EXAMPLES** John Steinbeck wrote *The Grapes of Wrath*.
     Mexico is south of the United States.

2. To ask a question
   - A **question** is a sentence that asks for information.
   - A question is also called an **interrogative sentence**.
   - A question ends with a question mark (?).
   - **EXAMPLES** Who wrote *The Grapes of Wrath*?
     Where is Mexico?

3. To give a command or make a request
   - A **command** tells or orders someone to do something.
   - A **request** politely asks someone to do something.
   - A request often includes the word *please*.
   - A command or request is also called an **imperative sentence**.
   - A command or request ends with a period (.).
   - **EXAMPLES** Please open the window.
     Play that CD for me, Tara.

4. To express strong feeling
   - An **exclamation** is a sentence that expresses strong feeling.
   - An exclamation is also called an **exclamatory sentence**.
   - An exclamation ends with an exclamation mark (!).
   - **EXAMPLES** Stop at once!
     What a hard question!

### Writing Complete Answers to Questions

You write the answers to questions on tests and assignments. When you apply for a job, you write answers to questions about yourself. Always write your answers as complete sentences. A complete sentence gives a complete idea. It has both a subject and a predicate. Answering questions in complete sentences shows that you have understood the question. To write the answer as a sentence, you repeat part of the question.

**Question:**  What kind of sentence asks a question?
**Answer:**  An interrogative sentence asks a question.
**Question:**  Why should Carl's Diner hire you?
**Answer:**  Carl's Diner should hire me because I am a hard worker.

**Step 1**  Look through one or two chapter tests from one of your subjects, or ask a teacher to loan you a chapter test he or she has given in the past. Find questions on the tests that ask you to write out an answer.

**Step 2**  Write three questions from these tests on the lines below.

**Step 3**  Decide the answer to each question. Talk to friends, family, or your teacher if you need help with the answer.

**Step 4**  Write a sentence that answers each question. Circle the part of the question and the answer that are the same.

**EXAMPLES** How many syllables are in the word *relaxation*?
There are four syllables in the word *relaxation*.

1. _____
2. _____
3. _____

# Writing Sentences

Composition is the act of writing. This book will help you become a better writer. Learning to write is a series of steps. First you learn the basic writing skills. Then you build on these skills.

Each chapter in this book begins with a photo. Each photo shows a different step in a typical student's day. As the photos take you on a "journey" through a student's day, the chapters take you through the steps to becoming a better writer. Learning to write well is another kind of journey.

The photo on the opposite page shows a good breakfast. A good breakfast gets your day started the right way. Chapter 1 will get you started in composition the right way. You will learn how to write sentences correctly. The sentence is the basic building block for writers.

## GOALS FOR LEARNING

- To find the beginning and ending of an idea
- To understand the four purposes of sentences
- To find the subject and predicate in a sentence
- To recognize and correct sentence fragments
- To recognize and correct run-on sentences

1

## Introducing the Chapter

Have students study the photo of a breakfast meal. Encourage them to discuss why they think a good breakfast is a good way to begin their day. Write some comments on the board. Ask volunteers to identify those that are sentences. Tell students that in Chapter 1 they will begin their study of writing by learning about sentences and how they are constructed.

Review and discuss the Goals for Learning on page 1.

## Notes

Ask volunteers to read the notes that appear in the margins throughout the chapter. Then discuss them with the class.

### TEACHER'S RESOURCE

The AGS Globe Teaching Strategies in English Transparencies may be used with this chapter. The transparencies add an interactive dimension to expand and enhance the *Basic English Composition* program content.

### WRITING PORTFOLIO

Ask students to write at least 10 sentences that describe or tell about themselves and their friends. Have them skip several lines between sentences. If students are unsure whether they are writing sentences, suggest that they write 10 important ideas about their subject. Encourage students to add symbols and sketches to help their ideas begin to flow. As they complete each lesson in the chapter, students can return to their sentences and revise them according to what they are learning. This project may be used as an alternative form of assessment for the chapter.

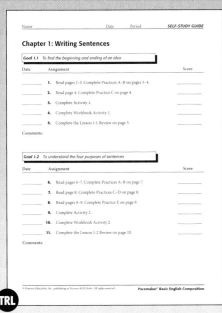

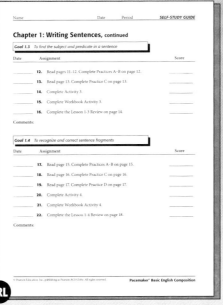

Chapter 1 Self-Study Guide, pages 1–3

## Reading Strategy: Summarizing

After students read the explanation, point out that they summarize when they tell a friend about a movie they have enjoyed. Model (or have a volunteer model) telling what a familiar movie is about in a few sentences. Suggest that students pause after reading paragraphs in the chapter and ask, *What is the main thing being said about this topic?*

........................................................

## Key Vocabulary Words

comma fault
compound sentence
conjunction
declarative sentence
exclamatory sentence
imperative sentence
interrogative sentence
noun
phrase
predicate
pronoun
run-on sentence
sentence
sentence fragment
simple sentence
subject
tense
verb
verb phrase

As you read aloud the words, have students read the definitions and ask any questions they have. If students are confused, provide an example or illustration for the term. Write the following headings on the board: *Kinds of Sentences, Parts of Speech (Jobs for Words), Sentence Parts, Sentence Mistakes.* Then ask students to identify the category under which each term can be written.

........................................................

# Reading Strategy: Summarizing

To summarize means to state a main idea briefly. You can ask questions to help you summarize what you read. As you read this chapter, ask yourself: What is this chapter about?

## Key Vocabulary Words

**Sentence** A group of words that expresses a complete thought

**Declarative sentence** A sentence that states a fact

**Interrogative sentence** A sentence that asks a question

**Imperative sentence** A sentence that gives a command or makes a request

**Exclamatory sentence** A sentence that expresses strong feelings

**Simple sentence** A sentence with one subject and one predicate

**Subject** The part of a sentence that names the person, place, thing, or idea that the sentence is about

**Noun** A word that names a person, place, thing, or idea

**Pronoun** A word that replaces a noun in a sentence

**Predicate** The part of a sentence that tells something about the subject; the predicate always contains a verb

**Verb** A word that expresses action or state of being; the main part of a predicate

**Tense** The time expressed by a verb

**Phrase** Two or more words that work together

**Verb phrase** A main verb and one or more helping verbs

**Sentence fragment** A group of words that does not express a complete thought; a part of a sentence

**Run-on sentence** Two or more ideas written as one sentence without correct punctuation or a conjunction

**Conjunction** A word that connects related words or groups of words

**Comma fault** The use of a comma instead of end punctuation to separate two sentences

**Compound sentence** Two or more related ideas that are connected with a conjunction

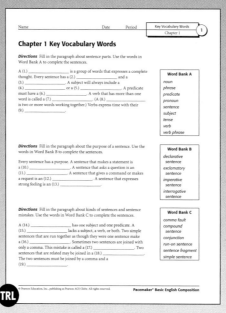

# Beginning and Ending a Sentence

## Objectives

- To write a complete sentence
- To move words around in a sentence without changing the meaning

**Sentence**

A group of words that expresses a complete thought

 **Brush Up on the Basics**

A sentence begins with a capital letter and ends with a punctuation mark. See Grammar 1 in Appendix A.

*Reading Strategy:* Summarizing

What are some important details that help you understand what a sentence is?

As a writer and a speaker, you have ideas to share. You express each idea with a group of words called a **sentence.** A sentence is a group of words that expresses a complete thought.

Here are two important rules for writing sentences.

**Rule 1** Use a capital letter to begin the first word of a sentence. A capital letter is the uppercase form of a letter. It tells the reader where a new idea begins.

**Rule 2** End each sentence with an end punctuation mark. The mark tells the reader where a complete idea ends. Use a period, a question mark, or an exclamation mark to end a sentence. The period is the most common end punctuation mark. Never end a sentence with a comma.

▶ **EXAMPLE 1**

| Incorrect | my friend Derek plays soccer |
| Correct | My friend Derek plays soccer. |

Get in the habit of reading your sentences aloud. You can hear where each idea begins and ends.

### Practice A

Find three sentences in this group of words. Add capital letters and end punctuation marks. Write the sentences on your paper.

in his junior year, Derek Anderson met Amber Choy and Sonia Moreno they liked him the three friends decided to work on fitness together

## Practice A

Have partners decide where each sentence begins and ends. Write the corrected sentences on the board. Have a volunteer read the sentences aloud and explain how he or she can tell when each idea begins and ends.

### Practice A Answers

In his junior year, Derek Anderson met Amber Choy and Sonia Moreno. They liked him. The three friends decided to work on fitness together.

**2** Teaching the Lesson

After students read page 3, have a volunteer summarize the rules for writing sentences. Read the example aloud and have students explain how to correct it. Ask a volunteer to tell what the sentence is about.

### *Reading Strategy:* Summarizing

A sentence expresses a complete thought. It begins wth a capital letter. It ends with an end punctuation mark.

## Lesson at a Glance

### Chapter 1 Lesson 1

**Overview** This lesson gives the rules for capitalizing and punctuating a simple sentence and discusses how word order affects sentence meaning.

### Objectives

- To write a complete sentence
- To move words around in a sentence without changing the meaning

### Student Pages 3–5

### Teacher's Resource Library

Activity 1

Modified Activity 1

Workbook Activity 1

## Vocabulary

sentence

Write the definition for *sentence* on the board as a sentence with blanks. Have students fill in the blanks to complete the definition.

## Background Information

In conversation and dialogue, complete sentences are not always necessary to communicate ideas. When these exchanges are written down, however, they are written as though they were sentences, using capital letters and end marks. Students should understand that for most assignments and work-related writing, they are expected to communicate ideas clearly. This means they must use complete sentences and capitalize and punctuate them correctly.

**1** Warm-Up Activity

Ask students to tell in their own words what makes a sentence "a complete idea." Read several word groups, such as *a very strong man* or *playing in the park* and have students explain what each group of words needs to make it a complete idea.

## Practice B

Suggest that students think about which words work together to complete a thought about what a subject is or does.

### Practice B Answers

In the past, Derek was a shy person. He spent a lot of time alone. Then he met Amber and Sonia. They were friendly. The girls and Derek quickly became friends.

### Reading Strategy: Summarizing

A sentence begins with a capital letter. It ends with an end punctuation mark.

## Practice C

Read the Example 2 sentences aloud. Point out that, in English, the subject usually comes before the verb in a sentence. However, some sentences begin with a word that is not the subject.

### Practice C Answers

**1.** Often Derek and Brandon go to the lake. **2.** Now it is too cold for camping. **3.** Instead they decided to hike. **4.** For three hours, the boys walked eagerly. **5.** Sometimes hikers see deer in the woods.

### 3 Reinforce and Extend

## Writing Practice

Have students review a written assignment and check for sentence completeness. Then have students experiment with changing the word order in some sentences. Pair students and have them read both versions.

### COMMON ERROR

Beginning writers often fail to vary the structure of their sentences. This makes writing monotonous. Point out that the subject does not have to be the first word in a sentence. Encourage students to try adding words to the following sentence and moving them around to vary it: *Dogs bark.*

---

### Reading Strategy:
Summarizing

What two rules do you need to know for Practice B?

## Practice B

Find five sentences in this group of words. Write them on your paper. Use capital letters and end punctuation marks.

in the past, Derek was a shy person he spent a lot of time alone then he met Amber and Sonia they were friendly the girls and Derek quickly became friends

### Word Order

When you write, think about the word order in each sentence. Sometimes you can move the words around without changing the meaning of the sentence. Read the three example sentences. Notice that they all begin differently. Notice that they all have the same meaning.

▶ **EXAMPLE 2**

The weather usually improves by noon.

Usually, the weather improves by noon.

By noon the weather usually improves.

## Practice C

Find a word in each sentence that you can move to the beginning. Rewrite each sentence on your paper. Capitalize the first word in each sentence.

1. Derek and Brandon go to the lake often.
2. It is too cold for camping now.
3. They decided to hike instead.
4. The boys walked eagerly for three hours.
5. Hikers sometimes see deer in the woods.

---

### LEARNING STYLES

**Logical/Mathematical**
Point out that end punctuation marks in written language work much like mathematical symbols. Ask students to name some mathematical signs, such as +, −, ×, ÷, <, >, and =. Write them on the board and discuss what they communicate to readers.

### LEARNING STYLES

**Interpersonal/Group Learning**
Have students copy a sentence of 12 words or less from a book. Then ask students to write each word of the sentence on a separate card, beginning all words with lowercase letters. Have students mix up their cards. Have students exchange cards and rearrange them into a sentence. Have them write each sentence, using correct capitalization and end punctuation.

# REVIEW

Change the order of the words in each sentence. Write the new sentence on your paper.

1. Brandon Tucker listens to music daily.

2. He prefers rock music lately.

3. He sometimes plays the music loudly.

4. His mother usually complains.

5. He turns the music down then.

Number your paper from 6 to 10. Find five sentences in the paragraph. Write them on your paper. Use capital letters and end punctuation marks.

sometimes one person can make a big difference have you ever heard of Rosa Parks she changed American history she refused to give up her seat on a bus the civil rights movement began with her brave action

## VOCABULARY BUILDER

### Using Context Clues to Find Meaning
Use context clues to help you figure out the meaning of a new word. Context clues are the words around the new word. What does the word *collided* mean in this sentence?

The car speeding north **collided** with the car heading south.

The word *collided* means "crashed together."
Use context clues to decide the meaning of the bold word in each sentence below. Write what you think it means. Then check a dictionary to see if your guess is correct.

1. The oil leak might **contaminate** the lake.

2. She had trouble seeing the chalkboard, so she went to an **optometrist**.

*Writing Sentences*    *Chapter 1*    **5**

---

| | | |
|---|---|---|
| Name    Date    Period | Activity<br>Chapter 1, Lesson 1 | 1 |

**Beginning and Ending a Sentence**

**Directions** Add capital letters and end punctuation to make the following words into three sentences. Write the sentences on the lines.

**EXAMPLE** School will end soon Laura is ready for summer her last day is June 12

    School will end soon. Laura is ready for summer.

    Her last day is June 12.

1. Amber received her yearbook today she wants her friends to autograph it together they look at the pictures and laugh.

2. the seniors will graduate at the Capital Center that is a huge building do you know where it is

3. Laura has a job at Pete's Grill Amber will be a lifeguard both girls hope to go to junior college in the fall

4. Laura is looking forward to her summer vacation she is going to see the Grand Canyon in June her parents and brother are going with her

5. graduating is bittersweet everyone is looking forward to moving on to the next phase of their lives everyone is also sad to be leaving behind old friends

**Pacemaker® Basic English Composition**

---

| | | |
|---|---|---|
| Name    Date    Period | Workbook Activity<br>Chapter 1, Lesson 1 | 1 |

**How a Sentence Begins and Ends**

**Directions** Read each group of words. Find the sentences and write them on a separate sheet of paper. Capitalize the first word in each sentence. Put a punctuation mark at the end.

**EXAMPLE** everyone in my family likes yogurt our favorite flavor is strawberry we often have yogurt for a snack

    Everyone in my family likes yogurt.

    Our favorite flavor is strawberry.

    We often have yogurt for a snack.

1. in the spring we planted a garden we planted green peppers and squash first later we planted tomatoes

2. my grandmother sent me a CD for my birthday I wrote a letter to thank her she was pleased

3. my friends and I started a singing group we practice five times a month I think we need more practice

4. today it rained the streets were flooded we could not get our car out of the garage

5. there was an announcement in the newspaper about an upcoming concert tickets go on sale next week I would love to go to that concert

6. yesterday my sister went to the bank she wanted to deposit her paycheck she also wanted to get some quarters for the machines at the laundry

7. I saw an announcement on the bulletin board the coach is having tryouts for the soccer team should I try out

8. every year the garden club has a sale the club members offer many different kinds of plants they tell visitors all about the plants

9. what two things must a writer do first a writer must think of an idea to write about he or she also must decide what to write about the idea

10. my new digital camera takes amazing pictures I love photography I would like to take a class to learn more about it

**Pacemaker® Basic English Composition**

---

Activity 1, pages 1–2            Workbook Activity 1

---

## Lesson 1-1 Review Answers

**1.** Daily Brandon Tucker listens to music. **2.** Lately he prefers rock music. **3.** Sometimes he plays the music loudly. **4.** Usually his mother complains. **5.** Then he turns the music down. **6.** Sometimes one person can make a big difference. **7.** Have you ever heard of Rosa Parks? **8.** She changed American history. **9.** She refused to give up her seat on a bus. **10.** The Civil Rights Movement began with her brave action.

## VOCABULARY BUILDER

Write the example sentence on the board and circle words that give clues to the meaning of *collided*. (*speeding north, heading south*) Invite a volunteer to diagram or model the meaning of the sentence and the new word.

### Vocabulary Builder Answers

Answers may vary but should be similar to those given. **1.** pollute, make dirty **2.** a person who examines eyes and prescribes glasses, an eye doctor

## LEARNING STYLES

**Body/Kinesthetic**
Invite students to walk around the room and select an object. Ask each student to use the word for the object in a sentence.

## ELL/ESL STRATEGY

**Language Objective:** *To read aloud sentences using capitals and punctuation as clues to expression*

Students learning English as a second language will benefit from reading aloud simple sentences containing mostly familiar vocabulary. Write sentences such as the following on the board: *I like this music. What is the answer? We got lost in the city. Can you help us, please?* Translate the sentences into a familiar language for students. Have students read aloud the familiar version, and then listen as you read the English version to compare inflection and rhythm.

*Writing Sentences*    **5**

### Chapter 1 Lesson 2

**Overview** This lesson classifies sentences based on their purpose (giving information, asking questions, making commands, and expressing feelings) and identifies the end mark each uses.

#### Objectives

- To identify the purpose of a sentence
- To choose the correct end punctuation for a sentence

**Student Pages** 6–10

**Teacher's Resource Library** 🌀

Activity 2

Modified Activity 2

Workbook Activity 2

Life Skills Connection 1

#### Vocabulary

declarative sentence
exclamatory sentence
imperative sentence
interrogative sentence

Explain the Latin beginnings of *declare* (to make clear), *exclaim* (to cry out), *imperative* (to command), and *interrogate* (to question or ask). Then read the vocabulary words aloud and have students read the definitions and predict the purpose of each kind of sentence.

#### Background Information

Exclamatory sentences should make up a very small percentage of written language. The exclamation point suggests strong feeling. It is not called for at the end of polite commands or requests. When it is overused, the exclamation point makes the writer's voice seem shrill or silly and the mark loses its ability to create excitement or feeling in the reader.

---

### LESSON 1-2

# Understanding the Purpose of a Sentence

#### Objectives
- To identify the purpose of a sentence
- To choose the correct end punctuation for a sentence

**Declarative sentence**
A sentence that states a fact

**Interrogative sentence**
A sentence that asks a question

**Imperative sentence**
A sentence that gives a command or makes a request

**Exclamatory sentence**
A sentence that expresses strong feeling

There are four main reasons for writing a sentence.

A **declarative sentence** gives information. It states a fact and ends with a period. A declarative sentence is also called a statement.

▶ **EXAMPLE 1**

Derek enjoys sports.

Annapolis is the capital of Maryland.

My friend saved a seat for me in class.

An **interrogative sentence** asks a question. It ends with a question mark.

▶ **EXAMPLE 2**

Are you going to the movies?

Where is Denver?

An **imperative sentence** is a command or request. It tells someone to do something. It ends with a period.

▶ **EXAMPLE 3**

Eat this sandwich if you are hungry. (command)

Please register to vote. (request)

An **exclamatory sentence** expresses strong feelings. It ends with an exclamation mark. Any kind of sentence can express strong feelings. The person who writes the sentence decides.

**6** Chapter 1 *Writing Sentences*

---

### 1 Warm-Up Activity

Write the sentence *Joey is here* three times on the board. End the sentence first with a period, then with a question mark, and finally with an exclamation mark. Have students discuss how the meaning changes depending on the end mark.

### 2 Teaching the Lesson

Ask volunteers to read the explanations for each kind of sentence aloud. Then have students make up their own sentences and punctuate them correctly. Point out that a request is a politely worded command. Discuss which kind of sentence students think occurs most.

### 3 Reinforce and Extend

#### IN THE COMMUNITY

Ask students to look closely at signs, billboards, and posters they see in business windows. Have them copy sentences from at least five different sources, making sure to write the correct end mark for each sentence. Assign students to groups and have them tally the number of declarative, interrogative, imperative, and exclamatory sentences they found in public places.

▶ EXAMPLE 4

I am so hungry! (statement)

Vote today! (command)

What are you doing! (question)

## Practice A

Read the following conversation between Derek Anderson and Amber Choy. Write the purpose of each sentence on your paper. Choose from these four purposes:

- To make a statement
- To ask a question
- To give a command or make a request
- To express strong feeling

1. Amber: What do you think of Mr. Lamar's music class?

2. Derek: I like the old recordings.

3. Amber: Wow, tell me more!

4. Derek: I wish I could have heard Louis Armstrong.

5. Amber: Wasn't he a jazz musician?

## Practice B

Read the conversation between Amber Choy and Sonia Moreno. The end punctuation marks are missing. Identify the purpose of each sentence. Then write the end punctuation mark that matches this purpose.

1. Sonia: Are you as hungry as I am

2. Amber: I'm starving

3. Sonia: Is it lunchtime yet

4. Amber: Look at your watch

5. Sonia: It's only ten o'clock

**Reading Strategy:**
Summarizing

What important idea about sentences does this lesson contain?

## Practice A

Ask volunteers to take the roles of Amber and Derek and read their conversation aloud. Then have students tell the purpose of each sentence and explain how they knew the purpose.

### *Practice A Answers*

1. to ask a question  2. to make a statement  3. to make a request and to express strong feeling  4. to make a statement  5. to ask a question

## Practice B

Ask volunteers to read a completed sentence aloud and explain why they chose its end punctuation mark.

### *Practice B Answers*

1. Are you as hungry as I am?  2. I'm starving!  3. Is it lunchtime yet?  4. Look at your watch.  5. It's only ten o'clock! (or .)

## ELL/ESL STRATEGY

**Language Objective:** *To write sentences with correct English syntax and punctuation*

Students whose first language is not English may be accustomed to other rules of syntax and punctuation. For example, in French, adjectives usually follow the nouns they describe. In Spanish, a question requires two question marks: one before and one after the sentence. Write several simple sentences in English on the board, putting each in its own column. Include at least one statement and one question. Identify the subject and verb in each sentence. Then invite volunteers to write the same sentence in their native language under the English version and identify the subject and verb. Remind students that the purpose of the sentence remains the same in each language. Discuss with students the differences in word order and punctuation.

## LEARNING STYLES

### Auditory/Verbal

Ask pairs of students to take turns making up and saying aloud complete sentences. Instruct students to include at least one question, one statement, one command, and one exclamation. Have partners identify the purpose of each sentence they hear: to make a statement, to ask a question, to give a command or make a request, or to show strong emotion.

## Writing Practice

Pair students and tell them they will interview each other. Have students write at least three questions they want to ask their partner. Explain that the questions should require more than a *yes* or *no* answer. Students can exchange questions and write answers that are complete sentences. Have students conduct their interviews using their questions and answers.

**Reading Strategy:** Summarizing

Different sentence types serve different purposes.

## TEACHER ALERT

Have volunteers read the example questions and answers. Point out the difference in inflection between a question and a statement. Have students note the way words are reordered to form a statement from a question.

## LIFE SKILLS CONNECTION

When students answer test questions, it is best for them to write the answers as complete sentences. This assures that they have internalized what the question is asking. Distribute copies of Life Skills Connection 1. Have students identify the words that appear in both the question and the answer in the example. You may choose to have students work in small groups to complete the worksheet. Then have students write one question they expect to see on a test. Students can exchange questions with a partner and write an answer to the question.

## Practice C

Have students read each sentence and point out the mistake in capitalization or punctuation. Encourage students to identify the kind of sentence each is.

## Practice C Answers

**1.** Have you ever eaten a mango? **2.** No, I haven't. **3.** What is a mango? **4.** A mango is a tropical fruit. **5.** It is sweet and juicy.

## Practice D

You may want to brainstorm a list of famous people and invite volunteers to talk about their achievements before having students write their questions.

## Practice D Answers

Questions will vary. Sample questions are given. **1.** Why did you fight in the Revolutionary War? **2.** Why were you chosen to lead the army? **3.** When did you believe the colonists would win the war? **4.** How did you feel when you became the first president of the United States? **5.** What was the hardest thing about being president?

## Punctuation: Questions and Answers

Always put a question mark at the end of a question. An answer to a question is a statement. Use a period at the end of an answer. Study the punctuation in Example 5.

▶ **EXAMPLE 5**

| Question | When did Abraham Lincoln become president of the United States? |
|---|---|
| Answer | Abraham Lincoln became president in 1861. |
| Question | Who invented the light bulb? |
| Answer | Thomas Edison invented the light bulb. |

### Practice C

Read the sentences. Find the mistakes. Write each sentence correctly on your paper.

1. have you ever eaten a mango?
2. No, I haven't?
3. What is a mango.
4. A mango is a tropical fruit?
5. it is sweet and juicy.

### Practice D

Think of five questions that you might use to interview a famous person. Write them on paper. Start each sentence with a capital letter. End each sentence with the correct punctuation mark.

**Reading Strategy:** Summarizing

What should you remember about exclamatory sentences?

## Punctuation: Exclamations

Say the sentences in Example 6 out loud. The words are the same, but the sentence with the exclamation mark expresses a stronger feeling. Use an exclamation mark only when you want to express extra emotion.

**Reading Strategy:** Summarizing

Exclamatory sentences express strong feelings and end with an exclamation mark.

▶ EXAMPLE 6

| Statement | It is very late. |
| Exclamation | It is very late! |
| Command | Write to me. |
| Exclamation | Write to me! |

### Practice E

Decide whether each sentence should end with a period or an exclamation mark. Choose an exclamation mark if the sentence shows strong feeling. If the sentence does not show strong feeling, choose a period. Write the end punctuation mark on your paper.

1. Amber is learning to drive
2. She took a lesson from her father
3. One lesson was enough
4. Oh, watch out
5. You're going too fast

*What a great day to practice driving!*

## Practice E

Have students work in pairs to decide which sentences logically express strong feeling. Then have them choose the appropriate end marks.

### *Practice E Answers*

1. . 2. . 3. . or ! 4. ! 5. !

## Lesson 1-2 Review Answers

**1.** to ask a question, ? **2.** to express strong feeling, ! **3.** to give a command or make a request, . **4.** to make a statement, . **5.** to make a statement, . **6.** What a great tennis player Arthur Ashe was! to express strong feeling **7.** He was more than that. to make a statement **8.** He was a true hero. to make a statement **9.** What book will Brandon choose for his report? to ask a question **10.** Derek is reading a biography. to make a statement

## WRITING PORTFOLIO

**Checkpoint** Have students check their 10 sentences for the following:

- Does each one express a complete thought?
- What is the purpose of each sentence?
- Does each sentence use the correct end mark?

As they answer the questions, have students improve their sentences.

---

Read each sentence. The end punctuation mark is missing. Decide the purpose of each sentence. Write the purpose of each sentence on your paper. Then write the punctuation mark that belongs at the end.

1. Did Ms. Ruiz assign books to read

2. What a fun assignment

3. Please choose a biography

4. It tells the story of someone's life

5. Derek's book is about Arthur Ashe

Look for mistakes in the following sentences. Rewrite each sentence with the correct capitalization and punctuation. Then write the purpose of each sentence.

6. What a great tennis player Arthur Ashe was?

7. He was more than that?

8. he was a true hero.

9. what book will Brandon choose for his report!

10. Derek is reading a biography?

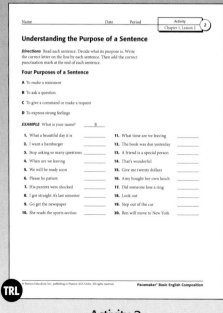

Activity 2

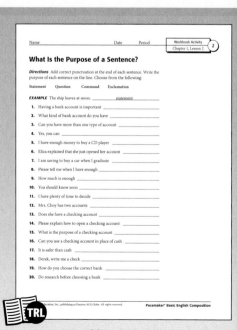

Workbook Activity 2

# Finding the Subject and Predicate

### Objectives

- To identify subjects and predicates in a sentence
- To find verbs or verb phrases in a sentence

**Simple sentence**
A sentence with one subject and one predicate

**Subject**
The part of a sentence that names the person, place, thing, or idea that the sentence is about

**Noun**
A word that names a person, place, thing, or idea

**Pronoun**
A word that replaces a noun in a sentence

**Predicate**
The part of a sentence that tells something about the subject; a predicate always contains a verb

A **simple sentence** has two parts: a subject and a predicate. The **subject** of a sentence is the person, place, thing, or idea that the sentence is about. Every sentence needs a subject. In Example 1, the subject of each sentence is in blue.

▶ **EXAMPLE 1**

The store opens at 6:00 AM.

Joel and his cousin have been working there.

He bags groceries.

She puts groceries on the shelves.

The subject is either a **noun** or **pronoun.** A noun is a word that names a person, place, thing, or idea. A pronoun is a word that replaces a noun. In the last two sentences in Example 1, the subject is a pronoun.

Every sentence also needs a **predicate.** The predicate tells something about the subject. A predicate always has a **verb.** A verb is a word that expresses action or state of being. In Example 2, each predicate is in blue. The verb is underlined.

▶ **EXAMPLE 2**

The store opens at 6:00 AM.

Joel and his cousin have been working there.

He bags groceries.

She puts groceries on the shelves.

In most sentences, the subject comes before the predicate.

### Chapter 1  Lesson 3

**Overview** In this lesson, students learn about subjects, understood subjects, and predicates. They also find the verb or verb phrase and identify its tense.

### Objectives

- To identify subjects and predicates in a sentence
- To find verbs or verb phrases in a sentence

**Student Pages** 11–14

**Teacher's Resource Library**

> **Activity** 3
>
> **Modified Activity** 3
>
> **Workbook Activity** 3

### Vocabulary

| | |
|---|---|
| noun | subject |
| phrase | tense |
| predicate | verb |
| pronoun | verb phrase |
| simple sentence | |

Read the definitions. Then present the following word pairs and have students tell how they are related: *subject/simple subject, predicate/verb, noun/pronoun, phrase/verb phrase.*

### Background Information

While most English sentences place the subject before the verb, there are several exceptions. Commands omit the understood subject *you.* (See the discussion on page 12.)

Questions often place a verb or the first word of a verb phrase before the subject: <u>Will</u> <u>you</u> <u>read</u> this? Where <u>shall</u> <u>we</u> <u>go</u>?

When a sentence begins with *there* or *here,* the subject follows the verb: Here <u>are</u> some good <u>ideas.</u>

Rarely, normal order is inverted to make the subject stand out: Up the street <u>marched</u> the <u>band.</u>

## 1  Warm-Up Activity

Write the following word groups on the board: *An angry storm with high winds and golf-ball-size hail. We stayed inside.* Ask students which word group is a sentence and why. Explain that every sentence must have a subject and a predicate.

## 2  Teaching the Lesson

Read the text explaining subjects. Have students read the example sentences and identify the subjects as nouns or pronouns. Then present the text explaining predicates and verbs. Ask students to use the example sentences to explain the difference between a predicate and a verb.

## TEACHER ALERT

Be sure students understand that the simple subject is a noun or pronoun. The complete subject is this word plus any modifiers. In the first example, *store* is the simple subject, and *the store* is the complete subject. Some subjects contain two important nouns or pronouns. In the second example, *Joel* and *cousin* are the simple subjects in a compound subject. The complete subject is *Joel and his cousin.*

## Practice A

Have a volunteer read the first sentence and identify the subject, predicate, and verb. Write the sentence on the board and model the correct way to indicate each part.

### Practice A Answers

1. Sonia Moreno (plays) the violin. 2. She (enjoys) the orchestra at school. 3. The orchestra (practices) four days a week. 4. Her mother (bought) her a violin. 5. Sonia (memorizes) many pieces of music.

### *Reading Strategy:* Summarizing

Imperative sentences give commands and have an understood subject.

## Practice B

Explain that commands are spoken directly to the person being asked to do something. The word *you* is not spoken, but it is the subject. Ask volunteers to identify the subject and verb in the example sentences.

Remind students to add the word *you* in parenthesis when they write commands.

### Practice B Answers

1. Derek (has) a job at a gas station. 2. He (likes) his boss. 3. The people (come) into the station all day. 4. (You) (fill) up the tank. 5. Derek (enjoys) the work.

## 3  Reinforce and Extend

### Speaking and Presenting Practice

Have pairs of students make a poster showing a picture of a job they would like to have. Beneath the picture, have them set up two columns headed *Subject* and *Predicate*. Then have students write five sentences about this job, placing the subject and the predicate in their respective columns. Last, have students explain their poster, read their sentences aloud, and identify the simple subject and verb in each sentence.

---

**Verb**
A word that expresses action or state of being; the main part of a predicate

**Reading Strategy:** Summarizing

In this lesson, what is the main idea about imperative sentences?

### Practice A

Write each sentence on your paper. Underline the subject of the sentence once. Underline the predicate twice. Then circle the verb.

1. Sonia Moreno plays the violin.
2. She enjoys the orchestra at school.
3. The orchestra practices four days a week.
4. Her mother bought her a violin.
5. Sonia memorizes many pieces of music.

### Imperative Sentences

An imperative sentence does not have a subject. The subject "you" is understood. When you give a command, the subject of the sentence is the person you are talking to.

▶ **EXAMPLE 3**

(You) Please fill up the tank.

(You) Fix my car.

### Practice B

Write each sentence on your paper. Underline the subject once. Underline the predicate twice. Circle the verb. If the subject "you" is understood, write that word on your paper.

1. Derek has a job at a gas station.
2. He likes his boss.
3. The people come into the station all day.
4. Fill up the tank.
5. Derek enjoys the work.

---

## LEARNING STYLES

**Body/Kinesthetic**

Have each student write five sentences using action verbs to tell about an exercise. Pair students and have them exchange sentences and read them aloud. As the sentences are read, have the partner identify the verb and model the action (for example, *lift, step, stretch, circle*).

## LEARNING STYLES

**Visual/Spatial**

Have students who need more visual input write subjects and predicates in different colors. Then have them use a third color to circle the verb.

## WRITING PORTFOLIO

**Checkpoint** Have students revise their Writing Portfolio sentences to be sure each has a subject and predicate.

**Reading Strategy:**
Summarizing

How do the details in
this paragraph help you
understand verbs and
tenses?

**Tense**
The time expressed by
a verb

**Phrase**
Two or more words
that work together

**Verb phrase**
A main verb and one
or more helping verbs

## Verbs and Tenses

The verb in a sentence tells what the subject did or will do.
The verb also expresses **tense.** Tense means time. The verb
tells you *when* the action happened or will happen. Past,
present, and future are examples of tenses.

A **phrase** is two or more words that work together. When
a verb is more than one word, you call it a **verb phrase.**
A verb phrase is the main verb and one or more helping
verbs. To form the future tense, you use the helping verb
*will.* The future tense of a verb is always a verb phrase.

▶ **EXAMPLE 4**

| | |
|---|---|
| Present Tense | Brandon studies Spanish now. |
| Past Tense | Brandon studied Spanish last year. |
| Future Tense | He will study Spanish next year also. |

### Practice C

Find the verb or verb phrase in each sentence. Write the
verb or verb phrase on your paper. Write the tense beside
it. The tense will be present, past, or future.

1. Yesterday Brandon called his friend Derek.

2. They will meet after school.

3. Both of them study Spanish.

4. They do their homework together.

5. Afterwards the two friends will watch TV.

*Writing Sentences    Chapter 1    **13***

---

## ELL/ESL STRATEGY

**Language Objective:**
*To speak and write the
simple tenses of* to be
*correctly*

Students who are learning English as a
second language often have difficulty
mastering the forms of *be,* which are
used often in speaking and writing.
Have students make a table showing
the principal parts for the simple tenses
of *to be.*

| Tense | Singular | Plural |
|---|---|---|
| Present | I am; you are; he, she, it is | We are, you are, they are |
| Past | I was; you were; he, she, it was | We were, you were, they were |
| Future | I will be; you will be; he, she, it will be | We will be, you will be, they will be |

Have students practice the tense forms
by reciting the table aloud. Then have
pairs of students write sentences using
each form to express time, for example:
*I am cold. I was cold. I will be cold.*
*You are cold. You were cold. You will be*
*cold.*

---

## Practice C

Have a student read the meaning of *tense.*
Ask volunteers to change sentence 1 in
Practice B to show past time and future
time. Point out the verb phrase in *Derek
will have a job at a gas station.*

Ask volunteers to read the example
sentences and tell how the basic verb
*study* changes in present, past, and future
tense.

Remind students that the verb or verb
phrase in Practice C is often only a part
of the whole predicate. Their answers
should be one or two words.

### *Practice C Answers*

1. called, past  2. will meet, future  3. study,
present  4. do, present  5. will watch, future

### ***Reading Strategy:*** Summarizing

The details explain how verbs tell when
the subject is or does something: in the
past, present, or future.

### Spelling Practice

Review with students the need to change
the *y* to an *i* before adding verb tense
suffixes if the verb ends in *-y: try + -ed =
tried.* However, if the suffix begins with
an *i,* the *y* is not changed: *try + -ing =
trying.*

Write the following verbs on the board
and have students write the past tense
form for each one and use it in a
sentence: *magnify, empty, spy,* and *pity.*

### TEACHER ALERT

Sometimes writers use the
helping verb *shall* to form
the future tense: *It shall be
done.*

### COMMON ERROR

Many students confuse
verb phrases with
predicates. Explain that
the predicate is all the
words that tell what the subject is or
does, including the verb and its
objects or modifiers. A verb phrase is
simply a verb with more than one
word.

## Lesson 1-3 Review Answers

Answers will vary. Possible answers are given. **1.** <u>We</u> are going to soccer practice. **2.** Amber and Sonia <u>will be at the practice</u>. **3.** <u>Sonia</u> ran quickly down the field. **4.** The muddy field <u>nearly ruined my shoes</u>. **5.** The final score <u>of our last game was 2–0</u>. **6.** <u>The friends</u> ⟨talked⟩ <u>about their favorite music</u>. **7.** <u>Sonia</u> ⟨plays⟩ <u>in the school band</u>. **8.** <u>She</u> ⟨likes⟩ <u>classical music best</u>. **9.** <u>Her friend Brandon</u> ⟨prefers⟩ <u>jazz</u>. **10.** <u>He</u> ⟨will loan⟩ <u>her one of his CDs</u>.

### GRAMMAR BUILDER

Model the difference between a simple subject and a compound subject:

Simple: *The tall girl is their best player.*

Compound: *Amber and Sonia are our best players.*

Point out that compound subjects are joined by a conjunction (*and, or,* or *but*). Explain that, since a compound subject names two or more people, places, or things, it must have a plural verb.

### *Grammar Builder Answers*

**1.** chooses (referee) **2.** writes (teacher) **3.** pick (brothers)

## Grammar Practice

Have students clip a magazine article that interests them and read it to identify at least five sets of subjects and verbs. Have students write these subjects and verbs on their papers in two columns. In a third column, have them identify the verb as singular or plural. Encourage students to use a dictionary to look up spellings of the principal parts of each verb.

### COMMON ERROR

Many students will use the singular form of a verb with compound subjects. They listen for what sounds right with the second half of the subject, as in *he and Megan eats lunch together.* Have students change the compound subject to a pronoun: *They eat lunch together.* The singular form will no longer "sound right."

---

Each group of words needs either a subject or a predicate. Add words to create a complete sentence. Write the sentence on your paper. Underline the words you added.

1. Are going to soccer practice.
2. Amber and Sonia.
3. Ran quickly down the field.
4. The muddy field.
5. The final score.

Write each sentence. Underline the subject once. Underline the predicate twice. Circle the verb or verb phrase.

6. The friends talked about their favorite music.
7. Sonia plays in the school band.
8. She likes classical music best.
9. Her friend Brandon prefers jazz.
10. He will loan her one of his CDs.

### GRAMMAR BUILDER

**Choosing the Right Verb for a Compound Subject**
The parts of a compound subject can be joined by the conjunction *or.* In these sentences, the verb should agree with the noun or pronoun closest to the verb.

**Singular**   Either the puppies or their **mother is** barking.
**Plural**      John or his **cousins work** at the store.

Write the verb that belongs in each sentence. After the verb, write the noun that helped you decide.
1. Either the players or the referee (choose, chooses) the field.
2. The students or their teacher (write, writes) the newsletter.
3. My mom or my brothers (pick, picks) me up from school.

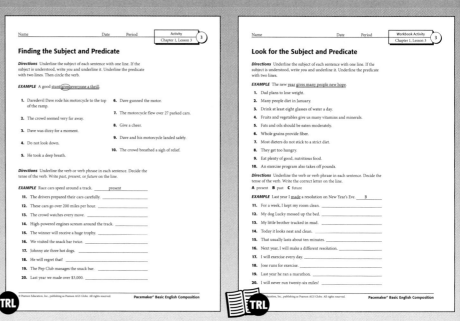

Activity 3                                        Workbook Activity 3

# Correcting Sentence Fragments

## Objectives

- To identify a sentence fragment
- To correct a sentence fragment

**Sentence fragment**
A group of words that does not express a complete thought; a part of a sentence

***Reading Strategy:***
Summarizing

Which information about sentence fragments is most important?

You have learned that a sentence has a subject and a predicate. A sentence also must express a complete thought. A group of words that does not express a complete thought is called a **sentence fragment.**

### Sentences vs. Fragments

The fragment in Example 1 begins with a capital letter and ends with a period. It looks like a sentence, but it does not express a complete idea. What was added to make the fragment a sentence?

▶ **EXAMPLE 1**

| Fragment | The team from Valley View. |
| Sentence | The team from Valley View is strong. |

### Practice A

Decide whether each group of words is a sentence or a fragment. Write *sentence* or *fragment* on your paper.

1. Running laps around the track after school.
2. Most of the other members of the track team.
3. A challenging race.
4. Anyone can enjoy running.
5. You should learn to stretch first.

### Practice B

Make the sentence fragments in Practice A into sentences. Add words to make each group of words express a complete idea. Then underline the words you added.

---

## 2  Teaching the Lesson

Read aloud the example fragment on page 15 and ask students why it is not a complete sentence. (*It lacks a predicate.*) Point out the missing element that has been added to make the fragment a sentence.

### Practice A

Remind students to look for groups of words that express complete ideas.

### *Practice A Answers*

1. fragment 2. fragment 3. fragment
4. sentence 5. sentence

### Practice B

Have students identify the element that is missing in each fragment.

### *Practice B Answers*

Students should correct items 1, 2, and 3 in Practice A. Their sentences will vary. Possible sentences are given. **1.** The team will be running laps around the track after school. **2.** Most of the other members of the track team will be in the weight room. **3.** I am looking forward to a challenging race.

### ***Reading Strategy:*** Summarizing

A sentence fragment does not express a complete idea.

---

## Lesson at a Glance

### Chapter 1  Lesson 4

**Overview**  In this lesson, students learn to identify and correct sentence fragments.

### Objectives

- To identify a sentence fragment
- To correct a sentence fragment

**Student Pages**  15–18

**Teacher's Resource Library**

Activity  4
Modified Activity  4
Workbook Activity  4

### Vocabulary

**sentence fragment**

Explain to students that the word *fragment* comes from a Latin word meaning "break." Have them read the definition for *sentence fragment* and tell how its meaning is related to the Latin meaning. (*It is a piece broken off of a sentence.*)

### Background Information

A common kind of sentence fragment is created when students use a phrase with an *-ing* form of a verb. Explain that verbs ending in *-ing* are not verbs when they are used alone. (They become verbals—they are used as adjectives or nouns.) To form a verb, the *-ing* form must be used with a helping verb.

Fragment: The barn roof *lying* on the ground.

Sentence: The barn roof *was lying* on the ground.

## 1  Warm-Up Activity

Write the following on the board:

*Dogs bark.*
*The dogs in the neighborhood.*

Ask students to identify which one is a complete sentence. (*the first*) Point out that the second group of words may be longer, but it does not express a complete idea.

# Practice C

Read the fragment in Example 2 and ask students what its subject is and what happens in the sentence. (Neither question is answered.) Point out that some fragments lack a subject and a predicate.

After students complete the items, have them tell whether they added a subject, a predicate, or both to each fragment.

## Practice C Answers

Sentences will vary. Possible sentences are given. **1.** The sick player decided to stay home. **2.** Our team will win most of its games with luck and hard work. **3.** The co-captains talk on the telephone every night. **4.** The best teams from Chicago, Detroit, and Toronto will compete for the title. **5.** sentence

**3** **Reinforce and Extend**

## ELL/ESL STRATEGY

**Language Objective:**
*To read word groups analytically to decide if subjects and predicates are present*

Many English language learners struggle with the word order of English sentences, which differs from that of their native language. Fragments are even more confusing because a crucial part of the sentence is missing. Remind students that a subject will contain a noun or pronoun—the *who* or *what* the sentence is about. A predicate will contain a verb, which tells what action the subject performed or describes the subject's state of being. Suggest that students use a chart like the following to help them determine whether a group of words is a fragment or a sentence:

| What does it say? | Who or what is it about? | What happens? |
|---|---|---|
| Decided to stay home. | MISSING | decided to stay home |

If the word group offers no answer to the first question, the subject is missing. If it gives no answer for the second question, the predicate or verb is missing.

---

A sentence fragment leaves the reader asking *what the subject is* or *what happened.* Compare the fragment in Example 2 with the sentence below it.

▶ **EXAMPLE 2**

| Fragment | In the van. |
|---|---|
| Sentence | Everyone rode in the van. |

## Practice C

Decide whether each group of words is a sentence or a fragment. If it is a sentence, write *sentence* on your paper. If it is a fragment, add words to make it a sentence. Write the new sentence on your paper.

1. Decided to stay home.
2. With luck and hard work.
3. Talk on the telephone.
4. From Chicago, Detroit, and Toronto.
5. Derek went to his first soccer tournament.

*Our team won second place in the tournament.*

## CAREER CONNECTION

Point out that writing sentences is a fundamental element of a newspaper writer's job. Explain that the headline for a news story may not express a complete idea. Have students work in small groups to find headlines that are fragments. Work with students to rewrite the headlines as sentences.

**Reading Strategy:**
Summarizing

In a sentence or two, summarize how to correct sentence fragments.

## Fragments in Speech

Speakers often use sentence fragments to answer questions. The person who asks the question usually understands the fragment answer. In Example 3, compare the fragment answer with the sentence answer.

▶ **EXAMPLE 3**

| Question | Which book did you like best? |
|---|---|
| Fragment Answer | The novel. |
| Sentence Answer | The novel was my favorite book. |

**Practice D**

Answer each question with a sentence. Write the sentence on your paper. Each answer should make sense to a reader who does not know what the question is. When you are finished, exchange papers with another student.

1. What is your full name?
2. How old are you?
3. What school do you attend?
4. What is the name of the town or city where you live?
5. What is your favorite TV program?

**LEARNING STYLES**

**Interpersonal/Group Learning**

Divide the class into groups of three. Ask each group to write six sentence fragments. Then ask them to make each sentence fragment into a complete sentence on a second sheet of paper. Have each group read its sentence fragments to the class. Ask the class to make these fragments into complete sentences. Then compare the group and the class sentences.

**Reading Strategy:** Summarizing

Decide what part of the complete idea is missing from a fragment. Add a subject or a predicate or both to make the fragment a sentence.

## Practice D

Ask volunteers to answer the following questions:

*What day of the week is it?*

*How many students are in this class?*

*When do you usually do your homework?*

Point out that people often use fragments to answer questions. However, it is best for students to write answers as complete sentences. Then their answers can stand alone as ideas.

Discuss with students how to identify key words in each question in Practice D and repeat these in their answers.

## *Practice D Answers*

Sentences will vary. Check to be sure that students answered each question with a complete sentence.

## Writing Practice

Ask students to write a list of five questions directed to classmates about interesting places they have been. Tell students to avoid questions that can be answered *yes* or *no.* Have them exchange lists of questions with a partner and then write complete sentences to answer the questions.

**GLOBAL CONNECTION**

Tell students that English speakers often use sentence fragments in common greetings and other salutations, such as *see you later* and *good morning.* Have students say some of these expressions, identify those that are fragments, and make each fragment into a complete sentence. For example, *Have a good morning.* Then have students who speak languages other than English share common salutations from those languages and decide whether each is a complete sentence or a fragment.

## Lesson 1-4 Review Answers

Sentences will vary. Possible sentences are given. **1.** fragment, The trip to the amusement park was fun. **2.** sentence **3.** fragment, "The next time I go there, I will get a pretzel," Amber said. **4.** sentence **5.** sentence **6–10.** Sentences will vary. Check that students answered each question with a complete sentence.

### WRITE ABOUT IT

You may want to offer the following goals to stimulate students' thinking:

• to win a contest

• to join the school newspaper staff

• to get a part in a play

• to volunteer each month

Suggest that before writing their descriptions, students outline information they want to include. Explain that in this prewriting stage they can add, delete, and rearrange details. When students exchange papers, have them look for the following:

• sentence fragments

• capitalized first words

• end marks

• spelling errors

Writers should correct any errors their partners find.

### Six Traits of Writing Focus

| | | | |
|---|---|---|---|
| | Ideas | | Word Choice |
| ✔ | Organization | | Sentence Fluency |
| | Voice | ✔ | Conventions |

## Conventions

As students proofread each other's writing, suggest that they read it several times and focus on only one element at a time. Encourage students to check spellings they are unsure of in a dictionary.

Students may also focus on organization. Discuss with students the need to begin with a statement of the goal and to organize sentences logically.

Refer students to page WPH1 for descriptions of the Six Traits of Writing.

---

# REVIEW

Decide whether each group of words expresses a complete idea. Write *sentence* or *fragment* on your paper. Then correct each fragment by writing a sentence.

**1.** The trip to the amusement park.

**2.** Brandon, Derek, Sonia, and Amber went together.

**3.** "The next time."

**4.** "I might try the roller coaster," said Derek.

**5.** Brandon had eaten five pretzels.

Answer each question with a sentence. Include a subject and predicate. Each answer should make sense to a reader who does not know what the question is.

**6.** What is your favorite book?

**7.** What is your address?

**8.** What is you favorite holiday and why?

**9.** What hobbies do you have?

**10.** What do you like to do for fun?

### WRITE ABOUT IT

**A Personal Goal**

Derek Anderson set a goal to run the 200-meter race. Think about some of your goals. Describe one goal that you would like to achieve. Tell what you are doing, or will do, to achieve your goal. Use complete sentences in your description. When you are finished, exchange papers with another student. Read your partner's description. Check to see if the sentences have correct capitalization and punctuation. Check for fragments and run-on sentences. Encourage your partner to reach his or her goal.

● **Six Traits of Writing:**
*Conventions* correct grammar, spelling, and mechanics

**18** *Chapter 1 Writing Sentences*

---

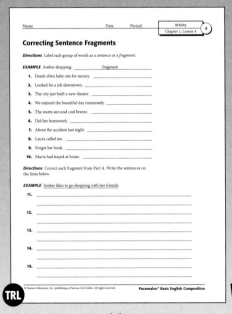

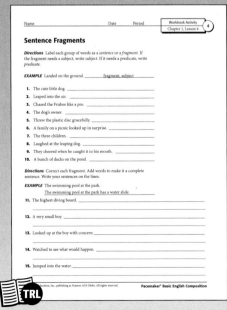

**Activity 4**

**Workbook Activity 4**

# Correcting Run-On Sentences

A **run-on sentence** has two or more ideas incorrectly written as one sentence. A run-on sentence often combines two or more sentences with no punctuation between them.

▶ **EXAMPLE 1**

| Run-On | Derek and Brandon like soccer they play as often as they can. |
| Correct | Derek and Brandon like soccer. They play as often as they can. |

## Dividing a Run-On Sentence

The easiest way to correct a run-on sentence is to divide it into separate sentences. Review these rules:

**Rule 1** Capitalize the first word in a sentence.

**Run-on sentence**

Two or more ideas incorrectly written as one sentence

**Rule 2** End a sentence with the correct punctuation mark. Periods, question marks, and exclamation marks are all end punctuation marks.

**Rule 3** Do not end a sentence with a comma.

### Practice A

**Reading Strategy:**
Summarizing

What main idea about run-on sentences does this paragraph contain?

Fix each run-on sentence by dividing it into two sentences. Capitalize the first word. Use correct end punctuation. Write the new sentences on your paper.

**1.** Do you have an extra soccer ball mine is lost.

**2.** Meet me at the field we can play for an hour.

**3.** Derek and Brandon practiced for several days they tried out for the school team.

**4.** Brandon is a fast runner he hopes to make the team.

**5.** Derek agreed with him he hopes to be chosen also.

---

Explain that the sentence on the board and the example sentence on page 19 are run-on sentences. They combine two or more ideas without punctuation or conjunctions. Have a volunteer split the sentence on the board into two sentences:

*Jody rides horses. Like me, she has taken lessons for several years.*

Review sentence punctuation. Point out that a sentence may end with a period, a question mark, or an exclamation mark.

## Practice A

When they have finished, have students read their corrected sentences.

### Practice A Answers

1. Do you have an extra soccer ball? Mine is lost. 2. Meet me at the field. We can play for an hour. 3. Derek and Brandon practiced for several days. They tried out for the school team. 4. Brandon is a fast runner. He hopes to make the team. 5. Derek agreed with him. He hopes to be chosen also.

### Reading Strategy: Summarizing

A run-on sentence is two or more sentences run together without punctuation between them.

## Lesson at a Glance

### Chapter 1 Lesson 5

**Overview** This lesson discusses how to recognize and repair run-on sentences.

### Objectives

■ To identify and correct a run-on sentence

■ To use a conjunction to connect related words, phrases, and sentences

■ To recognize and correct a comma fault

**Student Pages** 19–25

**Teacher's Resource Library**

Activity 5

Modified Activity 5

Workbook Activity 5

English in Your Life 1

Building Research Skills 1

......................................................

## Vocabulary

comma fault
compound sentence
conjunction
run-on sentence

Read each word and definition to students. Ask volunteers to provide an example illustrating each concept.
......................................................

## Background Information

Point out that conjunctions do more than join ideas. They also show the relationship between the joined parts. Review with students the meaning of *and*. It says to readers that the words, phrases, or sentences being joined are equal or similar in some way (as opposed to *but*, which contrasts parts and says that they are opposite). The word *and* adds sentences or sentence parts together.

Write the following on the board:

*Jody rides horses like me she has taken lessons for several years.*

Ask students where one idea ends and another idea begins. Point out that without correct punctuation, the way these two ideas are written is confusing.

## Practice B

Ask a volunteer to read aloud the example run-on sentence with too many *ands*. Point out that connecting too many ideas with *and* creates a childlike rhythm and does not give proper emphasis to each idea.

### Practice B Answers

Sometimes a song can have a strong effect on a listener. My eyes always fill up with tears when I hear "You Light Up My Life." It is so powerful. Listening to it makes me want to write a powerful song, too.

 **3** | **Reinforce and Extend**

### LEARNING STYLES

**Auditory/Verbal**
Ask volunteers to read aloud the paragraph in Practice B as it is punctuated. Discuss the difficulty in reading and understanding run-on sentences.

### LEARNING STYLES

**Logical/Mathematical**
Ask students to explain the difference in meaning between *and* and *but*. (*And* adds together similar ideas; *but* shows contrast between ideas.) Write these three sentences on the board:

*Amber practices hard every day.*

*She does not think she has improved much.*

*Her teacher sees great progress.*

Ask students to try joining two of the sentences with a comma and the word *and*. Then have them try joining two of the sentences with a comma and the word *but*. Point out that the relationship of the ideas makes these combinations sensible:

*Amber practices hard every day, and her teacher sees great progress.*

*Amber practices hard every day, but she does not think she has improved much.*

*She does not think she has improved much, but her teacher sees great progress.*

**Conjunction**
A word that connects related words or groups of words

**Comma fault**
The use of a comma instead of end punctuation to separate two sentences

 **NOTE**
Conjunctions are used to connect *related* words or groups of words. Do not use conjunctions to connect *unrelated* sentences. In the run-on sentence in Example 2, the conjunction *and* is used incorrectly.

Another kind of run-on sentence happens when you connect unrelated sentences with a **conjunction.** A conjunction is a word that connects related words or groups of words. Common conjunctions are *and*, *or*, and *but*.

▶ **EXAMPLE 2**

| Run-On | Friday's rehearsal was Amber's best and she will probably win an award for her performance and we can't wait to hear her sing at the talent show. |
| Correct | Friday's rehearsal was Amber's best! She will probably win an award for her performance. We can't wait to hear her sing at the talent show. |

### Practice B

Read the paragraph. Decide where each complete idea begins and ends. Find four sentences and write them on your paper. Take out the unnecessary conjunctions.

Sometimes a song can have a strong effect on a listener and my eyes always fill up with tears when I hear "You Light Up My Life" and it is so powerful and listening to it makes me want to write a powerful song, too.

### Fixing a Comma Fault

Another kind of run-on sentence happens when you separate two sentences with a comma. This mistake is a **comma fault.** A comma fault happens when a writer uses a comma instead of end punctuation to separate sentences.

▶ **EXAMPLE 3**

| Comma Fault | The coach is proud of Derek, he hopes that Derek will become the city finalist. |
| Correct | The coach is proud of Derek. He hopes that Derek will become the city finalist. |

### TEACHER ALERT

 Another common way to repair a comma fault is to substitute a semicolon for the comma. It shows that the ideas are closely related. Show this alternative way to correct run-on sentences to students who readily understand the two methods discussed. For example:

*The coach is proud of Derek; he hopes that Derek will become the city finalist.*

**Compound sentence**

Two or more related ideas that are connected with a conjunction

Sometimes you may want to show the connection between two related ideas. You can turn a comma fault into a **compound sentence**. A compound sentence is two or more related ideas that are connected with a conjunction. A comma is used before the conjunction. Notice the conjunction *and* in the following compound sentence.

▶ **EXAMPLE 4**

| Comma Fault | The coach is proud of Derek, he hopes that Derek will become the city finalist. |
| Correct | The coach is proud of Derek, and he hopes that Derek will become the city finalist. |

**Practice C**

Each run-on sentence has a comma fault. Decide how to fix the problem. Write the new sentence or sentences on your paper. Use the correct end punctuation.

1. What will you do today, please come to visit us.

2. The main character in this book is a sixteen-year-old boy, he dreams of becoming a boxer.

3. The weight room will be open after school until five o'clock, no one can come in without permission.

4. The detective tries to figure out who did the crime, the reader already knows who did it.

5. Derek started out running the mile, then he switched to sprinting.

 **Brush Up on the Basics**

A conjunction is a joining word such as *and* or *but*. It may be used to join two sentences. See Grammar 69 in Appendix A.

**Reading Strategy:** Summarizing

Summarize what you learned in this lesson about how to fix run-on sentences.

## Practice C

Remind students that two ideas must be closely related to be joined with the conjunction *and*.

## *Practice C Answers*

Some answers may vary. Possible answers are shown. **1.** What will you do today? Please come to visit us. **2.** The main character in this book is a sixteen-year-old boy, and he dreams of becoming a boxer. **3.** The weight room will be open after school until five o'clock. No one can come in without permission. **4.** The detective tries to figure out who did the crime, but the reader already knows who did it. **5.** Derek started out running the mile, and then he switched to sprinting.

## Grammar Practice

Have students join each pair of sentences two different ways by using two different conjunctions. Then ask volunteers to read their sentences and explain how the meanings differ.

• The tents are old. They are sturdy. (*and, but*)

• The band was excellent. It was really loud. (*and, but*)

• The yard work was boring. I did it quickly. (*but, so*)

 **WRITING PORTFOLIO**

**Checkpoint** Have students review their Writing Portfolio sentences to correct any run-on sentences they find.

## *Reading Strategy:* Summarizing

Run-on sentences can be corrected by separating them, adding the correct end mark, and capitalizing the second sentence. If they are closely related, they may be joined by a comma and a conjunction to form a compound sentence.

## ELL/ESL Strategy

**Language Objective:** *To identify subjects and verbs in order to correct run-on sentences in writing*

Students who are learning English as a second language may have difficulty recognizing when a sentence has two or more ideas and should be split into two or more sentences. Remind students that each complete sentence has a subject and a verb. Write the sentences from Example 2 on the board. Help students identify the subject and verb of each part of the sentences:

S1   V1
Friday's <u>rehearsal</u> <u>was</u> Amber's best
S2   V2 . . . . . . . . V2
and <u>she</u> <u>will</u> probably <u>win</u> an award
S3   V3 . .
for her performance and <u>we</u> <u>can't</u>
V3
<u>wait</u> to hear her sing at the talent show.

Pair students and ask them to identify subjects and verbs in Practices B and C.

## LESSON 1-5

# REVIEW

Read each group of words. If it is written correctly, write *correct* on your paper. If the group of words is a run-on sentence, rewrite it so that it is correct. There is more than one way to correct a run-on sentence. Use correct capitalization and end punctuation.

**1.** Brandon went to the soccer field alone, he practiced kicking.

**2.** Soon he and Derek would try out for the team, and they wanted to be chosen.

**3.** Eat at Anna's Restaurant, the salads are perfect, the dressings are super!

**4.** I purchased a toaster oven at Riley's Discount Store last November and the toaster oven stopped working last week and I returned it.

**5.** There are too many ideas in a run-on sentence you need to separate the ideas.

Decide whether each group of words is a correct sentence or a run-on sentence. Write *correct* or *run-on*.

**6.** Brandon went to the weight room with Derek, and they both worked out.

**7.** One afternoon Derek and Brandon met Sonia in the weight room, she was working out, too.

**8.** A track meet is exciting and suspenseful, have you ever gone to one?

**9.** Derek's friends want to go to the county meet, and they plan to cheer from the stands.

**10.** Some people enjoy team sports, and others like to exercise by themselves.

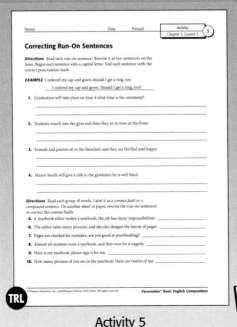

Activity 5

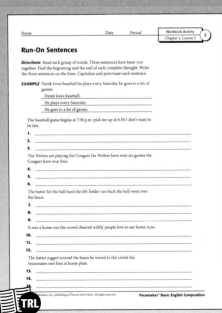

Workbook Activity 5

## Writing a Letter of Thanks

People often speak in sentence fragments: "Going to the game?" "Not sure yet." You know these fragments really mean "Are you going to the game?" and "I am not sure yet." Face to face, people understand what words have been left out of a thought. Written words are different. Your reader must understand your meaning when you are not there. In a letter, a report, or an e-mail, your goal is to be clear.

Julie wrote a thank-you letter to her aunt. She used complete sentences to make her meaning clear. Read Julie's letter carefully. Then follow the directions below.

*Dear Aunt Sue,*

*You are the best! Your package arrived today. It was right on time for my birthday. The denim jacket fits me perfectly! I especially love the style and brass buttons. I will wear it to the concert tonight. You always pick great gifts for me. How do you manage? Thank you so much.*

*Have a great week!*

*Love,*

*Julie*

1. For each sentence in Julie's letter, list the subject and predicate.

2. How many of each type of sentence did Julie write? Write the four types. Write the number after each type.

3. **CRITICAL THINKING** Why did Julie use a mix of different kinds of sentences? How did it help her writing?

 **SPEAKING AND LISTENING**

Think of a gift you received recently. A gift is not always a thing. It may be an action or someone's kind words. Write a letter of thanks to the person who gave you this gift. Be sure each sentence has a subject and a predicate. Work with a partner. Read your letters aloud and suggest improvements.

*Writing Sentences    Chapter 1    23*

---

Have several volunteers read the feature aloud. Remind students that most English rules exist to make sure people communicate their ideas to each other clearly. You may want to suggest that students set up a two-column chart with headings *Subject* and *Predicate* to answer question 1. Review the four types of sentences (declarative, interrogative, imperative, and exclamatory) and their purposes (see pages 6–7) before students complete question 2.

You may want to have students revise their letters of thanks and send them to the person thanked. Review the proper way to address an envelope and have students practice before writing on their envelopes.

### English in Your Life Answers

**1.**

| Subject | Verb in Predicate |
|---------|-------------------|
| You | are |
| package | arrived |
| It | was |
| jacket | fits |
| I | love |
| I | will wear |
| You | pick |
| you | do manage |
| (I) | thank |
| (You) | have |

**2.** statement: 6
question: 1
exclamation: 2
command: 1

**3.** Sample answer: Exclamations showed her feelings about her aunt and the gift. Statements explained why she liked it. A mix of different sentence types made the letter lively.

---

Name                Date            Period            English in Your Life
                                                          Chapter 1        1

**Writing a Letter of Thanks**

In a letter of thanks, use complete sentences. Be sure your ideas are clear. Begin every sentence with a capital letter. End every sentence with the correct punctuation mark.

Ben was happy when he got a B on a math test. He wrote a letter to thank his math tutor. Read Ben's letter. He made two mistakes. Find Ben's mistakes and circle them. Write these sentences correctly on the lines below.

Dear Mr. Ta,
Hurray! I got my algebra test back today I got a B on it! Your help paid off. The test did not even seem that hard to me. Thank you for making me study. And practice. I promise I won't complain any more!
Sincerely,
Ben

1. _____

2. _____

3. **CRITICAL THINKING** Tell what is wrong in each of the sentences you circled. What did Ben forget?

_____

_____

_____

**Pacemaker® Basic English Composition**

English in Your Life 1

*Writing Sentences    **23***

Inventory the types of encyclopedias available to students in your school library. Display one or two print encyclopedia volumes and model using guide words to look up an entry. Talk through the process of taking notes on the information in the entry. Remind students that they should summarize or paraphrase, not copy, information from any encyclopedia.

If possible, arrange to have students observe as you or someone in the media center models an online encyclopedia search. Point out the search window where they will need to enter the key words they are searching for.

### Building Research Skills Answers

Answers will vary. Possible answers are given. **1.** *World Book Encyclopedia Online*, "Parks, Rosa" **2.** Rosa Parks was born in 1913 in Tuskegee, Alabama. On December 1, 1955, she was arrested because she refused to give up her seat on a bus to a white passenger in Montgomery, Alabama. African-Americans boycotted the Montgomery bus line to protest. Parks became a leader in the African-American Civil Rights Movement. **3.** First, I went to the home page for *World Book Encyclopedia Online*. Then, I typed *Rosa Parks* into the search box. Next, I clicked on the title of the first article, "Parks, Rosa." Finally, I read the article.

## Using an Encyclopedia

Suppose you want to find information about Rosa Parks. One place to find information is in an encyclopedia. Encyclopedia articles are organized in alphabetical order by topic.

Some encyclopedias are available at a library as sets of books. Look for letters on the outside of each book. These letters tell what part of the alphabet it covers. First find the book that covers your topic. Then use the guide words at the top of each page to find the article you need.

You can also find an encyclopedia on CD-ROM or the Internet. To find an article on a CD-ROM or an online encyclopedia, use the search function. Enter keywords about the topic in the search box. Good keywords for a search on Rosa Parks might be *Rosa Parks, civil rights,* and *segregation.* Next, click on *Go* or press *Enter.*

Write the answer to each question.

1. Use an encyclopedia to look up information about Rosa Parks. Write the name of the encyclopedia you used. If you are using a print encyclopedia, write the volume (book number) and the page number. If you are using a computer encyclopedia, write the article title.

2. Read the article. List five facts from the article.

3. **CRITICAL THINKING** Explain how you found the information. Write the steps you took.

 **MEDIA AND TECHNOLOGY**

Do a computer search for the topic *Rosa Parks.* Scan the list that appears on the screen. These are the articles in which your topic is mentioned. Does your list show *Parks, Rosa; King, Martin Luther, Jr.;* and *Civil Rights Movement?* The articles with the most information on your topic are listed first. Choose three articles that sound interesting. Write the Web address for each site and the title of the article.

Name _____ Date _____ Period _____ Building Research Skills 1
Chapter 1

**Using an Encyclopedia**

An encyclopedia is a reference book. It gives facts and information about topics. The topics are listed in alphabetical order. Most encyclopedias have many volumes. The first volume might contain articles about topics beginning with A and B. The last volume might contain articles about topics beginning with W, X, Y, and Z.

Amber needs to find information about diamond mines. She decides to use the keywords *diamonds* and *mining.* She finds a set of encyclopedias to use for her research.

| Volume 1 A–Bre | Volume 2 Bri–Dam | Volume 3 Dan–Ful | Volume 4 Fun–Hab | Volume 5 Hac–Kil | Volume 6 Kim–Nym | Volume 7 Oak–Qui | Volume 8 Quo–Ris | Volume 9 Rit–Sal | Volume 10 Som–Tab | Volume 11 Tac–Waz | Volume 12 Wat–Zum | Volume 13 Index |

1. What volumes should Amber use to find *diamonds* and *mining*?
_____

2. Would the article titled "Diamonds" be in the first half or the second half of the volume?
_____

3. **CRITICAL THINKING** How could Amber use the last volume of the encyclopedia?
_____
_____

© Pearson Education, Inc., publishing as Pearson AGS Globe. All rights reserved.  **Pacemaker® Basic English Composition**

**TRL**

**Building Research Skills 1**

- Begin every sentence with a capital letter. End every sentence with a period, a question mark, or an exclamation point.

- Think about the purpose of a sentence before choosing a mark of end punctuation.

- Use a period at the end of a sentence that makes a statement.

- Use a period at the end of a sentence that makes a command or a request.

- Use a question mark at the end of a question.

- Use an exclamation mark at the end of a sentence that expresses strong feelings.

- Check that each sentence you write has a subject and a predicate. The subject of a sentence is a noun or pronoun. The predicate of a sentence includes a verb. The predicate tells something about the subject.

- Correct all sentence fragments by making them complete sentences. A sentence fragment is a group of words that does not express a complete idea.

- Correct all run-on sentences. Either divide a run-on sentence into separate sentences or use a conjunction. Conjunctions are words that connect two parts of a sentence or two related sentences.

## GROUP ACTIVITY

In a small group, discuss an upcoming school event. Write the important facts that tell *who, what, when, where,* and *why.* Then write an announcement about the event for the school bulletin board. Write at least five sentences. Be sure every member of the group writes at least one sentence.

Read the announcement aloud. Add any more information that you need. Take turns checking each other's sentences. Correct any sentence fragments or run-on sentences.

## Chapter 1 Summary

Have volunteers read aloud each Summary item on page 25. Ask volunteers to explain the meaning of each item.

### ONLINE CONNECTION

You may wish to locate the following Web sites for online encyclopedias:

*Encarta Encyclopedia*
www.agsglobepmbec.com/page25a

*World Book*
www.agsglobepmbec.com/page25b

### GROUP ACTIVITY

If possible, set up groups according to student interests or extracurricular activities. Suggest that students review their announcements to be sure that each sentence has a subject and predicate and sentences are correctly capitalized and punctuated. Remind students that a compound sentence joins two simple sentences with *both* a comma and a conjunction.

## Chapter 1 Review

Use the Chapter Review to prepare students for tests and to reteach content from the chapter.

## Chapter 1 Mastery Test

The Teacher's Resource Library includes two forms of the Chapter 1 Mastery Test. Each test addresses the chapter Goals for Learning. An optional third page of additional critical-thinking items is included for each test. The difficulty level of the two forms is equivalent.

### Review Answers

Part A

1. pronoun 2. sentence 3. verb phrase 4. tense 5. run-on sentence 6. conjunction 7. comma fault 8. predicate 9. subject 10. exclamatory sentence 11. noun 12. verb 13. sentence fragment 14. compound sentence 15. simple sentence

### Word Bank

comma fault

compound sentence

conjunction

exclamatory sentence

noun

predicate

pronoun

run-on sentence

sentence

sentence fragment

simple sentence

subject

tense

verb

verb phrase

**Part A** Find the word or words in the Word Bank that complete each sentence. Write your answer on your paper.

1. A _____ is a word that replaces a noun in a sentence.

2. A _____ is a group of words that expresses a complete thought.

3. Together, a main verb and any helping verbs form a _____.

4. The _____ of a verb tells when the action takes place.

5. Two or more ideas written as one sentence without correct punctuation or conjunctions is a _____.

6. A _____ connects related words or groups of words.

7. A _____ happens when you use a comma to separate two sentences.

8. The part of a sentence that always contains a verb is the _____.

9. The _____ of a sentence names the person, place, thing, or idea that the sentence is about.

10. An _____ expresses strong emotion.

11. A _____ names a person, place, thing, or idea.

12. A word that expresses action or state of being is a _____.

13. A _____ is a group of words that does not express a complete thought.

14. You create a _____ when you connect two related ideas with a conjunction.

15. A sentence with only one subject and one predicate is a _____.

---

Name _____ Date _____ Period _____ | Mastery Test A / Chapter 1 / Page 1

**Chapter 1 Mastery Test A**

**Part A** Circle the answer that best completes each sentence.

1. Every sentence expresses a complete _____.
   A thought  B question  C answer  D statement

2. A sentence should never end with a _____.
   A comma  C exclamation mark
   B period  D question mark

3. A _____ is a group of words written as a sentence but lacking a subject or predicate.
   A compound sentence  C simple sentence
   B sentence fragment  D comma fault

4. The _____ is a part of the predicate that tells what the subject did.
   A noun  B pronoun  C verb  D conjunction

5. A _____ is a word that joins related words or groups of words.
   A conjunction  B subject  C tense  D verb

**Part B** Read each sentence and identify its purpose. Write *statement, question, command or request,* or *strong emotion* on the line. Add the correct punctuation mark at the end of the sentence.

6. Stop bothering me please _____
7. Will we be staying long _____
8. Amber is coming with us _____
9. It's amazing _____
10. Bring your swimsuit _____
11. Reading is my favorite hobby _____
12. What is your favorite hobby _____
13. A good book is hard to beat _____
14. Pick a fun hobby _____
15. Which one will you choose _____

© Pearson Education, Inc., publishing as Pearson AGS Globe. All rights reserved.  **Pacemaker® Basic English Composition**

---

Name _____ Date _____ Period _____ | Mastery Test A / Chapter 1 / Page 2

**Chapter 1 Mastery Test A, continued**

**Part C** Read each word group. Write *complete sentence, fragment,* or *run-on.*

16. Tropical rain forests are home to large numbers of plants and animals. _____
17. Many of these plants and animals may never be found and studied. _____
18. The dense tree tops are easy to damage and they are in danger and the rain forests cannot be replaced. _____
19. An important source of oxygen for the earth. _____
20. Tropical rain forests help cool the entire earth. _____
21. By the release of billions of tons of water into the air. _____
22. As much as 400 inches of rain each year. _____
23. There are tropical rain forests in South America and Africa has rain forests and southeast Asia contains rain forests. _____
24. Sadly, very easy to damage. _____
25. Rain forests are disappearing fast. _____

**Part D** Rewrite each group of words on the lines. Correct any sentence mistakes.

26. The weather was dry the lawn needed to be watered often.
27. Juan bought a computer then he found better software.
28. What time does the basketball game start I want to go.
29. Almanacs are books of facts do you need to know the capital of Botswana you can find the answer in an almanac.
30. Canada is a huge country it stretches 3,326 miles from east to west the United States is on its southern border.

© Pearson Education, Inc., publishing as Pearson AGS Globe. All rights reserved.  **Pacemaker® Basic English Composition**

---

Name _____ Date _____ Period _____ | Mastery Test A / Chapter 1 / Page 3

**Chapter 1 Mastery Test A, continued**

**Part E** Write your answer to each question. Use complete sentences. Support each answer with facts and examples from the textbook.

31. How does a writer show a reader when each complete idea ends?

32. Why do run-on sentences make it hard to communicate ideas?

**Part F** Write a paragraph for each question. Include a topic sentence, body, and conclusion in the paragraph. Support your answers with facts and examples from the textbook.

33. Read the sentence below to find mistakes the writer made. Explain what is wrong and how to fix it.
    Today it is sunny tomorrow it will be cool and rainy.

34. How is a verb different from the predicate of a sentence?

© Pearson Education, Inc., publishing as Pearson AGS Globe. All rights reserved.  **Pacemaker® Basic English Composition**

Chapter 1 Mastery Test A, pages 1–3

**Part B** Decide on the correct end punctuation mark for each sentence. Write the letter of your answer.

16. Brandon listens to the radio every night

 A ! 　 B , 　 C . 　 D ?

17. Turn down the volume right now

 A ! 　 B , 　 C . 　 D ?

18. Who is your favorite musician

 A ! 　 B , 　 C . 　 D ?

**Part C** Read each group of words. Decide whether the words are a sentence fragment or a run-on sentence. Write *fragment* or *run-on*. Rewrite each group of words correctly.

19. Brandon has a new interest he is learning to cook.

20. Derek had trained hard, we were sure he would win.

21. For the 200-meter run.

**Part D** Read each sentence. Determine the kind of sentence it is. Write one of these: *declarative*, *exclamatory*, *interrogative*, or *imperative*.

22. Please think about joining the new art club.

23. When does the club meet?

24. It meets after school on Tuesdays.

**Part E**

25. Find five sentences in the paragraph below. Write the sentences, adding capital letters and end punctuation.

   Sonia Moreno enjoys singing rounds she taught her niece and nephew to sing "Row, Row, Row Your Boat" everyone sang a different line, and all three voices blended together they had fun several listeners clapped

## Test Tip

To prepare for a test, review a little each night for several nights. Do not wait until the night before the test. If it is a writing test, practice the kind of writing you expect to be on the test.

*Writing Sentences  Chapter 1*  **27**

## Review Answers

### Part B

**16.** C  **17.** A or C  **18.** D

### Part C

Sentences will vary. Possible sentences are given.  **19.** run-on, Brandon has a new interest. He is learning to cook.  **20.** run-on, Derek had trained hard, so we were sure he would win.  **21.** fragment, He came in first place for the 200-meter run.

### Part D

**22.** imperative  **23.** interrogative  **24.** declarative

### Part E

**25.** Sonia Moreno enjoys singing rounds. She taught her niece and nephew to sing "Row, Row, Row Your Boat." Everyone sang a different line, and all three voices blended together. They had fun. Several listeners clapped.

## WRITING PORTFOLIO

**Wrap-Up** Through the project, students should have written and revised sentences about themselves and their friends. Each student's project should contain at least 10 complete sentences that begin with a capital letter, end with the correct punctuation, and are not run-on sentences or fragments. Each sentence should have a subject and predicate and correctly use conjunctions and commas. This project may be used as an alternative form of assessment for the chapter.

Chapter 1 Mastery Test B, pages 1–3

*Writing Sentences*  **27**

| | Student Pages | Student Lesson | | | Language Skills | | | | |
|---|---|---|---|---|---|---|---|---|---|
| | | Vocabulary | Practice Exercises | Lesson Review | Identification | Writing | Punctuation & Capitalization | Grammar & Usage | Listening, Speaking, & Viewing |
| **Lesson 2-1** Making the Subject and Verb Agree | 31–35 | ✔ | ✔ | ✔ | ✔ | ✔ | ✔ | ✔ | ✔ |
| **Lesson 2-2** Using Irregular Verbs | 36–40 | ✔ | ✔ | ✔ | ✔ | ✔ | ✔ | ✔ | ✔ |
| **Lesson 2-3** Using Verbs and Verb Phrases | 41–45 | ✔ | ✔ | ✔ | ✔ | ✔ | ✔ | ✔ | ✔ |
| **Lesson 2-4** Using Conjunctions to Combine Ideas | 46–50 | | ✔ | ✔ | ✔ | ✔ | ✔ | ✔ | ✔ |
| **Lesson 2-5** Using Other Kinds of Conjunctions | 51–57 | ✔ | ✔ | ✔ | ✔ | ✔ | ✔ | ✔ | ✔ |

## Chapter Activities

**Teacher's Resource Library**
Life Skills Connection 2: Using
   Irregular Verbs in Everyday
   Writing
Writing Tip 2: Correcting Common
   Mistakes with Verbs
Writing on the Job 1: Sportswriter
Building Research Skills 2:
   Narrowing a Topic
Key Vocabulary Words 2

## Assessment Options

**Student Text**
Chapter 2 Review

**Teacher's Resource Library**
Chapter 2 Mastery Tests A and B

**Teacher's Edition**
Chapter 2 Writing Portfolio

| English in Your Life | Writing on the Job | Building Research Skills | Vocabulary Builder | Grammar Builder | Write About It | Group Activity | Reading Strategy | Six Traits | ELL/ESL Strategy | Background Information | Common Error | Life Skills Connection | Applications (Home, Career, Community, Global) | Online Connection | Teacher Alert | Speaking & Presenting Practice | Writing/Spelling/Grammar Practice | Auditory/Verbal | Body/Kinesthetic | Interpersonal/Group Learning | Logical/Mathematical | Visual/Spatial | Activities | Modified Activities | Workbook Activities | Self-Study Guide |
|---|---|---|---|---|---|---|---|---|---|---|---|---|---|---|---|---|---|---|---|---|---|---|---|---|---|---|
| | | | | 35 | | | 31, 34 | | 35 | 31 | 32, 34 | | 32, 35 | | | | 33 | 32 | 34 | | | | 6 | 6 | 6 | ✔ |
| | | | 40 | | | | 37, 39 | | 38 | 36 | 37 | 38 | 39 | | 37, 38 | | | | 39 | 37 | | | 7 | 7 | 7 | ✔ |
| | | | | | | | 44 | | 43 | 41 | 42, 44 | | | | 42 | 45 | 42, 45 | | | | | 43 | 8 | 8 | 8 | ✔ |
| | | | | | | | 46, 49 | | 49 | 46 | 47 | | 47 | | 48 | | 49 | | | | 48 | 49 | 9 | 9 | 9 | ✔ |
| 55 | 56 | | | | 54 | 57 | 52, 53 | 54 | 52 | 51 | 53 | | | 57 | 52 | | | 53 | | | | | 10 | 10 | 10 | ✔ |

## Pronunciation Key

| a | hat | e | let | ī | ice | ô | order | u̇ | put | sh | she | ə | a | in about |
|---|---|---|---|---|---|---|---|---|---|---|---|---|---|---|
| ā | age | ē | equal | o | hot | oi | oil | ü | rule | th | thin | | e | in taken |
| ä | far | ėr | term | ō | open | ou | out | ch | child | ᴛн | then | | i | in pencil |
| â | care | i | it | ȯ | saw | u | cup | ng | long | zh | measure | | o | in lemon |
| | | | | | | | | | | | | | u | in circus |

## Modified Activities

The Teacher's Resource Library (TRL) contains a set of lower-level worksheets called Modified Activities. These worksheets cover the same content as the standard Activities but are written at a lower reading level.

## Skill Track

Use Skill Track for *Basic English Composition* to monitor student progress and meet the demands of adequate yearly progress (AYP). Make informed instructional decisions with individual student and class reports of lesson and chapter assessments. With immediate and ongoing feedback, students will also see what they have learned and where they need more reinforcement and practice.

Writing Tip 2                    Life Skills Connection 2

# Writing Correct Sentences

**D**o you carry around a backpack? Look at the photo. A student has packed a backpack for the day. It contains pens and pencils, notebooks, folders of assignments, and a planner—everything the student needs for a successful day at school. When you have the right tools, your day moves ahead smoothly.

In Chapter 2, you will get the tools you need to write correct sentences. You will learn some rules for using words correctly in your sentences. You will learn how to use verb forms correctly. You will also learn ways to join related sentences. These tools will help you build sentences that express your ideas clearly.

## GOALS FOR LEARNING

- To make the subject of each sentence agree with the verb
- To use regular and irregular verbs correctly
- To understand verbs, verb phrases, and verb tenses
- To use conjunctions to combine related sentences and to connect related words and phrases
- To improve sentences with subordinating clauses

**29**

## Introducing the Chapter

Have students look at the photograph. Ask them to tell about how the student has organized the backpack. Write selected sentences on the board. Then read the text on page 29 aloud together. Model how the sentences on the board use verbs correctly and show how some of them could be joined to make ideas smoother. Explain that in this chapter, they will learn how to use subjects and verbs correctly in sentences and how to connect sentences to improve communication.

Review and discuss the Goals for Learning on page 29.

## Notes

Ask volunteers to read the notes that appear in the margins throughout the chapter. Then discuss them with the class.

## TEACHER'S RESOURCE

The AGS Globe Teaching Strategies in English Transparencies may be used with this chapter. The transparencies add an interactive dimension to expand and enhance the *Basic English Composition* program content.

## WRITING PORTFOLIO

Ask students to write a list of ways they get organized for their day in the morning. Explain that, as they read the chapter, they will refer to the list to write correct sentences about their organization plan. As they read through the chapter, have students check their sentences for subject-verb agreement and correct verb tense. In later lessons, ask them to combine some sentences to form compound and complex sentences. This project may be used as an alternative form of assessment for the chapter.

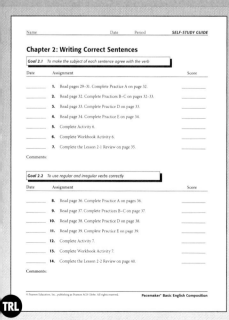

Chapter 2 Self-Study Guide, pages 1–3

## Reading Strategy: Questioning

Ask students to think about why they ask questions. Point out that asking questions about what they read helps students focus and get the answers they need to understand the text. Have a volunteer read the section aloud. Discuss how the answers to each bulleted point help a reader.

## Key Vocabulary Words

action verb
dependent clause
indefinite pronoun
independent clause
irregular verb
past participle
perfect tense
plural
regular verb
simple tense
singular
state-of-being verb
subordinating conjunction

Ask students to read through the words and their meanings. Pair students and give partners a pair of contrasting vocabulary words: *singular/plural, regular verb/irregular verb, simple tense/perfect tense, action verb/state-of-being verb, dependent clause/independent clause.* Have partners think of examples for each term and explain to the class how the two terms are different. Write *indefinite pronoun, past participle, and subordinating conjunction* on the board. Have students ask any questions they have about these vocabulary words. Then work together to brainstorm examples of each term.

# Reading Strategy: Questioning

As you read, ask yourself questions. Questioning the text will help you become a more active reader. It will also help you understand and remember more of the information. As you read this chapter, ask yourself:

- What is my reason for reading this chapter?
- What decisions can I make about the facts and details in this chapter?
- What connections can I make between this chapter and my own life?

## Key Vocabulary Words

**Singular** Referring to one person, place, thing, or idea

**Plural** Referring to more than one person, place, thing, or idea

**Indefinite pronoun** A pronoun that refers to people, places, things, or ideas in a general way

**Regular verb** A verb that forms its past tense and past participle by adding *-ed* or *-d* to the present tense

**Past participle** The verb form that you use to form the perfect tenses

**Irregular verb** A verb that does not form its past tense and past participle by adding *-ed* or *-d* to the present tense

**Perfect tense** The present perfect, past perfect, or future perfect tense of a verb; a verb form that is made from a past participle and a form of *have*

**Action verb** A verb that tells what the subject of a sentence did, does, or will do

**State-of-being verb** A verb that tells about the condition of the subject of a sentence

**Simple tense** The present, past, or future tense of a verb

**Independent clause** A group of words with a subject and a predicate that expresses a complete thought; a sentence

**Dependent clause** A group of words with a subject and a predicate that does not express a complete thought

**Subordinating conjunction** A conjunction that joins a dependent clause to an independent clause

**30** *Chapter 2 Writing Correct Sentences*

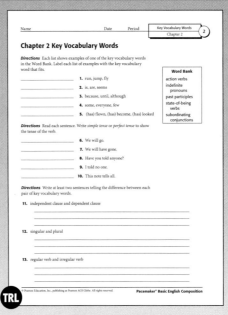

Name _____ Date _____ Period _____   Key Vocabulary Words  2
                                                            Chapter 2

**Chapter 2 Key Vocabulary Words**

*Directions* Each list shows examples of one of the key vocabulary words in the Word Bank. Label each list of examples with the key vocabulary word that fits.

_____ **1.** run, jump, fly
_____ **2.** is, are, seems
_____ **3.** because, until, although
_____ **4.** some, everyone, few
_____ **5.** (has) flown, (has) become, (has) looked

**Word Bank**
action verbs
indefinite pronouns
past participles
state-of-being verbs
subordinating conjunctions

*Directions* Read each sentence. Write *simple tense* or *perfect tense* to show the tense of the verb.

_____ **6.** We will go.
_____ **7.** We will have gone.
_____ **8.** Have you told anyone?
_____ **9.** I told no one.
_____ **10.** This note tells all.

*Directions* Write at least two sentences telling the difference between each pair of key vocabulary words.

**11.** independent clause and dependent clause
_____
_____

**12.** singular and plural
_____
_____

**13.** regular verb and irregular verb
_____
_____

© Pearson Education, Inc., publishing as Pearson AGS Globe. All rights reserved.     **Pacemaker® Basic English Composition**

**TRL**

Key Vocabulary Words 2

# Making the Subject and Verb Agree

## Objectives

- To make the subject of a sentence agree with the verb
- To identify the tense of a verb
- To decide if a subject is singular or plural
- To identify the number and gender of a pronoun

**Singular**
Referring to one person, place, thing, or idea

**Plural**
Referring to more than one person, place, thing, or idea

**Reading Strategy:** Questioning

Read the title of this lesson. What do you think you will learn?

The subject of the sentence can be **singular** or **plural**. A singular subject refers to one person, place, thing, or idea. A plural subject refers to more than one person, place, thing, or idea.

The verb is the main word in the predicate of a sentence. The verb must agree with the subject in number (singular or plural). The present tense of a verb has two forms. You use one form with a singular subject. You use the other form with a plural subject.

**Rule 1** When a subject is singular, add -s or -es to the present tense of the verb.

▶ **EXAMPLE 1**

The snow falls gently. (*Snow* is a singular noun.)

Sonia takes her violin to school. (*Sonia* is a singular noun.)

**Rule 2** When a subject is plural, do not add -s or -es to the present tense of the verb.

▶ **EXAMPLE 2**

The students run. (*Students* is a plural noun.)

The dancers whirl around the floor. (*Dancers* is plural noun.)

Sonia and Brandon enjoy music. (*Sonia and Brandon* is a plural noun.)

*Writing Correct Sentences* Chapter 2 **31**

## Chapter 2 Lesson 1

**Overview** This lesson explains how to make subjects and verbs agree.

### Objectives

- To make the subject of a sentence agree with the verb
- To identify the tense of a verb
- To decide if a subject is singular or plural
- To identify the number and gender of a pronoun

**Student Pages** 31–35

**Teacher's Resource Library**

Activity 6

Modified Activity 6

Workbook Activity 6

## Vocabulary

indefinite pronoun
plural
singular

Write the words on the board. Have students look in a dictionary to find the meaning of each vocabulary word.

## Background Information

To establish subject-verb agreement, a student must be able to recognize the subject. In many sentences, a phrase intervenes between the subject and verb. Then, if the phrase ends with a plural noun and the subject is singular, the student is likely to choose a plural verb form. You may want to give students several examples and highlight the subject and verb in each:

A *solution* to the problems *has been found*.

A *plate* of brownies *is sitting* on the counter.

*One* of the women *serves* the food.

**Reading Strategy:** Questioning

Students should conclude that they will learn how to make subjects and verbs agree.

## 1 Warm-Up Activity

Write the following sentence on the board:

*The man ride the bus every day.*

Help students recognize that the verb should be *rides* in order to agree with the subject *man*. Explain that this lesson will help them make sure that the subjects and verbs of their sentences agree.

## 2 Teaching the Lesson

After students read page 31, ask them to tell how a singular and a plural subject differ. Write the following sentences on the board:

*A verb ____ with its subject.*

*Make your verbs ____ with their subjects.*

Have students fill in the blanks correctly with *agree* or *agrees*.

## AT HOME

Ask students to write sentences stating the occupation or hobby of each of four family members. For example, "My grandmother volunteers at an animal shelter." Point out that the subject of each sentence will be singular. Have students share their sentences with a partner and ask partners to check to be sure each verb agrees with its subject.

## Practice A

Ask a volunteer to define the subject of a sentence in his or her own words.

### Practice A Answers

1. Sometimes Amber's dog runs away.
2. That dog jumps the fence. 3. His owners call him. 4. The neighbors chase him. 5. Finally the adventurer returns.

## Practice B

Have students look back at Practice A and find the verb in each sentence. Encourage them to use those sentences as models as they choose their answers for Practice B.

### Practice B Answers

1. singular 2. singular 3. plural
4. plural 5. plural

## COMMON ERROR

Often, students assume that the noun closest to the verb is the subject. Point out sentence 2 in Practice B. Explain that *knowledge* is the subject. *Of rules* is a phrase that describes the subject. Suggest that students look for the verb in a sentence first. Then they can ask themselves: *Who or what ___ (does the verb's action)?* For example: *Who or what helps his writing? Knowledge helps his writing.*

---

**Brush Up on the Basics**

The letter *s* is often used as a plural ending for nouns. However, an *s* added to a verb usually shows the singular form. See Grammar 28 in Appendix A.

The subject of each sentence is in bold. Choose the correct verb form in parentheses. Write the sentence on your paper.

1. Sometimes **Amber's dog** (run, runs) away.
2. That **dog** (jump, jumps) the fence.
3. His **owners** (call, calls) him.
4. The **neighbors** (chase, chases) him.
5. Finally the **adventurer** (return, returns).

**Rule 3** The past tense of a verb has only one form. All regular past-tense verbs end in *-ed*.

▶ **EXAMPLE 3**

Brandon played baseball yesterday. (*Brandon* is a singular noun.)

Several friends played baseball together. (*Friends* is a plural noun.)

**Practice B**

The subject of each sentence is in bold. Decide whether the subject is singular or plural. Write *singular* or *plural* on your paper.

1. The **snow** falls gently.
2. His **knowledge** of rules helps his writing.
3. The **answers** pop into my head.
4. My **friends** like music.
5. Those **dancers** whirl like tops.

---

## LEARNING STYLES

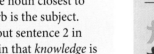

**Auditory/Verbal**

Saying and hearing correct subject-verb agreement will help students choose correct verbs in their writing. Have student pairs take turns reading aloud the correct sentences for Practice A. Then write the following on the board:

| | |
|---|---|
| *lamp glows* | *lamps glow* |
| *class begins* | *classes begin* |
| *flower blooms* | *flowers bloom* |
| *team practices* | *teams practice* |

Have partners make up sentences using each subject-verb pair.

## Practice C

Look at each subject in bold. Choose the correct verb form in parentheses. Write the sentence on your paper.

1. Derek's **friends** (run, runs) 30 miles each week.

2. The **girl** with the red shoes (dance, dances) well.

3. The **actors** in the school play (seem, seems) talented.

4. **They** (hope, hopes) for a big crowd on opening night.

5. The **students** (sell, sells) tickets in the cafeteria.

The subject of a sentence can be a noun or a pronoun. A pronoun is a word that replaces a noun.

**Rule 4** A singular pronoun replaces a singular noun. A plural pronoun replaces a plural noun.

**Rule 5** The verb must agree in number with the pronoun subject.

▶ **EXAMPLE 4**

Sonia crossed the street. (*Sonia* is a singular noun.)

She crossed the street. (*She* is a singular pronoun.)

The band members gather here. (*Band members* is plural.)

They gather here. (*They* is plural.)

## Practice D

Look at each subject in bold. Choose the correct pronoun in parentheses to replace the noun. Write the sentence using the pronoun.

1. **Amber Choy** has a dog named Rex. (She, They)

2. One day **the dog** ran away. (it, they)

3. **Amber and Sonia** looked for Rex. (She, They)

4. **The rain** started at about eight o'clock. (It, They)

5. **The girls** wondered if Rex was lost. (She, They)

*Writing Correct Sentences*    Chapter 2    **33**

## WRITING PORTFOLIO

**Checkpoint** Have students refer to the lists they made when the chapter was introduced. Ask them to write a sentence about getting organized for each item on the list. Remind them to check their sentences for subject-verb agreement.

## Practice C

Remind students that the subject is in bold; it is not the word closest to the verb. If they have trouble "hearing" which verb is correct, have them identify the subject as singular or plural and say the subject and verb together, ignoring any prepositional phrases. For example, in sentence 2, *girl dances* is correct, but saying "shoes dances" sounds wrong.

### *Practice C Answers*

1. Derek's friends run 30 miles each week. 2. The girl with the red shoes dances well. 3. The actors in the school play seem talented. 4. They hope for a big crowd on opening night. 5. The students sell tickets in the cafeteria.

## Practice D

Explain to students that the pronouns used in Example 4 are called personal pronouns. A personal pronoun replaces a specific noun: *She* refers to *Sonia; they* refers to *band members*. Help students recall which personal pronouns are singular and which are plural. Before students complete Practice D, have them identify each bold subject noun in the sentences as singular or plural.

### *Practice D Answers*

1. She has a dog named Rex. 2. One day it ran away. 3. They looked for Rex. 4. It started at about eight o'clock. 5. They wondered if Rex was lost.

### Writing Practice

Have students review a written assignment, identify the subjects and verbs, and correct any errors in subject-verb agreement. Then have students write several subject-verb pairs, such as *dogs run* and *cat climbs,* and exchange them with a partner. Challenge students to use the subjects and verbs in original sentences using adjectives, adverbs, and prepositional phrases. Remind them to keep the subject and verb in agreement. For example: *The crazy dogs from next door run loose all the time* or *A black cat with white spots climbs up a tree to escape them.*

## Practice E

Have students read the pronouns aloud from page 34. Invite students to offer sentences using each pronoun and a verb correctly. Encourage students to find each bold subject in Practice E in one of the three charts to help them choose the correct verb.

### Practice E Answers

**1.** Someone knocks at the door. **2.** The party is loud. No one hears the knocks. **3.** Several knocks make the door shake. **4.** Everybody looks at everybody else. **5.** A voice calls out, "Pizza delivery! Two kinds here!" Both smell wonderful.

### *Reading Strategy:* Questioning

Students should understand that a singular pronoun replaces a singular noun and must have the same singular verb.

---

**Indefinite pronoun**
A pronoun that refers to people, places, things, or ideas in a general way

***Reading Strategy:*** Questioning

Ask yourself: Did I understand what I just read? If not, read the material again.

---

**Indefinite pronouns** refer in a general way to people, places, things, and ideas. Some indefinite pronouns are singular. Some are plural. Some can be either, depending on how you use them.

### Singular Indefinite Pronouns

| | | | |
|---|---|---|---|
| anybody | either | neither | one |
| anyone | everybody | nobody | somebody |
| anything | everyone | no one | someone |
| each | everything | nothing | something |

### Plural Indefinite Pronouns

| | | | |
|---|---|---|---|
| both | few | many | several |

### Singular or Plural Indefinite Pronouns

| | | | | |
|---|---|---|---|---|
| all | any | most | none | some |

▶ **EXAMPLE 5**

Everybody works. (*Everybody* is a singular pronoun.)

Both need help. (*Both* is a plural pronoun.)

Most of the group walks to school. (*Most* is singular here.)

Most of the students want lunch. (*Most* is plural here.)

### Practice E

Look at the indefinite pronoun in bold. Decide if it is singular or plural. Then choose the correct verb form in parentheses. Write the sentence on your paper.

1. **Someone** (knock, knocks) at the door.
2. The party is loud. **No one** (hear, hears) the knocks.
3. **Several** knocks (make, makes) the door shake.
4. **Everybody** (look, looks) at everybody else.
5. A voice calls out, "Pizza delivery! Two kinds here!" **Both** (smell, smells) wonderful!

---

**34** Chapter 2 *Writing Correct Sentences*

---

## LEARNING STYLES

**Body/Kinesthetic**

Have students make a card for each indefinite pronoun and label it as *singular* or *plural*. The indefinite pronouns *all, any, most, none,* and *some* may be labeled with a bold question mark. Write the following on the board:

_____ (find/finds) it hard to wait.

_____ (want/wants) immediate attention.

_____ (look/looks) both ways.

Have students go to the board and hold various indefinite pronouns in the blank, then identify the verb that agrees with the subject. If students are confused, have them model the sentence actions: two students to model *both,* three to model *few* and *several,* and five or more to model *many.* For indefinite pronouns that can be singular or plural, discuss specific situations: *All of the team practices at once.* (The team is considered a group.) *All of the boys jump as high as they can.* (Each boy's jump is considered separately.)

---

The subject of each sentence is in bold. Choose the correct verb form in parentheses. Write the sentence on your paper.

1. Sonia's **grandparents** (visit, visits) often.

2. Derek's new **camera** (take, takes) great pictures.

3. The **students** in art class (paint, paints) murals.

4. **Everybody** (get, gets) a turn.

5. **Several** (leave, leaves) the building.

Decide whether the subject of each sentence is singular or plural. Then choose the correct verb form in parentheses. Write the sentence on your paper.

6. Derek (want, wants) good grades in English.

7. He (study, studies) every day.

8. All of his friends (encourage, encourages) him.

9. Someone (say, says) there will be a test on Monday.

10. The students (arrive, arrives) at nine o'clock every day.

## GRAMMAR BUILDER

### Using *Sit* and *Set* Correctly
Many people confuse *sit* and *set*.

| Present | Past | Past Participle | Verb Meaning |
|---------|------|-----------------|--------------|
| sit | sat | (has) sat | to rest with legs bent |
| set | set | (has) set | to put or place |

Write each sentence using the correct form of *sit* or *set*.
1. Kay ___ the dishes in the sink.
2. I usually ___ in the last row.
3. The boys have ___ the table for dinner.

---

## Lesson 2-1 Review Answers
**1.** Sonia's grandparents visit often. **2.** Derek's new camera takes great pictures. **3.** The students in art class paint murals. **4.** Everybody gets a turn. **5.** Several leave the building. **6.** Derek wants good grades in English. **7.** He studies every day. **8.** All of his friends encourage him. **9.** Someone says there will be a test on Monday. **10.** The students arrive at nine o'clock every day.

## GRAMMAR BUILDER

Write on the board *Please s_t down in your seats. You may s_t your books on the floor.* Have students read the sentences aloud, completing the verb as *sit* or *set*. Discuss how they chose the correct verb. Point out that the present and past tense of *set* are the same.

### Grammar Builder Answers
**1.** Kay set the dishes in the sink. **2.** I usually sit in the last row. **3.** The boys have set the table for dinner.

## GLOBAL CONNECTION

Verbs such as *sit/set*, *lie/lay*, and *rise/raise* are often confused because they have similar spellings or form tenses in similar ways. Have students send an e-mail to a penpal from a country whose principal language is not English. In the e-mail, have students explain how these three verbs confuse English speakers.

## ELL/ESL STRATEGY

**Language Objective:**
*To identify and use unusual singular nouns in sentences*

Some words are *collective nouns* (e.g., *audience, family*). Explain that they represent a group but usually refer to a unit and take a singular verb.

Other nouns are abstract (e.g., *advice, sugar*). Explain that these nouns that cannot be counted need a singular verb.

Have students make up sentences using as many collective and abstract nouns as they can.

---

### Making the Subject and Verb Agree

**Directions** Underline the form of the verb that agrees with the subject shown in bold.

**EXAMPLE** He (*is*, are) happy that he got the job.

1. **She** (wants, want) to ask a question.
2. **Both** of them (needs, need) to know the answer.
3. Your **friends** (says, say) you are a good listener.
4. **Everyone** (learns, learn) by asking questions.
5. **Paul** and **Rob** (brings, bring) extra water to practice.
6. **Eliza** (has, have) two bottles.
7. **Each** of the boys (carries, carry) running shoes.
8. **People** (is, are) afraid of different things.
9. **Some** students (hates, hate) spiders.
10. **Many** people (is, are) scared of snakes.

**Directions** Read each sentence. Write *singular* on the line if the subject shown in bold is singular. Write *plural* if the subject is plural. Then underline the form of the verb that agrees with the subject.

**EXAMPLE** Everyone (talks, talk) at once.     singular

11. **Few** of the bystanders (sees, see) what is happening. ___
12. **Dozens** of cameras (clicks, click) busily. ___
13. **Several** Hollywood **stars** (walks, walk) down the sidewalk. ___
14. **They** (causes, cause) a traffic jam. ___
15. This **city** (is, are) the site for a new film. ___
16. **Several** of the scenes (takes, take) place in this building. ___
17. **No one** in his or her right mind (goes, go) there. ___
18. A **movie** (makes, make) everyone "star crazy." ___
19. The **dream** of meeting stars (excites, excite) everyone. ___
20. **Movies** like these (gives, give) our city class. ___

### Activity 6

---

### Subject and Verb Agreement

**Directions** Read each sentence. The subject is in bold. If the subject is singular, circle *singular*. If it is plural, circle *plural*. Then underline the correct form of the verb to finish the sentence.

**EXAMPLE** Most **children** (like, likes) clowns.     singular   (plural)

1. **Eliza** (throws, throw) a party every year.     singular   plural
2. **Both** of my friends (is, are) going to the party.     singular   plural
3. **She** (makes, make) the best snacks you've ever tasted.     singular   plural
4. Her **house** (has, have) a recreation room.     singular   plural
5. **Jason and Eliza** (loves, love) parties.     singular   plural
6. **They** (dances, dance) well together.     singular   plural
7. **Brandon** always (gets, get) there early.     singular   plural
8. **Everyone** (knows, know) to come on time.     singular   plural
9. **Eliza's father** (comes, come) downstairs at 12.     singular   plural
10. **All** of Eliza's friends (goes, go) home then.     singular   plural

**Directions** Read each sentence. On each line, write the form of the verb in parentheses that agrees with the subject.

**EXAMPLE** He and I ___hope___ to receive many gifts. (hopes, hope)

11. **Both** Amber and Eliza _____ parties. (enjoys, enjoy)
12. **Everybody** _____ about the graduation party. (knows, know)
13. **Each** of the girls _____ very good cakes. (bakes, bake)
14. **One** of the soccer players _____ football, too. (likes, like)
15. The **dog** _____ over the gate all the time. (jumps, jump)
16. **Several** girls _____ Eliza every night. (calls, call)
17. **Many** people _____ to watch the parade. (stays, stay)
18. A **few** of them _____ along with the music. (claps, clap)
19. **Either** Derek or Brandon _____ to drive. (plans, plan)
20. **Neither** Amber nor Eliza _____ a ride. (wants, want)

### Workbook Activity 6

### Chapter 2 Lesson 2

**Overview** This lesson presents the present, past, and past participle forms of regular and irregular verbs and explains how to form perfect tenses.

### Objectives

- To form the past tense and past participle of a regular verb
- To write the perfect tenses of a regular verb
- To use the forms of *have* correctly
- To identify the correct forms of an irregular verb

**Student Pages** 36–40

### Teacher's Resource Library **TRL**

Activity 7

Modified Activity 7

Workbook Activity 7

Life Skills Connection 2

### Vocabulary

| | |
|---|---|
| irregular verb | perfect tense |
| past participle | regular verb |

Read the vocabulary words and definitions aloud. Write this chart on the board:

| Present | Past | Past Participle |
|---|---|---|
| *walk* | *walked* | *have walked* |
| *help* | *helped* | *have helped* |
| *eat* | *ate* | *have eaten* |

Have students identify verbs as regular or irregular. Point out that the third column shows one of the perfect tenses.

### Background Information

One reason students have difficulty with irregular verbs is that they form their tenses in different ways:

1. by changing a vowel (*ring/rang/have rung; come/came/have come*)
2. by changing a vowel and consonants: (*do/did/have done; see/saw/have seen*)
3. by making no change (*hurt/hurt/have hurt; put/put/have put*)

Suggest that students make a card for each irregular verb they encounter. They can write the principal forms for each verb, then make categories of verbs with like patterns.

**36** *Chapter 2*

---

### Objectives

- To form the past tense and past participle of a regular verb
- To write the perfect tenses of a regular verb
- To use the forms of *have* correctly
- To identify the correct forms of an irregular verb

**Regular verb**
A verb that forms its past tense and past participle by adding *-ed* or *-d* to the present tense

**Past participle**
The verb form that you use to form the perfect tenses

**Irregular verb**
A verb that does not form its past tense and past participle by adding *-ed* or *-d* to the present tense

Most of the verbs in English are **regular verbs.** To form the past tense or the **past participle** of a regular verb, you add *-ed* or *-d*. A past participle is a verb form. (Later in this lesson, you will see how to use past participles to form perfect tenses.)

The past tense and past participle of an **irregular verb** are created in a different way. In Example 1, *go* and *have* are irregular verbs. You do not add *-ed* to form their past tense or past participle.

▶ **EXAMPLE 1**

| | Present | Past | Past Participle |
|---|---|---|---|
| Regular | paint, paints | painted | (has) painted |
| Irregular | go, goes | went | (has) gone |
| Irregular | have, has | had | (has) had |

Use *has* with a singular subject. Use *have* with a plural subject.

▶ **EXAMPLE 2**

Derek has a job

The workers have a new schedule.

### Practice A

Choose the correct form of *have* . Rewrite the sentence.

1. Does Brandon (has, have) his homework?
2. The students (has, have) a new assignment.
3. Amber (has, have) a dog named Rex.
4. The girls (has, have) a new project.
5. Sonia (has, have) a list of directions.

---

### 1 Warm-Up Activity

Ask students if they have ever heard a child say a sentence such as "Grandma bringed me a present." Discuss with students why children might make such mistakes. Help them see that adding the *-ed* ending is the common way to form past tenses. Ask students how they think children learn the correct forms of irregular past tenses such as *brought*.

### 2 Teaching the Lesson

Discuss the forms of the verb *paint* on page 36, emphasizing that it is a regular verb. Then have students compare the forms of the irregular verb examples.

Explain that irregular verbs do not follow the regular pattern and must be memorized.

### Practice A

Be sure students understand that *has* and *have* are present tense forms and *had* is the past tense form.

### *Practice A Answers*

**1.** Does Brandon have his homework?
**2.** The students have a new assignment. **3.** Amber has a dog named Rex. **4.** The girls have a new project. **5.** Sonia has a list of directions.

## Perfect tense

The present perfect, past perfect, or future perfect tense of a verb; a verb form that is made from a past participle and a form of *have*

When you use *have* as a helping verb with a past participle, you form a **perfect tense** of the verb. The perfect tenses are present perfect, past perfect, and future perfect. Example 3 shows the perfect tenses of the verb *listen*. The past participle of *listen* is *listened*.

▶ **EXAMPLE 3**

| Present Perfect | Past Perfect | Future Perfect |
|---|---|---|
| I have listened. | They had listened. | You will have listened. |
| He has listened. | He had listened. | He will have listened. |

### Practice B

Write the three perfect tenses of each regular verb. Use the correct form of *have* plus the past participle of the verb.

1. recognize
2. struggle
3. tremble
4. look
5. enjoy

### Practice C

**Reading Strategy:**
Questioning

Ask yourself: Do I understand how to form the perfect tense of a verb? If not, reread the parts of this lesson that confuse you.

Complete each sentence with the perfect tense of the verb in parentheses. Add *has*, *have*, *had*, or *will have* to the past participle. Write the sentence on your paper. There may be more than one possible answer.

**Example:** The moon _____ behind the clouds. (disappear)
**Answer:** The moon has disappeared behind the clouds.

1. The students _____ at last. (arrive)
2. Amber and Derek _____ for several weeks. (exercise)
3. The band _____ the competition every year. (enter)
4. Mrs. Choy _____ a birthday party for Amber. (arrange)
5. "I _____ the project already," said Ms. Ruiz. (explain)

## TEACHER ALERT

Point out to students that the present perfect tense does not really express present time. The word *present* refers to the tense of the helping verb *has/have*. Present perfect tense expresses an action or condition that occurred at some time in the past: *The clock has stopped. They have caught the flu.* It may also reference an action that began in the past and is still occurring: *My brother has worked all summer.*

## LEARNING STYLES

**Interpersonal/Group Learning**

Ask students to work with a partner. Have each student write a list of five regular verbs. Have partners exchange words and write sentences using the present perfect tense of each verb (add *has* or *have* to the past participle form of the verb). Have partners read their sentences aloud to one another and discuss any difficulties.

## COMMON ERROR

Point out to students that the singular subject *I* uses *have* rather than *has* (otherwise, *have* is used with plural subjects), although singular pronouns *he* and *she* use *has*. Only the present perfect tense forms call for singular and plural forms.

## Practice B

Have students create a table like that in Example 3 to write the perfect tenses. Ask students to make up and say original sentences for each tense.

### Practice B Answers

1. have/has recognized, had recognized, will have recognized 2. have/has struggled, had struggled, will have struggled 3. have/has trembled, had trembled, will have trembled 4. have/has looked, had looked, will have looked 5. have/has enjoyed, had enjoyed, will have enjoyed

## Practice C

Have students refer to the table in Example 3 for ways of forming the perfect tenses. Review students' sentences with them. Point out the differences in meaning for different answers. For example: *The students had arrived at last.* (They arrived in the past later than they were expected.) *The students have arrived at last.* (They just now arrived, and they are later than expected.)

### Practice C Answers

Answers may vary. Reasonable answers are shown. 1. The students have arrived at last. 2. Amber and Derek have exercised for several weeks. 3. The band has entered the competition every year. 4. Mrs. Choy has arranged a birthday party for Amber. 5. "I have explained the project already," said Ms. Ruiz.

### Reading Strategy: Questioning

Students should understand that the perfect tenses are verb phrases that combine a form of *have* with the past participle.

## Practice D

Remind students that the sentence context may give clues to the time when an action occurred.

### Practice D Answers

Answers to items 2–5 may vary. Reasonable answers are shown. **1.** Brandon had gotten an A in health last year. **2.** He has made the tennis team. **3.** Each player has won a match for the team. **4.** Brandon has swung his racket to hit the ball. **5.** The coach had taught the players the rules.

**ELL/ESL STRATEGY**

**Language Objective:**
*To learn and use simple and perfect tenses of* be *and* have

It is vital for students learning English to know the forms of *be* and *have.* Provide the following nouns and pronouns: *I, you, Jim, pets.* Have students write the correct present, past, and past participle forms of *be* and *has* using these words as subjects.

Then have students form the perfect tenses for each verb and help them construct sentences:

*I have often been hungry. If we skip lunch, we will have been hungry for five hours by suppertime.*

There are many irregular verbs. Although there are more regular verbs than irregular ones, you use some irregular verbs very often.

For some irregular verbs, the past tense is the same as the past participle.

▶ **EXAMPLE 4**

| Present | Past | Past Participle |
|---|---|---|
| get, gets | got | (has) got (gotten) |
| make, makes | made | (has) made |
| swing, swings | swung | (has) swung |
| teach, teaches | taught | (has) taught |
| win, wins | won | (has) won |

**Practice D**

Complete each sentence with a perfect tense of the verb in parentheses. Add *has, have, had,* or *will have* to the past participle. Write the sentence on your paper. There may be more than one possible answer.

1. Brandon _____ an A in health last year. (get)
2. He _____ the tennis team. (make)
3. Each player _____ a match for the team. (win)
4. Brandon _____ his racket to hit the ball. (swing)
5. The coach _____ the players the rules. (teach)

*She swung her racket and returned the ball.*

Point out to students that people use irregular verbs constantly. Provide copies of Life Skills Connection 2 to students. Have them use the chart to fill in the appropriate form of each verb in these sentences:

*I _____ to the mall every weekend this month. (go)*

*Who _____ eating my porridge? (be)*

*Because you _____ to me, I _____ to you. (write)*

*Who _____ you that picture? (give)*

*She _____ what we did. (saw)*

Have students follow the steps on the worksheet to write their notes.

Reading Strategy:
Questioning

Think beyond the lesson text. Consider your own experience. Do you and others around you use irregular verbs correctly?

For some irregular verbs, the past tense is different from the past participle.

▶ **EXAMPLE 5**

| Present | Past | Past Participle |
|---------|------|-----------------|
| begin, begins | began | (has) begun |
| drive, drives | drove | (has) driven |
| know, knows | knew | (has) known |
| see, sees | saw | (has) seen |
| take, takes | took | (has) taken |

A few verbs are extremely irregular. The present, past, and past participle forms are all different.

▶ **EXAMPLE 6**

| Present | Past | Past Participle |
|---------|------|-----------------|
| do, does | did | (has) done |
| eat, eats | ate | (has) eaten |
| go, goes | went | (has) gone |

### Practice E

Complete each sentence with a perfect tense of the verb in parentheses. Add *has*, *have*, *had*, or *will have* to the past participle. Write the sentence on your paper. There may be more than one possible answer.

1. Sonia _____ that movie five times. (see)

2. Last week she _____ Amber to see it. (take)

3. They _____ to Amber's house afterwards. (drive)

4. Derek and Brandon _____ their dinner late. (eat)

5. Derek _____ to the movies tomorrow. (go)

## Practice E

Have students refer to the charts above to be sure of the past participle form as they complete the activity. Be sure they understand that they are to use perfect tenses in each sentence. Remind them to use context to decide when the action occurs.

### Practice E Answers

Some answers may vary. Reasonable answers are shown. **1.** Sonia has seen that movie five times. **2.** Last week she had taken Amber to see it. **3.** They had driven to Amber's house afterwards. **4.** Derek and Brandon have eaten their dinner late. **5.** Derek will have gone to the movies tomorrow.

### Reading Strategy: Questioning

Students should be (or become) aware of common incorrect usage in most informal speech, such as "I have ate" and "I seen."

### IN THE COMMUNITY

Have students select newspaper articles or brochures from local businesses and highlight any examples of perfect tense usage. Ask students to share their findings and identify each use as *present perfect*, *past perfect*, or *future perfect*.

### WRITING PORTFOLIO

**Checkpoint** Have students revisit their sentences about organizing for the day and check the verb tenses to be sure they have used the correct forms of regular and irregular verbs.

### LEARNING STYLES

**Body/Kinesthetic**

Have students model the difference between tenses of verbs such as *see*, *take*, *do*, and *eat*. Have two or three students work together and assign one of the verbs. Ask them to create a skit to act out while a narrator explains the action. For example: *Ed sees a UFO. They all see the UFO. They told their parents, "We saw a UFO!" The family wonders how many others will have seen it.*

## Lesson 2-2 Review Answers

Point out to students that they are not expected to create perfect tenses. Sentences that already include a form of *has* will require the past participle form of the verb to form perfect tenses. **1.** "Have you done your homework?" asked Derek. **2.** "I will have done it by Monday," Brandon said. **3.** Derek and Brandon went home. **4.** They did most of the assignment. **5.** "Have you eaten dinner?" asked Mrs. Tucker. **6.** "Yes, but we haven't had enough!" Derek said. **7.** Sonia and Amber did their homework last night. **8.** Amber's mother asked if they had gone to the library. **9.** Amber said that she did her work at Sonia's house. **10.** Amber and Sonia ate popcorn as they studied.

## VOCABULARY BUILDER

Have a volunteer read the explanation. Encourage students to name other words with multiple meanings and give sample sentences using them with different meanings.

### Vocabulary Builder Answers

Answers will vary. Possible answers are shown.
I filled a bowl with apples. They bowled over the pins. Let's play basketball at the park. People park their cars in the front lot. Professional athletes have a lot of drive. The golfer drives the ball down the greens.

# REVIEW

Complete each sentence with the correct form of the verb in parentheses. Write the sentence on your paper.

1. "Have you _____ your homework?" asked Derek. (do)

2. "I will have _____ it by Monday," Brandon said. (do)

3. Derek and Brandon _____ home. (go)

4. They _____ most of the assignment. (do)

5. "Have you _____ dinner?" asked Mrs. Tucker. (eat)

6. "Yes, but we haven't _____ enough!" Derek said. (have)

7. Sonia and Amber _____ their homework last night. (do)

8. Amber's mother asked if they had _____ to the library. (go)

9. Amber said that she _____ her work at Sonia's house. (do)

10. Amber and Sonia _____ popcorn as they studied. (eat)

## VOCABULARY BUILDER

### Using Parts of Speech to Find Word Meaning

Many words have several meanings. A word's meaning depends on how it is used in a sentence. For example, *sail* can be used as a noun or a verb.

**Noun**   He bought a boat with a yellow **sail**.

**Verb**   The girls **sail** across the harbor every weekend.

In the first sentence, *sail* means a piece of cloth used to catch the wind. In the second sentence, *sail* means "to move across water."

Write three sentences using each of these words as a noun: *bowl, park, drive.* Then write three sentences using each as a verb. Use a dictionary if you need help.

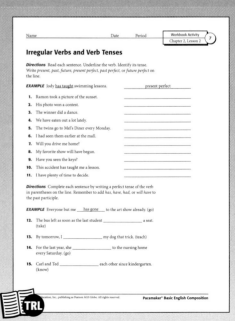

# Using Verbs and Verb Phrases

## Objectives

■ To use action verbs in sentences

■ To identify state-of-being verbs

■ To write verb phrases correctly

■ To use logical verb tense

**Action verb**

A verb that tells what the subject of a sentence did, does, or will do

**State-of-being verb**

A verb that tells about the condition of the subject of a sentence

*Reading Strategy:* Questioning

What do you already know about action verbs?

Every sentence must have a verb. A verb expresses an action or a state of being.

An **action verb** tells what the subject did, does, or will do.

▶ **EXAMPLE 1**

Derek runs five miles almost every day. (action verb)

Amber met Sonia at the corner. (action verb)

A verb can also express state of being. A **state-of-being verb** tells you something about the condition of the subject of a sentence. State-of-being verbs do not suggest action.

▶ **EXAMPLE 2**

Amber and Sonia are friends. (state-of-being verb)

Derek seems friendly, too. (state-of-being verb)

*Sonia will play a violin solo in the concert. Amber is excited to hear her friend play.*

## Chapter 2 Lesson 3

**Overview** This lesson explains action and state-of-being verbs as well as helping verbs used to create verb phrases. It also discusses the logic of selecting verb tense to suit the context.

### Objectives

■ To use action verbs in sentences

■ To identify state-of-being verbs

■ To write verb phrases correctly

■ To use logical verb tense

**Student Pages** 41–45

**Teacher's Resource Library** 📀

**Activity** 8

**Modified Activity** 8

**Workbook Activity** 8

## Vocabulary

action verb
simple tense
state-of-being verb

After students have read and discussed the words and their meanings, have them write each term on a card. Read a paragraph from a story, emphasizing the verbs. Have students hold up the appropriate card for each verb they hear. If a verb is both an action (or a state-of-being) verb and a simple tense, they hold up two cards.

## Background Information

Helping verbs are also known as *auxiliary verbs.* The parts of a verb phrase may be separated from one another, most often in questions and negative statements: *Have you seen that movie? I have not seen it yet.* The word *not* is never part of the verb or verb phrase. It is an adverb. Adverbs can move position in a sentence, so sometimes an adverb separates parts of a verb phrase: *You may well be right. Now you are just being silly.*

## 1  Warm-Up Activity

Ask volunteers to come to the board to write sentences about a seasonal event. Ask volunteers to come to the board and underline the verb in each sentence.

*Reading Strategy:* Questioning

Students may know that action verbs tell what the subject did and sometimes tell what the subject did to someone or something. They may suggest that actions may be mental or physical.

## 2  Teaching the Lesson

Point out that not all verbs express action. Some verbs express the condition of the subject: *I am busy. The cake smells good.* Define *helping verb* and *verb phrase.* Ask volunteers to write some sentences containing verb phrases on the board. Have other volunteers identify the helping verbs in the sentences.

## TEACHER ALERT

Point out to students that a verb phrase may have an action or a state-of-being verb as the main verb. In Example 3, *will jog* is an action verb and *have been* is a state-of-being verb.

## Practice A

Have students read the directions and define the term *verb phrase* before they begin the activity.

## *Practice A Answers*

**1.** has **2.** will find **3.** follows **4.** will write **5.** has found

## COMMON ERROR

Be sure students understand that the helping verbs *be, have,* and *do* may also serve as the main and only verb in a sentence. For example, *We are cold. I have the flu. You did it!*

Explain that these verbs have different roles they can play. The other helping verbs always occur with a main verb.

## Spelling Practice

Have students pronounce each helping verb on the list on page 42. Point out that some of the verbs have surprising spellings. For example, *would* and *wood* are pronounced the same. Explain that students must memorize the spellings of such words. Students can make a word bank of words that have each odd pattern, beginning with *would, could, should. Might* can be grouped with other words like *night, bright, sight.*

---

A verb can be more than one word. A main verb often has a helping verb. A helping verb combines with a main verb to form a verb phrase. In Example 3, *will* is a helping verb with *jog*. Together they form the verb phrase *will jog*.

▶ **EXAMPLE 3**

Brandon will jog in the morning.

Brandon and Derek have been friends for a long time.

### Practice A

Find the verb or verb phrase in each sentence. Write it on your paper.

1. Every sentence has a verb.
2. You will find a verb in every sentence.
3. Everyone follows the rules.
4. Soon you will write a better sentence.
5. Amber has found the verb in this sentence.

A verb phrase includes a helping verb and a main verb. The main verb expresses action or state of being. The helping verb helps express tense.

### Common Helping Verbs

| have | am | was | been | will | could | must |
|------|------|------|------|--------|-------|--------|
| has | is | were | do | would | shall | should |
| had | are | be | did | can | may | might |

A verb phrase has only one main verb. It may have one, two, or three helping verbs. The main verb is always last. In Example 4, each verb phrase is in blue. The helping verbs are underlined.

▶ **EXAMPLE 4**

By 1:00 in the afternoon, Derek had trained for two hours.

He has been running on the trail every morning.

**Simple tense**
The present, past, or future tense of a verb

Write the verb phrase in each sentence. Underline each helping verb.

1. Amber was writing a letter to her aunt.
2. Sonia has been playing in a band for a year.
3. The band is practicing now.
4. Amber has known Sonia for several years.
5. You should have left sooner!

People talk and write about events that happen at different times. In a sentence, the verb expresses tense. A verb tense tells the time when an action takes place. The three **simple tenses** are present, past, and future. The three perfect tenses are present perfect, past perfect, and future perfect.

▶ **EXAMPLE 5**

| | |
|---|---|
| Present | Derek starts his job today. |
| Past | Derek started his job last week. |
| Future | Derek will start his job on Monday. |
| Present Perfect | Derek has started his job. |
| Past Perfect | Derek had started his job earlier. |
| Future Perfect | Derek will have started by next week. |

**Practice C**

Write the verbs and verb phrases shown in bold. Next to each verb or verb phrase, write its tense.

Today Derek Anderson **announced** his training plan for the County Meet. When he **talked** with reporters, he already **had started** his training. Derek **runs** at least five miles every day. He **said** he **will have run** 30 miles by the end of this week. He **will enter** some local meets soon. Springfield High School **wishes** you luck, Derek!

## Practice B

Point out that a verb phrase has at least two verbs. It may have three or more.

### *Practice B Answers*

1. <u>was</u> writing 2. <u>has been</u> playing 3. <u>is</u> practicing 4. <u>has</u> known 5. <u>should have</u> left

## Practice C

Have students compare the simple and perfect tenses before they complete the practice. Ask a volunteer to explain how to tell simple and perfect tenses apart. (Perfect tenses use a form of *has*.)

### *Practice C Answers*

announced—past, talked—past, had started—past perfect, runs—present, said—past, will have run—future perfect, will enter—future, wishes—present

**LEARNING STYLES**

**Visual/Spatial**
Have students who need additional help write subjects and predicates in different colors. Then have them use a third color to highlight or circle the verb within the predicate.

**ELL/ESL STRATEGY**

**Language Objective:**
*To practice using simple and perfect tenses of common verbs*

Students may find the formation of English tenses confusing. Give students a list of useful, familiar English verbs. Have them make a chart showing the simple and perfect tenses of each verb in their own language. Then help them add the English equivalents in a row just below the native tenses. Pair ELL/ESL students with English-speaking students and have partners make up a sentence using each verb tense correctly. Partners can help each other learn the tenses of the verbs in each language.

Beginning writers can be inconsistent in their use of verb tense. Explain that, if the actions happen at the same time, tenses of all verbs should be the same. Write on the board:

*Derek and Brandon went to the gym. First they lifted weights. Then they run laps. Finally they took a shower.*

Have students read the sentences aloud, find the error in tense, and correct it. If students have difficulty with the tenses of irregular verbs, provide sheets with principal parts of common irregular verbs. Have them memorize the parts and practice them in original sentences.

## Practice D

Before students complete the practice, review the present, past, and past perfect forms of a regular verb. Remind them to consider when the actions in the sentences occur.

### Practice D Answers

**1.** A **2.** A **3.** B **4.** B **5.** A

### Reading Strategy: Questioning

Questions will vary. Possible questions are given.

What is the difference in the time when an action occurs if it is expressed in past perfect instead of simple past tense? How can future perfect tense represent future action when it uses the -ed form of the verb?

## Logical Verb Tense

As a writer, you must decide whether the tense of each verb is logical. Some sentences include more than one main verb. In general, all verbs should be the same tense if the actions occur at the same time. Use different tenses to show that actions happen at different times.

▶ **EXAMPLE 6**

Since Derek wanted to win, he practiced often.
(Both verbs are past tense.)

Every morning Amber gets up and feeds the cat.
(Both verbs are present tense.)

Brandon hopes that Derek will win the race.
(The tenses are different.)

In the last sentence above, the verb *hopes* is present tense. The verb phrase *will win* is future tense. The tenses tell you that *right now*, Brandon *hopes* that Derek will *win in the future*.

### Practice D

Read each pair of sentences. Study the verbs in bold. Decide which sentence shows correct use of tenses. Write the letter of the correct sentence on your paper.

1. **A** When Amber **smiles**, the room **seems** brighter.
   **B** When Amber **smiled**, the room **seems** brighter.

2. **A** The gun **fired**, and the runners **dashed** off!
   **B** The gun **fired**, and the runners **dash** off!

3. **A** As Derek **jogs**, he **waved** to his friends.
   **B** As Derek **jogged**, he **waved** to his friends.

4. **A** **Watch** verb tense, and your writing **improves**.
   **B** **Watch** verb tense, and your writing will **improve**.

5. **A** Because Derek **trains** hard, he **raced** well.
   **B** Because Derek **trained** hard, he **has raced** well.

**Reading Strategy:** Questioning

As you read, notice details that explain verb tenses. What questions can you ask yourself about these details?

# REVIEW

Check the tense of each verb in the sentences. Decide how to correct the tenses that are not logical. Write each sentence on your paper.

1. Last Saturday I look forward to my first big race.

2. That morning the alarm sounded, and I jump up.

3. My mother fixes me a good breakfast, and I ate it all.

4. I had already ask Ms. Lentz about having the day off.

5. "I believe that you will succeed," my mother remarks to me.

6. My stomach rumbles and I tensed up, too.

7. I never doubted that I want to win that race.

8. When I won, I celebrate.

9. Now I plan for next week's race, which I intended to win, too!

10. I practice every day next week.

*Writing Correct Sentences*  *Chapter 2*  **45**

1. Last Saturday I looked forward to my first big race. 2. That morning the alarm sounded, and I jumped up. 3. My mother fixed me a good breakfast, and I ate it all. 4. I had already asked Ms. Lentz about having the day off. 5. "I believe that you will succeed," my mother remarked to me. 6. My stomach rumbled and I tensed up, too. 7. I never doubted that I wanted to win that race. 8. When I won, I celebrated. 9. Now I will plan for next week's race, which I intend to win, too! 10. I will practice every day next week.

## Grammar Practice

Have students revise the following sentences to practice using past and past participle forms of verbs:

*I am sick.* [I was sick. I have been sick.]

*She does well.* [She did well. She had done well.]

*They have it.* [They had it. They have had it.]

*Someone gets it.* [Someone got it. Someone has gotten (or got) it.]

*He runs fast.* [He ran fast. He has run fast.]

Then have students write sentences using each verb from the sentences above in a verb phrase. For example, *I am sick* could become *I will be sick. She does well* could become *She could do well.*

## Speaking and Presenting Practice

Have students work with a partner and take turns reading the corrected sentences in "The Big Race" to each other. You may want to suggest that they emphasize verbs in each sentence. Have the listener check whether the verbs "match." Then have students work together to write a paragraph about an exciting event they have participated in. Ask pairs to check their sentences for correct use of verb tenses. Then have them read their paragraphs aloud to the class.

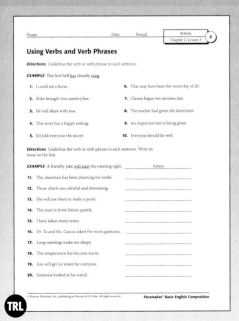

*Writing Correct Sentences*  **45**

## Lesson at a Glance

### Chapter 2 Lesson 4

**Overview** This lesson discusses the use of coordinating conjunctions and the correct punctuation of sentences that have these conjunctions.

### Objectives

■ To combine two sentences using a comma and a conjunction

■ To punctuate a series of three or more items

■ To use the conjunctions *and* and *but* correctly

■ To use conjunctions that work in pairs

**Student Pages** 46–50

**Teacher's Resource Library**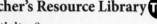

Activity 9

Modified Activity 9

Workbook Activity 9

### Background Information

Stress the importance of the connected items in a series being alike or similar. They should pair one part of speech with the same part of speech, a phrase with a phrase, and a clause with a clause. For example, *Jerry was tall, skinny, and did not stand up straight* is incorrect because it combines two adjectives and one predicate. *Jerry was tall, skinny, and slouchy* joins three adjectives, so it is well structured.

### *Reading Strategy:* Questioning

Students should notice their frequent use of *and* and *or* to add together or show a choice between elements: *you and I, fried eggs or scrambled eggs.*

### Objectives

■ To combine two sentences using a comma and a conjunction

■ To punctuate a series of three or more items

■ To use the conjunctions *and* and *but* correctly

■ To use conjunctions that work in pairs.

***Reading Strategy:***
Questioning

As you read, ask yourself: How does this lesson connect to my daily life? How do I use conjunctions when I speak?

 **NOTE**
A series is a list of three or more items.

# Using Conjunctions to Combine Ideas

You can combine short, choppy sentences about related ideas with a conjunction. A conjunction is a word that connects related words or groups of words. The most common conjunctions are *and*, *but*, *or*, *nor*, *yet*, and *so*.

## The Conjunction *And*

You can use the conjunction *and* to join words, phrases, and sentences.

▶ **EXAMPLE 1**

| Joining Words | I enjoy swimming and jogging. |
| Joining Phrases | She looked at work and at home. |
| Joining Sentences | Write well, and the world is yours! |

Here are some rules for using conjunctions.

**Rule 1** Connect only related ideas.

**Incorrect** Brandon plays tennis **and** eats lunch.
**Correct** Brandon plays tennis **and** jogs.

When you connect two words or phrases with a conjunction, no comma is needed. When you connect three or more words or phrases, commas are needed.

**Rule 2** Use commas to separate three or more words or phrases in a series.

**Incorrect** We like tennis swimming and golf.
**Correct** We like tennis, swimming, and golf.

**Rule 3** Place the last comma in a series before the conjunction.

**Incorrect** The children were lost, tired and, hungry.
**Correct** The children were lost, tired, and hungry.

## 1 Warm-Up Activity

Write these sentences on the board.

*Ben made sandwiches.*

*Carrie bought potato salad.*

*Darlene brought fresh fruit.*

Ask students how they might combine the three sentences into one sentence. Help them see that the word *and* can be used to join the three sentences.

## 2 Teaching the Lesson

Ask a volunteer to read aloud the sentences in Example 1. Have students identify the words, phrases, and sentences that are joined. Then have them tell what is alike about the parts. (They have the same form: *-ing* noun forms, prepositional phrases, simple sentences.) Read a sentence that lacks this structure: *I enjoy swimming and to go for a jog.* Have them comment on how it sounds to them.

When you connect two or more related sentences, you create a compound sentence.

**Rule 4** Use a comma before the conjunction when you combine two or more sentences.

**Incorrect**   Amber had a French test on Monday and she studied very hard.

**Correct**   Amber had a French test on Monday**,** and she studied very hard.

### Practice A

Combine each set of short sentences. Create one sentence using the conjunction *and*. Write the new sentence on your paper. Use commas to separate three or more items in a series. Be sure the new subject and verb agree.

1. Monday it rained. Tuesday it rained. Wednesday it rained.
2. I like running and cooking. I like listening to music.
3. The dog was lost. It was tired. It was hungry.
4. Amber is late. Sonia is late. Their friend Brandon is late.
5. We marched up the hill. We marched down the hill. We marched across a field.

### Practice B

Each sentence has at least one punctuation mistake. Write each sentence correctly on your paper.

1. Springfield is a large town and it is growing rapidly.
2. He signed up for a class in baking breads, and pies.
3. Luis speaks English, French and, Spanish.
4. She teaches at the school, and lives near it.
5. Toronto New York and Los Angeles are big cities.

## COMMON ERROR

Students may place a comma *after* coordinating conjunctions, especially if they have been told to insert commas for natural pauses in sentences. Explain that, although people may tend to pause after a conjunction when speaking, commas do not usually go after a conjunction.

## Practice A

Have students look for sentence parts that repeat in each item. Point out that the nonrepeating parts can be joined and the repeating part used only once.

### Practice A Answers

**1.** Monday, Tuesday, and Wednesday it rained.  **2.** I like running, cooking, and listening to music.  **3.** The dog was lost, tired, and hungry.  **4.** Amber, Sonia, and their friend Brandon are late.  **5.** We marched up the hill, down the hill, and across a field.

## Practice B

Emphasize that a comma is used to separate items in a series. It is also used between two sentences that have been joined.  Write the following sentence on the board. Have students explain why it does not need a comma:

*Jack washed the car and cleaned the garage.*

### Practice B Answers

**1.** Springfield is a large town, and it is growing rapidly.  **2.** He signed up for a class in baking breads and pies.  **3.** Luis speaks English, French, and Spanish.  **4.** She teaches at the school and lives near it.  **5.** Toronto, New York, and Los Angeles are big cities.

## Practice C

Have students highlight the comma in compound sentences (items 1, 3, 4, 5) to remind them that a comma goes before the conjunction. Ask what other way the ideas could be joined in sentence 5. (*A dictionary and a thesaurus are useful sources for writers.*)

### Practice C Answers

**1.** Amber has a dog, but Sonia does not. **2.** Both Amber and Sonia are Derek's friends. **3.** Amber wanted to go to dancing class, but it was canceled. **4.** Sonia plays in the orchestra, but she did not play tonight. **5.** A dictionary is one useful source for writers, and a thesaurus is another.

## The Conjunction *But*

You have learned that the conjunction *and* connects related ideas. You use the conjunction *but* to point out an exception to a statement. Study the use of *and* and *but* in Example 2.

▶ **EXAMPLE 2**

I like apples and pears.

I like apples but not pears.

I enjoy reading, and I have many books.

I enjoy reading, but I read only magazines.

### Practice C

Complete each sentence using *and* or *but*. Write the new sentence on your paper.

1. Amber has a dog, _____ Sonia does not.

2. Both Amber _____ Sonia are Derek's friends.

3. Amber wanted to go to dancing class, _____ it was canceled.

4. Sonia plays in the orchestra, _____ she did not play tonight.

5. A dictionary is one useful source for writers, _____ a thesaurus is another.

### The Conjunctions *Or*, *So*, and *Yet*

You have seen how the words *and* and *but* connect ideas in sentences. You can also use the conjunctions *or*, *so*, and *yet* to connect ideas. You can use conjunctions to connect two or more words or phrases. You can also use them to connect two sentences.

**Reading Strategy:** Questioning

Notice the details in what you read. What questions will help you to understand these details?

▶ **EXAMPLE 3**

I would like milk or juice.

Will he travel by plane, or will he take the train?

He said he would come by plane, yet he arrived by train.

The play had begun, so everyone hurried.

Look for the commas in the sentences in Example 3. Remember Rule 4 on page 47. When you join two sentences with a conjunction, use a comma before the conjunction.

## Conjunctions That Work in Pairs
Some conjunctions work in pairs:

- *either . . . or*
- *neither . . . nor*
- *not only . . . but also*

▶ **EXAMPLE 4**

You may choose to read either a novel or a play.

Neither Amber nor Brandon has arrived.

The kitten was not only tired but also wet and muddy.

**NOTE**

When you use *either/or* and *neither/nor* as conjunctions, the verb agrees with the last noun or pronoun in the pair. You would say, "Neither the children nor their mother likes strawberries."

**Practice D**

Find the conjunctions in the sentences. Write them on your paper.

1. The class will read a short story or several poems.
2. It was August, yet the weather grew cold.
3. The winds blew not only from the east but also from the north.
4. I will either phone you tonight or see you tomorrow.
5. The dog hid the keys, so Amber never found them.

*Writing Correct Sentences   Chapter 2*   **49**

---

**Reading Strategy:** Questioning

Questions will vary. Sample questions are given.

Why are these ideas (or phrases or words) joined? How is this conjunction used in this sentence?

## Practice D
After students complete the practice, write the sentences on the board. Have volunteers circle the conjunctions and underline the words, phrases, or clauses. Ask students to find subjects and verbs in compound sentences.

### *Practice D Answers*
**1.** or  **2.** yet  **3.** not only . . . but also
**4.** either . . . or  **5.** so

## Writing Practice
Point out that *either/or* points to a positive comparison, while *neither/nor* points to a negative one. *Neither Amber nor Brandon has arrived* means the same as saying *Amber has not arrived, and Brandon has not arrived*. Divide the class into pairs. Have partners brainstorm a list of pairs of items, such as *gloves and mittens* or *friends and acquaintances*. Have students write sentences using *neither/nor* and *either/or* with these items. For example:

*Either gloves or mittens will keep your hands warm.*

*Neither his friends nor his acquaintances visited him in the hospital.*

Ask pairs to share their sentences. Ask students to explain the meaning of what they hear.

---

**LESSON 2-4**

# REVIEW

Each sentence has one mistake. Write the sentence correctly on your paper.

**1.** Some plays are funny and others are sad.

**2.** She may choose a red hat or, she may choose a green hat.

**3.** The fruit tasted sweet, juicy and, fresh.

**4.** The dog ran around the tree, and jumped in the water.

**5.** Helen paints landscapes, and portraits.

Choose the correct conjunction in parentheses. Write the conjunction on your paper.

**6.** Most snakes are harmless, (and, but) many people fear them anyway.

**7.** The drivers honked their horns, (so, yet) the traffic did not move.

**8.** We have neither the time (or, nor) the patience for this.

**9.** Either the doorbell rang, (or, nor) I was hearing things.

**10.** The shoes were not only too small (or, but also) too worn.

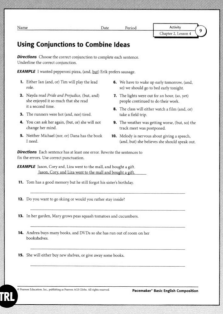

Activity 9

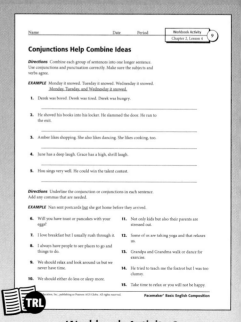

Workbook Activity 9

## LESSON 2-5

# Using Other Kinds of Conjunctions

**Objectives**

- To recognize independent and dependent clauses
- To identify a subordinating conjunction in a sentence
- To write a sentence using a subordinating conjunction

**Independent clause**

A group of words with a subject and a predicate that expresses a complete thought; a sentence

**Dependent clause**

A group of words with a subject and a predicate that does not express a complete thought

**Subordinating conjunction**

A conjunction that joins a dependent clause to an independent clause

A sentence is also called an **independent clause.** It has a subject and a predicate. It also expresses a complete thought.

You can also use a **dependent clause** in writing and speaking. A dependent clause has a subject and a predicate, but it does not express a complete thought.

▶ EXAMPLE 1

Independent Clause   Derek walked home.

Dependent Clause     Because he needed exercise.

A dependent clause begins with a **subordinating conjunction.** Here are some common subordinating conjunctions.

Subordinating Conjunctions

| | | |
|---|---|---|
| after | in order that | when |
| although | since | whenever |
| as | so that | where |
| because | unless | wherever |
| if | until | while |

A dependent clause begins with a subordinating conjunction. It has a subject and a predicate. A dependent clause can be at the beginning or end of a sentence. It is not a complete sentence by itself, however.

*Writing Correct Sentences    Chapter 2    **51***

---

## TEACHER ALERT

Point out that compound sentences require a comma before the coordinating conjunction. Complex sentences require no comma *before the subordinating conjunction.* (A comma in a complex sentence separates the clauses only when the conjunction begins the sentence.)

## Practice A

Tell students to read each half of the sentence by itself. The dependent clause begins with a subordinating conjunction and does not make sense standing alone because it is not a complete thought.

### Practice A Answers

**1.** If you want a puppy  **2.** because they were late  **3.** While the sun shines  **4.** When Sonia plays her violin  **5.** although the movie had not ended

## Practice B

Be sure students have understood the rule for punctuating sentences with subordinating conjunctions.

### Practice B Answers

**1.** Because she trained hard, Sarah won the race.  **2.** correct  **3.** While the other runners lift weights, Sarah runs sprints.  **4.** Although she feels ready, Sarah will not stop training.  **5.** correct

### Reading Strategy: Questioning

Both kinds of conjunctions (in Lessons 2-4 and 2-5) can be used to join two sentences.

---

### Practice A

Find the subordinating clause in each sentence. Write it on your paper.

1. If you want a puppy, try the animal shelter.
2. Everyone hurried because they were late.
3. While the sun shines, the temperature stays warm.
4. When Sonia plays her violin, everyone listens.
5. Everyone clapped although the movie had not ended.

Follow these rules for punctuating sentences with subordinating conjunctions.

**Rule 1**  If the sentence begins with a dependent clause, put a comma after the clause.

**Rule 2**  Do not use a comma if the dependent clause comes after the independent clause.

In Example 2, the dependent clauses are in blue.

▶ **EXAMPLE 2**

When we arrived, the play had already begun. (comma)

The play had already begun when we arrived. (no comma)

### Practice B

Each sentence contains a dependent clause. If the sentence needs a comma, write the sentence correctly on your paper. If the sentence is correct, write *correct.*

1. Because she trained hard Sarah won the race.
2. Sarah will keep training until the next track meet.
3. While the other runners lift weights Sarah runs sprints.
4. Although she feels ready Sarah will not stop training.
5. I will win the race if I can.

**Reading Strategy:**
Questioning

How do the ideas in this lesson compare to the ideas in Lesson 2-4?

---

## ELL/ESL STRATEGY

**Language Objective:** *To learn the meanings of subordinating conjunctions and to identify and write complex sentences*

Students learning English will have difficulty identifying dependent clauses if they do not know the meanings of subordinating conjunctions. These words set up an expectation in native

English speakers that more will follow. Have students look up each word on the list on page 51 in a dictionary. Suggest that they locate the example sentence for the word when used as a conjunction. Provide examples for the conjunctions students find confusing: *I cannot go to the movie until my homework is done.* When students know the meanings and "clues" offered by each subordinating conjunction, the words will act as signals to help them identify complex sentences.

---

**Reading Strategy:**
Questioning

What questions can you ask that will help you understand difficult sentences?

## Practice C

Write each sentence on your paper. Underline the dependent clause once. Underline the subordinating conjunction twice.

**Example:** James read a book <u>while I knitted</u>.

1. After the game was over, we were very tired.

2. Because everyone disagreed, we voted again.

3. The students studied before they took the test.

4. I couldn't get a job unless I filled out an application.

5. Although he likes tennis, Derek chose to join the soccer team.

## Practice D

Use four subordinating conjunctions to combine sentences in the paragraph. Write the new paragraph on your paper. Use correct punctuation. Use the chart on page 51 for help.

### Never Give Up!
by Brandon Tucker

I lost my first tennis match. I was not playing well. I expected to improve. I needed to practice every day. My friend Derek practiced with me. He gave me good pointers. The first defeat had been disappointing. I entered another tournament. I played my best. I won the first match! I continued to play well. I lost in the second round. I definitely had improved. I plan to keep trying.

## Practice E

Use each subordinating conjunction in a sentence.

1. because
2. while
3. unless
4. where
5. when

## COMMON ERROR

Students may mistake a word group that occurs after a word in the subordinating conjunctions list as a dependent clause. Point out that, just as most words have various meanings, they can also be used as different parts of speech. For example, *since* can be used as a conjunction (*It has been two years since he graduated.*), a preposition (*It has been two hours since lunch.*), or an adverb (*Those coupons have long since expired.*). Advise students to read carefully.

## LEARNING STYLES

**Auditory/Verbal**
Have students work with a partner after completing Practice D. Ask one student to read the original paragraph aloud and the other student to read the revised paragraph aloud. Then have the pairs discuss how each paragraph sounds, writing several adjectives to describe each. Bring the class together to discuss their conclusions.

## Practice C

Work through the example sentence with students. Write the sentence on the board. Explain why each part is marked the way it is.

### *Practice C Answers*

1. <u>After the game was over</u>, we were very tired. **2.** <u>Because everyone disagreed</u>, we voted again. **3.** The students studied <u>before they took the test</u>. **4.** I couldn't get a job <u>unless I filled out an application</u>. **5.** <u>Although he likes tennis</u>, Derek chose to join the soccer team.

### **Reading Strategy:** Questioning

Questions will vary. Sample questions are given.

When does adding a dependent clause require the use of a comma? How do you choose which subordinating conjunction to use when you join two related ideas?

## Practice D

Have students read the paragraph silently. Discuss ideas in it that could be combined. Then have students rewrite the paragraph.

### *Practice D Answers*

Paragraphs will vary. A possible paragraph follows.
Because I was not playing well, I lost my first match. If I expected to improve, I needed to practice every day. When my friend Derek practiced with me, he gave me good pointers. Although the first defeat had been disappointing, I entered another tournament. I played my best until I won my first match! I continued to play well, but I lost in the second round. Since I definitely had improved, I plan to keep trying.

## Practice E

Remind students to use each word as a subordinating conjunction only.

Subord. Conj.:   *We swam after we ate.*

Preposition:   *We swam after breakfast.*

### *Practice E Answers*

Sentences will vary. Check students' work.

## Lesson 2-5 Review Answers

**1.** Amber wanted to go to the game <u>because</u> it was the championship.
**2.** <u>Although</u> she was happy to see them, I was not. **3.** Luis gave Amber a big smile <u>whenever</u> he looked at her. **4.** We knew Brandon was mad <u>because</u> he was frowning. **5.** <u>When</u> Derek kicked the ball into the goal, the crowd cheered.
Sentences will vary. Possible sentences are shown. **6.** Until I get your permission, I will not go. **7.** No one has seen Derek since the game ended. **8.** Luis lived in Puerto Rico until he moved to Springfield. **9.** Amber is strong because she lifts weights.
**10.** Although Amber's dog Rex is loyal, he does not follow her to school.

### WRITE ABOUT IT

Have students jot down key verbs and describing words in a word web. Then instruct students to use the strongest verbs and images in their sentences about what happened.

## Six Traits of Writing Focus

| Ideas | | Word Choice | |
|---|---|---|---|
| Organization | ✔ | Sentence Fluency | |
| Voice | | Conventions | ✔ |

## Conventions

Suggest that students take their time when checking another student's work. Tell them to read for grammar, spelling, punctuation, and capitalization, and then review the errors with the author.

Tell students they can also focus on sentence fluency to determine if the writing is smooth and connected.

Refer students to page WPH1 for descriptions of the Six Traits of Writing.

---

# REVIEW

Find the punctuation mistake in each sentence. Write the sentence correctly on your paper. Underline the subordinating conjunction.

1. Amber wanted to go to the game, because it was the championship.
2. Although she was happy to see them. I was not.
3. Luis gave Amber a big smile, whenever he looked at her.
4. We knew Brandon was mad. Because he was frowning.
5. When Derek kicked the ball into the goal the crowd cheered.

Join each pair of sentences with a subordinating conjunction. Write the new sentence on your paper.

6. Until I get your permission. I will not go.
7. No one has seen Derek. The game ended.
8. Luis lived in Puerto Rico. He moved to Springfield.
9. Amber is strong. She lifts weights.
10. Amber's dog Rex is loyal. He does not follow her to school.

### WRITE ABOUT IT

**A School Event**
School events can create memories for a lifetime. Think about a school event that was important to you. It could be something recent or from long ago. Write several sentences about this event. Tell what happened and why you remember it. Use at least one conjunction. Use strong verbs. Check that each verb agrees with the subject. Share your writing with another student.

 **Six Traits of Writing:**
*Conventions* correct grammar, spelling, and mechanics

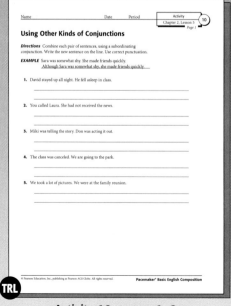

## Sportswriter

Hau Lin writes sports articles. He covers high school baseball, basketball, and football. Read Hau's article. Then answer the questions.

> The Lincoln Lions surprised their fans when they beat the Salem Bulldogs last night. The Lions met the Bulldogs on a wet field. The Lions passed and ran the ball well in a cold rain. Quarterback Lon Green threw for three touchdowns in the first half. However, the Bulldogs controlled the second half. With two minutes left, the teams were tied 21-21. The Lions marched the ball down the field, and kicker Jamal Jones drilled a field goal. The clock ran out on the Bulldogs, and Lions fans went wild. The Lions won 24-21.

### SPEAKING AND LISTENING

Find a newspaper or a sports magazine. Read an article about a sports event. Circle the action verbs. Underline conjunctions in compound sentences. Read your article to a partner. Discuss how action verbs and compound sentences make the article clear.

1. List five action verbs that describe what happened at the game.

2. The article has two compound sentences. Copy these sentences on your paper.

3. CRITICAL THINKING How do action verbs and compound sentences improve a sports article?

Ask a volunteer to read aloud the first paragraph. Discuss with students why sportswriters need to use verbs correctly and combine related ideas. Point out that the writer used simple past tense throughout the article.

Have on hand a sports article about an event at your school. Work with students to identify verbs in the article as action or state of being. Then write several subjects and verbs from article sentences on the board. Have students note whether they agree in number. Underline any verb phrases. Circle any perfect tenses.

### Writing on the Job Answers

**1.** Possible answers: surprised, beat, met, passed, ran, threw, controlled, marched, drilled, ran **2.** The Lions marched the ball down the field, and kicker Jamal Jones drilled a field goal. The clock ran out on the Bulldogs, and Lions fans went wild. **3.** Answers will vary. A sample answer is shown. Action words report what happened exactly. Compound sentences show how one thing led to another or how actions are connected.

## WRITING PORTFOLIO

**Checkpoint** Have students review their sentences about getting organized for the day. Challenge them to join some of the sentences using subordinating conjunctions and coordinating conjunctions (*and, but, so, or, yet*).

Name ___ Date ___ Period ___ Writing on the Job 1 — Chapter 2

**Sports Writer**

A sports writer uses strong verbs to catch the excitement of the action. He or she makes sentences as clear as possible so readers know what happened. For example, verb tense should be logical and clear.

Carlie wrote an article for the school paper. She covered a soccer game. Read the first paragraph of Carlie's article. Find the mistakes she made with verbs. Then follow the directions below.

> **Jets Defeat Stingers in Close Match**
> The Jets just squeaked by the Stingers in last night's match. Goalie Lynn Roman saves the day by stopping six shots on goal by the Stingers. Forward Natalie Beckman powered the ball for two goals in the first half. Then Beckman scored on a corner kick to break a 2–2 tie. The Stingers playing without their star forward Camie Sinjay, who sprained her ankle in the opening minutes. This break will be just enough for the Jets, who won the contest 3–2.

1. Find three mistakes in verb tense and circle them.

2. Rewrite the three sentences using the verbs correctly on the lines below.

3. **CRITICAL THINKING** Explain why you corrected one of the verbs the way you did. What was wrong with the tense?

© Pearson Education, Inc., publishing as Pearson AGS Globe. All rights reserved. **Pacemaker® Basic English Composition**

**TRL**

Writing on the Job 1

Explain that the size of a report topic should be small enough so all the important ideas can be covered in a few pages but large enough so you can find several resources on it.

If students struggle with the concept of narrowing a topic, work with a topic that they can relate to personally. For example:

*My personality and goals* (very broad—hundreds of aspects)

*What I like* (limited slightly; would require many pages to explore)

*Why I like riding horses* (limited enough—six or seven reasons can be explored in an essay)

### *Building Research Skills Answers*

**1.** safe cell phone use in vehicles
**2.** Answers will vary. A sample answer is given: "Global Warming Heats Up" by Jeffrey Kluger, *Time,* April 3, 2006, pages 17–23.
**3.** Answers will vary. A sample answer is given: Effects of global warming on polar ice caps; *National Geographic* magazine; *The New York Times* newspaper

### Narrowing a Topic

The topic of a written assignment should fit the length of the assignment. Most reports are two or more pages long. When you choose a topic, make sure it is focused on a limited subject. You may lose focus in a very broad subject.

Suppose you choose to write a report about cars. Your list of topics might look like this:

- cars in America
- the history of trucks
- how hybrid cars save gas

The first two topics are too broad. You could fill a room with all the information about cars in America. Several books could be written about the history of trucks. However, you could cover hybrid cars well in just a few pages. This topic is limited enough for a report.

1. Three writing topics are listed below. Which topic could you cover well in a short report? Write this topic on your paper.

   - a history of the computer
   - safe cell phone use in vehicles
   - cell phones today and tomorrow

2. Find a magazine article about a topic that interests you. Write the article title, author, and magazine title. Also list the date or issue of the magazine and the page numbers of the article.

3. **CRITICAL THINKING** Think of a report topic related to the article you found. Write your topic. Narrow your topic if necessary. List two places you can find information for your report.

### MEDIA AND TECHNOLOGY

Magazines are a good source of information about hybrid cars. The *Readers' Guide to Periodical Literature* is a good reference to check. It lists magazine articles by topic and by author. Use the *Readers' Guide* to look up an entry about hybrid cars. Write the author, article title, and magazine information for this entry. Check the Key to Abbreviations in the front of the *Readers' Guide* if you do not understand an abbreviation.

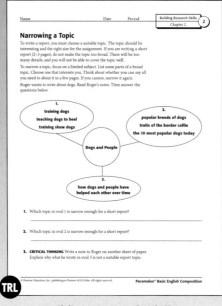

- The subject of a sentence can be singular or plural.

- Make sure the subject and verb of a sentence agree in number. The ending of a present-tense verb depends on whether the subject is singular or plural.

- Use indefinite pronouns (such as *anyone, both,* or *several*) to refer in a general way to people, places, and things.

- To form the past tense and past participle of a regular verb, add *-ed* to the present tense.

- To form the perfect tenses of a verb, use the helping verb *have* and the past participle.

- Irregular verbs form their past tense and past participle in different ways. Study irregular verbs and memorize their forms.

- Use conjunctions to connect related words, phrases, and sentences.

- Use the conjunction *but* to point out an exception to a statement.

- Use commas and one conjunction in a series of three or more words or phrases.

- Use a comma when a conjunction joins two related sentences. Put the comma before the conjunction.

- Do not use a dependent clause as a sentence. A dependent clause must be part of an independent clause.

- Use subordinating conjunctions to combine related ideas.

## GROUP ACTIVITY

Work with a group of students. Pick a topic that interests all of you. The topic might be music, cooking, or a game. Together, make a list of details about this topic. Tell what you like about it. Then write a paragraph

about the topic. Use action verbs to add interest. Try to improve the sentences you wrote. For example, join simple sentences that are related.

## Chapter 2 Summary

Have volunteers read aloud each Summary item on page 57. Ask volunteers to explain the meaning of each item.

### ONLINE CONNECTION

For a lesson in how to use the *Readers' Guide to Periodical Literature,* consult this site:

www.agsglobepmbec.com/page57a

Further suggestions for narrowing report subjects (with an emphasis on writing about technical subjects) appear at this site:

www.agsglobepmbec.com/page57b

### GROUP ACTIVITY

With the groups of students, brainstorm topics. If the groups have difficulty, help them brainstorm details or use a word web. Once this is complete, have the groups work together to write their paragraph. Remind them to use action verbs to make their sentences more interesting. Encourage them to look for ways to improve their sentences.

## Chapter 2 Review

Use the Chapter Review to prepare students for tests and to reteach content from the chapter.

## Chapter 2 Mastery Test

The Teacher's Resource Library includes two forms of the Chapter 2 Mastery Test. Each test addresses the chapter Goals for Learning. An optional third page of additional critical-thinking items is included for each test. The difficulty level of the two forms is equivalent.

### Review Answers

#### Part A

**1.** past participle **2.** irregular verb
**3.** singular **4.** state-of-being verb **5.** plural
**6.** regular verb **7.** subordinating conjunction
**8.** indefinite pronouns **9.** dependent clause
**10.** simple tenses **11.** perfect tenses
**12.** independent clause **13.** action verbs

---

**Word Bank**

action verbs
dependent clause
indefinite pronouns
independent clause
irregular verb
past participle
perfect tenses
plural
regular verb
simple tenses
singular
state-of-being verb
subordinating conjunction

**Part A** Find the word or words in the Word Bank that complete each sentence. Write your answer on your paper.

1. To form the perfect tenses of a verb, use the _____ of the verb with a helping verb.

2. An _____ does *not* form its past tense and past participle by adding *-ed* or *-d* to its present tense.

3. A noun or pronoun that names one thing is _____.

4. A verb that tells the condition of the subject is a _____.

5. A noun or pronoun that names two or more things is _____.

6. A _____ forms its past tense and past participle by adding *-ed* or *-d* to its present tense.

7. A _____ joins a dependent clause to an independent clause.

8. *Anyone* and *everyone* are examples of _____ because they refer to people in a general way.

9. A _____ is a group of words with a subject and a predicate that does *not* express a complete thought.

10. The three _____ are past, present, and future.

11. The three _____ are present perfect, past perfect, and future perfect.

12. A sentence is also an _____.

13. *Jog* and *think* are examples of _____ because they tell what someone is doing.

---

Name _____ Date _____ Period _____ | Mastery Test A / Chapter 2 / Page 1

### Chapter 2 Mastery Test A

**Part A** Underline the verb in parentheses that agrees with the subject of each sentence.

1. Spanish class (lasts, last) 50 minutes.
2. Derek, Amber, and Eliza all (takes, take) Spanish.
3. They (dreams, dream) of going to Spain.
4. The rain (falls, fall) hard.
5. The students (watches, watch) from the window.
6. Everyone (feels, feel) sleepy after lunch.
7. Most of the afternoon (goes, go) slowly as they fight off sleep.
8. Few of the windows (is, are) open.
9. None of the students (gets, get) much done.
10. Then the bell (rings, ring) and the boredom (disappears, disappear).

**Part B** Circle the letter of the correct form of the verb for each sentence.

11. She _____ painted a rosy picture.
   A has    B have    C is    D did
12. Last year, Derek _____ every episode of his favorite TV show.
   A seen    B had saw    C saw    D had taken
13. By next year, I _____ all the required courses for graduation.
   A took    B will have taken    C taked    D had taken
14. Call me after you _____ your dinner.
   A eats    B ated    C will be eating    D have eaten
15. Amber told me what she _____.
   A do    B had done    C doing    D done

© Pearson Education, Inc., publishing as Pearson AGS Globe. All rights reserved. | **Pacemaker® Basic English Composition**

---

Name _____ Date _____ Period _____ | Mastery Test A / Chapter 2 / Page 2

### Chapter 2 Mastery Test A, continued

**Part C** Write each verb phrase on the line. Circle each helping verb.

16. Mona has gone to the store. _____
17. She will return soon. _____
18. She will have bought fruit. _____
19. We should wash a bowl. _____
20. I can slice the apples. _____
21. Where did I put that knife? _____
22. The salad must be finished by noon. _____
23. Barb might cut the lemons. _____
24. Bill has peeled some oranges. _____
25. The fruit salad will be tasty. _____

**Part D** Join ideas from each set of sentences to make one smooth sentence. Use the conjunction in parentheses. Write your new sentence on the lines. Add any punctuation that is needed.

26. Today there was lightning. Today there was thunder. (and)
_____
27. Mom likes dancing. Dad refuses to dance at all. (but)
_____
28. You may write a poem. You may write a short story. (or)
_____
29. She was waiting for the bus. Amber read her book. (while)
_____
30. Moises moved his coat. Chantal could have a seat. (so that)
_____

© Pearson Education, Inc., publishing as Pearson AGS Globe. All rights reserved. | **Pacemaker® Basic English Composition**

---

Name _____ Date _____ Period _____ | Mastery Test A / Chapter 2 / Page 3

### Chapter 2 Mastery Test A, continued

**Part E** Write your answer to each question. Use complete sentences. Support each answer with facts and examples from the textbook.

31. How is an irregular verb different from a regular verb?
_____
32. When could an action verb also be part of a verb phrase?
_____

**Part F** Write a paragraph for each question. Include a topic sentence, body, and conclusion in the paragraph. Support your answers with facts and examples from the textbook.

33. Why do you think we need perfect tenses of verbs? Explain what they show.
_____
34. Read the clauses below. Explain why one of them is not a sentence. Then tell how you would join them and why this would improve them.
Until you apologize. I will be upset about your comment.
_____

© Pearson Education, Inc., publishing as Pearson AGS Globe. All rights reserved. | **Pacemaker® Basic English Composition**

Chapter 2 Mastery Test A, pages 1–3

**Part B** Choose the verb that agrees with the subject of the sentence. Write the letter of your answer.

14. Sonia _____ the violin.
   A play   B plays   C have played   D playing

15. Amber and Derek _____ soccer.
   A enjoys   B enjoy   C has enjoyed   D enjoying

16. Amber's dog _____ the fence.
   A jump          C jumping
   B have jumped   D has jumped

**Part C** Complete each sentence with a perfect tense of the verb in parentheses. Use the past participle with *has*, *have*, or *had*. Write the sentence on your paper.

17. "I _____ on it last week," Brandon said.  (work)

18. Derek and Brandon _____ home.  (go)

19. She _____ most of the assignment.  (do)

20. Yesterday my sister _____ her homework by suppertime.  (finish)

**Part D** Find the mistakes in each sentence. Make two sentences into one correct sentence. Write the new sentences on your paper.

21. Derek would like to drive or he can't.

22. Rex is barking. Rex is hungry.

23. Because Brandon practices daily. He is improving his game.

24. The test will cover Chapters 5 6 and 7.

25. The students can take the test again. If they got a low score.

**Test Tip**

Read test directions carefully. Find the key words. Ask yourself: What am I being asked to do? There may be several steps to complete.

*Writing Correct Sentences*  Chapter 2  **59**

## Review Answers

### Part B
**14.** B  **15.** B  **16.** D

### Part C
**17.** "I had worked on it last week," Brandon said.  **18.** Derek and Brandon have gone (or had gone) home.  **19.** She has done (or had done or will have done) most of the assignment.  **20.** Yesterday my sister had finished her homework by suppertime.

### Part D
Sentences will vary. Reasonable answers are shown.  **21.** Derek would like to drive, but he can't.  **22.** Rex is barking because he is hungry.  **23.** Because Brandon practices daily, he is improving his game.  **24.** The test will cover Chapters 5, 6, and 7.  **25.** The students can take the test again if they got a low score.

## WRITING PORTFOLIO

**Wrap-Up** Have students share their sentences about getting organized. Ask them how well they did in the following areas by rating themselves from 1 to 5, with 1 being best and 5 being worst:

- All my subjects and verbs agree.
- I have used the forms of regular and irregular verbs correctly.
- I have used conjunctions correctly to combine ideas.

This project may be used as an alternative form of assessment for the chapter.

---

Chapter 2 Mastery Test B, pages 1–3

*Writing Correct Sentences*  **59**

# PLANNING GUIDE

# Writing Better Sentences

| | | Student Lesson | | | Language Skills | | | | |
|---|---|---|---|---|---|---|---|---|---|
| | Student Pages | Vocabulary | Practice Exercises | Lesson Review | Identification | Writing | Punctuation & Capitalization | Grammar & Usage | Listening, Speaking, & Viewing |
| **Lesson 3-1** Replacing Nouns with Pronouns | 63–67 | ✔ | ✔ | ✔ | ✔ | ✔ | ✔ | ✔ | ✔ |
| **Lesson 3-2** Using Plural and Possessive Nouns | 68–71 | ✔ | ✔ | ✔ | ✔ | ✔ | ✔ | ✔ | ✔ |
| **Lesson 3-3** Adding Adjectives and Adverbs | 72–76 | ✔ | ✔ | ✔ | ✔ | ✔ | ✔ | ✔ | ✔ |
| **Lesson 3-4** Comparing with Adjectives and Adverbs | 77–80 | ✔ | ✔ | ✔ | ✔ | ✔ | ✔ | ✔ | ✔ |
| **Lesson 3-5** Adding Prepositional Phrases | 81–89 | ✔ | ✔ | ✔ | ✔ | ✔ | ✔ | ✔ | ✔ |

## Chapter Activities

**Teacher's Resource Library**
Life Skills Connection 3: Using
    Comparative Forms Correctly
    When You Speak
Writing Tip 3: Spicy Adjectives
English in Your Life 2: Explaining
    How to Do Something
Building Research Skills 3: Using a
    Dictionary
Key Vocabulary Words 3

## Assessment Options

**Student Text**
Chapter 3 Review

**Teacher's Resource Library**
Chapter 3 Mastery Tests A and B

**Teacher's Edition**
Chapter 3 Writing Portfolio

| English in Your Life | Writing on the Job | Building Research Skills | Vocabulary Builder | Grammar Builder | Write About It | Group Activity | Reading Strategy | Six Traits | ELL/ESL Strategy | Background Information | Common Error | Life Skills Connection | Applications (Home, Career, Community, Global) | Online Connection | Teacher Alert | Speaking & Presenting Practice | Writing/Spelling/Grammar Practice | Auditory/Verbal | Body/Kinesthetic | Interpersonal/Group Learning | Logical/Mathematical | Visual/Spatial | Activities | Modified Activities | Workbook Activities | Self-Study Guide |
|---|---|---|---|---|---|---|---|---|---|---|---|---|---|---|---|---|---|---|---|---|---|---|---|---|---|---|
| | | | | | | | 63, 66 | | 65 | 63 | 64, 66 | | 64 | | 65, 66 | | | | | | | | 11 | 11 | 11 | ✔ |
| | | | | | | | 68, 69 | | 69 | 68 | 69 | | 70 | | | | 71 | 69 | | | | | 12 | 12 | 12 | ✔ |
| | | | 76 | | | | 73, 75 | | 74 | 72 | 73 | | 73, 74 | | 73 | 75 | | 74 | | 74 | | | 13 | 13 | 13 | ✔ |
| | | | | 80 | | | 78, 79 | | 80 | 77 | 78 | 79 | 78 | | | | 78 | | | 77 | 79 | | 14 | 14 | 14 | ✔ |
| 87 | 88 | | | | 86 | 89 | 82, 85 | 86 | 83 | 81 | 82 | | | 89 | | 87 | 85 | | 82 | 81, 84 | | 83 | 15 | 15 | 15 | ✔ |

## Pronunciation Key

| | | | | | | | | | | | | |
|---|---|---|---|---|---|---|---|---|---|---|---|---|
| a | hat | e | let | ī | ice | ô | order | ù | put | sh | she | a in about |
| ā | age | ē | equal | o | hot | oi | oil | ü | rule | th | thin | e in taken |
| ä | far | ėr | term | ō | open | ou | out | ch | child | ᴛʜ | then | ə { i in pencil |
| â | care | i | it | ȯ | saw | u | cup | ng | long | zh | measure | o in lemon |
| | | | | | | | | | | | | u in circus |

## Modified Activities

The Teacher's Resource Library (TRL) contains a set of lower-level worksheets called Modified Activities. These worksheets cover the same content as the standard Activities but are written at a lower reading level.

## Skill Track

Use Skill Track for *Basic English Composition* to monitor student progress and meet the demands of adequate yearly progress (AYP). Make informed instructional decisions with individual student and class reports of lesson and chapter assessments. With immediate and ongoing feedback, students will also see what they have learned and where they need more reinforcement and practice.

(Answer Keys for the Teacher's Resource Library begin on page 446 of the Teacher's Edition.)

Writing Tip 3

Life Skills Connection 3

# Writing Better Sentences

**H**ow do you get to school? Do you walk, drive, or ride a bus? Look at the photo on the opposite page. Suppose you ride a bus to school. A bus will get you there more quickly and easily than if you walk.

In Chapter 3, you will learn to write better sentences by choosing better words. Better sentences will help your readers understand your ideas quickly and easily. Words that are carefully chosen move your writing in the right direction. Specific words add interest to this plain sentence:

*I rode the bus to school.*

*On Saturday, I rode the early bus to art school.*

The added words give details. They state the idea more clearly. As you read this chapter, you will learn to use nouns, pronouns, adjectives, adverbs, and prepositional phrases in your sentences.

## GOALS FOR LEARNING

- To replace nouns with pronouns
- To use plural and possessive nouns correctly
- To improve sentences by adding adjectives and adverbs
- To use adjectives and adverbs to make comparisons
- To use prepositional phrases in sentences

**61**

## Introducing the Chapter

Have students look at the photo on page 60. Ask them to state sentences telling about what is happening and why. (For example, students might say, "A student is getting on the bus to go to school.") Write several of the sentences on the board. Then have volunteers read the text. Point out that improving one's writing allows the writer to communicate ideas more easily. Model how choosing specific words sharpens and enlivens the sentences. For example, "A new high school student is timidly stepping up to the bus, clutching her books nervously." Tell students that Chapter 3 will focus on sentence elements that will make their writing more clear and correct.

Review and discuss the Goals for Learning on page 61.

## Notes

Ask volunteers to read the notes that appear in the margins throughout the chapter. Then discuss them with the class.

## TEACHER'S RESOURCE

The AGS Globe Teaching Strategies in English Transparencies may be used with this chapter. The transparencies add an interactive dimension to expand and enhance the *Basic English Composition* program content.

## WRITING PORTFOLIO

Ask students to write at least 10 sentences about a memorable trip or outing they took with family or friends. As they complete each lesson in the chapter, students can return to their sentences and revise them. Point out that the suggestions in each lesson can help them make their writing more specific and vivid. This project may be used as an alternative form of assessment for the chapter.

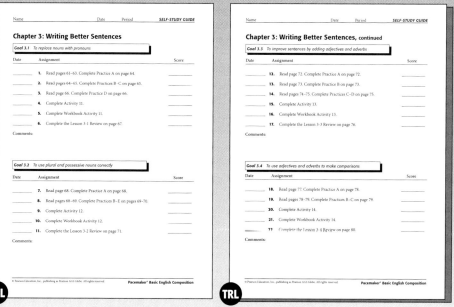

## Reading Strategy: Predicting

Ask students to name some predictions they have made and explain how they made them. Point out that writers give clues to help readers understand what is coming. Have students read the text about predicting. Discuss reasons why readers should be willing to change their predictions.

## Key Vocabulary Words

adjective
adverb
antecedent
apostrophe
comparative form
feminine
gender
masculine
personal pronoun
positive form
possessive noun
preposition
prepositional phrase
superlative form
synonym
thesaurus

Read aloud the words. Have volunteers define the terms they are familiar with in their own words. Write the unfamiliar words on the board. Then read the definition of each. Ask volunteers to write an example of each (as it applies to the English language) on the board except for *thesaurus*.

# Reading Strategy: Predicting

To preview a text means to take a quick look through it. Previewing a text helps readers predict what will come next. As you preview, think about what you already know about the subject. Look for new information. Then predict what will come next.

## Key Vocabulary Words

**Antecedent** The noun that a pronoun replaces

**Masculine** Relating to males

**Feminine** Relating to females

**Gender** Masculine or feminine

**Possessive noun** A word that shows ownership or a relationship between two things

**Personal pronoun** A pronoun that refers to a person or a thing

**Apostrophe (')** A punctuation mark that you use to show a noun is possessive

**Adjective** A word that describes a noun or pronoun

**Thesaurus** A book that lists words and their synonyms

**Synonym** A word that has the same meaning as another word

**Adverb** A word that answers questions about a verb, an adjective, or another adverb; it tells when, how, how often, where, or to what degree

**Positive form** The form of an adjective or adverb that you use to describe one person or thing

**Comparative form** The form of an adjective or adverb that you use to compare two people or things; formed by adding *-er* to the positive form or by adding the word *more*

**Superlative form** A form of an adjective or adverb that you use to compare three or more people or things; formed by adding *-est* to the positive form or by adding the word *most*

**Prepositional phrase** A group of words made up of a preposition and a noun or pronoun; it works like an adjective or an adverb in a sentence

**Preposition** A word that shows a relationship between a noun or pronoun (its object) and other words in a sentence

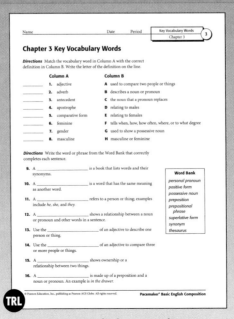

# Replacing Nouns with Pronouns

## Objectives

- To use pronouns to replace nouns in sentences
- To identify the antecedent of a pronoun
- To recognize the gender of a noun or pronoun
- To identify singular and plural nouns and pronouns

**Antecedent**
The noun that a pronoun replaces

**Reading Strategy:** Predicting
Preview the lesson title. Predict what you think you will learn in this lesson.

When you speak or write, you use nouns to name people, places, things, and ideas. It would be awkward to use the same noun several times in a sentence. Instead, you use a pronoun. A pronoun replaces a noun in a sentence. An **antecedent** is the noun that the pronoun replaces.

▶ EXAMPLE 1

Amber and Amber's mother go to pottery class.

Amber and her mother go to pottery class.

The pronoun *her* replaces *Amber's*. The antecedent is *Amber's*.

You cannot use a pronoun until you have identified the noun. If there is no antecedent, the listener or reader will not know who or what you are talking about.

▶ EXAMPLE 2

No Antecedent Given — Brandon saw it yesterday. (saw what?)

Antecedent Given — Brandon saw the movie yesterday. He liked it.

In the second sentence, you know what Brandon saw. The pronoun *it* has an antecedent. The antecedent is *movie*. The pronoun is not always in the same sentence as the antecedent.

There are two rules to remember:

**Rule 1** A pronoun must have an antecedent.

**Rule 2** A pronoun must agree with its antecedent.

*Writing Better Sentences* Chapter 3 **63**

## Chapter 3 Lesson 1

**Overview** This lesson discusses using pronouns to replace nouns in sentences. It discusses antecedents. It explains how to use pronouns clearly and correctly by making sure they agree with their antecedents in number and gender.

## Objectives

- To use pronouns to replace nouns in sentences
- To identify the antecedent of a pronoun
- To recognize the gender of a noun or pronoun
- To identify singular and plural nouns and pronouns

**Student Pages** 63–67

**Teacher's Resource Library**

Activity 11

Modified Activity 11

Workbook Activity 11

## Vocabulary

antecedent    masculine
feminine    personal pronoun
gender    possessive noun

Explain the meaning of each word in the context of pronouns. Then have students write a sentence containing an example of each word. For example, for *feminine* students might write, *She read her book.*

## Background Information

In the past it was correct to say, *Each passenger should carry his own ticket.* The masculine pronoun was used to agree with its antecedent *each passenger* although the gender of the passengers might be masculine, feminine, or both. Today, the correct way to express this idea is *Each passenger should carry his or her own ticket.* To avoid the wordy *his or her,* writers can make the subject plural: *All passengers should carry their own tickets.*

## 1 Warm-Up Activity

On the board write the sentence *Mike told Matt he liked his new haircut.* Ask students whether the meaning is clear and if not, why. Point out that it is not clear whom the two pronouns, *he* and *his,* refer to. Did Mike or Matt get the haircut? Explain that this lesson will help students recognize pronouns and use them correctly and clearly.

**Reading Strategy:** Predicting

Students should predict that they will learn how to use pronouns to replace nouns.

## 2 Teaching the Lesson

Read the definition of *pronoun* in the text and the two Example 1 sentences on page 63. Read the definition of *personal pronoun* on page 66. Ask students to look at the pronoun chart on page 66. Then call out a particular item from the chart. Ask a student to give a sentence using the appropriate pronoun from the chart. Continue until all the pronouns on the chart have been used correctly. Finally, read the definition of *antecedent* on page 63 and the Example 1 sentences again.

### COMMON ERROR

Students may use the pronoun *they* to refer vaguely to some authority, as in *They will fine you for littering*. Remind students that all pronouns must have a clear antecedent. The sentence above could be revised as *According to the law, you could be fined for littering*.

## Practice A

Ask a volunteer to define *antecedent* in his or her own words and give an example.

### *Practice A Answers*

**1.** it—national park **2.** he—Derek **3.** it—cave **4.** him—Brandon **5.** we—Brandon and Derek

### GLOBAL CONNECTION

Point out that English has fewer gender distinctions than other languages. Students who are familiar with Spanish, French, German, or any other language that has this feature may share examples of masculine and feminine nouns with classmates.

---

**Gender**
Masculine or feminine

**Masculine**
Relating to males

**Feminine**
Relating to females

 **NOTE**

Some nouns that name animals show gender. A mare is a female horse, and a stallion is a male horse. Nouns that name places, things, or ideas are usually neither masculine nor feminine.

---

Find the antecedent for each pronoun in bold. Write the pronoun and its antecedent on your paper.

1. Derek read about a national park in Kentucky. **It** is called Mammoth Cave.
2. "I would like to see this cave," **he** said.
3. "Tell me about **it**," Brandon said.
4. "A river runs through the cave's lowest level," Derek told **him.**
5. "**We** should plan to visit this cave," Brandon said.

### Gender and Number

Nouns are words that name people, places, things, or ideas. Some nouns that name people show **gender.** Gender tells if the noun is **masculine** or **feminine.** Masculine nouns refer to males. Feminine nouns refer to females. Some pronouns are also masculine or feminine.

▶ **EXAMPLE 3**

| Masculine | Brandon, man, boy, uncle, father, he, him, his |
|---|---|
| Feminine | Sonia, woman, girl, aunt, mother, she, her, hers |
| No Gender | table, mountain, city, pencil, it, they |

**Rule 3** A pronoun must agree with its antecedent in gender.

▶ **EXAMPLE 4**

Derek went to the movies. He saw a comedy.

Amber has a dog named Rex. She loves that dog!

The bell rang. It signaled that class had begun.

---

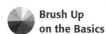

**Brush Up on the Basics**

Make sure the antecedent for a pronoun is clear. Unclear: When the snowball hit the window, it shattered. (What shattered?) Clear: The snowball shattered when it hit the window. See Grammar 41 in Appendix A.

Replace plural nouns with *they*, *them*, or *their*. It does not matter whether the noun is a group of men, women, or things.

▶ **EXAMPLE 5**

Ten families came. They brought their own food.

The store is open now. It stays open all night.

### Practice B

Change the words in bold to pronouns. Write the new sentence on your paper.

1. Amber and Sonia went to **Amber and Sonia's** class.

2. Ms. Ruiz had given **Ms. Ruiz's** class an assignment.

3. "Did everyone do **the assignment?**" asked Ms. Ruiz.

4. "Amber did," Sonia said. "Derek has **Derek's** work, too."

5. "Aren't **Amber and Derek** wonderful," laughed Luis.

**Rule 4** A pronoun must agree with its antecedent in number. If the antecedent is singular, the pronoun is singular. If the antecedent is plural, the pronoun is plural.

| | |
|---|---|
| **Singular Pronouns:** | I, you, he, she, it |
| **Plural Pronouns:** | we, you, they |

### Practice C

In each sentence, a pronoun does not agree with its antecedent. Write each sentence correctly on your paper.

1. Springfield has a park that their people love.

2. The park is off Main Street. They are behind the pool.

3. Three fields are there. It is for playing soccer.

4. The coaches are nice, and everyone likes it.

5. Each team should bring their own equipment.

---

## Practice B

Define masculine, feminine, and neuter genders. Ask students to give examples of pronouns in each. Discuss the use of *his or her*, emphasizing that it is correct although it can often be changed to a plural.

### *Practice B Answers*

**1.** Amber and Sonia went to their class. **2.** Ms. Ruiz had given her class an assignment. **3.** "Did everyone do it?" asked Ms. Ruiz. **4.** "Amber did," Sonia said. "Derek has his work, too." **5.** "Aren't they wonderful," laughed Luis.

### TEACHER ALERT

Another error students may make involves reflexive pronouns (*myself, yourself,* and so on). Ask volunteers to make up and say some sentences using these pronouns. For example, *I will go by myself.* Point out that it is incorrect to use these pronouns as subjects, as in *My sister and myself got tickets for the game.* The subject pronoun *I* should be used instead of *myself.* You may also need to point out to students that there is no such word as *theirselves.* The correct word is *themselves.*

## Practice C

Explain the concept of pronoun number. Ask volunteers to read the example sentences on page 65 and identify each pronoun and antecedent. Explain that students must first locate each pronoun and its antecedent to see if they agree in number. Point out that they may also have to change verbs to agree with the pronouns they change.

### *Practice C Answers*

**1.** Springfield has a park that its people love. **2.** The park is off Main Street. It is behind the pool. **3.** Three fields are there. They are for playing soccer. **4.** The coaches are nice, and everyone likes them. **5.** Each team should bring its own equipment.

Students may need extra help determining when to use subject pronouns and object pronouns. Write the following sentences on the board. Ask students to complete them with the pronoun *he, she, him,* or *her:*

_____ went to the park.
Stacy met _____ there.

Point out that a subject pronoun such as *he or she* must be used to complete the first sentence, since it is the subject of the sentence. An object pronoun such as *him* or *her* must be used to complete the second sentence since it is the object of the verb *met.* Have students complete the following sentences with an appropriate pronoun:

_____ go to the library each day.
The librarian helps _____ find books.
I always thank _____.
_____ knows how to research any topic.
The librarians are nice, so we don't hesitate to call on _____.

### Reading Strategy: Predicting

Students may refine their predictions to include learning how to use pronouns correctly with number and gender.

### Practice D

Read the definition of personal pronouns with the class. Point out that possessive pronouns should only be used in place of possessive nouns. Review the table of personal pronouns on page 66. Ask volunteers to use a personal pronoun in a sentence.

### Practice D Answers

**1.** Derek and Brandon are friends. They enjoy soccer. **2.** "What time should we leave?" asked Brandon. **3.** "What time is good for you?" Derek replied. **4.** "The coach told us to be at the field at 6:00." **5.** "He likes to start practice on time."

---

**Possessive noun**

A word that shows ownership or a relationship between two things

**Personal pronoun**

A pronoun that refers to a person or a thing

**NOTE**

A possessive noun acts as an adjective in a sentence. You will study adjectives in Lesson 3-3.

**Reading Strategy:**
Predicting

Think about your earlier prediction. Does it still work, or do you need to revise your prediction?

---

## Subject, Object, or Possessive Noun

Nouns have different purposes in sentences. The pronoun that replaces a noun depends on the noun's purpose. You can use a noun as a subject or an object. You can also use the possessive form of a noun. A **possessive noun** shows ownership or a relationship between two things.

▶ **EXAMPLE 6**

| | | |
|---|---|---|
| Subject | Sonia enjoys music. | She enjoys music. |
| Object | Amber e-mailed Sonia. | Amber e-mailed her. |
| Possessive | The violin is Sonia's. | The violin is hers. |

The table below lists **personal pronouns.** A personal pronoun refers to a person or a thing. Use the table to find the correct pronoun to replace a noun. A pronoun that replaces a possessive noun is called a possessive pronoun.

| | Subject | Object | Possessive |
|---|---|---|---|
| **Singular** | | | |
| First person | I | me | my, mine |
| Second person | you | you | your, yours |
| Third person | he, she, it | him, her, it | his, her, hers, its |
| **Plural** | | | |
| First person | we | us | our, ours |
| Second person | you | you | your, yours |
| Third person | they | them | their, theirs |

### Practice D

Decide which pronoun completes each sentence. Refer to the table above. Write the new sentence on your paper.

1. Derek and Brandon are friends. _____ enjoy soccer.
2. "What time should _____ leave?" asked Brandon.
3. "What time is good for _____?" Derek replied.
4. "The coach told _____ to be at the field at 6:00."
5. "_____ likes to start practice on time."

---

## COMMON ERROR

Students may incorrectly use object pronouns in place of subject pronouns, especially in sentences with a compound subject. For example, *Mark and me had fun at the game.* Tell students that when using a compound subject containing a pronoun, they can test the pronoun by trying it by itself in the sentence. Students will find that *Me had fun at the game* is clearly incorrect.

# REVIEW

Replace the noun in bold with the correct pronoun. Write the new sentence on your paper.

1. Until Derek was a junior in high school, **Derek** did not study enough.

2. Amber told **Derek** to study harder to get better grades.

3. **Amber** told him the work was worthwhile.

4. Derek found a quiet place where **Derek** liked to study.

5. With all of this effort, **Derek's** grades improved a lot.

Decide which pronoun completes each sentence. Write the sentence on your paper.

6. Derek and Brandon live in Springfield. _____ like their town.

7. Derek and _____ family have lived there for many years.

8. Sonia Moreno enjoys the violin. She plays _____ in the orchestra.

9. Amber, Derek, and Brandon love soccer. _____ play as much as possible.

10. Sonia's cousin Luis is fun to be around. _____ is always telling jokes.

*Writing Better Sentences* *Chapter 3* **67**

## Lesson 3-1 Review Answers

**1.** Until Derek was a junior in high school, he did not study enough. **2.** Amber told him to study harder to get better grades. **3.** She told him the work was worthwhile. **4.** Derek found a quiet place where he liked to study. **5.** With all of this effort, his grades improved a lot. **6.** Derek and Brandon live in Springfield. They like their town. **7.** Derek and his family have lived there for many years. **8.** Sonia Moreno enjoys the violin. She plays it in the orchestra. **9.** Amber, Derek, and Brandon love soccer. They play as much as possible. **10.** Sonia's cousin Luis is fun to be around. He is always telling jokes.

## WRITING PORTFOLIO

**Checkpoint** Students can continue working on their Writing Portfolio project. Check students' progress and address any questions or concerns they have.

---

*Writing Better Sentences* **67**

**Overview**  This lesson distinguishes between plural nouns and possessive nouns and describes the correct use of an apostrophe with the latter.

### Objectives

- To identify possessive nouns and plural nouns
- To write possessive nouns and pronouns correctly

**Student Pages**  68–71

**Teacher's Resource Library** **TRL**

Activity  12

Modified Activity  12

Workbook Activity  12

## Vocabulary

### apostrophe

Have students write the definition of *apostrophe.* Then ask pairs of students to find three examples of apostrophes in other books to indicate a possessive noun. Have them write the sentences.

## Background Information

Many languages, such as French and Spanish, do not have the equivalent of English possessives. Instead of using an apostrophe and an s to show possession, these languages use formations like *the book of my friend.*

### 1  Warm-Up Activity

Have students listen as you say each of the phrases below. Then have them say each phrase in the way that is more commonly used.

*the home of my aunt (my aunt's home)*
*the pencil of my classmate (my classmate's pencil)*
*the sister of David (David's sister)*

Explain that in this lesson students will review how to write these phrases correctly.

---

### LESSON 3-2

# Using Plural and Possessive Nouns

### Objectives

- To identify possessive nouns and plural nouns
- To write possessive nouns and pronouns correctly

**Apostrophe (')**
A punctuation mark that you use to show a noun is possessive

***Reading Strategy:***
Predicting

Based on what you have just read, predict what you think the next page will be about.

People often confuse the possessive and plural forms of a noun because they sound alike. A possessive noun shows ownership or a relationship between two things. Always use an **apostrophe** (') when you write a possessive noun.

▶ **EXAMPLE 1**

| Plural Noun | Possessive Noun |
|---|---|
| The members meet here. | A member's house is nearby. |
| My cousins live in Toronto. | My cousins' house is brick. |

### Practice A

Decide if each noun in bold is plural or possessive. Write *plural* or *possessive* on your paper.

1. Both **teams** met at the stadium.
2. Where is the **poodle's** leash?
3. Everyone in **Eliza's** class liked learning Spanish.
4. These are my running **shoes.**
5. **California's** weather is usually warm.

Here are the rules for writing possessive nouns:

**Rule 1**   Make a singular noun possessive by adding *'s.*

▶ **EXAMPLE 2**

Brandon's book is gone.

Ms. Ruiz's class meets in the morning.

The principal's office is a busy place.

---

### 2  Teaching the Lesson

Discuss the definition of a possessive noun. Have students read the examples silently as you read them aloud. Point out that the apostrophe is extremely important because it helps distinguish a possessive noun from a plural noun. Also point out each possessive phrase and emphasize that it shows ownership: the house belonging to the member and the house belonging to the cousins.

### Practice A

Write the phrases *the lunchroom for the students* and *the student's lunch* on the board. Have students identify the plural noun *(students)* and the possessive noun *(student's).* Then have students complete the activity.

### *Practice A Answers*

1. plural  2. possessive  3. possessive
4. plural  5. possessive

### *Reading Strategy:* Predicting

Students may predict that they will learn how to make a plural noun possessive.

**Reading Strategy:**
Predicting

Think about Rule 1 and Rule 2. Predict what you think Rule 3 will say.

**Rule 2** Make a plural noun possessive by adding only an apostrophe.

▶ **EXAMPLE 3**

The students' papers are not finished.

The boys' locker room needs to be cleaned.

Both cities' problems are the same.

**Rule 3** If a plural noun does not end in -s, add an s after the apostrophe.

▶ **EXAMPLE 4**

People's opinions about this vary.

Our children's jackets still fit them.

The women's team is practicing.

**Practice B**

Decide whether each bold possessive noun is singular or plural. Write *singular* or *plural* on your paper.

1. **Brandon's** room is painted green.

2. What time is the **teachers'** meeting?

3. The students answered the **teacher's** questions.

4. **Men's** shirts are on sale.

5. The **dancers'** feet hurt.

A possessive pronoun does not have an apostrophe.

▶ **EXAMPLE 5**

The dog's bone is buried.          Its bone is buried.

I love Brandon's house.            I love his house.

Amber and Sonia's friend came.     Their friend came.

## 3 Reinforce and Extend

### COMMON ERROR

Students may incorrectly use apostrophes in possessive pronouns: *it's* instead of *its*. Explain that apostrophes are used with pronouns only in contractions (*they're* for *they are*). Tell students that when they write a pronoun with an apostrophe, they should read the sentence aloud, saying both words of the contraction to see if it makes sense. For example, the sentence "The dog chased it's tail" does not make sense when read as "The dog chased it is tail."

**Reading Strategy:** Predicting

Students may predict that Rule 3 will say irregular plural nouns form the possessive in irregular ways.

## Practice B

Ask volunteers to read the rules and examples for forming singular and plural possessive nouns. Emphasize that they must only use these rules for creating possessive nouns, not plural nouns. If they need further help, ask volunteers to explain each example phrase; for example, *students' papers* are the papers completed by the students. Point out that by learning these rules, students can avoid common mistakes in writing possessives.

## *Practice B Answers*

**1.** singular **2.** plural **3.** singular **4.** plural **5.** plural

### LEARNING STYLES

**Auditory/Verbal**

Read the following sentences aloud to students. Ask them to write each sentence, deciding from context whether each noun is plural or possessive.

• *The cat's tail is stuck in the door.*
• *The cats are hungry.*
• *Sharon's trip was fun.*
• *Trips to Florida can be relaxing.*

### ELL/ESL STRATEGY

**Language Objective:** *To practice using possessive nouns*

Students may have difficulty with possessive nouns or may confuse possessive and plural nouns. All students will benefit from reviewing the rules for using plural nouns and possessive nouns correctly:

• Do not add an apostrophe to make a plural noun. Most of the time, just add s.

• Add 's to make a singular possessive noun.

• Add an apostrophe after the final s to make a plural possessive noun.

• If the plural noun is irregular, add 's to make it possessive.

Write the phrases below on the board. Have students identify the owner or owners and the thing or things possessed:

• *worker's wages*
• *singers' notes*
• *robin's wing*
• *students' assignment*
• *student's grades*

## Practice C

Ask volunteers to read the possessive pronouns on the chart on page 66. Then have volunteers read the example sentences using possessive pronouns. Ask them to identify the pronoun and antecedent in each example.

### Practice C Answers

**1.** Where are his running shoes? **2.** Brandon looked everywhere for her car keys. **3.** Their equipment was scattered everywhere. **4.** Rex lost his tennis ball. **5.** Their mothers are sisters.

## Practice D

Remind students that a possessive pronoun, like other pronouns, must agree with the noun it replaces in number and gender. Explain that they must identify the number and gender of each noun before replacing it with a pronoun.

### Practice D Answers

**1.** After school, Derek goes to his job at the gas station. **2.** It is a good job, and the workers like their boss. **3.** Ms. Lenz started her business five years ago. **4.** She has six employees on her staff. **5.** The station is open late. Its closing time is 10 PM.

## Practice E

Review the rules on pages 68 and 69 with students. After students have completed the exercise, you may wish to have them use one or more of the possessive nouns in a sentence.

### Practice E Answers

**1.** child's, children's **2.** man's, men's **3.** family's, families' **4.** shelf's, shelves' **5.** goose's, geese's

**CAREER CONNECTION**

Tell students that if they have a job that requires word processing, they may use spell-checking software to find misspellings. Explain that they cannot use a spell-checker to find mistakes in possessives and plurals. The software can only find words that are not real words; it does not find words that have been used incorrectly, such as using *there* instead of *their*.

---

### Practice C

Replace each bold possessive noun with the correct possessive pronoun. Refer to the table on page 66. Write the new sentence on your paper.

1. Where are **Derek's** running shoes?
2. Brandon looked everywhere for **Amber's** car keys.
3. **The players'** equipment was scattered everywhere.
4. Rex lost **Rex's** tennis ball.
5. **Luis's and Sonia's** mothers are sisters.

### Practice D

Write each sentence on your paper. Add the correct possessive pronoun. Refer to the table on page 66.

1. After school, Derek goes to _____ job at the gas station.
2. It is a good job, and the workers like _____ boss.
3. Ms. Lenz started _____ business five years ago.
4. She has six employees on _____ staff.
5. The station is open late. _____ closing time is 10 PM.

### Practice E

Read each pair of nouns. The first one is singular, and the second one is plural. Write the possessive form of each word on your paper.

**Example:** loaf, loaves
**Answer:** loaf's, loaves'

1. child, children
2. man, men
3. family, families
4. shelf, shelves
5. goose, geese

# REVIEW

Each sentence has a mistake in the use of possessive and plural nouns. Write the sentence correctly on your paper.

1. The Tuckers home is on Third Street.

2. Both team's were ready for the big event.

3. Childrens' toys were on the floor.

4. My neighbors cat climbed a tree.

5. The fire department brought some ladder's.

Replace each possessive noun in bold with the correct possessive pronoun. Write the new sentence.

6. **Amber's** dog Rex chased her neighbor's cat up a tree.

7. **The cat's** fur stood on end.

8. Derek heard **the cat's** meowing from across the street.

9. Mrs. Chin is **Amber and her mother's** neighbor.

10. The fire department will rescue **Mrs. Chin's** cat.

## Lesson 3-2 Review Answers

**1.** The Tuckers' home is on Third Street.
**2.** Both teams were ready for the big event.
**3.** Children's toys were on the floor. **4.** My neighbor's cat climbed a tree. **5.** The fire department brought some ladders. **6.** Her dog Rex chased her neighbor's cat up a tree. **7.** Its fur stood on end. **8.** Derek heard its meowing from across the street. **9.** Mrs. Chin is their neighbor. **10.** The fire department will rescue her cat.

## Grammar Practice

Have groups of students generate three singular nouns and three plural nouns on topics that interest them, such as *music* and *goalies*. Then have each member of the group write a sentence using each noun as a possessive. For example, *The goalies' skills were great.* Ask the group members to read their sentences aloud. Then have them exchange papers with a partner to see if each possessive noun is spelled correctly.

---

Name _____ Date _____ Period _____ | Activity 12 — Chapter 3, Lesson 2

**Using Plural and Possessive Nouns**

*Directions* Look at the singular form of each word. Write the singular possessive, plural, and plural possessive forms of the word in the columns.

*EXAMPLE*

| | Singular | Singular Possessive | Plural | Plural Possessive |
|---|---|---|---|---|
| | duck | duck's | ducks | ducks' |

| | Singular | Singular Possessive | Plural | Plural Possessive |
|---|---|---|---|---|
| 1. | bus | | | |
| 2. | city | | | |
| 3. | woman | | | |
| 4. | bike | | | |
| 5. | wolf | | | |
| 6. | child | | | |
| 7. | pony | | | |
| 8. | leaf | | | |
| 9. | dress | | | |
| 10. | goose | | | |
| 11. | country | | | |
| 12. | box | | | |
| 13. | week | | | |
| 14. | tree | | | |
| 15. | idea | | | |

*Pacemaker® Basic English Composition*

---

Name _____ Date _____ Period _____ | Workbook Activity 12 — Chapter 3, Lesson 2

**Plurals and Possessives**

*Directions* Decide whether each noun is singular or plural. Write *singular* or *plural* on the line beside each noun. Then write the possessive form of the noun.

*EXAMPLE* dogs _____ plural, dogs' _____

1. video _____          7. suitcases _____

2. wife _____          7. fox _____

3. people _____          8. coaches _____

4. men _____          9. feet _____

5. toothbrush _____          10. radios _____

*Directions* The apostrophes have been left out of these possessive phrases. Read each phrase and write it on the line. Put an apostrophe in the correct place.

*EXAMPLES* the ladys purse _____ the lady's purse _____
the mens club _____ the men's club _____

11. the wolfs howl _____          16. a books cover _____

12. the calves pen _____          17. the cities parks _____

13. Ambers dog Lucky _____          18. the peoples choice _____

14. the childrens room _____          19. the familys car _____

15. the Smiths vacation _____          20. two cats food _____

*Pacemaker® Basic English Composition*

# Lesson at a Glance

## Chapter 3  Lesson 3

**Overview**  This lesson focuses on the correct use of adjectives and adverbs as modifiers. It explains how to use a thesaurus to find specific words to replace vague words.

## Objectives

- To use adjectives and adverbs in sentences
- To choose specific adjectives and adverbs
- To know the purpose of a thesaurus

**Student Pages** 72–76

**Teacher's Resource Library** (TRL)

Activity 13

Modified Activity 13

Workbook Activity 13

## Vocabulary

adjective          synonym
adverb             thesaurus

Define each word. Have pairs of students make a set of flash cards containing the vocabulary words. Then ask the pairs to take turns holding up cards so partners can define each word.

## Background Information

Peter Mark Roget was a 19th century physician. For 50 years he compiled words in order to write a book that listed words and their synonyms. Reference books of synonyms had been published before. However, Roget's book, first published in 1852, differed in that it put words in six categories such as *matter* and *intellect*. *Roget's Thesaurus* is still a popular reference book.

## 1  Warm-Up Activity

Point to objects in the room and have students name one or two adjectives that describe each. Remind them that they can add interest to their writing by using adjectives.

---

# Adding Adjectives and Adverbs

## Objectives

- To use adjectives and adverbs in sentences
- To choose specific adjectives and adverbs
- To know the purpose of a thesaurus

**Adjective**
A word that describes a noun or pronoun

 **Brush Up on the Basics**

Adjectives and adverbs help you to add "color" to a description. They paint a picture for readers. They bring nouns and verbs to life. See Grammar 51 and 60 in Appendix A.

An **adjective** describes a noun or pronoun. An adjective tells how many, what kind, or which ones. Look at the adjectives in Example 1. Think about the question each adjective answers.

▶ **EXAMPLE 1**

| How Many? | one book, few athletes, three flowers |
| What Kind? | heavy book, strong athletes, purple flowers |
| Which Ones? | Mia's book, those athletes, other flowers |

*Mia's* is the possessive form of *Mia*. A possessive noun acts as an adjective.

Adjectives add details to sentences. Adjectives often appear in front of the words they describe.

▶ **EXAMPLE 2**

The teenager ate a plate of food in gulps.

The hungry teenager ate a huge plate of hot food in four gulps.

## Practice A

The nouns in each sentence are in bold. Write the sentence again. Add an adjective for each noun.

1. The **family** planted a **tree** in the **yard.**
2. In **class,** the **girl** did a **somersault.**
3. Sonia likes **apples** with **peanut butter** on them.
4. The **man** ate the **sandwich.**
5. The **dog** ate a **bowl** of **food.**

---

## 2  Teaching the Lesson

Ask volunteers to read the examples on pages 72 and 73. Ask them to identify the adjectives and nouns in the phrases and sentences. Emphasize that adjectives always describe a noun or a pronoun. Remind students that more than one adjective can be used to describe a noun, as in *sunny, breezy day.*

## Practice A

Make sure students understand the directions. Explain that you could use an adjective such as *large* or *cheerful* to describe the first noun in sentence 1, *family.* Encourage students to use interesting, specific adjectives.

## Practice A Answers

Sentences will vary. Possible sentences follow. **1.** The cheerful family planted a tiny tree in the front yard. **2.** In gym class, the athletic girl did a quick somersault. **3.** Sonia likes sweet apples with creamy peanut butter on them. **4.** The busy man ate the ham sandwich. **5.** The playful dog ate a huge bowl of dry food.

**Thesaurus**
A book that lists words and their synonyms

**Synonym**
A word that has the same meaning as another word

*Reading Strategy:*
Predicting

Think about what you have just read about adjectives. Now predict what the next page will tell you about adverbs.

**NOTE**

Most word-processing programs have a thesaurus. You can also find a thesaurus online. These resources allow you to type in a word you want to replace. They give you synonyms for the word. Sometimes they also provide definitions.

---

Help your readers form sharp pictures by using specific adjectives. *Specific* means exact or detailed. Avoid vague adjectives such as *good, nice, bad,* and *pretty. Vague* means general.

▶ **EXAMPLE 3**

| Vague | Specific |
|---|---|
| It was a nice day. | It was a sunny, breezy day. |
| The fruit tasted good. | The fruit tasted juicy and fresh. |

A **thesaurus** is a book that lists words and their **synonyms.** A synonym is a word with the same meaning as another word. A thesaurus can help you find more specific words to replace a vague word. Choose the synonym that has the meaning you want.

▶ **EXAMPLE 4**

| Vague | More Specific Synonyms for *Bad* |
|---|---|
| a bad storm | dangerous, threatening, severe |
| a bad dog | mischievous, stubborn, vicious |
| a bad taste | sickening, bitter, sour |

**Practice B**

Replace each adjective in bold with a more specific one. Use a thesaurus if possible. Write the new sentence on your paper. Use your imagination!

1. My best friend is **nice.**
2. The sky looks **nice.**
3. Write a **good** sentence.
4. The team had a **bad** game.
5. Those flowers are **pretty.**

---

## TEACHER ALERT

Write this sentence on the board:

*Joy ate a sweet, juicy, delicious orange.*

Point out that commas separate the three adjectives, but not the last adjective and the noun. Also explain that when the adjective closest to the noun is needed for the noun's meaning, a comma is not used:

*Pam has two small children.*

Tell students to test if a comma is needed between adjectives by replacing each comma mentally with the word *and.* If *and* fits, a comma should be used.

---

## COMMON ERROR

Students may use words from a thesaurus incorrectly. They may not know a word's part of speech or may not understand differences in meaning. Suggest that if they find an unfamiliar word in a thesaurus, students should check the word in a dictionary to be sure they understand it.

*Reading Strategy:* Predicting

Students may predict that the text will tell them adverbs describe verbs.

### Practice B

Show students a thesaurus. Ask a volunteer to suggest a common adjective. Show students how to find the word in the thesaurus and then read the synonyms. Have students pass one or more thesauruses around or share them in groups.

### *Practice B Answers*

Sentences will vary. Possible sentences follow. **1.** My best friend is charming. **2.** The sky looks glorious. **3.** Write an elegant sentence. **4.** The team had a miserable game. **5.** Those flowers are delightful.

## AT HOME

Ask students to visualize a room at home. Have them write five sentences that describe the room clearly. Have students underline the adjectives in their sentences.

**Adverb**
A word that answers questions about a verb, an adjective, or another adverb; it tells when, how, how often, where, or to what degree

 **NOTE**

Two adverbs that people use too much are *very* and *quite*. You can often remove these overused words without changing the meaning of your sentences.

An **adverb** tells more about a verb, an adjective, or another adverb. Adverbs often give details about actions. An adverb can tell when, how, how often, or where. Look at the adverbs in Example 5. Think about the question each adverb answers.

▶ **EXAMPLE 5**

| When? | Today we will shop early and eat later. |
| How? | Read slowly and carefully. Write clearly. |
| How Often? | Fees are paid weekly. Check in daily. |
| Where? | Put your umbrella there. We will go outside. |

Each adverb in Example 5 tells more about a verb. Adverbs also answer questions about an adjective or another adverb. Such adverbs tell about degree.

▶ **EXAMPLE 6**

| To What Degree? | Amber was extremely worried. Rex ran too quickly. He was almost lost. |

*Rex often runs off, but Amber always manages to find him.*

## Practice C

Each adverb is in bold. Decide what question each adverb answers. Write one of these choices on your paper: *when, how, how often, where,* or *to what degree.*

1. **Immediately,** the door slammed shut.

2. The bell rings **hourly.**

3. That group is **especially** busy.

4. The baby smiled **happily.**

5. We looked **everywhere** for the keys.

You can add variety to sentences by moving adverbs around. Notice the adverb in the sentences in Example 7.

▶ **EXAMPLE 7**

Turtles often move slowly.

Often, turtles move slowly.

Turtles move slowly, often.

## Practice D

Find the adverb in each sentence. Move the adverb to a different place in the sentence. Write the new sentence on your paper.

**The Tennis Tournament**
by Brandon Tucker

1. I entered the tennis tournament and actually thought I might win.

2. My serve has been strong lately.

3. "I will certainly win at least a few games," I told myself.

4. The match was over quickly.

5. I lost, but my friends immediately congratulated me for trying.

## Practice C

Discuss what an adverb is and what questions an adverb can answer in a sentence. Have volunteers read the Example 5 and 6 sentences on page 74. Have them identify each adverb and the word it tells more about.

### *Practice C Answers*

1. when 2. how often 3. to what degree 4. how 5. where

## Practice D

Read the Example 7 sentences on page 75. Discuss with students how rearranging adverbs can help them avoid using one sentence pattern too often.

### *Practice D Answers*

Sentences will vary. Possible sentences follow. 1. I entered the tennis tournament and thought I might actually win. 2. Lately, my serve has been strong. 3. "I will win at least a few games, certainly," I told myself. 4. The match was quickly over. 5. I lost, but my friends congratulated me immediately for trying.

### Speaking and Presenting Practice

Have pairs of students read their new sentences for Practice D to one another. Point out that listening to a sentence can help them decide whether the adverb placement "sounds right." Suggest that they try placing the adverb in different locations to see which placement they like best.

### **Reading Strategy:** Predicting

Students should revise their predictions to include questions that adverbs answer and other categories of words adverbs can describe.

### IN THE COMMUNITY

Ask students to attend a school or sports event or to watch one on television. Have them write a paragraph describing the players or the action. Tell students to use at least one adverb in each sentence and to underline the ones they use. Encourage them to use at least one adverb that answers each of the questions on page 74.

Complete the sentences by adding specific adjectives. Write the new sentences on your paper.

1. The _____ artist created a _____ sculpture.
2. I am looking for _____ shoes.
3. The morning air feels _____ and _____.
4. Would you like some _____ bread?
5. Some dancers can do _____ jumps.

Find the adverb in each sentence. Move the adverb to a different place in the sentence. Write the new sentence.

6. Amber gracefully danced across the stage.
7. Brandon sometimes does his homework in his room.
8. Rex, the beagle, bravely guarded the house.
9. The book disappeared mysteriously.
10. Sonia has not been to the movies lately.

### VOCABULARY BUILDER

**Using Synonyms**
A synonym is a word that means the same or about the same as another word. Choose the synonym with the meaning that fits the sentence. For example, *joyful* and *content* are synonyms for *happy*. Which word fits best in this sentence?
    Despite his simple life, the poor fisherman was ____.
*Joyful* means "filled with great happiness." *Content* means "happy enough not to complain." The word *content* fits best. For each bold word, write a synonym that fits the sentence.
1. The picture had a **pretty** frame.
2. The cook made **plain** food.

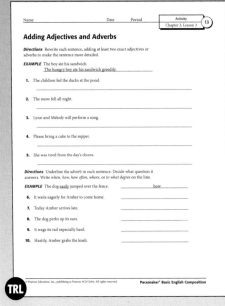

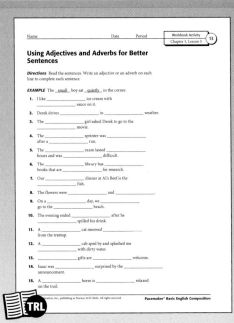

# Comparing with Adjectives and Adverbs

## Objectives

- To use adjectives and adverbs to make comparisons
- To use the comparative and superlative forms of adjectives and adverbs
- To recognize irregular adjectives and adverbs
- To avoid double comparisons

You can use adjectives and adverbs in your sentences to make comparisons. Each adjective and adverb has three forms: positive, comparative, and superlative.

**Rule 1** Use the **positive form** to describe one person or thing. Use the **comparative form** when you compare two people or things. Use the **superlative form** to compare more than two people or things.

| | |
|---|---|
| Positive | Brandon is **tall.** |
| Comparative | Brandon is **taller** than Derek. |
| Superlative | Brandon is the **tallest** one in his family. |

**Rule 2** For most one-syllable words, add -er or -est to the positive form.

| Positive | Comparative | Superlative |
|---|---|---|
| young | younger | youngest |
| wise | wiser | wisest |
| fast | faster | fastest |
| happy | happier | happiest |

**Rule 3** For words of more than one syllable, use *more* and *most* or *less* and *least*.

| Positive | Comparative | Superlative |
|---|---|---|
| beautiful | more beautiful | most beautiful |
| expensive | less expensive | least expensive |

**Rule 4** When an adjective ends in -*y*, change the *y* to *i* and add -*er* or -*est*.

| Positive | Comparative | Superlative |
|---|---|---|
| easy | easier | easiest |

### Positive form
The form of an adjective or adverb that you use to describe one person or thing

### Comparative form
The form of an adjective or adverb that you use to compare two people or things; formed by adding -*er* to the positive form or by using the word *more*

## Chapter 3  Lesson 4

**Overview** This lesson explains how to correctly make comparisons with adjectives and adverbs.

### Objectives

- To use adjectives and adverbs to make comparisons
- To use the comparative and superlative forms of adjectives and adverbs
- To recognize irregular adjectives and adverbs
- To avoid double comparisons

**Student Pages** 77–80

**Teacher's Resource Library**

- Activity **14**
- Modified Activity **14**
- Workbook Activity **14**
- Life Skills Connection **3**

## Vocabulary

comparative form
positive form
superlative form

Define each term. Write the word *nice* on the board. Have students write each vocabulary term followed by an example using the word *nice.*

## Background Information

Not all adjectives and adverbs have a comparative and superlative form. Some words, such as *unique, perfect,* and *dead,* are considered absolutes. Although something cannot be called *the most perfect,* it could be called *almost perfect.*

### 1 Warm-Up Activity

Ask these questions:

*Who is older, you or your brother?*

*Who is the funniest person in your family?*

*Can you run faster than your sister?*

Explain that all the questions compare you to other family members. Have students make up additional questions comparing family members.

### 2 Teaching the Lesson

Have volunteers read the examples of the positive, comparative, and superlative forms of adjectives and adverbs on page 77. Discuss the definitions of *positive form, comparative form,* and *superlative form.* Emphasize that when only two people, places, or things are being compared, the comparative form is used. Read aloud the one-syllable words and their comparative and superlative forms in Rule 2. Ask students to name additional words to which -*er* and -*est* are added.

### 3 Reinforce and Extend

#### LEARNING STYLES

**Interpersonal/Group Learning**

Have students work in groups of three. Ask each student to write five adjectives that are not in this lesson. One group member should read one of his or her words. Then a second group member should say the comparative form of the adjective. Then the third group member should say the superlative form.

## Practice A

Point out that for each sentence, students will need to decide whether one person or thing is being described, two persons or things are being compared, or more than two persons or things are being compared.

### Practice A Answers

**1.** That dress is the most beautiful one I have ever seen. **2.** That dress is more expensive than the other one. **3.** "Soccer is easier than tennis," said Brandon. **4.** Derek is the fastest runner on his team. **5.** Fruit is healthier than cookies.

### COMMON ERROR

Students may write a sentence such as *I felt badly about hurting my friend's feelings.* Point out that *badly* is an adverb, so it describes how an action is performed. The correct word in this sentence is *bad,* an adjective to describe the subject *I.* (*Felt* is a state-of-being verb, linking the subject and the predicate adjective *bad* in this sentence.)

### *Reading Strategy:* Predicting

Students may predict that irregular adverbs will not use *-er* or *-est* or *more* or *most* to form the comparative and superlative forms.

### IN THE COMMUNITY

Have students discuss their ideas about why superlative forms of adjectives are often used in ads: "Lowest Prices in Town," "Largest Selection of Sports Equipment," and so on. Ask students to make a list of examples of such superlatives from signs and ads. Ask students to share their lists.

---

**Superlative form**
The form of an adjective or adverb that you use to compare three or more people or things; formed by adding *-est* to the positive form or by using the word *most*

**NOTE**
*Good* and *well* have the same comparative and superlative forms.

***Reading Strategy:*** Predicting
You know something about irregular verbs. Predict what you will learn about irregular adjectives and adverbs.

 **Practice A**

Choose the correct form of the adjective in parentheses. Write the sentence on your paper.

1. That dress is the _____ one I have ever seen. (beautiful)
2. That dress is _____ than the other one. (expensive)
3. Soccer is _____ than tennis," said Brandon. (easy)
4. Derek is the _____ runner on his team. (fast)
5. Fruit is _____ than cookies. (healthy)

### Irregular Adjectives and Adverbs

A few adjectives and adverbs have irregular comparative and superlative forms.

| Positive | Comparative | Superlative |
| --- | --- | --- |
| good, well | better | best |
| bad, badly | worse | worst |
| many, much | more | most |
| little | less | least |

▶ **EXAMPLE 1**

| Incorrect | Today I feel even badder than yesterday. |
| --- | --- |
| Correct | Today I feel even worse than yesterday. |

The words *good* and *well* have different meanings as adjectives. You use *good* when you mean something is desirable or likeable. You use *well* when you mean the opposite of sick. *Well* is also an adverb. However, do not use *good* as an adverb. It is only used as an adjective.

▶ **EXAMPLE 2**

| The Adjective *Well* | I feel well today. |
| --- | --- |
| The Adjective *Good* | I thought the poem was good. |
| The Adverb *Well* | I played well in today's game. |
| Incorrect Use of *Good* | I played good in today's game. |

### Writing Practice

Have students write a short note to a friend describing a special place. Ask them to use at least three comparative or superlative adjectives. Help students brainstorm places to write about. Name categories such as *indoor places* and *outdoor places.* Ask students to give examples of each. Then give examples of statements students might use. For example, *I like the library because it is quieter and more peaceful than any other place.*

**NOTE**

When you use the comparative form of adjectives and adverbs, complete the comparison. Instead of "Jill writes better," say "Jill writes better than Emily."

**Reading Strategy:**
Predicting

Predict what *double comparison* might mean.

## Practice B

Choose the correct form of the word in parentheses. Write the sentence on your paper.

1. Of these three books by Agatha Christie, I liked this one _____. (good/well).

2. That was the _____ movie ever made! (bad)

3. Luis played very _____ in the chess tournament. (good/well)

4. _____ rain fell this month than last month. (little)

5. _____ rain falls in July than in December. (many/much)

## Avoiding Double Comparisons

Avoid double comparisons. Add either the ending *-er* or the word *more*, but not both. Add either the ending *-est* or the word *most*, but not both. Do not add an ending if you are using *less* or *least* to make a comparison.

▶ **EXAMPLE 3**

| Incorrect | This car is the most cleanest it's ever been! |
| Correct | This car is the cleanest it's ever been! |
| Incorrect | Which instrument is less noisier? |
| Correct | Which instrument is less noisy? |

## Practice C

Find the mistake in each sentence. Write the sentence correctly on your paper.

1. Today's lunch was more gooder than yesterday's.

2. Summer is the most laziest time of the year.

3. Which of these two brands is more cheaper?

4. The worst storm of the year hit the coast.

5. Stores hire more people for their most busiest season.

## Practice B

Ask students to study the chart of irregular adjectives and adverbs on page 78. Then have them respond to the following prompts in complete sentences.

Compare how well you play two sports.

Compare how well you felt the last time you had a bad cold to how you feel today.

## Practice B Answers

1. Of these three books by Agatha Christie, I liked this one best. 2. That was the worst movie ever made! 3. Luis played very well in the chess tournament. 4. Less rain fell this month than last month. 5. More rain falls in July than in December.

## Practice C

Read the section on avoiding double comparisons aloud to students. Then have volunteers read each example sentence and explain why the first and third are incorrect.

## Practice C Answers

1. Today's lunch was better than yesterday's. 2. Summer is the laziest time of the year. 3. Which of these two brands is cheaper? 4. The worst storm of the year hit the coast. 5. Stores hire more people for their busiest season.

**Reading Strategy:** Predicting

Students may say that *double* means "two". They may predict that a *double comparison* involves two comparisons.

## LIFE SKILLS CONNECTION

Ask students to explain why this sentence is wrong: *The West has the most beautifullest sunsets you have ever seen.* (It is incorrect to use *most* and *-est* together.) Distribute Life Skills Connection 3 and read through the directions. Have students work with a partner.

### LEARNING STYLES

**Logical/Mathematical**

Have students find five interesting facts about things that are highest, largest, smallest, and so on. They can research scientific, architectural, geographic, or other facts on the Internet or in the library. Then have students write a sentence stating each fact and using comparative or superlative forms.

## Lesson 3-4 Review Answers

**1.** Brandon's tennis serve is better than Derek's. **2.** Does Computer Village have the lowest prices? **3.** Which of these two computers is less expensive? **4.** Amber is older than Sonia, but Sonia is taller. **5.** "I just had the most horrible day of my life," announced Sonia. **6.** Celery tastes more delicious than broccoli. **7.** My puppy is young, but Amber's puppy is younger. **8.** Who is the wisest of them all? **9.** These decorations are the fanciest ones we've ever had! **10.** Amber writes better than most people do.

### GRAMMAR BUILDER

Read through the text with the class. Then write these sentences on the board:

*America lies among Canada and Mexico.*

*What are the differences among lions and tigers?*

*She is the smartest between all of us.*

Ask students if the sentences sound correct. Then have volunteers correct the sentences. Point out that *between* always compares two items. *Among* compares three or more. Once this warm-up is complete, have students write their own sentences.

### Grammar Builder Answers

Sample answers: **1.** We eat lunch between third and fourth period. **2.** When I am among my friends, I feel comfortable.

---

Find the mistake in each sentence. Write the sentence correctly on your paper.

1. Brandon's tennis serve is more better than Derek's.

2. Does Computer Village have the most lowest prices?

3. Which of these two computers is least expensive?

4. Amber is older than Sonia, but Sonia is the tallest.

5. "I just had the horriblest day of my life," announced Sonia.

6. Celery tastes deliciouser than broccoli.

7. My puppy is young, but Amber's puppy is youngest.

8. Who is the wiser of them all?

9. These decorations are the fancier ones we've ever had!

10. Amber writes more good than most people do.

### GRAMMAR BUILDER

**Knowing When to Use *Between* and *Among***
Careful writers use the prepositions *between* and *among* correctly. Each word has a different use.

• Use *between* when you discuss two people or things: *between you and me.*

• Use *among* when you discuss three or more people or things: *among the trees.*

Write a sentence using *between* correctly. Then write a sentence using *among* correctly.

---

**Language Objective:**
*To compare and contrast places around the world*

Ask all students to name places around the world. Suggest that students familiar with other countries should name places in those countries. Write the names on the board. Have students write sentences in which one place is compared to another (using adjectives and adverbs in the comparative form) and sentences in which one place is compared to all others (using adjectives and adverbs in the superlative form). Ask volunteers to read their sentences aloud.

---

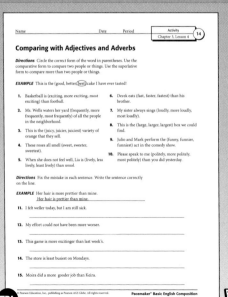

Activity 14

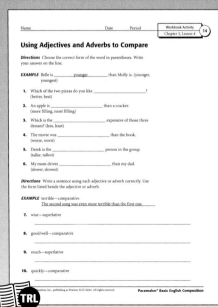

Workbook Activity 14

# Adding Prepositional Phrases

## Objectives

- To identify prepositional phrases in sentences
- To recognize the parts of a prepositional phrase
- To use prepositional phrases in sentences

**Prepositional phrase**

A group of words made up of a preposition and a noun or pronoun; it works like an adjective or an adverb in a sentence

**Preposition**

A word that shows a relationship between a noun or pronoun and other words in a sentence

A **prepositional phrase** is a group of words made up of a preposition and a noun or pronoun. A prepositional phrase works like an adjective or adverb in a sentence.

A prepositional phrase begins with a **preposition.** A preposition is a word that shows a relationship between a noun or a pronoun and other words in a sentence.

### Common Prepositions

| | | | |
|---|---|---|---|
| about | at | for | on |
| across | behind | from | out |
| after | between | in | over |
| against | beyond | into | to |
| among | by | near | under |
| around | during | of | with |

A prepositional phrase begins with a preposition. It ends with a noun or a pronoun.

▶ EXAMPLE 1

over the river    from a friend    in the middle

When you use a preposition with a pronoun, the pronoun must be the object form. The chart on page 66 shows the object form of some pronouns.

▶ EXAMPLE 2

to him    from them    with her

Other words may come between the preposition and the noun or pronoun.

▶ EXAMPLE 3

He woke up during the cold, dark, and rainy night.

*Writing Better Sentences*    *Chapter 3*    **81**

---

## 2   Teaching the Lesson

Write the phrase *at the beach* on the board. Explain that it is a phrase because it is two or more words that work together. Then point out that *at* is a preposition and have students find it on the list on page 81. Next, have students identify the noun in the phrase. Explain that this noun, *beach,* is the object of the preposition.

## 3   Reinforce and Extend

### LEARNING STYLES

**Interpersonal/Group Learning**

Have pairs of students look through newspapers for sentences with prepositional phrases. Ask students to change three sentences by moving their prepositional phrases in a way that causes confusion or humor. Have the partners read one of their sentences aloud. Then have a volunteer correct the sentence.

---

## Lesson at a Glance

### Chapter 3   Lesson 5

**Overview** This lesson discusses the use and placement of prepositional phrases in sentences.

### Objectives

- To identify prepositional phrases in sentences
- To recognize the parts of a prepositional phrase
- To use prepositional phrases in sentences

### Student Pages 81–89

### Teacher's Resource Library

**Activity** 15

**Modified Activity** 15

**Workbook Activity** 15

**English in Your Life** 2

**Building Research Skills** 3

---

## Vocabulary

preposition      prepositional phrase

Define each term. Have students write an example of each and then use each one in a sentence. Have them read their sentences aloud.

---

## Background Information

Prepositions may be especially difficult for English learners. Prepositions are often part of idiomatic expressions, as in *standing in line.* In addition, people in different regions use different prepositions in these expressions, for example *standing on line.* Hearing and using prepositions as well as doing other types of practice is helpful for these students.

## 1   Warm-Up Activity

Have each student take out a book and a pencil. Then make the following requests:

*Put the pencil on the book.*
*Put the pencil under the book.*
*Put the pencil behind the book.*
*Put the pencil inside the book.*

Students should recognize that only one word changed in each sentence. That one word, called a preposition, makes a big difference in meaning.

## Reading Strategy: Predicting

Students may predict that a prepositional phrase could answer the same questions as an adjective or adverb does.

## Practice A

Explain that many prepositional phrases contain words in addition to the preposition and object. Have students point out the additional words in the example sentences on page 82.

### Practice A Answers

**1.** in the middle, of that photo  **2.** for prepositional phrases, in this sentence  **3.** under the car, in the garage  **4.** at the gas station  **5.** for him, on his answering machine

## COMMON ERROR

Students who tend to use fragments may punctuate prepositional phrases as sentences. For example, *We went on a camping trip. At a national park.* Remind students that prepositional phrases alone are never sentences; they describe other words in a sentence. Make sure students familiarize themselves with the list on page 81 to help them avoid this.

## LEARNING STYLES

### Body/Kinesthetic

Ask volunteers to stand up and act out the list of prepositions on page 81. For example, a student might place a book *over* someone's head, *under* someone's desk, *near* someone's face, or *between* two desks. Ask other students to make up a sentence that describes each act.

---

**Reading Strategy:**
Predicting

You have just read what a prepositional phrase is. Now predict how a prepositional phrase could act as an adjective or adverb.

A sentence may include more than one prepositional phrase.

▶ **EXAMPLE 4**

A letter (from my cousin) (in Montreal) appeared (in my mailbox).

## Practice A

Write each prepositional phrase on your paper.  Some sentences have more than one.

**1.** The girl in the middle of that photo is my sister.

**2.** Look for prepositional phrases in this sentence.

**3.** Derek put his tools under the car in the garage.

**4.** He works at the gas station two days a week.

**5.** Sonia left a message for him on his answering machine.

### Adjective Phrases

Prepositional phrases are also called adjective phrases and adverb phrases. An adjective phrase describes a noun or pronoun in a sentence.

▶ **EXAMPLE 5**

| Adjective | The middle boy is my cousin. |
| Adjective Phrase | The boy in the middle is my cousin. |

The phrase *in the middle* describes the noun *boy*.

*After school, Luis talked to a friend on the phone.*

## Practice B

Each sentence contains an adjective phrase in bold. Find the noun that the adjective phrase describes. Write the noun on your paper.

1. We read a poem **by Edgar Allan Poe.**

2. The letter **from Karen** was short.

3. How often is the rodeo **in Centerville** held?

4. A house **near a highway** can be noisy.

5. Would you like fruit salad **with peaches?**

## Practice C

Think of a prepositional phrase to add after each noun in bold. The phrase must describe that noun. Write the new sentence on your paper.

**Example:**      That **man** is my uncle.

**Answer:**      That man in the blue suit is my uncle.

1. George Washington was the first **president.**

2. The **capital** is Quebec City.

3. The **man** won the race.

4. The **building** is 10 stories high.

5. Amber received a birthday **card.**

### Adverb Phrases

An adverb phrase answers a question about a verb, an adjective, or another adverb.

▶ **EXAMPLE 6**

| | |
|---|---|
| Adverb | He arrived later. (arrived when?) |
| Adverb Phrase | He arrived at night. (arrived when?) |

## Practice B

Review the function of adjectives. Have students identify the adjective, *middle,* in the Example 5 sentence on page 82. Then note how it is used as part of a prepositional phrase in the second sentence. Explain that the entire phrase is used as an adjective.

### *Practice B Answers*

1. poem 2. letter 3. rodeo 4. house
5. fruit salad or salad

## Practice C

Point out that a prepositional phrase used as an adjective tells *how many, what kind,* or *which one* about the noun it describes.

### *Practice C Answers*

Answers will vary. Possible answers follow.
1. George Washington was the first president of the United States. 2. The capital of Quebec is Quebec City. 3. The man in the red shirt won the race.
4. The building on the corner is 10 stories high. 5. Amber received a birthday card from her aunt.

---

## LEARNING STYLES

**Visual/Spatial**

Have students find a description they have written in which they used two or more prepositional phrases as adjectives. Ask them to circle each prepositional phrase. Then have students illustrate a sentence containing one of the phrases. For example, they could sketch or color a picture of *a robin's nest in the rosebush.*

---

## ELL/ESL STRATEGY

**Language Objective:** *To describe the meanings of common prepositions*

Pair students learning English with students who are proficient in it. Have the partners take turns making up sentences with each word from the list on page 81. Encourage partners to discuss their usage of prepositions.

## Practice D

Review the information that adverbs give about other words in a sentence: *where, when, how, how often,* or *to what degree.* Explain to students that prepositional phrases used as adverbs give the same kinds of information. Have volunteers read aloud the Example 6 sentences on page 83 and identify the word that the adverb and adverb phrase describe.

### Practice D Answers

**1.** by ourselves **2.** in 1492 **3.** to Centerville **4.** with a limp **5.** by plane

## Practice E

Review the information that adverb phrases give about other words in a sentence: *where, when, how, how often,* or *to what degree.* Tell students to make sure their prepositional phrases add this information and not information about a noun. For example, write the sentence *Brandon, in a silly mood, laughed.* In this sentence the prepositional phrase describes Brandon and therefore is an adjective phrase and not an adverb phrase.

### Practice E Answers

Sentences will vary. Possible sentences follow. **1.** Amber walked to the store. **2.** Her dog Rex barked in the yard. **3.** She arrived late on most evenings for dinner. **4.** Amber called Sonia after dinner. **5.** Their homework was difficult beyond belief!

### LEARNING STYLES

**Interpersonal/Group Learning**

Make word cards for the prepositions on page 81. Ask students to name several nouns and write their suggestions on the board. Distribute the preposition cards to students. Have each student combine his or her preposition with one of the nouns, adding other words as needed, to make a prepositional phrase. Student pairs can then exchange phrases and write a sentence using their partner's phrase.

---

**Practice D**

The verb of each sentence is in bold. Find the adverb phrase that answers a question about the verb. Write the adverb phrase on your paper.

**Example:**    Amber **met** Rene at the mall. (met where?)
**Answer:**    at the mall

1. We **read** the poem by ourselves.
2. Columbus **reached** the island in 1492.
3. The girls **drove** to Centerville.
4. The dog **walked** with a limp.
5. He **arrived** by plane.

An adverb phrase can also be an adverb of degree.

▶ **EXAMPLE 7**

| Adverb | We are very sorry. (sorry to what degree?) |
| Adverb Phrase | We are sorry beyond measure. (sorry to what degree?) |

**Practice E**

Think of a prepositional phrase to add after each verb or adjective in bold. The phrase must tell where, how, how often, when, or to what degree. Write the new sentence on your paper.

1. Amber **walked.**
2. Her dog Rex **barked.**
3. She arrived **late** for dinner.
4. Amber **called** Sonia.
5. Their homework was **difficult!**

Think about where you place prepositional phrases in your sentences. In general, place an adjective phrase close to the word it describes. Vary your sentences by putting adverb phrases in different positions.

▶ **EXAMPLE 8**

Amber Choy went to her locker between classes.

Between classes, Amber Choy went to her locker.

Place a prepositional phrase where it will not confuse the reader.

▶ **EXAMPLE 9**

| Confusing | We learned how to use a mirror to reflect light in our science class. |
| Clear | In our science class, we learned how to use a mirror to reflect light. |

**Reading Strategy:**
Predicting

Think about your last prediction. What details can you now add to make your prediction more specific?

**Practice F**

Find the prepositional phrase in each sentence. If the sentence is clear, write *clear* on your paper. If the sentence could be confusing, move the prepositional phrase and rewrite the sentence.

1. The smells are wonderful in Grandmother's kitchen.
2. The friends talked about the party in the hallway.
3. The audience left the theater after the first act.
4. The apartment has a big hall closet with two bedrooms.
5. A woman spoke to our class from Sweden.

## Practice F

Have volunteers read aloud the Example 8 sentences. Point out that not all prepositional phrases can be moved without affecting clarity. Have a volunteer read aloud the confusing Example 9 sentence and explain how it might confuse readers.

### *Practice F Answers*

1. clear  2. In the hallway, the friends talked about the party.  3. clear  4. The apartment with two bedrooms has a big hall closet.  5. A woman from Sweden spoke to our class.

### *Reading Strategy:* Predicting

Students might add details such as adjective phrases describe nouns or pronouns and adverb phrases describe verbs, adjectives, or other adverbs.

## Spelling Practice

Point out prepositions that students tend to misspell, such as *across, against,* and *during.* Also point out prepositions that have homophones such as *by (bye), for (four), in (inn),* and *to (too, two).* Dictate a few sentences containing these prepositions. Have students write the sentences and exchange papers with a partner to check their spelling.

## Lesson 3-5 Review Answers

**1.** at a store, in Springfield **2.** of words, in alphabetical order **3.** with similar meanings **4.** for each word **5.** with opposite meanings **6.** adverb phrase **7.** adjective phrase **8.** adverb phrase **9.** adverb phrase **10.** adverb phrase

## Write About It

Suggest that students consider some aspects of the career they choose: main responsibilities, possible job locations, a typical day, and fun elements. Encourage students to be as specific as possible. You may want them to research details they are unsure of.

## Six Traits of Writing Focus

| | | | |
|---|---|---|---|
| ✔ | Ideas | ✔ | Word Choice |
| | Organization | | Sentence Fluency |
| | Voice | | Conventions |

## Word Choice

Remind students to pay attention to verbs and adjectives as they listen. Have them assess whether the words create images that make the story interesting. If the words seem boring or bland, have them use a thesaurus to find alternatives.

Students can also focus on story content by listing other ideas that could spice up the writing.

Tell students to check page WPH1 for a description of the Six Traits of Writing.

---

# REVIEW

Find the prepositional phrases in the sentences. Some sentences have more than one. Write each phrase.

1. Amber bought a thesaurus at a store in Springfield.

2. A thesaurus has lists of words in alphabetical order.

3. Words with similar meanings are synonyms.

4. A thesaurus gives synonyms for each word.

5. It may list words with opposite meanings, too.

Each prepositional phrase is in bold. Decide whether it is an adjective phrase or adverb phrase. Write *adjective phrase* or *adverb phrase* on your paper.

6. Amber scored a goal **during the soccer game.**

7. The other players **on the team** cheered.

8. The team was happy **about winning.**

9. The coach took them **to a pizza place.**

10. They celebrated their victory **with joy.**

**Six Traits of Writing:**

*Word Choice* vivid words that "show, not tell"

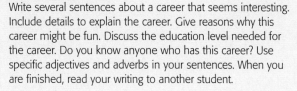

**WRITE ABOUT IT**

**An Interesting Career**
Write several sentences about a career that seems interesting. Include details to explain the career. Give reasons why this career might be fun. Discuss the education level needed for the career. Do you know anyone who has this career? Use specific adjectives and adverbs in your sentences. When you are finished, read your writing to another student.

# ENGLISH IN YOUR LIFE

## Explaining How to Do Something

Robby Jones made delicious French toast for a class breakfast. Everyone wanted the recipe. Robby put it on the bulletin board. Read his recipe. Notice how he used adjectives and adverbs to make his directions clear. Then answer the questions below.

| French Toast | (serves 6) |
|---|---|
| 12 slices bread | 1/2 cup milk |
| 4 eggs | 1 teaspoon cinnamon |

Beat the eggs, milk, and cinnamon briskly until the mixture is foamy. Pour it into a wide, flat bowl. Heat a little oil in a frying pan. When a drop of water sizzles in the pan, it is hot enough. Place the bread in the egg mixture, two pieces at a time. Remove when both sides are completely coated. Carefully place the slices in the hot oil. Brown each side for about 2 minutes. Serve hot with butter and powdered sugar.

1. Write five adjectives from the recipe.

2. Write three adverbs from the recipe.

3. **CRITICAL THINKING** How do adjectives and adverbs make directions clear?

### SPEAKING AND LISTENING

In a group, explain how to make your favorite snack. Describe one step at a time. Speak clearly and explain each step in order. Bring any equipment or pictures you need to demonstrate a step. Ask listeners if they have any questions. Find out how to make your explanation clearer next time.

Have several volunteers read the feature aloud. Remind students that one of the purposes of the English language is to give information. Have students share experiences they have had with written directions, especially those that were not clear.

Have students take turns reading some of the sentences and leaving out the adjectives and adverbs. Point out the difference these words make in the clarity of the recipe.

### English in Your Life Answers

**1.** Possible answers: foamy, wide, flat, little, hot, egg, two, both, each, 2, powdered **2.** Possible answers: briskly, enough, completely, carefully, about **3.** Possible answer: Adjectives make the nouns specific; adverbs make it clear what you are to do by telling *how, when,* or *to what extent* to do it. Adverbs can also clarify adjectives or other adverbs.

## Speaking and Presenting Practice

Have students meet in groups to decide on a snack recipe to explain. Suggest that after discussing all the steps as a group, each student might be in charge of explaining one or two steps. Point out that showing equipment or pictures is helpful in improving listeners' understanding.

*Writing Better Sentences*    Chapter 3    **87**

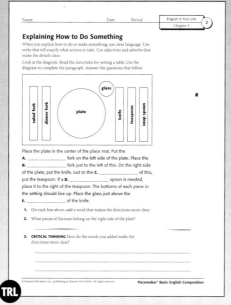

English in Your Life 2

*Writing Better Sentences*    **87**

Display a dictionary and review how to use guide words. Discuss the information shown in the sample entry on page 88. Discuss with students why it is important to know a word's part of speech (so they use it correctly in a sentence). Also discuss why it can be useful to learn a word's origin. For example, explain that several English words are based on the Latin word for *hand, manus*. This can help them learn the meanings of words such as *manual, manuscript,* and *manufacture.*

Take students to the library. Show them an assortment of dictionaries on the shelves and on the Internet.

### *Building Research Skills Answers*

**1.** \əd-'ven-ch(ə-)rər\ **2.** noun **3.** Possible answer: Read the sentence in which the word is used. Pick the meaning that fits this context.

## Using a Dictionary

The dictionary lists words in alphabetical order. Each word has an entry with many kinds of information. An entry gives a word's pronunciation, origin, part of speech, and meanings. For verbs, it also gives the main verb forms. For example, the entry for *write* shows the forms *wrote, written,* and *writing.*

Entry word          Pronunciation

Part of speech

**write** [rīt] v. **wrote, writ-ten, writ-ing** [ME, fr. OE *writan* to scratch, draw, inscribe] **1.** to form (letters or symbols) on a surface, usually with a pen or pencil **2.** to cover or fill with writing: to *write* ten pages every day **3.** to set down in writing: to *write* a will **4.** to tell by writing, usually a letter: she *wrote* that she would visit soon **5.** to show or make visible: guilt was *written* on his face

Origin

Meanings

Use a dictionary in your classroom. Write the answer to each question.

**1.** Look up the word *adventurer*. What is the pronunciation for this word? Write the pronunciation. Then use it to help you say the word aloud.

**2.** What part of speech is *adventurer*? (The abbreviations *n., v., adj.,* and *adv.* are used for noun, verb, adjective, and adverb.)

**3.** **CRITICAL THINKING** How could you choose which meaning of a word applies to your reading?

### TECHNOLOGY

Did you know dictionaries are also found on CD-ROMs and the Internet? The word-processing software on many computers also has a dictionary. Use a CD-ROM dictionary to find out how to spell a difficult word. Enter the spelling you think your word might have. Press *Search*. Were you correct? If not, try a different spelling and press *Spelling Help*. List the possible words that appear on the screen.

---

Name _____ Date _____ Period _____    Building Research Skills 3
Chapter 3

### Using a Dictionary

A dictionary is one of the most helpful tools a writer can have. Here are some of the bits of information about a word you can find in the dictionary:

- its spelling
- how many syllables it has
- its pronunciation
- the spellings of any other forms of the word (plurals, verb tenses, etc.)
- the parts of speech it may be
- its possible meanings
- example uses for each meaning
- its origin, or history

*Directions*  Read the entry for *aquarium*. Then answer the questions.

**a-quar-i-um** [ə kwâr′ e əm] n.,
*pl.* **a-quar-i-ums** or **a-quar-i-a**
1. a container such as a glass tank
or a manmade pond in which
water animals and plants live
2. a building where an aquatic
collection of this kind is displayed

**1.** How many syllables does *aquarium* have? Which syllable gets the strongest emphasis?

**2.** Which meaning of *aquarium* is used in this sentence:
*We enjoyed our visit to the city's beautiful aquarium.*

**3.** **CRITICAL THINKING** Explain what you learned from this dictionary entry about forming the plural of *aquarium.*

**TRL**

Building Research Skills 3

# SUMMARY

- Use pronouns to replace nouns in sentences when you have a clear antecedent.

- Check that a pronoun agrees with its antecedent in gender and number.

- Check that possessive pronouns also agree with their antecedents.

- Use an apostrophe with a possessive noun such as *men's*. However, do *not* use an apostrophe with a possessive pronoun such as *theirs*.

- Choose adjectives that add details to sentences. Sharp, specific adjectives are better than vague, general ones.

- Use adverbs to tell more about a verb, an adjective, or another adverb. Choose specific adverbs instead of vague ones. Adverbs tell the reader when, how, how often, where, or to what degree.

- Use adjectives and adverbs to make comparisons. Follow the rules for using positive, comparative, and superlative forms.

- Add prepositional phrases in sentences to provide the reader with details. Prepositional phrases are either adjective phrases or adverb phrases.

## GROUP ACTIVITY

Work with a group to write a description of an object in your classroom. Remember to use adjectives and adverbs. They will make your description clear and interesting. Compare the object to something else.

For example, you might write "This pen is shinier than a new dime." Check for nouns used over and over. Can you use pronouns instead? Trade papers with another group. Suggest ways to improve the other group's description.

## Chapter 3 Summary

Have volunteers read aloud each Summary item on page 89. Ask volunteers to explain the meaning of each item.

### ONLINE CONNECTION

 You may wish to locate the following Web sites for online dictionaries:

www.agsglobepmbec.com/page89a
www.agsglobepmbec.com/page89b

The second listing also contains a thesaurus.

### GROUP ACTIVITY

With students, brainstorm some common objects they might describe, such as a desk, a book, or a ruler. Point out that using specific words can make a description of a common object interesting. Students may also want to focus on a more complex object such as a plant or a work of art. Suggest that groups use a thesaurus to help them replace common adjectives and adverbs with more interesting ones.

## Chapter 3 Review

Use the Chapter Review to prepare students for tests and to reteach content from the chapter.

## Chapter 3 Mastery Test

The Teacher's Resource Library includes two forms of the Chapter 3 Mastery Test. Each test addresses the chapter Goals for Learning. An optional third page of additional critical-thinking items is included for each test. The difficulty level of the two forms is equivalent.

### Review Answers

Part A

**1.** thesaurus **2.** synonym **3.** prepositional phrase **4.** comparative form **5.** preposition **6.** apostrophe **7.** superlative form **8.** adjective **9.** possessive noun **10.** gender **11.** adverb **12.** antecedent **13.** personal pronouns **14.** masculine **15.** feminine

**Word Bank**

adjective
adverb
antecedent
apostrophe
comparative form
feminine
gender
personal pronouns
masculine
possessive noun
preposition
prepositional phrase
superlative form
synonym
thesaurus

**Part A** Find the word or words in the Word Bank that complete each sentence. Write your answer on your paper.

1. A _____ is a reference book that lists words and their synonyms.

2. A word that has the same meaning as another word is a _____.

3. A _____ includes a preposition and a noun or pronoun.

4. Use the _____ of an adverb or adjective to compare two things.

5. A _____ shows a relationship between a noun or pronoun and other words in a sentence.

6. The _____ is a punctuation mark used to create possessive nouns.

7. Use the _____ of an adjective or adverb to compare three or more things.

8. An _____ describes a noun or pronoun.

9. Use an apostrophe to form a _____.

10. Nouns and pronouns that show _____ are either masculine or feminine.

11. An _____ answers a question about a verb, an adjective, or another adverb.

12. A pronoun must agree with its _____ in gender and number.

13. *I, you, he, she, it, we,* and *they* are _____.

14. *He* and *him* are examples of _____ pronouns.

15. *She* and *her* are examples of _____ pronouns.

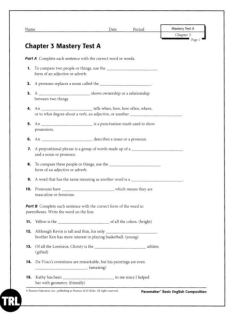

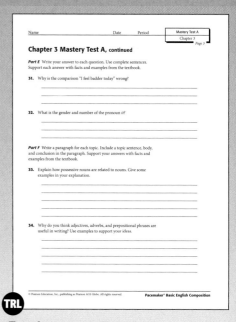

**Part B** Rewrite each sentence. Replace the word in bold with a more specific adjective. Then add one more adjective to each sentence.

**16.** The friends watched a **good** movie.

**17.** The lake is a **nice** place to visit.

**18.** The bread smells **great.**

**Part C** Rewrite each sentence. Add an *adjective* to one of the sentences. Add an *adverb* to one of the sentences. Add a *prepositional phrase* to one of the sentences.

**19.** The weather is hot.

**20.** The dog barked.

**21.** We will go on a trip.

**Part D** Write the letter of the word or words that correctly complete each sentence.

**22.** Luis arrived _____ than Brandon.
     **A** earliest   **B** early   **C** more earlier   **D** earlier

**23.** The water is _____ today than yesterday.
     **A** calm   **B** less calm   **C** least calm   **D** less calmer

**24.** That is the _____ music I have ever heard!
     **A** worstest   **B** worse   **C** worst   **D** most worst

**Part E**

**25.** Write each bold pronoun in the paragraph below. After each one, write its antecedent.

    Derek lost **his** lunch money yesterday. **He** borrowed money from **his** friend Brandon. Then **they** ate lunch together.

**Test Tip**

Answer the easy questions first. This can help you remember more information about the subject. Then go back and answer the harder ones.

*Writing Better Sentences   Chapter 3   **91***

## Review Answers

### Part B

Answers will vary. Possible answers are given. **16.** The old friends watched an excellent movie. **17.** The big lake is a quiet place to visit. **18.** The warm bread smells wonderful.

### Part C

Answers will vary. Possible answers are given. **19.** The weather is hot in the summer. **20.** The dog barked angrily. **21.** We will go on an exciting trip.

### Part D

**22.** D  **23.** B  **24.** C

### Part E

**25.** his — Derek's
He — Derek
his — Derek's
they — Derek and Brandon

## WRITING PORTFOLIO

**Wrap-Up** Students should complete their sentences about their memorable trips. The sentences should include pronouns that agree with their antecedents; possessive nouns and pronouns used correctly; adjectives and adverbs, including comparative and superlative forms; and prepositional phrases. This project may be used as an alternative form of assessment.

---

**Chapter 3 Mastery Test B, pages 1–3**

*Writing Better Sentences*   **91**

# CHAPTER 4 PLANNING GUIDE

# Writing Paragraphs

| | Student Pages | Vocabulary | Practice Exercises | Lesson Review | Identification | Writing | Punctuation & Capitalization | Grammar & Usage | Listening, Speaking, & Viewing |
|---|---|---|---|---|---|---|---|---|---|
| **Lesson 4-1** Planning to Write a Paragraph | 95–99 | ✔ | ✔ | ✔ | ✔ | ✔ | ✔ | ✔ | ✔ |
| **Lesson 4-2** Writing a Topic Sentence | 100–103 | ✔ | ✔ | ✔ | ✔ | ✔ | ✔ | ✔ | ✔ |
| **Lesson 4-3** Writing Supporting Details | 104–107 | ✔ | ✔ | ✔ | ✔ | ✔ | ✔ | ✔ | ✔ |
| **Lesson 4-4** Writing a Summary or Conclusion | 108–113 | ✔ | ✔ | ✔ | ✔ | ✔ | ✔ | ✔ | ✔ |

## Chapter Activities

**Teacher's Resource Library**
Life Skills Connection 4:
   Responding to a Writing Prompt
Writing Tip 4: Paragraphs
Writing on the Job 2: Office
   Assistant
Building Research Skills 4: Blending
   Ideas in Your Writing
Key Vocabulary Words 4

## Assessment Options

**Student Text**
Chapter 4 Review

**Teacher's Resource Library**
Chapter 4 Mastery Tests A and B

**Teacher's Edition**
Chapter 4 Writing Portfolio

| English in Your Life | Writing on the Job | Building Research Skills | Vocabulary Builder | Grammar Builder | Write About It | Group Activity | Reading Strategy | Six Traits | ELL/ESL Strategy | Background Information | Common Error | Life Skills Connection | Applications (Home, Career, Community, Global) | Online Connection | Teacher Alert | Speaking & Presenting Practice | Writing/Spelling/Grammar Practice | Auditory/Verbal | Body/Kinesthetic | Interpersonal/Group Learning | Logical/Mathematical | Visual/Spatial | Activities | Modified Activities | Workbook Activities | Self-Study Guide |
|---|---|---|---|---|---|---|---|---|---|---|---|---|---|---|---|---|---|---|---|---|---|---|---|---|---|---|
| | | 99 | | | | | 96, 97 | | 98 | 95 | 96, 97 | 96 | | | | | 97, 98 | | | | | | 16 | 16 | 16 | ✔ |
| | | | 103 | | | | 100, 102 | | 101 | 100 | | | 101, 102 | 102 | | | | 103 | | 101 | | | 17 | 17 | 17 | ✔ |
| | | | | | | | 104, 105 | | 107 | 104 | 106 | | 105 | | | | 106 | | 106 | | 106 | 105 | 18 | 18 | 18 | ✔ |
| 111 | 112 | | | | 110 | 113 | 108, 109 | 110 | 109 | 108 | 109, 111 | | 110, 111 | 113 | 109 | 111 | | | | | | | 19 | 19 | 19 | ✔ |

## Pronunciation Key

| | | | | | | | | | | |
|---|---|---|---|---|---|---|---|---|---|---|
| a | hat | e | let | ī | ice | ô | order | u̇ | put | sh she |
| ā | age | ē | equal | o | hot | oi | oil | ü | rule | th thin |
| ä | far | ėr | term | ō | open | ou | out | ch | child | ŦH then |
| â | care | i | it | ȯ | saw | u | cup | ng | long | zh measure |

ə { a in about / e in taken / i in pencil / o in lemon / u in circus }

## Modified Activities

The Teacher's Resource Library (TRL) contains a set of lower-level worksheets called Modified Activities. These worksheets cover the same content as the standard Activities but are written at a lower reading level.

## Skill Track

Use Skill Track for *Basic English Composition* to monitor student progress and meet the demands of adequate yearly progress (AYP). Make informed instructional decisions with individual student and class reports of lesson and chapter assessments. With immediate and ongoing feedback, students will also see what they have learned and where they need more reinforcement and practice.

## Chapter at a Glance

### Chapter 4:
### Writing Paragraphs

pages 92–115

### Lessons

**Skill Track for Basic English Composition**

### Teacher's Resource Library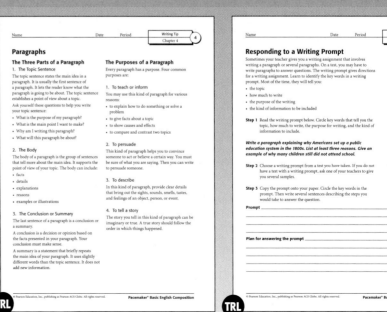

(Answer Keys for the Teacher's Resource Library begin on page 446 of the Teacher's Edition.)

---

**Paragraphs**

**The Three Parts of a Paragraph**

**1. The Topic Sentence**

The topic sentence states the main idea in a paragraph. It is usually the first sentence of a paragraph. It lets the reader know what the paragraph is going to be about. The topic sentence establishes a point of view about a topic.

Ask yourself these questions to help you write your topic sentence:

- What is the purpose of my paragraph?
- What is the main point I want to make?
- Why am I writing this paragraph?
- What will this paragraph be about?

**2. The Body**

The body of a paragraph is the group of sentences that tell more about the main idea. It supports the point of view of your topic. The body can include:

- facts
- details
- explanations
- reasons
- examples or illustrations

**3. The Conclusion or Summary**

The last sentence of a paragraph is a conclusion or a summary.

A conclusion is a decision or opinion based on the facts presented in your paragraph. Your conclusion must make sense.

A summary is a statement that briefly repeats the main idea of your paragraph. It uses slightly different words than the topic sentence. It does not add new information.

**The Purposes of a Paragraph**

Every paragraph has a purpose. Four common purposes are:

**1. To teach or inform**

You may use this kind of paragraph for various reasons:

- to explain how to do something or solve a problem
- to give facts about a topic
- to show causes and effects
- to compare and contrast two topics

**2. To persuade**

This kind of paragraph helps you to convince someone to act or believe a certain way. You must be sure of what you are saying. Then you can write to persuade someone.

**3. To describe**

In this kind of paragraph, provide clear details that bring out the sights, sounds, smells, tastes, and feelings of an object, person, or event.

**4. To tell a story**

The story you tell in this kind of paragraph can be imaginary or true. A true story should follow the order in which things happened.

**Pacemaker® Basic English Composition**

---

**Responding to a Writing Prompt**

Sometimes your teacher gives you a writing assignment that involves writing a paragraph or several paragraphs. On a test, you may have to write paragraphs to answer questions. The writing prompt gives directions for a writing assignment. Learn to identify the key words in a writing prompt. Most of the time, they will tell you:

- the topic
- how much to write
- the purpose of the writing
- the kind of information to be included

**Step 1** Read the writing prompt below. Circle key words that tell you the topic, how much to write, the purpose for writing, and the kind of information to include.

*Write a paragraph explaining why Americans set up a public education system in the 1800s. List at least three reasons. Give an example of why many children still did not attend school.*

**Step 2** Choose a writing prompt from a test you have taken. If you do not have a test with a writing prompt, ask one of your teachers to give you several samples.

**Step 3** Copy the prompt onto your paper. Circle the key words in the prompt. Then write several sentences describing the steps you would take to answer the question.

**Prompt** _____

_____

_____

**Plan for answering the prompt** _____

_____

_____

_____

_____

**Pacemaker® Basic English Composition**

---

Writing Tip 4                    Life Skills Connection 4

# Writing Paragraphs

Where do you start your day at school? One of your first stops is probably your locker. The lockers in the photo are lined up side by side. They are numbered according to a plan. Your locker helps you organize your things for the day. Perhaps you stand at your locker and think about what you need for your first, second, and third classes.

In Chapter 4, you will learn how to build a solid paragraph. You will place sentences side by side. You will organize them to tell about a topic. You will decide what needs to come first, second, and third.

First you will write a topic sentence to express the main idea. Next you will write sentences that support this idea. Then you will write a sentence to close the paragraph. This chapter will help you to write these three parts of a paragraph.

## GOALS FOR LEARNING

- To understand prewriting, and to understand the parts of a paragraph
- To write a topic sentence that expresses the main idea of a paragraph
- To write sentences that develop and support the main idea
- To end a paragraph with a conclusion or summary statement

93

## Introducing the Chapter

Have students examine the photograph on page 92. Ask them how they count on the organization of the lockers at school. Then have volunteers tell how they sort things in their locker. Point out that this plan helps them get through their day smoothly. Explain that careful writers also sort their ideas carefully. Throwing out sentences without any plan would be like throwing books and papers into a locker. The result would be confusion and mess. Point out that in Chapter 4 students will learn how to organize ideas effectively.

Review and discuss the Goals for Learning on page 93.

## Notes

Ask volunteers to read the notes that appear in the margins throughout the chapter. Then discuss them with the class.

## TEACHER'S RESOURCE

The AGS Globe Teaching Strategies in English Transparencies may be used with this chapter. The transparencies add an interactive dimension to expand and enhance the *Basic English Composition* program content.

## WRITING PORTFOLIO

Write the following topics on the board:

> What my locker shows about me
> The ups and downs of my day
> The unwritten rules of the lunchroom

Ask students to select a topic. Explain that, as they learn to write a paragraph, they will develop their ideas about this topic into their own paragraph. As students preview the chapter, point out that they will need to develop a main idea sentence, sentences to support the idea, and a sentence that closes the paragraph well. This project may be used as an alternative form of assessment for the chapter.

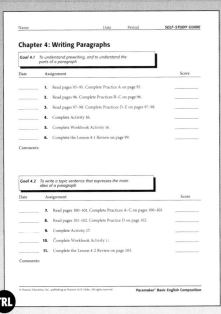

Chapter 4 Self-Study Guide, pages 1–2

**Reading Strategy:
Text Structure**

Have students look at a chapter
or lesson in a textbook as you
point out its headings, graphic
elements, and bold words. Explain
that readers can use the parts to
understand what a text is about
before they read it.

Read the text on page 94 with
students. Point out the bulleted list
and the boldface terms on page 95.
Have students use the heading to
predict what the bulleted list is for.

## Key Vocabulary Words

| | |
|---|---|
| audience | paragraph |
| body | prewriting |
| brainstorm | summary |
| conclusion | topic sentence |
| indent | writing prompt |

Ask volunteers to read each key word
and its definition. Explain that some
words have more than one meaning.
Read the following sentences. Have
students tell whether the key word in
each sentence has the meaning they
just read (starred sentences do not):

*I prepared to write a paper by
prewriting.*

* *The audience clapped.*

*I brainstormed some ideas for my
paragraph.*

*The last paragraph in the article is
interesting.*

*Indent the first line of a paragraph.*

*Tell your main idea in a topic sentence.*

*Exercise to take care of your body.*

*She wrote a summary of the movie.*

*My conclusion is that you are tired.*

For each starred sentence, challenge
students to write a different sentence
that uses the underlined word with
the chapter's meaning.

# Reading Strategy: Text Structure

A text is organized to help readers decide which
information is most important. Before you read this
chapter, look at how it is organized.

- Look at the chapter title, the lesson titles, and the bold
  vocabulary words.
- Ask yourself: How is the chapter organized? Does it
  describe parts of a sequence? Does it compare and
  contrast?
- Look at the pieces that make up a chapter in this
  book. What is on the first page of each lesson? What is
  at the end of each lesson?

## Key Vocabulary Words

**Prewriting** Preparing to write; the
planning step of the writing process

**Writing prompt** The directions for a
writing assignment

**Audience** The people who read your
writing

**Brainstorm** To think freely about a topic
and look for new, exciting ideas

**Paragraph** A group of sentences about
one idea

**Indent** To start a sentence a certain
distance from the left margin

**Topic sentence** A sentence that states
the main idea of a paragraph; usually the
first sentence of a paragraph

**Body** The sentences in a paragraph that
explain and support the main idea

**Summary** A sentence at the end of a
paragraph that repeats the main idea
using different words

**Conclusion** A logical decision or
opinion based on facts or evidence; the
sentence at the end of a paragraph

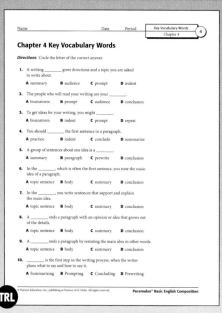

# Planning to Write a Paragraph

## Objectives

- To follow the directions in a writing prompt
- To identify the audience and purpose for your writing
- To brainstorm to get ideas to write about
- To write a paragraph about a topic

**Prewriting**
Preparing to write; the planning step of the writing process

**Writing prompt**
The directions for a writing assignment

Before you write, you have some work to do. You need to answer some basic questions. Answering these questions is **prewriting.** Prewriting is all about preparing to write. It is the first step in the writing process.

### Understanding Your Assignment

Your teacher may give you a **writing prompt.** A writing prompt is the directions for a writing assignment. During prewriting, read the prompt carefully. Then ask yourself these questions:

- What am I expected to do?
- What do I write about?
- Where should I start?
- What do I need to know?
- What is the purpose of my writing?

### Practice A

Read the prompt. Then answer the questions on your paper. (Do not actually write the paragraph.)

**Prompt:** Write a paragraph about your favorite type of movie. Explain why you like this type of movie. Give three reasons. Name one movie that belongs in this group.

1. How long should this writing assignment be?
2. What is the topic?
3. How many reasons does the writer need to give?
4. How many examples does the writer need to give?
5. Will the assignment explain something the writer likes or dislikes?

## 1  Warm-Up Activity

Ask students to describe how athletes get ready for a game. Explain that writers "warm up" by prewriting. Have students give their own definition of a paragraph. Draw a snake on the board. Use lines to label its head, body, and tail. Point out that a paragraph is like a snake: Both have a beginning, middle, and end.

## 2  Teaching the Lesson

Explain that *pre-* means "before." *Prewriting* is how writers get ready before they write. Ask volunteers to predict what should be done at this stage. Then read page 95 together.

## Practice A

Be sure students understand that a writing prompt tells them what and how to write. Read the prompt aloud. Then complete the exercise orally, having students skim the paragraph to find each answer.

## Practice A Answers

**1.** a paragraph  **2.** favorite type of movie
**3.** three  **4.** one  **5.** something the writer likes

# Lesson at a Glance

## Chapter 4  Lesson 1

**Overview**  This lesson gives prewriting suggestions about prompts, audience, purpose, and brainstorming. It describes the parts of a paragraph.

### Objectives

- To follow the directions in a writing prompt
- To identify the audience and purpose for your writing
- To brainstorm to get ideas to write about
- To write a paragraph about a topic

**Student Pages** 95–99

**Teacher's Resource Library**

**Activity** 16
**Modified Activity** 16
**Workbook Activity** 16
**Life Skills Connection** 4

## Vocabulary

| | |
|---|---|
| audience | paragraph |
| brainstorm | prewriting |
| indent | prompt |

Have students say the words and count the number of syllables in each. Together, divide each word into syllables. Ask volunteers to identify familiar word parts and their meanings. Then have students read the meanings of the words and use each in a sentence.

## Background Information

Some students will be able to explore a topic more easily by asking and answering questions about it. Have them begin with *who? what? where? when? why?* and *how?* Point out that identifying purpose and audience also helps writers narrow the topic and find direction.

## COMMON ERROR

Writers have trouble if they fail to establish a purpose and audience. When students choose a topic, have them change some bulleted points in Practice B into questions to help:

Do I want to teach readers something?

Do I want to change readers' minds?

**Reading Strategy:** Text Structure

The writer must determine what is expected, what topic to write about, where to get the information, and the reason for writing.

## Practice B

Read the directions with students. Suggest that they pick a specific audience for a specific topic to help them with the exercise.

### Practice B Answers

Answers will vary. Sample answers are shown. **1.** How much education or knowledge of English do my readers have? **2.** Are there any technical terms I need to define? **3.** What concepts will be hard for them to understand? **4.** What experiences of my readers can I draw on to help them understand? **5.** What style and tone will best suit this audience?

## Practice C

Invite students to give one example of writing they have done.

### Practice C Answers

**1.** to inform readers about a book **2.** to entertain readers by telling them about an incident **3.** to persuade readers that teens should vote **4.** to teach readers how to sew on a button **5.** to inform others about a vacation spot

---

**Audience**
The people who read your writing

**Reading Strategy:**
Text Structure

Preview this page. What is something a writer must decide before writing?

## Understanding Your Audience and Purpose

When you write, you write for one or more readers. The reader is your **audience.** During prewriting, ask yourself some questions about the reader. The answers will help you decide what to write.

- Who will read my writing?
- What does the reader want to know about the topic?
- What does the reader already know about the topic?
- What will the reader expect of my writing?

### Practice B

Make a list of five more questions that you might want to know about the person or people who will read your writing. Share this list with another student or the class.

You can write for many reasons. Here are some of them:

- You can write to teach or inform.
- You can write to entertain or tell a story.
- You can write to persuade someone to agree with your ideas.
- You can write to describe an object, event, person, or place.

### Practice C

Read each prompt. What seems to be the purpose of each one? Write the purpose of the prompt on your paper. There may be more than one good answer.

1. Write a report about a book that you have just read.
2. Write a story about something that happened to you.
3. Explain why teenagers should vote in presidential elections.
4. Explain the steps you must follow to sew on a button.
5. Tell about your favorite vacation spot.

---

**96**  *Chapter 4  Writing Paragraphs*

## LIFE SKILLS CONNECTION

Many tests will ask students to write paragraphs or essays. Ask students how they feel about writing essay answers on tests. Point out that responding to a writing prompt is a learned skill. They can learn how to turn the directions into a plan for writing. Distribute copies of Life Skills Connection 4. Read the first set of directions together. Then have students work independently to complete the page.

## Finding an Idea

When you need an idea to write about, try **brainstorming.** When you brainstorm, you write down every idea that pops into your head. You do not judge your ideas yet—you write them all. You will think of exciting ideas. You will have an amazing list of ideas to write about.

It is even more fun to brainstorm with a group of people. You choose a topic, and everyone in the group tells their ideas. Someone must write down the ideas. No one says an idea is good or bad. After you think of many ideas, the group can decide which one it likes best.

### Practice D

By yourself or in a small group, brainstorm about one of the topics below. Try to list at least five ideas that you could write about. There are no right or wrong answers.

- why people like to read about movie stars
- the popularity of camping
- stock car racing
- deciding on a career
- popular fashions of the past, present, or future

## Understanding the Parts of a Paragraph

Once you understand your assignment, know your audience and purpose, and have your idea, you have finished prewriting. Now you are ready to write.

A **paragraph** is a group of sentences about one idea. A paragraph has three parts:

- a topic sentence
- a body
- a conclusion or summary

Writers must practice putting their sentences together in paragraphs. For writing assignments, you should **indent** the first sentence in a paragraph.

*Writing Paragraphs* *Chapter 4* **97**

## Writing Practice

Have students use their ideas from Practice D to develop a plan for a paragraph. Suggest that they choose the idea for which they think they can generate at least three examples, facts, details, or reasons. Model an example:

*I think people like to read about movie stars mostly to feel they know them personally. Here are some details related to this idea:*

*I might meet the star and become a friend.*

*I can look for things I have in common with the star.*

*I have a crush on the star and want to know what he/she is doing all the time.*

Have students write their chosen idea on paper and then brainstorm three details that support the idea.

## Practice D

Emphasize to students that there are no right or wrong answers. Allow students to brainstorm alone for a minute on one topic. Then group students by topic and have them continue.

### *Practice D Answers*

Answers will vary, but students' ideas should be related to the topic they chose and have enough substance for writing a paragraph.

### COMMON ERROR

Beginning writers may concentrate on ideas and ignore form. Always have students write a draft of their paragraphs. When they edit, have them check to be sure its form is proper: first line indented and all other lines are flush left.

### *Reading Strategy:* Text Structure

The three parts of a paragraph are the topic sentence, body, and conclusion or summary.

## Practice E

Ask a volunteer to read the paragraph aloud as students listen to identify the topic sentence, examples, and conclusion.

### Practice E Answers

**1.** sentence 1 **2.** weather warm enough for outdoor games, trees leafing out, the approach of the end of school **3.** sentence 5 (last sentence)

## Spelling Practice

Write *brainstorm* on the board. Ask students how they would learn to spell this word. Point out that it is made up of two shorter words: *brain* and *storm*. By breaking compound words into their parts, students can analyze and spell one part at a time. Point out also that some compound words are separated by a space. Have students locate the compound word *movie stars* on page 97. Explain that a third kind of compound word includes a hyphen: *long-range*. Pair students. Have them skim a section of a textbook or article to find compound words. Ask them to write five compounds correctly on cards. Have them analyze each word's spelling and sounds. Then have partners quiz each other on the words.

Notice the three parts of the paragraph in Example 1. The first sentence states the main idea. The middle sentences are the body. They give examples of ways that people use computers. The last sentence is the conclusion.

▶ **EXAMPLE 1**

We use computers for many things. People play games with computers. People use computers to do math. Some people use computers to write letters. A computer is a very useful machine.

### Practice E

Read the paragraph. Then answer the questions.

Derek's favorite season is spring. The weather is warm enough to play soccer outside. The oak trees in Springfield turn green again. The end of the school year is near. When the month of April arrives, Derek is happy.

1. Which sentence tells the main idea?

2. What three examples does the writer give to explain the main idea?

3. Which sentence is the summary sentence?

*Computers help people to complete many kinds of tasks.*

# REVIEW

Read the prompt. Then answer the questions on your paper. (Do not actually write the paragraph.)

**Prompt:** Write a paragraph about the climate where you live. Imagine that you are explaining this to someone who just moved to the area. Give an example for each season. (*Climate* means the average yearly weather.)

1. How long should this writing assignment be?

2. What is the topic?

3. How many examples does the writer need to give?

4. Who is the audience?

5. What does *climate* mean?

Choose one of the topics below. Brainstorm about this topic. Number your paper from 6 to 10. List five ideas about the topic that you could put in a paragraph.

- a place in the world you would like to visit
- why people like roller coasters
- best ways to stay healthy
- getting along with family members

## VOCABULARY BUILDER

### Using Antonyms to Make Comparisons

Antonyms are words with opposite meanings. For example, *foolish* is an antonym for *wise*. *Exciting* is an antonym for *dull*. Antonyms can help you point out the differences between things. They can help you make comparisons.

Most dogs are **tame**, but a wolf is **wild**.

The last movie was **sad**, but this one is **funny**.

Write three sentences that compare. Use antonyms to compare two friends, two teachers, and two singers.

---

## Lesson 4-1 Review Answers

**1.** a paragraph **2.** climate where you live **3.** four examples, or one example per season in the area **4.** newcomers to the area **5.** average yearly weather Ideas will vary, but students' notes should be focused on the chosen topic and have enough substance to build a paragraph. **6–10.** Answers will vary.

## VOCABULARY BUILDER

Read the text with students and invite volunteers to list other examples of antonyms.

### Vocabulary Builder Answers

Answers will vary. Sample answers are shown. **1.** Alison is as quiet and reserved as her sister Christa is outgoing and excitable. **2.** Mr. Bakken is funny, but Ms. Wissing is serious. **3.** Cheryl has a sharp, cutting voice, but Bruce sings with a mellow, soothing tone.

## WRITING PORTFOLIO

**Checkpoint** Have students refer to their chosen topic for the Writing Portfolio and brainstorm ideas for a paragraph about the topic.

---

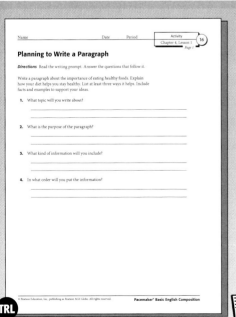

**Planning to Write a Paragraph**

*Directions* Read the writing prompt. Answer the questions that follow it.

Write a paragraph about the importance of eating healthy foods. Explain how your diet helps you stay healthy. List at least three ways it helps. Include facts and examples to support your ideas.

1. What topic will you write about?

2. What is the purpose of the paragraph?

3. What kind of information will you include?

4. In what order will you put the information?

**Understanding Writing Prompts and Paragraph Prompts**

*Directions* Read each writing prompt. Fill in the missing information in the chart.

| Writing Prompt | Purpose of Your Answer | Audience | Topic | Key Words |
|---|---|---|---|---|
| **1.** Write an essay to compare life in 1800 to life today. | | | | |

| Writing Prompt | Purpose of Your Answer | Audience | Topic | Key Words |
|---|---|---|---|---|
| **2.** Write a paragraph to describe the stories of Edgar Allan Poe. | | | | |

*Directions* The sentences below can be used to write a paragraph. Read the sentences. Decide how they should be ordered. Number the sentences in order.

_____ **3.** He first became popular as the star of comedies such as *Big*.

_____ **4.** His many awards prove that Hanks is among our most gifted actors.

_____ **5.** Later, he went on to star in many major dramas.

_____ **6.** Tom Hanks is one of Hollywood's finest, best-liked actors.

_____ **7.** He became the first actor since 1938 to win the Academy Award for Best Actor two years in a row.

## Lesson at a Glance

### Chapter 4   Lesson 2

**Overview**   This lesson discusses the purpose and placement of the topic sentence. It has students find the common topic represented by groups of supporting sentences.

### Objectives

- To choose a topic for a paragraph
- To begin a paragraph with a topic sentence

**Student Pages**   100–103

**Teacher's Resource Library**

Activity  17

Modified Activity  17

Workbook Activity  17

### Vocabulary

#### topic sentence

Have students read the definition for the term and search a textbook for examples. Ask volunteers why they chose their examples.

### Background Information

Beginning a paragraph with a topic sentence assists readers by giving them a clear idea of what will be discussed. However, a topic sentence may be placed elsewhere. It may be placed last to allow readers to think through details and reasons and compare their conclusion with the author's. Some paragraphs may simply imply the main idea.

### 1   Warm-Up Activity

Read these instructions, pausing briefly after each sentence:

Do not run in the hallways. I am going to tell you what to do in case of fire. Proceed to the nearest exit. Do not rush to the door when you hear the alarm. Leave the room in an orderly fashion.

Ask students what is wrong with these instructions. *(The sentences are out of order.)* Ask them which sentence should have been first. *(The third sentence is the topic sentence; it states the main idea.)*

---

## LESSON 4-2   Writing a Topic Sentence

### Objectives

- To choose a topic for a paragraph
- To begin a paragraph with a topic sentence

**Topic sentence**

A sentence that states the main idea of a paragraph; usually the first sentence of a paragraph

**Reading Strategy:**
Text Structure

Preview this lesson. Read its title and the meaning of *topic sentence*. What do you expect to learn in this lesson?

Begin a paragraph with a **topic sentence.** A topic sentence states the main idea of a paragraph. It is usually the first sentence of a paragraph.

Because you are the writer of the paragraph, only you know what its main idea should be. Think before writing the first sentence. Here are some questions to ask yourself:

- What is the purpose of this paragraph?
- What is the main point I want to make?
- Why am I writing this paragraph?
- What will this paragraph be about?

Read the paragraph in Example 1. The topic sentence is in blue. Think about how the topic sentence expresses the main idea.

▶ **EXAMPLE 1**

Adjectives can be words of power. Writers try to choose exact adjectives that express meaning sharply and clearly. Careful writers avoid adjectives such as nice and bad, which have little meaning. The best adjective is one that paints a clear picture. An adjective with a clear meaning is a word of power.

**Practice A**

Read the paragraph in Example 1 again. Write another topic sentence for it that states the main idea.

#### Recognizing a Topic Sentence

A topic sentence is a general statement. Examples and details appear in the rest of the paragraph. Read the paragraph in Example 2. The first sentence is the topic sentence. It states the main idea of the paragraph.

**100**   *Chapter 4   Writing Paragraphs*

---

### 2   Teaching the Lesson

Write these phrases on the board: *goes for days without water, survives great heat, able to walk swiftly across sand.* Have student pairs write a topic sentence for this information. (Example: *Camels are well adapted for desert life.*) Then ask volunteers to write specific details about a skill, a job, the weather, or another subject in phrases on the board. Ask the class to write a topic sentence to introduce the subject.

**Reading Strategy:** Text Structure

Students may suggest that they will read the lesson to find out how to write a topic sentence that introduces a paragraph.

### Practice A

Have a student read aloud the Example 1 paragraph. Discuss how the topic sentence prepares the reader for the main idea.

### *Practice A Answers*

Answers will vary. A possible answer is given: The right adjective can make a description come alive.

**NOTE**

Indent the first sentence of each paragraph.

▶ **EXAMPLE 2**

Springfield is a pleasant place to live. The weather is beautiful most of the year. The town has many parks, stores, museums, and restaurants. The townspeople have a friendly and helpful attitude. Springfield citizens are proud of their town.

**Practice B**

Read the four facts below. Suppose you want to write a paragraph that includes these facts. Write a topic sentence for this paragraph. It should state the main idea of the paragraph. (Do not write the whole paragraph.)

- Georgia O'Keeffe was an American painter.
- She painted landscapes and flowers.
- New Mexico was the subject of many of her paintings.
- She died in 1986 at the age of 98.

**Practice C**

Read the paragraph. The topic sentence is missing. Write a topic sentence that expresses the main idea.

Tennis players need good forehand strokes. Right-handed players use these strokes when the ball comes to their right side. They also need good backhand strokes. Right-handers use these strokes when the ball comes to their left. Tennis players use these two strokes most often.

**Identifying the Main Idea**

Some writing prompts give you the topic. They may even suggest the main idea. Other writing prompts are more general. You have to think of the topic and main idea. Before you write a topic sentence, you need to know the topic and main idea. Topics and main ideas come from:

- your past experiences
- your imagination
- things you have read or heard recently

*Writing Paragraphs* Chapter 4 **101**

## LEARNING STYLES

**Interpersonal/Group Learning**

Use books and magazines to find several short paragraphs with strong topic sentences. Give one paragraph to each group of students. The groups should read their paragraphs and write the topic sentences. Then have students cut their paragraphs into its sentences, mix them up, and exchange them with another group. Students should try to identify the topic sentence. Ask the groups to explain their choice.

## AT HOME

Discuss with students everyday print materials that are arranged in paragraphs—newspapers, magazines, brochures, and so on. Have students collect samples that show different arrangements. They should see that sometimes paragraphs are indented. Sometimes they are separated with extra space or set off in a frame. Emphasize that regardless of arrangement, a new paragraph signals a new idea.

## 3 Reinforce and Extend

### ELL/ESL STRATEGY

**Language Objective:** *To write topic sentences using familiar vocabulary*

To help students find a topic they can write about in English, provide frameworks for topic sentences. Be sure the sentences are on familiar subjects. An example might include "I would really like to learn to ____" or "My parents think I am ____, but really I am ____." Once students have chosen a topic sentence, have them brainstorm supporting details in their own language. Then have them use reference resources or English-speaking partners to translate their ideas. Students may want to use a framework like the following to organize their paragraph:

*Topic sentence:* _____
*Supporting detail 1:* _____
*Supporting detail 2:* _____
*Supporting detail 3:* _____
*Conclusion:* _____

## Practice B

Encourage students to think about what the four facts have in common before they try to write their topic sentence.

### *Practice B Answers*

Answers will vary. A possible topic sentence is given: Georgia O'Keeffe was a well-known artist.

## Practice C

Before students complete Practice C, have them reread Example 2. Discuss how the topic sentence makes a general introductory statement. Have a volunteer read aloud the paragraph before students write their topic sentences.

### *Practice C Answers*

Answers will vary. A possible topic sentence is given: Two strokes are basic to the game of tennis.

## TEACHER ALERT

Show students model paragraphs from published works. Use expository texts, such as informational articles. Preview them to make sure they contain enough good models. Experienced writers often choose not to place a topic sentence first in the paragraph or not to state it explicitly.

## Practice D

Choose one of the topics. Model a topic sentence you would write about it. Show students how you have limited the details you can include in your paragraph because of the topic sentence.

### Practice D Answers

Answers will vary. Sample answers are shown: **1.** The Lincoln Lions have the best record of any wrestling team in the state. **2.** Uncle Bob is both an interesting and a difficult man to talk to. **3.** I enjoy collecting horse figures. **4.** There is nothing more relaxing than fishing at Reamer's Pond. **5.** *The Andy Griffith Show* still makes us laugh.

## CAREER CONNECTION

Brainstorm with students a list of careers. Write them on the board. Then have student pairs select any three of the careers and write a topic sentence for each. Invite partners to write their favorite topic sentence on the board. Encourage interested students to find articles about a career and share a paragraph with classmates, identifying the topic sentence.

**Reading Strategy:** Text Structure

The example paragraphs show working topic sentences. They can be compared to the details used to support them to see how they summarize the paragraph's main idea.

---

**Brush Up on the Basics**

The topic sentence names the subject, which is often a noun. Avoid repeating this noun too many times in the sentences that follow. For example, replace a person's name with *he*, *she*, *you*, *I*, *me*, *her*, or *him*. Replace the name of a thing or idea with *it* or *they*. See Grammar 40 in Appendix A.

---

**Reading Strategy:** Text Structure

Look at the examples in this lesson. How do they help you understand what a topic sentence is?

---

Read the topics in Example 3. Notice how each topic suggests a topic sentence.

▶ **EXAMPLE 3**

| Topic | Possible Topic Sentence (Main Idea) |
|---|---|
| the police department | Our local police department helps the community in many ways. |
| hiking | Before you go hiking, you will need some equipment. |
| baseball | Each of the players on a baseball team has a different role. |

### Practice D

Write a topic sentence for each topic. Use Example 3 as a guide.

1. a sports team you like
2. a person in your family
3. the first hobby you ever had
4. someplace you enjoy going
5. a popular TV show

Think of a topic sentence for each set of details. Write the topic sentence on your paper.

**1.** Car owners should change their oil.
They should check the hoses for leaks.
They should also check the air pressure in the tires.

**2.** First, set the oven temperature.
Next, gather all the ingredients.
Finally, follow the steps in the recipe.

**3.** The wind blew down several trees.
The electricity was out for two hours.
The streets were flooded.

Think of a main idea for each topic. Then write a topic sentence that states this main idea.

**4.** music I like

**5.** if I were a millionaire

## GRAMMAR BUILDER

**Using Indefinite and Definite Articles**
*A* and *an* are indefinite articles. *The* is a definite article.
Remember these rules when using *a*, *an*, and *the*:
• Use *a* or *an* with the name of a general person, place, or thing.
• Use *an* if the next word begins with a vowel sound.
• Use *the* with the name of a particular person, place, or thing.

Write the article that belongs in each sentence.
1. We plan to buy ___ new automobile.
2. Mom thinks Mark's Auto Sales is ___ best place to buy one.
3. I want ___ black car, but Dad wants ___ apple-red one.

*Writing Paragraphs* Chapter 4 **103**

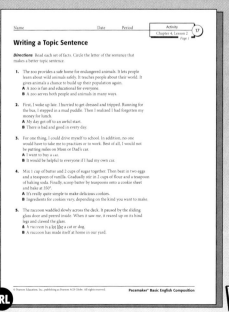

---

Answers will vary. Sample answers are shown: **1.** Car owners need to do regular checks and upkeep on their cars. **2.** If you are going to bake a cake, you must follow a set of steps. **3.** The thunderstorm yesterday caused problems around town. **4.** Nothing gets me moving at the gym like salsa music. **5.** If I were a millionaire, I would work hard to end hunger.

## GRAMMAR BUILDER

Have volunteers read aloud the rules for indefinite and definite articles. Read and discuss the sentences before students complete them.

*Grammar Builder Answers*
**1.** a **2.** the **3.** a, an

## WRITING PORTFOLIO

**Checkpoint** Have students read their ideas for the Writing Portfolio paragraph. Have them use it to write a topic sentence.

## LEARNING STYLES

**Auditory/Verbal**
Invite volunteers to suggest a topic for a paragraph. Ask other volunteers to turn this topic into a topic sentence and say their sentence aloud. Then have student pairs take turns naming a topic and writing a topic sentence. You may wish to have students record these topics and sentences on a tape for use when they begin writing reports.

## Lesson at a Glance

### Chapter 4 Lesson 3

**Overview** This lesson tells how to develop the body of a paragraph.

**Objectives**

- To write details to support a main idea
- To combine short paragraphs into one longer one

**Student Pages** 104–107

**Teacher's Resource Library**

Activity 18

Modified Activity 18

Workbook Activity 18

## Vocabulary

**body**

Have students look up the word in a dictionary and report how many different meanings it has. Ask them to point out the definition that fits in this chapter. Ask a volunteer to read this meaning aloud and use it in a sentence.

## Background Information

The elements for developing a paragraph usually fall into categories such as those listed in the text. However, students will find articles in magazines and newspapers that do not fit neatly into one of these categories. Explain to students that it is important to first learn how to organize information to make an idea clear. Beginning writers need to understand and use these basic elements as they develop paragraphs.

## 1 Warm-Up Activity

Write this sentence on the board: *There are many reasons to live in a city.* Ask students what they would expect to find in the rest of the paragraph. Elicit that the paragraph must have reasons that support the topic sentence.

---

## LESSON 4-3 Writing Supporting Details

**Objectives**

- To write details to support a main idea
- To combine short paragraphs into one longer one

**Body**

The sentences in a paragraph that explain and support the main idea

**Reading Strategy:**
Text Structure

Read this lesson's Objectives. How does this list help you understand the structure of this lesson?

What do you do after you have stated your main idea in a topic sentence? The next step is to develop that main idea. The sentences that tell more about the main idea make up the **body** of a paragraph. These sentences explain and support the main idea. In the body, you make the main idea clear to your reader.

Support the main idea with these details:

- facts
- quotations
- explanations
- reasons
- examples

### Practice A

Write the topic sentence below. Then use the details that follow to write three sentences. Each sentence must support the main idea stated in the topic sentence.

**Topic Sentence:** Springfield is a city with many places for recreation.

**Recreational Places in Springfield:**

- four city parks
- nine public tennis courts
- two public swimming pools
- three recreational centers
- a concert hall
- two golf courses
- a sports arena
- a museum
- an amusement park
- five movie theaters

### Sticking to the Main Idea

The sentences in the body of a paragraph must support the main idea. Remove any sentences that are not related to the topic sentence. You can also rewrite those sentences so that they support the main idea.

---

## 2 Teaching the Lesson

Write this topic sentence on the board: *Cafeteria food needs improvement.* Ask students to write sentences that they would include in a paragraph beginning with this sentence.

**Reading Strategy:** Text Structure

The objectives summarize what you should have learned by the time you have finished reading and completing the practices.

## Practice A

Tell students to choose three of the recreational places listed to write about in their supporting sentences.

### Practice A Answers

Answers will vary. A possible development is given: Springfield is a town with many places for recreation. People of all ages can enjoy walking among flowers and trees at four city parks. Young people spend time at three recreational centers and two public swimming pools. The sports arena and concert hall draw large crowds.

If a sentence in a paragraph is not related to the main idea, take it out. You might be able to use that sentence in a different paragraph. Or you might decide to write a new paragraph based on that sentence.

## Practice B

Read the paragraph. Find one sentence that does not belong. Write this sentence on your paper.

Summer is the best time of year for vacations. Children do not go to school. Freedom from classes allows time for sleeping late. Usually the weather is suitable for outdoor hobbies: tennis, running, gardening, or just lying lazily in the yard. Sometimes, spring is also a good time for a vacation. In summer, the beaches and the mountains have many activities for tourists. Vacationers can surf, swim, hike, or explore. It is no wonder that vacation spots do big business in the summer.

## Practice C

Read the paragraph. Find one sentence that does not belong. Write this sentence on your paper.

Regular exercise keeps a person fit. People who exercise may feel better and live longer than those who do not exercise. Exercise also helps people maintain a healthy weight. It stimulates the heart and lungs. After people exercise, they will probably be sore and tired. Everyone should try to exercise every day.

## Practice D

Read the paragraph. Find one sentence that does not belong. Write this sentence on your paper.

Our camping trip was simply awful! We froze at night and chased away bugs all day. No one caught a single fish! We enjoyed hiking through the woods. It took us an hour to start a fire, and the dinner burned. The strong winds overturned one canoe and blew down two tents. On top of it all, it rained. I am sure that we will never plan another camping trip.

**Reading Strategy:**
Text Structure

How does this lesson help you understand what supporting details do in a paragraph?

## LEARNING STYLES

**Visual/Spatial**

Have each student print a topic in the middle of a sheet of paper, for example, *cars, songs, pets, TV shows.* Have students make a web of related facts, feelings, details, examples, and thoughts about the topic. Ask them to draw lines from the topic to their ideas. Demonstrate on the board how this creates a web of information that students can use to expand a topic sentence into a paragraph or essay.

**Reading Strategy:** Text Structure

The lesson has a bulleted list of the types of details that support a topic sentence and the heading "Sticking to the Main Idea" to emphasize the importance of relevance of details.

### IN THE COMMUNITY

Have students work together to make a list of recreational attractions for their own town. A phone book or chamber of commerce listing might be used to check business types, names, and purposes. They may then use their list to write a paragraph about interesting things to do in their town.

## Practice B

Read the topic sentence aloud with students. Discuss what kinds of details should be expected in the paragraph. Then have volunteers read the sentences aloud.

### *Practice B Answers*

Sometimes, spring is also a good time for a vacation.

## Practice C

Remind students that the topic sentence appears first and states the main idea. They are looking for a sentence that does not tell anything about this main idea. If students have difficulty, have them repeat the topic sentence before reading each detail sentence.

### *Practice C Answers*

After people exercise, they will probably be sore and tired.

## Practice D

When students select the misfit sentence, have them explain why. Point out that it provides a detail about the writer's camping trip like all the other details. (They should explain that it tells about what the campers enjoyed, not about what was awful.)

### *Practice D Answers*

We enjoyed hiking through the woods.

## COMMON ERROR

Haste leads beginning writers to include details that do not belong in their paragraphs. Suggest that they set it aside for a day, then edit it to be sure all the details relate to the topic.

## Practice E

Ask volunteers to take turns reading the three steps in the directions and the two paragraphs in the activity. Make sure students understand what they are to do.

### *Practice E Answers*

Answers will vary. A sample paragraph is shown.

Springfield used to be a small town, but someday it may become a city. The population is growing as many people move to Springfield. Older people find that it is a quiet and pleasant place to live. Many recreational activities attract young, active families. Jobs are plentiful, and older homes are affordable. Springfield is now larger than some cities.

### WRITING PORTFOLIO

**Checkpoint** Have students write at least three supporting detail sentences for the topic sentence they wrote in Lesson 4-2.

### LEARNING STYLES

**Body/Kinesthetic**

Complete Practices B–D on page 105 as a game. Assign each student a sentence from one of the three paragraphs. Students should copy their sentences on a sheet of paper and get together with others who have sentences from the same paragraph. Then ask them to decide who has the sentence that does not belong. Have each group line up and read its sentences in order but not the one that does not belong. Have them explain why they did not include the sentence.

---

**Brush Up on the Basics**

Supporting details may include dates. Use a comma between the day and the year in a date: May 30, 2007. Do not use a comma between a month and a year: December 2006. See Punctuation 6 in Appendix A.

## Combining Short Paragraphs

The number of sentences in the body of a paragraph will vary. Sometimes you may find that you have written two or three short paragraphs about the same main idea. Combine those paragraphs into one longer paragraph.

### Practice E

Read the two short paragraphs. Both are about the same topic. Follow the directions below to combine the two paragraphs into one paragraph. Write the new paragraph on your paper.

Springfield used to be a small town. The population is growing. Springfield is now larger than some cities.

Many people are moving to Springfield. Older people find that it is a quiet and pleasant place to live. Many recreational activities attract young, active families. Jobs are plentiful. Large, older homes are affordable. Someday, Springfield may become a city.

1. Write a topic sentence. It should express the main idea for the new paragraph. Remember to indent this sentence.

2. Use details and facts from both paragraphs to write the body. These new sentences should support and explain the topic sentence.

*The town of Springfield attracts both young families and retired people.*

---

## Grammar Practice

Ask students how adjectives can help them write better details in their paragraphs. (*Adjectives make nouns more specific. They create pictures in the reader's mind.*) Have students locate adjectives in the first two sentences of paragraph 2, Practice E (like *many, older, quiet* and *pleasant*). Point out that adjectives usually come before a noun. Explain that adjectives may also follow a state-of-being verb. Have students read the rest of the paragraph and locate adjectives that follow verbs (like *plentiful* and *affordable*).

### LEARNING STYLES

**Logical/Mathematical**

Write this sentence on the board: *I lead a busy life.* Explain to students that you want them to organize information supporting this topic sentence. Ask them to make a time line divided into hours. Have them use it to show their activities on a typical day. Model a time line of your own day, if necessary. Invite volunteers to put their time lines on the board. Point out that all the information they need for the paragraph is on their time lines.

# REVIEW

In each paragraph, find one sentence that does not support the main idea. Write the sentence on your paper.

1.  Amber's mother likes to read. She also goes to dance class with Amber. Her favorite books are mysteries. She enjoys hunting for clues. Sometimes she likes to read short stories. They allow her to visit other times and places without leaving her house. She says that reading is relaxing, informative, and fun.

2.  Brandon's father is a great fisherman. He knows the best places to fish. He also enjoys hunting. Mr. Tucker has a large collection of fishing rods. He uses the rods that help him catch the biggest fish.

Combine the two paragraphs into one paragraph. Write the new paragraph on your paper.

3.  A piñata is a colorful decoration filled with toys or treats. A piñata is a fun thing to bring to a party.

    Party guests enjoy taking turns hitting the piñata with a stick. Each person swings at the piñata while blindfolded. When the piñata breaks, everyone rushes to grab the toys and treats that fall to the ground.

4.  Last night, Springfield had the biggest snowstorm of the year. The snow began falling at midnight and did not stop until late this morning. Springfield's last blizzard was not nearly as severe.

    Snowplows were unable to get into some of the neighborhoods. Most of the schools were cancelled today, and several businesses were closed. No cars were allowed downtown.

*Writing Paragraphs*   *Chapter 4*   **107**

## ELL/ESL STRATEGY

**Language Objective:** *To write detail sentences that are connected to a topic sentence by key words*

Students have many demands on them as they begin to write paragraphs: sentence structure and vocabulary in addition to the concepts of paragraphs. Give students a sample topic sentence with familiar words. For example, *We enjoy several festivals each year.* Have them highlight the key word *festivals.* Then have them write detail sentences in boxes and focus on related words or phrases, such as *the Festival of Lights* or *Oktoberfest.* They can connect the boxes to the topic sentence with lines and highlight the related words in each sentence.

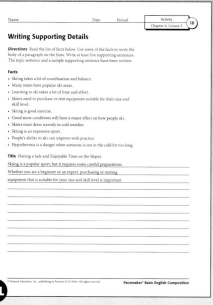

Activity 18        Workbook Activity 18

*Writing Paragraphs*   **107**

### Chapter 4  Lesson 4

**Overview**  This lesson tells how to end a paragraph well and how a conclusion and a summary differ.

### Objectives

- To write a summary or conclusion
- To choose facts that support a conclusion

**Student Pages**  108–113

### Teacher's Resource Library 🅣🅡🅛

Activity  **19**

Modified Activity  **19**

Workbook Activity  **19**

Writing on the Job  **2**

Building Research Skills  **4**

..................................................

## Vocabulary

conclusion           summary

Read the key words aloud and have volunteers read the definition for each. Ask students to write one way the two terms are alike and one way they are different.

..................................................

## Background Information

Not every paragraph ends with a neat conclusion. For example, some paragraphs build on each other. The final sentence creates a bridge or transition to the next paragraph. However, when writing a stand-alone paragraph, a conclusion is useful. Another way to explain its purpose might be that it summarizes main points, reveals an insight, or suggests a course of action.

### 1  Warm-Up Activity

Ask students if they have ever had to leave a movie before the end. Ask them how they felt. Point out that a paragraph without a good last sentence is like a movie without the ending.

---

## LESSON 4-4  Writing a Summary or Conclusion

### Objectives

- To write a summary or conclusion
- To choose facts that support a conclusion

**Summary**
A sentence at the end of a paragraph that repeats the main idea using different words

**Conclusion**
A logical decision or opinion based on facts or evidence; the sentence at the end of a paragraph

***Reading Strategy:***
Text Structure

This lesson explains two ways to end a paragraph. As you read, make a diagram that shows the difference between the two ways.

How do you end a paragraph?

### Writing a Summary

One way is to write a sentence that gives a **summary.** A summary sentence repeats the main idea in slightly different words. It is the last sentence of a paragraph. A summary sentence adds no new information to the paragraph. A summary is to a paragraph what a period is to a sentence. Both announce, "The end."

Read the paragraph in Example 1. The last sentence repeats the topic sentence using different words.

▶ **EXAMPLE 1**

Track is Derek Anderson's favorite activity. He runs five miles every day and practices regularly. He has won three races already. Derek will continue to improve his time, according to his coach. Derek works hard at track and enjoys it, too.

### Practice A

Write a summary sentence for the paragraph.

In today's world, education must never stop. New scientific discoveries appear daily. The jobs that people do keep changing. The amount of new information that people need to know is increasing rapidly!

### Writing a Conclusion

Another way to end a paragraph is with a **conclusion.** A conclusion is a decision that you make after thinking about facts or evidence. It is often an opinion. A conclusion must be logical—it must make sense to the reader. The facts in a paragraph must support the conclusion.

---

### 2  Teaching the Lesson

Point out to students that in a summary the ideas are repeated, not the words. Write this sentence on the board: *I feel great.* Ask students to think of similar sentences. (Examples: *Everything's wonderful. This is perfect.*)

Describe for students the following scene: Two people run out of a bank with guns and sacks. They drive off fast. An alarm inside the bank is ringing. Ask students what has happened. (*The two people just robbed the bank.*) Point out that a paragraph's final sentence sometimes does what they just did: it comes to a logical conclusion.

***Reading Strategy:*** Text Structure

Diagrams will vary. Sample diagrams are shown:

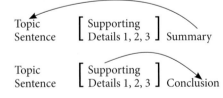

### Practice A

Discuss the similarity between the topic sentence and the last sentence in the Example 1 paragraph.

### *Practice A Answers*

Answers will vary. A sample answer is shown. Our information society will make lifelong students of us all.

Study the examples
in this lesson. How
do they help you
understand the
words *summary* and
*conclusion*?

**NOTE**

Do the facts support
the conclusion? When
you read and when you
write, this is an important
question to ask.

In Example 2, the last sentence of the paragraph is a logical conclusion.

▶ **EXAMPLE 2**

Track is Derek Anderson's favorite activity. He runs five miles every day and practices regularly. He has won three races already. Derek will continue to improve his time, according to his coach. Derek has a good chance to win a scholarship in track.

### Practice B

Read the paragraph and study the last sentence. Rewrite this conclusion so the details in the paragraph support it.

Last year, Amber's mother bought a computer. Amber and her mother enjoy playing computer games. Amber's mother uses the computer to keep track of spending. Amber uses it to learn Spanish. The computer was a waste of money.

### Practice C

Write a conclusion for the paragraph.

Sonia loves music. Every day, she listens to her favorite CDs. She also practices her violin and plays in the school orchestra.

### Practice D

Decide whether the last sentence of the paragraph is a summary or a conclusion. Write *summary* or *conclusion*.

Every day, Ms. Lentz listens to the weather report. Then she looks outside. One day the report called for sunny skies. The chance of rain was only 10 percent. When Ms. Lentz looked outside, she saw that it was raining. She decided that the weather report was wrong.

**NOTE**

When you talk about
yourself in a sentence,
put yourself last. For
example, write *Amber
and I met her. She told
Amber and me. The idea
was Amber's and mine.*

## Practice B

Have a volunteer read the paragraph aloud, pausing after every sentence to allow students to identify the topic and supporting sentences.

### Practice B Answers

Conclusions will vary. A sample conclusion is shown: The computer was a smart purchase for the family.

## Practice C

You may want to pair students to have them read the paragraph aloud and discuss conclusions for it.

### Practice C Answers

Conclusions will vary. A sample conclusion is shown: Sonia could become a professional musician one day.

## Practice D

Have a volunteer read aloud the paragraph. Then have students identify the final sentence as a summary or a conclusion.

### Practice D Answers

conclusion

## **3** Reinforce and Extend

### COMMON ERROR

Beginning writers may recast their topic sentence to end a paragraph. Emphasize that the final sentence should not be too similar to the topic sentence. Point out how the final sentence in Example 1 captures the main idea without repeating the topic sentence.

**Reading Strategy:** Text Structure

They illustrate how a summary and a conclusion for identical paragraphs might differ.

### TEACHER ALERT

The distinction between a summary and a conclusion is one that not all students may grasp. Emphasize that if a paragraph seems to just trail off, some kind of final sentence is needed to bring the main idea to a close.

### ELL/ESL STRATEGY

**Language Objective:**
*To read paragraphs to identify conclusions and summaries*

Students may need assistance and practice to understand the purpose of the final sentence in a paragraph. As students complete Practices B–D, suggest that they find the topic sentence first and use a picture to summarize its meaning. Then have them read the detail sentences and note how each is related to the topic sentence. Finally, ask students to read the last sentence and tell whether it repeats the idea in the topic sentence. If not, it should give an opinion. Have students tell whether they agree with the conclusion and why.

## WRITE ABOUT IT

Remind students to begin their process by prewriting. You may wish to hand out word web forms on which to make notes.

## Six Traits of Writing Focus

| | Ideas | ✔ | Word Choice |
|---|---|---|---|
| ✔ | Organization | | Sentence Fluency |
| | Voice | | Conventions |

## Organization

Suggest that students pay attention to the organization of their writing. Ask: *Does the topic sentence sum up the main point? Does the body support the topic? Does the conclusion restate the opinion?* Explain that these are "road signs" that guide readers through a piece.

Students can also work to improve word choice by replacing verbs or adjectives to add color to their writing.

Refer students to page WPH1 for descriptions of the Six Traits of Writing.

## GLOBAL CONNECTION

Encourage students to go online or use an almanac to look up information about the Olympics. Have them list facts about recent winners and their countries. Work together to develop a paragraph about it.

---

## LESSON 4-4

# REVIEW

Write a conclusion or a summary sentence for each paragraph.

1.  The Summer Olympic Games include a contest called the decathlon. The decathlon is 10 events. Athletes from all over the world run in 100-meter, 400-meter, and 1,500-meter races. They run a high hurdle race. They throw the discus, the javelin, and the shot put. They leap the high jump, the long jump, and the pole vault.

2.  Have you ever found a writer who makes you laugh aloud? I read everything I can find by Dave Barry. Every week, I read his column in the newspaper. If it is especially funny, I cut it out and save it. I have also bought two of Dave Barry's books.

3.  Last month, Derek met a girl on the track team. She runs the mile. She told him that she has played sports all her life. She also teaches an exercise class. She and Derek share many interests. Her name is Sarah.

4.  Amber and Sonia are worried about their friend Derek. Now that he has met Sarah, he looks dreamy all the time. He has stopped doing his homework. His old friends hardly ever see him.

## WRITE ABOUT IT

**Your Favorite Kind of Physical Exercise**
Write a paragraph about your favorite kind of exercise. Include details to explain this exercise to who has never tried it. Give one reason why this exercise is fun to do. Tell why you think other people should try this exercise. Be sure your paragraph has a topic sentence, a body, and a summary or conclusion.

● **Six Traits of Writing:**
*Organization* order, ideas tied together

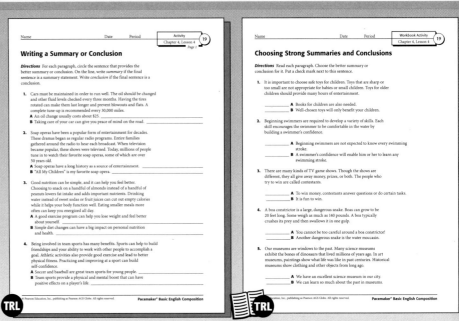

## Office Assistant

Valerie Hartman works in the sales office of a paper company. She answers the phone and files papers. She also sends messages for the office manager.

The company is getting ready for a big meeting. All sales people will meet for two days. The manager has given Valerie some facts about the meeting. Valerie is to write an e-mail telling about the meeting. Read her e-mail. Then answer the questions below.

| | |
|---|---|
| **To:** | All Sales Staff |
| **From:** | Valerie Hartman |
| Subject: | Sales Awards Meeting |

The time for our Sales Awards Meeting is nearly here. This year, it will be held in Lincoln on November 14 and 15. Please call the Lincoln Inn to reserve your room. I look forward each year to thanking you all for your hard work. We will also look ahead to next year. There are exciting new plans to share!

1. What is this e-mail message about?

2. Which sentence tells the topic? Write this sentence on your paper.

3. CRITICAL THINKING Why does Valerie include details about the place of the meeting? What is the purpose of the last three sentences?

## SPEAKING

In a large office, people talk face to face and in group meetings. They also communicate by e-mail, phone, fax, and online conferences. Practice leaving a phone message. Work with a partner. Speak clearly and slowly. Give your name, phone number, and the time you called. Tell why you called. Keep your message short.

*Writing Paragraphs* Chapter 4 **111**

Have students read the job title and look at the picture. Then have a volunteer read the opening paragraphs. Ask students to predict what the e-mail will contain. After students read the e-mail, ask them to point out any ways it differs from e-mails they send to friends or family. (For example, students probably do not use complete sentences and capitalize all proper nouns in their e-mails.)

Point out that the e-mail is a paragraph. Have them identify its topic sentence and supporting sentences.

### Writing on the Job Answers

**1.** the Sales Awards Meeting **2.** The time for our Sales Awards Meeting is nearly here. **3.** Details about the place tell attendees where they must go and that they need to reserve a room. The last three sentences tell that the meeting will thank sales staff and tell about plans for the next year.

## Speaking and Presenting Practice

Set up small groups of students who are interested in or have experience with the same kind of part-time job. Ask students to discuss the communication that takes place. Then have the group create a short skit that shows one kind of spoken communication at work. Give groups time to practice, then have them present their skits.

## COMMON ERROR

Many students have trained themselves to ignore punctuation, spelling, and capitalization when they e-mail. Point out that in the workplace, e-mail is as important as letters or memos. They are just as permanent and show the same skills. For this reason, students should apply their writing and grammar skills to workplace e-mails.

### Office Assistant

An office assistant must sometimes write e-mails and memos to other workers. These communications usually give information. They should use correct English and complete sentences. Sentences should be arranged in logical paragraphs.

Jeff Diemer is an office assistant at an insurance company. His boss had him write a letter to customers. The letter tells about a kind of insurance certain customers might want. Read Jeff's letter. Then answer the questions below.

Dear _____:

Thank you for choosing Bening Agency to insure your home. We welcome your business. From time to time, we will let you know about other products that might protect you in other ways.

Do you have special collections, jewelry, or other valuables worth more than $25,000? We are happy that we can offer you a personal articles policy that covers these kinds of items. For just a few dollars a month, you can have even more peace of mind about your personal treasures.

Sincerely,
Jeff Diemer

1. Which of the following sentences is the better topic sentence for paragraph 2?
   A Do you want to know about our monthly payment plan?
   B Many homeowners worry about the valuables in their homes.

2. Which of the following sentences is the better conclusion for paragraph 2?
   A For just a few dollars a month, you can have peace of mind about your personal treasures.
   B Call and ask about our policies for your car, boat, trailer, and RV, too.

3. CRITICAL THINKING What do you think is the purpose of paragraph 1?

Writing on the Job 2

## CAREER CONNECTION

Tell students that when they write a cover letter for a job, they might need a paragraph telling why they are qualified. Have them give examples of conclusions that they might write to end such a paragraph.

Ask students to tell what *blending* means. (*mixing together well*) Point out the note cards on page 112. Ask volunteers to read the notes aloud. Discuss what overall idea the facts suggest about wind farms. Then have students read the paragraph.

### *Building Research Skills Answers*

**1.** Wind farms can solve some of our energy problems. (Students may copy the first sentence of the paragraph as well.) **2.** Students may mention that wind energy is clean, cheap, and endless and that wind power already produces 8% of our nation's electricity on wind farms. **3.** They showed how wind energy is being used, how much is being used, and how it is better than fossil fuels.

## Blending Ideas in Your Writing

While doing some research on wind farms, a student wrote these notes on index cards:

> Wind power produces 8% of U.S. electricity.
> Wind energy is clean and cheap. It is endless.

> Farmers are putting wind machines on their farms.
> Oil and gas are costly and dirty energy sources.

> Wind farms use wind machines.
> They change wind energy into electricity.

These facts suggest a main idea about wind farms. The student blended the facts together and wrote a paragraph to support this idea. Read the paragraph below. Then answer the questions.

> Wind farms are a welcome answer to some of our energy problems. They use wind machines to change wind energy into electricity. They do it without making the air and water dirty. We will run out of oil and gas, but the wind is always there. Farmers are setting up wind machines on their farms. These wind farms already make 8 percent of the electricity in the United States.

1. What main idea does this paragraph express? Write it on your paper.

2. What are two details the writer used to support the main idea?

3. CRITICAL THINKING How did the notes help the writer conclude that wind farms are a good way to provide energy?

### TECHNOLOGY

Researching a topic helps you find details and draw conclusions. You can share your ideas in several ways. Instead of writing a report, you can make a poster, a model, or a project. Computer software can help you set up a slide show. You can combine pictures and words to show on a screen. Think of a subject you could research. Write a sentence telling how you would share the information you found and the conclusions you made.

---

Name _____ Date _____ Period _____

Building Research Skills 4
Chapter 4

### Blending Ideas in Your Writing

When you research a topic, you use different sources of information. You write notes about what you learn. Then you look at your notes. You find a way to combine the information to serve your purposes.

For example, Shar did research on diamonds. She decided to write a paragraph about how diamonds form. Look at her notes. Then read Shar's paragraph and answer the questions.

| A | B | C |
|---|---|---|
| • a crystal form of carbon<br>• usually clear<br>• cut surfaces are facets<br>• if flawless, has great value | • hardest known material in nature<br>• judged by the 4 Cs: carat, clarity, color, cut<br>• the hardest diamonds come from Australia | • shine with great brilliance when faceted<br>• form deep in the earth<br>• very great pressure and high temperatures |

Clear, sparkling diamonds and black, sooty coal are made of the same substance: carbon! Deep inside the earth, very high temperatures and very great pressure turn carbon into a crystal known as diamond. The result is a clear stone that is harder than any other material in nature. Unlike coal, diamonds have a brilliant sparkle when they are faceted, or cut.

1. Circle the notes that Shar used in her paragraph about how diamonds form.

2. What is the main idea of Shar's paragraph? Write it on the lines.

_____

3. CRITICAL THINKING What do all the notes you circled above have in common?

_____
_____
_____
_____

Pacemaker® Basic English Composition

TRL

**Building Research Skills 4**

# SUMMARY

- Before you begin writing, complete the prewriting stage of the writing process.

- Make sure you understand the writing assignment or prompt.

- Think about what the reader would like to know about your topic. Try to answer the reader's questions.

- Think about the purpose of your writing. Ask yourself: Why am I writing this? Am I trying to provide information? Am I trying to entertain or persuade someone?

- Find ideas by brainstorming alone or with other people.

- Write organized paragraphs. A paragraph is a group of sentences about one main idea.

- Start a paragraph with a topic sentence. It gives the main idea. It tells the reader what the paragraph is going to be about.

- In the body of a paragraph, write sentences that support the main idea. Include details such as facts, examples, explanations, and reasons.

- Take out sentences that are not about the main idea. Combine short paragraphs if they support the same main idea.

- End a paragraph with a summary or conclusion. Repeat the main idea using different words, or give a concluding opinion.

## GROUP ACTIVITY

In a group, make a list of several ways to save energy. (You might look at ways to save gas or electricity, or you might look at ways to use fewer resources.) Discuss what main idea your list supports. Together write a paragraph about your energy-saving plan.

Trade paragraphs with another group. Find the topic sentence and supporting details in the paragraph. Suggest ways to improve the other group's work.

## Chapter 4 Summary

Have volunteers read aloud each Summary item on page 113. Ask volunteers to explain the meaning of each item.

### ONLINE CONNECTION

For help in brainstorming, organizing, and writing, students may find these sites helpful:

www.agsglobepmbec.com/page113a
This interactive site guides writers through all developmental stages.

www.agsglobepmbec.com/page113b
This site includes organizers and advises how each is useful in writing.

### GROUP ACTIVITY

Have groups begin by brainstorming and recording ideas on a word web or a chart. Suggest that students evaluate their chosen topic to see if it is narrow enough. Remind students that they will need to plan not only the details to include but also the way they should be organized. As groups complete their paragraphs, encourage them to add a concluding or summarizing sentence.

## Chapter 4 Review

Use the Chapter Review to prepare students for tests and to reteach content from the chapter.

## Chapter 4 Mastery Test

The Teacher's Resource Library includes two forms of the Chapter 4 Mastery Test. Each test addresses the chapter Goals for Learning. An optional third page of additional critical-thinking items is included for each test. The difficulty level of the two forms is equivalent.

### Review Answers

#### Part A

1. prewriting  2. topic sentence
3. conclusion  4. body  5. summary
6. paragraph  7. brainstorming
8. audience  9. writing prompt  10. indent

#### Part B

Topic sentences will vary. Sample sentences are given. **11.** The hummingbird is a unique bird. **12.** Music has a strong effect on state of mind. **13.** Making your furniture glow is a simple process. **14.** We are ready for the big storm. **15.** We wanted to be ready for the baseball game.

#### Part C

**16.** Answers will vary. Sample notes are shown.

Saving money: Earn more or spend less. Drink water instead of other beverages. Get a job. Take money out of paycheck or allowance before doing anything else. Take a sack lunch to school. Have a goal.

### Word Bank

audience
body
brainstorming
conclusion
indent
paragraph
prewriting
summary
topic sentence
writing prompt

**Part A** Write the word or words from the Word Bank that complete each sentence.

1. The planning you do before you write is called _____.
2. A _____ states the main idea of a paragraph.
3. A logical decision or opinion based on facts is a _____.
4. The _____ of a paragraph contains supporting details.
5. A _____ repeats the main idea using different words.
6. A _____ is a group of sentences about one idea.
7. Writing down ideas as you think of them is _____.
8. The people who read what you write are your _____.
9. A _____ is the directions for a writing assignment.
10. You should _____ the first sentence in every paragraph.

**Part B** Write a topic sentence for each set of details.

11. A hummingbird can fly forward and backward. It is the smallest bird. It eats nectar and small insects.
12. Listening to music can be relaxing. A song can bring back happy memories. Music can change your mood.
13. First, find a dust cloth. Next, get a bottle of furniture polish. Then, dust and polish the furniture.
14. The survivor kit has matches and batteries. There is a flashlight and a radio. It also contains food and water.
15. We bought tickets to a baseball game. We got our gloves. We took a pencil to keep score.

**Part C**

16. Brainstorm about one of these topics: the weather, a gift, or saving money. Write five ideas or facts about it.

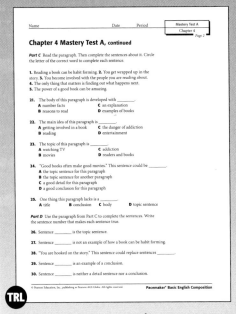

Chapter 4 Mastery Test A, pages 1–3

**Part D** Read the paragraph. Then answer the questions.

Luis Moreno is Sonia's favorite cousin. He has a great sense of adventure. Luis is fun and creative. He enjoys doing many things. Sonia is happy when Luis visits.

**17.** Which sentence tells the main idea?

**18.** What three examples support the main idea?

**19.** Which sentence is a summary?

**Part E** Use each set of facts to write a paragraph.

**20.** People use computers for word processing. People use computers to connect with others. Students do research using computers. People do their taxes on computers.

**21.** Visitors want to see the steep canyon walls. Rafting trips down the river are popular. Mules take riders to the bottom of the canyon. There are many hiking trails.

**Part F** Read the paragraph. Then write the letter of the answer that completes each sentence.

Owning a dog takes hard work. A dog needs food and water at least twice a day. A dog also needs a walk everyday. Sometimes, a dog needs a bath. Overall, the fun of playing with a dog outweighs the chore of caring for it.

**Test Tip**

In a writing test, watch how you use your time. Take some time to plan your writing and later revise it. However, spend most of your time writing.

**22.** *Overall, the fun of playing with a dog outweighs the chore of caring for it.* This sentence is a _____.
  **A** body   **B** detail   **C** conclusion   **D** topic

**23.** *Owning a dog takes hard work.* This is a _____.
  **A** body   **B** detail   **C** conclusion   **D** main idea

**24.** *Sometimes, a dog needs a bath.* This is a _____.
  **A** topic   **B** detail   **C** conclusion   **D** main idea

**25.** The _____ of this paragraph is dog care.
  **A** body   **B** detail   **C** conclusion   **D** topic

## Review Answers

**Part D**

**17.** Luis Moreno is Sonia's favorite cousin. **18.** Details include his sense of humor, fun and creative nature, and enjoyment of many things. **19.** Sonia is happy when Luis visits.

**Part E**

Paragraphs will vary. Sample paragraphs are given.

**20.** We could not get along without computers in our world. People use computers for word processing and to connect with others. Students rely on computers to do research. Many people do their taxes on the computer. If you want to see society screech to a halt, turn off the computers for a day.

**21.** Visitors to the canyon find different ways to enjoy the sights. Many visitors view the steep canyon walls from the top down. Others enjoy the changing views from the many hiking trails. Visitors can enjoy the view all the way down if they ride mules to the bottom of the canyon. Others prefer to see the view from the bottom up as they raft downriver through the canyon. No matter where you are, the canyon is spectacular to look at!

**Part F**

**22.** C  **23.** D  **24.** B  **25.** D

## WRITING PORTFOLIO

**Wrap-Up** Have students write a summary sentence for their Writing Portfolio paragraph.

---

**Chapter 4 Mastery Test B**

**Part A** Circle the correct letter of the item that correctly completes each sentence.

**1.** A _____ gives you directions for a writing assignment and often suggests the topic.
  **A** summary  **B** prompt  **C** paragraph  **D** topic sentence

**2.** When you _____, you think freely about a topic and get ideas for writing.
  **A** summarize  **B** brainstorm  **C** conclude  **D** indent

**3.** If a paragraph is _____, its first line is set in about an inch.
  **A** prompt  **B** prewriting  **C** indented  **D** summarized

**4.** A paragraph's final sentence is a _____ if it restates the main idea.
  **A** conclusion  **B** summary  **C** topic  **D** topic sentence

**5.** The sentences in the _____ of a paragraph tell more about the main idea.
  **A** topic  **B** body  **C** summary  **D** prompt

**Part B** Decide how these sentences should be ordered to form a paragraph. Write the order (1, 2, 3, 4, and so on) on the line before each sentence.

____ **6.** Wet the dog with warm water.
____ **7.** Rub the dog with towels.
____ **8.** Rinse the dog with water, using a bucket or shower head.
____ **9.** Gather shampoo, a sponge, and a bucket or shower head.
____ **10.** At the end, you are left with a clean, happy dog!
____ **11.** Apply shampoo and rub it in, using your fingers to scrub.
____ **12.** Let the dog shake off the excess water.
____ **13.** Wash the dog's face with a sponge dipped in water.
____ **14.** Comb the dog when its coat is dry.
____ **15.** Bathing a dog is easy if you follow the steps in my method.

---

**Chapter 4 Mastery Test B,** continued

**Part C** Read the paragraph. Then answer each question about it. Write your answers on the lines.

**1.** English has taken words from many languages. **2.** For example, *pretzel* is a German word. **3.** The words *ranch* and *plaza* are taken from Spanish. **4.** Italian gave us musical words, such as *piano*. **5.** Some animal names, including *chipmunk*, come from Native American languages. **6.** Many languages have given English a rich vocabulary.

**16.** Which sentence in the paragraph is the topic sentence? _____

**17.** Which 2 sentences are not examples of how a word came into English? _____

**18.** "Its large borrowed vocabulary is one reason English is so complex and hard to learn." This sentence could replace _____

**19.** What is the main idea of this paragraph? _____

**20.** Which sentence in the paragraph above could be replaced by this sentence: "The English language is a great borrower." _____

**Part D** Read each paragraph. Circle its topic sentence. Underline its summary or conclusion.

**21–22.** The snake dance of the Hopi people of Arizona is special. Hopi dancers carry live rattlesnakes in their mouths as they dance. They know how to handle the snakes, so they are rarely bitten. Watching a snake dance is a thrilling experience.

**23–24.** To take proper care of a horse, you need to buy all the right equipment. First, you need tools to groom the horse. Then, you should get a halter and lead rope for catching and leading your horse. Don't forget about hay, grain, and vitamins. To ride you need tack, including a saddle, and saddle blanket. Horse owners have empty wallets and happy horses!

**25.** Write a title for one of these paragraphs.

---

**Chapter 4 Mastery Test B,** continued

**Part E** Write your answer to each question. Use complete sentences. Support each answer with facts and examples from the textbook.

**26.** Write a topic sentence for the topic "My Idea of a Perfect Vacation."

**27.** What happens in the body of a paragraph?

**Part F** Write a paragraph for each topic. Include a topic sentence, body, and conclusion in the paragraph. Support your answers with facts and examples from the textbook.

**28.** Read the following paragraph. Then tell why the concluding sentence should be replaced.

My dog Boo is very shy. When the doorbell rings, he hides under the bed. On a walk, he stays as far as possible from other dogs and people. To be really relaxed, Boo prefers to have me all to himself. Now, my cat Jangles is another matter!

**29.** Name two ways to end a paragraph. Explain the difference between the two endings.

---

Chapter 4 Mastery Test B, pages 1–3

# Writing Better Paragraphs

| | Student Lesson | | | | Language Skills | | | | |
|---|---|---|---|---|---|---|---|---|---|
| | Student Pages | Vocabulary | Practice Exercises | Lesson Review | Identification | Writing | Punctuation & Capitalization | Grammar & Usage | Listening, Speaking, & Viewing |
| **Lesson 5-1** Writing an Interesting Topic Sentence | 119–122 | ✔ | ✔ | ✔ | ✔ | ✔ | ✔ | ✔ | ✔ |
| **Lesson 5-2** Using Sentence Variety | 123–126 | ✔ | ✔ | ✔ | ✔ | ✔ | ✔ | ✔ | ✔ |
| **Lesson 5-3** Adding Transitions | 127–130 | ✔ | ✔ | ✔ | ✔ | ✔ | ✔ | ✔ | ✔ |
| **Lesson 5-4** Revising a Paragraph | 131–134 | | ✔ | ✔ | ✔ | ✔ | ✔ | ✔ | ✔ |
| **Lesson 5-5** Editing Your Paragraph | 135–141 | ✔ | ✔ | ✔ | ✔ | ✔ | ✔ | ✔ | ✔ |

## Chapter Activities

**Teacher's Resource Library**
Life Skills Connection 5:
   Communicating Clearly in Writing
Writing Tip 5: Ways to Improve Your
   Paragraphs
English in Your Life 3: Writing to
   Solve a Problem
Building Research Skills 5: Using a
   Library's Online Catalog
Key Vocabulary Words 5

## Assessment Options

**Student Text**
Chapter 5 Review

**Teacher's Resource Library**
Chapter 5 Mastery Tests A and B

**Teacher's Edition**
Chapter 5 Writing Portfolio

| | Student Text Features | | | | | | | | | Teaching Strategies | | | | | | | | | Learning Styles | | | | | Teacher's Resource Library | | | |
|---|---|---|---|---|---|---|---|---|---|---|---|---|---|---|---|---|---|---|---|---|---|---|---|---|---|---|---|
| English in Your Life | Writing on the Job | Building Research Skills | Vocabulary Builder | Grammar Builder | Write About It | Group Activity | Reading Strategy | Six Traits | ELL/ESL Strategy | Background Information | Common Error | Life Skills Connection | Applications (Home, Career, Community, Global) | Online Connection | Teacher Alert | Speaking & Presenting Practice | Writing/Spelling/Grammar Practice | Auditory/Verbal | Body/Kinesthetic | Interpersonal/Group Learning | Logical/Mathematical | Visual/Spatial | Activities | Modified Activities | Workbook Activities | Self-Study Guide |
| | | | | | | | 119, 121 | | 121 | 119 | 121 | | 120 | 120 | | | | | | | 120 | | 20 | 20 | 20 | ✔ |
| | | | | 126 | | | 123, 125 | | 124 | 123 | 125 | | 124 | 124 | | | 128 | | 126 | 125 | | | 21 | 21 | 21 | ✔ |
| | | | | | 130 | | 127, 128 | 130 | 130 | 127 | | | 128 | 128 | | | 131 | 129 | | | | | 22 | 22 | 22 | ✔ |
| | | | 133 | | | | 131, 133 | | 133 | 131 | 132 | | | 132 | | | | | | | | 132 | 23 | 23 | 23 | ✔ |
| 139 | 140 | | | | | 141 | 136, 137 | | 138 | 135 | | 136 | | 141 | | 139 | 137 | | | | | | 24 | 24 | 24 | ✔ |

## Pronunciation Key

| | | | | | | | | | | | | |
|---|---|---|---|---|---|---|---|---|---|---|---|---|
| a | hat | e | let | ī | ice | ô | order | ù | put | sh | she | ə { a in about |
| ā | age | ē | equal | o | hot | oi | oil | ü | rule | th | thin | e in taken |
| ä | far | ėr | term | ō | open | ou | out | ch | child | ᴛʜ | then | i in pencil |
| â | care | i | it | ò | saw | u | cup | ng | long | zh | measure | o in lemon |
| | | | | | | | | | | | | u in circus |

## Modified Activities

The Teacher's Resource Library (TRL) contains a set of lower-level worksheets called Modified Activities. These worksheets cover the same content as the standard Activities but are written at a lower reading level.

## Skill Track

Use Skill Track for *Basic English Composition* to monitor student progress and meet the demands of adequate yearly progress (AYP). Make informed instructional decisions with individual student and class reports of lesson and chapter assessments. With immediate and ongoing feedback, students will also see what they have learned and where they need more reinforcement and practice.

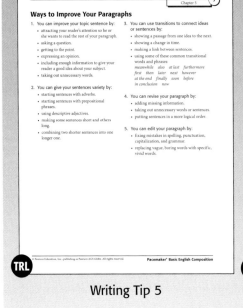

**Ways to Improve Your Paragraphs**

1. You can improve your topic sentence by:
   - attracting your reader's attention so he or she wants to read the rest of your paragraph.
   - asking a question.
   - getting to the point.
   - expressing an opinion.
   - including enough information to give your reader a good idea about your subject.
   - taking out unnecessary words.

2. You can give your sentences variety by:
   - starting sentences with adverbs.
   - starting sentences with prepositional phrases.
   - using descriptive adjectives.
   - making some sentences short and others long.
   - combining two shorter sentences into one longer one.

3. You can use transitions to connect ideas or sentences by:
   - showing a passage from one idea to the next.
   - showing a change in time.
   - making a link between sentences.
   - using some of these common transitional words and phrases:
     *meanwhile   also   at last   furthermore   first   then   later   next   however   at the end   finally   soon   before   in conclusion   now*

4. You can revise your paragraph by:
   - adding missing information.
   - taking out unnecessary words or sentences.
   - putting sentences in a more logical order.

5. You can edit your paragraph by:
   - fixing mistakes in spelling, punctuation, capitalization, and grammar.
   - replacing vague, boring words with specific, vivid words.

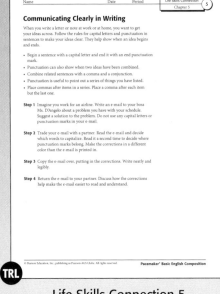

**Communicating Clearly in Writing**

When you write a letter or note at work or at home, you want to get your ideas across. Follow the rules for capital letters and punctuation in sentences to make your ideas clear. They help show when an idea begins and ends.

- Begin a sentence with a capital letter and end it with an end punctuation mark.
- Punctuation can also show when two ideas have been combined.
- Combine related sentences with a comma and a conjunction.
- Punctuation is useful to point out a series of things you have listed.
- Place commas after items in a series. Place a comma after each item but the last one.

**Step 1** Imagine you work for an airline. Write an e-mail to your boss Ms. D'Angelo about a problem you have with your schedule. Suggest a solution to the problem. Do not use any capital letters or punctuation marks in your e-mail.

**Step 2** Trade your e-mail with a partner. Read the e-mail and decide which words to capitalize. Read it a second time to decide where punctuation marks belong. Make the corrections in a different color than the e-mail is printed in.

**Step 3** Copy the e-mail over, putting in the corrections. Write neatly and legibly.

**Step 4** Return the e-mail to your partner. Discuss how the corrections help make the e-mail easier to read and understand.

# Writing Better Paragraphs

**H**ave you ever played a musical instrument? If you have, then you know that making music takes a lot of fine tuning. The saxophone player in the photo had to work hard before being able to play a song. He had to learn the keys to use. His wrong notes had to be corrected. Only after much practicing could he make pleasing music.

As a writer, you also can create something pleasing. But you need to work with what you write to make it pleasing to read. This means looking closely at sentences. It means improving a paragraph so each part of it counts.

In Chapter 5, you will learn to add interest to a topic sentence. You will learn how to use a variety of sentences and connect them smoothly. You will also learn how to review your writing and fix any mistakes. You will find many ways to make your writing better.

## GOALS FOR LEARNING

- To write interesting topic sentences
- To use sentence variety
- To make smooth transitions between sentences
- To revise paragraphs
- To edit paragraphs for mistakes

117

## Introducing the Chapter

Have students examine the photograph on page 116. Ask them to tell what the student is doing. Encourage students who have played musical instruments to tell what is involved in playing a musical instrument. Help students conclude that it takes time, practice, and knowledge of the techniques for playing the instrument for a musician to improve and play well. Extend the discussion to include writers and writing. Point out that in this chapter students will study and practice techniques a writer uses to improve writing.

Review and discuss the Goals for Learning on page 117.

## Notes

Ask volunteers to read the notes that appear in the margins throughout the chapter. Then discuss them with the class.

### TEACHER'S RESOURCE

The AGS Globe Teaching Strategies in English Transparencies may be used with this chapter. The transparencies add an interactive dimension to expand and enhance the *Basic English Composition* program content.

### WRITING PORTFOLIO

Have students choose one of the following topics and brainstorm details for a paragraph:

how to play a _____ (musical instrument)

my favorite kind of music

an instrument I would like to play

Have students generate a topic sentence and list at least three details related to the topic below this. Then have them write a rough draft of their paragraph. Explain that they will improve their paragraphs as they complete Chapter 5. This project may be used as an alternative form of assessment for the chapter.

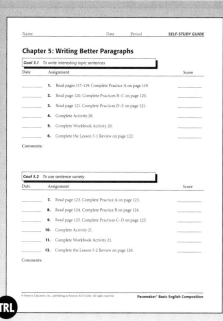

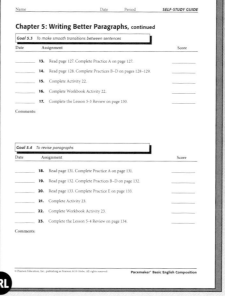

Chapter 5 Self-Study Guide, pages 1–3

## Reading Strategy: Visualizing

Ask students what goes on in their minds as they listen to a friend tell about something that happened. Invite students to tell when it is useful to visualize, or picture, something mentally. Have a volunteer read the reading strategy introduction, pausing after each question to allow classmates to respond.

### Key Vocabulary Words

| | |
|---|---|
| edit | rewrite |
| opinion | transition |
| revise | variety |

Write *revise* and *edit* on the board. Have volunteers read the meanings of the terms aloud. Write a sentence such as the following on the board: *Me and Bill become good friends.* Ask students to illustrate each of the operations using the sentence. Follow their directions and have students tell which operation led to each change. Have students read the other terms and their meanings, then write a sentence for each word.

# Reading Strategy: Visualizing

Visualizing is another way to better understand what you are reading. To visualize means to picture words as images. It is like creating a movie in your mind. Use the following ways to visualize the information in this chapter:

- Look at the vocabulary words listed below. What images do you think of when you read these words?
- Think about your own experiences. How do they add to these images?
- Look at the examples in the lessons. Which ones might help you remember the main ideas?

## Key Vocabulary Words

**Revise** To change a piece of writing to make it better

**Rewrite** To write again in a different way

**Opinion** The way a person thinks about something; a belief or viewpoint

**Variety** A collection of things that are different or vary in some way

**Transition** A change from one thing to another; often a change in time, place, situation, or thought

**Edit** To correct mistakes in a piece of writing; to check spelling, punctuation, capitalization, grammar, and word choice

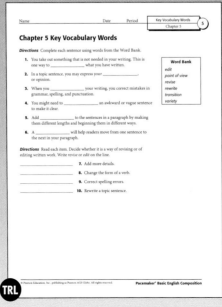

Key Vocabulary Words 5

## LESSON 5-1

# Writing an Interesting Topic Sentence

**Objectives**

■ To write a better topic sentence

■ To leave out unnecessary words

■ To get the reader's attention

■ To express an opinion in a topic sentence

**Revise**

To change a piece of writing to make it better

**Rewrite**

To write again in a different way

**Reading Strategy:**
Visualizing

What words on this page help you picture what you are reading?

A topic sentence introduces the reader to the main idea of the paragraph. It can also get a reader's attention. A lively topic sentence makes the reader want to find out more.

To improve a topic sentence, get to the point. Take out unnecessary words. Add words that will grab the reader's attention. Compare the topic sentences in Example 1.

▶ **EXAMPLE 1**

Poor    Let me begin by telling about Toronto, which is an interesting place to visit.

Better   Toronto is a one-of-a-kind city that offers visitors experiences they will never forget.

To be a good writer, you must always **revise** your writing. To revise means to make changes so that your writing is better. When you revise, you change what you have written. You might add something that is missing, take out something that is not needed, or **rewrite** something in a better way. To rewrite means to write again in a new way.

### Practice A

Copy each topic sentence on your paper. Cross out unnecessary words. Add words that will grab the reader's attention.

1. This paragraph is about a family vacation in Arizona.

2. I think I will begin this paragraph by telling you that I just got a new CD player.

3. Let me tell you about what I want to be: a musician.

4. I am going to write about the trip I took to a museum.

5. The topic I will tell about is Internet search engines.

*Writing Better Paragraphs*    Chapter 5    **119**

---

### Chapter 5  Lesson 1

**Overview** This lesson shows how to use attention-getting details, questions, and point of view to improve topic sentences.

### Objectives

■ To write a better topic sentence

■ To leave out unnecessary words

■ To get the reader's attention

■ To express an opinion in a topic sentence

**Student Pages** 119–122

**Teacher's Resource Library**

> Activity 20
>
> **Modified Activity** 20
>
> **Workbook Activity** 20

### Vocabulary

opinion          rewrite
revise

Write *revise* and *rewrite* on the board. Ask a volunteer to circle the parts of the words that are the same. Remind students that *re-* is a prefix that means "again." Therefore, to *rewrite* something is to write it again. Explain that *vis* is a root from Latin that means "to see," so when they revise something, students look at it again with fresh eyes in order to improve it. Have students make up sentences beginning with "My opinion about [an issue] is ____."

### Background Information

Some paragraphs—particularly narrative and descriptive paragraphs—have no topic sentence at all. Instead, they rely on strong details to *show* the main idea. At other times, writers may use two sentences to express the main idea of a paragraph. The first sentence introduces a general idea and a second one limits or focuses the idea.

### *Reading Strategy:* Visualizing

Students may say that the vocabulary words, the lesson title, and the Example 1 sentences help them visualize what they are reading.

---

## 1  Warm-Up Activity

Ask students why someone might want a speaker or writer to get to the point. Briefly discuss the meaning of the expression *to get to the point.*

## 2  Teaching the Lesson

After they have read the text on pages 119–120, ask students to comment about the type of information that grabs their attention. Have students tell why a topic sentence that is a question might make them keep reading.

### Practice A

Have students begin a new topic sentence on a separate line after they have crossed out the unnecessary words.

Then they can work the remaining words into any sentence position.

### *Practice A Answers*

Revised sentences will vary. Sample sentences are given. **1.** This paragraph is about a family vacation in Arizona. Revised: Our family vacation in Arizona was fabulous. **2.** I think I will begin this paragraph by telling you that I just got a new CD player. Revised: My new CD player rocks! **3.** Let me tell you about what I want to be: a musician. Revised: Someday I'll be onstage making music. **4.** I am going to write about the trip I took to a museum. Revised: My trip to the Museum of Art History inspired me. **5.** The topic I will tell about is Internet search engines. Revised: Internet search engines are your magic carpet to finding almost any kind of information.

## TEACHER ALERT

A well-written topic sentence also helps to make sure a topic is neither too narrow nor too broad. As a rule, students should consider whether their topic sentence can be developed in 3–5 detail sentences. If they cannot write that many relevant sentences, the topic is too narrow. If they cannot provide clear, precise information in one paragraph, the topic is too broad.

## Practice B

Have students decide which question in each pair does the better job of getting to the point and grabbing their attention. Ask students to explain their choices orally. They should conclude that the better topic sentence gives more specific information, uses livelier language, and involves the reader more personally.

### *Practice B Answers*

**1.** B **2.** B **3.** A **4.** A **5.** B

## Practice C

For more ideas for paragraphs, have students look at Chapter 4 for models of paragraphs that serve different purposes.

### *Practice C Answers*

Paragraphs will vary. Each topic sentence should be a question.

## LEARNING STYLES

**Logical/Mathematical**

Suggest that students use a word web to help them form questions about their topic in Practice C. After they have decided on a topic, have students write the topic in the center of a word web and details in the surrounding circles. They can use the word web for ideas to write their topic sentences and plan their paragraphs.

## GLOBAL CONNECTION

Review the Example 2 paragraph on page 120. Explain to students that the names of many American cities originated from the languages of Native Americans or explorers and settlers of the Americas. Suggest that students write a similar paragraph about the origin of another place name, such as *Chicago, Los Angeles, Baton Rouge, Pueblo, San Francisco, Pensacola, Chattanooga,* or *Corpus Christi.*

---

## Getting the Reader's Attention

One way to get your reader's attention is by asking a question. The topic sentence in Example 2 asks a question.

▶ **EXAMPLE 2**

Have you ever wondered how Toronto got its name? Toronto is one of the largest cities in Canada. Its name came from the Mohawk Indian word *tkaronto*. The word means "where there are trees standing in the water." The history of names is a fascinating subject.

### Practice B

Read each pair of questions. Decide whether *A* or *B* is a better topic sentence. Write the letter of your answer.

**1.** **A** Would you like me to tell you about our cat?
   **B** Have you met Harold, our family cat?

**2.** **A** Aren't some plants interesting?
   **B** Have you ever heard of a meat-eating plant?

**3.** **A** Would you like to live next door to a volcano?
   **B** What is a volcano?

**4.** **A** Are the foods you eat good for you?
   **B** Do you want me to tell you what foods are healthy?

**5.** **A** Poison ivy causes you to itch.
   **B** Have you ever had a bad case of poison ivy?

### Practice C

Choose a topic listed below, or choose your own topic. Write a paragraph about it. Begin with a question that gets to the point and grabs the reader's attention.

- your neighborhood
- decorating your room
- your favorite game

**Opinion**

The way a person thinks about something; a belief or viewpoint

*Reading Strategy:*
Visualizing

List the ways you can make a topic sentence more interesting. Picture how you can improve a topic sentence.

## Expressing Your Opinion

A topic sentence may express your **opinion.** Your opinion is the way you think about something. It is a belief or viewpoint.

▶ **EXAMPLE 3**

| Poor | Some TV shows are boring. |
| Better | TV shows about hospitals are all alike. |

### Practice D

Write a topic sentence for each topic. Express your opinion. Include enough information to lead the reader into the paragraph. (Do not write the whole paragraph.)

1. going to the doctor
2. a special family dinner
3. taking tests
4. oatmeal
5. personal computers

### Practice E

Revise each topic sentence. Change the sentence to make it better. Replace vague words with more specific or interesting words. Write the new sentence on your paper.

1. We took a trip last year.
2. Let me tell you about my cousin.
3. Apples are good food.
4. History is an interesting subject.
5. The song I heard on the radio was pretty.

Students may list asking a question, giving an opinion, and putting in attention-grabbing words.

## Practice D

Explain that a point of view is expressed as an opinion. Briefly discuss various opinions people might have about each of the topics listed.

### *Practice D Answers*

Answers will vary. Possible sentences are given. **1.** A visit to an optometrist can be an eye-opening experience. **2.** The best holiday of the year is Thanksgiving. **3.** Try my three-step plan for getting ready for tests, and you will get high scores every time. **4.** If you think oatmeal is boring, you've never tasted my special oatmeal surprise. **5.** Personal computers have made our lives less personal.

## Practice E

Encourage students to use all the methods discussed in the lesson to improve the topic sentences.

### *Practice E Answers*

Answers will vary. Sample answers are given. **1.** Our trip to Italy last year was the best vacation we have ever taken. **2.** There was never a funnier comedian than my cousin Dickie. **3.** Do you know why "an apple a day keeps the doctor away"? **4.** No one makes history come to life like Doris Kearnes Goodwin. **5.** Have you ever been haunted for days by a song you happened to hear on the radio?

## COMMON ERROR

Beginning writers often reuse *and* and *but* monotonously, a practice which often fails to show the relationship of ideas. Help students practice choosing conjunctions to show contrast, cause and effect, chronological order, and other relationships.

## ELL/ESL STRATEGY

**Language Objective:**
*To write correct, interesting questions as topic sentences*

Students who are learning English as a second language may have difficulty with word order. They have learned that in English, the subject precedes the verb. However, in English questions, the subject often follows the verb or helping verb(s). All students will benefit by identifying the subject and verb in their sentences. Have students change the following sentences into questions:

*You have had chicken pox.*

*You can play a saxophone.*

Then encourage students to add details to their questions that add specific details and interest, for example: *Have you ever suffered through the agony of chicken pox?*

## WRITING PORTFOLIO

**Checkpoint** Have students reword the topic sentence of their Writing Portfolio paragraph draft to add interest.

---

Read each pair of topic sentences. Which one is better? Write *A* or *B* on your paper.

1. **A** This paragraph is going to be about our cat.
   **B** Our cat Harold rules our home with an iron paw.

2. **A** Did you know there was an Earl of Sandwich?
   **B** Sandwiches are a popular lunch choice.

3. **A** Have you ever read a book with 1,037 pages?
   **B** *Gone with the Wind* is a story about the Civil War.

4. **A** Derek runs track at Springfield High School.
   **B** Meet Derek Anderson, a shining star of Springfield's track team.

Revise each topic sentence to make it better. Include your opinion.

5. We saw a movie not long ago.

6. Let me tell you about a funny dream I had once.

7. Do you know what is really boring?

8. Science can be an interesting subject.

9. The book I read was about motorcycles.

10. Rock collecting is fun.

---

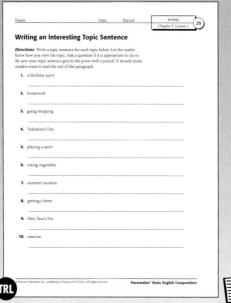

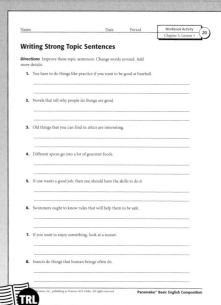

# LESSON 5-2

## Using Sentence Variety

### Objectives

- To use different lengths of sentences
- To start some sentences with adverbs and adverb phrases
- To start sentences in a paragraph with different words

**Variety**
A collection of things that are different or vary in some way

**Reading Strategy:** Visualizing

How does the bulleted list on this page help you understand sentence variety?

Spice up your paragraphs by giving your sentences **variety.** Variety is a collection of things that are different. Sentences with variety are more interesting to read. Here are some ways to add variety to a paragraph:

- Make sentences different lengths. Some can be short. Others can be long and include more details.
- Start some sentences with adverbs.
- Start some sentences with adverb phrases.

You can create a long sentence by combining two short sentences that are related. Use a comma followed by a conjunction such as *and, but,* or *so.*

### Practice A

Combine each pair of sentences into one longer sentence. Use a comma and a conjunction. Write the new sentence.
**Example:** Brandon was excited about the tennis match. Derek was worried.
**Answer:** Brandon was excited about the tennis match, but Derek was worried.

1. After the tennis match, Brandon was happy. Derek was tired.

2. Derek wanted to rest. Brandon wanted to celebrate.

3. Brandon wants to play in another tournament. Derek does not.

4. Derek and Brandon are good friends. Derek just does not love tennis.

5. Brandon had worked up an appetite. Derek was hungry.

---

## 2 Teaching the Lesson

Write the word *conjunction* on the board and have students name examples of conjunctions. (Refer students to pages 46 and 51 in Chapter 2 if they have difficulty recalling conjunctions.) Copy your paragraph onto the board and invite volunteers to use conjunctions listed on the board to combine ideas in the Warm-Up paragraph.

### Practice A

Remind students to refer to the list of conjunctions on the board as they combine sentences. If necessary, review the punctuation required for joining clauses.

### Practice A Answers

Answers will vary. Possible sentences are given. **1.** After the tennis match, Brandon was happy, but Derek was tired. **2.** While Derek wanted to rest, Brandon wanted to celebrate. **3.** Brandon wants to play in another tournament, but Derek does not. **4.** Although Derek and Brandon are good friends, Derek just does not love tennis. **5.** Brandon had worked up an appetite, and Derek was hungry, too.

## Lesson at a Glance

### Chapter 5 Lesson 2

**Overview** This lesson focuses on ways to vary sentences and make them more interesting.

### Objectives

- To use different lengths of sentences
- To start some sentences with adverbs and adverb phrases
- To start sentences in a paragraph with different words

**Student Pages** 123–126

**Teacher's Resource Library**

Activity 21
Modified Activity 21
Workbook Activity 21

### Vocabulary

**variety**

Have students read the meaning of *variety.* Then have them point out sets of objects in the room that illustrate variety.

### Background Information

Sentences may also be varied by using a mix of declarative, interrogative, imperative, and exclamatory sentences in writing. Using inventive language such as metaphors and similes also introduces variety.

### 1 Warm-Up Activity

Have students read the first few paragraphs and bulleted items. Ask students if they would like to wear the same clothes or eat the same foods every day. Make up and read aloud a paragraph using short, monotonous sentences. Have students comment on the paragraph's effect.

**Reading Strategy:** Visualizing

Students may point to the words *short, long, adverbs,* and *adverb phrases.*

## 3 Reinforce and Extend

## IN THE COMMUNITY

Have students obtain a local newspaper and examine the articles for sentence variety. Students may list different beginning words or phrases, note different sentence lengths, and point out ideas that have been combined. Discuss students' observations about whether the sentences begin in varied and pleasing ways.

## Practice B

Read the directions aloud and refer students to Example 1 for models. Remind them to think about the answers to the questions *why, how,* and *when* as they add variety using adverbs and adverb phrases.

### Practice B Answers

Answers will vary. Possible sentences are given. **1.** Fortunately, Brandon is a fast runner. **2.** With loud voices, their friends cheered when Brandon and Derek won. **3.** After the match, the tournament director gave them a trophy. **4.** Proudly, Brandon has been showing everyone the trophy. **5.** Surprisingly, Derek hopes that this tournament is his last.

## TEACHER ALERT

Point out to students that adverb phrases add variety to sentences as well as information.

**Brush Up on the Basics**

A compound subject that includes the word *and* is a plural subject. It calls for a plural form of the verb. This verb form does not end in -s. See Grammar 29 in Appendix A.

Here is another way to add variety. Begin a sentence with an adverb or an adverb phrase.

▶ **EXAMPLE 1**

Derek can run a mile in five minutes.

**Adverb** Surprisingly, Derek can run a mile in five minutes.

**Adverb Phrase** With great effort, Derek can run a mile in five minutes.

## Practice B

Begin each sentence with an adverb or an adverb phrase. Add new words or use words from the sentence. Write the new sentence on your paper.

1. Brandon is a fast runner.
2. Their friends cheered when Brandon and Derek won.
3. The tournament director gave them a trophy.
4. Brandon has been showing everyone the trophy.
5. Derek hopes that this tournament is his last.

## ELL/ESL STRATEGY

**Language Objective: To identify and use adverbs appropriately for sentence variety**

Students who are learning English may have trouble differentiating between adverbs and adjectives. Point out that many adjectives become adverbs when -ly is added: *happy/happily, angry/angrily, serious/seriously,* *regular/regularly.* Explain, however, that some adjectives end in -ly: *hourly* pay, *friendly* neighbors, *lively* music. Have students construct sentences using the adverbs above. They can write each word on a separate slip of paper, place the adverb next to the word it modifies, then rearrange the words to place the adverb first. Have students read the sentences aloud with both word order arrangements.

Start the sentences in a paragraph with different words. Do not start every sentence with *The* or *I*.

## Practice C

Revise Brandon's paragraph by following the steps below. Write the new paragraph on your paper.

### The Tennis Match
#### by Brandon Tucker

The story that I am about to tell is about an important tennis match. The match began at noon. The sun was very hot that day. The hopes were high that Derek and I would win. The opponents were weak and out of shape. The match ended differently from the others. The victory this time was ours!

1. Begin two sentences with an adverb or adverb phrase.

2. Combine two short sentences into one long sentence.

3. Remove words that are not necessary.

4. Add or change words to make the sentences livelier.

5. Improve the topic sentence.

## Practice D

*Reading Strategy:*
Visualizing

Make a list to help you visualize what this lesson is about. How does this list help you remember?

Here is a story about the same event from the local newspaper. Read the story. Then change the words around or combine sentences. Add sentence variety. Write the new story on your paper.

### Tucker and Anderson Win Tennis Tournament

The annual Springfield Tennis Tournament had a surprise ending. The Lopez twins were the defending champions. The guys looked tired and out of shape. The challengers were a new pair named Brandon Tucker and Derek Anderson. They took command immediately. The final scores were 6-0, 6-2.

## Practice C

Have a volunteer read Brandon's paragraph aloud. Invite students to give ideas about improvements they could make by following the five directions below it.

### Practice C Answers

Paragraphs will vary. A sample paragraph is given. Would you like to hear about a memorable tennis match? At noon, the match began. The sun blazed overhead. All our friends had high hopes that Derek and I would win. Because our opponents were weak and out of shape, this match ended differently from the others. This time, the victory was ours!

### COMMON ERROR

Caution students against joining unrelated sentences simply to create long sentences. Instead of adding variety, the long sentences become monotonous. Explain that they must consider how two sentences are related, then choose an appropriate conjunction to show the relationship.

## Practice D

Read the paragraph with students. Point out how its point of view differs from Brandon's. Discuss with students which sentences are related and could be combined with conjunctions.

### Practice D Answers

Paragraphs will vary. A possible paragraph is given.
It was a surprise ending for the annual Springfield Tennis Tournament. Although the Lopez twins were the defending champions, the guys looked tired and out of shape. The challengers were a new pair named Brandon Tucker and Derek Anderson. From the start, they took command. The final scores were 6-0 and 6-2.

### *Reading Strategy:* Visualizing

Student lists will vary but should address sentence variety and interest level.

---

## LESSON 5-2

# REVIEW

Begin each sentence with an adverb or an adverb phrase. Write the new sentence on your paper.

1. Sonia is a better singer than anyone.
2. Amber enjoys being in front of a crowd.
3. Sonia and Amber tried out for the school musical.
4. Sonia got the lead role.
5. Amber wasn't disappointed.

Follow the directions to write a paragraph with sentence variety.

6. Choose a prompt below, or choose your own topic. Write a paragraph about it. Begin some sentences with adverbs and adverb phrases. Combine short sentences by using a conjunction.
   - Tell about your favorite sport or hobby.
   - Explain why you prefer a particular kind of music.
   - Describe a movie that you have seen recently

### GRAMMAR BUILDER

**Using Appositives**

An appositive appears next to a noun to rename or explain it. An appositive may be a noun, a noun phrase, or a noun clause. Long appositives are set off by commas.

Mr. Poli, **our next-door neighbor,** is a teacher.

Some one-word appositives do not need commas.

Our neighbor **John** is a teacher.

Write each sentence. Underline the appositive. Add commas if needed.

1. Kelly trained her dog Ranger to fetch.
2. Ranger is a pug an Asian breed.

---

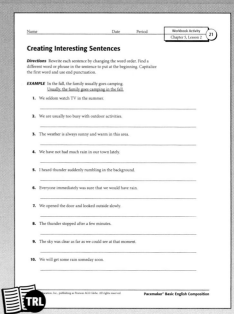

# Adding Transitions

### Objectives

- To use transitional words and phrases
- To use conjunctions as transitions

**Transition**

A change from one thing to another; often a change in time, place, situation, or thought

**NOTE**

When you tell a story, use transitions that show time.

**Reading Strategy:**
Visualizing

What could you draw to represent the idea of a transition? Think of what a transition does in a paragraph.

A **transition** is a change from one thing to another. When you read from one sentence to the next, transitional words and phrases help you follow along. A writer's goal is to make transitions as smooth as possible for the reader.

## Using Transitions That Show Time

Here are some transitional words and phrases that show a change in time.

### Time Transitions

| | | | |
|---|---|---|---|
| afterwards | at this time | in the meantime | now |
| at first | before | later | soon |
| at last | during | meanwhile | then |
| at the end | finally | next | while |

▶ **EXAMPLE 1**

No rain fell for three months. Storm clouds appeared.

No rain fell for three months. At last, storm clouds appeared.

### Practice A

Read the paragraph. Find four transitional words or phrases, and write them on your paper. (Not every sentence has a transition.)

A computer has many uses. Sonia got hers a year ago. At first, she used her computer to play computer games. Then, Sonia began to write letters on her computer. Recently, she used her computer to print photos. Now, Sonia's computer is part of her daily life.

## Chapter 5  Lesson 3

**Overview**  This lesson introduces transitions, expressions that connect related ideas within and between sentences.

### Objectives

- To use transitional words and phrases
- To use conjunctions as transitions

### Student Pages  127–130

### Teacher's Resource Library **TRL**

**Activity** 22
**Modified Activity** 22
**Workbook Activity** 22

## Vocabulary

**transition**

Ask students what it means to be "in transition." Then have a volunteer read the meaning of *transition* and predict what words of transition do in a paragraph.

## Background Information

Transitions can be sorted by type of relationship:

*Time:* after, first, before, meanwhile
*Place:* above, below, beside, here
*Importance:* first, second, mainly
*Cause and effect:* as a result, therefore
*Comparison/contrast:* although, similarly
*Example:* for instance, likewise

**1  Warm-Up Activity**

Write the following words and phrases on the board: *second, after that, finally, first.* Ask students to decide in what order they would use the words to teach someone how to do something.

**2  Teaching the Lesson**

Have students read the lesson text and explain why transitional words and phrases are called connectors. Ask volunteers to make up examples for transitions.

## Practice A

Point out that not all language that expresses time is a transition. *A year ago* functions as an adverb in the second sentence. However, it helps set up the time framework.

## Practice A Answers

At first, Then, Recently, Now

## Reading Strategy: Visualizing

Students might draw a bridge or a chain link to represent something used to connect two objects or places.

## 3  Reinforce and Extend

### TEACHER ALERT

The words in the list on page 128 are conjunctive adverbs. They clarify the relationship between clauses of equal weight. Unlike subordinating conjunctions, which always appear as the first word in a dependent clause, conjunctive adverbs may move to the middle or the end of the clause. Explain that conjunctive adverbs are stronger and more precise than coordinating conjunctions. They require a semicolon between joined clauses and are set off by a comma. The clauses may also stand as separate sentences.

## Practice B

Have a volunteer read the paragraph aloud. Have students match the transitions they find to the chart on page 128. Encourage students to tell what kind of relationship each transition shows.

### Practice B Answers

For example, In addition, Furthermore, As a result, however

### *Reading Strategy:* Visualizing

Students may picture symbols such as an addition sign for *in addition* or picture themselves writing a sentence using one of the transitions.

### AT HOME

Have students imagine they are going to have a party at home. Ask them to diagram the room where the party would be held and plan how the room would be changed for the party. Changes might include rearranging furniture; decorating; or setting up special stations for activities. Ask students to write a paragraph telling their plan for the party and use at least three linking transitions from the list on page 128.

---

*Reading Strategy:*
Visualizing

Study this list of transitional words and phrases. How do they help you remember what to do to make paragraphs smoother?

---

**Brush Up on the Basics**

A transitional word is usually placed at the beginning of a sentence. Set the transitional word off with a comma. See Punctuation 10 in Appendix A.

---

## Using Transitions That Link Ideas

Transitional words and phrases can also show how two ideas are related. These transitions are conjunctions. For example, transitions such as *also* and *however* point out how two things are alike or different. Transitions such as *therefore* link a cause and its effect.

### Transitions That Link Ideas

| also | for that reason | in conclusion |
|------|------|------|
| as well as | furthermore | nevertheless |
| as a result | however | such as |
| for example | in addition | therefore |

▶ **EXAMPLE 2**

The Internet has many uses. Students use it to do research.

The Internet has many uses. For example, students use it to do research.

### Practice B

Read the paragraph. Find five transitional words or phrases that link related ideas. Write them on your paper.

**Planning a Party**
by Amber Choy

Planning a party for my friends was a big job. For example, my first task was making a guest list. In addition, I had to create a menu as well as a plan for activities. Furthermore, I had to decide how to pay for the expenses. As a result of good planning, however, I expect my party to be a big success.

**128**  *Chapter 5   Writing Better Paragraphs*

---

### CAREER CONNECTION

List on the board a variety of careers suggested by students. Ask them to choose one career and write a paragraph in which they tell about its advantages and disadvantages. They should use transition words and phrases such as *for example, on the other hand, however,* and *in conclusion.*

## Spelling Practice

Write the word *information* on the board and have students pronounce it. Have a volunteer circle the letters that spell the /shən/ sound *(tion)*. Have students scan pages 127 and 128 for words that have this sound, spelled *tion.* Brainstorm other words with a /shən/ ending.

Point out how the suffix with the /shən/ sound may be spelled *-sion*. Also explain that some words add *-ation* as the ending. Have students find the base word to which the endings have been added. Explore ways the base word may change spelling before the suffix is added.

## Practice C

Rewrite the paragraph. Add some of the transitional words or phrases that show a change in time (see page 127).

### The History of Sacramento
by Sonia Moreno

Sacramento, California, has a colorful history. John Augustus Sutter founded the first permanent settlement in this state in 1839. James Marshall discovered gold nearby in 1848. The Pony Express and the Central Pacific Railroad were both part of Sacramento's early history.

## Practice D

Rewrite the paragraph. Add some transitional words or phrases that link ideas.

### A Good Night's Sleep
by Derek Anderson

Would you like to improve the quality of your sleep? Give yourself a bedtime routine. Do something relaxing. Read a book. Listen to soothing music. Take a bath. Go to bed at the same time each night. Wake up at the same time each morning. You will feel more rested.

*Reading a few pages from a good novel is relaxing.*

## Practice C

Have a volunteer read the paragraph aloud. After students have revised it, ask other volunteers to read their revisions aloud and compare them to the original.

### Practice C Answers

Paragraphs will vary. A sample paragraph is given. Sacramento, California, has a colorful history. First, John Augustus Sutter founded the first permanent settlement in this state in 1839. Then, James Marshall discovered gold nearby in 1848. In addition, the Pony Express and the Central Pacific Railroad were both part of Sacramento's early history.

## Practice D

Have a volunteer read the paragraph aloud. Help students understand that the short, choppy sentences do not clearly show connections among ideas. Invite students to give their ideas about transitions and sentence combinations that might be helpful.

### Practice D Answers

Answers will vary. A sample paragraph is given. Would you like to improve the quality of your sleep? Then give yourself a bedtime routine. Read a book, for example, or listen to soothing music. You may also take a bath. In addition, go to bed at the same time every night, and wake up at the same time every morning. As a result, you will feel more rested.

### LEARNING STYLES

**Auditory/Verbal**
Have students listen to an explanation, directions, or a description that has been recorded on audiotape or videotape. Ask them to write down the transitional words and phrases they hear. Then provide students with a paragraph of story text from which the transitional words and phrases have been removed. Ask a volunteer to read it aloud. Discuss problems listeners have following the text. Finally have students practice reading the same text aloud with the transition words and phrases restored. Encourage them to use expression with transitions to add meaning.

## Lesson 5-3 Review Answers

**1.** Students should provide four of the six transitional words or phrases. Sample answers: First, At least once a day, Next, Then, At last, Tomorrow **2.** Answers will vary. Paragraphs should deal with a recent local event and include at least three transition words or phrases.

### WRITE ABOUT IT

Model describing how you met a friend. As you talk, capture key words and phrases on a graphic organizer. Then have students brainstorm details using their own graphic organizers.

Student paragraphs should follow an organizational plan, include some vivid details, and suggest feelings. Have students revisit this work when they learn to revise and edit in the coming lessons.

### Six Traits of Writing Focus

| | Ideas | | Word Choice |
|---|---|---|---|
| ✔ | Organization | ✔ | Sentence Fluency |
| | Voice | | Conventions |

### Sentence Fluency

Remind students to use transitions to connect their sentences. Suggest that they read their paragraph to a partner. Partners should listen for smooth rhythm and flow. If they do not hear it, have them recommend more fluid transitions.

Partners should also pay attention to the organization. Lack of organization can also make an essay sound choppy or disjointed.

Refer students to page WPH1 for further instruction on the Six Traits of Writing.

### ELL/ESL STRATEGY

**Language Objective:**
*To identify transitions*

Students who are learning English may have difficulty identifying transitions, let alone using them. Provide practice in identifying transitions in use by reading aloud passages that contain transitions. Point out the relationship each transition establishes and have students draw a graphic to help them visualize the relationship each shows.

---

# REVIEW

**1.** Read the paragraph. Find four transitional words or phrases that show changes in time. Write them on your paper.

### Sarah
#### by Derek Anderson

Everyone I know wants to meet Sarah. First, there is my mom. At least once a day, she asks me when she will meet Sarah. Next, there are my friends Sonia and Amber. All they talk about is Sarah. Then, there is my best friend Brandon, who keeps asking, "When, Derek, when?" At last, their lucky day is almost here! Tomorrow, at the last track meet of the year, they will all meet Sarah.

**2.** Practice using transitional words and phrases. Write a paragraph about a recent event in your town or city. Include at least three transitional words or phrases. Remember to use sentence variety, too.

### WRITE ABOUT IT

**A Friend**
Having a friend is important. You meet new people nearly every day. Only some of them become good friends. Think about one of your best friends. Write a paragraph about how you met. Include these details:
- when and where you met
- why the meeting was special
- why you continued to stay in touch with this person
- what about this person made you develop a friendship
When you are finished, revise and edit your paragraph. Then read it to another student.

**Six Traits of Writing:**
*Sentence Fluency*
smooth rhythm and flow

---

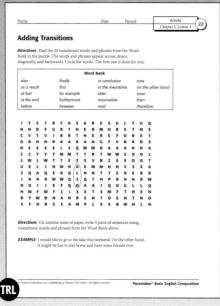

Activity 22

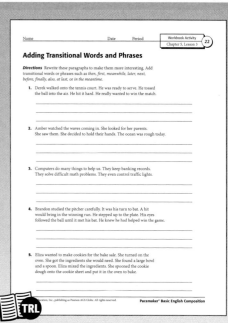

Workbook Activity 22

# Revising a Paragraph

## Objectives

- To read a writing prompt carefully
- To add missing words and take out extra words
- To revise a topic sentence
- To check for transitions

**Reading Strategy:** Visualizing

Make a diagram or list that will help you remember what to do when you revise.

**NOTE**

Always revise what you write. Your first draft is not your best work.

After you have written a paragraph, look for ways to improve it. Making changes in your paragraph is called revising. Follow the steps in this lesson to revise a paragraph.

**Step 1** First, consider the content of the paragraph. The content is the information in the paragraph. Does the content match the writing prompt?

Read the prompt in Example 1. Then read the paragraph. Does the content match the prompt?

▶ **EXAMPLE 1**

Prompt    Write about how you got your first job.

Paragraph    My first job was mowing lawns. I used my father's lawn mower. It was hard work. I enjoyed earning money.

The paragraph does not give the right kind of information. It tells *about someone's first job*. It does not tell *how the person got the job*. When you revise a paragraph, make sure the content fits the prompt.

### Practice A

Read the prompt. Then write a paragraph that matches the prompt.

**Prompt:**    Write about how you got your first job. It can be a volunteer job or a paid job.

## Chapter 5  Lesson 4

**Overview** This lesson explains revising a paragraph for focus, completeness, relevance, order, and smoothness.

### Objectives

- To read a writing prompt carefully
- To add missing words and take out extra words
- To revise a topic sentence
- To check for transitions

**Student Pages** 131–134

**Teacher's Resource Library**

Activity 23

Modified Activity 23

Workbook Activity 23

## Background Information

During the revision process, writers consider the content, organization, tone, language, and style of what they have written. Most writers can look at their work more objectively if they have set it aside for a time before reviewing it. Do not have students write and revise a paragraph on the same day, if possible.

### 1  Warm-Up Activity

Ask students what they think an artist does after making a rough sketch for a painting. Explain that, for a writer, a first written version is like a rough sketch. By revising, a writer improves the text. Have students read the objectives on page 131, then predict ways a writer might improve a paragraph.

### 2  Teaching the Lesson

Remind students that in reading a prompt, they should highlight and think about all the key words.

### 3  Reinforce and Extend

#### WRITING PORTFOLIO

**Checkpoint** Have students check their Writing Portfolio paragraphs to see whether transitions will make their writing smoother.

#### Grammar Practice

Have students reread the paragraph in item 1 of the Review on page 130. Ask them to find the subject of the second sentence. Guide students to understand that in sentences beginning *There is . . .,* the subject follows the verb.

### Practice A

Discuss with students some volunteer jobs. Point out the value of such jobs in building skills and responsibility and learning how to deal with people.

#### Practice A Answers

Paragraphs will vary but should list a series of steps in chronological order.

#### Reading Strategy: Visualizing

Answers will vary. A sample diagram is given.

| Main Idea | ✔ |
|---|---|
| Detail 1 | ✔ |
| Detail 2 | ✔ |
| Detail 3 | ✔ |

## Practice B

Discuss the topic sentence. Have volunteers suggest more details that could be added to the paragraph.

### Practice B Answers

Answers will vary. Sample additions to the paragraph are given. It is also important to eat nutritious food, especially fresh fruits and vegetables. In addition, you should limit your intake of foods high in fat and sugar.

## Practice C

Have a volunteer read the paragraph aloud. Discuss why the topic sentence is true but not suitable for the details. Have students point out what all the details have in common.

### Practice C Answers

Sentences will vary. A possible sentence is given. The vast Grand Canyon is a breathtaking sight.

**NOTE**

Remember to indent the first sentence in a paragraph.

**Step 2** Look at the entire paragraph. Have you written enough, or do you need to write more?

### Practice B

Read the paragraph. Add two more examples or details to the body. Write the new paragraph on your paper.

Healthy eating is a good habit to develop. You can begin by eating breakfast. This way of eating should continue all your life.

**Step 3** Read your paragraph out loud. If possible, read it to another person. Ask these questions:

- Does the topic sentence express the main idea?
- Does it show your opinion?
- Will it get someone's attention?
- Do the sentences in your paragraph have variety?

### Practice C

Read the paragraph. Look at the topic sentence. Write a better topic sentence on your paper.

The Grand Canyon is a national park in Arizona. The Colorado River formed this canyon. The canyon is 277 miles long. It is 10 to 18 miles wide at the rim. It is the most spectacular canyon in the United States.

**Step 4** Look for transitional words and phrases in your paragraph. Be sure your paragraph has at least one or two.

### Practice D

Read the paragraph. Add transitional words or phrases. Write the new paragraph. Underline the words you added.

Every great book begins with a single sentence. The writer has an idea. The writer puts down the first word. More words follow. A great book has begun!

## Practice D

Students may refer to the list of transitions on page 127 if necessary.

### Practice D Answers

Paragraphs will vary. A sample paragraph is given. Every great book begins with a single sentence. First, the writer has an idea. Next, the writer puts down the first word. Then, more words follow. A great book has begun!

## LEARNING STYLES

### Visual/Spatial

Read the paragraph in Practice C aloud. Have students close their eyes and visualize the details they hear. Then have them explain what all the details have in common. Display a picture of the Grand Canyon and ask students to add two more details that could be added to the paragraph. Then have students write an improved topic sentence.

**Reading Strategy:**
Visualizing

What image might help you remember that revising includes adding and cutting content?

**Step 5** Get rid of words that clutter up your paragraph. Take out words that do not support your main idea. Take out vague words and replace them with more specific ones.

▶ **EXAMPLE 2**

| Wordy | I think that watching football on Sunday with my family is my favorite thing to do. |
| Clear | Watching football on Sunday with my family is my favorite activity. |

### Practice E

Rewrite each sentence on your paper. Take out the unnecessary words.

1. The storm last night you know was just really bad.

2. Wow, the lightning was like so amazing.

3. Our dog well he hates loud noises.

4. I know he gets frightened in a storm.

5. I was thinking that I find storms exciting myself.

## VOCABULARY BUILDER

### Using Root Words

A root word is a word from which other words are made. Word parts may be added to the beginning or ending of a root word. Add *mis-* to the root word *place*. This makes *misplace*. Add *-ment* to *place* to make *placement*. Look at each pair of words. Write the root word used to make them.

1. opening, reopen
2. mistake, taken
3. trusted, distrust
4. remove, mover

**Reading Strategy:** Visualizing

Answers will vary. Students might suggest images such as a plus and a minus sign or a needle and thread and a scissors.

## Practice E

Review the wordy sentence in Example 2. Point out that the phrase *I think that* adds no meaning to the sentence. It is simply deleted. The general phrase *thing to do* is replaced by the more specific *activity*.

### Practice E Answers

Sentences may vary. Sample answers are given. **1.** The storm last night was really bad. **2.** The lightning was amazing. **3.** Our dog hates loud noises. **4.** He becomes frightened in a storm. **5.** On the other hand, I find storms exciting.

## VOCABULARY BUILDER

After students complete the activity, ask them to identify the prefixes and suffixes that have been added to each root word. Then provide examples with both a prefix and suffix, such as: *unhelpful, disappeared, prehistoric.* Ask students to identify the root word in each.

### Vocabulary Builder Answers

**1.** open **2.** take **3.** trust **4.** move

## ELL/ESL STRATEGY

**Language Objective:**
*To increase vocabulary by learning roots and building word families*

Students who are learning English may share some native vocabulary based on Latin and Greek roots. For example, *viv* means "life" and can be used to build the words *vivid, revive,* and *vivacious.* The French word *vive* ("long live") and the Spanish word *vivido* ("vivid") are derived from *viv* as well.

Encourage students to build word families for *sci* ("know") and *man* ("hand") and to write meanings and example sentences for each word they collect. As they share their word families, ask students to teach classmates about words in their native language that are derived from these same roots.

## Lesson 5-4 Review Answers

Paragraphs will vary but should explain how the pet was acquired and introduced to the home and family. Events should be presented in order using time transition words. The paragraph should include an interesting topic sentence and at least three detail sentences with no irrelevant details. A sample paragraph is given.

The day our dog Sir Nibbs came to live with us is unforgettable. We picked him from all the others at the animal shelter because he sat quietly in his cage and wagged his tail whenever we looked at him. On the way home, he pressed so close to me he was sitting on my toes. When we opened the door, he leaped out and raced away. My heart raced as I chased after him. That was when we found out we had adopted a hunting dog.

## WRITING PORTFOLIO

**Checkpoint** Have students revise their Writing Portfolio paragraphs using the checklist on page 134.

---

## LESSON 5-4 REVIEW

1. Read the prompt. Then write a paragraph on your paper.

   **Prompt:** Write about your first pet. Tell how you got it and what happened next. If you have not had a pet, write about someone else's pet.

2. Use the checklist below to revise the paragraph you just wrote. Write the new paragraph on your paper.

### Checklist for Revising a Paragraph

1. Check your assignment. Does your paragraph match the prompt?

2. Does your topic sentence express the main idea? Will it get someone's attention?

3. Have you given enough details, facts, reasons, or examples to support the main idea?

4. Does every sentence in the body support the main idea?

5. Does your paragraph contain transitions to help the reader?

6. Do your sentences contain unnecessary or vague words? Cut any extra words.

7. Can you add specific adjectives, adverbs, or prepositional phrases?

8. Does every sentence begin with the same word? Change some words to add variety.

9. Are all of your sentences about the same length? Can you combine any short, related sentences?

10. Did you end with a good conclusion or summary?

---

Name _____ Date _____ Period _____

Activity
Chapter 5, Lesson 4 **23**
*Page 1*

### Revising a Paragraph

**Directions** Read the paragraph. First, write a better topic sentence on the line provided. Then cross out any sentence that does not support the main idea. Think of ways to combine short, choppy sentences using transitions. Then rewrite sentences on the lines that match the sentence numbers.

**1.** This is about the difference between a moth and a butterfly. **2.** Moths have fat bodies. **3.** They are not colorful. **4.** Butterflies have thinner bodies and are colorful. **5.** Butterflies have round things on the ends of their antennae. **6.** Moths do not. **7.** Butterflies fly in the day. **8.** Moths fly after sundown. **9.** Moths will fly into a flame or a light bulb. **10.** Moths rest with wings spread out flat. **11.** Butterflies rest with them pressed together overhead.

Improved topic sentence:

1. _____

Combined sentences and transitions:

2–4. _____

5–6. _____

7–8. _____

9–11. _____

© Pearson Education, Inc., publishing as Pearson AGS Globe. All rights reserved.

**Pacemaker® Basic English Composition**

**Activity 23, pages 1–2**

---

Name _____ Date _____ Period _____

Workbook Activity
Chapter 5, Lesson 4 **23**

### Improving Paragraph Drafts

**Directions** Read each paragraph. Cross out a sentence that does not belong. Add two new sentences to give each paragraph enough support. Write the new sentences on the lines.

**1.** I try hard to keep my room organized. All my clothes are neatly folded and put away. My little brother, on the other hand, is a slob.

2. _____

3. _____

**4.** My friend Carrie really cares about others. She enjoys singing. Carrie works every Saturday at a homeless shelter.

5. _____

6. _____

**7.** With just a little effort, you can make friends. It is not pleasant to have enemies. When you meet someone, smile and give the person a compliment.

8. _____

9. _____

**10.** There is much to see in the night sky. The moon changes through the month, growing full and then narrow. You should not look at the sun directly.

11. _____

12. _____

**13.** A dictionary is loaded with all sorts of useful information. It gives the meanings of words as well as their spellings and pronunciations. A thesaurus lists synonyms and antonyms for many words.

14. _____

15. _____

© Pearson Education, Inc., publishing as Pearson AGS Globe. All rights reserved.

**Pacemaker® Basic English Composition**

**Workbook Activity 23**

## LESSON 5-5 — Editing Your Paragraph

### Objectives
■ To catch mistakes in your writing
■ To edit a paragraph

**Edit**
To correct mistakes in a piece of writing; to check spelling, punctuation, capitalization, grammar, and word choice

After you have revised a paragraph, you are ready to **edit** it. When you edit, you correct mistakes in spelling, punctuation, capitalization, and grammar. You also make any final changes in your choice of words.

#### Mistakes to Fix When You Edit
misspelled words
missing punctuation or wrong punctuation
sentences that do not start with a capital letter
proper nouns that are not capitalized
pronouns with no clear antecedents
subjects and verbs that do not agree
wrong verb tenses or the incorrect use of irregular verbs
poor word choices
paragraphs that are not indented

Spelling mistakes will make a bad impression on your reader.

### Practice A

Find five spelling mistakes in the paragraph. Write each word correctly on your paper.

**The Tennis Match**
by Brandon Tucker

My friend, Derek Anderson, and I had been practiceing tennis for several weeks. At first, we were mostly chaseing the ball around. Finally, we decided that we were good enough to make a challenge. There was a lot of excitement in Springfield as the news got around. That day we saw several of our friends arriveing to watch us play. To make a long story short, we were not exactly blazeing the ball. No one confusd us with Pete Sampras and Andre Agassi.

**Brush Up on the Basics**
For verbs that end in -e, remove the e before adding -ing or -ed. Race becomes racing or raced. See Spelling 37 in Appendix A.

*Writing Better Paragraphs* Chapter 5 **135**

---

### 1 Warm-Up Activity

Ask students how they would go about finding and fixing mistakes in a paragraph they had written. Help students realize that a set of questions or checklist is helpful to be sure that every error is addressed.

### 2 Teaching the Lesson

Ask students to provide an example of each of the categories of mistakes in the list on page 135. Review any categories that students do not recall.

### Practice A

Have students read the Brushing Up on the Basics note in the margin before they begin the practice.

### Practice A Answers

practicing, chasing, arriving, blazing, confused

---

## Lesson at a Glance

### Chapter 5 Lesson 5

**Overview** This lesson gives students practice in fixing spelling, punctuation, capitalization, grammar, and word choice errors.

### Objectives
■ To catch mistakes in your writing
■ To edit a paragraph

### Student Pages 135–141

### Teacher's Resource Library
Activity 24
Modified Activity 24
Workbook Activity 24
Life Skills Connection 5
English in Your Life 3
Building Research Skills 5

### Vocabulary
**edit**

Write the following sentence on the board: *phil and me cherred for them until we was horse.* Ask volunteers to correct one mistake at a time. For each mistake they correct, write *spelling, punctuation, capitalization,* or *grammar* on the board and put a check mark for the kind of mistake corrected. When the sentence is correct, tell students they have just edited a piece of writing.

### Background Information

For the final version of a paper, students should follow acceptable manuscript form. If they will handwrite paragraphs and essays, the following list will be helpful:

1. Write only on lined, 8½ × 11 paper.
2. Write only on one side of the paper.
3. Use blue or black ink.
4. Leave margins of about an inch at the top, sides, and bottom of the page.
5. Write legibly and neatly.
6. Be sure the left margin is straight.

*Writing Better Paragraphs* **135**

## LIFE SKILLS CONNECTION

Point out to students that the writing they do as adults, such as letters, notes, and memos, should use correct capitalization and punctuation in order to communicate ideas clearly. Distribute Life Skills Connection 5 and have students work in pairs to complete it.

## Practice B

Write the following punctuation marks on the board and review with students their uses: period, question mark, exclamation mark, comma. Have students explain why they added each mark in the paragraph.

### Practice B Answers

An almanac is a book that contains facts, statistics, and general information. Some almanacs have information about baseball, and others have facts about the weather. When you use an almanac, check its date.

## Practice C

Invite volunteers to list as many rules for capitalizing as they can. List them on the board. After students complete the practice, refer to the list to find the rule for each correction students have made (or add the rule to the list).

### Practice C Answers

The problem with lunch at Springfield High School is time. We just do not have enough of it. So we have to eat in a big hurry. Brandon's big complaint is portion size. He says that he could eat three times as much. I say Brandon and I are both right.

### Reading Strategy: Visualizing

They give you experiences in which you see corrections made. You can remember these images as you edit other paragraphs.

**NOTE**

Proofreading is part of the editing process. To proofread means to mark mistakes while you read something. See page WPH24 near the front of this book.

### Reading Strategy:
Visualizing

Complete the Practices in this lesson. How do they help you picture what it means to edit your writing?

Punctuation is important. Always end a sentence with an end punctuation mark. Use commas where you need them.

### Practice B

Copy the paragraph on your paper. Find the punctuation mistakes. Add seven missing punctuation marks to the paragraph.

An almanac is a book that contains facts statistics and general information Some almanacs have information about baseball and others have facts about the weather When you use an almanac check its date

Capitalization is also important. Capitalize the first word in every sentence. Capitalize proper nouns and the pronoun *I*.

### Practice C

Copy the paragraph on your paper. Find the ten capitalization mistakes and fix them.

*The students wish they had an hour to eat lunch with their friends.*

the problem with lunch at springfield high school is time. we just do not have enough of it. so we have to eat in a big hurry. brandon's big complaint is portion size. He says that he could eat three times as much. i say brandon and i are both right.

Remember these rules about pronouns:

- A pronoun must have a clear antecedent.
- A pronoun must agree with its antecedent in gender and number.
- Personal pronouns that act as subjects are different from pronouns that act as objects.

### Practice D

**Reading Strategy:**
Visualizing

Think about what you do to fix mistakes in your writing. How does this help you understand the editing checklist on page 138?

Copy the paragraph on your paper. Find three pronoun mistakes and fix them.

Derek and him friend Brandon are on a soccer team. Derek enjoys this activity very much. He likes to play goalie. She also plays forward. Brandon likes playing any position. "It is all fun for I," he said.

Good writers check that their subjects and verbs agree. When a singular subject has a present-tense verb, it usually ends in -s. The verb *be* is very irregular and has several different forms. The personal pronoun chart on page 66 can help you with the next practice.

### Practice E

Copy the paragraph on your paper. Underline the five mistakes in subject-verb agreement. Then fix them in the paragraph.

Amber's dog Rex always run away. He are not a bad dog. Rex are just adventurous. Amber call him every night. The neighbors chase him. So far, he always come home.

Editing involves fixing many kinds of mistakes. It is also the final opportunity to choose better words.

Look through Appendix A, which begins on page 376. It is a helpful editing handbook. It lists tips on grammar, capitalization, punctuation, and spelling. Refer to this handbook as you write.

## Practice D

Have students brainstorm with you to list personal and possessive pronouns on the board, or have them refer to pages 63–66 to review.

### *Practice D Answers*

Derek and his friend Brandon are on a soccer team. Derek enjoys this activity very much. He likes to play goalie. He also plays forward. Brandon likes playing any position. "It is all fun for me," he said.

## Practice E

Refer students to Lesson 1 of Chapter 2 if they need review of subject-verb agreement, especially of *be* verbs, before completing the practice.

### *Practice E Answer*

Amber's dog Rex always runs away. He is not a bad dog. Rex is just adventurous. Amber calls him every night. The neighbors chase him. So far, he always comes home.

### *Reading Strategy:* Visualizing

As you read the list, you can picture each kind of correction and see yourself making each kind.

## Writing Practice

Have students choose a piece of writing from their portfolio and review the sentences for subject-verb agreement and correct pronoun usage. Students may refer to pages 31–34 and 63–66 to review subject-verb agreement and pronoun usage. Have students correct any errors they find and rewrite the paragraph.

## LESSON 5-5

# REVIEW

1. Choose a topic listed below, or choose your own topic. Write a paragraph about it. Your paragraph should have a topic sentence, a body, and a conclusion or summary. Possible topics:

   • things to do at a water park
   • a person you admire
   • how you like to celebrate your birthday

2. Use the checklist below to edit your paragraph. Make corrections and rewrite the paragraph.

---

### Checklist for Editing a Paragraph

**1.** Did you indent the first sentence in the paragraph?

**2.** Are any words spelled wrong? Use a dictionary or the spelling checker on a computer.

**3.** Is there a punctuation mark at the end of each sentence? Do questions end with question marks? Did you use commas to separate words in a series?

**4.** Did you capitalize the first word in each sentence? Did you capitalize proper nouns?

**5.** Does each pronoun have a clear antecedent? Does each pronoun agree with its antecedent in gender and number? If a pronoun is a subject, use the subject form. If it is an object, use the object form.

**6.** Does each possessive noun have an apostrophe?

**7.** Does each verb agree with the subject?

**8.** Is the tense of each verb correct? Did you use the correct form of irregular verbs?

**9.** Are there any vague words? Choose more specific ones.

---

## Writing to Solve a Problem

Ben Varberg takes care of his neighbor's dog. After school, he walks Oso and then feeds her. Today Ben hurt his ankle and should stay off it. How can he care for Oso? He wrote Ms. Mendoza a note to explain the problem and how it could be fixed. Read his note. Then answer the questions below.

Dear Ms. Mendoza,

For the next week, I will not be able to walk Oso. Today I hurt my ankle. The doctor says I should rest it. It will be easy for me to feed Oso, but I know she needs to get out. Because she loves to run and play, I cannot keep up with her. Is it okay if my sister Sue helps me out? She is 13 and loves dogs. Oso likes her, too. I think Sue would do a good job.

Ben

1. How many sentences begin with an adverb or prepositional phrase?

2. How many long sentences (more than 10 words) does Ben use? How many short sentences (5 to 10 words)?

3. **CRITICAL THINKING** Why does using a variety of sentences make Ben's note better?

### SPEAKING AND LISTENING

In a small group, choose a problem or issue in your school or community. How do you think it should be fixed? Discuss the problem and ways to solve it. Then take turns explaining one possible solution. Clearly state your solution. Give details to support how and why it will work. Answer any questions your listeners ask.

---

**ENGLISH IN YOUR LIFE**

Ask students to think about a time when they had to solve a problem or resolve a conflict. Have them imagine that they needed to write to someone with whom they must resolve an issue. Discuss why it would be important to write clearly and correctly. Have a volunteer read the introductory paragraph of English in Your Life. Invite students to predict how Ben will solve his problem. Then have them read Ben's note and answer the questions.

### English in Your Life Answers

**1.** 2 **2.** 3 long; 6 short **3.** Answers will vary. A possible answer is given. The longer sentences combine ideas that are related so they make more sense. The shorter sentences contrast and communicate simple statements and questions directly.

## Speaking and Presenting Practice

Ask students to think about a time when they solved a problem in a humorous or dramatic way. Give students time to make notes about the incident, including the problem, the cause, and descriptive details that capture the feelings and incidents involved in solving the problem. Suggest that students create note cards or an outline as a guide and practice delivering their talks. They may practice before a friend or family member or record their practice. Then have students share their solutions in a humorous or dramatic style.

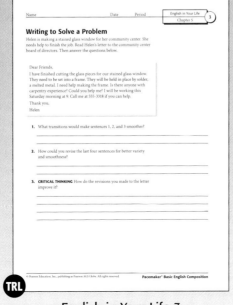

English in Your Life 3

Have students practice finding information online. Ask them to think of the title and author of a publication that they are familiar with. Then have students look for the same work online using title, author, and subject searches. Point out that many systems have keyword searches, which are useful when they are unsure of an exact subject or title.

### Building Research Skills Answers

1. author  2. subject; stock car racing, history  3. It can point out specific books that are suitable for your topic. It saves you the time of wandering the stacks looking for books on the right topic.

## Using a Library's Online Catalog

How do you find what you need in a library? One way is to use the online catalog. A library's online catalog can help you find books, magazines, and other materials about a topic.

With most online catalogs, you can search by author, title, or subject. For example, you may click on *Search by Author*. If you enter Charles Dickens, the system will list all the books by Charles Dickens that are in the library. If you click on *Search by Subject*, you can enter a subject. Then the system will list books on that subject.

Some libraries loan books to other libraries. If your library has a loan program, then the catalog results may list books in other libraries. These books can be ordered, but they may take a week or more to arrive.

1. You want to find books by Maya Angelou. Should you search by author, title, or subject?

2. You want to read about the history of stock car racing. Should you search by author, title, or subject? What should you enter in the search box?

3. CRITICAL THINKING How does an online catalog search save you research time?

### TECHNOLOGY

Choose an author, book title, or subject. Use an online catalog to run a search on it. When the screen shows a list of books, click on one that looks helpful. Then the computer will show you more facts about this book, including a description of its contents. The sample screen below shows facts about the book *Oliver Twist.* The information on this screen helps you see if the book is what you want. To return to the list of books, click the *Back* arrow.

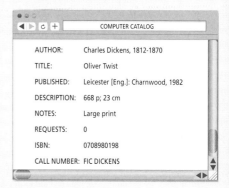

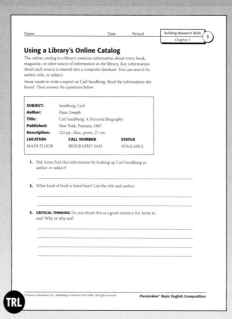

# SUMMARY

- Use the topic sentence to get your reader's attention. Asking a question is one way to get the reader's attention.

- Express your opinion in your topic sentence.

- Give your sentences variety by beginning some of them with adverbs and adverb phrases.

- Use a variety of sentence lengths.

- Add transitional words and phrases to help your reader. Transitions can show a change in time. They can connect one idea to another.

- Always revise your work. The first draft is not your best work.

- Make sure your content matches the assignment or prompt.

- Check that you have enough supporting details in the body. End your paragraph with a good conclusion or summary.

- Cross out words you do not need. Cross out sentences that do not support the main idea.

- Edit your work. Fix spelling, punctuation, capitalization, and grammar mistakes. Improve poor word choices. Replace vague words.

- Writing that is revised and edited will make a good impression on your reader.

## GROUP ACTIVITY

In a group, write a paragraph about the plot of a movie or TV show you have seen. Begin with an interesting topic sentence. Tell what happened in the story, in order. Include transitions. Work together to revise your paragraph.

Leave out details that repeat or are not important to the action. Trade paragraphs with another group. Find mistakes in spelling and grammar. Suggest changes you think would improve the paragraph.

## Chapter 5 Summary

Have volunteers read aloud each Summary item on page 141. Ask volunteers to explain the meaning of each item.

### ONLINE CONNECTION

Explain that editors and professional writers are familiar with a standard set of marks for marking errors in writing. Students may find the lists of proofreading marks at the sites listed below to be helpful. Also remind students of the proofreading marks on page WPH24.

www.agsglobepmbec.com/141a
www.agsglobepmbec.com/141b

### GROUP ACTIVITY

Remind groups to begin by prewriting. They might list important plot events and then number events in order. Next, they could use a word web to collect strong descriptive words and phrases about events and characters. Remind groups that they should revise their rough drafts, using the checklist on page 134. When students edit another group's paragraph, have them refer to the checklist on page 138.

# Chapter 5 Review

Use the Chapter Review to prepare students for tests and to reteach content from the chapter.

## Chapter 5 Mastery Test  (TRL)

The Teacher's Resource Library includes two forms of the Chapter 5 Mastery Test. Each test addresses the chapter Goals for Learning. An optional third page of additional critical-thinking items is included for each test. The difficulty level of the two forms is equivalent.

## *Review Answers*

### Part A

1. transition  2. opinion  3. variety  4. edit
5. revise  6. rewrite

### Part B

Answers will vary. Sample answers are given. 7. Usually, Brandon can run faster than the other players. 8. Amazingly, the soccer team won every game this season. 9. To our surprise, Brandon scored three goals yesterday. 10. Proudly, the soccer coach gave a speech after the victory.

### Part C

Sentences will vary. Sample sentences are given. 11. With a few changes to your diet, you can eat healthful foods that will boost your energy. 12. *I find country music relaxing. 13. As our population ages, it will demand even more workers in the medical field. 14. *Our lazy boat ride down the river was the perfect way to de-stress. 15. How would you like to spend a day with baboons, koalas, and manta rays? 16. A successful camping trip begins with careful packing.

### Word Bank

edit
opinion
revise
rewrite
transition
variety

**Part A** Find the word or words in the Word Bank that complete each sentence. Write your answer on your paper.

1. A _____ is a change from one thing to another.
2. The way you think about something is your _____.
3. Things that are different in some way show _____.
4. To _____ means to fix mistakes in spelling, punctuation, capitalization, and grammar.
5. To _____ means to make your writing better by changing it.
6. To _____ means to write something again.

**Part B** Begin each sentence with an adverb or an adverb phrase. Write the new sentence on your paper.

7. Brandon can run faster than the other players.
8. The soccer team won every game this season.
9. Brandon scored three goals yesterday.
10. The soccer coach gave a speech after the victory.

**Part C** Rewrite each topic sentence so that it grabs a reader's attention. Then place a star in front of each sentence that expresses an opinion.

11. This paragraph will be about eating healthful foods.
12. Some kinds of music are great.
13. I think it would be good to have a job in the medical field.
14. The boat ride down the river was fun.
15. We spent the whole day at the zoo.
16. I want to tell you what to pack when you go camping.

---

**Part D** Read each pair of topic sentences. Which one is better? Write *A* or *B* on your paper.

**17.** **A** This paragraph is going to be about my funny dog.
   **B** Our dog Rex rules the house like a king.

**18.** **A** I am going to write about alligators.
   **B** What do you know about large reptiles?

**19.** **A** Sonia Moreno plays the violin in the orchestra.
   **B** Talented is the best way to describe Sonia Moreno.

**Part E** Decide which transition belongs in each sentence. Write the letter of your answer.

**20.** The cake will bake for an hour. _____, I will clean up.
   **A** While  **B** Meanwhile  **C** Usually  **D** Sometimes

**21.** Our team won every game. _____, we are champions!
   **A** Usually  **B** Sometimes  **C** At last  **D** Meanwhile

**22.** The sky is turning black. _____ it will begin to rain.
   **A** Soon  **B** First  **C** Finally  **D** Meanwhile

**23.** _____ going to sleep, Derek always brushes his teeth.
   **A** Later  **B** Before  **C** First  **D** After

**24.** First Amber walks her dog, and _____ she feeds him.
   **A** then  **B** before  **C** while  **D** now

**Part F**

**25.** Revise and edit the paragraph. Then rewrite it.

Have you ever seen the Grand Canyon? The canyon is a national park. It is in Arizona. Thousands of people visits it. the people come mainly in the summer. The Colorado River formed this canyon. The canyon is 277 miles long. It is the most spectacular canyan in the united states?

**Test Tip**

When studying for a test, work with a partner to write your own test questions. Then answer the questions together.

*Writing Better.Paragraphs*  **143**

## Review Answers

**Part D**
**17.** B  **18.** B  **19.** B

**Part E**
**20.** B  **21.** C  **22.** A  **23.** B  **24.** A

**Part F**

**25.** Paragraphs will vary. A possible paragraph is given.
Have you ever seen Grand Canyon National Park? Every year, thousands of people visit this beautiful spot in Arizona. They gaze at the steep, colorful cliffs of the canyon. Over a mile below, they see the rushing Colorado River, which formed this canyon over millions of years. Stretching over 277 miles, the Grand Canyon is the most spectacular canyon in the United States.

### WRITING PORTFOLIO

**Wrap-Up** Have students make a clean final copy of their revised and edited paragraphs. You may want to collect the paragraphs and read them anonymously to the class, or have classmates share their paragraphs in small groups. This project may be used as an alternative form of assessment for the chapter.

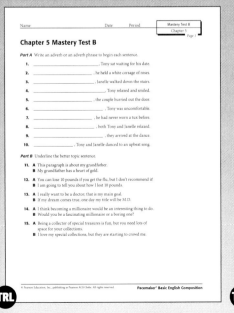

Chapter 5 Mastery Test B, pages 1–3

# CHAPTER 6

## PLANNING GUIDE

# Writing to Explain

| | Student Pages | Vocabulary | Practice Exercises | Lesson Review | Identification | Writing | Punctuation & Capitalization | Grammar & Usage | Listening, Speaking, & Viewing |
|---|---|---|---|---|---|---|---|---|---|
| **Lesson 6-1** Explaining How to Do Something | 147–149 | | ✔ | ✔ | ✔ | ✔ | ✔ | ✔ | ✔ |
| **Lesson 6-2** Giving Information | 150–153 | | ✔ | ✔ | ✔ | ✔ | ✔ | ✔ | ✔ |
| **Lesson 6-3** Comparing and Contrasting | 154–158 | ✔ | ✔ | ✔ | ✔ | ✔ | ✔ | ✔ | ✔ |
| **Lesson 6-4** Showing Cause and Effect | 159–161 | ✔ | ✔ | ✔ | ✔ | ✔ | ✔ | ✔ | ✔ |
| **Lesson 6-5** Explaining a Solution to a Problem | 162–167 | ✔ | ✔ | ✔ | ✔ | ✔ | ✔ | ✔ | ✔ |

Columns span **Student Lesson** and **Language Skills**.

## Chapter Activities

**Teacher's Resource Library**
Life Skills Connection 6: Solving Problems
Writing Tip 6: Writing Clear Explanations
Writing on the Job 3: Hospital Kitchen Helper
Building Research Skills 6: Using Your Own Words
Key Vocabulary Words 6

## Assessment Options

**Student Text**
Chapter 6 Review

**Teacher's Resource Library**
Chapter 6 Mastery Tests A and B

**Teacher's Edition**
Chapter 6 Writing Portfolio

| | Student Text Features | | | | | | | | | Teaching Strategies | | | | | | | | | Learning Styles | | | | | Teacher's Resource Library | | | |
|---|---|---|---|---|---|---|---|---|---|---|---|---|---|---|---|---|---|---|---|---|---|---|---|---|---|---|---|
| English in Your Life | Writing on the Job | Building Research Skills | Vocabulary Builder | Grammar Builder | Write About It | Group Activity | Reading Strategy | Six Traits | ELL/ESL Strategy | Background Information | Common Error | Life Skills Connection | Applications (Home, Career, Community, Global) | Online Connection | Teacher Alert | Speaking & Presenting Practice | Writing/Spelling/Grammar Practice | Auditory/Verbal | Body/Kinesthetic | Interpersonal/Group Learning | Logical/Mathematical | Visual/Spatial | Activities | Modified Activities | Workbook Activities | Self-Study Guide |
| | | | 149 | | | | 147, 148 | | 147 | 147 | 148 | | 149 | 148 | | | 149 | | 148 | | | | 25 | 25 | 25 | ✔ |
| | | | | 152 | | | 150, 151 | | 152 | 150 | 152 | | 153 | | | | | 153 | | 151 | | | 26 | 26 | 26 | ✔ |
| | | | | | | | 155, 157 | | 158 | 154 | 155 | | | | 156 | 156 | | | | | | 157 | 27 | 27 | 27 | ✔ |
| | | | | | | | 160 | | 161 | 159 | 160 | | 160 | | | | 161 | | | | 160 | | 28 | 28 | 28 | ✔ |
| 165 | 166 | | | | 164 | 167 | 162, 163 | 164 | 166 | 162 | | 163 | | 167 | | | 163 | | | | | | 29 | 29 | 29 | ✔ |

---

## Pronunciation Key

| | | | | | | | | | | | |
|---|---|---|---|---|---|---|---|---|---|---|---|
| a | hat | e | let | ī | ice | ô | order | ü | put | sh | she |
| ā | age | ē | equal | o | hot | oi | oil | ü | rule | th | thin |
| ä | far | ėr | term | ō | open | ou | out | ch | child | ŦH | then |
| â | care | i | it | ȯ | saw | u | cup | ng | long | zh | measure |

ə { a in about / e in taken / i in pencil / o in lemon / u in circus }

## Modified Activities

The Teacher's Resource Library (TRL) contains a set of lower-level worksheets called Modified Activities. These worksheets cover the same content as the standard Activities but are written at a lower reading level.

## Skill Track

Use Skill Track for *Basic English Composition* to monitor student progress and meet the demands of adequate yearly progress (AYP). Make informed instructional decisions with individual student and class reports of lesson and chapter assessments. With immediate and ongoing feedback, students will also see what they have learned and where they need more reinforcement and practice.

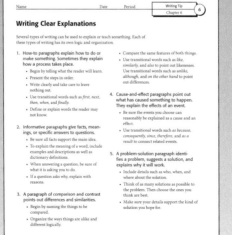

Writing Tip 6

Life Skills Connection 6

# Writing to Explain

A computer is a useful tool. In the computer lab shown in the photo, identical computers sit side by side. Imagine students working at the computers. They all use the same tools. However, they use the computers to do very different things. They find information or send e-mail messages. They write paragraphs and essays or fill out job applications.

Just as a computer can be used to do many things, you can use your writing skills in many ways. You can write for different purposes. You can create different kinds of writing.

In Chapter 6, you will learn to write for the purpose of explaining something. For example, you can explain the steps in a process. You can give facts, explain a meaning, or compare two things. You can show how one event causes another. You can also explain how to solve a problem.

## GOALS FOR LEARNING

- To write a paragraph that tells how to do something
- To write a paragraph that gives information
- To write a paragraph that compares and contrasts
- To write a paragraph that shows cause and effect
- To write a paragraph that explains a solution to a problem

**145**

## Introducing the Chapter

Have students examine the photograph on page 144 and describe what it shows. Ask them to name different tasks they have done using a computer. Discuss computers as a tool for managing information. Point out that a writer uses his or her writing skills as a tool for different purposes, such as informing, explaining, persuading, describing, or telling stories. Encourage volunteers to talk about their approach to writing. Explain that this chapter will discuss how to write paragraphs that explain.

Review and discuss the Goals for Learning on page 145.

## Notes

Ask volunteers to read the notes that appear in the margins throughout the chapter. Then discuss them with the class.

### TEACHER'S RESOURCE

The AGS Globe Teaching Strategies in English Transparencies may be used with this chapter. The transparencies add an interactive dimension to expand and enhance the *Basic English Composition* program content.

### WRITING PORTFOLIO

Have students list things they know how to do well and enjoy doing. Ask them to choose one of these topics and brainstorm details about it for several minutes. Suggest that students write a sentence telling what they would like to explain about the topic. Have students save their papers in their portfolios. Explain that they will develop their ideas as they complete the chapter. This project may be used as an alternative form of assessment for the chapter.

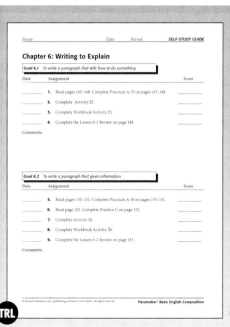

## Reading Strategy:
Inferencing

Read the following to students:

*Sean's mother sat down slowly with a sigh. She slipped off her shoes and began rubbing her feet and groaning. She asked Sean to make her a cup of tea.*

Ask students what Sean might conclude about asking his mother to take him to the mall now. (*She is tired and her feet hurt. She will not want to go anywhere. He should not ask her right now.*)

Explain to students that they constantly make inferences, or good guesses, about things that have not been said. Have students read the text about inferencing on page 146.

............................................................

## Key Vocabulary Words

cause and effect    contrast
compare          solution

Display two items that have similarities and differences, for example, a third-cut folder and an accordion folder. Ask students to point out ways they are the same and different. Explain that this is called comparing and contrasting. Then have students talk about why they would use one of the folders. Point out that they are giving a cause. List some effects of using folders to organize. Then have students talk about what kind of problem they could solve using the folders. Have volunteers read the key vocabulary words and their meanings. Ask other volunteers to make up sentences about the folders using these terms.

............................................................

# Reading Strategy: Inferencing

Sometimes the meaning of what you read is suggested but not stated. You have to infer—or make an inference—to figure out the meaning. To make an inference, you must "read between the lines." You must combine what you already know with what you are reading:

What You Know + What You Read = Inference

Here are some strategies for making inferences:

- Think about what you already know about the subject.
- Think of ideas that are related to the subject.
- Predict what will happen next.
- Read the text again to see if you can understand the meaning.

## Key Vocabulary Words

**Compare** To point out how two things are alike or different

**Contrast** To point out how two things are different

**Cause and effect** Something that happens (effect) because of something else (cause)

**Solution** An answer to a problem; a way of making a situation better

**146**   *Chapter 6   Writing to Explain*

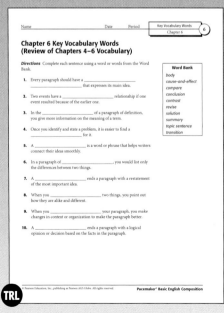

# Explaining How to Do Something

## Objectives

■ To write a how-to paragraph

■ To use words like *next* and *finally* to make the steps clear

■ To revise and edit the paragraph

*Reading Strategy:*
Inferencing

What do you already know about teaching someone to do something?

How-to books and articles are very popular. They explain how to do something. You can tell your readers how to do something, too.

In a how-to paragraph, the topic sentence tells the readers what they will be learning. The body of the paragraph takes them through the steps. The body includes words such as *first, next, then, when*, and *finally*. The last sentence is either a conclusion or a summary.

### Practice A

Read the how-to paragraph. Then answer the questions.

**Getting in Shape**

Before you begin a new sport, take time to get in shape. To avoid injury, you need to improve your flexibility, strength, and endurance. To improve flexibility, try a yoga class. Yoga provides the stretching you need. Next, work on your strength with weight training. Most schools and community centers have weight-training equipment. Talk to the trainer to find out the right weight training for you. Finally, you need to develop endurance. Aerobics classes or even long walks will increase your staying power. These three things—flexibility, strength, and endurance—will help you perform your best in any sport.

1. What is the main idea of this paragraph?
2. What three steps are described?
3. What words help the reader know when to take certain steps?
4. Is the last sentence a summary or a conclusion?
5. What is another way of stating the final sentence?

## Practice A

Have a volunteer read the paragraph. Answer any questions students have about the information before they answer the questions.

### Practice A Answers

Answers will vary. Possible answers are given. **1.** The main idea of this paragraph is to explain how to get in shape for playing a sport. **2.** The three steps in getting in shape are improving flexibility, gaining strength, and developing endurance. **3.** The words *Before, Next*, and *Finally* help the reader know when to take certain steps. **4.** The last sentence is a summary. **5.** Another way of stating the final sentence is "Getting in shape will prepare you for any sport."

### 3 Reinforce and Extend

#### ELL/ESL STRATEGY

**Language Objective:** *To prepare how-to directions*

Have students select a familiar task and ask them to make a set of numbered steps. Then let them follow the steps to see if they give the correct information.

*Reading Strategy:* Inferencing

Students may know from teaching friends that directions have to be specific, organized, and sometimes modeled.

## Chapter 6  Lesson 1

**Overview** This lesson focuses on paragraphs that explain how to do or make something.

### Objectives

■ To write a how-to paragraph

■ To use words like *next* and *finally* to make the steps clear

■ To revise and edit the paragraph

**Student Pages**  147–149

**Teacher's Resource Library**

**Activity** 25

**Modified Activity** 25

**Workbook Activity** 25

## Background Information

Writing that explains how to do something or how something occurs is called *process writing*. One kind of process writing is a set of instructions. Another is a process analysis—for example, how legislation is passed or how thunderstorms form. Process writing calls for a topic sentence and details in linear (time) order.

### 1  Warm-Up Activity

Ask students to imagine that someone has asked them for directions to a place several miles away. Have volunteers give directions to the place. Students can discuss the effectiveness of the directions: Would the visitor be able to find the place? Connect the explanation process to writing. Ask why it is important to be precise when writing a paragraph that tells how to do something.

### 2  Teaching the Lesson

Invite students to tell where they would find written explanations of how to do something. Then let volunteers identify some of the things they do well. Ask them how they would go about writing a paragraph telling someone else how to do these things.

## COMMON ERROR

When giving directions, people can omit details that are obvious to them. Tell students when they give directions, they should consider if the listener is unfamiliar with the area.

## Practice B

Discuss distance and direction words—*north, left, blocks, miles, yards*—students might want to use. Point out that descriptions of landmarks can be useful. For example, *turn left as soon as you pass the bright yellow house.*

## *Practice B Answers*

Answers will vary. Students' paragraphs should state the departure and arrival points.

## Practice C

Review the revising checklists on pages 134 and 138. Also review terms such as *subject, verb,* and *run-on sentence.* Then have students read the directions.

## *Practice C Answers*

Revisions of the paragraph will vary. A sample paragraph is given.
To have a successful garden, you must do several things. First, you must choose the right spot. The garden will need plenty of sunshine. It helps to have a slight slope for good drainage. Next, be sure to buy and plant good seeds. Then you should fertilize, weed, and water your garden. Later, you will enjoy the fruits of your labor.

## Practice D

Students may select a paragraph written earlier if their Practice B paragraphs are not suitable. Be sure partners understand that they are not to revise their own work.

## *Practice D Answers*

You may want to have each student rewrite his or her own paragraph based on the changes suggested. Then have students read their revised paragraphs aloud.

## *Reading Strategy:* Inferencing

Transitions are important to help the reader easily understand the order of the directions.

---

 **Brush Up on the Basics**

In a how-to paragraph, use strong action verbs that tell the exact thing to do. Also use specific adverbs. *Stir the eggs quickly until smooth* is exact. *Mix the eggs* is not. See Grammar 60 in Appendix A.

---

*Reading Strategy:* Inferencing

After reading this lesson, what can you conclude about using transitions in a how-to paragraph?

---

In a how-to paragraph, you are teaching your reader something new. You need to give the steps in the correct order. Do not forget a step, and do not assume the reader already knows about a step. Make the content clear.

### Practice B

Suppose you invite a friend home for dinner. Write a paragraph that gives directions from school to your home.

When you write a how-to paragraph, define any words your reader might not understand.

### Practice C

Revise and edit the how-to paragraph. Change the order of some sentences. Combine short sentences into longer ones. Fix the mistakes. Write the new paragraph on your paper. Use the checklists on pages 134 and 138.

**How to Start a Vegetable Garden**

To have a successful vegetable garden you must do several things. First, you must chose the right spot, the garden will need plenty of sunshine. It helps to have a slight slope for good drainage. Its also a good idea to add fertilizer. A fertilizer is a substance you add to the soil to make plants grow better be sure to buy good seeds. Water and weed your garden. plant your seeds. Later, you will enjoy the fruits of your labor.

### Practice D

Sometimes a friend can give you helpful writing advice. Choose one of the paragraphs you already wrote in this lesson. Trade paragraphs with a partner. Revise and edit your partner's paragraph. Then share the changes you made. Did your partner improve your paragraph?

---

**148**   *Chapter 6   Writing to Explain*

---

## LEARNING STYLES

 **Body/Kinesthetic**

Collect sources of information, such as cookbooks and financial guides. Ask students to use them to write paragraphs for a demonstration. Remind students to use words like *first, next,* and *finally* for sequence. Have them present their demonstrations to the class.

## TEACHER ALERT

Make the point that all writers can be sensitive about having their work criticized. Emphasize that good criticism is positive, not negative. Discuss the importance of commenting on strengths in the writer's work as well as parts that need further work.

---

# REVIEW

1. The following details explain one way to become more physically fit. Use the details to write a how-to paragraph. Write a topic sentence. Use words such as *first* and *finally* in the body. End with a conclusion or summary. Use the checklists on pages 134 and 138 to revise and edit your paragraph.

   - Build the activity into your schedule.
   - Start with a short walk around the block.
   - Take the walk several times a week.
   - Gradually increase your walking speed.
   - Work up to a two-mile walk three times a week.

2. Think of something that you know how to do, make, or fix. Write a how-to paragraph about it. Make the first sentence your topic sentence. Use words such as *first*, *next*, and *finally* in the paragraph body. End with a summary sentence. Use the checklists on pages 134 and 138 to revise and edit your paragraph.

# VOCABULARY BUILDER

## Using Prefixes

A prefix is a group of letters added to the beginning of a word. A prefix changes the meaning of the word. For example, the prefix *un-* means "not." When you are unhappy, you are not happy. Below are some common prefixes. Each prefix is followed by its meaning and an example.

*re-* ("again") regain     *mis-* ("wrongly") misspell
*dis-* ("opposite") displease     *sub-* ("under") subtopic
*non-* ("not") nonsense     *pre-* ("before") preview

Write a word that begins with each of the prefixes listed above.

*Writing to Explain*    Chapter 6    **149**

---

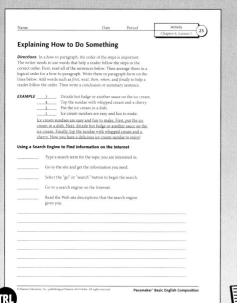

Activity 25

Workbook Activity 25

---

## Lesson 6-1 Review Answers

Paragraphs will vary. A possible paragraph is given. **1.** Would you like to build your physical fitness? The most important thing to do is to make physical activity a regular part of your schedule. First, start with a short walk around the block. Repeat the walk the next day or the day after. Try to take the walk several times a week. After you are used to the walk, gradually increase your walking speed. Finally, work up to a fast two-mile walk three times a week. You will see a big improvement in your fitness level. **2.** Students' how-to paragraphs should have a topic sentence, at least three sentences of supporting details, and a summary sentence. The steps should be clearly organized and use logical transitions.

# VOCABULARY BUILDER

Ask volunteers to explain what they already know about prefixes. Write students' examples on the board. Then have students read the paragraph of text and study the prefixes in the chart.

## Vocabulary Builder Answers

You may want to brainstorm an example of a word beginning with each prefix before students generate their own lists. Remind students that they can look up the prefixes in the dictionary if they need to. Lists will vary. Sample lists are given.

renew, remind, relive, rewrite
disappear, dislike, dismiss, disobey
nonfat, nonconformist, nonfiction, nonbeliever
misuse, mislead, misinform, misplace
submarine, subway, sublease, subdivide
precaution, preschool, prehistoric, prepay

## Spelling Practice

When adding prefixes, do not change the spelling of the base word:
mis- + spell = misspell

Have students make new words by combining the following sets of prefixes and base words:

mis- + spent
un- + necessary
im- + mobile
il- + logical

Students may check their words in a dictionary.

*Writing to Explain*    **149**

## Lesson at a Glance

### Chapter 6 Lesson 2

**Overview** This lesson focuses on the informative paragraph, such as one that explains a definition or an answer to a specific question.

### Objectives

- To write a paragraph that provides information
- To write a paragraph based on a definition
- To write a paragraph that answers a question

**Student Pages** 150–153

**Teacher's Resource Library**

Activity 26

Modified Activity 26

Workbook Activity 26

### Background Information

A paragraph of definition is more than an expanded dictionary definition. It develops the meaning of a term by providing examples and details that elaborate to a greater extent than a dictionary does. In addition to examples, a paragraph of definition often includes narrative and description.

### 1 Warm-Up Activity

Ask students to describe any written answers to questions they have completed recently, such as essay tests or work applications. Discuss the importance of writing a clearly organized paragraph when giving information.

### 2 Teaching the Lesson

Write these two sentences on the board: *When threatened, the hognose snake can play dead. Animals have varied ways of defending themselves.* Ask students to tell which sentence could be the topic sentence of a paragraph and why. *(The second sentence because it is more general; the first sentence gives a detail that belongs in the body.)* Have students tell the difference between a topic sentence and a detail.

---

# Giving Information

### Objectives

- To write a paragraph that provides information
- To write a paragraph based on a definition
- To write a paragraph that answers a question

**Reading Strategy:** Inferencing

This lesson talks about giving information. What kinds of information do you give to others each day?

When you write to inform, you are trying to make something clear. You want to help your reader understand something. You might do this by:

- providing facts about a topic
- explaining the meaning of something
- answering a question

Like all paragraphs, your topic sentence prepares the reader for your main idea. The body of your paragraph gives facts and explanations. Your final sentence may be a summary or a conclusion.

### Providing Facts

The purpose of many paragraphs is to provide facts about a topic. The facts support the main idea.

**Practice A**

Read the paragraph. Then answer the questions.

Personal computers are appearing in more homes. Even the smallest personal computers are more powerful than those of the 1960s. Computers have become easy and fun to use. Families use them to surf the Internet, send e-mail, do homework, play games, and keep track of checkbook balances. Soon, people will find it difficult to remember a time when they did not have computers at home.

1. What is the topic of this paragraph?
2. What is the main idea? State it in your own words.
3. What facts and reasons support the main idea?
4. What conclusion does the writer give?
5. Write a different conclusion for this paragraph.

---

### Practice A

Read the paragraph aloud as students follow along. Then have them analyze its parts by answering the questions.

### Practice A Answers

Wording of answers will vary. Possible answers are given. **1.** Personal computers are the topic of this paragraph. **2.** Personal computers have become popular. **3.** Personal computers are powerful, fun, and easy to use. Their uses include surfing the Internet, sending e-mail, doing homework, playing games, and tracking finances. **4.** Soon, people will find it difficult to remember a time when they did not have computers at home. **5.** Computers will soon be a necessary part of every home.

### Reading Strategy: Inferencing

Students may say that they give information about how they feel, what time it is, what they did or plan to do, what someone else said or did, and where they went or are going.

**Reading Strategy:**
Inferencing

What new idea does this lesson give about using a dictionary?

## Explaining a Definition

You may need to write a paragraph that develops a definition. A definition is the meaning of a word or phrase. You can use details from dictionaries and encyclopedias to write a paragraph that informs and explains. In Example 1, compare the definition with the paragraph.

▶ **EXAMPLE 1**

| Definition | Krakatau (*n.*) a volcanic island in Indonesia |
|---|---|
| Paragraph | Have you ever heard of Krakatau? It is a volcanic island in Indonesia. In 1883, the volcano erupted and destroyed part of the island. Krakatau would be an interesting place to visit. |

### Practice B

Use each definition to write a paragraph about the word. Include a topic sentence and a summary or conclusion.

1. **glockenspiel** (*n.*) an instrument with flat, level bars set in a frame; the metal bars are tuned to produce bell-like tones when struck with two small hammers.

2. **paisley** (*adj.*) a colorful pattern of flowers or designs; originally used on wool shawls; named after Paisley, Scotland, where it was designed.

3. **leotard** (*n.*) a tight-fitting garment made of a stretchy fabric worn by dancers, gymnasts, and other people who exercise; named for a nineteenth-century French acrobat, Jules Léotard.

4. **doodle** (*v.*) to wander aimlessly, without purpose; to scribble designs on a piece of paper. Originally, to doodle meant to play a bagpipe.

5. **grace period** (*n.*) extra time allowed, as for payment of a bill or for handing in an assignment after it is due.

*Writing to Explain    Chapter 6    **151***

---

## Practice B

Use the example definition and paragraph to help students see how the details in the definition are expanded to sentences that form a paragraph. Provide dictionaries so that students can find more information about each term.

### *Practice B Answers*

Answers will vary. Sample paragraphs are given. **1.** A glockenspiel is a percussion instrument. Like all percussion instruments, it makes its music by being struck. Glockenspiels used to be made of bells or tubes. Today a glockenspiel is made of flat, level bars that are hit with two small hammers. The notes of a glockenspiel sound like bells. A glockenspiel resembles a more familiar percussion instrument, the xylophone. **2.** If you would like to see paisley, look at men's ties and women's scarves. Paisley is a pattern of colorful flowers or other designs that originated in Scotland. Paisley was originally a cloth used to make soft wool shawls. Today paisley designs come in many colors and fabrics. **3.** When you exercise wearing a stretchy, one-piece outfit, do you ever wonder why it is called a leotard? The first leotard was worn by a French acrobat more than one hundred years ago. He invented a garment he could move around in easily. His name was Jules Léotard. **4.** Do you find yourself drawing designs or silly pictures when you talk on the telephone? Many people doodle while talking on the telephone or sitting in a meeting. Doodling is a way to occupy your hands when your mind is elsewhere. To doodle originally meant to play a bagpipe. Maybe people once thought that playing a bagpipe was a mindless, silly way to pass the time. **5.** If you have ever owed money to a friend and found you could not pay it back on time, you might have appreciated a grace period. Credit card companies and understanding teachers often allow a grace period. Companies and teachers realize that there may be times when payments or assignments require a little extra time to complete.

### *Reading Strategy:* Inferencing

It suggests using dictionary information to write a paragraph-long explanation of a term or a concept.

---

*Writing to Explain    **151***

## Practice C

Be sure students understand that they are to answer only one of the questions.

### Practice C Answers

Paragraphs will vary. Students should write a paragraph including explanation, reasons, or other details to develop the response.

### GRAMMAR BUILDER

Write *Cause* and *Effect* on the board. Under *Cause* write *Why?* Then ask the class to vote on a favorite food. Under *Effect*, write a statement based on their choice: *You like* _____. Have students give reasons why they like the food. Under *Cause*, list the reasons on the board. Then emphasize the connection between the reasons and the statement of effect.

Use a cause-effect graphic organizer to help students see the relationship between each pair of actions or conditions in the sentences.

### Grammar Builder Answers

Sentences will vary. A sample cause-effect sentence is given.
I saved the money I received as gifts. As a result, I have enough to get a car.

### COMMON ERROR

Point out to students that some conjunctive adverbs (*as a result, therefore, however, consequently*) must be set apart from the clauses that precede them by more than a comma. They require a semicolon or a period. A comma follows these transitional expressions.

## Answering a Question

Informative paragraphs can answer questions. If a question asks why, you can answer it with an explanation. You use facts and reasons to support your answer.

In Example 2, notice how the paragraph answers the question. It also supports the answer with an explanation.

▶ **EXAMPLE 2**

| Question | Why did Othello kill Desdemona? |
|---|---|
| Paragraph | In Shakespeare's play, Othello killed his wife, Desdemona, because of a mistake. Othello's false friend, Iago, lied to him. Iago told Othello that Desdemona was in love with another man. To get revenge, Othello smothered his innocent wife. He later found out that he had been misled. |

### Practice C

Choose a question below. Write a paragraph that answers it.

- How have cell phones changed the way teenagers communicate?
- Why is it important to be on time?
- What is the weather like in October where you live?

### GRAMMAR BUILDER

**Using Cause-and-Effect Transitions**
Transitional words can show how one thing causes another.
- The belt broke *because* it was worn out.
- Inez did not study. *As a result*, she failed the test.
- The car window was open, *so* the seat got wet.
- Several bad accidents have happened at the corner. *For this reason*, we should put a stoplight there.

Write a sentence showing a cause and effect. Use one of the italic transitional words above.

### ELL/ESL STRATEGY

**Language Objective:**
*To compare literary figures across cultures*

Some students may have no cultural background for understanding who William Shakespeare or Othello are (in Example 2). Provide some background information. Explain that William Shakespeare was an English poet and playwright during the late 1500s and early 1600s. He is considered one of the world's greatest playwrights. *Othello* is a tragic play he wrote. It tells about the personal tragedy of Othello, a military officer serving in Venice. He marries a much younger woman. His own weaknesses, insecurities, and jealousy result in his wife's murder and his own suicide. Invite students to describe a character from their native literature who shares some of Othello's traits.

# REVIEW

Read the paragraph. Then answer the questions on your paper.

### Who's Who

When you write about a famous person, you may want to get information from *Who's Who*. This reference book lists famous living people. It is in alphabetical order. You will find a short paragraph about each person. This paragraph is a brief biography that gives a few facts about the person's life. *Who's Who* gives a little information about many people.

1. What is the main idea of this paragraph?

2. What information would you find in *Who's Who*?

3. What are three things you know about *Who's Who*?

4. What is the purpose of the last sentence?

5. What is the purpose of this paragraph?

Choose one of the topics below.

- uses for a dictionary
- kinds of calendars you can buy
- the meaning of *silhouette*
- features on new cars

6. Write a paragraph of five sentences about the topic you chose. State the main idea in the first sentence. Then write three sentences that give facts and reasons to support the main idea. End with a summary or a conclusion.

7. Revise and edit your paragraph. Then write the final copy.

*Writing to Explain*  Chapter 6  **153**

## AT HOME

Students may look through magazines and newspapers for question-and-answer features such as "Ask the Doctor" or "Smart Money." Have students clip examples of one-paragraph answers written in response to a question. Ask students to identify the main idea, either by underlining it in the article or by writing it.

## CAREER CONNECTION

Have students make up a *why* question about a job they are considering. For example, *Why do I want to become a nurse? Why would Woodrow's hire me as a salesperson?* Then ask them to develop reasons in a clearly organized paragraph.

## LEARNING STYLES

### Auditory/Verbal

Have students choose a specialized term relating to a hobby or activity they pursue. Ask students to make notes about the term's meaning and prepare to explain it to classmates. Encourage students to use diagrams, models, or actions to help them explain the term.

---

**Giving Information**

**Directions** On the lines, write a short paragraph to answer the question. Remember that the purpose of your paragraph is to inform a reader about this topic.

**Is physical exercise important? Why or why not?**

**Directions** Answer these questions about the paragraph you wrote.

1. What is the main idea of your paragraph? State the main idea in another way.

2. Identify three facts or reasons you used to support the main idea.

3. What is your conclusion? Does it support the information you have provided?

4. Read the paragraph again. Is the main idea clear? Does your body support the main idea? How could you improve your paragraph?

5. Write a title for your paragraph.

**Explaining What Something Means**

**Directions** Read the paragraph. Then answer the questions below it.

A convertible is a car with a top that can be removed or lowered. In every other way, a convertible is a typical car. It has four wheels, a windshield, seats, and so on. Yet, unlike a regular car, it makes the driver feel adventurous. There is something glamorous and thrilling about the idea of speeding along with the wind in your hair. When you think about a convertible, what do you picture? You probably think of a sporty, red little car that zips along. You picture yourself in sunglasses, enjoying a beautiful spring or summer day. A car may just be transportation, but a convertible sounds like a good time.

1. What does this paragraph define?

2. What is the dictionary definition for this thing?

3. What are three details the writer added that explain what sets this thing apart from all others of its kind?

4. How does your imagination help you understand the meaning of the thing?

5. Does the paragraph end with a summary or a conclusion?

## Chapter 6  Lesson 3

**Overview**  This lesson discusses techniques for developing a comparison by pointing out how things are alike and different.

### Objectives

- To develop a topic by making comparisons
- To explain how two things are alike
- To explain how two things are different
- To use transitional words in comparisons

**Student Pages**  154–158

### Teacher's Resource Library **TRL**

Activity  27

Modified Activity  27

Workbook Activity  27

...................................................

## Vocabulary

compare          contrast

After students have read the meanings for the terms, display a catalog page or sales ad from a newspaper or magazine. Point out two items that appear together, such as two pairs of jeans. Ask students to compare the items, then contrast them.

...................................................

## Background Information

In comparison writing, the writer should describe the same features or aspects of the two things compared. Second, the writer should develop a logical plan. Block format means comparing all the aspects of Subject A, then addressing Subject B. Alternating format involves switching back and forth between subjects as you examine each aspect.

### 1  Warm-Up Activity

Explain that writers use comparison and contrast to show the ways two things are alike and different. Ask students to name some occasions when this approach would be helpful. *(to compare two characters, two books, or two cities, for example)*

---

## LESSON 6-3  Comparing and Contrasting

### Objectives

- To develop a topic by making comparisons
- To explain how two things are alike
- To explain how two things are different
- To use transitional words in comparisons

**Compare**
To point out how two things are alike or different

Making a comparison is one way to develop a topic. A comparison is a statement that **compares** two or more things. To compare means to point out how two things are alike or different.

You can write a paragraph based on a comparison. In the topic sentence, name the things you are comparing. Each topic sentence in Example 1 sets up a comparison.

▶ **EXAMPLE 1**

Amber's dog Rex is friendlier than most dogs.

Sonia and her cousin Luis both like music.

New Orleans and Miami are two cities that have warm winters.

### Practice A

Compare the two items in each set. Write one topic sentence for each set. Point out how the items are different or how they are alike.

*This shirt is less expensive than that one.*

1. a banana and an orange
2. a mountain and a hill
3. a hamburger and a hot dog
4. spring and fall
5. two people in your family

---

### 2  Teaching the Lesson

Point out that a topic must have several similarities or differences to be suitable for a comparison.

## Practice A

You may want to copy a Venn diagram onto the board and model collecting information about two subjects on it. Students can then note if the similarities or differences should be compared.

## Practice A Answers

Topic sentences will vary. Sample sentences are given. **1.** How can two fruits be more different than a banana and an orange? **2.** You could call a hill a "chip off the old block"—a hill is "chip-sized" compared to a mountain. **3.** Two all-time American favorite sandwiches, the hamburger and the hot dog, have a great deal in common. **4.** Spring and fall are both seasons of change, but how remarkably different those changes are! **5.** Though they are brothers, Hal and Hank look very different.

The chart in Example 2 shows some differences between modern and early automobiles.

▶ **EXAMPLE 2**

| Modern Automobiles | Early Automobiles |
|---|---|
| start quickly with key | harder to start |
| fast: up to 100 mph | slow: up to 30 mph |
| dependable | broke down often |
| comfortable | cold, wet |
| purpose: transportation | purpose: transportation |

**Practice B**

Write a paragraph comparing modern automobiles with early automobiles. Use the details in Example 2. Add other details if you can. Begin with a topic sentence. Give supporting details in the body. End with a summary or conclusion. When you are finished, read your paragraph to your class or to another student.

You may use comparisons to explain why one thing is better or worse than another. Example 3 compares two sports.

▶ **EXAMPLE 3**

Basketball provides more exercise than golf.

**Practice C**

Choose a topic listed below. Write a paragraph that explains why one thing is better or worse than the other. Give examples that support your main idea.

- two movies that you have seen
- two TV shows that you watch
- two places where you have lived or visited
- two characters in a book that you have read

## COMMON ERROR

Students may fail to compare similar elements in the objects or people they are writing about. Point out in Example 2 that every characteristic mentioned in column 1 is also described in column 2. Students may benefit by making a chart of details on each feature they are comparing in Practice C. As they write supporting sentences, they can cross off the items in the chart.

## Practice B

Have two volunteers read the lists in Example 2. Point out how the same aspects of each automobile category are described in the same order. Discuss how students might organize the details using block or alternating format.

### *Practice B Answers*

Paragraphs will vary. A sample paragraph is given.
Modern automobiles are much improved compared to the earliest models. In the early days, automobile drivers had to spend time and energy hand cranking a car to start it. Today, a turn of the key makes an engine roar. Long ago, motorists spent much longer driving from place to place. Although today's cars can easily go 100 miles per hour, the early cars were racing at 30! When today's drivers start on a trip, they can count on a reliable ride. On the other hand, the pioneers of motoring never knew if their new invention would make it. When it comes to comfort, modern drivers expect heat and cooling at a touch. In contrast, drivers of early cars, which were open to the weather, had to carry blankets for warmth and often got wet when it rained. As different as cars of the past and of today are, they both got people where they wanted to go.

### *Reading Strategy:* Inferencing

Students might suggest listing qualities that are similar and that are different in both subjects.

## Practice C

Have students describe other differences between basketball and golf in Example 3.

### *Practice C Answers*

Paragraphs will vary but should include a topic sentence that sets up a comparison of the two chosen items, detail sentences that point out differences between the two, and a concluding sentence.

## Practice D

Encourage students to use conjunctions to show differences or opposites: *but, unlike, although, while.*

### Practice D Answers

Sentences will vary. Sample sentences are given. **1.** While Saturdays are busy with chores and shopping, Sundays are a time for resting and relaxing. **2.** Watching TV keeps my eyes on the story, but reading a book involves my whole mind and all my senses in the story. **3.** Although applesauce tastes good, yogurt comes in many delicious flavors. **4.** Unlike a time-consuming novel, a magazine provides entertainment in easy bites. **5.** A motorcycle may get you places faster, but a bicycle exercises your body without hurting your ears.

## Practice E

Read the directions with students. Remind them that they need at least three differences between the subjects to develop a paragraph. Suggest that students begin by brainstorming differences between the parts of their chosen topic.

### Practice E Answers

Paragraphs will vary. Students should write a topic sentence that names both items and sets up their contrasting nature. They should develop contrasts using a reasonable sequence of details and examples and end their paragraph with a summary or a conclusion.

### Reading Strategy: Inferencing

Students may say that you can first tell how two things are alike, then how they are different. Also, you can address one subject completely, then the other one. Or you can alternate between subjects, telling about one difference at a time.

---

**Contrast**
To point out how two things are different

**Reading Strategy:** Inferencing

What different ways can you organize the information in a paragraph that compares two things?

## Using Contrast

In a paragraph that compares two things, you may want to say how the things are different. To **contrast** is to point out how two things are different.

▶ EXAMPLE 4

A lemon is sour. An orange is sweet.

Dogs are pals. Cats are independent.

### Practice D

Contrast the two things in each set. Write one sentence for each set. Point out how the two things are different.

1. Saturdays and Sundays
2. reading a book and watching TV
3. applesauce and yogurt
4. magazines and novels
5. bicycles and motorcycles

### Practice E

Choose one topic below. Write a paragraph that contrasts the two things. Begin with a topic sentence. Add a body of supporting details. End with a summary or conclusion. When you are finished, read your paragraph to your class or to another student.

- two kinds of music
- two restaurants where you have eaten
- a beach and a desert
- two regions in your country

## Speaking and Presenting Practice

Have students use their paragraphs from Practice E as the basis for a class presentation. Suggest that students add visuals or recordings to make the contrasts they describe easy to understand.

## Using Transitions

A transitional word or phrase shows a connection between one sentence and the next. The following transitions are especially useful in a paragraph of comparison.

### Transitions Used to Compare

| | | |
|---|---|---|
| unlike | on the other hand | but |
| in comparison | although | nevertheless |
| on the contrary | similarly | now |
| in like manner | in the same way | still |
| also | for example | in addition |
| as a result | furthermore | in conclusion |
| consequently | however | therefore |
| at last | first | next |
| at the end | in the meantime | soon |
| before | later | then |
| finally | meanwhile | while |

### Practice F

Find the words you do not know in the list above. Use a dictionary to look up the meanings of these words. Write their definitions on your paper.

### Practice G

Make two lists on your paper. In the first list, write five transitions that show how two things are alike. In the other list, write five transitions that show how two things are different. Use the transitions in the list above or think of others. Start with these lists:

| Things That Are Alike | Things That Are Different |
|---|---|
| *similarly* | *although* |

## Practice F

Suggest that students write the part of speech as well as the meaning. For a phrase such as *on the contrary,* students should look up *contrary.* The phrase is listed at the end of the entry, as an idiomatic expression.

### Practice F Answers

Words chosen by students will vary. Meanings should match the part of speech of the transition. For example, *still* can be an adjective, a verb, an adverb, or a conjunction. *While* may be a noun, verb, or conjunction. As a conjunction, it can have three different meanings. The meanings suitable for comparison are "although" and "whereas."

## Practice G

Encourage students to refer to their meanings from Practice F to help them decide where to place their chosen transitions.

### Practice G Answers

Lists will vary. Sample lists are given.

| Alike | Different |
|---|---|
| also | unlike |
| in like manner | although |
| in addition | but |
| in the same way | in contrast |
| similarly | however |

### LEARNING STYLES

**Visual/Spatial**

Set up pairs of objects (or pictures of the objects) that belong to the same category but have differences. Have pairs of students spend a minute or two with each pair of objects. Have them write sentences telling how they are alike and different. Encourage students to use transitional words and phrases from the list on page 157.

## Lesson 6-3 Review Answers

1. However 2. In comparison 3. Unlike
4. Although 5. but
Sample answers are given. 6. Two
amusement parks—Wonder World and The
Great Getaway—are compared. 7. They
differ in atmosphere and the kind of crowd
they attract. Fanciful, slower-paced Wonder
World is for dreamers. Scary, fast-paced
Great Getaway is for the daring. Wonder
World offers a boat trip while The Great
Getaway features the world's largest roller
coaster. 8. Both are amusement parks, and
both are large. 9. but, On the other hand,
while, In comparison 10. Answers will vary
but should be supported with a logical
reason.

## WRITING PORTFOLIO

**Checkpoint** Have
students look over their
Writing Portfolio
paragraphs to see if they
would benefit from a
comparison or contrast. If their topic
is better suited for comparison than
for a how-to paragraph, they should
write their complete rough draft
now.

## ELL/ESL STRATEGY

**Language Objective:**
*To use synonyms
to show subtle
differences*

Students may have difficulty
choosing or understanding
descriptive words that have slight
differences in meaning. For example,
students may know that *gigantic* and
*vast* are synonyms for *big*. However,
*vast* suggests an immense expanse,
such as "the vast Sahara desert,"
while *gigantic* is used to compare
the size of other like things: "a
gigantic stadium." Have students use
dictionaries or thesauruses to list
synonyms. Have them work with
English-speaking partners to learn
differences in meaning. Then ask
students to write example sentences
using the synonyms for comparisons.

---

## LESSON 6-3 REVIEW

In each set, find the transitional word or phrase. Write it on your paper.

1. Derek is quiet. However, his little brother can be loud.

2. Last spring was warm and dry. In comparison, this spring was rainy and cool.

3. Unlike Brandon, Sonia has musical talent.

4. Although her dog Rex is difficult, Amber loves him.

5. Chicago is a crowded, noisy city, but Springfield is still a peaceful, sleepy town.

Read the paragraph. Then answer the questions on your paper.

Wonder World and The Great Getaway are both large amusement parks, but each draws a different crowd. Wonder World is a park for people who love to dream and imagine. It is a land full of elves, princesses, and fantasy characters. On the other hand, The Great Getaway is a place for the daring. Wonder World offers a boat trip through a fantasyland, while The Great Getaway offers a scary trip on the world's largest roller coaster. Visitors to Wonder World come away saying, "Wasn't that delightful?" In comparison, when visitors leave The Great Getaway, they are barely able to speak at all.

6. What two things are being compared?

7. Name three ways these places are different.

8. Name two ways these places are alike.

9. What four transitional words or phrases are used?

10. Which place would you want to visit? Give one reason for your choice.

---

Name _____ Date _____ Period _____ Activity [27] Chapter 6, Lesson 3

**Comparing and Contrasting**

*Directions* Read the following paragraph. Then answer the questions below it.

Like the St. Bernard, the English sheepdog is a long-haired dog that weighs more than 100 pounds. First bred in England, the sheepdog is gray and white. By contrast, the St. Bernard comes from Switzerland and is black, tan, and white. Both the English sheepdog and the St. Bernard were bred to do specific jobs. The sheepdog's original job, of course, was to herd sheep. On the other hand, the St. Bernard was used to aid accident victims in the snowy mountains.

**1–4.** Underline the four transitional words that show comparisons.

**5–7.** List three ways the St. Bernard and the English sheepdog are alike.

_____
_____
_____

**8–10.** List three ways the dogs are different.

_____
_____
_____

*Directions* Choose one of the three categories listed below. On the lines, list five items that fit in this category. On another sheet, write three sentences comparing the items you listed.

| musical groups | funny movies | athletic teams |
|---|---|---|

11. _____
12. _____
13. _____
14. _____
15. _____

Pacemaker® Basic English Composition

**Activity 27**

---

Name _____ Date _____ Period _____ Workbook Activity [27] Chapter 6, Lesson 3

**Understanding How Two Things Are Alike and Different**

*Directions* Read each sentence below. Think about how the words in italic type are related. Find a word in the Word Bank that is related to the underlined word in the same way. The first sentence has been done for you.

*EXAMPLE* *Hat* is to *head* as *glove* is to *hand*.

1. *Colt* is to *horse* as *calf* is to _____

2. *Saw* is to *carpenter* as *pen* is to _____

3. *Pilot* is to *airplane* as *driver* is to _____

4. *Blood* is to *veins* as *water* is to _____

5. *Hand* is to *wrist* as *head* is to _____

| Word Bank |
|---|
| automobile |
| cow |
| hand |
| neck |
| riverbed |
| writer |

*Directions* Write a sentence about each item above. In your sentence, use the four related words. Compare how two things are alike.

*EXAMPLE* To stay warm, it is just as important to wear a hat on your head as it is to wear gloves on your hands.

6. _____
7. _____
8. _____
9. _____
10. _____

Pacemaker® Basic English Composition

**Workbook Activity 27**

# Showing Cause and Effect

## Objectives

■ To understand a
cause-and-effect
relationship

■ To determine if a
cause-and-effect
relationship is
reasonable

■ To write a paragraph
to explain why
something happened

**Cause and effect**

Something that
happens (effect)
because of something
else (cause)

**Cause and effect** means that something happens because
of something else. The reason why something happens is
the *cause*. The result of the cause is the *effect*.

▶ **EXAMPLE 1**

| First Happening (Cause) | Second Happening (Effect) |
|---|---|
| It rained last night. | The grass is wet. |
| Luis liked the music. | He bought the new album. |

When you write a paragraph explaining a cause and its
effect, make sure the cause-and-effect relationship is
reasonable. It must make sense that the first event causes
the effect to occur. In Example 2, each cause is in black.
Each effect is in blue.

▶ **EXAMPLE 2**

| Reasonable | Sonia practices the violin every day. She is a very good violinist. |
|---|---|
| Not Reasonable | Derek's team won a soccer match. They will win the championship. |

If Sonia practices every day, it is likely that she
plays her violin well. This cause and effect makes
sense. Derek's team won one match. Whether the
team will win the championship is unknown. This
is not a reasonable cause-and-effect relationship.
There are too many facts about the team that you
do not know.

*If you practice your writing skills,
you will become a better writer.*

*Writing to Explain*    Chapter 6    **159**

---

## Chapter 6 Lesson 4

**Overview** This lesson explains
the cause-and-effect relationship
and has students write a paragraph
explaining a cause and effect.

### Objectives

■ To understand a cause-and-effect
relationship

■ To determine if a cause-and-
effect relationship is reasonable

■ To write a paragraph to explain
why something happened

**Student Pages** 159–161

**Teacher's Resource Library**

  **Activity** 28

  **Modified Activity** 28

  **Workbook Activity** 28

## Vocabulary

**cause and effect**

Explain that a cause makes something
happen. An effect is what happens
because of an earlier event. Put a cause/
effect graphic organizer on the board:

Give an example sentence, such as *I got
a ticket because I was speeding.* Have
volunteers write the cause (speeding) in
the first box and the effect (got a ticket)
in the second.

## Background Information

Cause-and-effect relationships are
complex. A single event can lead to
numerous effects. Some events have
many causes. And some effects become
causes in a cause-and-effect chain of
events. Invite students to name effects
of going without sleep. List these in a
graphic organizer. Discuss with students
which effects are immediate and which
happen later. This can also be shown
graphically.

---

## 1   Warm-Up Activity

Discuss with students how they can
decide if two events are related as cause
and effect. Suggest that they use the
organizer from the Vocabulary activity to
help them.

## 2   Teaching the Lesson

Ask students to find the cause and the
effect in each sentence:

Cause first: *It snowed, so the streets were
slippery.*

Effect first: *The streets were slippery
because it snowed.*

Explain that either the cause or the effect
may come first. Suggest to students that
they find the part of the sentence that
tells why something happened. That
is the cause. The part that tells what
happened is the effect.

## 3  Reinforce and Extend

### COMMON ERROR

Assuming that one thing must have caused another because it happened earlier is a common mistake. Another is seeing a situation as the result of a single cause. Students must learn to think critically about cause-and-effect relationships, asking "Is it likely that A causes B?"

### Practice A

Encourage students to think through these relationships. Have them ask themselves: *What does event A have to do with event B?*

### Practice A Answers

1. not reasonable  2. reasonable
3. reasonable  4. reasonable
5. not reasonable

### Practice B

Have volunteers read events 1–5. Have students think about what might cause each event. Then have them choose the cause.

### Practice B Answers

1. D  2. B  3. E  4. A  5. C

### Practice C

Have students rephrase their chosen topic sentence as a question in order to list causes. Have students make a word web and list at least three answers to the question.

### Practice C Answers

Paragraphs will vary but should give three causes for the event or develop a reason through three supporting sentences.

### Reading Strategy: Inferencing

Students may mention that a cause-and-effect paragraph should begin by presenting the cause(s) first. Explain that, in some cases, it may make sense to present the effect(s) first.

---

**Brush Up on the Basics**

When the dependent clause comes first, set it off from the independent clause with a comma. *Because you waited the longest, you get the first ticket.* See Punctuation 10 in Appendix A.

**Reading Strategy:**
Inferencing

After reading this lesson, what can you infer about how to organize writing that shows cause and effect?

---

### Practice A

Decide if each cause-and-effect relationship is reasonable. Write *reasonable* or *not reasonable*. Discuss the reason for your choice with another student.

1. It is cold today, so tomorrow will be warmer.
2. There are many fire hazards in that building. Someday a fire might result.
3. Amber Choy studies hard. She will get good grades.
4. Brandon lost his watch. He arrived late for work today.
5. Sonia likes her cousin Luis. He will be class president.

In a cause-and-effect paragraph, you explain why something happened.

### Practice B

Match each event (effect) in the first column with a cause in the second column. Write the letter of the cause.

| Events | Causes |
|---|---|
| 1. The birds flew south. | **A** Luis got paid today. |
| 2 There is a storm warning. | **B** A hurricane is coming. |
| 3. Sonia is playing a solo. | **C** Derek's brother is sick. |
| 4. Luis bought a new CD. | **D** The weather turned cold. |
| 5. Derek has a cold. | **E** The music calls for a solo. |

### Practice C

Choose a topic sentence below. Write a paragraph that explains what caused the event in the topic sentence. Use your imagination. Include three supporting sentences and a conclusion or summary.

- Derek hopes to receive money when he graduates.
- Luis won the election for class president.
- Our school's football team did well this year.

**160** Chapter 6 *Writing to Explain*

---

### LEARNING STYLES

**Logical/Mathematical**

Students should evaluate cause-and-effect claims in advertising. Have students clip an ad from a magazine or newspaper, tape it to a sheet of paper, and draw a diagram below it. In the diagram, have them write what effect the ad suggests this product will have. Then have them write what is supposed to cause this. Have students explain whether the ad is reasonable or not.

### GLOBAL CONNECTION

Ask students to use a newspaper or the Internet to list issues that concern nations of the world. Have the class choose one of these issues and brainstorm some of its causes and effects. Finally, have students create an artwork, a piece of creative writing, or a song that expresses their feelings about these causes and effects.

Decide if the relationship between the two events is reasonable. Write *reasonable* or *not reasonable* on your paper.

1. Luis doesn't like to write, but he thinks he can write a novel.

2. There is no battery in the smoke detector, so it will not work if there is a fire.

3. The band is popular. The concert tickets will sell fast.

4. Summer is the dry season, so the farmers need to water their crops.

5. Brandon spends all of his money. He expects to save money to buy a car.

Match each event (effect) in the first column with a reasonable cause in the second column. Write the letter of the cause.

| Events | Causes |
|---|---|
| 6. There are branches on our lawn. | **A** I forgot to take a sweatshirt to the game. |
| 7. I got cold when the sun went down. | **B** Derek studied for the Spanish test. |
| 8. Rex won first place. | **C** There was a strong wind last night. |
| 9. Derek got a B in Spanish. | **D** Sonia filled the glass too full. |
| 10. The juice spilled on the table. | **E** Amber entered Rex in a contest. |

*Writing to Explain* Chapter 6 **161**

**1.** not reasonable **2.** reasonable
**3.** reasonable **4.** reasonable **5.** not
reasonable **6.** C **7.** A **8.** E **9.** B **10.** D

## Grammar Practice

Have students write complex sentences combining causes and effects from items 6–10 in the Lesson 6-4 Review. Explain that they will need to choose a conjunction to join the sentences and make some changes in capitalization and punctuation. Work through one example with students and have them underline changes:

*Because there was a strong wind last night, there are branches on our lawn today.*

### WRITING PORTFOLIO

**Checkpoint** Have students revisit their Writing Portfolio notes. Have them star any notes that express a cause-and-effect relationship. Encourage them to revise their paragraphs to include this explanation. If their chosen topic fits best with a cause-and-effect pattern, have them develop their complete rough draft.

### ELL/ESL STRATEGY

**Language Objective:** *To practice using cause-effect transitions*

Give students extra practice using the expressions *as a result, because, consequently, since, so, therefore,* and *if/then* to establish that one event causes another. Present a familiar situation, such as being late for school. Have students suggest some causes and effects related to this. Show the relationship on the board:

| Cause | Effect |
|---|---|
| I overslept. | I was late. |

Then work with students to form sentences using some of the transitions listed. Point out appropriate punctuation.

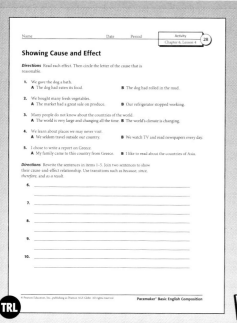

Activity 28      Workbook Activity 28

*Writing to Explain* **161**

## Lesson at a Glance

### Chapter 6 Lesson 5

**Overview** This lesson focuses on developing a reasonable solution to an identified problem in writing.

### Objectives

- To identify a problem
- To explain a solution to a problem
- To use brainstorming to solve a problem

### Student Pages 162–167

### Teacher's Resource Library

Activity 29

Modified Activity 29

Workbook Activity 29

Life Skills Connection 6

Writing on the Job 3

Building Research Skills 6

......................................................

## Vocabulary

**solution**

Have students look up the word in a dictionary and read the meanings it can have. Ask students to choose the meaning that fits this context: *Have you found a solution to your problem?*

......................................................

## Background Information

An effective problem-solution paper is limited to a problem narrow enough to be discussed in several paragraphs. A graphic organizer can be used to guide students to find solutions:

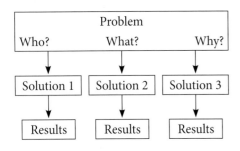

---

### LESSON 6-5

# Explaining a Solution to a Problem

### Objectives

- To identify a problem
- To explain a solution to a problem
- To use brainstorming to solve a problem

**Solution**
An answer to a problem; a way of making a situation better

***Reading Strategy:***
Inferencing

What must a writer do before explaining the solution to a problem?

Sometimes you write to explain a **solution** to a problem. A solution is an answer to a problem. In this kind of writing, you identify a problem and give one or more solutions. You also explain why your solution might work. Begin by choosing a topic and writing a topic sentence. The topic sentence should state the problem.

▶ **EXAMPLE 1**

| | |
|---|---|
| Problem | paying for my trip |
| Topic Sentence | To pay for my trip, I need to find a job. |

### Practice A

For each problem, write a topic sentence on your paper. Each sentence should state the problem. Use first-person point of view.

1. getting along with your family
2. finding time to study
3. eating healthy food
4. making the team
5. getting a ride

After you choose the problem and state your topic sentence, you need to think of one or more solutions. The body of the paragraph gives details about solving the problem.

162    *Chapter 6    Writing to Explain*

---

## 1   Warm-Up Activity

Invite volunteers to offer advice to an imaginary student who is always late. Summarize students' suggestions on the board. Point out that many problems have more than one possible solution.

## 2   Teaching the Lesson

Have students focus on Example 1. Point out that a clear statement of the problem is essential before solutions can be suggested.

***Reading Strategy:*** Inferencing

Before explaining the solution to a problem, a writer must state the problem clearly.

## Practice A

Read aloud the phrases with students. Encourage them to change the topic sentences to their own situations.

### *Practice A Answers*

Topic sentences will vary. Sample answers are given. **1.** To make things less stressful at home, I need to find a way to stop arguing with my sister. **2.** In order to get my homework done, I need to find at least an hour each night to study. **3.** I want to start eating healthier snacks. **4.** If I am going to make the team, then I have to start practicing every day. **5.** To be able to take part in after-school activities, I will have to find a ride home from school.

**162**   *Chapter 6*

## Practice B

Follow the steps to write a paragraph about a solution to a problem.

*Prewriting*

1. Choose one of the problems in Practice A.

2. Brainstorm possible solutions. Write several ways to solve the problem. Include ideas about who will solve the problem and when and where it should be solved. Also try to answer why the solutions will work.

3. Look at your list of ideas. Choose the solution(s) you like best. To help you decide, think about what kind of conclusion or summary you want to make.

*Drafting*

4. Use the topic sentence you wrote for Practice A or write a new one. It should state the problem.

5. Write the paragraph body. Explain the solution(s) to the problem. Refer to your brainstorming list for details. The details should support the conclusion or summary you want to make.

6. Write a summary or conclusion. It should sum up the solution(s) or make a closing judgment. You might want tell why the solution(s) will work.

*Revising and Editing*

7. Read the paragraph aloud. How does it sound? Revise your sentences. Use the checklist on page 134.

8. Edit your paragraph. Use the checklist on page 138. Use a dictionary to check spelling.

*Publishing*

9. Write the finished paragraph on a new sheet of paper.

10. Share your paragraph with another student or with your class.

*Reading Strategy:*
Inferencing

You already know something about solving problems. How does your knowledge add to what you have just read?

*Writing to Explain    Chapter 6    **163***

## Practice B

Review the steps in the writing process as you read through the steps together.

### *Practice B Answers*

Paragraphs will vary. Have students write a clean copy of their paragraphs after they have revised them. A sample paragraph is given.

In order to get my homework done, I need to find at least an hour each night to study. Most nights, by the time I have eaten dinner, relaxed, and talked to my friends, it is 9:30. Then I am too tired to study. I could change this around so that I study for an hour either before dinner or after dinner, but before I talk to my friends. Then the phone calls would be my reward. In about a week, I should see better scores at school.

### *Reading Strategy:* Inferencing

Students may say that their past experiences helped them know why it is important to identify the problem before you can solve it.

### LIFE SKILLS CONNECTION

Explain to students that problem-solving is a skill they will need all their lives. Point out that steps 1–3 on page 163 help them get ideas and plan a solution. Steps 4–6 help them work out the details. Steps 7–10 help them fix any flaws in their plan. Pass out the Life Skills Connection 6 worksheet and have students read the directions. After students ask any questions they have, have them complete the activity.

### Writing Practice

Have students read newspaper headlines and choose a problem. Write several choices on the board, phrasing them as problems to be solved. Have students form groups based on interest in a problem and write sentences that suggest solutions. As groups offer sentences, write them under the problems. Elicit from students which sentences could serve as a topic sentence and which could provide support.

*Writing to Explain*    **163**

Paragraphs will vary. They should include a clear statement of the problem, at least three sentences explaining a solution, and a summary or conclusion. Remind students to refer to the checklists on pages 134 and 138 to revise their work. Ask students to attach their notes and their rough drafts to their final copies.

### WRITE ABOUT IT

Students will need access to appropriate reference books or the Internet to complete the exercise. Explain that some references or sites deal with first names and others with surnames, or last names. See the Online Connection feature on page 167 for two possible Web sites to use. Instruct students to take notes.

## Six Traits of Writing Focus

| | | | |
|---|---|---|---|
| ✔ | Ideas | | Word Choice |
| | Organization | | Sentence Fluency |
| ✔ | Voice | | Conventions |

### Ideas

In this activity, students' ideas should focus on fulfilling their purpose: explaining the meaning of their name.

Suggest that students also work to establish a unique voice in their writing. Tell them a voice can be funny or serious depending on the subject, but, just like their speaking voice, it should be all their own.

Tell students to check page WPH1 for more instruction on the Six Traits of Writing.

---

## LESSON 6-5

# REVIEW

Write a paragraph that offers a solution to a problem. Follow these steps.

1. Write down a problem that you have now. This is your topic.

2. Brainstorm about your topic. Write down details and facts about the problem. Write down ideas for solving it. Then decide what solution(s) you want to focus on. Decide what conclusion or summary you want to make.

3. Write your paragraph. State the problem in the topic sentence. Write three sentences explaining how you can solve this problem. Use your details from brainstorming. Then write a summary or conclusion.

4. Revise and edit the paragraph. Use the checklists on pages 134 and 138. Write the final paragraph.

5. Publish your work in one of these ways:
   • Give your final paragraph to your teacher.
   • Read the paragraph to the class.
   • Exchange paragraphs with another student.

### WRITE ABOUT IT

**The History of Your Name**

Most names have a history. The name James comes from the Hebrew name Jacob, which means "grasps by the heel." This name appears in different forms in many languages, including Jakob (Afrikaans), Jacques (French), Kimo (Hawaiian), Giacomo (Italian), and Santiago (Spanish). Use a dictionary, a book of names, or the Internet to look up your name. Use the name of a relative if you cannot find your own name. Write a paragraph about its history.

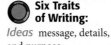

**Six Traits of Writing:**
*Ideas* message, details, and purpose

---

**164** *Chapter 6 Writing to Explain*

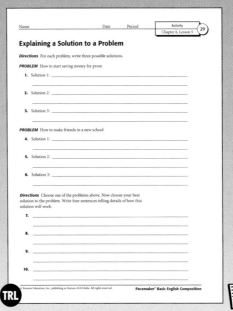

Activity 29

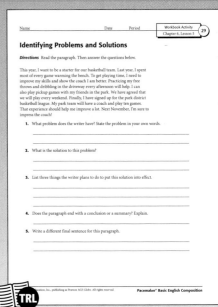

Workbook Activity 29

## Hospital Kitchen Helper

Andre Morris works as a helper in a hospital kitchen. He washes dishes and helps to prepare food. The hospital must prepare special foods for some patients. A new patient is allergic to nuts and bananas. Andre's supervisor wrote a note for Andre. Read the note below. Then answer the questions.

Mr. Winters, in Room 220A, cannot eat any nuts or bananas. He cannot have a food that contains nuts or has been touched by nuts. When you make today's fruit salad, make his special. First, wash the apples and celery on the counter. Then chop them. Next, wash the grapes and cut them in half. Mix the apples, celery, and grapes with spinach leaves. Set aside 2 cups of salad for Mr. Winters. Then add chopped nuts and bananas to the rest of the salad.

**1.** What does this paragraph explain?

**2.** What transitional words have been used to show the order of steps?

**3.** CRITICAL THINKING Why is it important for the writer to put the information in a special order?

### SPEAKING AND LISTENING

Work with a partner to give directions for how to make a book cover or tie a shoelace. Choose who will start. Demonstrate as you explain how to do the task. Be sure to include all the steps in order. Then switch roles. Listen and watch as your partner explains and demonstrates. Carefully follow your partner's directions.

*Writing to Explain    Chapter 6*    **165**

# WRITING ON THE JOB

Have students read the feature title and predict what a hospital kitchen helper does. Then ask students to read the feature and answer the questions.

### Writing on the Job Answers

**1.** The paragraph explains why a patient's salad must be prepared specially and gives directions for preparing it. **2.** When, First, Then, Next, Then **3.** The ingredients must be washed before cutting to get rid of germs. The nuts and bananas must be added last, after Mr. Winters' salad is set aside, or Andre will have to start over.

Writing on the Job 3

*Writing to Explain*    **165**

Talk with students about plagiarism. Emphasize the importance of putting ideas in their own words. Explain that this is not only right but also smart. Ideas that they can paraphrase are ideas that they have understood. Lead a discussion about specific problems students have in taking notes. Have other students offer methods that have worked for them. Then have students read the feature.

### Building Research Skills Answers

**1.** Martin Luther King Jr. civil rights, African-Americans, rights, Nobel Peace Prize, 1964 **2.** He worked to end the separation of black and white people. **3.** If you copy, you break the law. If you use your own words, you will be sure you understand what the source said.

## ELL/ESL Strategy

**Language Objective:** *To practice taking notes*

Students may find it challenging to paraphrase in English. Suggest that they retell important ideas from a source in their own language. Then they can work with an English-speaking partner to express their notes in English.

## Using Your Own Words

As you do research, you will want to take notes. If you use another writer's exact words, these words must be in quotation marks (" "). Usually, you use your own words to rewrite or summarize the ideas from a reference source. This is called paraphrasing.

As you read, ask yourself: What does this mean? What is another way to say this? Suppose you read these sentences:

> Martin Luther King Jr. was awarded the Nobel Peace Prize in 1964 to recognize his work in the Civil Rights Movement. Under his leadership, African Americans made progress toward gaining equal rights. The civil rights movement tried to end segregation.

You might rewrite these ideas in your own words like this:

> Martin Luther King Jr. was a civil rights leader who helped African Americans gain more rights. He worked to end the separation of black and white people. For his work, he won the Nobel Peace Prize in 1964.

Write the answer to each question.

**1.** What key words and phrases appear in both the source and the notes?

**2.** Which sentence in the notes puts "The civil rights movement tried to end segregation" into other words?

**3.** CRITICAL THINKING Why is it important to put ideas from a source into your own words?

 **MEDIA AND TECHNOLOGY**

Computers make it easy to copy, cut, and paste paragraphs from a source. Copying another writer's words without using quotation marks is called plagiarizing. It is against the law. If you do not want to quote a source, make sure you paraphrase the information. Practice summarizing information in your own words. Choose a paragraph from a textbook and summarize it.

# SUMMARY

- Use a how-to paragraph to explain how to do, make, or fix something. A reader who does not know anything about the topic should be able to understand your steps.

- Use transitional words and phrases to help order your steps.

- When you write to give information, your goal is to make something clear. You might do this by giving facts, explaining a meaning, or answering a question.

- When you write to compare, set up the comparison in the topic sentence. Use transitional words and phrases to help make the comparison.

- Compare two things by telling how they are alike and how they are different. When you contrast two things, you are telling how they are different.

- Use a comparison paragraph to explain why one thing is better or worse than another.

- Explain relationships between two related events in a cause-and-effect paragraph. First make sure the cause-and-effect relationship is reasonable.

- When you write to give a solution, your topic sentence should state the problem. The paragraph's body should explain the solution and give details about how and why it will work.

- Include these basic parts in all paragraphs: a topic sentence, a body, and a conclusion. The details in the body should support the main idea. The last sentence should sum up the paragraph or give a conclusion that makes sense.

## GROUP ACTIVITY

Work with a group to write a lesson. In the lesson, teach other students about an interesting animal. Gather information about the animal from an encyclopedia. Decide which facts you want to teach.

Tell how the animal acts and what causes it to act in this way. Practice teaching your lesson. Use pictures and activities to make it fun.

*Writing to Explain    Chapter 6*    **167**

## Chapter 6 Summary

Have volunteers read aloud each Summary item on page 167. Ask volunteers to explain the meaning of each item.

### ONLINE CONNECTION

To complete the Write About It activity on page 164, students may choose to find out about their given name, their surname, or both. The following site gives the history of first names from many different cultures:

www.agsglobepmbec.com/page167a

This site offers information about the meanings and origins of last names:

www.agsglobepmbec.com/page167b

### GROUP ACTIVITY

Provide encyclopedias, reference works on animals, and natural science magazines to groups. After they take notes, have groups make a plan, including activities for their "students" and any aids they will use. You may want to suggest that students use an outline and note cards for their presentation.

### WRITING PORTFOLIO

**Wrap-Up** Have students review their explanation draft and read it to a partner. The partner can ask questions and suggest revisions. Have students revise their paragraphs before writing a final, clean copy. This project may be used as an alternative form of assessment for the chapter.

## Chapter 6 Review

Use the Chapter Review to prepare students for tests and to reteach content from the chapter.

## Chapter 6 Mastery Test

The Teacher's Resource Library includes two forms of the Chapter 6 Mastery Test. Each test addresses the chapter Goals for Learning. An optional third page of additional critical-thinking items is included for each test. The difficulty level of the two forms is equivalent.

## *Review Answers*

### Part A

**1.** compare **2.** contrast **3.** cause-and-effect **4.** solution

### Part B

**5.** to compare **6.** to inform **7.** to show cause and effect **8.** to teach how to do something **9.** to explain a solution to a problem

### Part C

**10.** A **11.** A **12.** B

---

### Word Bank

cause-and-effect

compare

contrast

solution

### Answer Bank

to teach how to do something

to inform

to compare

to show cause and effect

to explain a solution to a problem

**Part A** Find the word or words in the Word Bank that complete each sentence. Write your answer on your paper.

1. To _____ is to tell how two things are alike or different.

2. To _____ is to show how two things are different.

3. A _____ paragraph explains how one event is related to another.

4. An answer to a problem is a _____.

**Part B** Read each topic sentence. Think about the purpose of a paragraph that might follow it. Write one of the purposes from the Answer Bank.

5. Pandas and bears are actually very different.

6. Standard time zones were set up in 1883.

7. A paragraph full of mistakes makes a bad impression.

8. The writing process involves five main steps.

9. There is no recycling program at my school.

**Part C** Read each event. Choose the cause that is reasonable. Write the letter of your answer.

10. Derek's soccer team won the game.
    **A** Derek scored three goals.
    **B** The other team was fast.
    **C** The team celebrated with a party.
    **D** It was the last game of the year.

11. Brandon found a part-time job.
    **A** Brandon saw a "Help Wanted" sign.
    **B** Brandon is a good student.
    **C** The gas station is closing.
    **D** Brandon quit his job.

**168** *Chapter 6 Writing to Explain*

---

**12.** A bill came in the mail for Luis.
- **A** Luis pays his bills on time.
- **B** Luis has a credit card.
- **C** Luis needs a new jacket.
- **D** Luis always checks the mail.

**Part D** Decide if each transitional word could be used to show how two things are alike or different. Write *alike* or *different* on your paper.

**13.** similarly     **16.** also

**14.** however     **17.** although

**15.** but     **18.** likewise

**Part E** Brainstorm ways to solve each problem. Then write a topic sentence stating the problem.

**19.** finishing an assignment on time

**20.** settling an argument with a friend

**21.** finding time to exercise

**22.** throwing a surprise party

**23.** starting a new club

**Test Tip**

In a writing test, carefully read and follow each prompt or direction. As you plan what to write, think back to class discussions. Use your own experiences to get details.

**Part F** For each prompt, write a paragraph of five sentences.

**24.** Write a paragraph that explains how to do something. Choose your own topic or choose one of these:
- how to cook an egg
- how to fix a flat tire
- how to go to a Web site

**25.** Write a paragraph about yourself. Explain why you are like or different from someone else.

## Review Answers

### Part D

**13.** alike **14.** different **15.** different **16.** alike **17.** different **18.** alike

### Part E

Topic sentences will vary. Sample answers are given. **19.** Researching and writing a report for history in just one week is a huge challenge. **20.** Ed and I have to settle our argument about which of us should try out for the lead in the class play. **21.** Although I don't seem to have enough time to sleep, I must somehow find time to exercise every day. **22.** This year is Dad's fortieth birthday, and we really want to surprise him with a big party. **23.** How could I interest other Springfield High students in starting a rock climbing club?

### Part F

**24.** Paragraphs will vary. All should include a topic sentence that states the process being explained, at least three detail sentences that outline the steps in order using time transitions, and a concluding or summarizing statement. **25.** Paragraphs will vary. All should include a topic sentence that names the things or people compared and a basis for comparison. They should organize three to five details that show likenesses and/or differences in a logical order using either a block or an alternate organization plan consistently. They should end with a summary or conclusion.

Chapter 6 Mastery Test B, pages 1–3

# Writing to Persuade

| | Student Pages | Student Lesson | | | Language Skills | | | | |
|---|---|---|---|---|---|---|---|---|---|
| | | Vocabulary | Practice Exercises | Lesson Review | Identification | Writing | Punctuation & Capitalization | Grammar & Usage | Listening, Speaking, & Viewing |
| **Lesson 7-1** Stating an Opinion | 173–175 | | ✔ | ✔ | ✔ | ✔ | ✔ | ✔ | ✔ |
| **Lesson 7-2** Separating Facts from Opinions | 176–180 | ✔ | ✔ | ✔ | ✔ | ✔ | ✔ | ✔ | ✔ |
| **Lesson 7-3** Supporting Your Opinion | 181–184 | ✔ | ✔ | ✔ | ✔ | ✔ | ✔ | ✔ | ✔ |
| **Lesson 7-4** Writing an Advertisement | 185–191 | ✔ | ✔ | ✔ | ✔ | ✔ | ✔ | ✔ | ✔ |

## Chapter Activities

**Teacher's Resource Library**
Life Skills Connection 7: Judging
  Advertisements
Writing Tip 7: Using Opinions and
  Facts to Persuade
English in Your Life 4: Writing a
  Cover Letter
Building Research Skills 7: Using
  Periodicals
Key Vocabulary Words 7

## Assessment Options

**Student Text**
Chapter 7 Review

**Teacher's Resource Library**
Chapter 7 Mastery Tests A and B
Chapters 1–7 Midterm Mastery Test

**Teacher's Edition**
Chapter 7 Writing Portfolio

| | Student Text Features | | | | | | | | | Teaching Strategies | | | | | | | | | Learning Styles | | | | | Teacher's Resource Library | | | |
|---|---|---|---|---|---|---|---|---|---|---|---|---|---|---|---|---|---|---|---|---|---|---|---|---|---|---|---|
| | English in Your Life | Writing on the Job | Building Research Skills | Vocabulary Builder | Grammar Builder | Write About It | Group Activity | Reading Strategy | Six Traits | ELL/ESL Strategy | Background Information | Common Error | Life Skills Connection | Applications (Home, Career, Community, Global) | Online Connection | Teacher Alert | Speaking & Presenting Practice | Writing/Spelling/Grammar Practice | Auditory/Verbal | Body/Kinesthetic | Interpersonal/Group Learning | Logical/Mathematical | Visual/Spatial | Activities | Modified Activities | Workbook Activities | Self-Study Guide |
| | | | | | | | | 173, 174 | | | 173 | | | 174 | | 174 | | | | | | 174 | | 30 | 30 | 30 | ✔ |
| | | | | 179 | 180 | | | 176, 179 | | 179 | 176 | 178, 179 | | 178 | 178 | | | 177, 180 | | 178 | 177 | | | 31 | 31 | 31 | ✔ |
| | | | | | | | | 181, 183 | | 182 | 181 | | | 183 | | | 183 | | 182 | | | | | 32 | 32 | 32 | ✔ |
| | 189 | | 190 | | | 188 | 191 | 185, 187 | 188 | 187, 190 | 185 | 186 | 186 | 189 | 191 | | | | | | | | 187 | 33 | 33 | 33 | ✔ |

## Pronunciation Key

| | | | | | | | | | | | | | |
|---|---|---|---|---|---|---|---|---|---|---|---|---|---|
| a | hat | e | let | ī | ice | ô | order | ů | put | sh | she | ə { | a in about |
| ā | age | ē | equal | o | hot | oi | oil | ü | rule | th | thin | | e in taken |
| ä | far | ėr | term | ō | open | ou | out | ch | child | ᵺ | then | | i in pencil |
| â | care | i | it | ȯ | saw | u | cup | ng | long | zh | measure | | o in lemon |
| | | | | | | | | | | | | | u in circus |

## Modified Activities

The Teacher's Resource Library (TRL) contains a set of lower-level worksheets called Modified Activities. These worksheets cover the same content as the standard Activities but are written at a lower reading level.

## Skill Track

Use Skill Track for *Basic English Composition* to monitor student progress and meet the demands of adequate yearly progress (AYP). Make informed instructional decisions with individual student and class reports of lesson and chapter assessments. With immediate and ongoing feedback, students will also see what they have learned and where they need more reinforcement and practice.

## Chapter 7:
## Writing to Persuade

**Skill Track for Basic English Composition**

**Teacher's Resource Library** TRL

**Activities**  30–33

**Modified Activities**  30–33

**Workbook Activities**  30–33

**Life Skills Connection**  7

**Writing Tip**  7

**English in Your Life**  4

**Building Research Skills**  7

**Key Vocabulary Words**  7

**Chapter 7 Self-Study Guide**

**Chapter 7 Mastery Tests A and B**

**Chapters 1–7 Midterm Mastery Test**

(Answer Keys for the Teacher's Resource Library begin on page 446 of the Teacher's Edition.)

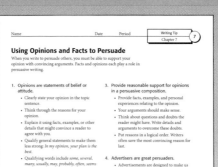

Name _____ Date _____ Period _____  Writing Tip 7 / Chapter 7

### Using Opinions and Facts to Persuade

When you write to persuade others, you must be able to support your opinion with convincing arguments. Facts and opinions each play a role in persuasive writing.

1. Opinions are statements of belief or attitude.
   - Clearly state your opinion in the topic sentence.
   - Think through the reasons for your opinion.
   - Explain it using facts, examples, or other details that might convince a reader to agree with you.
   - Qualify general statements to make them less strong: *In my opinion, my plan is the best.*
   - Qualifying words include *some, several, many, usually, may, probably, often, seems to, in some cases,* and others.

2. Facts are statements that can be proven.
   - There is evidence that a fact is true.
   - Broad generalizations are usually not facts. Show you know statements are not facts by qualifying them.
   - In persuasive writing, use facts to support your opinion.

3. Provide reasonable support for opinions in a persuasive composition.
   - Provide facts, examples, and personal experiences relating to the opinion.
   - Your arguments should make sense.
   - Think about questions and doubts the reader might have. Write details and arguments to overcome these doubts.
   - Put reasons in a logical order. Writers often save the most convincing reason for last.

4. Advertisers are great persuaders.
   - Advertisements are designed to make us want to buy a product.
   - Ads may promise benefits, suggest problems if the product is not bought, or show one product is better than another.
   - Clever, attention-getting words and pictures have a powerful persuasive effect.
   - Advertising slogans stick in the mind because they are short and clever.

**Pacemaker® Basic English Composition**

TRL

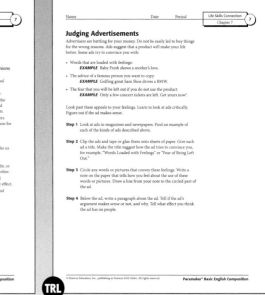

Name _____ Date _____ Period _____  Life Skills Connection 7 / Chapter 7

### Judging Advertisements

Advertisers are battling for your money. Do not be easily led to buy things for the wrong reasons. Ads suggest that a product will make your life better. Some ads try to convince you with:

- Words that are loaded with feelings:
  **EXAMPLE** Baby Fresh shows a mother's love.
- The advice of a famous person you want to copy:
  **EXAMPLE** Golfing great Sam Shoe drives a BMW.
- The fear that you will be left out if you do not use the product:
  **EXAMPLE** Only a few concert tickets are left. Get yours now!

Look past these appeals to your feelings. Learn to look at ads critically. Figure out if the ad makes sense.

**Step 1** Look at ads in magazines and newspapers. Find an example of each of the kinds of ads described above.

**Step 2** Clip the ads and tape or glue them onto sheets of paper. Give each ad a title. Make the title suggest how the ad tries to convince you, for example, "Words Loaded with Feelings" or "Fear of Being Left Out."

**Step 3** Circle any words or pictures that convey these feelings. Write a note on the paper that tells how you feel about the use of these words or pictures. Draw a line from your note to the circled part of the ad.

**Step 4** Below the ad, write a paragraph about the ad. Tell if the ad's argument makes sense or not, and why. Tell what effect you think the ad has on people.

**Pacemaker® Basic English Composition**

Writing Tip 7

Life Skills Connection 7

# Writing to Persuade

**W**hat do you think about ___? Teachers often ask students to tell their feelings and opinions. The students in the photo want to respond to something the teacher has asked. Perhaps they want to express their opinion and give reasons for it. In other words, perhaps they want to persuade. Every day, teachers and students try to persuade each other with actions and ideas.

You can also write to persuade your readers. In this kind of writing, you state your opinion clearly. Then you support it with strong reasons. Your goal is to convince your readers that you are right. In Chapter 7, you will learn how to recognize and state opinions. You will also learn to write a paragraph that persuades.

## GOALS FOR LEARNING

- To state an opinion and explain it
- To separate facts from opinions, and to qualify opinion statements
- To write a persuasive paragraph that includes supporting details
- To write an advertisement and a slogan

**171**

## Introducing the Chapter

Have students examine the photograph on page 170 and tell about what is happening. Ask students what kinds of questions the students might be answering. Will they give facts or opinions for answers? If they give opinions, how will they support them? Point out that writers sometimes must write to persuade—that is, to give an opinion and back it up with reasons. Have volunteers read the opening paragraphs aloud. Then encourage students to predict what a persuasive paragraph will contain.

Review and discuss the Goals for Learning on page 171.

## Notes

Ask volunteers to read the notes that appear in the margins throughout the chapter. Then discuss them with the class.

## TEACHER'S RESOURCE

The AGS Globe Teaching Strategies in English Transparencies may be used with this chapter. The transparencies add an interactive dimension to expand and enhance the *Basic English Composition* program content.

## WRITING PORTFOLIO

Ask students to think of an issue about which people disagree. The issue may apply to the school, the community, the state, the nation, or the world in general. Once they choose an issue, have students freewrite about their feelings on it. The writing may include questions, opinions, facts, reasons, or examples. Encourage students to read more about the issue in order to answer their questions. Have students keep their writings in their portfolio. Explain that they will develop their ideas into a letter to the editor as they complete the chapter. This project may be used as an alternative form of assessment for the chapter.

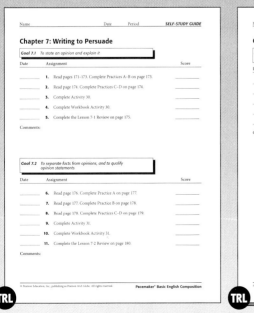

Chapter 7 Self-Study Guide, pages 1–3

## Reading Strategy: Metacognition

Ask students if they sometimes finish reading a page and realize they do not know what it was about. Explain that learning what reading strategies work best for them and thinking about how to use those strategies will help them become good readers. Using metacognition means asking themselves questions like these before reading: *What is my purpose for reading this lesson? What is the topic? What do I already know about the topic?* And questions like these during and after reading: *What am I doing to be sure I understand this? If it isn't working (or did not work), what else can I do?*

## Key Vocabulary Words

| | |
|---|---|
| advertisement | persuade |
| advertiser | qualify |
| fact | slogan |

Pair students. Have partners read and discuss the meanings of the words. Then ask them to clip a magazine or newspaper advertisement that includes both images and words. Have partners write sentences about the ad. They should use each key word in a different sentence giving an example from their ad. Invite partners to share their ads and sentences.

# Reading Strategy: Metacognition

Metacognition means "thinking about your thinking." To become a better reader, keep track of whether you understand what you read. To get more meaning from what you read, do these things:

- Preview the lesson.
- Make predictions. Ask yourself what you already know about the topic.
- Write the main idea, details, and any questions you have.
- Picture what is happening in the chapter.
- If something does not make sense, stop. Go back and read it again.

## Key Vocabulary Words

**Fact** A piece of information that is known to be true

**Qualify** To make a statement less strong; to limit the meaning of a statement

**Persuade** To convince someone to agree with an opinion, an idea, or a request; to change someone's opinion about something

**Advertisement** A message designed to attract the public's attention; also called an ad

**Advertiser** A person who uses an advertisement to sell a product or service

**Slogan** A short phrase or sentence designed to catch the public's attention

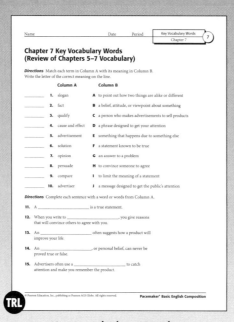

# Stating an Opinion

## Objectives

■ To write a sentence stating your opinion

■ To list reasons for your opinion

**Reading Strategy:**
Metacognition

Notice the structure of this lesson. Look at the lesson's Objectives. Look at the Example and Practices. Notice the blue subheadings on the next page.

In Chapter 5, you learned that an opinion is the way someone thinks about something. It is a belief or a viewpoint. Sometimes, you write to give your opinion on a topic.

▷ **EXAMPLE 1**

*Kidnapped,* a novel by Robert Louis Stevenson, is a great book.

Watching a play is more fun than seeing a movie.

Rock music is better than jazz.

### Practice A

Finish each sentence so that it states your opinion. Write the word or words on your paper.

1. The food in the school cafeteria is _____.

2. The city where I live needs _____.

3. To me, _____ is a waste of time.

4. People under age 25 are _____ drivers.

5. No one should buy _____ because _____.

### Practice B

Choose one of the sentences you completed in Practice A. Make a list of reasons for your opinion. Brainstorm by yourself or with another student.

## Chapter 7  Lesson 1

**Overview**  This lesson has students form opinions and explain them.

## Objectives

■ To write a sentence stating your opinion

■ To list reasons for your opinion

**Student Pages**  173–175

**Teacher's Resource Library** 🆀

Activity  30

Modified Activity  30

Workbook Activity  30

## Background Information

Most persuasive writing (and speaking) contains a mix of facts, statistics, and opinions. For this reason, it is crucial for students to be able to distinguish between facts and opinions. Encourage students to ask themselves questions such as *Is this accurate? Has it been proven true? How can I check it?* to determine whether statements presented as fact actually are fact. Any opinion, regardless of how well it is supported by evidence, is still a personal belief. People will have different views about it.

## 1  Warm-Up Activity

Write these sentences on the board:

*Chocolate is the world's best food.*

*Chocolate contains antioxidants.*

Ask students which statement is an opinion. *(the first one)* Have students tell how it differs from the second statement.

Now ask students to express their opinions about using cell phones in cars. Write the majority opinion on the board. Ask students to tell why the sentence on the board is an example of an opinion. Then ask them to give you a statement about cell phones that is not an opinion. Write one of these statements on the board.

## Practice A

Use sentence 1 to model opinion versus fact:

Opinion: *The food in the school cafeteria is delicious.*

Fact: *The food in the school cafeteria is $1 to $3 per item.*

## Practice A Answers

Answers will vary. Possible answers are given.  **1.** too salty  **2.** more activities for teens  **3.** being angry  **4.** dangerous  **5.** bottled water . . . tap water is perfectly healthy

## Practice B

Suggest that students select an opinion from Practice A for which they can list at least three reasons. Have students write their reasons as complete sentences.

## Practice B Answers

Answers will vary but should have a logical and reasonable connection to the viewpoint.

## Reading Strategy: Metacognition

Students may use the objectives, examples, practices, and blue subheadings to set a purpose for reading.

## 2 Teaching the Lesson

Write this sentence on the board: *Students today have too much homework.* Ask students to give their opinions, but tell them they must follow their opinions with at least one reason or fact that supports their opinion. Remind students that in persuasive writing, opinions must be supported with reasons and facts.

## 3 Reinforce and Extend

### TEACHER ALERT

Watch for circular reasoning in students' reasons. Explain that a statement that simply repeats the opinion in other language is not a reason: *Driver education classes should last longer because they are too short.*

## Practice C

Remind students that their opinions involve their beliefs or attitudes, not facts, which can be proven true. For example, *Eating vegetables is one way to get fiber* is a fact.

### Practice C Answers

Answers will vary. Sample answers are given. **1.** Eating vegetables is a delicious way to get your vitamins. **2.** Country music is better than opera. **3.** Playing computer games is a way to get valuable skills. **4.** Driver education classes should last one year, not one semester. **5.** Our family holiday parties are a lot of fun.

## Practice D

Students may find that the Practice C opinion about which they have the strongest feelings will be easiest to generate reasons for. Have students write a minimum of three reasons.

### Practice D Answers

Answers will vary. Sample answers are given. Eating vegetables is a delicious way to get your vitamins. Many vegetables, such as carrots and peppers, are sweet and have a satisfying crunch. Scientists have shown that your body can use the vitamins in whole foods better than the vitamins in a pill. There are dozens of kinds of vegetables, so you are sure to be able to find some you like at the store.

---

### Stating Your Opinion

It is important to be able to state your opinion. Think about the ideas that your friends and family believe are important. What do they feel strongly about? They probably have an opinion about these topics:

- having a pet
- foods they like
- the best car to drive

### Practice C

Write a sentence that states your opinion about each topic.

**Example:** dogs as pets
**Answer:** Most dogs are very loyal pets.

1. eating vegetables
2. country music
3. playing computer games
4. driver education classes
5. family holiday parties

### Explaining Your Opinion

Consider the reasons for your opinion. If you want someone to understand your opinion, you can explain it with facts, examples, or other details. Your explanation might convince the person to agree with you.

### Practice D

Choose one of the sentences that you wrote in Practice C. Make a list of reasons for this opinion.

**Example:** Most dogs are very loyal pets.
**Answer:** They bark whenever there is a noise.
They growl at strangers.
They comfort you when you are lonely or sad.
They are happy to see you when you come home.

> **Reading Strategy:** Metacognition
>
> What was this page about? If you do not know, reread the page and look for specific information.

---

### LEARNING STYLES

**Logical/Mathematical**

Have students clip a letter to the editor or an editorial from a local paper. Have them make a word web and write the writer's opinion in the center circle. Then have them list reasons, facts, and examples in the letter that explain the opinion. Ask students to place a star beside the details they find most convincing.

### AT HOME

Have students ask several family members and friends their opinions about two or three current-events issues. Students can write opinions about one issue in a group and compare their wording to note which opinions seem most strongly held. Ask students to write several sentences telling what they learned.

**Reading Strategy:** Metacognition

Students should find that the page was about how to state an opinion and explain reasons for it.

# REVIEW

Write a sentence on your paper that states your opinion about each topic.

1. cafeteria food

2. rock music

3. summer vacation

4. teenage drivers

5. getting a job

Read the paragraph. Then answer the questions.

The Mohawk 5000 is the safest car on the road today. Most cars have fiberglass bodies. The Mohawk is made of a new, secret material. It is harder than steel and impossible to dent. The Mohawk 5000 also has wider tires than those on most cars. The wide tires give a smooth ride. The Mohawk 5000 costs more than other cars, but its safety record makes it today's best automobile.

6. Who is the writer trying to persuade?

7. What is the writer's opinion of this car?

8. What is one way that this car is better than others?

9. Is the last sentence a summary or a conclusion?

10. Has the writer persuaded you? Why or why not?

*Writing to Persuade    Chapter 7*    **175**

## Lesson 7-1 Review Answers

Sentences 1–5 will vary. Possible opinions are given. **1.** Cafeteria food is bound to be boring. **2.** The world is a better place because of rock music. **3.** Summer vacation is too long and should be spread throughout the year. **4.** Teenage drivers should drive with an experienced adult driver in the car. **5.** Serious students should not get a job during the school year.

Answers 6–10 will vary in wording. Sample answers are given. **6.** The writer is trying to persuade adults that the Mohawk 5000 is the best car to buy. **7.** The writer feels that it is the safest and best automobile available. **8.** Answers may include that its body is hard and will not dent, that it has wider tires and a smoother ride than other cars, and that it has a (presumably) very good safety record. **9.** The last sentence is a conclusion. **10.** The writer has not considered enough factors. Nor has the writer given statistics or facts with specific comparisons to other cars. In addition, smoothness of ride does not show safety.

## WRITING PORTFOLIO

**Checkpoint** Have students refer to their freewriting notes about their chosen issue. Ask them to write their opinion about the issue on a new sheet of paper. They can look through their notes to find reasons to support their opinion and list these below the opinion.

Activity 30

Workbook Activity 30

*Writing to Persuade*    **175**

## Chapter 7 Lesson 2

**Overview** This lesson explains how to make opinions more reasonable by adding qualifying words and how to distinguish facts from opinions.

### Objectives

- To understand the difference between a fact and an opinion
- To use qualifying words in an opinion statement without changing the meaning

**Student Pages** 176–180

**Teacher's Resource Library**

Activity 31

Modified Activity 31

Workbook Activity 31

........................................

## Vocabulary

fact               qualify

Have students use each word in a sentence. Explain that *qualify* has a second meaning, "to limit or restrict in some way." Read the text definitions aloud, then ask students to give an example of a fact and a qualified remark.

........................................

## Background Information

In what ways can a fact be proved true? First, personal experience may prove a fact. (*It is raining outside*.) Second, an authoritative source such as a reference book or expert can provide proof. (*Washington became president in 1789*.) A statement may be framed as a fact and yet be false. Students need to learn to check facts to be sure they are accurate.

### 1   Warm-Up Activity

Return to the sentences from the Lesson 1 Warm-Up. Have students explain how they could find out whether *Chocolate contains antioxidants* is a fact.

---

# Separating Facts from Opinions

### Objectives

- To understand the difference between a fact and an opinion
- To use qualifying words in an opinion statement without changing the meaning

**Fact**
A piece of information that is known to be true

**Qualify**
To make a statement less strong; to limit the meaning of a statement

*Reading Strategy:*
Metacognition

Before you go on, stop and think. Do you understand what it means to qualify an opinion? If not, reread this page.

When you write a statement of opinion, make it clear that it is not a **fact.** A fact is something that is known to be true. When you give your opinion, you can **qualify** your statement or limit its meaning. When you qualify a statement, you make it less strong.

▶ **EXAMPLE 1**

| Not Qualified | Mrs. Lentz is a terrific boss. |
| Qualified | In my opinion, Mrs. Lentz is a terrific boss. |

The phrase *In my opinion* qualifies the statement. It lets the reader know that the statement is your opinion. It is not a fact.

When you make a general statement, decide if it is *always* true. If it is *not* always true, you can show this by qualifying the statement.

▶ **EXAMPLE 2**

| General | Teenagers are safe drivers. |
| Qualified | Many teenagers are safe drivers. |

You cannot prove that *all* teenagers are safe drivers. *Many* is a qualifying word. You might find facts to show that many teenagers are safe drivers.

---

### 2   Teaching the Lesson

Point out Example 1 to students. Ask them which opinion is more reasonable. Point out that qualifying words show the writer or speaker understands that the sentence is a personal belief, not a fact.

***Reading Strategy:*** Metacognition

Students' responses should depend on their understanding the concept of limiting meaning. If they have difficulty, suggest that they think of a fence that limits cows to a smaller area. A qualifying word or phrase limits an opinion so that it applies only to the writer.

## Practice A

Each sentence expresses someone's opinion. Find the qualifying word or phrase in each one. Write it on your paper.

1. Cafeteria food is usually too salty for me.

2. Some people think rock music is too loud.

3. People often take a vacation during the summer.

4. In my opinion, teenage drivers should take driver education classes.

5. For many people, getting a job for the first time is scary.

Sometimes an opinion statement is too general. If a statement does not apply to all situations, add words to limit it.

▶ EXAMPLE 3

| Not Qualified | Qualified |
| --- | --- |
| It will rain tomorrow. | It will probably rain tomorrow. |
| Dogs bark at cars. | The dogs I know bark at cars. |

Here are some words that you can use to qualify opinions or general statements.

### Qualifying Words

| | | | |
| --- | --- | --- | --- |
| some | apparently | seems to | in my opinion |
| several | probably | most | frequently |
| many | almost | might | in some cases |
| usually | often | it seems | approximately |
| may | sometimes | regularly | typically |

---

## Practice A

Have students list the qualifying words and phrases they read on page 177 before they complete the practice.

### Practice A Answers

1. usually  2. Some  3. often  4. In my opinion  5. For many people

## 3  Reinforce and Extend

### LEARNING STYLES

**Interpersonal/Group Learning**

Group students. Have them generate five sentences beginning "Everybody knows that ____." Then groups can play a game. Each team has a turn reading one of its sentences. If the sentence is too general, the opposing teams must add qualifying words. If the sentence is a fact, they must identify it as such. (For example, *Men are better drivers than women* is too general, but *You have to have a driver's license to drive a car by yourself* is a fact.) A team gets a point for every correction or identification of a fact.

## Spelling Practice

Have students write each qualifying word or phrase from the list on page 177 on a note card and divide words into syllables. In pairs, students can practice spelling the words by syllables. Encourage partners to think of mnemonics, or tricks, for learning difficult spellings. For example, *Al has the most (almost)*. Have students quiz each other on the words and focus extra attention on those that are most difficult.

## Practice B

Have a volunteer read the directions aloud. Point out that if a statement can be proved true, it is a fact and does not need to be qualified. Have students refer to the list of qualifying words on page 177 to make good choices.

### Practice B Answers

Answers will vary. Sample answers are given. **1.** not needed **2.** You will probably need to replace that car in five years. **3.** Many women love to dance. **4.** Some people love Judy Garland's singing. **5.** Dogs frequently chase mail carriers.

### COMMON ERROR

Have students avoid begging the question—assuming that an opinion is true. *Everyone knows that driver education is the best way to learn to drive.* Sentences that begin with "Everyone knows that . . ." often are not facts at all.

### LEARNING STYLES

**Body/Kinesthetic**
Write simple statements of fact and statements of opinion on note cards. Label two areas of the classroom "Fact" and "Opinion." Have each student draw a card, read the sentence aloud, and identify it as a fact or opinion. If the class agrees, the student moves to the correct labeled area. If the class does not agree, the student gives reasons. The class responds until a correct identification is reached.

### TEACHER ALERT

Not all fact-based statements turn out to be facts. Tell students that as readers they must not only separate facts from opinions but also be alert for misinformation. The Internet is rife with misinformation, some of which is accidental and some of which is intentional.

---

Decide if each statement needs to be qualified. If a statement needs to be qualified, rewrite it with a qualifying word or phrase. If it does not need qualifying words, write *not needed*.

1. Sonia parked the car in the garage.
2. You will need to replace that car in five years.
3. Women love to dance.
4. Everyone loves Judy Garland's singing.
5. Dogs chase mail carriers.

### Facts and Opinions

A fact is something that is known to be true. You can look up some facts in reference books such as almanacs.

You can recognize when a statement is an opinion and not a fact. Here are some words that often appear in opinion statements:

### Words That Show Opinion

| | | |
|---|---|---|
| best | favorite | always |
| never | good | bad |
| unimportant | important | worst |

▶ **EXAMPLE 4**

| | |
|---|---|
| Fact | Amber's family gets eight cable TV channels. |
| Opinion | Amber's family gets the best cable TV channels. |

*These friends do not agree on which flavor of frozen yogurt is best.*

### IN THE COMMUNITY

Have students work in small groups to brainstorm sentences for a tourism brochure for your town. Then have groups check their factual sentences. Finally, have students create a simple brochure using both facts and opinions. Have them add photos or drawings to illustrate.

## Practice C

Read each sentence. Decide if the writer is stating a fact or giving an opinion. Write *fact* or *opinion* on your paper.

1. The highest mountain is Mount Everest.
2. Strawberry ice cream tastes the best.
3. I received my high school diploma in June.
4. Summer is the nicest season of the year.
5. Being able to sing well is important.

## Practice D

Rewrite the opinion statements in Practice C. Change them to statements of fact.

**Reading Strategy:**
Metacognition

What is the most important idea in this lesson? Summarize what you have read to be sure you understand it.

## VOCABULARY BUILDER

### Using Euphemisms

A euphemism is a word or phrase that makes something bad sound better. Euphemisms try to persuade you that things are not really so bad. They may also be used to avoid sounding harsh. For example, company might say it was *letting people go* instead of saying it was *firing* them.

What do the following euphemisms really mean? Write your answers on your paper.

1. He **stretched the truth**.
2. She **passed away**.
3. Where is the **restroom**?

*Writing to Persuade    Chapter 7*    **179**

## Practice C

Before students complete the practice, have them explain why one sentence in Example 4 is a fact and the other is an opinion.

### *Practice C Answers*

1. fact 2. opinion 3. fact 4. opinion
5. opinion

## Practice D

You may also want to have students recast the statements of fact in Practice C as opinions.

### *Practice D Answers*

Answers will vary. Sample answers are given.
2. Strawberry ice cream contains more calories than strawberry sorbet. 4. Summer lasts from June 21 to September 21.
5. Most people need voice lessons to sing well.

### *Reading Strategy:* Metacognition

Sample answer: Distinguish facts, which are known to be true, from broad opinions, which are not always true, by using qualifying words.

## VOCABULARY BUILDER

Ask students to tell the difference between these sentences: *Grandfather was laid to rest. / Grandfather was buried.* Read the title of the activity and have students pronounce *euphemisms*. After they have read the text, ask students for examples of euphemisms. (*custodial engineer* for *janitor, strategic withdrawal* for *retreat*)

### *Vocabulary Builder Answers*

1. lied 2. died 3. toilet or bathroom

## COMMON ERROR

Many young people lack skill in evaluating language for logic. In addition, they hold strong opinions. Point out to students that broad generalizations (e.g., *teenagers are better drivers than old people*) left unqualified show bias, not logic.

## Lesson 7-2 Review Answers

**1.** Most **2.** Some **3.** In my opinion
**4.** Usually **5.** For many people **6.** fact
**7.** opinion **8.** opinion **9.** fact **10.** opinion

### Writing Practice

Have students write a paragraph explaining how they tell the difference between a fact and an opinion. Point out to students that their paragraphs should contain a topic sentence that states the main idea, at least three sentences that explain their procedure, and a conclusion or summary sentence.

### GRAMMAR BUILDER

Review the functions of adverbs. (See page 74.) Remind students that a prepositional phrase can act as an adverb. Then explain that a clause can do the same.

### Grammar Builder Answers

Answers will vary. Sample answers are given. Our family goes to Green Lake every summer for a week because we enjoy it. Although I was tired, I stayed up to finish my homework.

### Grammar Practice

Have students rewrite the following sentences, replacing the adverb with an adverb clause.

*Luis should win the election _easily_.*

*_Sometimes_, Mia eats lunch at home.*

### WRITING PORTFOLIO

**Checkpoint** Have students review their opinion and reasons to be sure the opinion is qualified. If possible, have them include facts in their support.

---

Each sentence expresses someone's opinion. Find the qualifying word or phrase in each one. Write it on your paper.

**1.** Most desserts are too sweet for me.

**2.** Some of my friends enjoy jazz music.

**3.** In my opinion, a vacation in the mountains is better than one at the beach.

**4.** Usually, the most current news is on television.

**5.** For many people, reading a newspaper starts their day.

Read each sentence. Decide if the writer is stating a fact or giving an opinion. Write *fact* or *opinion* on your paper.

**6.** Lesson 2 is about opinions and facts.

**7.** Everyone loves peanut butter.

**8.** Blue is a beautiful color.

**9.** Harvard University is in Massachusetts.

**10.** Everyone should buy this new CD.

### GRAMMAR BUILDER

**Punctuating Adverb Clauses**

An adverb clause works just like a one-word adverb. It answers a question about a verb, an adjective, or another adverb. At the beginning of a sentence, an adverb clause is set off with a comma. If it is placed later in the sentence, no comma is needed.

When practice is over, Brandon will go home.

Brandon will go home when practice is over.

Write two sentences using the adverb clauses below. Use one adverb clause at the beginning of a sentence. Use the other at the end of a sentence.

• because we enjoy it
• although I was tired

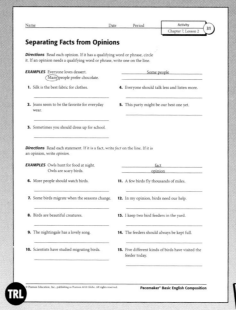

Activity 31

Workbook Activity 31

# LESSON 7-3

# Supporting Your Opinion

## Objectives

■ To support your opinion with facts and other details

■ To persuade other people to accept your ideas

**Persuade**

To convince someone to agree with an opinion, an idea, or a request; to change someone's opinion about something

Do you have a good idea? Would you like to **persuade** someone that your idea will work? Persuade means to cause someone to agree with an opinion, idea, or request. It means to convince. When you write to persuade, you give reasons that will convince someone to agree with you.

When you write a persuasive paragraph, keep these points in mind:

- Clearly state your opinion, idea, or request.
- Use reasons such as facts, examples, and personal experiences to support your opinion.
- Make sure your supporting details are reasonable. Your argument should make sense.
- Think about your reader's doubts. Try to overcome those doubts.

Suppose that Derek is applying for a scholarship to Western College. The application form asks, "Why do you deserve this scholarship?" Example 1 gives Derek's response.

▶ **EXAMPLE 1**

**Reading Strategy:**
Metacognition

Make a prediction about the content of a paragraph that persuades. Check your prediction at the end of the lesson.

   I think that I deserve a scholarship to Western College. I participate fully in school events. I am on the Springfield High School track team. I intend to continue running track in college. I know that Western College has high academic standards, and I look forward to the opportunity to learn. Although I was only a fair student when I began high school, I began to challenge myself at the end of my sophomore year. My grades have improved steadily. I work hard and take my studies seriously. I need this scholarship to continue my education. I hope you agree that I would be a successful and involved student at Western College.

*Writing to Persuade    Chapter 7    **181***

---

## 2  Teaching the Lesson

Have students name different kinds of writing and speaking that try to persuade others. *(political ads and letters, letters from charities, advertisements, issue-driven letters to the editor)* Discuss some ways these persuasive items try to influence people. Guide students to express that knowing when an argument is well reasoned is in their best interest.

---

## Lesson at a Glance

### Chapter 7  Lesson 3

**Overview**  This lesson explains how to build a good persuasive paragraph.

### Objectives

■ To support your opinion with facts and other details

■ To persuade other people to accept your ideas

**Student Pages**  181–184

**Teacher's Resource Library**

Activity 32

Modified Activity 32

Workbook Activity 32

..........................................................

## Vocabulary

**persuade**

Have a volunteer read the meaning of the term. Ask other volunteers to use *persuade* in a sentence.

..........................................................

## Background Information

Generally, a persuasive composition should be based on a debatable issue—one for which arguments can be made on both sides. Personal preferences express opinions but they cannot be resolved by presenting evidence. Once a topic has been selected, the writer should write a clear, specific position statement—one that leaves the reader certain of exactly where the writer stands.

## 1  Warm-Up Activity

Write a sentence like the following on the board: *Mom could not persuade Uncle Tim to stay for dinner.* Ask students to tell what Mom might have done or said to try to change Uncle Tim's mind. Explain that these words or actions are persuasive techniques.

### *Reading Strategy:* Metacognition

After previewing the lesson, students may predict that a persuasive paragraph will contain an opinion and sensible reasons for the opinion.

*Writing to Persuade*    **181**

## Practice A

Read the paragraph in Example 1 on page 181 aloud after students have read the directions for Practice A and previewed the questions.

### Practice A Answers

Wording of answers will vary. Possible answers are given. **1.** Derek is trying to persuade the scholarship committee of Western College. **2.** He wants the committee to award him a scholarship to the college. **3.** He explains that he is active in track, has worked hard to improve his grades, is a serious student, and needs a scholarship to be able to attend college. **4.** Derek improved his rather poor grades of early high school by studying hard. **5.** He concludes that he would be successful and involved in college life.

## Practice B

Discuss the six reasons Brandon has for playing with Derek in the tournament. Ask students for ideas about how to list the reasons in paragraph form. Point out that many persuasive writers like to end with their strongest reason.

### Practice B Answers

Answers will vary. Each paragraph should begin with a topic sentence in which Brandon states his goal—persuading Derek to join him in the next tournament. Each paragraph should also include the reasons from the list, a sentence that summarizes or concludes, and a title.

**3** **Reinforce and Extend**

### LEARNING STYLES

**Auditory/Verbal**

On slips of paper, print things a student might want to persuade someone to do—for example, play golf, bake cookies, join the drama club, or buy a new dress. Ask volunteers to draw a slip and then present a persuasive speech to the class for the chosen topic. After each persuasive speech, encourage students to suggest additional reasons the speaker could have used.

---

### Brush Up on the Basics

Make sure each sentence in a paragraph is a complete sentence. It must have a subject and predicate. It must express a complete idea. A dependent clause such as *if I go* cannot stand alone. See Grammar 2 in Appendix A.

### Practice A

Answer the questions about Derek's paragraph in Example 1.

1. Who is Derek trying to persuade?
2. What is he trying to persuade his readers to do?
3. What reasons does Derek give to support his topic sentence?
4. What problem did he overcome in high school?
5. What conclusion about himself does Derek make?

### Practice B

Brandon thinks that he and Derek can win the next tennis tournament. Imagine that you are Brandon. You want to persuade Derek to be your partner in the tennis tournament. Here are your reasons:

- I have been practicing.
- I have developed a better serve.
- I will practice with you every day.
- We both have experience. We will not be as nervous as we were last time.
- The other players are not very good.
- I have a strong wish to enter the tournament.

Write a paragraph that you will send to Derek. Use the above reasons. Follow these directions:

1. Write a topic sentence. State your request or position.
2. Use the list of reasons to write the body.
3. End your paragraph with a summary or conclusion.
4. Use the checklists on pages 134 and 138 to revise and edit your paragraph.
5. Write the final paragraph. Give it a title.

### ELL/ESL STRATEGY

**Language Objective:** *To increase conversational skills and to give advice*

Introduce the concept of asking for and giving advice. Together, brainstorm a list of problems students face in school. Provide some common sentence patterns used to give advice: *If I were you, I would . . ., I think you should . . ., Why don't you . . .?* Have students provide answers to a hypothetical student using the sentence patterns.

## Practice C

Derek does not want to be Brandon's partner in the next tennis tournament. Derek wants to persuade Brandon to find a different partner. Imagine that you are Derek. Write a paragraph to support your opinion. Follow these directions:

1. Begin your paragraph with a topic sentence.
2. Think of logical reasons why Brandon should find another tennis partner. Be convincing. Be creative. Use these reasons to write the body.
3. End your paragraph with a summary or a conclusion.
4. Use the checklists on pages 134 and 138 to revise and edit your paragraph.
5. Write the final paragraph. Give it a title.

## Practice D

Follow the directions to write a paragraph that persuades.

1. Choose one of the following main ideas, or make up your own.

   - Every school should have a computer center.
   - Everyone should exercise.
   - I should be hired for the job of (name of job).

2. Write your paragraph. State the main idea in a topic sentence. Persuade the reader by giving facts and other details in the body of your paragraph. End with a summary or a conclusion.
3. Edit and revise your paragraph. Use the checklists on pages 134 and 138.
4. Rewrite the final paragraph. Give it a title.
5. Read your paragraph to another student or to the class.

### Speaking and Presenting Practice

Ask students to create a one-minute speech based on the persuasive paragraph they wrote for Practice D. Explain that students should make an outline or note cards with key phrases and prompts for their main idea and for each reason, fact, or detail. After students have an opportunity to practice, have them present their speeches in class.

## Practice C

Have students offer ideas about why Derek, who prefers track to tennis, might not want to play in another tournament with Brandon.

### *Practice C Answers*

Answers will vary. Each paragraph should include a topic sentence, facts and logical reasons, a summary or conclusion, and a title.

## Practice D

Review the directions in steps 1–5 with students. Then have them write their paragraphs independently.

### *Practice D Answers*

Paragraphs will vary. Students may choose one of the topics listed or make up one of their own. Opinion statements should be supported by at least three supporting sentences of facts or reasons. Students should proofread, revise, and rewrite to make sure they have met the requirements listed.

### *Reading Strategy:* Metacognition

Students might ask themselves: *What do I already know about this? Does this make sense? What do I picture when I read this?*

## GLOBAL CONNECTION

Discuss some of the international issues that are currently in the news. Have students look over editorial pages of newspapers or magazines to find opinion essays. Together identify the writer's position. Evaluate the effectiveness of the written argument.

## WRITING PORTFOLIO

**Checkpoint** Have students write an editorial or letter to the editor using the opinions and reasons they generated in earlier lessons.

---

1. Read the topic sentence. Then choose at least five facts from the list that support the topic sentence. Write the sentences on your paper.

   **Topic sentence:** An atlas is a valuable book to have around the house.

   **Facts:**

   • An atlas has colorful maps.

   • An atlas has geographical facts.

   • An atlas might have statistics. It might tell the size of a country or how many people live there.

   • Some maps in an atlas show you where mountains, rivers, and lakes are.

   • We have our atlas on our coffee table.

   • The maps in an atlas usually give names of cities and towns.

   • I got an atlas for my birthday.

   • An atlas might have maps of only one country. Or, it might have maps of all countries.

   • Some atlases contain only road maps. You can use them to find a driving route.

2. Write the topic sentence shown above on your paper. Then write at least three more sentences that give details to support the topic sentence. Use some of the facts above or add facts of your own. Write a conclusion or summary sentence. Revise and edit your paragraph. Rewrite it if necessary.

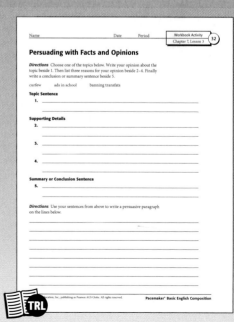

# Writing an Advertisement

### Objectives

■ To recognize messages that are advertisements

■ To create an advertisement

■ To create a slogan

**Advertisement**

A message designed to attract the public's attention; also called an ad

**Advertiser**

A person who uses an advertisement to sell a product or service

**Advertisements** make you want things you never knew you wanted. An advertisement, or ad, is a message designed to attract the public's attention. **Advertisers** are some of the greatest masters of persuasion. They use ads to persuade the public to buy a certain product or service.

An ad often tells or shows how a product will improve your life. The ad may not say, "Buy this! It will make your life better." Instead, the ad will suggest that idea. For example, an ad might suggest that a certain athletic shoe will make a person run very fast.

The quick track to speed and success
Wherever you go

QTrakk

### Practice A

Look at the advertisement above. Then answer the questions on your paper.

**1.** What is the main picture in this ad?

**2.** What product is the ad selling?

**3.** What is the reason for having wings in the logo?

**4.** What does the advertiser want the reader to think?

**5.** What does the advertiser want the reader to do?

*Reading Strategy:*
Metacognition

How does the example advertisement help you understand the purpose of advertising?

---

## 1   Warm-Up Activity

Invite students to tell about their favorite advertisement, describing why they find it persuasive. Ask students to try to identify the persuasive techniques in their chosen ad as they read the section.

## 2   Teaching the Lesson

Point out that their experiences with advertising illustrate making inferences. Since ads usually do not state the purpose directly ("Buy this product"), the audience takes in the suggestions and converts them into a decision that the product is valuable.

## Practice A

Have students describe what they see in the advertisement. Encourage them to explain why these specific details are used, that is, why do they influence viewers?

## *Practice A Answers*

Answers will vary. Samples are given.
**1.** The main picture is of a runner racing in a high, rugged, but beautiful area. **2.** The ad is selling running shoes. **3.** Wings in the logo suggest that the shoes make a runner "fly" or run very fast. **4.** The advertiser wants readers to think that the shoes will make them successful because they will be able to run faster. **5.** The advertiser wants the reader to buy the shoes.

### Chapter 7 Lesson 4

**Overview** This lesson looks at the persuasive art of advertising and has students try their hand at creating an ad and a slogan for a product.

### Objectives

■ To recognize messages that are advertisements

■ To create an advertisement

■ To create a slogan

### Student Pages 185–191

### Teacher's Resource Library

Activity 33

Modified Activity 33

Workbook Activity 33

Life Skills Connection 7

English in Your Life 4

Building Research Skills 7

......................................................

## Vocabulary

advertisement      slogan
advertiser

Have students identify the base word in the first two terms. *(advertise)* Point out that it is a verb. The endings *-er* and *-ment* change verbs to nouns. Have students predict the meaning of the two terms, then read all three terms' meanings. Finally, have students use each word in a sentence.

......................................................

## Background Information

The wings on the heels of the shoes in the ad are an allusion to the Roman god Mercury (to the Greeks, Hermes). Jupiter made Mercury chief messenger and cup-bearer to the gods and gave him wings for his heels (called *talaria*). These wings enabled him to fly faster than lightning to any place he wished.

### *Reading Strategy:* Metacognition

Students may say that the ad shows how details can be appealing or how words and images make the product appealing.

## Practice B

Have magazines and newspapers on hand for students to use. Suggest that students use questions like those in Practice A to analyze their ads. Have students mount their ads on paper or posterboard with enough space around the ad to label details that are persuasive.

### *Practice B Answers*

Answers will vary. Encourage students to use the text criteria of telling benefits of having the product, telling drawbacks of not having the product, or comparing a product favorably to another.

## Practice C

Set guidelines for the ads before assigning the practice. Point out, for example, that TV and radio ads require a script, actors, sound effects, and so on. Encourage students to be creative.

### *Practice C Answers*

Ads will vary greatly but should have words and images that attract attention and make clear why the product should be purchased.

**3**    **Reinforce and Extend**

### COMMON ERROR

Most people fail to look at ads critically. Point out to students that they need to evaluate the reasons the ad gives for buying the product. They are often not logical.

### LIFE SKILLS CONNECTION

Point out to students that understanding persuasive techniques will help them become smart consumers. Distribute copies of Life Skills Connection 7. After reading the directions and answering any questions, have students complete the activity in small groups.

---

**Slogan**

A short phrase or sentence designed to catch the public's attention

 **NOTE**

Advertisers also use ads to promote an idea or cause a certain action. Some ads try to persuade people to attend an event or vote a certain way.

---

Advertisers place their ads in various places. You see ads on TV. You hear ads on the radio. You read ads in magazines and newspapers. You receive ads in the mail. Web sites on the Internet also have ads.

Advertisers try to sell products in different ways. Some ads tell the benefits of having or using a product. Some ads tell what might happen if you do not have the product. Other ads tell why one product is better than a competing product.

### Practice B

Cut three ads out of a newspaper or magazine. For each one, explain how the advertiser is trying to sell the product. Look at the words and illustrations in the ad.

### Practice C

Create an ad for one of these products. It can be a TV, radio, magazine, or Internet ad. Share your ad with the class.

- a new cereal
- a new cleaning product
- a new movie
- a new car

### Slogans

Advertisers often use **slogans** to sell a product. A slogan is a short phrase designed to catch your attention.

▶ **EXAMPLE 1**

Super Smoothie hits the spot!

The new Tiger: car of the century

---

Slogans usually have these characteristics:

- Slogans are easy to remember. They may rhyme.
- Slogans are short.
- They say something that the advertiser wants you to remember.

### Practice D

Think of a slogan from an ad. Answer the questions on your paper.

1. What is the slogan?
2. What product is it trying to sell?
3. What facts does the slogan give about the product?
4. What is the main message of the slogan?
5. Why do you think you remembered this slogan?

### Practice E

Write a slogan for a product of your choice. It can be a real product or one you make up. Follow the guidelines below. Share your slogan with the class.

- Limit your slogan to 10 words or less.
- Make your slogan sound exciting.
- Use exaggeration.
- Use sharp, vivid words.
- Make it funny, inspirational, or both.
- Mention something that might make someone remember a happy memory.

## Practice D

Together with students, brainstorm a list of some well-known slogans, past and present. Invite volunteers to suggest why the slogans are so famous.

### *Practice D Answers*

Answers will vary. A sample answer is given. **1.** "Campbell's soup is M'm M'm good." **2.** It is trying to sell soup. **3.** It states that this brand of soup tastes good. **4.** The slogan's main message is to buy Campbell's soup because it is delicious. **5.** It is sung to a catchy tune and it uses a sound (mmm) that people make when they smell or taste something they really like.

## Practice E

Develop a slogan using the guidelines. Think aloud as you choose words that will stand out and associate the product with positive things.

### *Practice E Answers*

Slogans will vary. A sample slogan is given. "Come back to an old friend." (for a hotel chain) "The best air freshener ever." (for an air freshener)

---

**LEARNING STYLES**

**Visual/Spatial**

Have students analyze the ads they chose for Practice B. Students may copy and cut apart the ads or sketch elements of each ad onto grids of the same size. On one grid, students may place words in their original position. On another, they can sketch or paste in the central image. On a third, they can place any other elements, such as symbols. With a partner, students should discuss each element's effects and why it was placed as it was.

*Reading Strategy:* Metacognition

An ad should make the public want to buy a product in the fewest words and images possible. It should include only information that increases the product's appeal.

---

## ELL/ESL STRATEGY

**Language Objective:**
*To understand slogans*

Many ad slogans contain idioms or figurative expressions that give English language learners trouble. Have students copy the following slogans:

*You're <u>in good hands</u> with Allstate.*

*<u>Reach out</u> and <u>touch</u> someone.*

*Nothing <u>runs</u> like a Deere.*

*<u>Say it with flowers</u>.*

*Sometimes you <u>feel like a nut</u>, sometimes you don't.*

Have students use a dictionary and consult with other classmates to understand the meanings of the underlined words in the slogan's context. Students can make sketches or write brief explanations for the phrases beside the slogans to help them remember their meanings.

## Lesson 7-4 Review Answers

**1.** Paragraphs will vary. A sample paragraph is given.

The harder you work, the luckier you get. Most of us envy the lucky ones who succeed in life. In fact, most people who succeed in their chosen field have earned their success. A movie star is "born" overnight, it seems. An NFL quarterback becomes a sensation on the TV screen. A 21-year-old sets up an Internet business and becomes a millionaire. Usually, these successes occur because the person set a goal and worked hard for years to achieve it. Most successful people make their own "luck." **2.** Ads will vary but should include a script and any description or sketches needed for readers to understand what will appear in the ad.

## WRITE ABOUT IT

Read a local editorial to students. Help them identify the issue and the writer's opinion and reasons. If students decide to choose their own topic, help them brainstorm a list of school issues or problems that affect them, such as school space needs, scheduling, or lunch options. Refer students who will write a problem-solution paragraph to the guidelines on page 163.

## Six Traits of Writing Focus

| | | | |
|---|---|---|---|
| | Ideas | ✔ | Word Choice |
| | Organization | | Sentence Fluency |
| ✔ | Voice | | Conventions |

### Voice

Explain to students how using lively and heartfelt language can help them convince readers to care about their opinion. Tell them that if their voice comes across as half-hearted or insincere, no one will listen.

Point out to students that their editorials will be strengthened by careful word choice: precise nouns, strong verbs, and vivid adjectives.

Students can also refer to page WPH1 for more information on the Six Traits of Writing.

---

# REVIEW

1. People use slogans and sayings for inspiration. Choose a slogan from the list below. Write a persuasive paragraph. Use the slogan as your topic sentence or as your conclusion. (Do not write an ad.)

   - Take life one day at a time.
   - United we stand; divided we fall.
   - The pen is mightier than the sword.
   - The greater the obstacle, the more glory in overcoming it.
   - Be yourself. Who else is better qualified?
   - The harder you work, the luckier you get.

2. Choose one slogan listed above, or make up your own slogan. Use the slogan to write an ad for a product. The ad should include the slogan. Use your imagination. You can change the slogan to fit your product.

## WRITE ABOUT IT

### Your Opinion

In daily newspapers, you will find editorials. An editorial is an essay about a current event. The writer gives an opinion about the event or a related issue. Think of an issue that involves you and other students at school. Write a paragraph to explain the issue, your opinion about it, and your reasons. If the issue is a problem, explain how it should be solved. Support your opinion with facts, examples, or personal experiences. Choose your own topic or one of these:

- using cell phones in school
- standardized tests
- dress codes

Carefully revise and edit your editorial. Then share it with another student or give it to the editor of your school newspaper.

**Six Traits of Writing:**

*Voice*  the writer's own language

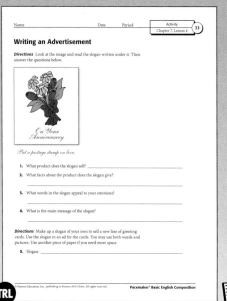

Activity 33

Workbook Activity 33

## Writing a Cover Letter

Zoey Luca is applying for a job at Fred's Foods. She has filled out a job application. To go with it, she wrote a cover letter. The cover letter introduces Zoey to the owner, Adam Miller. Its purpose is to persuade him that she should get the job. Read Zoey's letter. Then answer the questions below.

Dear Mr. Miller:

You advertised that you need someone to stock shelves. My experience fits this job well. I live only two blocks from Fred's Foods. Because I know your store very well, I know where everything goes on the shelves. Working summers for my dad's construction business has made me strong. I can carry heavy boxes. My dad and my teachers say I am dependable and work hard. I hope you agree I am right for the job.

Sincerely,

*Zoey Luca*

Zoey Luca

1. Why is knowing about the store a reason to hire Zoey?

2. Why does Zoey mention that she is strong?

3. **CRITICAL THINKING** Which of Zoey's reasons do you think is the best? Why?

 **VIEWING**

Look through the Help Wanted ads in a newspaper. Choose a job you would like to have one day. Read the ad carefully. Circle facts about the job. Make a list of traits and experiences you should have to do the job well. Then write reasons why you would be good for this job.

Explain to students that a cover letter is written by a job applicant. Like an advertisement, it should make the reader want the "product"—the person applying for the job. It is short but gives a summary of the applicant's strengths and qualifications for the job. Have students read the introductory paragraph and look at the picture. Ask a volunteer to read Zoey's letter aloud. Have students read along to identify reasons Zoey uses to convince Mr. Miller that she is the one for the job.

### English in Your Life Answers

Answers will vary. Sample answers are given.
**1.** Zoey would not have to be trained about store layout or type of merchandise.
**2.** Many products at the grocery store, such as canned goods, are heavy. She would have to carry boxes of these products to the aisles and place them on shelves of different heights. **3.** I think Zoey's reputation for being a dependable, hard worker is most important. This is a quality every boss hopes for in an employee.

### CAREER CONNECTION

 Ask interested students to locate facts about jobs in advertising. They can report on what the job is like, what it requires (education and skills), and personality types suited for the job.

Name _____ Date _____ Period _____    English in Your Life    4
Chapter 7

**Writing a Cover Letter**
Jim Tally is applying for a job in the library. He wrote the following letter to send with his application. He wants to convince the librarian, Ms. Coover, that he is the best person for the job. Read Jim's letter. Then answer the questions below.

Dear Ms. Coover:
I am applying for the job of library assistant. My school librarian, Mr. Hadley, suggested that this job is right for me. Here is why.
1. As a school library worker, I have learned how libraries are organized.
2. You need someone Wednesday evenings and Saturday mornings. I have this time free and live close to the library. I can easily walk to work in five minutes.
3. My teachers say I am pleasant to work with and eager to learn.
4. I really love books and think they are important.
I look forward to talking with you soon.
Sincerely,
*Jim Tally*
Jim Tally

1. Why is his work at the school library a good reason to hire Jim?

2. Why is living near the library an advantage?

3. **CRITICAL THINKING** Do you think it will be important to Ms. Coover that Jim loves books? Why or why not?

© Pearson Education, Inc., publishing as Pearson AGS Globe. All rights reserved.    **Pacemaker® Basic English Composition**

**TRL**

English in Your Life 4

Invite students to name their favorite magazines and tell why they enjoy reading them. Have volunteers read the text aloud. Ask students to explain how to read the partial table of contents on page 190 and predict what the articles are about. Display a magazine or journal and leaf through it so that students can see the pages. Ask them to identify it as a magazine or a journal and comment about the types of ads they notice.

### Building Research Skills Answers

**1.** A magazine lists its contents in the table of contents. **2.** A journal is more focused on one type of article, especially science and job-related information. **3.** The magazine prints ads because the advertisers have paid for space in the magazine. The editors have not approved or disapproved of the product.

## ELL/ESL STRATEGY

**Language Objective:** *To use pictures and words in ads in an oral vocabulary review*

Ads from Practice B on page 186 may be used to teach, practice, or review the vocabulary for the chapter and other words. Have students use the terms *advertisement, advertiser, slogan, opinion, fact, qualify,* and *persuade* as they describe and analyze the ads orally. Depending on their confidence, you may choose to provide sentence frameworks for them to fill in: *This (advertisement) is selling ____. It is trying to (persuade) you to ____. One (opinion) stated in the ad is ____.*

## Using Periodicals

A periodical is printed material that is published at regular times, such as every month. Magazines and journals are periodicals. A magazine includes articles, stories, photos, and more. A magazine focuses on one subject. For example, news magazines focus on the important news of the week. A journal usually reports on scientific research or presents ideas related to a certain type of job.

Like a book, a periodical has a table of contents, such as the sample below. It lists articles and the page number on which each one begins.

**CONTENTS**

SCIENCE AND TECHNOLOGY

| 37 | A Condo on the Moon |
| 52 | The FDA's Painkiller Warning: How to Avoid Taking Too Much |
| 71 | A New Alzheimer's Test? |

Periodicals include advertisements. The ads help pay to print the periodical. Remember, ads try to persuade you. Do not assume ads are facts. Look at the reasons they give for buying something. Are they reasonable? Are they fair?

Write the answer to each question below.

1. Where will you find a list of what is in a magazine?
2. What is one way a journal is different from a magazine?
3. CRITICAL THINKING An ad appears in a magazine. Does this mean the magazine thinks this is a good product for you to buy? Explain.

 **MEDIA**

Advertisements are made to sell products or services. Ads are all around you. You see them in periodicals and newspapers. You see and hear them on the Internet, TV, and radio. Write an advertisement to sell a product. The product can be real or imaginary.

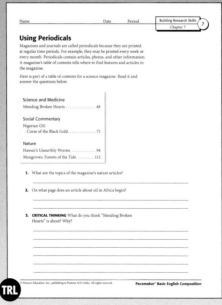

- State your opinion clearly.

- Explain your opinion with facts, examples, and personal experiences.

- Recognize when a statement is an opinion. Recognize statements of fact.

- When you write a statement of opinion, use qualifying words. Make it clear that the statement is not a fact.

- Qualify general statements of opinion if they do not apply to all situations.

- When you write a paragraph that persuades, you want to convince your reader to agree with you. Express your opinion in the topic sentence. In the body, give strong reasons that support your opinion. End with a summary or conclusion.

- Make sure your supporting reasons make sense.

- Try to overcome the doubts your reader might have.

- Advertisers create ads. An ad is a message designed to attract attention and sell something.

- When you write an ad, your goals are to attract attention and to persuade.

- Advertisers use slogans. A slogan is a short phrase designed to catch your attention.

- When you write a slogan, make it short and easy to remember. Say something you want your reader to remember.

## GROUP ACTIVITY

With a group, choose a favorite vegetable and write an advertisement for it. Tell why people should eat this vegetable. Begin by giving an opinion. Then give reasons, facts, and examples to support the opinion. Add art or photos cut from a magazine.

Make your vegetable sound as tempting as possible. Get together with another group and read your ads to each other. As you listen, pay attention to the reasons and facts that you think are best. Offer ideas for improving the ads.

## Chapter 7 Summary

Have volunteers read aloud each Summary item on page 191. Ask volunteers to explain the meaning of each item.

### ONLINE CONNECTION

 This Web site presents statements for students to identify as fact or opinion. It also provides scoring feedback.

www.agsglobepmbec.com/page191a

This site provides many links to other Web sites on persuasive writing. It is designed for secondary teachers and students.

www.agsglobepmbec.com/page191b

### GROUP ACTIVITY

Brainstorm and list on the board the names of vegetables students might use. Encourage students to use creativity, humor, and vivid language in their ads.

# Chapter 7 Review

Use the Chapter Review to prepare students for tests and to reteach content from the chapter.

## Chapter 7 Mastery Test

The Teacher's Resource Library includes two forms of the Chapter 7 Mastery Test. Each test addresses the chapter Goals for Learning. An optional third page of additional critical-thinking items is included for each test. The difficulty level of the two forms is equivalent.

The Teacher's Resource Library includes the Midterm Mastery Test. This test is pictured on page 443 of this Teacher's Edition. The Midterm Mastery Test assesses the major learning objectives for Chapters 1–7.

## *Review Answers*

### Part A
**1.** persuade **2.** qualify **3.** fact
**4.** advertisement **5.** slogan **6.** advertiser

### Part B
**7.** opinion **8.** opinion **9.** fact **10.** opinion
**11.** fact **12.** opinion **13.** opinion

### Part C
Answers will vary. Sample answers are given.
**14.** A little of the tropics in a bottle **15.** Hold your huddle at the hut with our new Team Pizza. **16.** The biggest screens at the lowest prices **17.** Because it's the SUPER Bowl, that's why! **18.** Alohas and luaus and leis, oh my!

---

### Word Bank
advertisement
advertiser
fact
persuade
qualify
slogan

**Part A** Find the word in the Word Bank that completes each sentence. Write your answer on your paper.

**1.** To _____ means to convince someone to agree with you.

**2.** When you _____ a statement, you make it less strong.

**3.** A piece of information that is known to be true is a _____.

**4.** To sell a product or service, you might create a public message called an _____.

**5.** A _____ is a short phrase or sentence that catches your attention.

**6.** An _____ is someone who uses an ad to sell something.

**Part B** Decide if each sentence is a statement of fact or an opinion. Write *fact* or *opinion* on your paper.

**7.** Floor hockey is more fun to play than ice hockey.

**8.** Rex is the world's greatest dog.

**9.** Amber is studying to become a lawyer.

**10.** People who have suffered write the best songs.

**11.** Sonia plays the violin in the orchestra.

**12.** You will need to replace that car in two months.

**13.** You should vote for Luis in the school election.

**Part C** Write a slogan to advertise each product or event.

**14.** a new fruit drink     **17.** the Super Bowl

**15.** a special pizza     **18.** a vacation to Hawaii

**16.** a sale on big-screen TVs

---

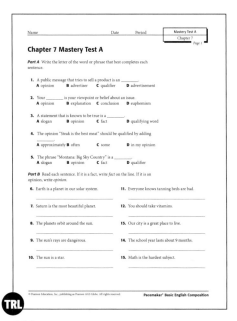

**Part D** Choose the word or phrase that qualifies, or *limits*, the statement. Write the letter of your answer.

19. When Rex barks at night, he _____ wakes up Amber.
    - **A** usually
    - **B** might
    - **C** always
    - **D** approximately

20. _____ broccoli is the best vegetable.
    - **A** Some
    - **B** Everyone thinks
    - **C** Regularly
    - **D** In my opinion

21. Derek _____ practices soccer after school.
    - **A** in my opinion
    - **B** often
    - **C** always
    - **D** may

22. _____ high school students have busy schedules.
    - **A** Most
    - **B** All
    - **C** Probably
    - **D** Approximately

**Part E** Follow the directions for each item.

23. Choose one of the opinion statements in Part B. (Do not choose a statement of fact.) Think about why someone might have that opinion. Write two reasons that support the opinion. Use your imagination.

24. Choose one of the products or events in Part C. Why might someone buy the product or go to the event? Write two reasons that an advertiser might use.

25. Choose one of the prompts below. Write a five-sentence paragraph that persuades.

    **Prompt A** Choose a topic and explain your opinion about it. State your opinion and give details to support it.

    **Prompt B** Think of something that you want. Persuade someone to give it to you. Give reasons why you deserve the item.

**Test Tip**

Look for key words in a test question or a writing prompt. These words may tell you the length or format of the answer.

## Review Answers

Part D

**19.** A **20.** D **21.** B **22.** A

Part E

Answers will vary. Sample answers are given. **23.** You should vote for Luis in the school election. The volunteer recycling program he started shows his strong leadership ability. Luis works well with adults and teenagers and can bring teachers and students together to resolve issues. **24.** People would go to the Super Bowl because it is exciting and full of drama. Also, it decides the best team, so it is historic. **25.** I should be allowed to get a part-time job after school. I could get my homework done in study hall or when I get home, so my grades would not suffer. The money I would earn would let me buy my own clothes and save for college, too. Most important, a job would teach me to be responsible and work with others. It is time for me to enter the adult world of work, at least part of each week.

## WRITING PORTFOLIO

**Wrap-Up** Have students read their editorial draft to a partner and get feedback. After they make any needed revisions, they can edit their editorials and make a clean copy. You may wish to have students publish their editorials in a classroom newspaper or send them to the school or local newspaper. This project may be used as an alternative form of assessment for the chapter.

---

**Chapter 7 Mastery Test B**

*Part A* Write the correct word from the Word Bank to complete each sentence.

1. A public message that tries to sell a product is an _____.

2. A catchy, short phrase or sentence that keeps a product in your mind is a _____.

3. Your _____ is your viewpoint or belief about an issue.

4. A statement that is known to be true is a _____.

5. If a statement is not always true, you should add words that _____ it.

6. To _____ is to convince someone to agree with you.

7. A persuasive paragraph should give good _____ for an opinion.

8. Someone who uses advertisements to sell products is an _____.

9. If something is not _____ true, it is not a fact.

10. An advertisement may tell you the _____ of having a product.

**Word Bank**
advertisement
advertiser
always
benefits
fact
opinion
persuade
qualify
reasons
slogan

*Part B* Read each sentence. If it is a fact, write *fact* on the line. If it is an opinion, write *opinion*.

11. People need to drink water.

12. Bottled water is a waste of money.

13. Your body is about 70% water.

14. Cherry lemonade is the best drink.

15. Everyone should take vitamins.

---

**Chapter 7 Mastery Test B,** continued

*Part C* Read the paragraph. Then circle the word that completes each sentence below.

1. People should not drive a car if they have been drinking alcohol. 2. For one thing, alcohol weakens your ability to react quickly to make good judgments. 3. Sadly, many people die every year because of drunk drivers. 4. Don't drink and drive. 5. The life you save may be your own.

16. Sentence 1 of the paragraph gives (an opinion, a slogan).

17. In sentence 3, the word *many* is (a qualifier, an opinion).

18. Sentence 5 of the paragraph is (a fact, a slogan).

19. The purpose of this paragraph is to (persuade, tell a story).

20. A sentence that gives a reason is sentence (3, 4).

*Part D* Follow the directions for each item.

Write your opinion about each topic.

21. cell phones

22. dating

23. the color purple

24. homework

25. reality TV

Write a slogan for each product.

26. a new cereal

27. a coat

28. an electric car

Pick one product from **26–28**. Write two reasons people should buy it.

29.

30.

---

**Chapter 7 Mastery Test B,** continued

*Part E* Write your answer to each question. Use complete sentences. Support each answer with facts and examples from the textbook.

31. When should you use words such as *usually* and *in my opinion* in a statement?

32. How can you tell if a statement is a fact?

*Part F* Write a paragraph for each topic. Include a topic sentence, body, and conclusion in the paragraph. Support your answers with facts and examples from the textbook.

33. List three ways advertisers persuade you to buy products.

34. Explain why it is important to be able to write persuasive paragraphs.

# Writing to Describe

| | Student Pages | Student Lesson | | | Language Skills | | | | |
|---|---|---|---|---|---|---|---|---|---|
| | | Vocabulary | Practice Exercises | Lesson Review | Identification | Writing | Punctuation & Capitalization | Grammar & Usage | Listening, Speaking, & Viewing |
| **Lesson 8-1** Choosing Words That Appeal to the Senses | 197–201 | ✔ | ✔ | ✔ | ✔ | ✔ | ✔ | ✔ | ✔ |
| **Lesson 8-2** Choosing Specific Words | 202–205 | ✔ | ✔ | ✔ | ✔ | ✔ | ✔ | ✔ | ✔ |
| **Lesson 8-3** Using Figures of Speech | 206–209 | ✔ | ✔ | ✔ | ✔ | ✔ | ✔ | ✔ | ✔ |
| **Lesson 8-4** Developing a Writing Style | 210–215 | ✔ | ✔ | ✔ | ✔ | ✔ | ✔ | ✔ | ✔ |

## Chapter Activities

**Teacher's Resource Library**
Life Skills Connection 8: Using
Specific Words in Directions
Writing Tip 8: Using Vivid, Exact
Words to Describe
Writing on the Job 4: Pet Store
Worker
Building Research Skills 8:
Using Graphs and Tables
Key Vocabulary Words 8

## Assessment Options

**Student Text**
Chapter 8 Review

**Teacher's Resource Library**
Chapter 8 Mastery Tests A and B

**Teacher's Edition**
Chapter 8 Writing Portfolio

| English in Your Life | Writing on the Job | Building Research Skills | Vocabulary Builder | Grammar Builder | Write About It | Group Activity | Reading Strategy | Six Traits | ELL/ESL Strategy | Background Information | Common Error | Life Skills Connection | Applications (Home, Career, Community, Global) | Online Connection | Teacher Alert | Speaking & Presenting Practice | Writing/Spelling/Grammar Practice | Auditory/Verbal | Body/Kinesthetic | Interpersonal/Group Learning | Logical/Mathematical | Visual/Spatial | Activities | Modified Activities | Workbook Activities | Self-Study Guide |
|---|---|---|---|---|---|---|---|---|---|---|---|---|---|---|---|---|---|---|---|---|---|---|---|---|---|---|
| | | | 201 | 199 | | | 197, 200 | | 199 | 197 | | | 199 | | 198 | 200 | 200 | 198 | | | | | 34 | 34 | 34 | ✔ |
| | | | | | 205 | | 202, 204 | 205 | 204 | 202 | 203, 204 | 203 | 205 | | 203 | | | | 204 | | 203 | | 35 | 35 | 35 | ✔ |
| | | | | | | | 207, 208 | | 207 | 206 | 207 | | 208 | | 208 | | 209 | | | 208 | | 209 | 36 | 36 | 36 | ✔ |
| 213 | 214 | | | | | 215 | 211 | | 211 | 210 | 211 | | 212 | 215 | | | 213 | | | | | | 37 | 37 | 37 | ✔ |

## Pronunciation Key

| | | | | | | | | | | | |
|---|---|---|---|---|---|---|---|---|---|---|---|
| a | hat | e | let | ī | ice | ô | order | u̇ | put | sh | she |
| ā | age | ē | equal | o | hot | oi | oil | ü | rule | th | thin |
| ä | far | ėr | term | ō | open | ou | out | ch | child | ₮H | then |
| â | care | i | it | ȯ | saw | u | cup | ng | long | zh | measure |

ə { a in about / e in taken / i in pencil / o in lemon / u in circus }

## Modified Activities

The Teacher's Resource Library (TRL) contains a set of lower-level worksheets called Modified Activities. These worksheets cover the same content as the standard Activities but are written at a lower reading level.

## Skill Track

Use Skill Track for *Basic English Composition* to monitor student progress and meet the demands of adequate yearly progress (AYP). Make informed instructional decisions with individual student and class reports of lesson and chapter assessments. With immediate and ongoing feedback, students will also see what they have learned and where they need more reinforcement and practice.

**Using Vivid, Exact Words to Describe**

When you write to describe, you want your writing to be crystal clear. This clearness comes from using exactly the right words and just enough words. The subject of a good description comes to life for the reader.

1. Use sensory images.
   - Appeal to the senses of smell, hearing, touch, taste, and sight. This makes readers pay attention with all their senses.
   - Details that appeal to the senses are sensory images.
   - Alliteration creates interesting sound effects by repeating the first sound in several words.

2. Use specific words to create a clear and correct picture in the reader's mind.
   - Specific nouns name particular things: "We ate *chili*," not "We ate *food*."
   - Specific verbs tell exactly what the subject did: "The wolf *snarled*," instead of "The wolf *made a noise*."
   - Specific adjectives focus the picture you paint with words: "a *friendly, talkative* woman," not "a *nice* woman"

3. Appeal to the imagination with vivid figures of speech.
   - Metaphors compare two things directly: The ice was glass.
   - Similes compare two things indirectly using *like* or *as*: He leaped off the starting blocks like a bullet.
   - Personification gives nonhuman things human qualities: The willows wept.
   - Exaggeration adds fun and color to writing by making things sound greater than they really are: a diamond the size of Texas. A little exaggeration goes a long way. Don't overdo it.

4. Develop your writing style with many elements.
   - Choose specific, vivid words.
   - Use figures of speech.
   - Vary sentence lengths and kinds for interest and rhythm.
   - Choose a topic that interests you and show your interest.
   - Include enough descriptive detail.
   - Use exactly the right words. Do not be wordy.

Pacemaker® Basic English Composition

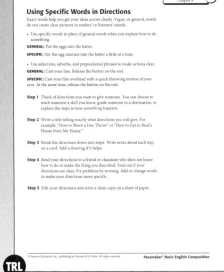

**Using Specific Words in Directions**

Exact words help you get your ideas across clearly. Vague, or general, words do not create clear pictures in readers' or listeners' minds.

- Use specific words in place of general words when you explain how to do something.

**GENERAL:** Put the eggs into the batter.

**SPECIFIC:** Stir the egg mixture into the batter a little at a time.

- Use adjectives, adverbs, and prepositional phrases to make actions clear.

**GENERAL:** Cast your line. Release the button on the reel.

**SPECIFIC:** Cast your line overhead with a quick throwing motion of your arm. At the same time, release the button on the reel.

**Step 1** Think of directions you want to give someone. You can choose to teach someone a skill you know, guide someone to a destination, or explain the steps in how something happens.

**Step 2** Write a title telling exactly what directions you will give. For example, "How to Shoot a Free Throw" or "How to Get to Brad's House from My House."

**Step 3** Break the directions down into steps. Write notes about each step on a card. Add a drawing if it helps.

**Step 4** Read your directions to a friend or classmate who does not know how to do or make the thing you described. Find out if your directions are clear. Fix problems by revising. Add or change words to make your directions more specific.

**Step 5** Edit your directions and write a clean copy on a sheet of paper.

Pacemaker® Basic English Composition

Writing Tip 8

Life Skills Connection 8

# Writing to Describe

Lunchtime! When hungry students get their lunch, they can't wait to dig in. Can you imagine how the lunch in this photo tastes and smells? The bread looks fresh and soft. The milk might be ice cold. The orange slices will no doubt taste tangy and sweet. Your enjoyment of food comes through your senses.

When you write to describe something, your goal is to create a vivid mental picture. To do this, you need to use words that appeal to the senses. You also need to use specific words, not general ones. If you described the lunch in the photo as *good*, no one could tell exactly what you meant. Words like *fresh* and *tangy* are more specific.

In Chapter 8, you will learn how to choose specific words and make vivid comparisons. You will learn how to write a good description.

## GOALS FOR LEARNING

- To choose words that appeal to the senses
- To choose specific words instead of general words
- To use metaphors, similes, personification, and exaggeration
- To develop a writing style

**195**

## Introducing the Chapter

Have students examine the photograph on page 194 and describe it. If students limit their descriptions to visual cues only, ask them to imagine being there. Have them add details about the tastes, smells, sounds, and feelings they would get from the food. Explain that descriptive writing uses details that make you feel as though you are really there. This means using details that involve all of the senses.

Have students read the introductory paragraphs and Goals for Learning. Then have them predict what they will find out as they read the chapter.

## Notes

Ask volunteers to read the notes that appear in the margins throughout the chapter. Then discuss them with the class.

## TEACHER'S RESOURCE

The AGS Globe Teaching Strategies in English Transparencies may be used with this chapter. The transparencies add an interactive dimension to expand and enhance the *Basic English Composition* program content.

## WRITING PORTFOLIO

Have students choose an object they know well and like. Explain that they will be writing a description of it for a person who has never seen it before. Have students write their topic in a word web and brainstorm interesting details about the object. Ask students to save their work and add to it as they complete the chapter. This project may be used as an alternative form of assessment for the chapter.

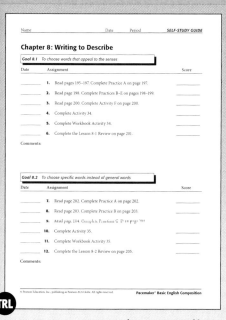

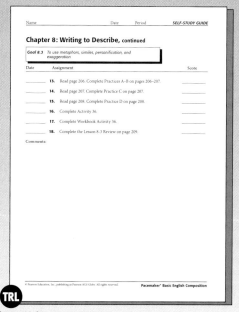

Chapter 8 Self-Study Guide, pages 1–3

## Reading Strategy: Visualizing

Ask students what part they think imagination plays in reading. (*They may suggest that it makes the words "come to life" or makes them feel as though they are inside the action.*) Explain that good readers notice details in writing and try to picture them. Have students read the text to learn tips for visualizing, then tell which of the tips they have used when reading.

........................................................

## Key Vocabulary Words

alliteration          personification
connotation          sensory image
exaggeration         simile
figure of speech     style
metaphor

Say the words aloud and have students repeat them before they read the meanings. Point out mnemonics students might use to learn the words: *A simile will put an extra* i *in your smile.* Encourage them to think of their own mnemonics. Read each meaning aloud and have students identify the matching word.

........................................................

# Reading Strategy: Visualizing

When you read, try to picture what the writer is describing or explaining. Use your imagination to picture whatever the words say. For example, you might:

- Look for words that remind you of your own experiences. Also look for words that help you to create a mental picture.
- Think of pictures to go with what the writer is talking about.
- Use pictures and diagrams to help you understand and organize the main ideas.

## Key Vocabulary Words

**Sensory image**  A word, phrase, or sentence that appeals to one or more senses

**Alliteration**  Two or more words in the same sentence that begin with the same sound

**Connotation**  An idea or feeling associated with a word

**Figure of speech**  An expression that a writer uses for a particular purpose

**Metaphor**  An expression that shows that two things are alike in some way

**Simile**  An expression using *like* or *as* that shows that two things are alike in a certain way

**Personification**  Giving human qualities to animals or objects

**Exaggeration**  An overstatement that says something is greater than it is

**Style**  A writer's individual way of using words

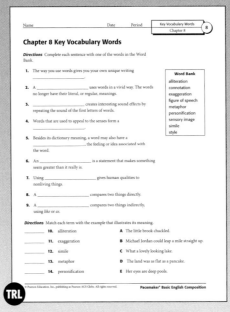

# Choosing Words That Appeal to the Senses

**Objectives**

- To recognize sensory images
- To use sensory images in your writing
- To recognize and use alliteration

**Sensory image**

A word, phrase, or sentence that appeals to one or more senses

**Reading Strategy:**
Visualizing

What words in the example help you picture what you are reading?

Good writers use **sensory images.** A sensory image is a word, phrase, or sentence that appeals to one or more senses. Sensory images appeal to the reader's touch, sight, taste, smell, and hearing. A writer uses sensory images to create a mental picture for the reader.

▶ **EXAMPLE 1**

| Touch | The puppy's nose was cold and wet. |
| Sight | Streaks of red and orange glow in the sky. |
| Taste | Luis gulped ice water after eating the spicy chili. |
| Smell | The baking bread drew Amber to the kitchen. |
| Hearing | The cheers of the crowd grew loud and angry. |

## Practice A

Read each sentence. Choose the sense to which the writer is trying to appeal. Write *touch, sight, taste, smell,* or *hearing* on your paper.

1. The hummingbird's wings hummed quietly.
2. The sweet sugar syrup drew the bird to the feeder.
3. The tiny birds enjoy the fragrance of the flowers in the garden.
4. The feathers of the hummingbird look soft and smooth.
5. The bright red patch at the throat gives the ruby-throated hummingbird its name.

*Writing to Describe* Chapter 8 **197**

---

## Lesson at a Glance

### Chapter 8  Lesson 1

**Overview** This lesson explains the use of sensory images and alliteration in descriptive writing.

### Objectives

- To recognize sensory images
- To use sensory images in your writing
- To recognize and use alliteration

### Student Pages 197–201

### Teacher's Resource Library

Activity 34

Modified Activity 34

Workbook Activity 34

### Vocabulary

alliteration          sensory image

Write on the board *The snow fell soft as silk.* Have students identify the beginning sound that repeats. *(s)* Explain that this technique, called alliteration, produces a kind of sound effect. Compare the words *sense* and *sensory.* Point out that something is sensory if it comes to us through our senses. Have volunteers read the meanings of the terms aloud and suggest examples.

### Background Information

Most people use the sense of sight most often to get information about an object. They rely primarily on visual images to describe. Though the other senses don't seem as important, it is all the senses working together that allow us to provide complete descriptions. Science has shown that smell is a very powerful trigger of memories. Beginning writers need to be encouraged to add more sensory images involving the four underused senses.

---

## 1  Warm-Up Activity

Ask students to name the five senses. Invite volunteers to suggest one detail from each sense to describe a hot slice of cinnamon bread.

## 2  Teaching the Lesson

Use the Reading Strategy question in the margin on page 197 with Example 1 to pinpoint descriptive words in the sentences. Ask students to identify the part of speech of each word. Point out that sensory images are sharpened by specific adjectives.

## Practice A

Answer any questions students may have about Example 1 before assigning this practice. If a sentence appeals to more than one sense, have students write the sense that has the stronger appeal.

## Practice A Answers

1. hearing  2. taste  3. smell  4. touch
5. sight

## Reading Strategy: Visualizing

Students may mention *cold, wet, red, orange, glow, ice water, spicy, baking bread, cheers, loud, angry.*

## Practice B

Explain that students should keep their chosen objects secret. Their descriptions will make readers focus on the object's details to guess what it is.

### Practice B Answers

Answers will vary but should include details that involve all the senses. A sample answer is given.
It can lie flat like a snowy blanket. Papery thin and soft, it whispers when I bunch it up. Balled up in the fist, it waits to comfort the distressed. It tickles the nose as though dust had settled there. (tissue)

## Practice C

Encourage students to choose a place about which they have vivid impressions from all their senses, not just sight.

### Practice C Answers

Paragraphs will vary but should include a topic sentence that names the place described, supporting detail sentences with sensory images that appeal to several senses, and a conclusion or summary sentence.

## 3 Reinforce and Extend

### TEACHER ALERT

Writing is seldom purely descriptive. More often, description is sprinkled in narrative, expository, and persuasive writing to enliven it. However, when students write a description, encourage them to organize its details spatially, moving logically from one side (region, or feature) to another. For example, one's home could be described from roof to ground or from entry to back door.

---

**Alliteration**
Two or more words in the same sentence that begin with the same sound

When you write to describe something, use all of your writing skills. Use words to create a picture in the reader's mind.

### Practice B

1. Choose an object in the room where you are. Write a description of it, but do not name the object. Answer some of these questions in your description:

   - How big is it compared to other things in the room?
   - What is it used for?
   - What sound does it make? What sound could it make?
   - How would it feel if you touched it?
   - How does it smell or taste?
   - What color is it? What does it look like?

2. When you are finished, exchange papers with another student. See if that person can guess what you described.

### Practice C

Write a paragraph to describe one of the places listed below. Use sensory images to help your reader imagine the place. Include details about the way it looks, feels, tastes, smells, or sounds.

   - your home
   - your school or classroom
   - a park
   - a shopping mall or restaurant

When two or more words in the same sentence start with the same sound, this is **alliteration.** Alliteration appeals to the reader's sense of sound.

▶ **EXAMPLE 2**

It was a soft spring day.

The sleeping city sidewalks disappeared in the fog.

They jumped headlong into the huge haystack.

### LEARNING STYLES

**Auditory/Verbal**
Have students select a poem, jingle, or lyric that uses alliteration to create an effect. After they have practiced reading their selections aloud, ask volunteers to recite them to the class. The audience should listen for beginning sounds that repeat and jot these down. Ask students to describe the effect of the alliteration in each presentation.

## Practice D

Find the alliteration in each sentence. On your paper, write the words that create the alliteration.

1. The title of the play was *The Sweet Smell of Success.*
2. The scent of salt filled the air near the ocean.
3. The red rose attracted his attention.
4. The frown was frozen on her face.
5. The farmer told him to dig deeper into the dirt.

## Practice E

Create five examples of alliteration to describe how you feel today. Use your own words or start with these: *lively, friendly, nervous, proud, confident, peaceful,* or *puzzled.*

**Example:** I was so surprised by Sunday's storm!

### GRAMMAR BUILDER

**Using the Information in a Dictionary Entry**
A dictionary helps you use and say words. It shows a word's spelling and syllables. In addition, a dictionary entry gives the part of speech and different forms of the word. Look at the sample entry for the word *choose.*

choose \chüz\ *v.* chose, cho-sen, choos-ing
1. to select from a group: choose an answer  2. to decide or prefer to do something: chose to remain  choos-er *n.*

Use the sample entry to answer these questions.
1. What part of speech is the word *choose*?
2. How do you make *choose* into a noun?
3. How many syllables does *chosen* have?

---

## Practice D

Ask students to explain in their own words what alliteration is. Then have them read the directions and complete the practice.

### Practice D Answers
**1.** *Sweet Smell, Success*  **2.** scent, salt  **3.** red rose  **4.** frown, frozen, face  **5.** dig deeper, dirt

## Practice E

Students might brainstorm a list of words that begin with the same sound as a key word in each example. They could also use a thesaurus to find synonyms that begin with the desired letter.

### Practice E Answers
Answers will vary but should be sentences including at least three words that begin with the same sound. A sample answer is given: It was Lucy's lively look that led me to love.

### GRAMMAR BUILDER

Have students examine a dictionary with a partner to compare its presentation with that in the text. Point out that inflectional forms (such as *chose, chosen, choosing*) are included where a change in form or the addition of other letters causes spelling to change.

### Grammar Builder Answers
**1.** verb  **2.** Drop the final *e* and add *-er.* [*Choice* is also a correct answer.]  **3.** two

### GLOBAL CONNECTION

Ask students to investigate the foods of another culture. They may use cookbooks, the Internet, library books, or ethnic restaurants to learn about several foods. Have students select one food to try, either by making it or ordering it. Then ask students to write a description using sensory words to explain its smell, taste, texture, and sounds. Have students summarize why the food is popular in its original culture.

---

### ELL/ESL STRATEGY

**Language Objective:**
*To use sensory images in your writing*

Write the following sentence on the board: *I heard a very loud noise.* Read the sentence and ask students to explain what the sentence tells them and what sense is used to

hear something. Continue with these senses to identify sight, smell, touch, and taste: *I saw the huge jet in the sky. I smelled the beautiful flowers. I felt the soft, furry cat. I tasted the new chips.* Then have students create a sentence that uses several of the senses to tell about something and make the explanation more appealing to the class.

## Practice F

Review the purpose of each step in the writing process with students. For example, prewriting is a chance to gather ideas and think about how to organize them. Have students bookmark the checklists for revising and editing on pages 134 and 138.

### Practice F Answers

Paragraphs will vary but should include a variety of sensory images, a topic sentence with a point of view, at least three supporting sentences with specific details, and a conclusion or summary sentence.

### Reading Strategy: Visualizing

Pictures could show organs of sense beside the words *sight, hearing,* etc. A diagram might show a stick figure in a center circle and five lines leading to outer circles naming the senses.

### Grammar Practice

When they edit their paragraphs for Practice F, have students identify the adjectives they have used and check their placement. Remind students that adjectives may be placed before the noun or pronoun they describe or after a state-of-being verb. *(The reading room is cozy. A fresh loaf of bread smells heavenly.)* Then have them decide if the words are well chosen, or if any should be replaced by more specific descriptive words.

### Speaking and Presenting Practice

Invite students to present their descriptive paragraphs orally to the class. To prepare, have students practice reading their paragraphs to a partner. The partner's role is to question unclear passages and offer constructive feedback about tone, pace, and expression. After making any needed changes, students can then present their paragraphs.

**Brush Up on the Basics**

An adjective adds to the meaning of a noun or pronoun. Adjectives can appeal to the senses. An adjective goes before a noun or after a state-of-being verb: *This is a warm room. The room is warm.* See Grammar 51 in Appendix A.

**Reading Strategy:** Visualizing

Make a picture or diagram to show the main idea of this lesson. How will you show the five senses?

---

Organize a descriptive paragraph just like other types of paragraphs.

### Practice F

Write a descriptive paragraph. Follow the steps below.

*Prewriting*

1. Think of an object that you would enjoy describing. Write it down. Here are some ideas:
   - a sofa or chair in your home
   - a favorite food
   - the library in your community

2. Brainstorm about your topic. Quickly make a list of words that come to your mind when you think about the topic. Write fast! Don't worry about spelling. Think about how the object looks, sounds, tastes, smells, and feels.

*Drafting*

3. Write a topic sentence that tells the main idea. Include your point of view. It is okay to express your opinion in this sentence. Use your brainstorming list to help you.

4. Write three sentences with details that support the topic sentence. Use your brainstorming list.

5. Write a conclusion or summary sentence at the end.

*Revising and Editing*

6. Read the paragraph aloud. How does it sound? Revise it to make it better. Use the checklist on page 134.

7. Edit your paragraph. Use the checklist on page 138.

8. Write the final paragraph. Give it a title.

*Publishing*

9. Share your description. Read it to another student.

# REVIEW

Read each sentence. Choose the sense to which the writer is trying to appeal. Write *touch, sight, taste, smell,* or *hearing* on your paper.

1. This lemonade is too sour and tart for me.
2. The bright blue kayak rocked back and forth on the choppy waves.
3. The Labrador retriever's ears are velvety smooth.
4. Raindrops beat hard against the window.
5. The kitchen smells of burnt toast.

Choose one of the topics below. Write five sentences about it. Include one sentence about the way it looks, feels, tastes, smells, or sounds. Use vivid descriptions in each sentence.

- a lake, river, or ocean
- your school building
- a car or bike
- someone you know

## VOCABULARY BUILDER

### Using Suffixes

A suffix is a group of letters added at the end of a word. A suffix changes the meaning of the word. Often, it also changes the word's part of speech. When *-ly* is added to the end of an adjective, the adjective becomes an adverb. *Sad* is an adjective; *sadly* is an adverb.

The clown had a sad face. He shook his head sadly.

Add the suffix *-ly* to each of these adjectives: *quick, strange, safe.* Then use each adverb in a sentence.

*Writing to Describe    Chapter 8    201*

---

## Lesson 8-1 Review Answers

1. taste  2. sight  3. touch  4. hearing
5. smell
Sentences will vary. Sample sentences are given.
The lake's surface looks glassy and unruffled. Its cool water slips like silk over the swimmers' skin. It tastes of metal and silt. A fishy odor rises around the dock. The water calmly laps at the shore.

## VOCABULARY BUILDER

Review the meanings of *suffix* and *part of speech* with students. Have students list words to which they think *-ly* can be added. (Examples might include *happy, noisy, bright, warm, slow,* and so on.) Ask students to tell what question each adverb answers in their sentences.

### Vocabulary Builder Answers

quickly, strangely, safely
Sentences will vary. Sample sentences are given. The spilled water flowed quickly over the floor. The wind whistled strangely in the chimney. We were safely tucked in our sleeping bags.

## WRITING PORTFOLIO

**Checkpoint** Have students add sensory details to their notes about their objects covering all five senses. Encourage students to create an alliterative phrase about their objects.

---

**Activity 34**                    **Workbook Activity 34**

**Overview**  This lesson explores the value of using specific nouns, adjectives, and verbs to make descriptions precise.

### Objectives

- To improve your writing with specific nouns and adjectives
- To use action verbs in your writing
- To identify the connotations of words

**Student Pages**  202–205

**Teacher's Resource Library**

  Activity  35

  Modified Activity  35

  Workbook Activity  35

  Life Skills Connection  8

### Vocabulary

**connotation**

Ask students how they would use the following pairs of synonyms in writing: *stink/fragrance, wailing/weeping, beg/implore*. Explain that many words affect people because of the emotions associated with them. Read the meaning of *connotation*. Have students explain the connotations of the listed words.

### Background Information

Clear description calls for concrete, specific language. Concrete words describe real things *(flag, ring)*, as opposed to abstract words, which do not *(patriotism, devotion)*. Like sensory words, concrete words allow readers to picture scenes and objects clearly. Concrete words help writers show rather than tell.

### 1  Warm-Up Activity

Write on the board *The girl ran home.* Challenge students to change the noun and verb and add adjectives and adverbs to create a clearer picture.

---

## LESSON 8-2  Choosing Specific Words

### Objectives

- To improve your writing with specific nouns and adjectives
- To use action verbs in your writing
- To identify the connotations of words

**Reading Strategy:** Visualizing

Look at the example. How did the picture in your mind change when a more specific word was used?

You can improve your sentences by using specific nouns. *Specific* means exact and detailed, not general. A noun is the name of a person, place, or thing. A specific noun is a particular type of person, place, or thing.

▶ **EXAMPLE 1**

| General | Specific |
|---------|----------|
| house   | cottage, mansion, townhouse, residence |
| flower  | marigold, rose, sunflower, pansy, daisy |

Writing is more interesting when the nouns are specific. Specific nouns provide more information than general nouns.

▶ **EXAMPLE 2**

Sonia plays a musical instrument.  (general)

Sonia plays the violin.  (specific)

### Practice A

Replace each noun in bold with a more specific word or phrase. Write the new sentence on your paper. There are many possible answers.

1. Derek does not like that **food.**
2. The **car** was parked in the road.
3. Luis put his **things** into his locker.
4. The girl is from **another country.**
5. Amber took her **dog** for a walk.

---

### 2  Teaching the Lesson

Have students rank words within a class: *blue, light blue, azure; truck, SUV, Chevy Tahoe; move, walk, pace.* Have students report how the mental image they have changes as the words become more specific. Then have students practice making these general words more specific by degrees: *say, eat, box, light.*

**Reading Strategy:** Visualizing

The mental image becomes clearer, more accurate, and more detailed.

### Practice A

Encourage students to use phrases including adjectives or adverbs in addition to nouns and verbs to make the sentences more specific.

### Practice A Answers

Answers will vary. Sample answers are given.
**1.** Derek does not like that greasy chili.
**2.** The rusty old Cadillac was parked in the road. **3.** Luis put his load of heavy textbooks into his locker. **4.** The girl is from sunny Spain. **5.** Amber took her nervous little terrier for a walk.

You can improve your writing with specific action verbs. They tell what the subject of the sentence is doing.

▶ **EXAMPLE 3**

| General | Specific |
|---------|----------|
| walk | stroll, amble, march, stride, pace |
| bark | yap, howl, growl, snarl, woof |

Writing is more interesting when verbs are specific or unusual.

▶ **EXAMPLE 4**

Rex barked at the neighbor.

Rex yapped at the neighbor.

### Practice B

Replace each verb in bold with a more specific or unusual verb. Write the new sentence on your paper. You may use a dictionary or thesaurus to help you.

1. Amber's Spanish class **meets** every day.
2. The boat **went** into the harbor.
3. Do not **eat** that cake.
4. Do you **like** mashed potatoes?
5. Luis **walked** to school this morning.

*Between classes, the hallways are crowded. Sarah calls it "jam-packed." Luis says, "It's one big shoulder-to-shoulder student body."*

*Writing to Describe*    Chapter 8    **203**

### TEACHER ALERT

 A specific action verb can often stand in for a general verb and its modifiers, making sentences clear and less cluttered. *They walked slowly, in a leisurely way* can be replaced by *They strolled.*

### COMMON ERROR

 Beginning writers frequently seesaw between writing that is too general *(He yelled)* and writing that contains far too many modifiers *(He screamed with horror in a high-pitched, terrified, trembling voice).* Encourage students to use descriptive language, but rein them in by having them choose one or two well-focused adjectives rather than six that drown the reader.

## Practice B

Make dictionaries and thesauruses available to students. Have students learn the meanings of unfamiliar synonyms rather than use them indiscriminately in their sentences.

### Practice B Answers

Answers will vary. Sample answers are given.
**1.** Amber's Spanish class convenes every day. **2.** The boat chugged into the harbor. **3.** Do not wolf that cake. **4.** Do you enjoy mashed potatoes? **5.** Luis strode to school this morning.

*Writing to Describe*    **203**

## Practice C

Ask students to find examples of objects with the red shades listed in Example 5. Challenge them to add more specific or unusual shades of red to the list (*rose, blush, rouge*) or to list more specific words for *green* (*emerald, jade, olive, lime, sea green*).

### Practice C Answers

Answers will vary. Sample answers are given. **1.** A rust-colored cat with scruffy fur and a drooping tail stood at the door. **2.** Slim and neatly dressed, Mr. Bauer eyed his small frame in the mirror and combed his bushy white hair carefully. **3.** The tiny living room bristled with hot pink balloons and crepe paper streamers. **4.** Ben's surprise birthday party left him speechless. **5.** The jet black stone had been worn to a shining black disc by the river's current.

### COMMON ERROR

Many students pay little attention to the connotations of words they choose. Use humor to make them aware of contrasting connotations among synonyms: *The rowing team was (swamped, defeated). The new hybrid cars are (tight-fisted, economical) with gas.*

## Practice D

Have students tell about their associations for the word *scent*, then for the word *stink* in Example 6. Repeat for the word pair *curious* and *nosy*.

### Practice D Answers

Sentences will vary. Sample sentences are given. **1.** An active girl carried the heavy tray. **2.** Pete smiled whenever he remembered his winning shot. **3.** That bird has an unusual beak. **4.** The chef has prepared his specialty for us. **5.** Mom and Dad agreed to discuss my punishment later.

### Reading Strategy: Visualizing

Students might draw a smiling face and a frowning face beside the word *connotation*.

---

**Connotation**
An idea or feeling associated with a word

---

**Brush Up on the Basics**

A verb is a word that shows action or state of being. Use action verbs that show exactly what happened. Specific verbs make descriptions clear. See Grammar 19 in Appendix A.

---

**Reading Strategy:** Visualizing

Read the explanation of connotation. To help you remember its meaning, think of your own example.

---

You can improve your writing with more specific adjectives. Instead of saying that a flower is pretty and red, you could use more specific or unusual words.

▶ **EXAMPLE 5**

| General | Specific or Unusual |
|---------|---------------------|
| red | crimson, scarlet, ruby, cherry, burgundy |
| pretty | attractive, beautiful, appealing, lovely |

### Practice C

Write a sentence to describe each person, place, or thing. Use specific adjectives.

  **1.** an animal    **3.** a room    **5.** a rock

  **2.** a neighbor    **4.** a party

Words have meanings. They also have **connotations**. A connotation is an idea or feeling associated with a word. Connotations make people think of good or bad things.

▶ **EXAMPLE 6**

*Scent* is a positive word for smell.

*Stink* is an unpleasant word for smell.

When you choose a word, think about its connotation. The connotation is part of the message to the reader.

### Practice D

Read each pair of words. Choose the word with the more positive connotation. Write a sentence using this word.

  **1.** wild, active        **4.** chef, cook

  **2.** smiled, grinned    **5.** argue, discuss

  **3.** unusual, strange

---

## LEARNING STYLES

**Body/Kinesthetic**

Write general directions on index cards, using purposefully vague words. Have students draw a card and read it to a partner, who tries to follow the directions. Partners can talk about how to improve the directions, rewrite them, and read them to another student. Have partners assess whether more revision is needed based on the second student's response.

## ELL/ESL STRATEGY

**Language Objective:** *To listen closely for specific details*

Display four pictures that have common elements. For example, all might be landscapes or children. Tell students you will describe one picture. Begin by describing things that are similar. By degrees, begin describing small differences in more specific language. When students have guessed which picture you are describing, they can take turns describing a different picture.

Replace each word in bold with a more specific word. Write the new sentence on your paper. There are many possible answers.

1. The **journey** lasted three weeks.

2. The leaves turned a bright **red.**

3. Amber got cold walking home in the **rain.**

4. Luis is reading a **book** in the library.

5. A **girl** called Sonia on the telephone.

Read each pair of words. Choose the word with the more positive connotation. Write it on your paper.

6. job, career

7. proud, conceited

8. shy, quiet

9. say, yell

10. remind, nag

## WRITE ABOUT IT

### Your Feelings

Every day, you use language to express your ideas and feelings to others. Figures of speech can help you describe your feelings. Write a paragraph that describes how you feel about your home and the area where you live (your city, town, or rural area). Use metaphors, similes, personification, and exaggeration to help your reader understand your feelings. When you are finished, share your writing with another student or a family member.

**Six Traits of Writing:**

*Word Choice* vivid words that "show, not tell"

*Writing to Describe*    Chapter 8    **205**

---

## Lesson 8-2 Review Answers

Answers for 1–5 will vary. Sample answers are given. **1.** The European tour lasted three weeks. **2.** The leaves turned a bright scarlet. **3.** Amber got cold walking home in the sudden downpour. **4.** Luis is reading a murder mystery in the library. **5.** A girlfriend called Sonia on the telephone. **6.** career **7.** proud **8.** quiet (Students may have good reasons to support either choice.) **9.** say **10.** remind

## WRITE ABOUT IT

Have students complete this activity after they have read Lesson 8-3 on figurative language. Have students write a word or phrase that summarizes their feelings about their home and hometown. They can write in a word web and fill in the spaces with images, comparisons, and emotion-evoking words.

## Six Traits of Writing Focus

| Ideas | | ✔ | Word Choice |
|---|---|---|---|
| | Organization | | Sentence Fluency |
| ✔ | Voice | | Conventions |

## Word Choice

Students should choose precise, vivid words and figures of speech to suggest their feelings. Encourage students to use descriptive words and phrases that depict emotion. For example, have them replace common words like *lonely* and *happy* with *there's not another person within a thousand miles* or *smiling ear to ear.*

Tell students they should work to develop a distinctive voice in their paragraphs as well.

Refer students to page WPH1 for descriptions of the Six Traits of Writing.

## IN THE COMMUNITY

Have students collect brochures from local businesses and organizations. In small groups, have students highlight specific nouns, action verbs, and vivid adjectives. Then have them read each brochure again to locate words with positive connotations. Have groups read their brochures aloud and discuss the effects of specific language.

---

TRL

 TRL

**Activity 35**                    **Workbook Activity 35**

*Writing to Describe*    **205**

### Chapter 8 Lesson 3

**Overview** This lesson shows how metaphors, similes, personification, and exaggeration can add interest to a description.

### Objectives

- To use metaphors and similes in your writing
- To use personification in your writing
- To use exaggeration in your writing

**Student Pages** 206–209

**Teacher's Resource Library**

Activity 36

Modified Activity 36

Workbook Activity 36

## Vocabulary

exaggeration     personification
figure of speech     simile
metaphor

Write *figure of speech* in the center of a word web and the other vocabulary words in circles around this. Ask students to read the definitions for the words, then explain why you arranged the words in this way.

## Background Information

Figurative language suggests meaning through comparison. It helps writers express concepts in fresh and imaginative ways. For example, an abstraction becomes immediate for a reader when it is expressed in concrete terms: *Historians sift the ashes of the past. The mind is a house of many mirrors.* Good figures of speech are neither flowery nor snobby.

---

## LESSON 8-3

# Using Figures of Speech

### Objectives

- To use metaphors and similes in your writing
- To use personification in your writing
- To use exaggeration in your writing

**Figure of speech**
An expression that a writer uses for a particular purpose

**Metaphor**
An expression that shows that two things are alike in some way

**Simile**
An expression using *like* or *as* that shows that two things are alike in a certain way

 **NOTE**

A figure of speech is also called *figurative language*.

**Figures of speech** help you write strong descriptions. A figure of speech is an expression that a writer uses for a particular purpose. It creates a vivid picture in the reader's mind.

▶ **EXAMPLE 1**

The sound of the wind was like a rushing river. It sent chills up Amber's spine.

Using a figure of speech inspires the reader's imagination.

## Metaphors and Similes

**Metaphors** and **similes** are figures of speech that compare. Both show that two things are alike. However, a simile uses the word *like* or *as*, and a metaphor does not. In Example 2, the figures of speech compare a desert to a sea.

▶ **EXAMPLE 2**

| | |
|---|---|
| Metaphor | The Sahara Desert is a sea of sand. |
| Simile | The Sahara Desert is like a sea of sand. |
| Simile | The Sahara Desert is as wide as a sea. |

### Practice A

Decide whether each sentence contains a metaphor or a simile. Write *metaphor* or *simile* on your paper.

1. That neighbor is a puzzle to me.
2. The child eats like a bird.
3. These instructions are as clear as mud.
4. Derek is a breath of fresh air.
5. Amber is as sweet as honey!

---

## 1   Warm-Up Activity

Say the following comparisons, having students fill in the ending. Then challenge them to complete each simile with a more original ending. Discuss the meaning of each phrase:

*as big as a . . . (house)*
*as quiet as a . . . (mouse)*
*as sharp as a . . . (tack)*

## 2   Teaching the Lesson

Explain that in figures of speech, the words no longer have their simple dictionary definitions. Discuss the following figurative expression:

*a long, hard road ahead (a difficult challenge to meet)*

## Practice A

Point out that metaphors do not contain the word *like* or *as* but simply state *X is Y.* As students read the sentences, have them tell what two things are being compared in each.

### Practice A Answers

1. metaphor 2. simile 3. simile
4. metaphor 5. simile

**Personification**

Giving human qualities to animals or objects

**NOTE**

A metaphor is a direct comparison. A simile is an indirect comparison.

*Reading Strategy:*
Visualizing

Do the sensory images in Example 3 help you understand personification?

**Practice B**

Rewrite each sentence to include a metaphor or simile.

**Example**: The desert is very large.
**Answer**: The desert is as wide as an ocean.

1. When I stood before the audience, I felt nervous.
2. Derek talks about Sarah constantly.
3. Some basketball players are tall.
4. The TV announcer spoke fast.
5. Sonia has a beautiful singing voice.

### Personification

**Personification** is another figure of speech. It means giving human qualities to animals or objects.

▶ **EXAMPLE 3**

The ocean roared.

My heart was singing for joy.

**Practice C**

Find an example of personification in each sentence. Write the figure of speech on your paper.

1. The moon smiled down on the sleepy town.
2. The pen flew out of my hand.
3. The storm cloud thundered its unhappiness.
4. The school building extended its welcoming arms.
5. The alarm clock told me it was time to get up.

*Writing to Describe    Chapter 8*    **207**

---

### ELL/ESL STRATEGY

**Language Objective:**
*To understand figurative language*

Students may find comparisons with nonliteral meanings baffling. Use exercises such as the following to help them understand metaphors:

1. Identify whether each sentence has a good or bad connotation

*Things are looking up.* (good)
*Since last year, things have gone downhill steadily.* (bad)
*He's in top shape.* (good)
*She fell ill.* (bad)

2. Each sentence below is based on one of these metaphors: love is magic; love is war; love is madness. Identify the metaphor.

*He fled from her advances.* (war)
*I'm crazy about him.* (madness)
*She was spellbound.* (magic)

---

## Practice B

As students write their own metaphors and similes, ask them to be original and avoid familiar sayings like those in Practice A.

### Practice B Answers

Answers will vary. Sample answers are given. **1.** When I stood before the audience, I trembled like a leaf in a windstorm. **2.** When Derek starts talking about Sarah, he's like a runaway train. **3.** Basketball players loom like telephone poles. **4.** The TV announcer jabbered like a tape recorder set on fast forward. **5.** Sonia's singing voice is as beautiful as a shimmering sunset.

## Practice C

Have students read the sentences in Example 3. Point out that a personification is an indirect comparison similar to a metaphor. For example, the ocean is compared to an angry person because both make a roaring noise.

### Practice C Answers

**1.** moon smiled; sleepy town **2.** pen flew **3.** cloud . . . unhappiness **4.** building extended its welcoming arms **5.** clock told me

### Reading Strategy: Visualizing

Students may point out that the sensory images give human qualities to the ocean and to a person's heart.

**3** **Reinforce and Extend**

### COMMON ERROR

Some students have trouble differentiating literal and figurative statements: *My car is a four-door sedan* is literal. *My car is a thunderbolt* is nonliteral. Some qualities of the second object help us understand the first object. (*The car is remarkably fast and loud.*)

## TEACHER ALERT

Students may be most familiar with exaggeration through tall tales. You might read brief excerpts from a tall tale to illustrate the effect of exaggeration.

### *Reading Strategy:* Visualizing

Students may say they realized no one can be on the phone every minute of the day.

## Practice D

Review the exaggerations in Example 4, then ask students to offer their own examples of exaggerations.

### *Practice D Answers*

Sentences will vary. Sample sentences are given. **1.** Winning this argument is worth a million dollars to me. **2.** When I got the college acceptance letter, my spirits flew as high as an astronaut. **3.** The announcement of the award came like a sudden clap of thunder. **4.** How can Raymond drive that tiny car? He is as tall as a tree! **5.** When he heard that I broke his favorite game, my brother Thomas blew up like a volcano.

## LEARNING STYLES

**Interpersonal/Group Learning**

Have students form three groups. Give each group one of the following ideas to act out. Ask them to use exaggeration to make their points clear.

1. A teenager comes in late and finds parents waiting.
2. A group of friends talk each other into riding on a new hair-raising roller coaster.
3. Students try to convince buyers at a bake sale how great the goodies are.

**Exaggeration**
An overstatement that says something is greater than it is

### *Reading Strategy:* Visualizing

What did you picture as you read Example 4? How did this picture help you understand what exaggeration is?

 **NOTE**

When people use a phrase too often, it becomes a cliché. A cliché is an overused phrase such as *I'm so hungry, I could eat a horse!* Avoid clichés. Use words and phrases in unique ways.

## Exaggeration

Sometimes **exaggeration** can improve your writing. An exaggeration is an overstatement. You say that something is greater than it is. An exaggeration helps readers understand your feelings. It can also entertain readers.

▶ **EXAMPLE 4**

Sarah is the most interesting person who ever lived.

They talk on the phone every minute of the day!

### Practice D

Add words to complete each exaggeration. Write the new sentence on your paper.

**Example**: _____ bigger than Paul Bunyan!
**Answer**: That football player is bigger than Paul Bunyan!

1. _____ worth a million dollars to me.
2. _____ flew as high as an astronaut.
3. _____ like a sudden clap of thunder.
4. _____ as tall as a tree.
5. _____ blew up like a volcano!

*Thanks! Without your help, I'd be stuck here forever!*

**208** *Chapter 8    Writing to Describe*

## AT HOME

Exaggeration is a staple of TV sitcoms. Discuss the sitcoms that students watch. Suggest that they select one program to watch with a notepad. They can jot down jokes that rely on exaggeration. Set aside time for students to share their findings.

**208** *Chapter 8*

# REVIEW

Match each group of words in Column 1 with a group of words in Column 2. Write the new sentence on your paper. Then write whether the figure of speech is a *metaphor*, a *simile*, or *personification*.

*Column 1*

1. I was so nervous that my hands
2. The snowflakes
3. The unexpected compliment
4. Driving in Brandon's old car
5. We settled down as happily as

*Column 2*

A danced through the sky.

B is like riding on a two-humped camel.

C chicks in a nest.

D was a rainbow appearing suddenly overhead.

E fluttered like butterflies with no place to land.

Write a sentence to describe each thing. Use exaggeration in each sentence.

6. the tallest building you have ever seen
7. the most delicious meal you have ever eaten
8. the most difficult task you have ever completed
9. the most exciting day of your life
10. the most beautiful song that you have ever heard

## Lesson 8-3 Review Answers

In addition to matching the sentence parts, students should be able to explain orally what each comparison means.
**1.** E—simile **2.** A—personification **3.** D—metaphor **4.** B—simile **5.** C—simile Answers 6–10 will vary. Sample answers are given. **6.** When I looked up at the building, I was sure it was touching the sun. **7.** Tasting that pasta was like falling in love. **8.** That job was like counting grains of sand on a beach. **9.** By the end of that day, I was dancing on the ceiling. **10.** That song is so touching, it could make a stone cry.

## LEARNING STYLES

### Visual/Spatial

Challenge students to create pictures to show the five comparisons in the review on this page. Encourage students to draw a picture illustrating one of their comparisons. When they finish, invite students, one by one, to display their pictures. Ask the class to identify which comparison has been illustrated.

## WRITING PORTFOLIO

**Checkpoint** Have students revisit their draft about an object to sharpen the description with figures of speech.

## Spelling Practice

Students' descriptive sentences for items 6–10 of the review will include degrees of comparison. Point out that, when adding -er and -est to adjectives, students may have to change the spelling of the base word.

Explain that if the word ends in *e*, drop the *e* before adding -er or -est: *late* + -est = *latest*.

Explain that if the word ends in -y, change the y to an *i* before adding -er or -est: *lovely* + -est = *loveliest*.

Have students spell the superlative forms of these adjectives and adverbs: *friendly, large, gentle, happy, noisy, lonely, loose.*

Activity 36

Workbook Activity 36

### Chapter 8 Lesson 4

**Overview** This lesson explains some elements that characterize writing styles and encourages students to develop their own style.

### Objectives

- To recognize the characteristics of style
- To develop your own writing style

**Student Pages** 210–215

**Teacher's Resource Library**

## Vocabulary

**style**

Have several volunteers tell what it means to say that someone has style. Read the meaning of style in this lesson. Ask students what words they might use to describe their favorite writer's style.

## Background Information

A writer's style is like a fingerprint—unique. However, every writer should aim to develop a clear, concise style; the techniques for doing that are universal. First, be specific but brief. Use active voice whenever possible; it makes sentences shorter and brisker. Make your writing reader-friendly; this means saying things in a way that is easy to follow.

## 1 Warm-Up Activity

Read paragraphs from several different books that illustrate very different styles. Ask students to describe what the writing is like in each, for example, choppy or smooth, lively or quiet, simple or complex.

---

## LESSON 8-4

# Developing a Writing Style

### Objectives

- To recognize the characteristics of style
- To develop your own writing style

**Style**
A writer's individual way of using words

Every writer has a special **style**. Style is a certain way of doing something. A writing style is a person's unique way of using words. Some characteristics of a writer's style are:

- use of figures of speech
- choice of words
- length of sentences
- choice of topics
- amount of description

As you read what someone else has written, try to recognize some characteristics of the writer's style.

### Practice A

Read the paragraph. Then answer the questions below.

The wind howled as it whipped through the trees in the front yard. Inside the sturdy brick home, the family slept soundly. Suddenly a loud crash jolted them awake. The wind had uprooted a huge oak tree and tossed it against the house. Shattered glass from broken windows scattered inside the house and out on the lawn. It was a nightmare!

1. Choose three words and write them on your paper. For each one, write a different word that you might have chosen if you had written this story.

2. Count the number of words in each sentence. Write these numbers on your paper. Does this writer like long or short sentences?

3. Give one example of alliteration from the paragraph.

4. Does this writer like to describe people, places, or events? Give an example to support your conclusion.

5. Write one sentence to describe this writer's style.

---

## 2 Teaching the Lesson

Point out that style, the overall effect of a writer's words, results from the way many elements are combined: sentence variety, original expression, ability to "get to the point." Their goal is to make their style more mature by choosing words well and saying things as clearly as they know how.

## Practice A

Read the paragraph aloud as students listen. Talk about the overall effect of the writing on listeners.

### Practice A Answers

Some answers will vary. Sample answers are given. **1.** *Blasted* instead of *whipped through*; *unaware* instead of *soundly*; *massive* instead of *huge* **2.** 13, 9, 7, 14, 14, 4; Both long and short sentences are used. **3.** *slept soundly* **4.** This writer likes to describe events: the wind lashing the trees, the crash of the tree into the house. **5.** This writer's style seems clear and dramatic.

As you write more, you will develop your own style.

## Practice B

Follow the steps to write a descriptive paragraph.

*Prewriting*

1. Choose a topic and write it on your paper. It can be a person, place, or object. Here are some suggestions:
   - a favorite family member
   - a place where you spent a vacation or holiday
   - a special item such as a trophy or gift

2. Brainstorm about your topic. Quickly make a list of words that come to your mind when you think about your topic. Don't worry about spelling. Think about how the topic looks, sounds, tastes, smells, and feels.

3. Write a metaphor or simile about the topic. Write a sentence with personification or exaggeration.

*Drafting*

4. Write a topic sentence that tells the main idea. Express your opinion. Look at your brainstorming list and the figures of speech that you wrote.

5. Write three sentences with details that support the topic sentence. Use your brainstorming list and your figures of speech. Check that you used alliteration.

6. Write a conclusion or summary sentence at the end.

*Revising and Editing*

7. Read the paragraph aloud. How does it sound? Revise it to make it better. Use the checklist on page 134.

8. Edit your paragraph. Use the checklist on page 138.

*Publishing*

9. Write the final paragraph. Give it a title.

10. Read your paragraph to another student.

**Reading Strategy:**
Visualizing

Create a chart to show the characteristics of your writing style. This will help you visualize what style means.

---

### Practice B

Take time to read through the steps with students, answering their questions. As they select their topics and prewrite, remind them to use specific words and sensory images.

### Practice B Answers

Paragraphs will vary but should show understanding of paragraph parts and organization, specific words, and sensory and figurative language. Students should submit a clean, edited copy with their prewriting notes and first drafts.

## 3  Reinforce and Extend

### COMMON ERROR

Beginning writers often confuse wordiness and flowery language with good style. Point out that the best writers communicate in the most efficient way. They choose words carefully and use no more words than necessary. Their sentences are crystal clear. Suggest that students read their work aloud (or have a partner read it aloud to them). Sentences that sound awkward, flat, or boring need revision.

### Reading Strategy: Visualizing

Charts may use elements listed on page 210 in the form of a checklist. For example, *choice of words* might be represented by questions such as *Do my words create clear, correct pictures? Have I used strong action verbs? Is the language interesting and lively?*

---

## ELL/ESL STRATEGY

**Language Objective:**
*To describe and compare foods of two cultures*

Ask students to clip pictures or bring photographs of foods popular in their native culture. Provide similar images of popular U.S. foods, such as hamburgers and pizza. Ask students to write sentences describing the familiar foods. They may begin by writing in their native language, then work with a partner for help in translating. Have students listen to a prerecorded description of one or more of the U.S. foods. Then hold a discussion with students to have them compare how some foods of the two cultures differ.

## Lesson 8-4 Review Answers

**1.** E **2.** B **3.** D **4.** C **5.** A
Answers for 6–10 will vary. Sample answers are given. **6.** The Statue of Liberty welcomes immigrants to America with an image of strength and mercy. She stands firm and tall, holding up a lighted torch. She looks indestructible. The look on her face seems to say, "I welcome you. You will be free from tyranny and suffering here." For over a hundred years, the Statue of Liberty has been a powerful symbol of a free, compassionate people.
**7.** My sentences are varied in length.
**8.** Answers will vary (immigrants, indestructible, tyranny). **9.** Answers will vary (The look on her face seems to say, "I welcome you . . . "). **10.** I would describe my writing style as clear and admiring.

### WRITING PORTFOLIO

**Checkpoint** Have students read their paragraphs to a partner. Partners should listen for the style elements listed on page 210, then give feedback on the writer's strengths and areas that need improvement.

### CAREER CONNECTION

Have students select a career that interests them and research it on the Internet. Ask them to find out what sorts of writing the career involves and describe the typical style of that writing (technical, direct, colorful, or humorous). Students can get samples of writing by workers in the field to read to classmates.

---

# REVIEW

Match each writing choice in Column 1 with a feature of style in Column 2. Write the letter of your answer.

*Column 1*

**1.** using many adjectives and adverbs

**2.** using unfamiliar words

**3.** writing about danger

**4.** using conjunctions to create long sentences

**5.** using metaphors and similes

*Column 2*

**A** use of figures of speech

**B** choice of words

**C** length of sentences

**D** choice of topics

**E** amount of description

Follow the directions below. You will write a paragraph and then answer questions about your writing style.

**6.** Write a paragraph that describes one of these topics. Try to use sensory images, specific words, and figures of speech. Create a word picture for the reader.
   • the Statue of Liberty
   • a wrapped present
   • a blue jay
   • a laptop computer

**7.** Read the sentences you wrote. Are they short or long?

**8.** What specific words did you use? Circle them.

**9.** Does your paragraph include alliteration, a sensory image, or a figure of speech? Underline each one.

**10.** How would you describe your writing style?

---

### Developing a Writing Style

**Directions** Read the paragraph below. Then answer the questions about it.

The catfish looked as big as a whale lying in the boat. Its slippery, dark skin was striped with scars. Its fins twisted as the stout body thrashed. The wide mouth gulped at air. A set of funny, old-man whiskers twitched. But the fish's situation was about as funny as a house fire.

**1.** How many figures of speech does the paragraph have?

**2.** What kind of figures of speech are they?

**3.** List two specific nouns in the paragraph.

**4.** List two specific verbs in the paragraph.

**5.** To which sense does the paragraph most appeal?

**6.** Write a sentence that uses alliteration. Underline the part that uses alliteration.

**7.** How long is each sentence? Are there more long sentences or short sentences?

**8.** Why do you think the writer used mostly (long/short) sentences?

**9.** What is the effect of words like *scars, twisted, thrashed, gulped, twitched*?

**10.** Write a sentence to describe this writer's style.

**Activity 37**

---

### Writing Choices for Style

**Directions** Read the topic sentence below. Add three detail sentences and a conclusion to make a paragraph. Then answer the questions below.

Joe and Mandy thought that Miss Iris, who lived in the old house on the hill, was a witch.

**1.** Find three specific words you used. Write them on the line.

**2.** What are two words you could make more specific? Underline them. Then write replacement words on the line.

**3.** Count the words in each sentence. How many long sentences (more than 10 words) are there? How many short sentences?

**4.** Have you used figures of speech? If so, circle them. If you have not, add at least one to the paragraph.

**5.** What is your paragraph about? Have you described it well? If not, add more description on these lines.

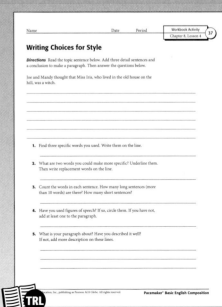

**Workbook Activity 37**

## Pet Store Worker

Nita Suarez works at a pet store. Her job is to unload delivery trucks and help customers. This evening she unloaded an order of cat beds and play towers. She noticed a problem. She wrote the following note to her boss to describe the problem. Read Nita's note. Then answer the questions below.

Ms. Parker,

Our order of Krazy Kat beds and towers came yesterday. The carpet on them is wet and stinky. They smell like chemicals and mold mixed. The driver said that they were not left out in the rain. I put the beds and towers in the east corner of the storeroom. I covered them with plastic so the odor will not get in bags of food.

Nita

1. What words did Nita use that appeal to the senses?

2. List five specific words that help make Nita's description clear.

3. **CRITICAL THINKING** Why is it important to use specific words such as *yesterday*, *east*, and *storeroom* in this description?

## SPEAKING AND LISTENING

Suppose you work at a pet store. A customer wants to buy a fish. Work with a partner. One person describes two kinds of fish for sale. The other person listens carefully and writes the descriptions. Then switch roles. Work together to add specific words to each description.

*Writing to Describe* Chapter 8 **213**

# WRITING ON THE JOB

Have students read the title and look at the photo. Invite volunteers to predict what kinds of tasks a pet store worker does. Talk about reasons why a pet store worker should be able to describe things clearly (*to direct customers to products and animals; to explain care and feeding; to describe proper setup*). Then have students read the text and answer the questions.

### Writing on the Job Answers

**1.** wet, stinky, smell, chemicals, mold, left out in the rain, covered with plastic **2.** Krazy Kat beds and towers, yesterday, carpet, east corner, storeroom **3.** Ms. Parker needs to know when the problem was noticed, what the driver reported, and where to find the products so she can evaluate the situation.

## Writing Practice

Have students research an animal often sold in pet stores. They may use the Internet, encyclopedias, brochures, and primary sources at a pet store. If possible, have students observe the animal. Then have students write a description of the animal using specific language, descriptive words, and varied sentences. Explain that their goal is to help readers understand the animal through a clear, interesting style.

Writing on the Job 4

*Writing to Describe* **213**

Read the feature title and have students identify a graph and a table on the page. Ask students to describe times when they used graphic features to understand text. Together, read the text. Invite volunteers to explain the purpose of the graph and the chart and interpret their labels. Then have students answer the questions.

### Building Research Skills Answers

**1.** 17 million birds were household pets in 2004. **2.** There were more cats than dogs. **3.** Answers will vary. A sample answer is given. A graph or table is useful to show number facts concisely for comparison.

## Using Graphs and Tables

A graph is a picture that shows relationships among numbers. It may show the relationships as lines or as bars. The bar graph below shows the number of pets owned in the United States in 2004. The bar heights are easy to compare.

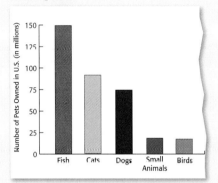

A table is another way to organize information so it is easy to compare. The information is put in rows and columns. The table below shows the same information as the graph above.

| Number of Pets Owned in U.S. in 2004 | |
| --- | --- |
| Pet Type | Number (in millions) |
| Fish | 149 |
| Cats | 91 |
| Dogs | 74 |
| Small animals | 18 |
| Birds | 17 |

A graph or table is a good way to describe certain kinds of information. Sometimes, a graph or table can show a main idea better than words.

Use the graph or table to answer the following questions.

**1.** How many birds were household pets in the United States in 2004?

**2.** Compare the number of cats to the number of dogs. Which were there more of?

**3.** CRITICAL THINKING Give an example of when it might be helpful to include a table or graph with your writing.

### MEDIA AND TECHNOLOGY

Have you heard the saying "a picture is worth a thousand words"? A photo sends a powerful message. Some cameras use light and chemicals to catch images on film. Today, digital images are widely used. A digital camera uses electrical impulses to catch images. You probably view photos or videos every day. They appear in printed media and on the Internet and TV. People use computers to store and share their own photos and videos.

---

**Using Graphs and Tables**

Graphic elements help readers understand a text. Writers use graphs to picture how two sets of information are related. The sets of information may be related using bars, lines, or a series of points. Tables list related facts in columns and rows so they can easily be located and compared. Photos, diagrams, and illustrations show how something looks.

Look at the graph and table below. Then answer the questions.

**Pet Dogs and Cats in U.S., 2007**

| | CATS | DOGS |
| --- | --- | --- |
| Percent of U.S. households that own one | 34% | 39% |
| Percent of owners with more than one | 50% | 39% |

**1.** How many more pet cats than pet dogs were there in 2007?

**2.** What percent of U.S. households own dogs?

**3.** CRITICAL THINKING In households that own two or more pets, which pet is more popular? Why do you think that might be?

- Use sensory images to appeal to your reader's touch, sight, taste, smell, and hearing. Create a mental picture by using words.

- Use alliteration to appeal to your reader's sense of hearing.

- Improve your sentences by using specific nouns, verbs, and adjectives.

- Think about the connotations of the words you use. A word's connotation can make your readers think of good things or bad things.

- Add metaphors, similes, personification, and exaggeration to make your writing exciting. These figures of speech will help you write a strong description. They will give the reader a sharp, interesting mental picture.

- Use metaphors and similes to show that two things are alike. A simile includes the word *like* or *as*.

- Describe an animal or object using human qualities. This is personification.

- Use exaggeration to entertain your readers and get their attention.

- Replace clichés with unusual figures of speech and specific words.

- Develop your own style of using words.

- When you read what someone else has written, see if you can recognize a certain writing style.

## GROUP ACTIVITY

Work with a group to describe a funny or scary experience. First talk about the details. Then write a draft of your description. Use nouns, verbs, adjectives, and adverbs that tell exactly what happened. Include words that appeal to the senses. Use funny or exciting figures of speech. Get together with another group and read your descriptions aloud. Use a tone of voice that fits the mood. After you listen, tell what stood out in what you heard.

## Chapter 8 Summary

Have volunteers read aloud each Summary item on page 215. Ask volunteers to explain the meaning of each item.

## ONLINE CONNECTION

Students will find useful resources to help them understand figurative language at this site:

www.agsglobepmbec.com/page215a

The site gives an easy and hard tutorial. It also has links to a number of Internet resources on figurative language. Students can also find many poems online. Have them find one they like and use it to provide examples of metaphors and similes.

The following Web site for teachers provides links to resources on poetry and figurative language.

www.agsglobepmbec.com/page215b

## GROUP ACTIVITY

Instruct groups to choose a leader and two recorders before they choose an experience to describe. The leader can draw responses from all members. The recorders can take prewriting notes for details. Remind groups to consider the mood of their description as they make word choices. As an alternative presentation, you may suggest that groups record their descriptions, with sound effects, then play them for the class.

## Chapter 8 Review

Use the Chapter Review to prepare students for tests and to reteach content from the chapter.

## Chapter 8 Mastery Test

The Teacher's Resource Library includes two forms of the Chapter 8 Mastery Test. Each test addresses the chapter Goals for Learning. An optional third page of additional critical-thinking items is included for each test. The difficulty level of the two forms is equivalent.

### Review Answers

Part A

1. metaphor  2. style  3. connotation
4. simile  5. alliteration  6. personification
7. figures of speech  8. exaggeration
9. sensory image

Part B

10. A  11. D  12. C  13. B

---

**Word Bank**

alliteration
connotation
exaggeration
figures of speech
metaphor
personification
sensory image
simile
style

**Part A** Write the word or words from the Word Bank that complete each sentence.

1. A comparison that does not use *like* or *as* is a _____.
2. Your special way of writing is your _____.
3. An idea or feeling associated with a word is a _____.
4. A comparison that uses *like* or *as* is a _____.
5. Words that start with the same sound create _____.
6. Saying that the ocean roared is an example of _____.
7. Metaphors, similes, personification, and exaggeration are _____.
8. Saying that someone talks constantly is an example of _____.
9. A word or phrase that appeals to the senses is a _____.

**Part B** Read each sentence. Choose the sense to which the writer is trying to appeal. Write the letter of your answer.

10. The sand felt rough beneath her feet.
    **A** touch     **B** taste     **C** smell     **D** hearing

11. Sonia tapped her foot to the loud beat of the drums.
    **A** touch     **B** taste     **C** smell     **D** hearing

12. The fragrance of the roses reminded her of spring.
    **A** touch     **B** taste     **C** smell     **D** hearing

13. The cherries in the pie were both tart and sweet.
    **A** touch     **B** taste     **C** smell     **D** hearing

---

Name _____ Date _____ Period _____  | Mastery Test A / Chapter 8 / Page 1

**Chapter 8 Mastery Test A**

*Part A* Circle the letter of the word or phrase that best completes each sentence.

1. A metaphor is a comparison that does not use _____.
   A personification   C *like* or *as*
   B style             D description

2. The idea or feeling associated with a word is its _____.
   A connotation       C metaphor
   B sensory image     D meaning

3. A _____ is words used with a meaning different from their dictionary meanings.
   A style             C figure of speech
   B description        D alliteration

4. _____ means objects or animals are given human qualities.
   A Exaggeration      C Metaphor
   B Simile            D Personification

5. An _____ says that something is greater than it actually is.
   A simile            C exaggeration
   B alliteration      D image

*Part B* Find the special use of words in each sentence. Write *metaphor, simile, exaggeration, personification,* or *alliteration* on the line.

6. I jumped 50 feet in the air.
7. Ashley is as limber as a willow branch.
8. Your smile is my sunshine.
9. The wind moaned and whistled sorrowfully.
10. Nighthawks have nested in the north field.

---

Name _____ Date _____ Period _____  | Mastery Test A / Chapter 8 / Page 2

**Chapter 8 Mastery Test A,** continued

*Part C* Decide to which sense each sentence appeals. Write *sight, touch, taste, smell,* or *hearing* on the line.

11. The children squealed and giggled wildly.
12. The full moon glowed brightly.
13. The odor of cinnamon and nutmeg rose from the oven.
14. Abe savored the rich stew and buttery biscuit.
15. The wool pants itched Juan.

16. The bitter nutshell puckered my mouth.
17. The ticking of the clock filled the room.
18. The kitten chased its tail, then fell down.
19. A moldy, musty smell came from the basement.
20. As I rubbed its tummy, the puppy relaxed.

*Part D* Read each sentence. Choose the most specific word in parentheses to complete the sentence. Underline this word.

21. Ryan went to the (supermarket, store) for his mom.
22. After lunch, we can (cook, bake) a cake.
23. Elise (dances, moves) very well.
24. Today's special is baked (fish, trout).
25. Letters were mailed to everyone in the (county, region).
26. Read the (instrument, thermometer) to see how cold it is.

27. A lonesome coyote (made noise, howled) all night.
28. Have you read any good (nonfiction, books) lately?
29. They live in a (house, mansion) on Easy Street.
30. Our family (goes, drives) to Florida every spring.

---

Name _____ Date _____ Period _____  | Mastery Test A / Chapter 8 / Page 3

**Chapter 8 Mastery Test A,** continued

*Part E* Write your answer to each question. Use complete sentences. Support each answer with facts and examples from the textbook.

31. What are three things that help create your writing style?

32. Why are specific words better than general words in writing?

*Part F* Write a paragraph for each topic. Include a topic sentence, body, and conclusion in the paragraph. Support your answers with facts and examples from the textbook.

33. Compare and contrast metaphors and similes.

34. Why do you think sensory images improve writing?

Chapter 8 Mastery Test A, pages 1–3

**Part C** In each sentence, replace at least one word with a more specific word. Write the new sentence.

14. Derek runs fast.

15. This math problem is hard.

16. The house is old.

**Part D** Add words to each sentence to create alliteration. Write the new sentence.

17. I liked that new sandwich.

18. Amber was happy.

19. The moon glowed in the sky.

**Part E** Find the sensory image in each sentence. Write *metaphor*, *simile*, *exaggeration*, or *personification*.

20. The elephant looked as big as a mountain.

21. The sun smiled down upon the garden.

22. My stomach is growling louder than thunder!

23. At the dance class, I was a fish out of water.

24. The tired, old house stood on the top of a hill.

**Part F**

25. Improve the following paragraph. Add a sensory image. Add a figure of speech. Choose more specific words. Write the improved paragraph on your paper.

   Border collies work very hard. They round up flocks of sheep. They find sheep that have wandered away. They are very dependable workers. If you have ever seen a border collie at work, you would be amazed.

## Test Tip

You can work with a partner or a small group to get ready for a test. Ask each other questions about the material that will be on the test.

## Review Answers

### Part C

Answers will vary. Sample answers are given.
14. Derek sprints with lightning speed.
15. This algebra problem is confusing.
16. The cottage is historic and quaint.

### Part D

Answers will vary. Sample answers are given.
17. The brand-new bacon burger just tastes better. 18. Amber was pleased as punch. 19. The moon glimmered ghostlike in the sky.

### Part E

20. simile 21. personification
22. exaggeration 23. metaphor
24. personification

### Part F

25. Paragraph revisions will vary. A sample answer is given.
Border collies are the workaholics of the dog world. These go-getters can round up flocks of sheep as quick as a wink. They also sniff out the wanderers and shoo them back to the flock. Year in and year out, the border collie gives its best effort and seems to thrive on the job. If you ever see one at work, you will be amazed.

## WRITING PORTFOLIO

**Wrap-Up** Have students revise and edit their paragraphs, then share them with classmates orally. This project may be used as an alternative form of assessment for the chapter.

---

Chapter 8 Mastery Test B, pages 1–3

# PLANNING GUIDE

# Writing to Tell a Story

| | Student Pages | Student Lesson | | | Language Skills | | | | |
|---|---|---|---|---|---|---|---|---|---|
| | | Vocabulary | Practice Exercises | Lesson Review | Identification | Writing | Punctuation & Capitalization | Grammar & Usage | Listening, Speaking, & Viewing |
| **Lesson 9-1** Telling a Story | 221–223 | ✔ | ✔ | ✔ | ✔ | ✔ | ✔ | ✔ | ✔ |
| **Lesson 9-2** Putting Events in Order | 224–226 | ✔ | ✔ | ✔ | ✔ | ✔ | ✔ | ✔ | ✔ |
| **Lesson 9-3** Deciding on Point of View | 227–229 | ✔ | ✔ | ✔ | ✔ | ✔ | ✔ | ✔ | ✔ |
| **Lesson 9-4** Using Verb Tense Correctly | 230–232 | | ✔ | ✔ | ✔ | ✔ | ✔ | ✔ | ✔ |
| **Lesson 9-5** Writing Dialogue | 233–237 | ✔ | ✔ | ✔ | ✔ | ✔ | ✔ | ✔ | ✔ |
| **Lesson 9-6** Using Direct and Indirect Quotations | 238–243 | ✔ | ✔ | ✔ | ✔ | ✔ | ✔ | ✔ | ✔ |

## Chapter Activities

**Teacher's Resource Library**
Life Skills Connection 9:
  Understanding Order of Events
Writing Tip 9: Writing Good Stories
English in Your Life 5: Telling a Story
Building Research Skills 9: Reading
  a Newspaper
Key Vocabulary Words 9

## Assessment Options

**Student Text**
Chapter 9 Review

**Teacher's Resource Library**
Chapter 9 Mastery Tests A and B

**Teacher's Edition**
Chapter 9 Writing Portfolio

| English in Your Life | Writing on the Job | Building Research Skills | Vocabulary Builder | Grammar Builder | Write About It | Group Activity | Reading Strategy | Six Traits | ELL/ESL Strategy | Background Information | Common Error | Life Skills Connection | Applications (Home, Career, Community, Global) | Online Connection | Teacher Alert | Speaking & Presenting Practice | Writing/Spelling/Grammar Practice | Auditory/Verbal | Body/Kinesthetic | Interpersonal/Group Learning | Logical/Mathematical | Visual/Spatial | Activities | Modified Activities | Workbook Activities | Self-Study Guide |
|---|---|---|---|---|---|---|---|---|---|---|---|---|---|---|---|---|---|---|---|---|---|---|---|---|---|---|
| | | | | | | | 221 | | 222 | 221 | | | 222 | | | 223 | 223 | | | | | | 38 | 38 | 38 | ✔ |
| | | | | | | | 224, 225 | | 226 | 224 | | 225 | | 224 | | | | | 226 | | 225 | | 39 | 39 | 39 | ✔ |
| | | | | | | | 227, 228 | | 229 | 227 | | | 228 | | | | | 229 | | | | 228 | 40 | 40 | 40 | ✔ |
| | | | | 232 | | | 230, 231 | | 231 | 230 | | | | | 232 | | 231 | | | | | | 41 | 41 | 41 | ✔ |
| | | 237 | | | | | 234 | | 235 | 233 | 233, 235, 236 | | 235 | | | 236 | | | | 234 | | | 42 | 42 | 42 | ✔ |
| 241 | 242 | | | | 240 | 243 | 238, 239 | 240 | 239 | 238 | 239 | | 242 | | 243 | | 241 | | | | | | 43 | 43 | 43 | ✔ |

**Student Text Features** | **Teaching Strategies** | **Learning Styles** | **Teacher's Resource Library**

## Pronunciation Key

| | | | | | | | | | | | |
|---|---|---|---|---|---|---|---|---|---|---|---|
| a | hat | e | let | ī | ice | ô | order | ů | put | sh | she |
| ā | age | ē | equal | o | hot | oi | oil | ü | rule | th | thin |
| ä | far | ėr | term | ō | open | ou | out | ch | child | ŦH | then |
| â | care | i | it | ȯ | saw | u | cup | ng | long | zh | measure |

ə { a in about / e in taken / i in pencil / o in lemon / u in circus }

## Modified Activities

The Teacher's Resource Library (TRL) contains a set of lower-level worksheets called Modified Activities. These worksheets cover the same content as the standard Activities but are written at a lower reading level.

## Skill Track

Use Skill Track for *Basic English Composition* to monitor student progress and meet the demands of adequate yearly progress (AYP). Make informed instructional decisions with individual student and class reports of lesson and chapter assessments. With immediate and ongoing feedback, students will also see what they have learned and where they need more reinforcement and practice.

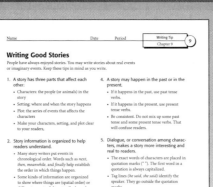

**Writing Good Stories**

People have always enjoyed stories. You may write stories about real events or imaginary events. Keep these tips in mind as you write.

1. A story has three parts that affect each other:
   - Characters: the people (or animals) in the story
   - Setting: where and when the story happens
   - Plot: the series of events that affects the characters
   - Make your characters, setting, and plot clear to your readers.

2. Story information is organized to help readers understand.
   - Many story writers put events in chronological order. Words such as *next, then, meanwhile,* and *finally* help establish the order in which things happen.
   - Some kinds of information are organized to show where things are (spatial order) or different aspects of character (looks and actions).

3. A story's point of view controls who tells the story and how much information readers get.
   - First-person point of view stories are told by a character who reports events using *I, me, my, mine, we, our, ours, us.*
   - Third-person point of view stories are told by someone who is outside of the story. This storyteller uses *she, her, hers, he, him, his, they, their, theirs* to report what happens.

4. A story may happen in the past or in the present.
   - If it happens in the past, use past tense verbs.
   - If it happens in the present, use present tense verbs.
   - Be consistent. Do not mix up some past tense and some present tense verbs. That will confuse readers.

5. Dialogue, or conversation among characters, makes a story more interesting and real to readers.
   - The exact words of characters are placed in quotation marks (" "). The first word in a quotation is always capitalized.
   - Tag lines (*he said, she said*) identify the speaker. They go outside the quotation marks.
   - The punctuation at the end of a quotation belongs inside the closing quotation mark ("). Which mark you use depends on where the tag lines fall. However, if a quotation is a question it always ends with a question mark. An exclamation ends with an exclamation mark.
   - Every time the speaker changes in a dialogue, begin a new paragraph.
   - If you report what someone said without using the speaker's exact words, do not use quotation marks.

**Pacemaker® Basic English Composition**

TRL

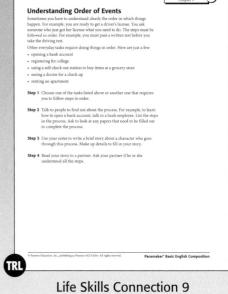

**Understanding Order of Events**

Sometimes you have to understand clearly the order in which things happen. For example, you are ready to get a driver's license. You ask someone who just got her license what you need to do. The steps must be followed in order. For example, you must pass a written test before you take the driving test.

Other everyday tasks require doing things in order. Here are just a few:
- opening a bank account
- registering for college
- using a self-check out station to buy items at a grocery store
- seeing a doctor for a check up
- renting an apartment

**Step 1**  Choose one of the tasks listed above or another one that requires you to follow steps in order.

**Step 2**  Talk to people to find out about the process. For example, to learn how to open a bank account, talk to a bank employee. List the steps in the process. Ask to look at any papers that need to be filled out to complete the process.

**Step 3**  Use your notes to write a brief story about a character who goes through this process. Make up details to fill in your story.

**Step 4**  Read your story to a partner. Ask your partner if he or she understood all the steps.

**Pacemaker® Basic English Composition**

# Writing to Tell a Story

Our lives are full of stories. Look around and you will see them everywhere. For example, look at the photo on the opposite page. What story does it suggest?

Derek arrived late for the tennis match. He changed quickly and hurried onto the court. He left his gym bag and water bottle on the bench in the locker room. Will he win the match? What will happen next?

This is an imaginary story. Like all stories, it has a setting, at least one character, and a plot. You can write about the real stories in your life. You can also write about made-up people and events. In Chapter 9, you will learn to write stories. You will learn how to put a story together, choose a point of view, and write dialogue.

## GOALS FOR LEARNING

- To write a paragraph that tells a story
- To put events in logical or chronological order
- To choose a point of view for writing a story
- To use verb tense consistently and logically
- To write dialogue
- To distinguish between direct and indirect quotations

**219**

## Introducing the Chapter

Have students examine the photo on page 218. Ask them what story they could make up about the student who owns this bag. As volunteers offer suggestions, encourage them to tell what events and characters they would put in their stories.

Read the paragraphs and Goals for Learning on page 219 aloud. Have students write questions about any terms or goals they do not understand. They can answer the questions as they read the chapter.

## Notes

Ask volunteers to read the notes that appear in the margins throughout the chapter. Then discuss them with the class.

## TEACHER'S RESOURCE

The AGS Globe Teaching Strategies in English Transparencies may be used with this chapter. The transparencies add an interactive dimension to expand and enhance the *Basic English Composition* program content.

## WRITING PORTFOLIO

Ask students to choose an exciting or funny experience they have had. Explain that they will be writing a story about this experience. Then have students brainstorm details. Suggest to students that they write sensory images to capture feelings, moods, or details. Have students keep their notes in a folder for easy reference. They will develop their stories as they read the chapter. This project may be used as an alternative form of assessment for the chapter.

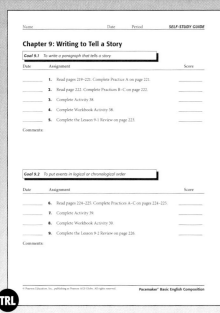

## Reading Strategy: Predicting

Invite volunteers to tell about predictions they have made, such as who will win a game or what the weather will be. Ask students to explain how they make such predictions. Explain that readers also predict what will happen next in a text on the basis of clues, logic, and past experience.

## Key Vocabulary Words

anecdote
character
chronological order
dialogue
direct quotation
fiction
indirect quotation
nonfiction
novel
plot
point of view
quotation
quotation marks
setting
short story

Have students read the vocabulary words and identify the ones that are familiar. Then read the words and meanings aloud. Group students and have groups write one card for each word. Then have them sort the cards into categories such as *kinds of stories, elements that make up a story,* and *ways of handling spoken words in writing.* Ask students to analyze each card and try to find a category for it.

# Reading Strategy: Predicting

Predicting is telling what you think will happen next. When you preview a chapter or lesson, it is a good idea to predict what the main ideas will be. When you predict:

- Make your best guess. Base your prediction on clues you have noticed.
- Add details about why you think your prediction will happen.
- Keep your prediction in mind as you read. What you read may cause you to change your prediction.

## Key Vocabulary Words

**Fiction** A piece of writing about imaginary people and events

**Short story** A short work of fiction

**Novel** A long work of fiction

**Nonfiction** A piece of writing about real people and actual events

**Plot** The events in a story

**Character** A person in a story

**Setting** The location and time of a story

**Anecdote** A very short story about a funny or interesting event

**Chronological order** An arrangement of events according to time, usually from the earliest event to the most recent event

**Point of view** The position of the storyteller in a story; either first-person or third-person point of view

**Dialogue** The words that people or story characters say to one another; conversation

**Quotation** Someone's exact spoken or written words; quotation marks are needed at the beginning and end of a quotation

**Quotation marks (" ")** The marks placed at the beginning and end of a direct quotation

**Direct quotation** A quotation that reports someone's exact words; quotation marks are required

**Indirect quotation** A quotation that reports what someone said without using the speaker's exact words; quotation marks are not used

**220**   *Chapter 9   Writing to Tell a Story*

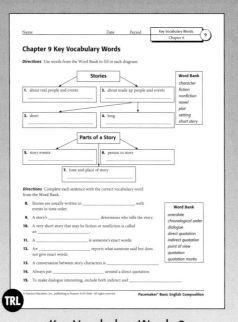

# Telling a Story

**Objectives**

■ To identify types of fiction and nonfiction
■ To write a story that includes a setting, plot, and characters
■ To write an anecdote

**Fiction**
A piece of writing about imaginary people and events

**Short story**
A short work of fiction

**Novel**
A long work of fiction

**Nonfiction**
A piece of writing about real people and actual events

***Reading Strategy:***
Predicting

Preview the lesson title, headings, and bold vocabulary words in this lesson. Predict what the lesson will teach you.

When you write a story, you are answering a basic question: What happened? Stories come in different lengths. A story may be a thousand pages or only one paragraph.

**Fiction** is a story about imaginary people and events. A short work of fiction is a **short story.** A long fictional story is a **novel.**

A story can also be about real people and actual events. True stories are **nonfiction.** Short works of nonfiction are essays and articles. They appear in magazines and newspapers. Nonfiction books cover many different topics. In a library or bookstore, you find them arranged by subject.

### Practice A

Read the paragraph. Then answer the questions below.

**The Day I Almost Drowned**
by Sonia Moreno

When I was eight years old, I almost drowned in the Gulf of Mexico. My cousin Luis and I were playing with a raft. The raft started to drift out to sea. As I swam toward the raft, the wind took it out farther and farther. People were yelling, but I could not hear them. A man on shore swam out to rescue me. When I got back to the beach, my mom and Luis were crying. We all thanked the man who saved me. Almost drowning was an unforgettable experience!

**1.** Who is the "I" in this story?

**2.** What event is described?

**3.** Sonia is a real person. Is her story fiction or nonfiction?

**4.** What information does the topic sentence give you?

**5.** Is the last sentence a conclusion or a summary?

## Chapter 9  Lesson 1

**Overview** This lesson identifies kinds of real and imaginary stories and describes story elements.

### Objectives

■ To identify types of fiction and nonfiction
■ To write a story that includes a setting, plot, and characters
■ To write an anecdote

**Student Pages** 221–223

**Teacher's Resource Library**

**Activity** 38
**Modified Activity** 38
**Workbook Activity** 38

### Vocabulary

| | |
|---|---|
| anecdote | novel |
| character | plot |
| fiction | setting |
| nonfiction | short story |

Display familiar stories as examples. Work with students to identify each as fiction or nonfiction. Then identify the stories as novels, short stories, or anecdotes. Finally, ask volunteers to describe the plot, setting, and a character in one favorite story.

### Background Information

This chapter includes a broad range of narrative writing in its definition of *story,* unlike a literature text, which would focus on short stories. Students will write anecdotes, narrative paragraphs, and one journalistic narrative.

### 1  Warm-Up Activity

Ask students to think about a good storyteller. Draw from students what makes the person's stories interesting.

***Reading Strategy:*** Predicting

Students may predict that the lesson will define different kinds of stories or describe what makes up a story.

### 2  Teaching the Lesson

Ask students to tell what kind of story each of the following would be:

a true story about getting lost (*nonfiction*)
a story about living on Mars (*fiction*)
the story of your life (*nonfiction*)

Ask students to invent and describe a hypothetical setting, characters, and plot of one of these stories.

### Practice A

Read the story aloud while students identify the characters, setting, and events.

### Practice A Answers

1. Sonia Moreno 2. The story tells how Sonia was swept out to sea and then rescued. 3. nonfiction 4. The topic sentence tells who was involved, how old she was, where she was, and what happened to her. 5. conclusion

## Practice B

Ask students who know *The Legend of Sleepy Hollow* to explain its plot in more detail. When students understand plot, characters, and setting, have them read the questions in Practice B and turn back to Practice A to answer them.

### Practice B Answers

Answers will vary in wording. Sample answers are given. **1.** Sonia is an eight-year-old girl at a beach. Luis is her cousin. Sonia's mom is a worried parent. An unnamed swimmer is the hero. **2.** The story is set at a beach on the Gulf of Mexico when Sonia was much younger. **3.** Sonia and Luis played with a raft. The raft drifted out to sea. Sonia swam after it and got too far out. Her mom and Luis were upset. A man swam out and rescued her. They all thanked the man.

### Practice C

Encourage students to choose a small event that can be described in a paragraph. You may want to have students copy a story map for gathering their notes about characters, setting, and plot events. Explain that this is to help them prewrite. They will also write a draft and a clean copy after they revise and edit.

### Practice C Answers

Anecdotes will vary but should show understanding of character, plot, and setting. They should also use specific details and sensory images.

### ELL/ESL STRATEGY

**Language Objective:**
*To write a story that includes a setting, a plot, and characters*

Students who are learning English may benefit from talking through a story together before they begin to write. Have them identify and describe the setting, plot, and characters and provide details about the story. Then have students write about these elements for their own story.

---

**Plot**
The events in a story

**Character**
A person in a story

**Setting**
The location and time of a story

**Anecdote**
A very short story about a funny or interesting event

 **NOTE**

A true story about someone's life is called a biography. When a writer writes a true story about his or her own life, it is called an autobiography.

---

 **Brush Up on the Basics**

An adjective adds to the meaning of a noun or a pronoun. Choose specific adjectives to describe your characters. See Grammar 51 in Appendix A.

---

## The Parts of a Story

When you write a story, you will include these things: **plot, character,** and **setting.** The plot is the events in the story. The characters are the people in the story. The setting is where and when the story takes place. Example 1 summarizes these three parts in Washington Irving's short story, *The Legend of Sleepy Hollow*.

▶ **EXAMPLE 1**

| | |
|---|---|
| Characters | Ichabod Crane, a school teacher<br>Katrina van Tassel, the woman Ichabod loves<br>Brom Bones, Ichabods rival |
| Plot | Brom defeats Ichabod and wins Katrina. |
| Setting | Tarry Town, a village in New York state, 1700s |

### Practice B

Read the story in Practice A. Then answer these questions.

1. Name the people in the story. Describe each person.
2. Where and when did this story take place?
3. List the events in the order they happened.

### Anecdotes

An **anecdote** is a very short story about an interesting or funny event. Anecdotes are often only one paragraph.

### Practice C

Write an anecdote about a funny or interesting event. It can be real or made up. First, list the characters involved in the event. Then list the details of the event in order. Next, use these lists to write your story. Finally, revise and edit your story. Add sensory images, specific words, and transitions. Read your anecdote to another student or to the class.

### GLOBAL CONNECTION

Challenge students to locate stories written by authors from countries around the world and read one by a chosen author. Students should write a summary of the story and its characters along with a few sentences about the author.

Match each word in Column 1 with a meaning in
Column 2. Write the letter of the meaning on your paper.

*Column 1*

1. anecdote
2. fiction
3. plot
4. characters
5. setting

*Column 2*

**A** a story about imaginary people

**B** what happens in a story

**C** the place and time of a story

**D** the people in a story

**E** a very short story about an
interesting event

6. Write a story about something that happened. It
can be fiction or nonfiction. Include one or more
characters. Write one sentence about the setting and
a few sentences about the plot. Write a conclusion or
summary at the end. Here are some suggestions to get
you started:

- Amber's dog gave her a big scare again.
- Derek receives a surprise gift.
- A popular band is coming to town, and Brandon
wants tickets.
- Last night Sonia got an interesting phone call.

*Writing to Tell a Story*   Chapter 9   **223**

*Lesson 9-1 Review Answers*

**1.** E **2.** A **3.** B **4.** D **5.** C **6.** Stories will vary
but should include a character or characters,
describe a setting, and involve a series of
events. Stories should also contain a topic
sentence and summary or conclusion
sentence.

## Speaking and Presenting Practice

Ask students to practice and read their
anecdote from Practice C or their story
from the Lesson 9-1 Review aloud to the
class. Instruct students to think about the
mood they want to create and practice
reading with appropriate expression,
tone, and pace.

## WRITING PORTFOLIO

**Checkpoint** Have
students consult their
portfolio notes about a
personal experience. They
can use a story map to
organize these notes and any other
details they wish to add.

## Spelling Practice

Have students reread the story in Practice
A to find words with a long *a* sound.
*(eight, playing, saved)* Ask students to
identify the letters that have the long *a*
sound in each word, then brainstorm
more words that spell the sound in this
way. Combine students' lists in a chart on
the board.

| *ei* | *ay* | *aCe* |
|------|------|-------|
| eight | play | save |
| freight | sway | gave |
| sleigh | may | brave |
| weigh | spray | date |
| neigh | clay | blaze |
| | say | make |
| | pay | chase |

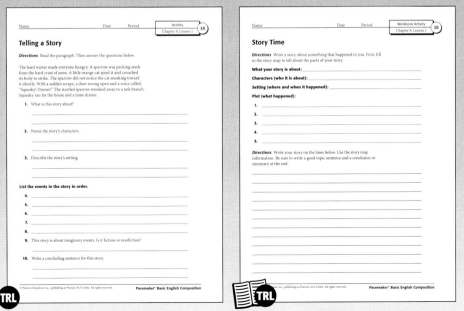

**Activity 38**          **Workbook Activity 38**

*Writing to Tell a Story*   **223**

### Chapter 9  Lesson 2

**Overview**  This lesson tells about ways of ordering plot events, primarily by chronological order.

### Objectives

- To put a series of events in chronological order
- To arrange details in a paragraph in different ways

### Student Pages  224–226

### Teacher's Resource Library

Activity  39

Modified Activity  39

Workbook Activity  39

Life Skills Connection  9

..............................................

## Vocabulary

**chronological order**

Write *chronos* on the board. Explain that this is the Greek word for *time*. Then have a volunteer explain what chronological order has to do with time. (*It is the technique of putting something in time order, from what happened first to what happened last.*)

..............................................

## Background Information

While most stories students will read use chronological order to organize events, individual paragraphs of description may use spatial, cause-and-effect, or compare-and-contrast order. Some stream of consciousness works purposefully distort the sense of time, instead organizing text around the way a character's mind works.

## 1  Warm-Up Activity

Have students suggest the best way to order or organize each of the following:

sentences describing someone
sentences describing a room
sentences telling about an accident

Point out that the details in stories must be organized logically and are usually in chronological order.

---

## LESSON 9-2  Putting Events in Order

### Objectives

- To put a series of events in chronological order
- To arrange details in a paragraph in different ways

**Chronological order**
An arrangement of events according to time, usually from the earliest event to the most recent event

**Reading Strategy:** Predicting

Predict what this lesson will say about the order of events in a story. What clues helped you make your prediction?

When you tell a story, think about the order of events. Think about which detail to tell first.

Often, you will tell about events in **chronological order.** Chronological order is the order in which events happened in time. You start with the earliest event and end with the most recent. Transitional words help show the order of events.

The events in Example 1 are in chronological order. Notice the transitions that help show this order.

▶ **EXAMPLE 1**

#### How I Met Sarah
by Derek Anderson

Last month I was running laps at the track. I was not watching where I was going. As a result, I ran into another runner. We both fell. Then each of us saw the other's surprised face and started laughing. I noticed immediately that the other runner had a beautiful smile. She told me her name was Sarah. When we finished our laps, we started talking. We decided to meet at the track after school twice a week.

### Practice A

Read the story in Example 1. Then answer the questions.

1. When did the event take place?
2. What happened after they bumped into each other?
3. Why did they both start laughing?
4. What did Derek like about Sarah?
5. What was the last thing that happened?

---

**224**  *Chapter 9  Writing to Tell a Story*

---

## 2  Teaching the Lesson

Ask students why transitions help make the order of details clear. Review transition words and phrases with students. Refer students to the lists on pages 127 and 128.

### TEACHER ALERT

 Students may think of details they want to add to their stories at odd moments. You may suggest having them write each event on a card, then putting the cards in chronological order, so that they can reorganize events easily.

## Practice A

Have a volunteer read the Example 1 paragraph aloud as students note the sequence of events and transitions that signal time order.

### Practice A Answers

**1.** The event took place last month.
**2.** They fell down.  **3.** They laughed because they saw each other's surprised expressions.
**4.** Derek liked Sarah's beautiful smile.
**5.** Derek and Sarah talked and agreed to meet twice a week after school.

### Reading Strategy: Predicting

Students may predict that story events will be organized in *chronological order* since the lesson emphasizes it.

**Reading Strategy:**
Predicting

Think about the prediction you made earlier. Is it still useful? Or do you need to change your prediction?

**Practice B**

Put these facts in chronological order. Start with the earliest event, and end with the most recent. Then use the facts to write a paragraph about St. Paul, Minnesota.

- St. Paul became a city in 1854.
- The name of the settlement was changed to St. Paul in 1841, when Lucien Galtier built St. Paul's Chapel.
- It became a town in 1849.
- The settlement was first called Pig's Eye after its first European settler, Pierre "Pig's Eye" Parrant.

## Other Kinds of Order

There are other ways to arrange the information in a story besides chronological order. When you describe a place, you might arrange the details from near to far. When you describe characters, you might tell how they look, then how they act.

**Practice C**

Read the details about a town. Arrange them in a logical order. Write a paragraph about this place. Use your imagination to add details. Use transitions and figures of speech.

*Most visitors want to see the beach first. Then they explore the town.*

- The edge of the town is on the ocean.
- The town is one square mile in size.
- All of the streets start at the ocean and head away from it.
- There is a beach on the ocean that people enjoy.
- Along the main street are many shops and restaurants.

*Writing to Tell a Story*   Chapter 9   **225**

## Practice B

Remind students that some stories are nonfiction. If they are historical in nature, then chronological order becomes even more important. Have students add transitions to the paragraph they write.

## *Practice B Answers*

Paragraphs will vary somewhat in wording. A sample paragraph is given.
The city of St. Paul didn't always have its "heavenly" name. It began as a settlement called Pig's Eye, after its first European settler, Pierre "Pig's Eye" Parrant. In 1841, when Lucien Galtier built St. Paul's Chapel, its name was changed to St. Paul. The name change seemed to draw people like a charm. By 1849 it had grown into a town. In 1854, just five years later, it was officially a city.

## Practice C

Have students suggest how they would order details in a story about their town. Sketch a simple map showing your town and point out logical ways to set up spatial order. Then have students read the directions and bulleted list.

## *Practice C Answers*

Paragraphs will vary. A sample paragraph is given.
The best day of our trip was spent in a fishing village on the Atlantic. The charming village is about one square mile in size, and we wanted to see it all. We began at the edge of town that looks onto the ocean. For an hour or so, we strolled along the beach in bare feet, peeking down street after street—for all the streets ran from the beach into the town. Choosing the street that looked busiest, we turned toward the heart of town, stopping to browse at many shops and restaurants. By lunchtime, we had picked our favorite restaurant and gratefully rested our feet.

**3** **Reinforce and Extend**

### LIFE SKILLS CONNECTION

 Distribute copies of Life Skills Connection 9. Talk about situations in which it is important to understand the order of events. Then have students work in pairs to complete the activity.

### *Reading Strategy:* Predicting

Students may predict that there are many ways to organize story events, but chronological order is the method used most often.

### LEARNING STYLES

 **Logical/Mathematical**

If students have difficulty ordering events, suggest that they create a time line, measured in appropriate units of time (weeks, days, hours, minutes, or seconds, for example). Then have students think through an incident, asking *What happened next?* They can plot the events in the incident along the time line.

**1.** a dog named Rex **2.** at the Choy home in the town of Springfield **3.** seven years ago and now **4.** *seven years ago, Now, Whenever* **5.** The final sentence concludes Rex's story of his life so far. **6.** Anecdotes will vary but should include at least one character, a setting, and a series of events that elaborate a situation. They should use transitions and logical order. **7.** Final copies should be clean and show effort to fix errors in grammar, spelling, and punctuation.

## WRITING PORTFOLIO

**Checkpoint** Have students look at their story map of a personal experience, add any other events they may have forgotten, and number events in chronological order.

## LEARNING STYLES

### Body/Kinesthetic

Have students write each sentence of their anecdote on a separate index card. Instruct students to put the cards in random order. In small groups, have students work through one set of cards at a time, putting them in order. Then have each group choose one story to act out for the class.

## ELL/ESL STRATEGY

### Language Objective:
*To create chrono-logical order in events and use transitional words*

Students may have difficulty creating chronological order in events, writing sentences, and using transitions. Suggest that they create simple sketches that show the events in the narrative. Have students cut the sketches apart and set them out in order. Working with an English-proficient partner, students can list transitional words useful to lead from one sketch to the next.

---

## LESSON 9-2

# REVIEW

Read the paragraph. Then answer the questions.

### Rex's Story

My life began in Springfield about seven years ago. I had three sisters, but Mrs. Choy sold them. Amber begged to keep me, so I was not sold. Now I spend my days eating, sleeping, and barking. Whenever I get a chance, I jump the fence and run away. Everyone chases me and yells, "Rex!" It is a lot of fun. All in all, I'm a happy dog.

**1.** Who is the "I" in this story?

**2.** Where does the story take place?

**3.** The story takes place at two different times. What are they?

**4.** What words point out chronological order?

**5.** What is the purpose of the last sentence?

Read each sentence. Does one make you think of a story?

- I had a strange experience.
- Did I do the right thing?
- This incident made everyone laugh.

**6.** Use one sentence as a guide to write an anecdote.

**7.** Revise, edit, and rewrite your story. Use the checklists on pages 134 and 138.

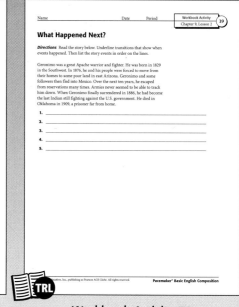

# Deciding on Point of View

## Objectives

■ To write a story using first-person or third-person point of view

■ To identify the point of view in a story

**Point of view**

The position of the storyteller in a story; either first-person or third-person point of view

***Reading Strategy:***
Predicting

Stop after reading Example 1. Make a prediction about what *third-person point of view* means.

Every story has a **point of view.** It is the position of the storyteller. When you identify a story's point of view, you know who is telling the story.

There are two main points of view: first person and third person. A writer chooses one of these to tell a story.

- You are writing from a first-person point of view when you use these pronouns: *I, me, my, mine, we, our,* or *ours.*
- You are writing from a third-person point of view when you use these pronouns: *she, her, he, him, his, they, their,* or *theirs.*

▶ EXAMPLE 1

| First Person | Last year I visited Yellowstone Park. |
| Third Person | Last year Derek visited Yellowstone Park. |
| First Person | We went out to dinner with our family. |
| Third Person | They went out to dinner with their family. |

### Practice A

Each sentence uses a first-person point of view. Write the sentence using third-person point of view. You can use your name, another name, or a third-person pronoun.

**1.** I drank a cup of tea with my lunch.

**2.** I put sugar in my tea.

**3.** Also, this time I used lemon.

**4.** There are many kinds of tea that I like.

**5.** What kind of tea should I drink with dinner?

## Chapter 9 Lesson 3

**Overview** This lesson explains and illustrates the use of first- and third-person points of view.

## Objectives

■ To write a story using first-person or third-person point of view

■ To identify the point of view in a story

**Student Pages** 227–229

**Teacher's Resource Library** TRL

**Activity** 40

**Modified Activity** 40

**Workbook Activity** 40

## Vocabulary

### point of view

Have students predict the difference in meaning of *point of view* in these two contexts:

From my *point of view,* Darius is being selfish.

An autobiography is told from first-person *point of view.*

Have students read the text definition and predict the meaning of *first-person point of view.*

## Background Information

Point of view influences a story greatly because it controls how information is perceived and understood. First-person storytellers create great interest because they report their thoughts and feelings from inside the story. However, their perceptions are limited by the inability to see inside other characters' heads. A third-person storyteller exists outside the story (and so has a less immediate impact), but can reveal all characters' thoughts and actions.

### *Reading Strategy:* Predicting

Students may predict that third-person point of view means telling about something someone else did, not something they personally experienced.

## 1 Warm-Up Activity

Have two volunteers act out an accident while a third observes. Then have each volunteer tell what happened from his or her point of view. Talk about how each version differs and why.

## 2 Teaching the Lesson

After students have read page 227, read aloud several paragraphs from familiar stories. Have students identify the storyteller's point of view as first-person or third-person.

## Practice A

Have students point out the words that change in Example 1 when a sentence changes from first-person to third-person point of view.

## *Practice A Answers*

Names used will vary. Sample answers are given. **1.** Britney drank a cup of tea with her lunch. **2.** She put sugar in her tea. **3.** Also, this time she used lemon. **4.** There are many kinds of tea that Britney likes. **5.** What kind of tea should she drink with dinner?

## Practice B

Have students find the words that change when the point of view changes in Examples 2 and 3. Ask students to explain how they need to change the story for Practice B.

### Practice B Answers

Stories will vary. A sample story is given. His name is Rex, and he loves mud puddles. He has white fur so his owner Amber can always see the mud. There was a big mud puddle in their yard. Amber let Rex out and he ran right for it. He splashed around with glee. To Rex's surprise, Amber was mad. She gave him a bath before he went inside. Rex doesn't know why, but he hates baths!

## Practice C

Talk about differences in how Amber would see the story in Practice B before students rewrite the paragraph from Amber's point of view.

### Practice C Answers

Stories will vary. A sample story is given. My dog Rex loves mud puddles. He has white fur, so I can always see the mud. There was a big mud puddle in our yard. I let Rex out, and he ran right for it. He splashed around with glee. Rex seemed surprised that I was mad! I had to give him a bath before he could come inside. It was too bad because Rex really hates baths!

### Reading Strategy: Predicting

Students may predict that point of view controls readers' attitude toward characters and events because it determines what is reported.

### WRITING PORTFOLIO

**Checkpoint** Have students choose a point of view for their stories about a personal experience, then write a first draft using their story maps.

---

**NOTE**

Fiction writers often use third-person point of view, but they also use first-person point of view.

**Reading Strategy:** Predicting

Based on the meaning of point of view, predict what effect it has on a story. Why do you think this?

When you are telling your own story, you usually use first-person point of view. Example 2 is written in first person.

▶ **EXAMPLE 2**

Thanksgiving dinner at our house is an important event. My aunts, uncles, and cousins spend all day helping us get ready for the meal. Thirty minutes later, we are too full to eat another bite. We stay around the table talking until we have room for dessert!

Example 3 is written in third person.

▶ **EXAMPLE 3**

Thanksgiving dinner at the Anderson house is an important event. Derek's aunts, uncles, and cousins spend all day helping the family get ready for the meal. Thirty minutes later, they are too full to eat another bite. Derek's family stays around the table talking until they have room for dessert!

When you change a story's point of view, some subjects and verbs change. Each verb must agree with its subject.

### Practice B

Change the story below from first-person to third-person point of view. Write the new paragraph on your paper.

My name is Rex, and I love mud puddles. I have white fur so my owner Amber can always see the mud. There was a big mud puddle in our yard. Amber let me out and I ran right for it. I splashed around with glee. To my surprise, Amber was mad! She gave me a bath before I came inside. I don't know why, but I hate baths!

When you write a story, you decide which character tells the story.

### Practice C

Rewrite the story in Practice B. This time use first-person point of view as if Amber is telling the story.

---

### LEARNING STYLES

**Visual/Spatial**

Have students create a diagram that represents the difference in point of view with a first-person and a third-person narrator. For example, students might draw a circle labeled "Story" and put a pair of eyes inside labeled "first-person point of view" to show this narrator is inside the story. A pair of eyes outside the circle could represent "third-person point of view" to show this narrator is not part of the story. Have students explain their diagrams to a partner.

### AT HOME

Have students take notes on an episode of a fiction TV program. Have them notice who the camera follows and what information viewers are allowed to have. This control establishes the way characters are perceived. Ask students to talk about how stories on TV use point of view.

# REVIEW

Each sentence uses first-person point of view. Write the sentence using third person. You can use your name, another name, or a third-person pronoun. Pay attention to subject-verb agreement.

**Example:** I like to go to the movies.

**Answer:** Luis likes to go to the movies.

1. I read a good book last week.

2. I could hardly put it down.

3. My mother gave it to me as a gift.

4. I like adventure stories.

5. Whenever I can, I look for an exciting activity.

Follow the directions in each item to rewrite the story.

6. The story below is written in third-person point of view. Rewrite it in first-person point of view. You can tell the story from either Sonia's or Amber's point of view. Be sure each pronoun has a clear antecedent.

> Last week Sonia asked her friend Amber to go kayaking. Amber had never been kayaking before. Sadly, the water in the lake was choppy. The wind was quite rough that day. Amber got into the kayak with help from Sonia. She paddled around the edge of the lake for a while. Then the wind picked up. "Let's get to shore!" Sonia said. "We will try again on a calmer day."

7. Read the story below. Choose one character: Mr. Peters or a student. Rewrite the story in first person from that character's point of view.

> Mr. Peters wanted to surprise his students. One day, he brought apples to school. Before class, he put one apple on each student's desk. When the students walked in, they all smiled.

*Writing to Tell a Story*   *Chapter 9*   **229**

---

## Lesson 9-3 Review Answers

Answers will vary. Sample answers are given. **1.** Derek read a good book last week. **2.** He could hardly put it down. **3.** His mother gave it to him as a gift. **4.** Sonia likes adventure stories. **5.** Whenever she can, she looks for an exciting activity. **6.** Last week I asked my friend Amber to go kayaking. She had never been kayaking before. Sadly, the water in the lake was choppy. The wind was quite rough that day. She got into the kayak with my help. She paddled around the edge of the lake for a while. Then the wind picked up. "Let's get to shore!" I said. "We will try again on a calmer day." **7.** The following sample is written from the teacher's point of view: I wanted to surprise my students. One day, I brought apples to school. Before class, I put one apple on each student's desk. When the students walked in, they all smiled.

## LEARNING STYLES

### Auditory/Verbal

Provide blind excerpts of stories that students have not read. Give each student an excerpt from a different story to practice reading aloud. In small groups, have students read their excerpts while the group listens to identify the storyteller and the point of view.

## ELL/ESL STRATEGY

### Language Objective:
*To practice using pronouns correctly to indicate point of view*

Provide a blank personal pronoun chart.

|  | Singular | Plural |
|---|---|---|
| 1st person |  |  |
| 2nd person |  |  |
| 3rd person |  |  |

Have students work together to complete the chart, referring back to Lesson 3-1 if needed. Then, as they complete this lesson's practices, have students refer to the chart.

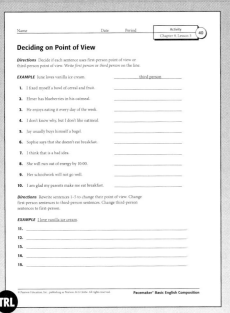

Activity 40

Workbook Activity 40

## Lesson at a Glance

### Chapter 9 Lesson 4

**Overview** This lesson demonstrates why verb tense should be consistent in a story.

### Objectives

■ To use verb tense correctly in your stories

■ To recognize incorrect tense changes

■ To tell a story in either present or past tense

**Student Pages** 230–232

**Teacher's Resource Library**

Activity 41

Modified Activity 41

Workbook Activity 41

### Background Information

Verb tense becomes more complicated in a story that is not linear. For example, a flashback may cause a change in tense as the narrator recalls past action. Tense becomes still more complex if, from a changing vantage point, the narrator who has leapt back in time then looks forward during the flashback. For example: *I raced to the site of the wreck and opened the car door. Later, I would regret this instinctive rush to help.*

### 1  Warm-Up Activity

Write the following sentence on the board:

*I stayed up late watching a movie, and I get scared.*

Ask students to find an error and explain what makes it wrong. *(Past and present tense are combined in one sentence.)*

### 2  Teaching the Lesson

Review the simple tenses of verbs with students, including the *be* verbs and several irregular verbs, such as *begin* and *hear* (which appear in Examples 1 and 2).

---

# Using Verb Tense Correctly

### Objectives

■ To use verb tense correctly in your stories

■ To recognize incorrect tense changes

■ To tell a story in either present or past tense

**Reading Strategy:** Predicting

Read the lesson title. Predict what correct verb tense has to do with writing a story.

As a writer, you must decide when your story happens. You must decide what tense the verbs will be. You can tell the story in the past or in the present.

▶ **EXAMPLE 1**

I began my first night in the wilderness. I watched the sun set in the sky. I snuggled down in my sleeping bag and watched the stars twinkle. Then I heard the howl of a wolf. I pulled the sleeping bag around my head. It was going to be a long night.

▶ **EXAMPLE 2**

I begin my first night in the wilderness. I watch the sun as it sets in the sky. I snuggle down in my sleeping bag and watch the stars twinkle. Then I hear the howl of a wolf. I pull the sleeping bag around my head. It is going to be a long night.

### Practice A

Read Examples 1 and 2. The verbs are in blue. What is the difference between these examples? Write your answer.

Verb tense usually stays the same throughout a story. In Example 3, the writer changed the tense in the middle of the story. Past-tense verbs are in blue. Present-tense verbs are underlined.

▶ **EXAMPLE 3**

The elevator stopped between two floors. The people inside the elevator looked worried. One man pushes the buttons nervously. The other man tries to open the door. The woman in the elevator banged on the door. Then they all yelled for help.

---

### Practice A

Have volunteers read Examples 1 and 2 aloud. You may want to have them alternate sentences to make differences clearer.

### Practice A Answers

Example 1 is told in past tense, so it has already happened, but Example 2 is told in present tense, as though the action is happening right now.

### Reading Strategy: Predicting

Students should understand that switching tenses within a story confuses readers about when events take place.

Write the paragraph in Example 3 on your paper. Then edit it so all the verbs have the same tense.

Some sentences have more than one verb. If the actions happen at the same time, the tenses should be the same.

▶ **EXAMPLE 4**

The parade began while the air was still cool. (past tense)

The band plays loudly as the crowd cheers. (present tense)

Different tenses show the actions happen at different times.

▶ **EXAMPLE 5**

They hope the temperature will get warmer tomorrow.

The verb *hope* is present tense. The verb phrase *will get* is future tense. Today they hope for a warmer tomorrow.

**Practice C**

In each pair, choose the sentence that shows the correct use of tenses. Write the letter of your answer.

1. **A** Luis **plays** chess when he **has** time.
   **B** Luis **played** chess when he **will have** time.

2. **A** He **learned** to play chess because his father **enjoyed** it.
   **B** He **learns** to play chess because his father **enjoyed** it.

3. **A** Players **learn** when they **find** good opponents.
   **B** Players **learn** when they **find** good opponents.

4. **A** **Pay** attention to your opponent, and you **will win.**
   **B** **Pay** attention to your opponent, and you **won.**

5. **A** Because Luis **studied** chess, he **played** well.
   **B** Because Luis **will study** chess, he **has played** well.

**Reading Strategy:**
Predicting

Remember your earlier prediction. Now you have read more of the lesson. What details can you add to your prediction?

*Writing to Tell a Story    Chapter 9    **231***

---

## Practice B

Ask students whether they think the verbs in Example 3 should all be past tense or present tense.

## *Practice B Answers*

Paragraphs may use either past tense or present tense. The sample uses past tense. The elevator stopped between two floors. The people inside the elevator looked worried. One man pushed the buttons nervously. The other man tried to open the door. The woman in the elevator banged on the door. Then they all yelled for help.

## Practice C

Ask volunteers to think of a sentence to add to Example 3 that would use past, present, and future tense. *(The woman told them, "I will get hysterical soon. I suffer from claustrophobia.")*

## *Practice C Answers*

**1.** A **2.** A **3.** B **4.** A **5.** A

**3   Reinforce and Extend**

## ELL/ESL STRATEGY

**Language Objective:**
*To practice using verb tense correctly*

Ask students to change the names and verbs in the sentences in Practice C and create five new sentences that show the correct use of tenses. Pairs of students can work together to create the sentences and share them with the rest of the group.

## Grammar Practice

Provide a list showing principal parts of common irregular verbs, such as *begin, break, bring, choose, come, do, drink, drive, eat, give, go, know, ride, run, see, speak, take, write.* Have partners use five of the verbs in sentences that report a series of events using present tense. Then have pairs exchange sentences, underline the verbs, and rewrite the sentences using past tense.

## *Reading Strategy:* Predicting

Students might predict that mistakes in verb tense would confuse story readers.

## Lesson 9-4 Review Answers

**1.** Paragraphs will vary but should involve a character or characters, a setting, and a series of events. Students should underline each verb. Revised and rewritten paragraphs should be free of verb tense errors and inconsistencies. A sample paragraph is given.

I was determined not to oversleep like I usually do on Monday morning. Before I went to bed, I set my alarm clock for 6:30. Then I worried that I might have set it for 6:30 PM. So I got up to check. It was 12:00 then. I woke up three times that night—at 3:00 AM, 4:00 AM, and 5:45 AM—wondering if it was time for the alarm to go off. By 6:30, I felt "Sleepless on Sunday!"

### WRITING PORTFOLIO

**Checkpoint** Have students review their story drafts for verb tense consistency and make any needed corrections.

### GRAMMAR BUILDER

Have students read the text. Write a template on the board for sentences with a direct object: S-V-DO. Add several examples: *Jeff ate a big steak. Daniel paid the waiter. Jeff thanked Daniel.* Have students substitute *whom* for *the waiter* in the second sentence and *Daniel* in the third sentence to hear correct use of *whom.*

### Grammar Builder Answers

**1.** Who  **2.** Whom

### TEACHER ALERT

Inverted subject-verb order in questions confuses many students. Have them reword questions as statements, for example *I would pick ____ for team captain.* Then it becomes clear that the blank is to be filled with a direct object, not a subject.

---

# REVIEW

1. Choose a topic below. Write a paragraph that tells a story. The story can be fiction or nonfiction. You can write from either first-person or third-person point of view. Underline each verb in your paragraph.
   - getting up in the morning
   - getting lost
   - the first day of school
   - buying shoes

2. Exchange paragraphs with another student. Edit the other person's story. Check the verb tenses.

3. When you are finished, exchange papers again. Revise and rewrite your story.

## GRAMMAR BUILDER

**Using *Who* and *Whom***
The pronouns *who* and *whom* confuse many people. These rules will help you.
- Use *who* as the subject of a sentence or clause.
   **Who** was with Joe?
- Use *whom* as a direct object or the object of a preposition. A direct object receives the action of the verb.
   She is the teacher **whom** students like best. **Whom** do you think is best?

Write *who* or *whom* to complete each sentence.
1. _____ won today's soccer game?
2. _____ would you pick for team captain?

---

Name _____ Date _____ Period _____  Activity  Chapter 9, Lesson 4  41

**Using Verb Tense Correctly**

***Directions*** The paragraph below uses past tense verbs. It contains some mistakes. Cross out verbs that use the wrong tense. Write the verb correctly above each one.

Brandon wanted to buy Sarah a valentine. He stopped by a drug store after school. He reads card after card. None of the cards seems exactly right for Sarah. At last he found one that he liked. All the way home, he hummed cheerfully.

***Directions*** Read each pair of sentences. Circle the letter of the sentence that shows correct use of verb tense.

1. **A** Sarah made a cake when she gets home from school.
   **B** Sarah made a cake when she got home from school.
2. **A** Because it was Valentine's Day, she baked it in a heart-shaped pan.
   **B** Because it is Valentine's Day, she baked it in a heart-shaped pan.
3. **A** Sarah waited for Brandon, who said he would stop by.
   **B** Sarah will wait for Brandon, who said he would stop by.
4. **A** She invites him in and had showed him the cake.
   **B** She invited him in and showed him the cake.
5. **A** It was a deep red color, and it had white frosting.
   **B** It is a deep red color, and it had white frosting.
6. **A** Sarah cutting a piece of cake and offered it to Brandon.
   **B** Sarah cut a piece of cake and offered it to Brandon.
7. **A** He thought that it was delicious.
   **B** He will think that it being delicious.
8. **A** Then Brandon gives Sarah the card he will buy for her.
   **B** Then Brandon gave Sarah the card he had bought for her.
9. **A** She liked the card because it was funny.
   **B** She will like the card because it was funny.
10. **A** They watched a movie, and then Brandon goes home.
    **B** They watched a movie, and then Brandon went home.

**Pacemaker® Basic English Composition**

**Activity 41**

---

Name _____ Date _____ Period _____  Workbook Activity  Chapter 9, Lesson 4  41

**When Did It Happen?**

***Directions*** Read the paragraphs below. They tell a story using present tense verbs. Rewrite the story on the lines. Change the verbs to past tense.

Adam has a job interview at Ben's Bookstore. He introduces himself to the store manager, Ms. Lorenzo. They talk about his work experience. Adam tells about his job at the library. Ms. Lorenzo thanks Adam. She says that she will call him soon.

As he leaves, Adam feels good about the interview. The next day, he receives a call. Ms. Lorenzo asks him to start work that weekend. Adam is happy to have the job.

_____
_____
_____
_____
_____
_____
_____
_____
_____
_____
_____
_____
_____
_____

**Pacemaker® Basic English Composition**

**Workbook Activity 41**

# Writing Dialogue

### Objectives

- To use dialogue to tell a story
- To understand quotations and quotation marks
- To punctuate dialogue correctly

**Dialogue**
The words that people or story characters say to one another; conversation

**Quotation**
Someone's exact spoken or written words; quotation marks are needed at the beginning and end of a quotation

**Quotation marks ("  ")**
The marks placed at the beginning and end of a direct quotation

**Dialogue** is conversation. It is the words that people or story characters say to each another. A **quotation** is someone's exact written or spoken words. You can use quotations in many types of writing. Here are the rules for writing quotations:

**Rule 1** Put **quotation marks** (" ") at the beginning and end of a quotation.

▶ EXAMPLE 1

Amber asked, "Where are you going?"

**Rule 2** Capitalize the first word of a quotation even when the quotation is in the middle of a sentence.

▶ EXAMPLE 2

Sonia answered, "Now I'm going to lunch."

**Rule 3** Identify the speaker at the beginning or end of a quotation. Use a comma to separate the speaker from the quotation. If the quotation ends the sentence, use an end punctuation mark at the end of it.

▶ EXAMPLE 3

"I'll see you at the bus stop," said Sonia.

Amber said, "I will see you later."

*Writing to Tell a Story*    *Chapter 9*    **233**

---

## Lesson at a Glance

### Chapter 9  Lesson 5

**Overview** This lesson shows how to write dialogue correctly.

### Objectives

- To use dialogue to tell a story
- To understand quotations and quotation marks
- To punctuate dialogue correctly

### Student Pages  233–237

### Teacher's Resource Library

Activity  42

Modified Activity  42

Workbook Activity  42

### Vocabulary

dialogue                    quotation marks
quotation

After they have read the key vocabulary words and their meanings, ask students to find examples of each in a book of stories.

### Background Information

Dialogue brings the story to life for readers by plunging them into character interaction. Dialogue also helps advance plot. For example, an argument between two characters reveals what happened to make them argue. It also reveals their personalities.

### COMMON ERROR

It may seem wrong to students to end sentences of dialogue with a comma because they are complete sentences. Point out that the tag line (such as *he said*) provides the rest of the meaning, so it must be attached to the quotation. If the tag line follows the quotation (and it is a statement), then the quotation will end with a comma.

---

## 1  Warm-Up Activity

Display a comic strip or page of a comic book. Ask students how the words would be different if they were placed in a short story format. (*Words in speech balloons would be placed in quotation marks and tagged with words of saying such as* he said. *Description and narration would be written in paragraph form with no quotation marks.*)

## 2  Teaching the Lesson

Have volunteers act out a scene with heavy dialogue from a familiar story as classmates follow along in their books. Point out that the characters only say the words that are in quotation marks. Words outside the quotation marks give clues as to how the characters speak.

# Practice A

Ask students to summarize Rules 1–3 in their own words and use Examples 1–3 to illustrate. Have students find the comma in each illustration. Then have them identify the spoken words in item 1 of Practice A and explain where they will put a comma and quotation marks.

## Practice A Answers

1. Sonia said, "I am going to Centerville."
2. Amber asked, "Why are you going there?"
3. "I want to see a rodeo," answered Sonia.
4. Amber said, "Take me with you." 5. "Sure, come along," replied Sonia.

# Practice B

Have students use Examples 4 and 5 to explain where a question mark and an exclamation point belong in a quote. Use the last sentence in Example 5 to point out that the quotation begins with a capital, even though it is preceded by words of saying.

## Practice B Answers

1. "How far are we from Centerville?" asked Amber. 2. "About 200 miles," said Sonia.
3. Amber asked, "When does the rodeo begin?" 4. "The rodeo begins at noon," Sonia answered. 5. Sonia said, "The first event is the barrel-racing event."

## 3 Reinforce and Extend

### LEARNING STYLES

**Interpersonal/Group Learning**

Copy dialogue from stories, leaving out punctuation and capital letters. Give small groups of students each a dialogue and have them work together to figure out who is speaking and which words represent the speaker's words. After rewriting the dialogue correctly, have students check it against the original. Then have group members take roles and read the dialogue aloud.

**Reading Strategy:** Predicting

Students should predict that this page will have them practice using the rules they learned on page 233 for writing quotations.

---

*Reading Strategy:* Predicting

Based on what you have just read, predict what this page will be about.

## Practice A

Write each sentence. Punctuate the dialogue.

1. Sonia said I am going to Centerville.
2. Amber asked Why are you going there?
3. I want to see a rodeo answered Sonia.
4. Amber said Take me with you.
5. Sure, come along replied Sonia.

**Rule 4** If a quotation is a question, use a question mark at the end of it instead of a comma. If the speaker's sentence expresses strong feeling, use an exclamation mark.

▶ **EXAMPLE 4**

"Will you be on time?" asked Amber.

"Of course I will!" Sonia said.

**Rule 5** Put the punctuation mark at the end of a quotation inside the closing quotation marks.

▶ **EXAMPLE 5**

"I want to see the barrel-racing event!"

"I want to see the bull-riding event," said Sonia.

Amber asked, "How long will we be there?"

## Practice B

Write each sentence. Punctuate the quotations. Capitalize the first word in a quotation.

1. How far are we from Centerville asked Amber.
2. About 200 miles said Sonia.
3. Amber asked when does the rodeo begin.
4. The rodeo begins at noon Sonia answered.
5. Sonia said the first event is the barrel-racing event.

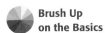
Find the mistakes. Write each sentence correctly.

1. "let's buy a postcard for Derek," suggested Amber.
2. "Which card do you like best," asked Sonia.
3. I like them all, "said Amber."
4. Sonia added. "Let's buy one of each."
5. That's a good idea, Amber agreed.

**Rule 6** Start a new paragraph with each new speaker. You do not always need to identify the speaker.

▶ EXAMPLE 6

"Here we are at last!" said Sonia.

"I am glad we came to the rodeo," said Amber.

"Me, too!"

**Rule 7** The speaker may say several sentences. Use quotation marks at the start and end of the entire speech.

▶ EXAMPLE 7

"Just think, only yesterday we were back home in Springfield. Now we are in Centerville. Soon we will be seeing a rodeo," Amber said to Sonia.

*These friends are talking excitedly. If you wrote their dialogue, you would have a long series of quotations.*

*Writing to Tell a Story    Chapter 9*    **235**

## Practice C

Remind students to refer to Rules 1–5 on pages 233–234 if they are uncertain how to punctuate and capitalize any item in the practice.

### *Practice C Answers*

1. "Let's buy a postcard for Derek," suggested Amber. 2. "Which card do you like best?" asked Sonia. 3. "I like them all," said Amber. 4. Sonia added, "Let's buy one of each." 5. "That's a good idea," Amber agreed.

### COMMON ERROR

Many students are perplexed about where to place a question mark or exclamation point in a quotation. Point out that the words of saying do not do the asking or exclaiming. They are always followed by a comma (at the beginning or middle of a quotation) or a period (at the end of a quotation).

### CAREER CONNECTION

Ask students to research a career that interests them. They may gather information using the Internet, a career guide book from a guidance counselor, or interviews with family members or neighbors. Have students use what they learn to write a dialogue. Ask students to use their dialogues to create a scene in which they are interviewed for a job in this field.

### ELL/ESL STRATEGY

**Language Objective:** *To dictate dialogue and explain differences in recording dialogue*

Students who are learning English may have stronger speaking skills than writing skills. Have them first dictate their dialogue to an English-proficient partner, who records it and explains possible improvements. Provide opportunities for these students to teach their classmates about differences in the way dialogue is presented in their native language.

## Practice D

Have students read each sentence first to determine which words are spoken. Then have them decide where capital letters and punctuation belong.

### Practice D Answers

**1.** "Which rider will win?" asked Amber. **2.** "The first rider will be Rudy Mendez," said the announcer. **3.** Sonia called out, "Come on, Rudy!" **4.** "That was a great ride," Amber said. **5.** "Give Rudy a big cheer!" said the announcer.

---

### COMMON ERROR

 Some students want to capitalize the second half of an interrupted quote even if it continues a sentence. Have them cover the words of saying and decide if the quotation contains more than one sentence before they punctuate.

---

## Practice E

Have students explain why *We* is capitalized but *or* is not in Example 8.

### Practice E Answers

**1.** "When is the next event?" Sonia asked. **2.** "I am not sure," Amber answered. "Let's ask someone." **3.** "When is the next event?" Amber asked the man at the booth. **4.** The man replied, "The next event is in 60 minutes." **5.** "I can hardly wait!" shouted Sonia.

### Speaking and Presenting Practice

Have students select a page of dialogue from a familiar story and work with a partner or a small group to practice presenting the scene as a reader's theater. Students should omit tag lines *(he said, she said)* and use expression, tone, and volume to communicate emotions. After each performance, invite the audience to tell how the scene helped them understand something new about the story or characters.

---

Write each sentence on your paper. Add the correct punctuation and capitalization.

1. which rider will win asked Amber
2. the first rider will be Rudy Mendez said the announcer
3. Sonia called out come on, Rudy
4. that was a great ride Amber said
5. give Rudy a big cheer said the announcer

**Rule 8** You can identify a speaker within a quotation. If the second part of the quotation finishes a sentence, begin it with a small letter. If the second part of the quotation is a new sentence, begin it with a capital letter.

▶ **EXAMPLE 8**

"We can see the bull-riding event," suggested Amber, "or the barrel-racing event."

"I want to see every event," Sonia replied. "We should stay longer."

**Practice E**

Write each sentence on your paper. Punctuate the dialogue correctly.

1. When is the next event Sonia asked
2. I am not sure Amber answered Let's ask someone
3. When is the next event Amber asked the man at the booth
4. The man replied The next event is in 60 minutes
5. I can hardly wait shouted Sonia

---

# REVIEW

Write each sentence on your paper. Then fix the mistakes.

1. We can put the postcards in our journals, Sonia said.

2. "Let's go," "The show is about to begin," Amber said.

3. "I hope we have good seats" Sonia said.

4. "I would like to be in the front row", Amber added.

5. "I know I will enjoy this, said Sonia."

Follow the directions to correct and rewrite the story.

6. Rewrite the story. Begin a new paragraph when someone different begins to speak. Add the correct punctuation and capitalization.

What do you want to do today Brandon asked his friends. Derek said I think we should go to the mall. I need a new pair of shoes. Let's go to the movies instead said Amber. That's a great idea Sonia replied. I want to see a comedy Brandon told them. Will you come with us asked Sonia. Yes Derek said I can go to the mall later. then it's decided laughed Sonia.

## VOCABULARY BUILDER

**Using the Word *Said***
In a dialogue, the words a character says are often followed by the words *he said* or *she said*. Sometimes, choose other verbs in place of *said*. Words such as *shouted* and *whispered* describe how a character spoke and show mood.

Think about what a character might say to match each verb below. Then write a short dialogue using three of the verbs.

| shouted | whispered | mumbled | questioned | bawled |
|---------|-----------|---------|------------|--------|

*Writing to Tell a Story* Chapter 9 **237**

---

## Lesson 9-5 Review Answers

**1.** "We can put the postcards in our journals," Sonia said. **2.** "Let's go. The show is about to begin," Amber said. **3.** "I hope we have good seats," Sonia said. **4.** "I would like to be in the front row," Amber added. **5.** "I know I will enjoy this," said Sonia. **6.** "What do you want to do today?" Brandon asked his friends.
Derek said, "I think we should go to the mall. I need a new pair of shoes."
"Let's go to the movies instead," said Amber.
"That's a great idea," Sonia replied.
"I want to see a comedy," Brandon told them.
"Will you come with us?" asked Sonia.
"Yes," Derek said. "I can go to the mall later."
"Then it's decided," laughed Sonia.

## WRITING PORTFOLIO

**Checkpoint** Have students revise their stories to include several lines of dialogue. Then have students check their dialogue for correct use of punctuation and capitalization.

## VOCABULARY BUILDER

Ask students to think of words they could use to replace *said* in a dialogue. (Some examples include *cried, exclaimed, whimpered, yelled, begged, crowed*.) After students read the text, ask what moods each of the bold words could suggest. (For example, *shouted* might suggest excitement, fear, or anger.)

### Vocabulary Builder Answers

Dialogues will vary. A sample dialogue is given.
"There's the light," whispered the spy.
"That's our signal. Let's go."
At the sound of footsteps, the guard bawled, "Halt! Who goes there?"
"Run! Now!" shouted Captain Hamilton.

---

**Writing Dialogue**

**Directions** Read each sentence. Find the mistakes in punctuation and capitalization. Write the sentences correctly on the lines.

**EXAMPLE** do you like jokes asked Anne
"Do you like jokes?" asked Anne.

1. a man downtown just ran over himself said Anne

2. oh no exclaimed Rita how did he do that

3. the man asked me to run across the street and mail a letter for him explained Anne

4. I could not do it Anne continued because I was already late

5. what happened then Rita asked eagerly

6. he ran over himself, of course giggled Anne

7. Rita rolled her eyes and said that is a real groaner.

8. well you laughed, didn't you replied Anne

9. Rita responded I owe you one

10. good said Anne I love a good joke

© Pearson Education, Inc., publishing as Pearson AGS Globe. All rights reserved.   **Pacemaker® Basic English Composition**

**Activity 42**

---

**Creating Dialogue**

**Directions** Rewrite the conversation below. Each time someone different begins to speak, start a new paragraph. Add the correct punctuation and capitalization.

did you see that asked Derek I sure did said Sonia and I could not believe my eyes Derek continued why would anyone wear his glasses hanging from just one ear? maybe he started to take them off said Sonia and forgot halfway. or maybe laughed Derek that is how he keeps from losing his glasses

© Pearson Education, Inc., publishing as Pearson AGS Globe. All rights reserved.   **Pacemaker® Basic English Composition**

**Workbook Activity 42**

*Writing to Tell a Story* **237**

### Chapter 9 Lesson 6

**Overview** This lesson shows the difference between direct and indirect quotations.

**Objectives**

- To recognize a direct quotation
- To recognize an indirect quotation
- To write a direct quotation
- To write an indirect quotation

**Student Pages** 238–243

**Teacher's Resource Library**

Activity 43

Modified Activity 43

Workbook Activity 43

English in Your Life 5

Building Research Skills 9

### Vocabulary

direct quotation    indirect quotation

Talk about the meaning of the adjective *direct. (having nothing between, straightforward)* Remind students that the prefix *in-* means "not." Invite students to predict the meanings of this pair of terms. Then have students read the meanings and adjust their predictions.

### Background Information

If students have difficulty distinguishing indirect and direct quotations, explain that indirect quotations state the general meaning of what a person said or thought. They do not use the person's exact words.

### 1  Warm-Up Activity

Have two volunteers role-play these parts:

SPEAKER: My fellow Americans, we must move forward without hesitation or fear.

REPORTER: Senator Smith said that we must move forward without hesitation or fear.

Talk about why one quote is direct and the other is indirect.

---

**Objectives**

- To recognize a direct quotation
- To recognize an indirect quotation
- To write a direct quotation
- To write an indirect quotation

**Direct quotation**
A quotation that reports someone's exact words; quotation marks are required

**Indirect quotation**
A quotation that reports what someone said without using the speaker's exact words; quotation marks are not used

*Reading Strategy:*
Predicting

Look at the Examples in this lesson. Predict the difference between direct quotations and indirect quotations.

# Using Direct and Indirect Quotations

A quotation can be either direct or indirect. In Lesson 9-5, you wrote **direct quotations.** You reported a speaker's exact words and placed quotation marks around them. An **indirect quotation** reports what someone said, but it does not use the speaker's exact words. When you write indirect quotations, you do not use quotation marks. The word *that* often introduces an indirect quotation.

▶ **EXAMPLE 1**

| Direct | "I enjoy rodeos," Amber said. |
| Indirect | Amber said that she enjoys rodeos. |

### Practice A

Decide if the quotation is a direct quotation or an indirect one. Write *direct* or *indirect* on your paper.

1. "Do you come to the rodeo often?" Sonia asked.
2. "Yes, I enjoy rodeos," answered the woman.
3. The woman added that she lives nearby.
4. "Do you live in Centerville?" she asked Sonia.
5. Sonia explained that she and Amber live in Springfield.

Sometimes you will want to change an indirect quotation to a direct quotation. To do this, you will need to change or rearrange some words.

▶ **EXAMPLE 2**

| Indirect | She asked if they enjoyed the rodeo. |
| Direct | "Did you enjoy the rodeo?" she asked. |

---

### 2  Teaching the Lesson

Give students this rule of thumb for distinguishing direct and indirect quotations:

*Direct quotation:* The words are being spoken by the person at that moment. Use quotation marks.

*Indirect quotation:* The words someone said earlier are being reported later, preceded by *that.* Do not use quotation marks.

### *Reading Strategy:* Predicting

Students may predict that indirect quotations tell what someone else said earlier and direct quotations tell what someone said at a particular moment.

### Practice A

Ask students to explain the difference between the Example 1 quotations. Point out that the practice is a dialogue between Sonia and a woman at the rodeo. Have students work in pairs to decide which words are spoken directly by the person.

### *Practice A Answers*

**1.** direct **2.** direct **3.** indirect **4.** direct **5.** indirect

**Reading Strategy:**
Predicting

What have you learned about punctuating dialogue? Did you predict that quotation marks are needed in direct quotations?

**NOTE**

A false quotation in nonfiction writing is called a *misquote*. A misquote in the media can have serious effects.

### Practice B

Change each indirect quotation to a direct quotation. Write the direct quotation on your paper. You will need to change some pronouns to first person.

1. Sonia said that she enjoyed the rodeo.
2. The woman said that the girls should come again.
3. Amber told her that they would definitely return.
4. Sonia said that she liked the bull-riding event best.
5. The woman said that she liked it best, too.

Sometimes you will want to change a direct quotation to an indirect quotation. You will need to change or rearrange some words.

▶ **EXAMPLE 3**

Direct      "There is a rodeo every month," she said.

Indirect    She said that there is a rodeo every month.

### Practice C

Write each direct quotation as an indirect quotation.

1. "Next time let's bring Derek," Amber said.
2. Sonia agreed, "He would enjoy the rodeo."
3. "Who is Derek?" the woman asked.
4. "He is a friend of ours from school," Amber told her.
5. The woman said, "Bring him when you come again."

When you are writing a story, use both direct and indirect quotations. This creates variety. If you are writing nonfiction, make sure your direct quotations are accurate. The words must be exact. If you are not sure of someone's exact words, then use an indirect quotation.

*Writing to Tell a Story    Chapter 9    **239***

## Practice B

Have students look at Example 2 and explain how the direct quotation was created from the first sentence. Talk about why the pronoun *they* must be changed to *you*. (*Because the woman herself is speaking to Amber and Sonia, she must use the pronoun* you.) Point out that some verbs will change slightly, too.

### *Practice B Answers*

Answers will vary somewhat in wording and word order. **1.** Sonia said, "I enjoyed the rodeo." **2.** "You girls should come again," commented the woman. **3.** Amber replied, "We will definitely return." **4.** "I liked the bull-riding event best," said Sonia. **5.** The woman agreed, "I liked it best, too."

## Practice C

Use Example 3 to point out that, to change a direct quotation to an indirect quotation, students will reverse the process they just learned.

### *Practice C Answers*

Answers will vary somewhat in wording and order. **1.** Amber said that they should bring Derek next time. **2.** Sonia agreed that he would enjoy the rodeo. **3.** The woman asked them who Derek is. **4.** Amber explained that he is a friend of theirs from school. **5.** The woman suggested that they should bring him when they came to the rodeo again.

**3** | **Reinforce and Extend**

### COMMON ERROR

Remind students that quotation marks must always be used in pairs. Some writers forget to add the end quotation marks.

### *Reading Strategy:* Predicting

Students may say they have learned where to place quotation marks and the punctuation marks that accompany them.

## Lesson 9-6 Review Answers

**1.** direct **2.** indirect **3.** indirect **4.** direct
**5.** direct
Answers 6–10 may vary somewhat in wording or order. **6.** "You can leave work early, Derek," said Ms. Lentz.
**7.** "Thank you, Ms. Lentz," replied Derek.
**8.** He told her that he had a big test to study for. **9.** He explained that he had to go to the library. **10.** He confessed that he was hoping for an A on the test.

### WRITE ABOUT IT

Display a short story to point out conventions such as beginning each speaker's words of dialogue on a new line. Suggest that students make a separate pass through their story for each type of correction: spelling, verb tense consistency, punctuation, and so on.

## Six Traits of Writing Focus

| Ideas | ✔ | Word Choice |
|---|---|---|
| Organization | ✔ | Sentence Fluency |
| Voice | | Conventions |

### Sentence Fluency

Inform students that readers will not find a story engaging if it is choppy and difficult to read. Have students read their story aloud to a partner to make sure it flows well. Have partners recommend smoother transitions.

Tell students that word choice can help make a story funny. Suggest that they choose a word with multiple meanings to create an amusing play on words.

Also tell students to check page WPH1 for more instruction on the Six Traits of Writing.

---

LESSON
## 9-6

# REVIEW

Identify each sentence as either a direct quotation or an indirect quotation. Write *direct* or *indirect* on your paper.

1. "Do you work today?" Mrs. Anderson asked Derek.
2. Derek said that he had to work but could leave early.
3. Mrs. Anderson asked Derek if he was ready for his test.
4. "I have some more studying to do," Derek said.
5. Mrs. Anderson said, "I am sure you will do well."

Change each indirect quotation to a direct quotation. You can change or rearrange some words.

6. Ms. Lentz told Derek that he could leave work early.
7. Derek thanked Ms. Lentz.

Change each direct quotation to an indirect quotation. You can change or rearrange some words.

8. "I have a big test to study for," Derek told her.
9. "I am going to the library," Derek said.
10. "I am hoping for an A on this test," he said.

### WRITE ABOUT IT

**A Funny Thing That Happened**
Write a short story about a funny thing that happened to you. Tell your story in five paragraphs. Make the first paragraph an introduction. Use the next three paragraphs to give details. Include at least three sentences of dialogue. Use both direct and indirect quotations. Make the last paragraph a conclusion. Think of it as the "punch line." When you are finished, check verb tenses, spelling, and punctuation. Then pair up with another student and read each other's stories.

**Six Traits of Writing:**
*Sentence Fluency*
smooth rhythm and flow

**240** Chapter 9 Writing to Tell a Story

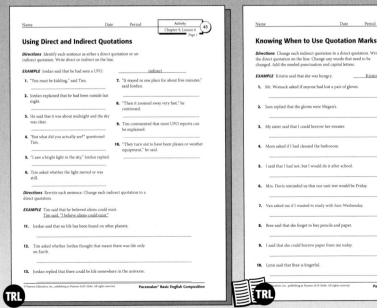

Activity 43, pages 1–2

Workbook Activity 43

## Telling a Story

Lea Hiatt had an automobile accident in a parking lot. She reported the accident to the police. The officer had her tell how the accident happened. It was important for Lea to speak clearly and put events in order when she told the story. Read Lea's story carefully. Then answer the questions below.

### Accident Report Form

*I pulled into the parking lot at Fairmart. I was going about 10 miles per hour. There was an empty parking space on the right up ahead. As I started to pull into the space, a red van came toward me very fast. It was going the wrong way. It hit the left rear of my car. This impact pushed my car into the blue truck that was parked to the right. Now my neck hurts.*

1. What caused the accident?

2. Why did Lea say how fast she was going?

3. **CRITICAL THINKING** Why is it important to tell the events of a story in the order they happened?

## SPEAKING AND LISTENING

Think about an unforgettable event from your childhood. What happened? Why? What was the experience like? Tell your story to a partner. Then switch roles. As you listen to your partner's story, take notes and ask questions about any part that is not clear. Use your notes to retell your partner's story to a group. Be sure to tell the events in order.

Explain that when someone has an automobile accident, he or she reports the accident to the police, who write a report about it. Have students read the opening paragraph of text and tell why they think Lea needs to be accurate and clear about how the accident happened. (*Fault will be assigned according to the report, and insurance will make judgments based on it.*) Then have students read the accident report and answer the questions.

### English in Your Life Answers

1. A red van was speeding the wrong way in a parking lot and hit Lea's car. 2. She wanted to make it clear that she was not being reckless or at fault for causing the accident. 3. The story must be clear to the listener or reader. If events are out of order, the story will be confusing.

## Writing Practice

Have students practice what they have learned about writing stories by rewriting the accident report on this page. Their revisions should develop a plot and include dialogue. Remind students to keep point of view and verb tense consistent.

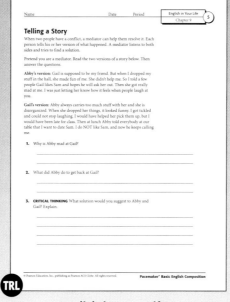

English in Your Life 5

Survey your students about their newspaper habits. How many see a paper every day? Which sections do they read? If they do not read a newspaper, what is their primary source of information? Have copies of a variety of different newspapers on hand. Talk about their sections and organization. When students complete the activity, provide them a newspaper or have partners share one.

## Building Research Skills Answers

Answers will vary depending on the newspaper. Reasonable answers are given. **1.** The index should be found on page 1 or 2 of the first section. **2.** Many newspapers have sections for major news, editorials, sports, business, and classified advertisements. Some also have sections for travel, leisure, and arts. **3.** Readers can see what is on the front page immediately.

## IN THE COMMUNITY

Ask interested students to learn about the production of a local newspaper either by asking for an interview and tour or by researching the paper's Web site. Students should try to answer questions such as *What departments does the paper have? What does a worker in each department do? How do you find out about news stories? Who decides which stories go where? When does writing for the next day's paper have to be complete?* Ask students to report what they learned to the class.

---

## Reading a Newspaper

A newspaper reports all kinds of stories. The front page has news stories. The sports page tells what happened in games. A travel section might tell about someone's trip to China.

How can you find your way around a newspaper? Suppose you want to read what happened at the baseball game last night. You would look in the sports section of the newspaper.

Most newspapers are organized in sections—A, B, and so on. They often have an index on the first or second page. It tells where to find each section of the newspaper. Here is a sample index:

| | |
|---|---|
| COUNTY EVENTS | A2 |
| LOCAL AND STATE NEWS | A3 |
| OBITUARIES | A4 |
| NATIONAL AND WORLD NEWS | A5 |
| OPINIONS | A6 |
| SPORTS | B1 |

---

Find a local or national newspaper at home or in the library. Answer the questions below using this newspaper.

1. Where is the index of the newspaper located?

2. How many sections does the newspaper have? What are they?

3. CRITICAL THINKING Why doesn't the newspaper's index list what is on the front page?

## MEDIA AND TECHNOLOGY

News stories are also found on radio, TV, and the Internet. Some radio and TV stations present news all day and night. Other stations give the news once an hour or several times a day. Most networks give news online as well as on the air. Find one of these news sources. List how and when it gives the news.

---

TRL

**Building Research Skills 9**

- Stories can be fiction or nonfiction. They can be long or short. An anecdote is a very short story that is interesting or funny.

- When you write a story, describe the setting, characters, and plot.

- Put the events in a story in chronological order. Use transitions to help you tell the story.

- Think about the order of other story details.

- Decide on the best point of view for a story. Use first-person point of view to tell about a true experience that you had.

- If you change a story's point of view, watch the subject-verb agreement.

- Use verb tense correctly in your writing. The verbs in a story usually have the same tense. They are either all in past tense or all in present tense.

- Use dialogue in your story. Use correct punctuation and capitalization in quotations. Follow the rules listed in Lesson 9-5.

- For variety, use both direct and indirect quotations in your writing. Indirect quotations do not have quotation marks.

- In nonfiction, when you do not know someone's exact words, use an indirect quotation.

## GROUP ACTIVITY

Work with a group to write a story about a local hero. Pick someone who has done something brave or unselfish. Tell about the person's good deed or deeds. Put events in order. Use examples, description, and dialogue to show the person's character. Read the story aloud. Have each member of the group read a part of the story. Use expression and tone of voice to show the mood you want.

## Chapter 9 Summary

Have volunteers read aloud each Summary item on page 243. Ask volunteers to explain the meaning of each item.

## ONLINE CONNECTION

Students who are interested in learning more skills for writing short stories will find these sites useful:

www.agsglobepmbec.com/page243a ("How to Write a Short Story")

www.agsglobepmbec.com/page243b ("Short Story Writing: Plot")

www.agsglobepmbec.com/page243c ("How to Write a Better Weblog")

## GROUP ACTIVITY

Groups will need time and access to information to gather news stories and interviews. If possible, students should consult at least one primary source, such as a witness to the heroic action. Encourage students to include facts and details that inspire them or make them admire the hero. Remind groups that specific words and sensory images will make their descriptions vivid.

## Chapter 9 Review

Use the Chapter Review to prepare students for tests and to reteach content from the chapter.

## Chapter 9 Mastery Test

The Teacher's Resource Library includes two forms of the Chapter 9 Mastery Test. Each test addresses the chapter Goals for Learning. An optional third page of additional critical-thinking items is included for each test. The difficulty level of the two forms is equivalent.

### Review Answers

#### Part A

1. nonfiction  2. chronological order
3. fiction  4. dialogue  5. direct quotation
6. indirect quotation  7. setting  8. plot
9. character  10. anecdote  11. novel
12. short story  13. point of view
14. quotation marks

#### Part B

15. Paragraphs will vary somewhat in wording. A sample paragraph is given. His name is Luis Moreno, and he loves chess. He has a good teacher. He learned chess from his father. Mr. Moreno taught Luis everything he knows. Luis has been winning a lot of matches.

---

**Word Bank**

anecdote
character
chronological order
dialogue
direct quotation
fiction
indirect quotation
nonfiction
novel
point of view
plot
quotation marks
setting
short story

**Part A** Find the word or words in the Word Bank that complete each sentence. Write your answer on your paper.

1. A _____ story is about real people and actual events.
2. The arrangement of events according to time is _____.
3. A story about imaginary people and events is _____.
4. The conversation between people or story characters is _____.
5. A _____ is someone's exact words in quotation marks.
6. When you tell what someone said without using the exact words, you are using an _____.
7. The location and time of a story make up the _____.
8. The events of a story make up the _____.
9. A person in a story is a _____.
10. A very short story about a funny event is an _____.
11. A long work of fiction is a _____.
12. A short work of fiction is a _____.
13. The _____ of a story is either first person or third person.
14. Use _____ around a direct quotation.

**Part B** Follow the directions to rewrite the story.

15. Change the point of view to third person. Write the new sentences. Pay attention to subject-verb agreement.

   My name is Luis Moreno, and I love chess. Luckily, I have a good teacher. I learned chess from my father. He taught me everything he knows. I have been winning a lot of matches.

---

**244**   *Chapter 9   Writing to Tell a Story*

---

### Chapter 9 Mastery Test A

Name _____ Date _____ Period _____ | Mastery Test A / Chapter 9 / Page 1

**Part A** Write the word or phrase that best completes each sentence.

1. The words that characters say to each other in a story is _____.
2. A _____ story tells about imaginary people and events.
3. A story takes place at a certain time and place called the _____.
4. A long work of fiction is a _____.
5. Put _____ at the beginning and end of a direct quotation.
6. The events in a story make up its _____.
7. A _____ reports someone's exact words.
8. An _____ is a very short story about a funny event.
9. True stories, such as essays and articles, are _____.
10. The storyteller determines whether a story is told from first-person or third-person _____.

**Part B** Read the story. Then answer the questions below.
Some explorers became lost in a cave. They had no food and little water. After wandering for several days, they became weak. Then a dog finds them and leads them to safety.

11. How is the story organized? _____
12. What happened after the explorers became lost? _____
13. How does the plot end? _____
14. What is the story point of view? Circle one:   first person   third person
15. What sentence contains a mistake in verb tense? _____

© Pearson Education, Inc., publishing as Pearson AGS Globe. All rights reserved.   **Pacemaker® Basic English Composition**

---

### Chapter 9 Mastery Test A, continued

Name _____ Date _____ Period _____ | Mastery Test A / Chapter 9 / Page 2

**Part C** Rewrite each sentence. Change the point of view from third person to first person. Fix any mistakes in verb tense.

16. Pam cleaned out the stalls and polishes her tack.
17. She worked at the stables every weekend.
18. Her horse was an Appaloosa, and it stays in a corral.
19. Pam wanted to win a contest, so she practices often.
20. When it is raining, she will ride indoors.

**Part D** Fix mistakes in punctuation and capitalization. Then rewrite the dialogue as an indirect quotation.

21. can I take the car to practice pat asked.
22. _____
23. yes you may mom said but be careful
24. _____
25. it is supposed to rain she added
26. _____
27. thanks said pat I should be home by 7
28. _____
29. goodbye called mom have fun
30. _____

© Pearson Education, Inc., publishing as Pearson AGS Globe. All rights reserved.   **Pacemaker® Basic English Composition**

---

### Chapter 9 Mastery Test A, continued

Name _____ Date _____ Period _____ | Mastery Test A / Chapter 9 / Page 3

**Part E** Write your answer to each question. Use complete sentences. Support each answer with facts and examples from the textbook.

31. How does a writer show when events happened in a story?
32. How are direct and indirect quotations different?

**Part F** Write a paragraph for each topic. Include a topic sentence, body, and conclusion in the paragraph. Support your answers with facts and examples from the textbook.

33. Explain the difference between first-person and third-person point of view.
34. What should you include in a paragraph that tells a story?

© Pearson Education, Inc., publishing as Pearson AGS Globe. All rights reserved.   **Pacemaker® Basic English Composition**

---

Chapter 9 Mastery Test A, pages 1–3

**Part C** Complete each sentence. Choose the verb with the same tense as the verb in bold. Write the letter of your answer.

**16.** Rex **barked** fiercely when the mailman _____ the gate.
 A opens
 B will open
 C opened
 D opening

**17.** The mailman **jumps** when he _____ Rex barking.
 A heard
 B hearing
 C hears
 D will hear

**18.** Sonia **throws** a ball because it _____ Rex.
 A amusing
 B has amused
 C amused
 D amuses

**Part D** Find the punctuation and capitalization mistakes. Write the dialogue correctly.

**19.** "where is your homework, Derek" asked Ms. Ruiz.

**20.** Derek replied it must be at home on my desk.

**21.** "your book report is due today" Ms. Ruiz said. I know Derek replied

**Part E** Change each indirect quotation to a direct quotation. Change each direct quotation to an indirect quotation. Write the new sentences on your paper. Capitalize and punctuate each sentence correctly.

**22.** Sonia told Derek that she had gone to Centerville to see a rodeo.

**23.** Derek asked who had gone with her.

**24.** Sonia told him that she had gone with Amber.

**25.** "Are you going again?" Derek asked.

**Test Tip**

Read test directions more than once. Underline key words that tell you what to do. For example, *explain, describe,* and *give two examples* are key words.

## Review Answers

### Part C

**16.** C **17.** C **18.** D

### Part D

**19.** "Where is your homework, Derek?" asked Ms. Ruiz. **20.** Derek replied, "It must be at home on my desk." **21.** "Your book report is due today," Ms. Ruiz said. "I know," Derek replied.

### Part E

Sentences may vary slightly in wording. Sample answers are given. **22.** "Derek, I went to Centerville to see a rodeo," said Sonia. **23.** "Who went with you?" Derek asked. **24.** "I went with Amber," Sonia told him. **25.** Derek asked whether Amber and Sonia would be going again.

**WRITING PORTFOLIO**

**Wrap-Up** Have students work with a partner to revise and edit their stories about a personal experience. Have students publish their stories by reading them aloud or collecting them in a class book. This project may be used as an alternative form of assessment for the chapter.

---

# PLANNING GUIDE

# Writing for School

| | Student Pages | Vocabulary | Practice Exercises | Lesson Review | Identification | Writing | Punctuation & Capitalization | Grammar & Usage | Listening, Speaking, & Viewing |
|---|---|---|---|---|---|---|---|---|---|
| | **Student Lesson** | | | | **Language Skills** | | | | |
| **Lesson 10-1** Answering Test Questions | 249–252 | | ✔ | ✔ | ✔ | ✔ | ✔ | ✔ | ✔ |
| **Lesson 10-2** Writing an Essay | 253–257 | ✔ | ✔ | ✔ | ✔ | ✔ | ✔ | ✔ | ✔ |
| **Lesson 10-3** Writing a Report About a Book, Movie, or TV Show | 258–265 | ✔ | ✔ | ✔ | ✔ | ✔ | ✔ | ✔ | ✔ |

## Chapter Activities

**Teacher's Resource Library**
Life Skills Connection 10:
   Answering Essay Questions
Writing Tip 10: Improving Your
   Essay Answers
Writing on the Job 5: Children's
   Librarian
Building Research Skills 10: Judging
   Information Sources
Key Vocabulary Words 10

## Assessment Options

**Student Text**
Chapter 10 Review

**Teacher's Resource Library**
Chapter 10 Mastery Tests A and B

**Teacher's Edition**
Chapter 10 Writing Portfolio

| Student Text Features | | | | | | | | | Teaching Strategies | | | | | | | | | Learning Styles | | | | | Teacher's Resource Library | | | |
|---|---|---|---|---|---|---|---|---|---|---|---|---|---|---|---|---|---|---|---|---|---|---|---|---|---|---|
| English in Your Life | Writing on the Job | Building Research Skills | Vocabulary Builder | Grammar Builder | Write About It | Group Activity | Reading Strategy | Six Traits | ELL/ESL Strategy | Background Information | Common Error | Life Skills Connection | Applications (Home, Career, Community, Global) | Online Connection | Teacher Alert | Speaking & Presenting Practice | Writing/Spelling/Grammar Practice | Auditory/Verbal | Body/Kinesthetic | Interpersonal/Group Learning | Logical/Mathematical | Visual/Spatial | Activities | Modified Activities | Workbook Activities | Self-Study Guide |
|  |  |  | 251 |  |  |  | 249, 251 |  | 250 | 249 | 250 |  | 250 |  |  |  |  |  | 250 |  | 251 |  | 44 | 44 | 44 | ✔ |
|  |  |  |  | 257 |  |  | 254, 256 |  | 254 | 253 | 255, 256 | 255 | 254 | 256 |  | 257 | 256 | 255 |  |  |  | 254 | 45 | 45 | 45 | ✔ |
| 263 | 264 |  |  |  | 262 | 265 | 259, 260 | 262 | 259 | 258 | 259, 261 |  | 260, 261 | 265 | 260 |  | 259, 261 |  |  | 260 |  |  | 46 | 46 | 46 | ✔ |

## Pronunciation Key

| | | | | | | | | | | | |
|---|---|---|---|---|---|---|---|---|---|---|---|
| a | hat | e | let | ī | ice | ô | order | ù | put | sh | she |
| ā | age | ē | equal | o | hot | oi | oil | ü | rule | th | thin |
| ä | far | ėr | term | ō | open | ou | out | ch | child | ᴛʜ | then |
| â | care | i | it | ȯ | saw | u | cup | ng | long | zh | measure |

ə { a in about, e in taken, i in pencil, o in lemon, u in circus }

## Modified Activities

The Teacher's Resource Library (TRL) contains a set of lower-level worksheets called Modified Activities. These worksheets cover the same content as the standard Activities but are written at a lower reading level.

## Skill Track

Use Skill Track for *Basic English Composition* to monitor student progress and meet the demands of adequate yearly progress (AYP). Make informed instructional decisions with individual student and class reports of lesson and chapter assessments. With immediate and ongoing feedback, students will also see what they have learned and where they need more reinforcement and practice.

## Chapter 10:
## Writing for School

## Skill Track for Basic English Composition

## Teacher's Resource Library TRL

**Activities** 44–46

**Modified Activities** 44–46

**Workbook Activities** 44–46

**Life Skills Connection** 10

**Writing Tip** 10

**Writing on the Job** 5

**Building Research Skills** 10

**Key Vocabulary Words** 10

**Chapter 10 Self-Study Guide**

**Chapter 10 Mastery Tests A and B**

(Answer Keys for the Teacher's Resource Library begin on page 446 of the Teacher's Edition.)

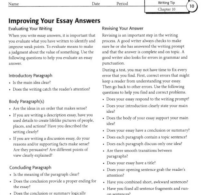

### Improving Your Essay Answers

**Evaluating Your Writing**

When you write essay answers, it is important that you evaluate what you have written to identify and improve weak points. To evaluate means to make a judgment about the value of something. Use the following questions to help you evaluate an essay answer.

**Introductory Paragraph**
- Is the main idea clear?
- Does the writing catch the reader's attention?

**Body Paragraph(s)**
- Are the ideas in an order that makes sense?
- If you are writing a description essay, have you used details to create lifelike pictures of people, places, and actions? Have you described the setting clearly?
- If you are writing a discussion essay, do your reasons and/or supporting facts make sense? Are they persuasive? Are different points of view clearly explained?

**Concluding Paragraph**
- Is the meaning of the paragraph clear?
- Does the conclusion provide a proper ending for the essay?
- Does the conclusion or summary logically fit with the main idea and supporting paragraph(s)?

**Entire Essay**
- Are there any grammar, spelling, or punctuation errors?
- Does the essay answer the writing prompt logically and completely?

**Revising Your Answer**

Revising is an important step in the writing process. A good writer always checks to make sure he or she has answered the writing prompt and that the answer is complete and on topic. A good writer also looks for errors in grammar and punctuation.

During a test, you may not have time to fix every error that you find. First, correct errors that might keep a reader from understanding your essay. Then go back to other errors. Use the following questions to help you find and correct problems.

- Does your essay respond to the writing prompt?
- Does your introduction clearly state your main idea?
- Does the body of your essay support your main idea?
- Does your essay have a conclusion or summary?
- Does each paragraph contain a topic sentence?
- Does each paragraph discuss only one idea?
- Are there smooth transitions between paragraphs?
- Does your essay have a title?
- Does your opening sentence grab the reader's attention?
- Have you combined short, awkward sentences?
- Have you fixed all sentence fragments and run-on sentences?
- Have you crossed out unnecessary words?
- Do your verbs agree with your subjects?
- Does each pronoun agree with its antecedent?
- Have you used correct punctuation and spelling?

### Answering Essay Questions

An essay is a short piece of writing about a single subject or topic. Essay questions usually begin with the words *describe*, *compare*, *explain*, or *discuss*. An essay answer is one or more paragraphs. It has a topic sentence, a body, and a summary or conclusion. Descriptions and discussions are two kinds of essay questions. A description essay question asks you to tell about something. A discussion essay question asks you to tell more than one point of view about the subject.

Writing good essay answers takes practice. Follow these steps to practice answering essay questions.

**Step 1** Think of something that interests you that you would like to learn more about such as a sport, a hobby, a place, or a job.

**Step 2** Think of two essay questions about this subject. Make sure that you do not know the answers to the questions. Write one of the questions so that it asks for a description. Write the other question so it asks for a discussion. Write the questions below.

1. _____
2. _____

**Step 3** Find answers for your questions. Interview someone who knows something about the subject. You can also find information by looking in encyclopedias, books, and magazines at the library.

**Step 4** Use another sheet of paper to answer your essay questions. Be sure to include a topic sentence. Write a body that supports your topic sentence. Then write a summary or conclusion.

**Step 5** After you write each essay answer, underline the topic sentences.

**Step 6** Share your essay questions and answers with the class.

# Writing for School

**W**hat is the person in the photo doing? He or she may be working on a school assignment. Perhaps the person is taking a test. On many occasions, you have to write for school. You probably take notes, do writing assignments, and write test answers. If you are like most students, you would rather do something else.

However, there are things you can do to make writing for school easier. For example, you can prepare. If you learn to answer test questions properly, you can do better on tests. If you learn how to write essays and reports, you will feel more confident.

In Chapter 10, you will learn how to answer test questions, plan and write essays, and write book reports. You will learn how to write your best in school.

## GOALS FOR LEARNING

- To answer test questions using sentences
- To plan and write an essay, and to improve an essay
- To write a report about a book, movie, or TV show

247

## Introducing the Chapter

Have students examine the photograph on page 246 and describe what it shows. Ask them to name different ways the person could be using writing. Have students create a list of all the things they do each day that involve writing. Point out that a writer uses his or her writing skills to write essays or reports, take notes, or answer test questions in almost every school subject. Explain that this chapter will discuss how to write for school tasks.

Review and discuss the Goals for Learning on page 247.

## Notes

Ask volunteers to read the notes that appear in the margins throughout the chapter. Then discuss them with the class.

## TEACHER'S RESOURCE

The AGS Globe Teaching Strategies in English Transparencies may be used with this chapter. The transparencies add an interactive dimension to expand and enhance the *Basic English Composition* program content.

## WRITING PORTFOLIO

Ask students to write an essay describing their favorite movie and explaining why it is their favorite. As they complete each lesson in the chapter, students can return to their essays and revise them according to what they are learning. Point out that they should discuss each story element of the movie: characters, conflict, plot, resolution, and setting. This project may be used as an alternative form of assessment for the chapter.

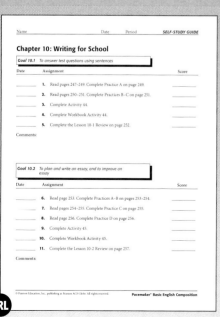

Chapter 10 Self-Study Guide, pages 1–2

## Reading Strategy: Questioning

Have students read the explanation and the questions aloud. Point out that asking these and other questions while reading can help students anticipate test questions. Questioning also improves understanding of fiction. Have students write a question they might ask as they read a story. For example, *Why is this character behaving like this? Why do I like or dislike this character? What might happen next?* Encourage students to use sticky notes for writing questions as they read.

·········································

## Key Vocabulary Words

conflict          resolution
essay

Read the words and definitions aloud. Have students write an example of each term. For instance, have them describe an essay they have written or read, the conflict in a story they are familiar with, and the resolution in that story. Have students share their examples with the class.

·········································

# Reading Strategy: Questioning

Good readers ask themselves questions as they read. The questions may be "I wonder" questions such as: I wonder why that happens? Or they may be routine questions such as: Did that make sense? Here are useful questions to ask as you read:

- Why am I reading this? What do I hope to learn?
- Is there anything I need to know to make sense of this text?
- How is this connected to my own experiences?

## Key Vocabulary Words

**Essay** A short piece of writing about one topic

**Conflict** A problem or struggle at the center of a story

**Resolution** A solution; an end to the conflict in a story

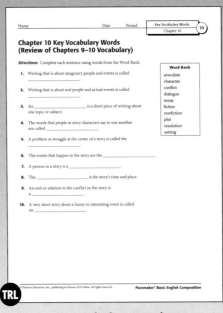

# Answering Test Questions

## Objectives

■ To answer a
test question in
sentences
■ To describe or
identify a person,
place, or thing
■ To use reference
books to answer
questions

**Reading Strategy:**
Questioning

Ask yourself: What do
I already know about
writing answers to test
questions?

Some test questions require a short or long written answer. Answer these test questions in complete sentences, not fragments. Remember that a sentence expresses a complete idea. It must include both a subject and a predicate. Study the answers in Example 1.

▶ **EXAMPLE 1**

| Question | Who is Pearl Buck? |
|---|---|
| Answer | Pearl Buck was an American novelist who won the Nobel Prize for literature. Her most famous novel is *The Good Earth*, a story about China. |
| Question | What activities are popular in the winter? |
| Answer | Many activities are popular in the winter, including skiing, skating, and sledding. |

### Practice A

Answer each question with a sentence. You can find the answers in a dictionary, encyclopedia, or almanac.

1. In which state is the Statue of Liberty located?
2. Why do pictures of Cupid often appear on valentines?
3. What is a Nobel Prize?
4. Denver is the capital city of what state?
5. At what temperature on the Fahrenheit scale will water boil?

*Writing for School    Chapter 10    **249***

## Chapter 10  Lesson 1

**Overview**  This lesson discusses using complete sentences and important details to answer test questions.

## Objectives

■ To answer a test question in sentences
■ To describe or identify a person, place, or thing
■ To use reference books to answer questions

**Student Pages**  249–252

**Teacher's Resource Library** TRL

Activity  44
Modified Activity  44
Workbook Activity  44

## Background Information

Dictionaries, encyclopedias, and almanacs offer some of the same kinds of information. Researchers can choose one based on how much specific information they need. For example, in researching a person, writers can find a brief description in the biographical section of a dictionary. For more detailed information, an encyclopedia is useful. An encyclopedia provides the most detailed and complete information. An almanac is especially useful for finding current facts such as population statistics. All of these resources are offered online.

## **2**  Teaching the Lesson

Ask a volunteer to read each example question aloud; then read the answer and identify the subject and verb in each sentence. Point out that the facts of the answers follow the subject and verb. To be sure they use complete sentences, students should practice using the subject and, often, the verb in their responses. This practice has the benefit of focusing the writer's attention on the subject.

## Practice A

Provide the reference sources named in the directions, or give students the opportunity to do this activity in the library.

## *Practice A Answers*

Wording of answers will vary. Possible answers follow. **1.** The Statue of Liberty is located in the state of New York. **2.** Pictures of Cupid often appear on valentines because Cupid was the ancient Roman god of love. **3.** A Nobel Prize is an international award given each year for major achievements in science, medicine, literature, economics, and world peace. **4.** Denver is the capital of Colorado. **5.** Water boils at 212 degrees Fahrenheit.

## **1**  Warm-Up Activity

Ask students what type of test items they expect to see if the teacher announces a "short-answer test." They may note such test formats as fill in the blank, matching, and multiple choice. Explain that in this lesson, they will focus on short answers that are given in complete sentences.

**Reading Strategy:** Questioning

Possible response: I know I should write complete sentences.

## LEARNING STYLES

**Body/Kinesthetic**

Invite students to select a person named in Practice C or another famous historic figure. Have them present a mini-pantomime that shows what made the person famous. When the audience correctly identifies the person, he or she reads a complete sentence identifying the person.

## IN THE COMMUNITY

Tell students that information about people, past and present, can be found in special reference books such as *Who's Who*. Write the term *biographical dictionary* on the board. Have volunteers find biographical reference sources in a library. Ask them to copy the title and call number of each source and to report to the class the kinds of information the source contains.

## COMMON ERROR

Students may pad test answers with vague, general statements or may state facts in a wordy fashion. This is especially true when they are unsure of the lesson content. Explain to students that teachers always recognize worthless padding, and it will not improve their grade. Emphasize that test answers should always state specific facts with no wordiness.

**Brush Up on the Basics**

Remember that a sentence has a subject and a predicate. It expresses a complete thought. See Grammar 1 in Appendix A.

A test item may ask you to identify or describe a certain person, place, or thing. When you identify or describe something, you give its important characteristics. Ask yourself: What makes this person famous? What is unusual about this place? What are the special characteristics of this thing?

Read Example 2. Do you see why the second answer is better?

▶ **EXAMPLE 2**

| | |
|---|---|
| Test Item | Describe Mount Elbert. |
| Poor Answer | Mount Elbert is a big mountain in Colorado. |
| Better Answer | Mount Elbert is the highest mountain in Colorado with an altitude of 14,433 feet. |

*Visitors to Mount Elbert enjoy hiking and snowshoeing.*

## ELL/ESL STRATEGY

**Language Objective:** *To identify prewriting methods for test questions*

Students may need to review and practice ways to brainstorm details to answer a test question and to plan the answer. Have a student read aloud the Example 2 test item on page 250. On the board, start a word web with *Mount Elbert* in the center circle. Ask students to name kinds of details that might be used to describe the topic, such as definition, location, height, and unusual features. Write these in circles connected to the center of the web. Point out that when taking a test, students could fill in these circles with specific details, such as *14,433 feet*. Also point out that students might not have time for this kind of prewriting for every test question, but it would be worthwhile for essay questions. Have students create a web for the following essay prompt: *What would you say to persuade someone not to litter?*

## Practice B

Describe each person, place, or thing by writing one or two sentences about it. You can find information in this book on the pages given in parentheses. Write your answers on your paper.

1. St. Paul, Minnesota (page 225)
2. Othello (page 152)
3. *Who's Who* (page 153)
4. Georgia O'Keeffe (page 101)
5. Krakatau (page 151)

## Practice C

Write a sentence that identifies each person. You can find information in a dictionary, almanac, or other reference book.

1. Sandra Day O'Connor
2. Simon Bolivar
3. Rosa Parks
4. Clara Barton
5. Nelson Mandela

## VOCABULARY BUILDER

### Learning New Words

A new word is a chance to make your vocabulary grow. Look up a word you do not know in the dictionary. Learn how to say the word. Write a definition for it. Then use it in a sentence.

Read the paragraph. Find two new words. Write a definition for each word. Use each word in a new sentence.

Dan and Slim, two prisoners, were digging a tunnel to freedom. The only implement they had was a rusty old spoon. For six months, they had burrowed through the earth. One night, Dan called out in a voice hoarse with anticipation.

**NOTE**

Dictionaries list real people by their last name. To find Joe Louis, look under "Louis." Dictionaries list fictional characters by their first name. To find Robin Hood, look under "Robin."

**Reading Strategy:**
Questioning

How can the information in this lesson help you on a test?

*Writing for School    Chapter 10*    **251**

---

## LEARNING STYLES

### Logical/Mathematical

Have students make cards for each person, place, or thing identified in this lesson's activities and review. Students should write the name on one card. On another card, they should write a sentence describing the person, place, or thing. Students can then use the cards in a variety of mix-and-match games.

## VOCABULARY BUILDER

Ask volunteers to read aloud the introductory material and the paragraph. Ask students to suggest words in the paragraph that are new to them. After students have completed the activity, have volunteers read their definitions and sentences aloud.

### Vocabulary Builder Answers

Answers will vary. Possible answers: *implement*: a tool. A spatula is a useful cooking implement. *burrowed*: progressed by digging. The animal burrowed a hole in the ground. *anticipation*: the act of looking forward. The students discussed their upcoming graduation with anticipation.

## Practice B

Help students find the relevant information on the pages cited. Point out that a complete answer may call for more than one sentence.

### Practice B Answers

Answers will vary. Possible answers follow. **1.** St. Paul is a city in Minnesota named for St. Paul's Chapel, which was built on the site in 1841. **2.** Othello is the main character in Shakespeare's play of the same name. In a jealous rage, Othello mistakenly kills his wife. **3.** *Who's Who* is a reference book that gives information about noteworthy living people. The book includes a short paragraph about each person. **4.** Georgia O'Keeffe was an American artist known for her paintings of nature in the American Southwest. **5.** Krakatau is a volcanic island in Indonesia.

## Practice C

Review the names on the list, inviting students to identify people they already know. Discuss what is probably most important to include when identifying famous people.

### Practice C Answers

Answers will vary. Possible answers follow. **1.** Sandra Day O'Connor was the first woman to serve as an associate justice of the Supreme Court of the United States, serving from 1981 until 2006. **2.** Simon Bolivar was a South American general who led armies in victories over Spain, gaining independence for Bolivia, Colombia, Ecuador, Peru, and Venezuela. **3.** Rosa Parks was an African-American woman who helped bring about the civil rights movement in the United States when she refused to give up her bus seat to a white passenger in Montgomery, Alabama. **4.** Clara Barton was a nurse during the Civil War and the founder of the American Red Cross. **5.** Nelson Mandela was a leader in the black protest movement against the white government of South Africa, the first democratically elected president of South Africa, and a winner of the Nobel Peace Prize.

### Reading Strategy: Questioning

Students may identify these main ideas as helpful: Test answers should be written in sentences. When identifying or describing someone or something, give important characteristics and specific facts.

## Lesson 10-1 Review Answers

**1.** no **2.** no **3.** yes **4.** no **5.** yes
Wording of answers will vary. Each answer must be a complete sentence. Possible answers follow. **6.** Robinson Crusoe was the main character, a castaway on an island, in the novel of the same name by Daniel Defoe. **7.** Ontario is a Canadian province that lies between the Great Lakes and Hudson Bay, covering an area of 363,282 square miles. **8.** Frida Kahlo was a Mexican artist, known for her surrealistic paintings and unique style of dress. **9.** Eleanor Roosevelt was a human-rights supporter and the wife of President Franklin D. Roosevelt. **10.** Mammoth Cave is the world's longest known cave, located in south central Kentucky.

## WRITING PORTFOLIO

**Checkpoint** Students can continue working on their Writing Portfolio project. Check students' progress and address any questions or concerns they may have.

---

### LESSON 10-1

# REVIEW

Read each question and answer. Decide whether the answer is a sentence. Write *yes* or *no* on your paper.

1. How many rooms are in your home?

   Three bedrooms, a living room, a dining room, and a kitchen.

2. Why is there a picture of Cupid on many valentines?

   Because Cupid was the god of love in Roman mythology.

3. Identify Zachary Taylor.

   Zachary Taylor was an American general and the twelfth president of the United States.

4. Identify Centerville.

   A town in Texas.

5. What is a llama?

   A llama is an animal that people use to carry cargo in the Andes Mountains of South America.

Identify each character, person, or place. Write your answer as a sentence. You may use a dictionary or other reference book.

6. Robinson Crusoe

7. Ontario

8. Frida Kahlo

9. Eleanor Roosevelt

10. Mammoth Cave

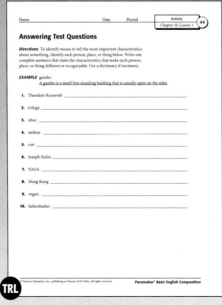

Activity 44

Workbook Activity 44

# Writing an Essay

## Objectives

- To write an essay for an assignment or test
- To respond to a prompt that asks you to discuss a topic
- To improve an essay

**Essay**
A short piece of writing about one topic

 **NOTE**

If you are writing a long essay, start with a topic paragraph. Then write one or more paragraphs for the body. End with a summary paragraph.

An **essay** is a short piece of writing about one topic. An essay can be one or more paragraphs. You might write an essay for an assignment or as part of a test.

## Writing an Essay

When you are asked to write an essay, you are given an essay question or a writing prompt. The prompt may begin with a word such as *describe, compare, explain,* or *discuss.* The question may ask *why, what,* or *how.* Your answer will be one or more paragraphs.

Before you write an essay, reread the question or prompt. Think about your audience and the details you want to include. Then organize your information.

For a one-paragraph essay, begin with a topic sentence. Include supporting details in the body. Explain these details so your reader will understand. End with a summary or conclusion.

### Practice A

Read the question and each topic sentence. Decide which topic sentence is the best. Explain why you chose it.

**Question:**  How do people celebrate Valentine's Day?
**Topic Sentences:**
**A** There are many ways to celebrate this day.
**B** People celebrate Valentine's Day in many ways.
**C** It is a day for giving cards and having parties.
**D** I do not celebrate Valentine's Day, but many people do.

---

## Lesson at a Glance

### Chapter 10  Lesson 2

**Overview**  This lesson outlines how to read a prompt and gather and organize ideas to plan an essay response.

### Objectives

- To write an essay for an assignment or test
- To respond to a prompt that asks you to discuss a topic
- To improve an essay

### Student Pages  253–257

### Teacher's Resource Library

Activity  45

**Modified Activity**  45

**Workbook Activity**  45

**Life Skills Connection**  10

····················································

## Vocabulary

**essay**

Have students write the definition of *essay*. Then ask students to write summaries of three essays they have written. Have pairs of students share and discuss their summaries.
····················································

## Background Information

Prewriting is a useful step in writing an essay, even when the essay is for a timed test. Writers can use graphic organizers such as a word web to show how ideas are connected. They might also use a T-chart, especially in writing a comparison/contrast essay. Aids like these are good tools for both brainstorming for an essay and organizing the ideas.

### 1  Warm-Up Activity

Encourage volunteers to describe how they approach an essay test. Explain that careful organization is important when writing within a time limit. In this lesson, students will learn steps to plan an essay answer, which will make them more comfortable with writing essay answers.

### 2  Teaching the Lesson

Encourage students to explain the steps they use to write a paragraph. They may mention writing a topic sentence, thinking of supporting details, and organizing them according to a plan. Then have students read the paragraphs on page 253 and compare this information to their own writing process.

## Practice A

Read the question to students. Have them suggest their own topic sentences before reading the choices given.

### Practice A Answers

Topic Sentence B is the best because it responds to the question.

## Practice B

You may wish to have students brainstorm ways of celebrating various holidays and list them on the board. As they develop their essays, students can refer to the list.

### Practice B Answers

Paragraphs will vary. A sample paragraph follows.

In the United States, people celebrate Valentine's Day in many ways. Sending cards is probably the most common custom. Some cards are handmade, and others are purchased in a store. They may be funny, or they may be romantic. A person can send a card to his or her sweetheart, but people also send cards to teachers, relatives, and friends. In addition to cards, people give each other gifts. Men and women may send each other flowers, too. A couple may go to a restaurant for a romantic dinner. However people choose to celebrate Valentine's Day, it is a time to show others that they are cared for and appreciated.

### Reading Strategy: Questioning

Possible response: I will to learn how to write better essays.

### ELL/ESL STRATEGY

**Language Objective:**
*To learn about and use transitional words*

Students who are learning English will benefit from practice with transitional words. Have them make a card listing transitional words for chronological order (*next, now, as soon as, finally, until, immediately*), order of importance (*first, second, further, particularly, most important*), and spatial order (*above, below, on the right, on the left, under, beyond*). Provide a topic for each method of organization. Have students talk about one of these topics, using words from the appropriate card to connect ideas.

*Reading Strategy:*
Questioning

Think about the purpose of this lesson. Ask yourself: What will I learn by reading it?

## Practice B

Choose a holiday. Write a one-paragraph essay about how people celebrate this holiday. Use your own experiences as examples. You may also use a reference book. Include supporting details in the body of your paragraph. End your paragraph with a conclusion or a summary.

### Discussing a Topic

Sometimes an essay question will ask you to discuss a topic. When you discuss something, you talk about it. You give details about it. The paragraph in Example 1 discusses jogging. The writer was given this prompt: Discuss jogging as a form of exercise.

▶ **EXAMPLE 1**

To jog means to run slowly. Usually, jogging is good exercise. It is an inexpensive form of exercise. You do not need special equipment other than proper shoes. Although you can jog year-round, it is not so enjoyable in hot, cold, or stormy weather. Because of its numerous benefits, many people jog to improve their physical fitness.

*It is fun to jog with friends.*

### CAREER CONNECTION

Point out that interviewers ask questions that call for essay-type responses from job seekers. Examples: *Why do you think you will make a contribution to this company? What kind of work are you especially good at? Where did you get your training?* Have students analyze each question and use it to create a statement or "topic sentence" that will lead to a complete and specific answer.

### LEARNING STYLES

**Visual/Spatial**

Have students choose a magazine picture and write a test prompt based on it. Then have them exchange prompts with partners and identify the topic, audience, and purpose of the writing activity. Have partners verify each other's response.

Read every essay question or prompt carefully. Follow the directions exactly. Even if your answer contains correct information, it will be marked wrong if it does not answer the question.

Practice C

Read each writing prompt and answer. Each answer is incorrect. Explain what the writer did wrong. Write your reasons in sentences.

1. Tell how people celebrated Valentine's Day long ago.

    Some people celebrate Valentine's Day by sending cards. These cards often say "be my valentine." In this phrase, a *valentine* is a special friend. People usually enjoy receiving Valentine's Day cards.

2. Discuss the achievements of Millard Fillmore.

    Millard Fillmore was the thirteenth president of the United States. He became president after Zachary Taylor died in office. Fillmore had been the vice president. He did not serve a second term.

3. Describe the Grand Canyon.

    Many people visit the Grand Canyon every year. Some visitors walk on the trails to the bottom of the canyon. Others ride on mules or horses to the bottom. In the summer, the Grand Canyon is very crowded.

4. Why do many people plant vegetable gardens?

    Vegetable gardening is becoming more popular every year. In a small area, people can grow vegetables as well as flowers. Even people in apartments often have small gardens. They can grow tomatoes in flowerpots on a balcony.

5. Give three reasons why exercise is good for people.

    People need to exercise every day. Sometimes they pull muscles. It makes them tired. It takes discipline to exercise daily.

*Writing for School*    *Chapter 10*    **255**

## Practice C

Read each test item with students, asking them how the question should be answered. Then proceed with reading the "wrong" responses and developing critiques.

### Practice C Answers

Wording of answers will vary. Possible answers follow. **1.** This paragraph does not tell how people celebrated Valentine's Day long ago. Instead, it tells general information about how people celebrate Valentine's Day today. **2.** This paragraph tells who Millard Fillmore was, but it does not give any specific information about his achievements. **3.** This paragraph does not include enough details to help readers picture the Grand Canyon. The only descriptive words are *very crowded*. **4.** The topic sentence sticks to the subject, but the other sentences do not tell why people plant vegetable gardens. **5.** This paragraph does not give reasons why exercise is good for people. Instead, it makes vague statements about exercising.

### LEARNING STYLES

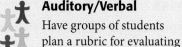

**Auditory/Verbal**

Have groups of students plan a rubric for evaluating a paragraph. Categories may include topic sentence, supporting details, unity (no irrelevant information), organization, and grammar and punctuation. Ask groups to present their rubric and explain why they included these rules. As a class, develop a final rubric including the best suggestions from each group. Have students use it to evaluate a paragraph from their portfolio.

### LIFE SKILLS CONNECTION

Explain to students that the skills used with essay writing are the same skills used with other types of writing: newspaper articles, job applications, stories, research papers, and more. Provide copies of Life Skills Connection 10 to students. Read the instructions with them. Answer any questions they may have. If they have difficulty with step 2, divide the class into pairs. Then have students describe their essay topics to their partners and have partners suggest essay questions.

### COMMON ERROR

Instead of simply using a personal experience as an example in a factual essay, students may end up writing a personal narrative. Emphasize that an essay is usually fact-based, while a personal narrative tells the story of a personal experience. Point out that facts are statements that readers can look up in reference books.

## Practice D

Have a volunteer read the prompt aloud. Discuss what it is asking students to write about and what they think the essay should include. Point out that to compare and contrast, some writers first present one subject and then the other. Other writers may combine them and present ways they are alike and then ways they are different.

### Practice D Answers

Revisions may vary somewhat. A possible revision follows.

Sonia and Derek
by Amber Choy

My two best friends, Sonia and Derek, could not be more different. They are both special in their own way.

Sonia is very outgoing. She has a wonderful sense of humor and a beautiful voice. She loves getting in front of a crowd to perform. I always enjoy being around Sonia.

Before I met Derek, he was very shy and spent most of his time working. As I got to know him, I realized that he was special. He is a great listener and very dependable. He is always there when I need someone to talk to.

Even though Sonia and Derek are different, they are both great friends. I don't know what I would do without them. I hope I am as good a friend to Sonia and Derek as they are to me.

### COMMON ERROR

 Students may put a comma after the word *and* when punctuating a series of items or a compound sentence. Point out that in both cases, a comma goes only before *and*.

### TEACHER ALERT

Some students may have difficulty allocating their time when writing essays on tests. Suggest that they divide their time into fourths. They can use one-fourth of the time to organize their essay, two-fourths to write the essay, and one-fourth to revise it.

### *Reading Strategy:* Questioning

Encourage students to share their interpretation of what they read.

---

*Reading Strategy:* Questioning

Did you understand what you just read? If not, read the material again. This time, look for clues and key words.

## Improving an Essay

If your essay is an assignment, always take time to revise and edit it. If your essay is a test answer, you often have some extra time before turning in the test. Use this time to revise and edit your essay. Go over your writing to improve the weak points.

### Practice D

Read the prompt and then the essay. Look for mistakes in the essay. Edit and rewrite the essay on your paper.

**Prompt:** We make friends with people for different reasons. Some friends are very different from one another, and others have a lot in common. Compare and contrast two of your friends. Discuss what makes each one special.

**Sonia and Derek**
by Amber Choy

My too best friends, Sonia and Derek, could not be more different, they are both special in they're own way. Sonia is very outgoing. She has a wonderful sense of humor. Sonia also has a beautiful voice. She loves getting in front of a crowd to perform. I always enjoy be around Sonia.

Before I met Derek, he was very shy and spent most of his time working. As I got to know him, I relized that he was special. He is a great listener and is always there when I need someone to talk to. He is very dependable. Even though Sonia and Derek are different, they are both great friends. I don't know what I would do without them. I hope I am as good a freind to Sonia and Derek as they are to me.

## Writing Practice

Pair students. Ask them to write a topic sentence for each of the following essay prompts:

*Describe the Golden Gate Bridge.*

*Compare summer activities with winter activities.*

*Discuss the pros and cons of recycling.*

Then ask partners to select one item and brainstorm details to include in a paragraph they would write. Finally, have pairs organize the details in an outline based on chronological, logical, spatial, or importance order.

# REVIEW

1. Read the prompt and then the essay. Look for mistakes in the essay. Edit and rewrite the essay.

   **Prompt:** People have pets for many reasons. Write an essay to explain why people own and care for pets. Include at least two reasons in your essay.

   The two common reasons are for help and for companionship. For example, pets such as seeing-eye dogs help those who are blind. Specially trained animals can help people with special needs complete tasks they would not usually be able to complete. Most people own pets for companionship, pets provide friendship and loyalty. No matter what their purpose, pets give there owners enjoyment.

2. Read the prompt. Then write a five-sentence essay.

   **Prompt:** Describe your best friend's most important characteristic. Explain why this characteristic is important in your friendship.

## GRAMMAR BUILDER

### Using Commas in a Series
Follow these rules when you list items in a series:
- A comma follows each item before the word *and*.
  *Bring a ball, bat, and glove to practice.*
- A comma separates adjectives before a noun.
  *What a muddy, rocky field.*
- If two adjectives express one idea, do not use a comma.
  *That is a great Chinese restaurant.*

Write each sentence. Add commas where needed.
1. Danika Ted and Wes practiced marching for the parade.
2. They wore new soft jackets and carried bright red flags.

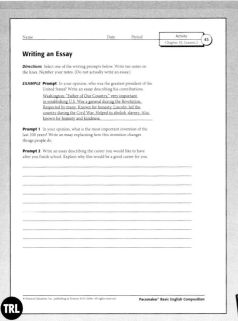

---

## Lesson 10-2 Review Answers

**1.** Essays will vary. A sample revised essay follows.

The Purpose of Pets
by Brandon Tucker

The two most common reasons people own and care for pets are for help and for companionship. Specially trained animals can help people with special needs complete tasks they would not usually be able to complete. For example, pets such as seeing-eye dogs help those who are blind. Most people own pets for companionship. Pets provide friendship and loyalty. No matter what their purpose, pets give their owners enjoyment.

**2.** Essays will vary. Students should show that they have revised and edited their essays.

## Speaking and Presenting Practice

Have pairs of students read their essays from item 2 in the review to one another. Ask partners to tell the readers whether they have answered the prompt and whether the essay gives a specific answer.

## GRAMMAR BUILDER

Ask volunteers to read the rules and examples. As you discuss the third example, point out that a test can be performed to determine whether to put a comma between adjectives. Tell them to silently insert *and* between the adjectives. If the sentence could be said in this way, a comma should be used. For example, you would not say "a great *and* TV program," so there should be no comma.

### Grammar Builder Answers

**1.** Danika, Ted, and Wes practiced marching for the parade. **2.** They wore new, soft jackets and carried bright red flags.

## Lesson at a Glance

### Chapter 10 Lesson 3

**Overview** This lesson defines some key elements of stories. It describes how to write a report about a story in a book, movie, or TV show.

### Objectives

- To identify the conflict in a story
- To explain the resolution of a conflict
- To write a report about a book, movie, or TV show

**Student Pages** 258–265

**Teacher's Resource Library**

Activity 46

Modified Activity 46

Workbook Activity 46

Writing on the Job 5

Building Research Skills 10

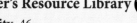

### Vocabulary

conflict          resolution

Have students read the definitions of each word. Then have them use a dictionary to find another common definition of each word. Have them write sentences using each word in a literary context and then in another common context. Have students work in pairs and read their sentences aloud.

### Background Information

In addition to characters, conflict, plot, and resolution, setting is an important feature in narratives. Sometimes the setting is merely a backdrop, as in the suburban home in the TV show *Everybody Loves Raymond*. Other times the setting is essential to the plot, as in the desert island in *Robinson Crusoe*. The setting includes not only where but when a story occurs.

### 1 Warm-Up Activity

Ask students to recall a story in a book, movie, or TV show. Encourage them to think about how characters, setting, or plot affected their enjoyment.

---

# Writing a Report About a Book, Movie, or TV Show

### Objectives

- To identify the conflict in a story
- To explain the resolution of a conflict
- To write a report about a book, movie, or TV show

**Conflict**

A problem or struggle at the center of a story

**NOTE**

When you write about a novel, movie, or TV show, you cannot tell everything that happened. It is not important to tell the entire story. It is important, however, to show that you understand the main parts of the story.

Discussing a book, movie, or TV show can add to your enjoyment of it. Sometimes, it is interesting to stop and think about why you liked it so much.

### Conflict

Every story has a **conflict.** The conflict is the problem at the center of the story. It is what the characters struggle to solve. Example 1 describes the conflict in *Jurassic Park*.

▶ **EXAMPLE 1**

A wealthy man secretly creates a theme park featuring living dinosaurs. Before the grand opening, he invites some people to go there. When things go wrong, their park visit is full of unexpected danger.

#### Practice A

Choose a TV show, movie, or book you have seen or read recently. Write one or two sentences describing the conflict in the story.

### Plot

What happens to the characters because of the conflict is the plot. You learned about plot in Chapter 9. In some stories, the events lead to the solution of the problem. In other stories, the events make the situation worse, increase the problem, and heighten the suspense.

#### Practice B

Think about a TV show, movie, or book that you have seen or read recently. Write several sentences about the things that happened. Share your writing with your class.

---

### 2 Teaching the Lesson

Define and discuss each element of a story. Ask students to give examples of each element: conflict, plot, characters, and resolution.

### Practice A

Point out that the main conflict of a story usually involves one main character. A character may have a conflict with another character, with himself or herself, or with nature.

### *Practice A Answers*

Answers will vary. Students should clearly state only the conflict of the story and not other elements of the plot.

### Practice B

Ask students to name a movie with which most class members are familiar. Ask volunteers to name main events of the plot. Note the events on the board.

### *Practice B Answers*

Answers will vary. Students' sentences should state only main events and not insignificant ones.

## Characters

The people in the story are the characters. In most stories, the characters are very important. People often watch a show or read a book because they like the characters. Example 2 explains why some characters have been popular.

▶ **EXAMPLE 2**

Arthur Conan Doyle wrote 60 stories about a detective named Sherlock Holmes. These books were popular because people liked the character and his best friend Dr. Watson. The conflict was the same from book to book. Sherlock solved a mystery that no one else could. The plot was how he solved the mystery.

*Everybody Loves Raymond* was a successful TV show. Viewers liked to watch Raymond, his older brother Robert, his wife Debra, and his weird parents Frank and Marie. People tuned in every week to see what these characters were doing.

### Practice C

Choose one character from a book, movie, or TV show. Write a paragraph about that character. Describe his or her personality and appearance. Explain what it is about the character that you find interesting. Include the name of the book, movie, or TV show.

## Resolution of Conflict

People read a book or watch a movie or TV show until the end. They want to find out how the conflict is resolved, or ended. The solution to a conflict is the **resolution.** The main character in the story usually resolves the conflict. Example 3 describes one conflict and its resolution.

## Spelling Practice

Discuss the terms *conflict, characters,* and *resolution*. Point out that each word helps illustrate a spelling rule that is helpful when spelling other words. For example, students may tend to omit the final *t* in *conflict.* Explain that pronouncing the word correctly will help them spell it correctly. Point out that *characters* begins with a *k* sound spelled *ch,* such as the words *chemical* and *chrome.* Finally, point out that the schwa sound in the middle of *resolution* is spelled with an *o,* as in *revolution* and *isolation.* You may wish to give students a spelling test on these lesson words.

## COMMON ERROR

When summarizing a plot, students often retell each thing that happens no matter how insignificant it may be. Point out how boring it is to listen to someone recite an entire plot: "*and then . . . and then. . .*" Remind students that summarizing consists of stating only the main idea and not all the supporting details. Likewise, in summarizing a plot, students should state only the main events and not the minor ones.

## Practice C

Have a volunteer read Example 2 on page 259 aloud. Write the chart headings *Book, Movie,* and *TV* on the board. With students, brainstorm several fictional characters. Write their names beneath the proper headings on the board. Ask students to name one or two specific character traits of each character. Write these in a separate list. Point out that when describing a character, students should name specific traits such as these and illustrate them with examples.

## Practice C Answers

Answers will vary. Students' paragraphs should name specific traits and illustrate them with examples.

**Reading Strategy:** Questioning

Answers will vary depending on the reports completed for assignments.

**3** | **Reinforce and Extend**

## ELL/ESL STRATEGY

**Language Objective:** *To learn and use words to describe character traits*

Students may need help finding words to describe characters. First of all, point out that describing a character's physical appearance is a good place to start. However, a good review focuses more on the person's inner traits. On the board, write the words *kind, generous, selfish, confused, clever, inventive,* and *loyal.* Ask students to give an example of an action that would show each trait. For example, a character who made a house out of palm branches could be called *inventive.* Then have students name some familiar fictional characters and brainstorm adjectives to describe them. Finally, have students use a dictionary and a thesaurus to look up synonyms for these character words and also find several new words to describe characters.

## Practice D

Ask a volunteer to read Example 3 aloud. Point out that the first sentence specifically states the conflict. Ask one or two volunteers to describe another conflict from a popular movie.

### Practice D Answers

Answers will vary. Students' paragraphs should specifically state the conflict and describe its resolution.

## Practice E

Have students take turns reading the book report on page 261 aloud. Point out that the book *Robinson Crusoe* is several hundred pages long, yet the plot summary consists of only a few sentences. It describes only the most important events. Point out that each part of the book report is objective, giving facts about each part of the book. Only the last section of the report states the writer's opinion. Ask students to summarize the opinion and the reasons the writer gives for it.

### Practice E Answers

Answers will vary. Students' reports should contain each section shown in the sample report on page 261.

### Reading Strategy: Questioning

Remind students that they may need to reread to gather relevant information.

**AT HOME**

Ask students to keep a chart on their TV viewing for several days. Have them write the name of each story-type TV program they watch. Then have them note the show's characters, conflict, and a one-sentence plot summary. Students can use their notes as they complete the assignments in the lesson. They also may want to discuss their viewing habits in small groups. Encourage them to evaluate the quality of some shows based on what they learn about character, plot, and conflict.

▶ **EXAMPLE 3**

Episodes I, II, and III of the Star Wars movies involve a conflict between the Jedi and the evil Sith. In the third movie, the conflict ends when the Jedi lose to the Sith, who form the Galactic Empire. However, the audience knows something important. Twin children born in secrecy will grow up to become Luke Skywalker and Princess Leia Organa. Perhaps the Jedi will rise again.

### Practice D

Choose any book, movie, or TV show. Write one sentence that describes the main conflict of the story. Write a few sentences explaining how the conflict was resolved. If you choose a TV show, use one episode as an example.

### A Report or Review

You may be asked to write a report about a book, movie, or TV show. Such a report might be called a review. In it, you discuss the main parts of the story: the plot, characters, and setting. You explain the conflict and its resolution. You also give your opinion. A review can be one or several paragraphs. Read the sample book report on the next page.

### Practice E

Write a report about a TV show, movie, or book. Use the book report about Robinson Crusoe on the next page as your guide.

 **NOTE**

Newspapers regularly print reviews of new books and movies.

**Reading Strategy:**
Questioning

What important ideas from this Lesson should I remember?

**LEARNING STYLES**

 **Interpersonal/Group Learning**

Have students work in three groups. Have each student find an example of a review in a magazine. Have one group find movie reviews, one book reviews, and one TV show reviews. Ask students to bring copies of their reviews to class and discuss them with their groups. Have each group present their findings to the rest of the class.

**TEACHER ALERT**

Even after reading and discussing well-written book reports, students may write a rambling plot summary instead of a review. Discuss in detail the report on page 261, emphasizing that the plot summary is only one small part of the entire report. Also, challenge students to limit their plot summaries to four or five sentences.

**A Book Report on *Robinson Crusoe***

**Author:** Daniel Defoe

**Setting:** The story takes place in the 1600s on a desert island. There are only a few native people living on the island.

**Main characters:** The main character is Robinson Crusoe. The other important character is Friday, a native about 26 years of age that Crusoe describes as "handsome and tall."

**Conflict:** Will Robinson Crusoe survive after being shipwrecked on an island? His enemies are the cannibals on the island, the weather, hunger, and loneliness.

**Plot:** After a shipwreck, Robinson Crusoe lands on a desert island. The only people living there are cannibals. The book is about Crusoe's adventures on the island. With a few supplies from the wrecked ship, he builds a small boat and a house for himself. He saves the life of one of the natives. The man became his servant, whom he names Friday. After many years, the crew from a passing ship rescues Crusoe.

**Important event:** One important event is when Robinson Crusoe rescues Friday from other natives who want to kill him. Crusoe takes him to his home. He gives him food and water. The two men communicate using sign language. Soon they become friends, and Crusoe is less lonely.

**Resolution of conflict:** The story explains how Robinson Crusoe survives. The author tells how he builds a home and a boat. The book describes how he finds food. At the end, the crew from a passing ship rescues him and he returns home.

**Opinion:** This book is about survival. The characters are very vivid. At first, Robinson Crusoe has no friends. He has only a few tools. Somehow, he uses what he has to survive. It is interesting that he finds a friend on the island. They cannot talk to each other, but they still communicate. Now that I have read this book, I understand what it takes to survive. I recommend this book to anyone.

## COMMON ERROR

Students may state a very vague opinion, such as *I liked this book because it was great.* Suggest that students focus on the specific elements of a story—conflict, plot, characters, and setting—when formulating and writing their opinions. Also point out that each opinion must be supported by details in the book.

## Grammar Practice

Explain that in a book or movie review, the plot is summarized using present-tense verbs. Present tense should be used consistently throughout the review. For example, "After a shipwreck, Robinson Crusoe *lands* on a desert island." Write the following sentences on the board. Have students supply the correct verbs.

*A tornado (struck, strikes) the farm in Kansas. Dorothy (found, finds) herself in a strange land. She (met, meets) three friends who help her.*

## GLOBAL CONNECTION

Explain that Daniel Defoe was a British writer who lived from 1660 to 1731. He is known for being one of the first realistic novelists. He wrote about ordinary people who are influenced by the social and economic circumstances in which they live. Point out that many novels by British writers of the 17th, 18th, and 19th centuries are still popular today. Students might want to find out more about books by the following British authors: Jane Austen, Charles Dickens, Emily Bronte, and Charlotte Bronte.

Sentences will vary. Possible sentences follow. **1.** Daniel Defoe wrote *Robinson Crusoe*. **2.** The setting is a desert island in the 1600s. **3.** The main character is Robinson Crusoe, a man stranded by a shipwreck who must learn survival skills. **4.** One problem Crusoe must solve is finding food. **5.** Crusoe meets Friday when he rescues him from other natives who want to kill him. **6.** D **7.** A **8.** E **9.** C **10.** B

## WRITING PORTFOLIO

**Checkpoint** Students can continue working on their Writing Portfolio project. Check students' progress and address any questions or concerns they may have.

## WRITE ABOUT IT

Remind students that a paragraph has a topic sentence, supporting details, and a conclusion. Encourage them to think about conflict and resolution, plot, and characters while prewriting. You may wish to hand out word web templates or have students copy a word web from the board on which to gather details. Have them use a blank word web when they write the one-paragraph report on their own book.

## Six Traits of Writing Focus

| | | | |
|---|---|---|---|
| ✔ | Ideas | ✔ | Word Choice |
| | Organization | | Sentence Fluency |
| | Voice | | Conventions |

## Ideas

Have students ask themselves what message they hope to express in their report. Suggest that they discuss their ideas with a partner, who can help them decide which points will help convey their message.

Remind students of the importance of word choice when describing something for an audience. Ask them how saying *The book was good* is different from saying *It tied my stomach in knots*.

Direct students to page WPH1 for more about the Six Traits of Writing.

---

<image name="lesson box">**LESSON**<br>**10-3**</image>

# REVIEW

Use the sample book report on page 261 to answer the questions. Write your answers in sentences.

1. Who wrote *Robinson Crusoe*?
2. What is the setting of this story?
3. Name and describe the main character in the story.
4. Name one problem that Crusoe has to solve.
5. How does Crusoe meet Friday?

Match each word in the first column with a definition in the second column. Write the letter of the definition.

6. conflict     **A** all of the events in a story
7. plot     **B** one happening in a story
8. characters     **C** how the characters solve the problem
9. resolution     **D** the main problem in a story
10. event     **E** the people in a story

## WRITE ABOUT IT

**A Book**
Read this essay about Jack Londons novel, *Call of the Wild*.

Jack London's *Call of the Wild* was an outstanding book. London made me understand the feelings of the main character, a big dog named Buck. I wanted Buck to survive. I worried about him when he fought other dogs and fell into the hands of cruel masters. London described the frozen Arctic setting so clearly that I could see it in my mind. *Call of the Wild* is an exciting adventure story that I would recommend.

1. Does the writer give a clear picture of what the novel is about? Give three examples to support your answer.
2. Write a short essay on a book that you have enjoyed.

**Six Traits of Writing:**
*Ideas* message, details, and purpose

---

Name    Date    Period    **Activity**   46
Chapter 10, Lesson 3

**Writing a Report About a Book, Movie, or TV Show**

**Directions** You can write a report about a book, movie, or TV show by remembering a few easy pointers.

- Remember to write about the conflict—a problem or struggle at the center of the story.
- Write about the characters—the people who the story is about.
- Write about the plot—what happens to the characters in the story.
- Write about the resolution to the conflict. Describe an ending to the conflict in the story.
- Always revise and edit your work.

Select a book, movie, or TV show you have read or seen. Write a 15-sentence first draft on the lines below. Revise and edit your report. Then write your final draft on another sheet of paper.

© Pearson Education, Inc., publishing as Pearson AGS Globe. All rights reserved.    **Pacemaker® Basic English Composition**

**Activity 46**

---

Name    Date    Period    **Workbook Activity**   46
Chapter 10, Lesson 3

**Writing a Report**

**Directions** Use the writing clues to write a report about a book, movie, or TV show. Choose a book, movie, or show that you have read or seen.

1. Give the title of the book and the author. For a movie or TV show, just give the title.
2. Describe the setting. Tell where and when the story or show took place.
3. Describe the major characters.
4. Tell something about the plot, the events that happen in the story or show.
5. Give your opinion of the book, movie, or show. Tell why you think it is interesting, what you liked about it, or what you did not like about it.

© Pearson Education, Inc., publishing as Pearson AGS Globe. All rights reserved.    **Pacemaker® Basic English Composition**

**Workbook Activity 46**

## Children's Librarian

Ann McCoy works in the children's department at the public library. One of her jobs is to review new books. She writes a paragraph about each book to put with a display. She wants children to learn a little about the book. It is important to Ann to create interest in the book. Read one of Ann's reviews. Then answer the questions below.

Book: The Awesome Aquarium Mystery!
Author: Carole Marsh
Do you love to watch fish swim? Just how big can a fish tank get? Christina and Grant take their grandparents to the world's largest aquarium. Mysterious things happen to Christina, who is 10. Grant, who is 7, finds clues. The characters have fun meeting whales, an octopus, and the world's largest fish. Along the way, they solve a mystery. Who will go into the tank? Read this fun book to find out!

1. What is the setting of the book? When does Ann identify it in her review?

2. What characters does Ann describe?

3. CRITICAL THINKING Why do you think Ann used questions and exclamations in the review?

### VIEWING, LISTENING, AND SPEAKING

A librarian knows where to find any kind of book, movie, or music in the library. He or she has looked at these materials. People ask librarians many questions: Where can I find information on _____? Do you have the newest book by _____? Librarians listen carefully and speak clearly to help people find what they want. Look through a library book. With a partner, practice telling what the book is about.

---

Have several volunteers read the feature aloud. Ask students to summarize the traits of a good children's librarian. Help students recognize that the librarian is familiar with the main elements of a story and knows how to evaluate it. Ask students to describe positive experiences they have had with librarians in their school and/or library.

### *Writing on the Job Answers*

**1.** The setting of the book is the world's largest aquarium. Ann describes it in the third sentence of the review. **2.** Ann describes two children, Christina and Grant. **3.** Possible answer: The questions make readers actively participate in the review and increase their suspense about the book. The exclamation communicates excitement about the book.

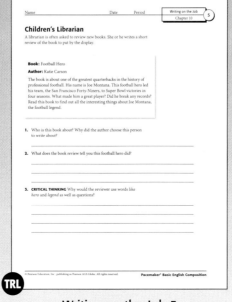

Writing on the Job 5

Display a nonfiction book on a specific topic. Demonstrate looking up a subtopic in the book's table of contents and in its index. Ask students whether the book would be a good source for a report on the topic. Point out that looking at a book's copyright date might also be an important indication of whether the source is a useful one. For example, for a report on global warming, a book published 20 years ago would not offer the most up-to-date information.

## Building Research Skills Answers

**1.** By looking up a topic in an index, you can tell whether that topic is discussed in the book and to what extent. **2.** A source is not dependable if its author is biased or plays favorites or presents opinions as facts. A source that is old may or may not be dependable. **3.** When you use a biased source, you may report someone's opinions as facts.

## Judging Information Sources

Finding sources of information may be easy. The hard part may be deciding which sources are really useful. Information may be found in books, articles, and on the Internet. To judge whether to use a source, ask the two bulleted questions below:

- **Does the source have the information I need?**

Suppose you need to find out about seeing-eye dogs. You find a book about dogs. Check in the index at the back of the book. The index lists topics in the book in alphabetical order. If the index does not list seeing-eye dogs, this source will not help you.

- **Does the source give information that is accurate and fair?**

Some information is not accurate. Be sure the facts you use are correct. Check them against other sources, such as a recent encyclopedia. If a source is old, the facts in it may no longer be true. Newly published sources have up-to-date information. Also, some authors may be biased—they may be trying to persuade their readers. Try to decide whether the source gives a fair, true picture. Are opinions presented as facts?

Answer the following questions.

1. How can an index help you find out if a source will be helpful?

2. When is a source not dependable?

3. **CRITICAL THINKING** What is the problem with using a biased source?

### TECHNOLOGY

Check Internet sources carefully. Look at the name of the site. Look at the person or group who wrote or sponsors it. Ask yourself: Is this site written by an expert? Does it give facts or opinions? Look at the Internet site address. Addresses ending with .com are doing business. These sites may try to convince you to buy something. Addresses that end in .org, .gov, or .edu are good sources to use.

---

Name _____ Date _____ Period _____ Building Research Skills / 10 / Chapter 10

**Judging Information Sources**

Sources can contain specific types of information. Some sources may or may not be appropriate for the type of information you seek.

**Directions** Choose a reference source from the box that goes with each description. Write the name of the source on the line.

encyclopedia  magazine  newspaper  dictionary  Internet  glossary

1. Contains general information on many subjects; a good starting place when writing a report

2. Gives information about words used in a specific book

3. Contains detailed information about recent events on specific topics that fit the scope of its content

4. Contains current information about news, events, sports, weather, schedules

5. Gives the spelling, pronunciation, meaning, and use of thousands of words

6. Contains access to a variety of information but each source must be evaluated for correctness and accuracy

© Pearson Education, Inc., publishing as Pearson AGS Globe. All rights reserved.     **Pacemaker® Basic English Composition**

TRL

# SUMMARY

- Answer test questions in sentences. Show that you understand the question and know the answer.

- Use any extra time at the end of a test to improve your answers.

- If you are asked to identify or describe something, state the most important characteristics.

- If you are asked to discuss a topic, give details about the topic.

- Carefully read the question or prompt before you write an essay. Follow the directions exactly.

- To write a one-paragraph essay, first write a topic sentence. Then give supporting details. End with a conclusion or summary.

- In a report about a book, movie, or TV show, discuss the setting, characters, plot, conflict, and resolution. Include your opinion.

- Think before you write. Make sure you understand the question, prompt, or directions. Complete prewriting activities. Plan your details. Then write for your audience.

- Revise and edit your writing.

## Chapter 10 Summary

Have volunteers read aloud each Summary item on page 265. Ask volunteers to explain the meaning of each item.

### ONLINE CONNECTION

 Ask students to select one of the test items in Practice C on page 255 and write an extended essay response. Suggest that they go to the library and use an online encyclopedia such as *World Book* (www.agsglobepmbec.com/page265a) or *Encyclopedia Britannica* (www.agsglobepmbec.com/page265b) to locate supporting facts for their essays.

### GROUP ACTIVITY

With students, brainstorm some topics for test questions. Remind students that their questions should clearly state the topic and the kind of answer called for.

## GROUP ACTIVITY

Work with a group to write an essay test question. You may write a question for a test you will be having soon. Ask students to describe, discuss, or explain something. Then write a sample answer of one or more paragraphs. Be sure each paragraph has a topic sentence, supporting details, and a conclusion. Ask another group to answer your question. Compare their answer to yours.

# Chapter 10 Review

Use the Chapter Review to prepare students for tests and to reteach content from the chapter.

## Chapter 10 Mastery Test

The Teacher's Resource Library includes two forms of the Chapter 10 Mastery Test. Each test addresses the chapter Goals for Learning. An optional third page of additional critical-thinking items is included for each test. The difficulty level of the two forms is equivalent.

## Review Answers

### Part A

**1.** essay **2.** conflict **3.** resolution

### Part B

Wording of answers will vary. Possible answers follow. **4.** Marie Curie discovered radium. **5.** Pearl Harbor is an inlet of the Hawaiian Islands, west of Honolulu. **6.** A caterpillar is a small wormlike larva that turns into a butterfly or moth. **7.** Charles Schulz created the popular comic strip *Peanuts*. **8.** Nova Scotia consists of a peninsula and an island off the eastern coast of Canada on the Atlantic Ocean.

### Part C

**9.** Gardening is a common hobby. **10.** Gardens can be grown in small or large spaces. **11.** Many people grow vegetables such as corn, peppers, and beans. **12.** Other people might choose to grow colorful and sweet-smelling flowers. **13.** All plants need sun, water, and good soil to survive. **14.** Some plants grow well in shady areas, while others need direct sunlight. **15.** Any garden makes a yard look beautiful.

---

**Word Bank**

conflict

essay

resolution

**Part A** Write the word from the Word Bank that completes each sentence.

**1.** An _____ is a short piece of writing on one subject.

**2.** The main problem in a story is the _____.

**3.** The _____ is how the problem in a story ends.

**Part B** Write a sentence to answer each question. You can find information in a reference book. Check that your sentence answers the question.

**4.** What did Marie Curie accomplish?

**5.** Where is Pearl Harbor?

**6.** What is a caterpillar?

**7.** What did Charles Schultz create?

**8.** Where is Nova Scotia?

**Part C** Number your paper from 9 to 15. Read the prompt and then the essay. Look for mistakes in the essay. Write each sentence in the essay correctly.

**Prompt:** Discuss the hobby of gardening.

Gardening is a comon hobby. Gardens can be grown in small or largest spaces. Many people grow vegetables such as corn peppers and beans. Other people might chose to grow colorful and sweet-smelling flowers. All plants needs sun, water, and good soil to survive. Some plants grow well in shady areas, While others need direct sunlight. Any garden make a yard look beautiful.

**Part D**

**16.** Write one paragraph to describe a book or movie character. Include a topic sentence, details, and a conclusion. Give your opinion. Revise and edit your essay.

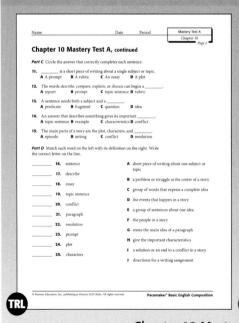

Chapter 10 Mastery Test A, pages 1–3

## Answer Bank

characters

conflict

opinion

plot

resolution

setting

**Part E** The sentences below are from a report on a play. Choose a word from the Answer Bank that describes each sentence. Write the word.

**17.** Romeo and Juliet are young people who fall in love.

**18.** The story takes place in Verona, Italy.

**19.** This is definitely one of Shakespeare's best plays.

**20.** Romeo's family and Juliet's family are bitter enemies.

**21.** First Romeo falls in love, then he drinks the poison.

**22.** The play has a tragic end since both main characters die for love.

**Part F** Choose the best topic sentence for each essay question or prompt. Write the letter of your answer.

**23.** What qualities did Thomas Edison have that made him successful?
   **A** Thomas Edison was a famous inventor.
   **B** Thomas Edison was creative and hardworking.
   **C** He was very successful.
   **D** I am going to tell you about Thomas Edison.

**24.** Describe the planet Mercury.
   **A** It is a very weird planet.
   **B** The planet Mercury is not as big as Earth.
   **C** The planet Mercury has several interesting features.
   **D** Here are some features of the planet.

**25.** Identify Edgar Allan Poe.
   **A** He is a poet.
   **B** Edgar Allan Poe wrote short stories.
   **C** I have read several of Poe's stories and poems.
   **D** Edgar Allan Poe is a well-known American poet.

## Test Tip

When you study for a test, use the titles and subtitles in a chapter to help you. Titles and subtitles show main ideas.

## Review Answers

Part D

**16.** Essays will vary. Students should follow the instructions to write their essays.

Part E

**17.** characters **18.** setting **19.** opinion **20.** conflict **21.** plot **22.** resolution

Part F

**23.** B **24.** C **25.** D

### WRITING PORTFOLIO

**Wrap-Up** Students should complete their essays describing their favorite movie. Have them write a test question based on their essay. Then have pairs of students exchange essays and answer one another's test questions. Student essays should discuss each of these story elements: characters, conflict, plot, resolution, and setting. Essays should also include an explanation of why the movie was chosen as the student's favorite. This project may be used as an alternative form of assessment for the chapter.

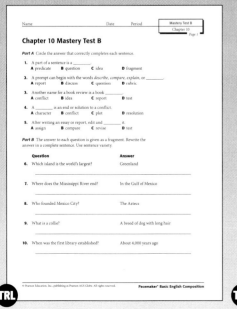

# PLANNING GUIDE

# Writing for Yourself

| | | Student Lesson | | | | Language Skills | | | |
|---|---|---|---|---|---|---|---|---|---|
| | Student Pages | Vocabulary | Practice Exercises | Lesson Review | Identification | Writing | Punctuation & Capitalization | Grammar & Usage | Listening, Speaking, & Viewing |
| **Lesson 11-1** Writing a Personal Letter | 271–273 | ✔ | ✔ | ✔ | ✔ | ✔ | ✔ | ✔ | ✔ |
| **Lesson 11-2** Writing a Message | 274–277 | ✔ | ✔ | ✔ | ✔ | ✔ | ✔ | ✔ | ✔ |
| **Lesson 11-3** Writing an E-Mail Message | 278–283 | ✔ | ✔ | ✔ | ✔ | ✔ | ✔ | ✔ | ✔ |

## Chapter Activities

**Teacher's Resource Library**
Life Skills Connection 11: Writing a
  Letter
Writing Tip 11: Writing Messages
English in Your Life 6: Writing an
  Invitation
Building Research Skills 11: Using a
  Phone Book
Key Vocabulary Words 11

## Assessment Options

**Student Text**
Chapter 11 Review

**Teacher's Resource Library**
Chapter 11 Mastery Tests A and B

**Teacher's Edition**
Chapter 11 Writing Portfolio

| | Student Text Features | | | | | | | | | Teaching Strategies | | | | | | | | | Learning Styles | | | | | Teacher's Resource Library | | | |
|---|---|---|---|---|---|---|---|---|---|---|---|---|---|---|---|---|---|---|---|---|---|---|---|---|---|---|---|
| | English in Your Life | Writing on the Job | Building Research Skills | Vocabulary Builder | Grammar Builder | Write About It | Group Activity | Reading Strategy | Six Traits | ELL/ESL Strategy | Background Information | Common Error | Life Skills Connection | Applications (Home, Career, Community, Global) | Online Connection | Teacher Alert | Speaking & Presenting Practice | Writing/Spelling/Grammar Practice | Auditory/Verbal | Body/Kinesthetic | Interpersonal/Group Learning | Logical/Mathematical | Visual/Spatial | Activities | Modified Activities | Workbook Activities | Self-Study Guide |
| | | | | | 273 | | | 272 | | 272 | 271 | 272 | | 272, 273 | | 272 | | | | | 272 | 273 | | 47 | 47 | 47 | ✔ |
| | | | 277 | | | | | 274, 276 | | 275 | 274 | 275, 276 | | 276 | | | | 275, 277 | 275 | 276 | | | | 48 | 48 | 48 | ✔ |
| | 281 | | 282 | | | 280 | 283 | 279 | 280 | 279 | 278 | 279 | 282 | 281 | 283 | 278 | 282 | 280 | | | | | 279 | 49 | 49 | 49 | ✔ |

### Pronunciation Key

| | | | | | | | | | | | | | | |
|---|---|---|---|---|---|---|---|---|---|---|---|---|---|---|
| a | hat | e | let | ī | ice | ô | order | ů | put | sh | she | ə | a | in about |
| ā | age | ē | equal | o | hot | oi | oil | ü | rule | th | thin | | e | in taken |
| ä | far | ėr | term | ō | open | ou | out | ch | child | ᴛʜ | then | | i | in pencil |
| â | care | i | it | ȯ | saw | u | cup | ng | long | zh | measure | | o | in lemon |
| | | | | | | | | | | | | | u | in circus |

## Modified Activities

The Teacher's Resource Library (TRL) contains a set of lower-level worksheets called Modified Activities. These worksheets cover the same content as the standard Activities but are written at a lower reading level.

## Skill Track

Use Skill Track for *Basic English Composition* to monitor student progress and meet the demands of adequate yearly progress (AYP). Make informed instructional decisions with individual student and class reports of lesson and chapter assessments. With immediate and ongoing feedback, students will also see what they have learned and where they need more reinforcement and practice.

## Chapter at a Glance

### Chapter 11:
### Writing for Yourself

### Skill Track for Basic English Composition

### Teacher's Resource Library **TRL**

(Answer Keys for the Teacher's Resource Library begin on page 446 of the Teacher's Edition.)

---

Name _____  Date _____  Period _____  | Writing Tip  Chapter 11  11 |

**Writing Messages**

Messages are any kind of written or spoken communication. When you write messages, you usually write them by hand. To make messages helpful, you should write neatly so they are readable. You can help the person the message is for by including:

• The time you wrote the message
• The date you wrote the message
• The name of the person who called or gave you the information
• Information that the person who gets the message needs to know
• Your name, to show who wrote the message

Reread your message to:
• Make sure the information is complete
• Make sure nothing is missing
• Make sure the information is correct
• Make sure it is written neatly

Pretend you are taking a phone message for someone in your family. Use the checklist above to write the message on the lines below.

_____
_____
_____
_____
_____

© Pearson Education, Inc., publishing as Pearson AGS Globe. All rights reserved.    **Pacemaker® Basic English Composition**

**TRL**   Writing Tip 11

---

Name _____  Date _____  Period _____  | Life Skills Connection  Chapter 11  11 |

**Writing a Letter**

The final step in mailing a letter is correctly preparing the envelope. A complete envelope will include the return address, or the address of the person sending the letter, in the top left corner. The mailing address, or the person and place where the letter is being sent, is in the center of the envelope and a little to the right. The postage stamp is placed in the top right-hand corner.

Now that you know what to do to write and send letters, practice doing so. Follow the steps below.

**Step 1**  Think of a person to whom you could write a letter. You may like to write a personal letter to a relative or friend. Or maybe you are writing to a new pen pal for the first time.

**Step 2**  On another piece of paper, write your personal letter.

**Step 3**  Imagine that the box below is an envelope. Address the envelope for your letter. Draw your own postage stamp in the correct place.

[ box ]

© Pearson Education, Inc., publishing as Pearson AGS Globe. All rights reserved.    **Pacemaker® Basic English Composition**

**TRL**   Life Skills Connection 11

# Writing for Yourself

There will be times when you will want to write to someone. Like the person in the photo, you might want to send an e-mail. Your e-mail might be a quick message to a friend or a reminder about the next club meeting.

Sometimes you will want to write a letter or note by hand. You might write a letter to a family member while you are at camp. You might write a letter to thank someone for a gift or a favor.

Whatever your reason for writing, you need to know the important information to include. You also need to know the right format for letters, notes, and e-mails. In Chapter 11, you will learn how to write personal messages.

## GOALS FOR LEARNING

- To identify the five parts of a personal letter, and to write a personal letter
- To write a clear message that includes the necessary information
- To identify the parts of an e-mail message, and to write an e-mail message

**269**

## Introducing the Chapter

Have students examine the photograph on page 268. Help them recognize that the student is writing an e-mail. Encourage students who have used e-mail to discuss how they have used it. From whom have they received e-mails? Have students discuss how e-mails and letters are different and alike. When might it be better to write a letter? Point out that in this chapter students will study and practice types of personal writing.

Review and discuss the Goals for Learning on page 269.

## Notes

Ask volunteers to read the notes that appear in the margins throughout the chapter. Then discuss them with the class.

### TEACHER'S RESOURCE

The AGS Globe Teaching Strategies in English Transparencies may be used with this chapter. The transparencies add an interactive dimension to expand and enhance the *Basic English Composition* program content.

### WRITING PORTFOLIO

Explain to students that they will write three items in this chapter: a personal letter, a message, and an e-mail message. Have students think of ideas for a short personal letter to a family member, a friend, or a role model. Students can tell about school, a recent vacation, or other experiences. They can also ask questions of the person they are writing to. Students can use a fictional phone call or other purpose for writing a message. Their e-mail message can be similar to their written messages. These items can be used as an alternative form of assessment for the chapter.

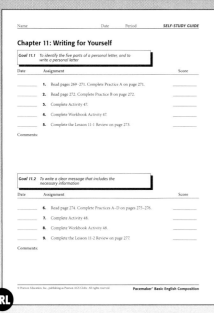

Chapter 11 Self-Study Guide, pages 1–2

Ask students if they always understand what they are reading. Invite students to tell what strategies they can use to understand text better. Have them discuss situations when they might use the reread or summarize strategies. Have students preview the lesson and make predictions about what they will learn.

## Key Vocabulary Words

e-mail
Internet service provider (ISP)
message
personal letter
postscript (P.S.)
screen name

As you read the words, have students read the definitions and ask any questions they may have. If students are confused, provide an example or illustration for the term.

# Reading Strategy: Metacognition

Good readers are always thinking while they are reading. As you read, be aware of whether you are understanding what you read. Ask yourself: How can I change the way I am reading to understand this text better? Use these strategies:

- Preview the text.
- Make predictions. Think about what you already know.
- Write the main idea and details.
- Picture what is happening.
- Reread anything you do not understand.
- Summarize what you have read.
- Make conclusions about what the writer means.

## Key Vocabulary Words

**Personal letter** An informal letter to a friend or relative

**Postscript (P.S.)** A short message at the end of a personal letter

**Message** Any communication; a message may be written, spoken, or shown visually

**E-mail** An electronic message that you send from one computer to another

**Screen name** A name that you use as identification when sending and receiving e-mail

**Internet service provider (ISP)** A company that connects a computer to the Internet

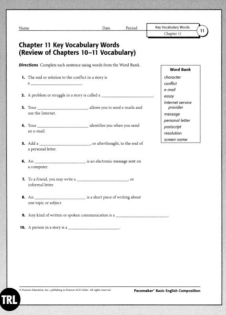

# Writing a Personal Letter

## Objectives

■ To identify the five parts of a personal letter

■ To write a personal letter

**Personal letter**

An informal letter to a friend or relative

When you write a **personal letter,** you share news and feelings with a friend or family member. A personal letter is an informal letter that you write to a friend or relative. It has five parts. Study the five parts of the following letter.

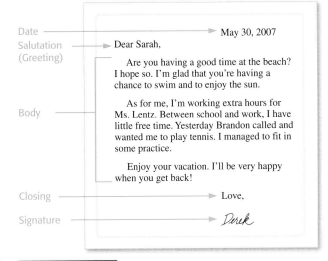

Date — May 30, 2007
Salutation (Greeting) — Dear Sarah,

    Are you having a good time at the beach? I hope so. I'm glad that you're having a chance to swim and to enjoy the sun.

Body —

    As for me, I'm working extra hours for Ms. Lentz. Between school and work, I have little free time. Yesterday Brandon called and wanted me to play tennis. I managed to fit in some practice.

    Enjoy your vacation. I'll be very happy when you get back!

Closing — Love,
Signature — Derek

**Brush Up on the Basics**

Capitalize proper nouns. Titles and names of people are proper nouns. Also begin the names of streets, highways, cities, states, and countries with a capital letter. See Capitalization 5 in Appendix A.

### Practice A

Use the sample letter above to answer each question.

1. What mark of punctuation follows the salutation?
2. What closing does Derek use in this letter?
3. What mark of punctuation follows the closing?
4. Which part of a letter contains the message?
5. What is another name for the greeting?

*Writing for Yourself    Chapter 11*    **271**

---

## Lesson at a Glance

### Chapter 11  Lesson 1

**Overview**  This lesson discusses the purposes and format of a personal, or friendly, letter.

### Objectives

■ To identify the five parts of a personal letter

■ To write a personal letter

**Student Pages**  271–273

**Teacher's Resource Library**

Activity  47

Modified Activity  47

Workbook Activity  47

## Vocabulary

personal letter      postscript (P.S.)

Write *personal* and *postscript* on the board. Tell students that a personal letter is friendly and informal. Tell students that *post-* is a prefix that means "after" and that *script* means "something written." Therefore, a *postscript* is written after something else.

## Background Information

There are two common formats for letters: block style and modified block style. In this lesson, modified block style is shown. In this style, the date, closing, and signature are aligned near the center of the paper. The beginning of each paragraph is indented. In letters, both the greeting and the closing are capitalized.

### 1  Warm-Up Activity

Ask students why a personal letter should include questions. Discuss why adding questions is better than simply making statements about themselves.

---

### 2  Teaching the Lesson

After they have read the text on pages 271 and 272, ask students to summarize the parts of a personal letter. Ask them how a writer separates ideas in the letter's body. Ask them how a writer separates the different parts of the letter. Discuss closings with students and make a list of closings on the board.

### Practice A

Have a volunteer read aloud the sample personal letter before students answer the questions. Remind students to use complete sentences.

### Practice A Answers

1. A comma follows the salutation. 2. Derek uses the closing "Love." 3. The closing is followed by a comma. 4. The message is contained in the body. 5. The salutation is also called the greeting.

## Practice B

After reading the sample letter on page 272, have students write a thank-you letter to someone who has given them a gift or done them a favor. Make sure they are specific about what they are thanking the person for. Remind students to be polite and make positive remarks. Encourage them to ask a question in the letter. Have them revise and edit their letters.

### Practice B Answers

Thank-you letters will vary but must include the five parts of a letter.

**3** **Reinforce and Extend**

### TEACHER ALERT

 Emphasize to students that the word *personal* refers to the informal tone of the letter and does not necessarily mean "private" or "secret." Another name for a personal letter is "friendly letter."

### *Reading Strategy:* Metacognition

Students may say that each sample clearly shows all five parts of a letter.

### COMMON ERROR

 When using a computer to write a letter, students are wise to use an electronic spelling checker. However, most programs are not without flaws. Stress to students the importance of proofreading their work or having someone else proofread it for them.

### IN THE COMMUNITY

 Ask students whether and when they have used thank-you cards. Briefly discuss how a written thank-you letter, such as the one shown on page 272, differs from a store-bought card. When might a letter be better than a thank-you card?

---

**Postscript (P.S.)**
A short message at the end of a personal letter

### *Reading Strategy:*
Metacognition

Study the sample letters in this lesson. How do they help you remember the parts of a letter?

 **NOTE**
If you want someone to reply to a written invitation, write RSVP at the bottom. RSVP is an abbreviation for the French phrase *répondez s'il vous plaît*, which means please reply. "

---

## Thank-You Letters

It is always polite to say thank you for a gift or a favor. Read the sample letter below. The writer describes her gift in detail. Comments like these show the writer's appreciation for the gift.

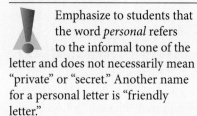

August 6, 2007

Dear Aunt Marie,

   Thank you for the wonderful soft sweater that you sent. It was so thoughtful of you to remember my birthday. How did you guess that the sweater was exactly what I wanted? It fits perfectly. Blue is my favorite color, too.

Love,
Carolyne

P.S. The rest of the family says hello.

### Practice B

Write a thank-you letter to someone who has given you a gift or done a favor for you. Be specific. Make positive comments. When you are finished, revise and edit.

### Postscripts

Sometimes a letter will include the letters P.S. below the closing. P.S. is the abbreviation for **postscript,** which means "after the writing." You can use P.S. to add a short message after you have completed a personal letter.

▶ **EXAMPLE 1**

   P.S. I forgot to mention that I miss you.

---

### LEARNING STYLES

 **Interpersonal/Group Learning**

Divide the class into pairs. Give each pair a catalog with pictures. Invite the partners to page through the catalog and find something they would each like to receive as a gift. Ask them to imagine that their partner has given them the item. Then ask each partner to write a thank-you letter to the other partner.

### ELL/ESL STRATEGY

**Language Objective:** *To write a personal letter*

   Letter writing may be useful in coaxing ESL students to express themselves. Given an opportunity to express an opinion or communicate with a favorite personality, students might be influenced to express themselves as well as they can. Their interest may be sparked further by the intention to actually mail the letter.

# REVIEW

1. Read the thank-you letter. Find three mistakes in its format. Write the letter correctly on your paper.

> *DEREK*
>
> Dear Aunt Harriet
>
>    It was so thoughtful of you to remember my birthday. You are so generous! I really needed the money. I need new running shoes for the next track meet. Thanks! Love,
>
>                     Derek

2. Write a personal letter to a friend or a relative. It may be an invitation, a thank-you note, or just a letter to keep in touch. Remember to include the five parts.

## GRAMMAR BUILDER

### Using Hyphens

A hyphen is a punctuation mark. It is used in many places:

- Between words in a compound number: *twenty-one*
- In a fraction used as an adjective: *one-fourth cup of flour*
- Between words in a compound adjective: *a ten-year-old girl*
- At the end of a line to divide a word between syllables: *train-ing*

Rewrite each phrase below. Add a hyphen where it is needed.

1. forty five tickets
2. a two thirds majority
3. a well designed house

*Writing for Yourself*    Chapter 11    **273**

---

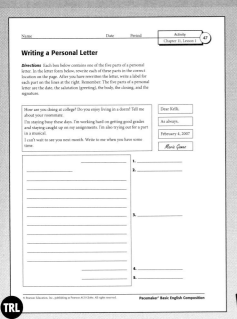

Activity 47

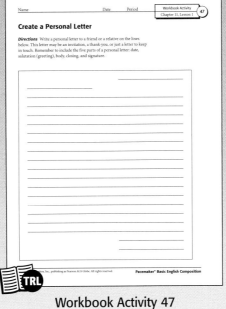

Workbook Activity 47

---

## Lesson 11-1 Review Answers

## AT HOME

Using the sample letters on pages 271–272 as guides, have students write their own letters. Students can choose someone who lives in their house or building. For example, a student could write a letter to her father, asking if he had a busy day. Students may want to share their letters with the class.

## LEARNING STYLES

### Logical/Mathematical

Have students bring a letter from home or print a letter from the Internet. Discuss with students the sequential organization of ideas in the letters. Have them create an outline of each part of the letter: date, salutation, ideas in the body, closing, and signature. Then have students use this outline as a model for creating their own letter.

## GRAMMAR BUILDER

Discuss with students where and why hyphens are used. Encourage students to ask questions they may have about hyphens.

### Grammar Builder Answers

1. forty-five tickets 2. a two-thirds majority
3. a well-designed house

## Chapter 11 Lesson 2

**Overview** This lesson focuses on reasons and ways to write a message.

### Objectives

- To write a clear message to inform someone about a phone call
- To write a clear message to inform someone of your plans
- To include the important details in a message

**Student Pages** 274–277

**Teacher's Resource Library** **TRL**

Activity 48

Modified Activity 48

Workbook Activity 48

## Vocabulary

**message**

Have students read the meaning of *message*. Then encourage them to help you make a list of reasons you might write a message.

## Background Information

It isn't always necessary to ask a person for a callback number. For instance, if you take a message from a close family friend, you probably have that friend's number already. However, remind students to always take a callback number from someone they don't know well.

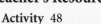

## 1 Warm-Up Activity

Read the sample message in Example 1 on page 274. Express to students that the message is written in complete sentences. Discuss with them why it might be better to use complete sentences in a message.

## 2 Teaching the Lesson

Have students imagine that they have answered the phone in the school office and are taking a message for a teacher. Ask them what information they should include in order for the message to be complete.

---

# Writing a Message

### Objectives

- To write a clear message to inform someone about a phone call
- To write a clear message to inform someone of your plans
- To include the important details in a message

**Message**
Any communication; a message may be written, spoken, or shown visually

**Reading Strategy:**
Metacognition

Remember to ask yourself questions as you read this lesson. For example, ask: What are the parts of a message?

A **message** is any type of communication. Everyday messages are usually written or spoken. Friends and family members often leave messages to inform each other of plans. Writing phone messages is an important job in many places of work. When writing a message, make your handwriting readable. Sometimes it is better to print so that you communicate clearly.

Include the following information in a message:

- the time and date that you wrote the message
- the name of the person who called or gave you the information
- the information you want the person who gets the message to know
- a phone number if the person is supposed to call someone back
- your name, to show that you wrote the message

The message in Example 1 is complete and correct. The message gives the person receiving it the information she needs to know.

▶ **EXAMPLE 1**

Sonia,

Amber called at 3:00 PM. Call her at home before 4:30 PM. She will be at the dog training class from 4:30 until 5:30 PM. Then, she will be home again.

Love,

Mom

---

**Reading Strategy:** Metacognition

Students may include time and date, name of person calling, important details, callback number, and own name.

## Practice A

Use the message in Example 1 to write the answer to each question.

1. What time did Amber call?
2. Who took this message?
3. Who is this message for?
4. What is Sonia supposed to do?
5. It is now 5:00 PM. Is Amber home?

**NOTE**

Messages can also be presented visually. A facial expression or gesture can communicate a message. TV or magazine ads may use strong images and few words to express a message. Often, written or spoken words are used along with visual messages.

## Practice B

Read each message. Decide what important information the writer left out. Write what is missing. There may be more than one thing missing.

1. Mom, I am going out. I will be home later. Amber
2. Derek, Brandon called you. Call him back by 5 PM. Mom
3. Monday, 2 PM. Brandon, you are supposed to play tennis with Luis.
4. Friday, 6 PM. Dad, someone called about the car. Luis
5. Mr. Martin, I stopped by during second period to ask about my homework. I will be back. Sonia

## Practice A

Have a volunteer read aloud the sample message in Example 1 on page 274. Students should refer to it as they answer questions 1–5. Instruct students to write their answers in complete sentences.

### *Practice A Answers*

**1.** Amber called at 3:00 PM. **2.** Sonia's mother took the message. **3.** This message is for Sonia. **4.** Sonia should call Amber before 4:30 or after 5:30. **5.** No, Amber is not home.

## Practice B

Tell students to use their imagination in order to complete the information in each message. Refer them to the list on page 274 of their book.

### *Practice B Answers*

**1.** Add the date and time. Be more specific about the time "later." **2.** Add the date and time. **3.** Add the writer's name. Add more specific information about where and when the tennis game is being held. **4.** Add the name and phone number of the caller. **5.** Add the date and a detail about when Sonia will be back.

---

**3** | **Reinforce and Extend**

### COMMON ERROR

Some students may live in a household in which two people have the same first name, specifically, fathers and sons. When taking a message, students should always clarify which person the caller is asking for. Express to them that the same rule would apply in any situation where people share the same first name.

### Writing Practice

Divide the class into pairs. Have students write short messages to one another. Messages should include some sentence fragments. Partners will revise the fragmented messages and read the finished messages aloud.

---

## ELL/ESL STRATEGY

**Language Objective:**
*To take and leave phone messages*

Students will be divided into callers and receivers. Callers can imitate a phone ringing and tap the receiver. The receiver "answers" the call. Callers ask for a friend or family member. The receiver responds that the friend is not in and asks if he or she can take a message. Callers practice leaving necessary information for their "friends," while receivers learn to record information and ask for details.

## LEARNING STYLES

**Auditory/Verbal**

Write down a short message you want to give to the class. Then whisper this message into the ear of the student nearest you. Ask that student to whisper the same message into the ear of the next student. Continue around the room until everyone has listened to the message. Ask the last student who heard the message to write it on a slip of paper. Then compare your written message with the one the student wrote down.

## Practice C

Have students read the sample message and answer the questions on their paper. Direct them to write complete sentences.

### Practice C Answers

1. The message is for Brandon.
2. Brandon's mother took the message.
3. Sonia called at 2:00 PM on Saturday.
4. The party was on Saturday. **5.** Sonia canceled the party because everyone has the flu.

### COMMON ERROR

Some people may be difficult to understand on the telephone. They may tend to speak very quickly or not speak clearly. Students should be encouraged to ask callers to slow down or repeat parts of a message that are unclear.

## Practice D

Have students visualize the easiest route from school to their home. If students are unsure of street names, use your own knowledge or a simple map to assist them.

### Practice D Answers

Directions will vary but should include a definite order between school and home.

### Reading Strategy: Metacognition

Student predictions will vary but may include using accurate and specific words and a correct sequence.

### LEARNING STYLES

**Body/Kinesthetic**

Divide the class into several groups. Each group will be divided into "callers" and "answering service." Students will model actions of dialing, answering, speaking into, and listening on a telephone throughout the exercise. Callers "call" the answering service and practice leaving a message for a friend, relative, or teacher. Students in the answering service practice taking messages.

---

**Reading Strategy:**
Metacognition

Use what you have learned to make a prediction about how to write good driving directions.

 **NOTE**

Make your handwritten messages easy to read. Use a clean sheet of paper with no other writing on it. Write in careful cursive or print neatly. Check punctuation and spelling.

---

### Practice C

Read the message and then answer the questions. Write your answers on your paper.

2:00 PM Saturday

Brandon,

Sonia called to say she canceled the party tonight. Everyone has the flu. She will see you at school on Monday.

Mom

1. Who is this message for?
2. Who took this message?
3. When did Sonia call?
4. What day was the party?
5. Why did Sonia cancel the party?

### Practice D

Write a message that gives driving directions from the school to your house.

*"Let me read these details back to you. I want to make sure I wrote them down correctly."*

---

### GLOBAL CONNECTION

Have students imagine that a visitor is coming from another country. Their job is to make sure the visitor is met at the airport. List the critical information to include on a message to the person who is meeting the visitor: date and time of arrival, airline, flight number, meeting place, and any other important details. Have students create a message that is complete and concise.

### WRITING PORTFOLIO

**Checkpoint** Have students edit their Writing Portfolio messages using the checklist on page 274.

# REVIEW

1. Write a message to a member of your family. Explain that you went to the store and will be home in time for dinner. Include the date and time, the name of the person who will receive the message, and your name.

2. Assume that Derek is walking past the coach's office at 2:30 PM. The phone rings, and Derek answers it. Read the phone dialogue below. Write the message that Derek should write for Coach Jones. Use today's date.

Derek: Hello. This is the Springfield Phy Ed Department. The coach is not here. May I help you?

Woman on phone: Yes, this is Springfield Sporting Goods. Coach Jones ordered 10 baseball bats. The bats are ready. He can pick them up anytime between 9:00 AM and 6:00 PM.

Derek: May I please ask your name?

Woman on phone: Yes. My name is Ms. Handley. He can call me at 312-555-8900.

## VOCABULARY BUILDER

### Making New Words with Suffixes

Adding a suffix, or word ending, to a base word can change the part of speech. A suffix can change an adjective into a noun:

happy + -ness = happiness

The suffixes -ion, -er, -ist, -or, and -ant change verbs into nouns:

act + -ion = action

1. Add -ness to these adjectives: quick, nervous. Then write a sentence using each new noun.
2. Write a sentence using each new noun below.

operate + -ion        assist + -ant        act + -or

*Writing for Yourself* Chapter 11    **277**

---

## Lesson 11-2 Review Answers

**1.** Answers will vary. A sample message is given.

January 4, 4:00 PM

Sheila,

I've gone to Mahoney's. I'll be back by 6:00 for dinner.

Davis

**2.** Answers will vary. A sample message is given.

April 5, 2:30 PM

Coach Jones,

Ms. Handley of Springfield Sporting Goods called. The 10 bats you ordered are ready. You can pick them up between 9:00 AM and 6:00 PM. If you have questions, call her at 555-8900.

Derek Anderson

## VOCABULARY BUILDER

If necessary, review parts of speech with students. Remind them that an adjective describes a noun.

### Vocabulary Builder Answers

Sample answers are shown. **1.** A soccer player needs quickness to succeed. A speaker shows nervousness by speaking too fast. **2.** The doctor told her she needed an operation. Pete is an assistant for a veterinarian. An actor must memorize lots of dialogue.

## Spelling Practice

There are a number of rules related to hyphens and compound modifiers. Below are a few such rules.

Use a hyphen when the modifier is before the noun.
Incorrect: This is a well written paper.
Correct: This is a well-written paper.

Do not use a hyphen when the modifier is after the noun.
Incorrect: This paper is well-written.
Correct: This paper is well written.

Do not use a hyphen when the modifier ends in -*ly*.
Incorrect: This is a badly-typed sentence.
Correct: This is a badly typed sentence.

Following these rules, have students write several sentences with compound modifiers. Direct them to tell which rule each sentence follows.

---

Activity 48                    Workbook Activity 48

# Lesson at a Glance

## Chapter 11  Lesson 3

**Overview**  This lesson introduces students to electronic mail, or e-mail.

## Objectives

- To identify the parts of an e-mail
- To write and send an e-mail

**Student Pages**  278–283

**Teacher's Resource Library** (TRL)

Activity  49

Modified Activity  49

Workbook Activity  49

English in Your Life  6

Building Research Skills  11

Life Skills Connection  11

........................................................

## Vocabulary

e-mail
Internet service provider (ISP)
screen name

Ask students with e-mail accounts what their *screen name* is. If they are unsure, have them write their e-mail address on the board. Explain that the first part of the address is the screen name. To illustrate electronic communication, make a simple diagram outlining the path from *ISP* to *screen name* and *e-mail,* back to *ISP.*

........................................................

## Background Information

When a student writes an e-mail and clicks the *send* button, the message is sent instantly to the recipient. It takes mere seconds. However, several things must happen before the message arrives on the recipient's computer. The electronic mail must first go through the Internet service provider's mail server. The server will decide how to properly route the message by observing the ending of the address. The message is then sent via the Internet to the mail server of the recipient's ISP. The message will be stored in an electronic mailbox until the recipient opens his or her e-mail account. The message will then appear in the recipient's personal mailbox.

---

# Writing an E-Mail Message

## Objectives

- To identify the parts of an e-mail
- To write and send an e-mail

**E-mail**
An electronic message that you send from one computer to another

**Screen name**
A name that you use as identification when sending and receiving e-mail

**Internet service provider (ISP)**
A company that connects a computer to the Internet

**NOTE**

Most ISPs offer e-mail programs with an address book. An address book allows you to save the e-mail addresses of your friends.

An **e-mail** is an electronic message that you send from one computer to another. *E-mail* is an abbreviation for electronic mail.

### E-Mail Addresses

When you get an e-mail account, you choose a **screen name**. This is the name that you use as identification when sending and receiving e-mail. The first part of your e-mail address is your screen name. In your e-mail address, the name of the **Internet service provider (ISP)** follows your screen name. An ISP is a company that connects your computer to the Internet. Following the name of the ISP is one of these endings: *.com, .net, .edu, .gov,* or *.org.* Schools and universities usually use the ending *.edu.*

### Practice A

Write the answer to each question.

1. What does the word *e-mail* stand for?
2. What is a screen name?
3. What is an Internet service provider?
4. What kind of organization uses the ending *.edu*?
5. What endings follow the ISP in an e-mail address?

### Writing and Sending E-Mail

The exact format for e-mail depends on the Internet service provider. Most e-mail programs have similar features. Notice the features of the e-mail program in the sample e-mail on the next page. You can send an e-mail "now," or you can send it "later." Before you send an e-mail, check that you have entered the correct e-mail address. Check that you have entered a subject in the subject field.

---

## 1  Warm-Up Activity

Read the sample e-mail on page 279. Express to students that the message is written in complete sentences. Discuss with them why it might be better to use complete sentences in a message.

## 2  Teaching the Lesson

Discuss the sample message on page 279. How is an e-mail message like a personal letter? When might it be useful to send an e-mail? When would it be better to write a letter?

## Practice A

Have students recall the information from page 278 to answer the questions.

### Practice A Answers

**1.** electronic mail **2.** a name you choose as the first part of an e-mail address **3.** a company that connects a computer to the Internet **4.** a school or university **5.** .com, .net, .edu, .gov, or .org

### TEACHER ALERT

Emphasize that clicking the *send* button is akin to submitting a finished writing project for a grade. When writing an e-mail message, students should make sure they've checked for spelling, punctuation, and grammatical errors. Express to students that a message cannot be retrieved after it has been sent.

**Reading Strategy:**
Metacognition

Look at the format of the sample e-mail. How does it compare with the format you are familiar with?

---

**Brush Up on the Basics**

An electronic spelling checker does not catch all misspelled words. For example, it may not catch *piece* when you meant to write *peace*. See Spelling 1–12 in Appendix A.

---

**NOTE**

A symbol used in a computer program is called an *icon*. A blank space designed for entering information is a *field*. A row of tool icons shown at the top of a computer screen is a *toolbar*.

You must connect your computer to the Internet to send an e-mail. When you are connected, you are *online*. When you are not connected, you are *off-line*.

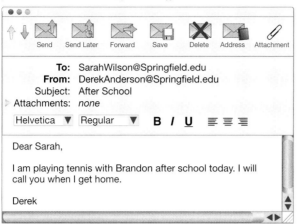

To: SarahWilson@Springfield.edu
From: DerekAnderson@Springfield.edu
Subject: After School
Attachments: *none*

Dear Sarah,

I am playing tennis with Brandon after school today. I will call you when I get home.

Derek

## Practice B

Use the sample e-mail above to answer each question.

1. To whom did Derek send this e-mail?
2. What is the subject of the e-mail?
3. What is Sarah's screen name?
4. What is Sarah's complete e-mail address?
5. What icon would you click to find e-mail addresses?

When you write an e-mail message, use sentences and check your spelling. Many e-mail programs have a spell checker. Its icon often appears in a toolbar.

Most e-mail programs allow you to attach documents. An attachment can be a word processing document, a photo, or another type of file.

A formatting toolbar gives you options for changing the format in your message. This toolbar has fields for font and font size. It has icons for bold, italic, and underlined fonts.

*Writing for Yourself   Chapter 11*   **279**

## Practice B

Have students use the sample e-mail on page 279 to answer the questions.

### Practice B Answers

1. Sarah Wilson  2. After School
3. SarahWilson  4. SarahWilson@Springfield.edu  5. Address

### Reading Strategy: Metacognition

Students might draw comparisons to the format of the e-mail program they use at school or at home.

 **3  Reinforce and Extend**

## COMMON ERROR

Students experienced with e-mail may want to use the Cc:, or "carbon copy," function to e-mail several people at once. Remind students that recipients of these e-mails will also be able to see the e-mail addresses of people listed in the Cc: field. Most people do not want their e-mail address given out to people they don't know.

## ELL/ESL STRATEGY

**Language Objective:** *To compare and contrast letters*

Have ELL/ESL students bring envelopes addressed and sent from other countries. Encourage discussion regarding the differences in address format on an envelope, parts of a personal letter, and postage. Students who may not understand ZIP codes, rural routes, or post office boxes may benefit by discussing what the numbers and abbreviations mean.

## WRITING PORTFOLIO

**Checkpoint** Have students revise their Writing Portfolio e-mails using the samples on pages 279 and 280.

## COMMON ERROR

Students may sometimes want to type messages using all capital letters. Guide them to understand that using capital letters tends to give the reader the impression that the writer is shouting at them. Express to students that use of capital letters should be limited. Extra exclamation points should also be avoided.

## LEARNING STYLES

**Visual/Spatial**

Seat students or groups at a computer with e-mail access. Have them examine the sample e-mail on page 279. Encourage students to compare the sample to a real e-mail. If possible, have students send a simple message to each other. They can print their messages and trade with other students. Students who are unfamiliar with e-mail will benefit from a hands-on e-mail experience.

**1.** DerekAnderson **2.** DerekAnderson@
Springfield.edu **3.** History Test **4.** Amber
**5.** Springfield

## Grammar Practice

Have students reread the sample e-mail in
the review on page 280. Ask them to find
the subject of the closing *c u later*. Discuss
with students how this popular form of
quick, short writing is grammatically
incorrect. Ask a volunteer to correct this
closing on the board.

### WRITE ABOUT IT

Describe a part-time job you have had.
As you talk, capture key words and
phrases on a graphic organizer such as
a word web on the board. Be sure to
include details from the list on page 280.
Then have students brainstorm details
using their own graphic organizers.

### *Write About It Answers*

Student paragraphs should follow an
organizational plan, include some vivid
details, and suggest feelings.

## Six Traits of Writing Focus

|   |              |   |                  |
|---|--------------|---|------------------|
|   | Ideas        |   | Word Choice      |
| ✔ | Organization |   | Sentence Fluency |
| ✔ | Voice        |   | Conventions      |

## Voice

Remind students to use words and style
that are reminiscent of their own voice.
Suggest that they read their paragraph
aloud to a partner. Partners should
listen for a voice that is unique and true
to the writer and make suggestions for
improvement.

Tell students that organization is key
to engaging the reader. Without logical
flow in a piece of writing, the reader will
become confused and disinterested.

Tell students to check page WPH1 for
more instruction on the Six Traits of
Writing.

---

## LESSON 11-3 REVIEW

Use the sample e-mail to answer each question.

**1.** What is Derek's screen name?

**2.** What is Derek's complete e-mail
address?

**3.** What is the subject of this e-mail?

**4.** Who sent this e-mail?

**5.** What is the name of the ISP in both
addresses?

### WRITE ABOUT IT

**A Part-Time Job**
Many people have had interesting part-time jobs. Write a
paragraph about a part-time job that you have had. Include
these details:

- why you wanted a job
- how you got the job
- what your job responsibilities were
- any interesting experiences on the job
- what you liked best about the job
- what you did not like about the job

Be sure that each sentence starts with a capital letter and ends
with an end punctuation mark. Include a topic sentence, at least
two details in the body, and a summary or conclusion. Read
what you wrote to the class.

 **Six Traits
of Writing:**
*Voice* the writer's own
language

---

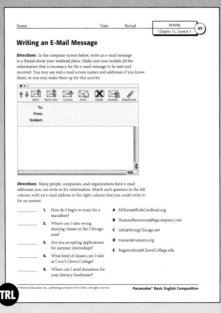

**Activity 49**

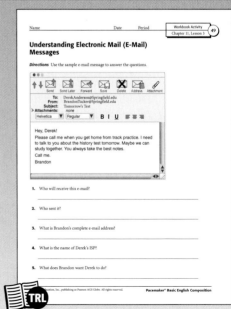

**Workbook Activity 49**

## Writing an Invitation

The Spanish Club is having a dinner for parents of club members. Nick Garcia sent the invitation as an e-mail attachment. He was careful to include all the details people might need. Read Nick's invitation. Then answer the questions.

### YOU ARE INVITED

April 25, 2007

Dear parents of Spanish Club members,

We appreciate your support and help this year. To thank you, we are having a dinner and program in your honor. Please join us for an "Evening in Spain" on May 3 at 6:30 PM.

The evening will begin with a Spanish dinner in the school commons. We will serve the dishes we learned about in club meetings. Then we will present a program of Spanish music and dancing. To get in the spirit, you may want to add Spanish touches to the outfit you wear!

I am looking forward to seeing you!

Nick Garcia
Spanish Club President

RSVP to the School Office: 555-4262.

1. Where and when will "Evening in Spain" be held?

2. What will happen at the event?

3. **CRITICAL THINKING** Why does Nick need to hear from the parents?

## SPEAKING AND LISTENING

When asked to RSVP to an invitation, call as soon as you can. Let the person know your plans. Also ask any questions you may have. For example, you might ask: Should I bring something? What should I wear? Work with a partner to role-play the phone call that a parent might make to Nick. One partner is the parent responding to Nick's invitation. The other is Nick taking the response. Then switch roles.

---

Ask students to think about a time when they have sent or received an invitation. Have them recall the invitation and what kinds of information were included. Discuss why it would be important to include any certain details. Have a volunteer read the introductory paragraph of English in Your Life. Invite students to predict three basic details that should be included in the invitation. Then have them read Nick's invitation and answer the questions.

### *English in Your Life Answers*

**1.** It will be held in the school commons on May 3 at 6:30 PM. **2.** Club members will serve a Spanish-theme dinner and perform Spanish music and dances. **3.** The club needs to know how many will attend so they know how much food to prepare.

### CAREER CONNECTION

Encourage students to think of one or more careers that they might consider. Have them write a paragraph citing ways that e-mail might be used in that career. If students are unsure, allow them to use the Internet to research how e-mail is used in the workplace.

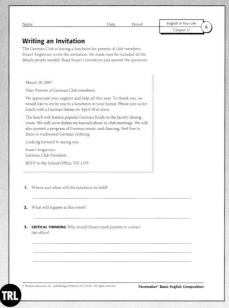

**English in Your Life 6**

Have students practice finding information in a phone book. Ask them to find their parents or a friend in the white pages or a certain business in the yellow pages. Then have students look for the same listings using an Internet directory. Have students read the selection and answer the questions.

### *Building Research Skills Answers*

**1.** It gives you the street address for each person or residence. **2.** It has listings of businesses in the area by type, maps, and advertisements. **3.** The yellow pages could help them find schools, grocery stores, insurance offices, and other businesses they need. The maps could help them get around town.

## Speaking and Presenting Practice

Ask students to think of advertisements they have seen or heard that sound like invitations. Perhaps they have seen on television or heard on the radio someone inviting people to come to a special event. Give students time to make notes about the invitation, such as the event, benefits, location, and date. Suggest that students create note cards or an outline as a guide and practice "advertising" their invitations. They may practice before a friend or family member or record their practice. Then have students share their advertisements in a humorous or dramatic style.

### LIFE SKILLS CONNECTION

Discuss with students what information they need to include on an envelope. Explain the importance of a return address as well as proper postage. Distribute Life Skills Connection 11 and have students complete it.

---

## Using a Phone Book

A phone book lists the names, addresses, and phone numbers of people and businesses in an area or city.

The white pages of a phone book list people by their last name.

> **Marsh Sarah**  609 Cloverlane Dr Syc........**815-555-3791**

In this entry, *Dr* and *Syc* are abbreviations for Drive and Sycamore. Sycamore is the name of a town.

Each phone book also has yellow pages. These pages may be in the back of the white pages or in a separate book. The yellow pages list businesses by type. To find a moving company, you would look in the *M*s. Each moving company in the area is listed alphabetically under "Movers." Many businesses also put advertisements in the yellow pages.

Phone books contain other useful information. Many have street maps of the town or towns they cover. They may also show area codes. This kind of information is found in the white pages.

Answer the following questions.

**1.** How could the phone book help you address invitations to friends?

**2.** What is found in the yellow pages of the phone book?

**3.** CRITICAL THINKING How might the phone book help someone who is new in town?

### TECHNOLOGY

Besides a phone book, a town or area puts out other documents. For example, the chamber of commerce may publish a list of interesting things to do and see. The local government may make certain documents available to the public. These materials—and phone books—are often posted online. In online white page listings, you can find information for people all over the world. However, you must know a person's name and location to find a phone number.

---

Name _____ Date _____ Period _____  Building Research Skills  Chapter 11  **11**

### Using a Phone Book

Phone books list names, addresses, and phone numbers of people and places in a town or city. Many also contain street maps. Some phone books separate the book into sections. The White Pages list information of residents. The Yellow Pages list businesses. Schools and government buildings are often listed in another part of the phone book.
Use the sample phone book below to answer the questions.

> **JANITORIAL SERVICES**
> **A1 CLEANERS**
> 678 Redding Av Black Spring........ (773) 555-9041
> **BEST MAIDS**
> 3080 Hwy 1 Kenwood ...............(815) 555-4862

**1.** What does Hwy stand for?

**2.** Do these businesses have the same area code?

**3.** CRITICAL THINKING How might the phone book help you if you wanted to go to A1 Cleaners?

© Pearson Education, Inc., publishing as Pearson AGS Globe. All rights reserved.   **Pacemaker® Basic English Composition**

**TRL**

Building Research Skills 11

- When you write a personal letter to a friend or relative, use the five-part format. Include the date, a salutation, the body, a closing, and your name.

- When you write a thank-you letter, use the same format as a personal letter. Describe the gift you received in detail.

- If you forget to include a detail in the body of a personal letter, you can add a postscript at the end.

- When you leave a message for someone, include the date and time. At the end, give your name to show that you wrote the message.

- When you write a phone message, give the name of the person who called, their message, and their phone number.

- Write neatly so your messages are easy to read.

- Check the punctuation, subject-verb agreement, and spelling in everything you write.

- Write e-mail messages as carefully as any other message. Write in sentences.

- Before you send an e-mail, check that you have entered the receiver's correct e-mail address. It should have a screen name, an ISP name, and an ending. Check that you have entered a subject in the subject field.

- Learn about the features of your e-mail program. Learn to use the spelling checker on your e-mail program. Learn how to attach a file to an e-mail. Learn how to change the format in your message.

## GROUP ACTIVITY

Work with a group to write directions from your school to a popular meeting place. You may want to look at a map of your town or neighborhood. Write clearly and simply.

Be sure to capitalize the names of streets and buildings. Trade directions with another group. Suggest how the other group could improve their directions.

## Chapter 11 Summary

Have volunteers read aloud each Summary item on page 283. Ask volunteers to explain the meaning of each item.

### ONLINE CONNECTION

 Some Web sites can assist in the letter-writing process. They offer standard guidelines, templates, and creative suggestions for writing different types of letters. The following sites may help:

www.agsglobepmbec.com/page283a
www.agsglobepmbec.com/page283b

### GROUP ACTIVITY

Provide enough phone books for each group to share one. Remind groups to begin by prewriting. They might compile a list of popular meeting places. You might stress to students the importance of order when writing directions. Remind groups that they should revise their rough drafts.

## Chapter 11 Review

Use the Chapter Review to prepare students for tests and to reteach content from the chapter.

## Chapter 11 Mastery Test

The Teacher's Resource Library includes two forms of the Chapter 11 Mastery Test. Each test addresses the chapter Goals for Learning. An optional third page of additional critical-thinking items is included for each test. The difficulty level of the two forms is equivalent.

### Review Answers

#### Part A

**1.** personal letter **2.** e-mails **3.** Internet service provider **4.** message **5.** screen name **6.** postscript

#### Part B

**7.** ATurner **8.** ATurner@Springfield.edu **9.** Permission slips **10.** Ms. Hall **11.** Springfield **12.** Helvetica **13.** BHall

**Word Bank**

e-mails

Internet service provider

message

personal letter

postscript

screen name

**Part A** Write the word or words from the Word Bank that complete each sentence.

**1.** A _____ is written to a friend or relative.

**2.** People send _____ from one computer to another.

**3.** Your _____ connects your computer to the Internet.

**4.** A _____ can be written, spoken, or shown visually.

**5.** A _____ is the identification you use when sending and receiving e-mail.

**6.** A _____ is a short message at the end of a letter.

**Part B** Read the sample e-mail. Then write the answer to each question.

Send   Send Later   Forward   Save   Delete   Address

To: ATurner@Springfield.edu
From: BHall@Springfield.edu
Subject: Permission slips
Attachments: none

Helvetica ▼   Regular ▼   **B** *I* U

Dear Ms. Turner,

Each student going on the Art Club field trip must provide a signed permission form by Thursday, May 8. Members who do not provide a form will not be allowed to go on the trip.

Sincerely,

Ms. Hall

**7.** What is Ms. Turner's screen name?

**8.** What is Ms. Turner's e-mail address?

**9.** What is the subject of the e-mail?

**10.** Who sent the e-mail?

**11.** Who is Ms. Turner's ISP?

**12.** What font is Ms. Hall using?

**13.** What is Ms. Hall's screen name?

**Part C** Suppose you are babysitting a child named Tanya at the Jefferson home. You answer the phone at 6:00 PM, and the caller says:

"My name is Denise Smith. I am Tanya Jefferson's aunt. I cannot meet Mrs. Jefferson tomorrow evening. I will call Mrs. Jefferson tomorrow at 9:00 AM."

Based on this information, answer questions 14–18.

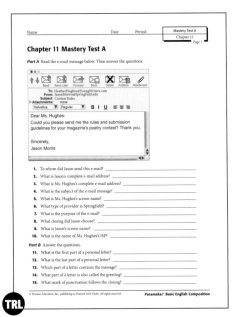

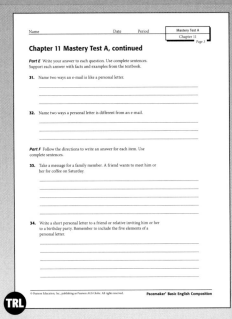

Chapter 11 Mastery Test A, pages 1–3

For questions 14–17, write the letter of your answer.

**14.** Who is Denise Smith?
   **A** Mr. Jefferson's aunt  **C** Mrs. Jefferson's aunt
   **B** Tanya's aunt      **D** Tanya's sister

**15.** What time did Denise Smith call?
   **A** 6:00 PM  **B** 9:00 PM  **C** 6:00 AM   **D** 9:00 AM

**16.** Who is this message for?
   **A** Denise Smith    **C** Mrs. Jefferson
   **B** Tanya Jefferson  **D** Mr. Jefferson

**17.** Why did Denise Smith call Mrs. Jefferson?
   **A** to make plans    **C** to say hello
   **B** to talk to Tanya  **D** to change plans

**18.** Use the information from the caller to write a message for Mrs. Jefferson, Tanya's mother.

**Part D** Write the answer to each question.

**19.** What is the first part of a personal letter?

**20.** What mark of punctuation follows the salutation and closing of a letter?

**21.** "Dear Mia," is an example of what part of a letter?

**22.** "Sincerely," is an example of what part of a letter?

**23.** What is another word for the main part of a letter?

**Part E** Follow the directions in each writing prompt.

**24.** Write a personal letter to a friend, family member, or teacher. It can be a thank-you letter or a letter just to keep in touch. Include the five parts in your letter.

**25.** Write a message that you might e-mail to another student about a school project. It may be a real or imaginary project. Include the subject line.

**Test Tip**

In a writing test, strong, well-organized ideas count the most. However, your handwriting should be clear enough to read.

## Review Answers

### Part C

**14.** B **15.** A **16.** C **17.** D **18.** Responses will vary, but should include the time of the call, the name of the person the message is for, the name of the person who took the message (the student's name), and the content of the message.

### Part D

**19.** date **20.** comma **21.** salutation **22.** closing **23.** body

### Part E

**24.** Responses will vary but should include date, greeting, body, closing, and signature.
**25.** Responses will vary but should include the subject line, greeting, body, closing, and student's name.

---

**WRITING PORTFOLIO**

**Wrap-Up** Have students make a clean final copy of their revised and edited products. You may want to collect and read them anonymously to the class, or have classmates share their products in small groups. This project may be used as an alternative form of assessment for the chapter.

---

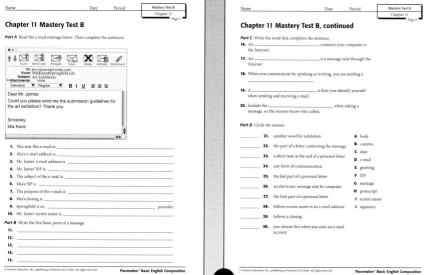

Chapter 11 Mastery Test B, pages 1–3

# Chapter 12 Planning Guide

# Writing for the Workplace

| | Student Lesson | | | | Language Skills | | | | |
|---|---|---|---|---|---|---|---|---|---|
| | Student Pages | Vocabulary | Practice Exercises | Lesson Review | Identification | Writing | Punctuation & Capitalization | Grammar & Usage | Listening, Speaking, & Viewing |
| **Lesson 12-1** Writing a Business Letter | 289–294 | ✔ | ✔ | ✔ | ✔ | ✔ | ✔ | ✔ | ✔ |
| **Lesson 12-2** Addressing an Envelope | 295–298 | | ✔ | ✔ | ✔ | ✔ | ✔ | ✔ | ✔ |
| **Lesson 12-3** Writing a Business Memo | 299–305 | ✔ | ✔ | ✔ | ✔ | ✔ | ✔ | ✔ | ✔ |

## Chapter Activities

**Teacher's Resource Library**

Life Skills Connection 12: Comparing Business and Personal Letters

Writing Tip 12: Business Letters

Writing on the Job 6: Customer Service Representative

Building Research Skills 12: Developing Inquiry Skills

Key Vocabulary Words 12

## Assessment Options

**Student Text**

Chapter 12 Review

**Teacher's Resource Library**

Chapter 12 Mastery Tests A and B

**Teacher's Edition**

Chapter 12 Writing Portfolio

| English in Your Life | Writing on the Job | Building Research Skills | Vocabulary Builder | Grammar Builder | Write About It | Group Activity | Reading Strategy | Six Traits | ELL/ESL Strategy | Background Information | Common Error | Life Skills Connection | Applications (Home, Career, Community, Global) | Online Connection | Teacher Alert | Speaking & Presenting Practice | Writing/Spelling/Grammar Practice | Auditory/Verbal | Body/Kinesthetic | Interpersonal/Group Learning | Logical/Mathematical | Visual/Spatial | Activities | Modified Activities | Workbook Activities | Self-Study Guide |
|---|---|---|---|---|---|---|---|---|---|---|---|---|---|---|---|---|---|---|---|---|---|---|---|---|---|---|
| | | | | 293 | 294 | | 290, 293 | 294 | 292 | 289 | 293 | 293 | 290, 291 | | 292 | | 289 | 291 | | | | | 50 | 50 | 50 | ✔ |
| | | | | | | | 295, 297 | | 297 | 295 | 295, 297, 298 | | 295, 296, 297 | | 296 | 298 | 296 | | | 296 | 297 | 298 | 51 | 51 | 51 | ✔ |
| 303 | 304 | 301 | | | | 305 | 299, 300 | | 300 | 299 | 300, 303 | | | 305 | | | 301 | | 300 | | | | 52 | 52 | 52 | ✔ |

## Pronunciation Key

| | | | | | | | |
|---|---|---|---|---|---|---|---|
| a hat | e let | ī ice | ô order | ù put | sh she | | a in about |
| ā age | ē equal | o hot | oi oil | ü rule | th thin | ə { | e in taken |
| ä far | ėr term | ō open | ou out | ch child | ŦH then | | i in pencil |
| â care | i it | ȯ saw | u cup | ng long | zh measure | | o in lemon |
| | | | | | | | u in circus |

## Modified Activities

The Teacher's Resource Library (TRL) contains a set of lower-level worksheets called Modified Activities. These worksheets cover the same content as the standard Activities but are written at a lower reading level.

## Skill Track

Use Skill Track for *Basic English Composition* to monitor student progress and meet the demands of adequate yearly progress (AYP). Make informed instructional decisions with individual student and class reports of lesson and chapter assessments. With immediate and ongoing feedback, students will also see what they have learned and where they need more reinforcement and practice.

## Chapter 12: Writing for the Workplace

**Skill Track for Basic English Composition**

**Teacher's Resource Library** (TRL)

(Answer Keys for the Teacher's Resource Library begin on page 446 of the Teacher's Edition.)

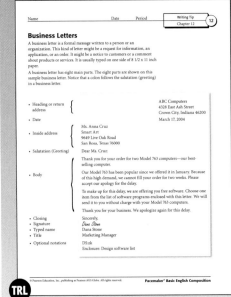

Writing Tip 12

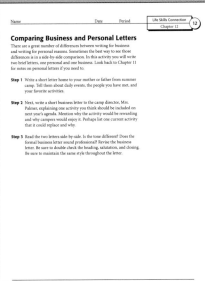

Life Skills Connection 12

# Writing for the Workplace

**A**fter school, your day continues. Many students work at a part-time job. Perhaps you work at a grocery store like the one in this photo. Perhaps you work at a restaurant or in an office.

As a worker, there are times when you will need to write. Writing for your workplace is different than writing personal notes and letters. Business letters and memos are two kinds of messages that you might write for work. The words in these messages sound more formal. They have a certain format.

Chapter 12 will explain how to write a business letter correctly. It will show you the proper way to address an envelope. It will also explain how to write a memo.

## GOALS FOR LEARNING

- To identify the eight parts of a business letter, and to write a business letter
- To write an address correctly, and to address an envelope
- To write a memo using the correct format

**287**

## Introducing the Chapter

Have students examine the photograph on page 286. Ask them to suggest some tasks that workers in a grocery store might do. Encourage students with job experience to describe some of their specific work responsibilities. Help students conclude that it takes commitment, dedication, and the development of certain skills to succeed in the workplace. Extend the discussion to explain that writing knowledge is an important skill in any job. Point out that in this chapter students will learn how to write business letters and memos as well as address envelopes.

Review and discuss the Goals for Learning on page 287.

## Notes

Ask volunteers to read the notes that appear in the margins throughout the chapter. Then discuss them with the class.

## TEACHER'S RESOURCE

The AGS Globe Teaching Strategies in English Transparencies may be used with this chapter. The transparencies add an interactive dimension to expand and enhance the *Basic English Composition* program content.

## WRITING PORTFOLIO

Have students brainstorm ideas for the perfect summer job. Once they have chosen their dream job, have each student draft a sample letter to the company/ organization they would most like to work for. Instruct students that each letter should explain what they would like to do and why they would be a good choice for the position. Explain that they should use professional language in the letter and should support their statements with details. Tell students that as they learn more throughout Chapter 12, they will be able to improve their letters. This project may be used as an alternative form of assessment for the chapter.

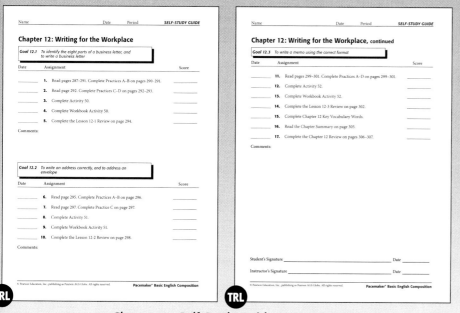

Chapter 12 Self-Study Guide, pages 1–2

## Reading Strategy: Inferencing

Ask students if they have ever been able to figure out someone's opinion without the person actually saying it. Perhaps a friend described a movie as being really long. Or maybe a sibling said they were having spaghetti . . . again. Tell students that understanding what isn't actually being said, or reading between the lines, is inferencing. Pair students. Have each student describe a show they watched or a book they read recently without giving their opinion. Ask the partners if they were able to infer if the student liked it or not.

## Key Vocabulary Words

block style
business letter
memorandum
modified block style

As you read the words aloud, have students read the definitions and ask questions. If students are confused, show them an example of the style or letter. Then write *block style* on one side of the board and *modified block style* on the other. Show students an example of each format and have them categorize it correctly.

---

# Reading Strategy: Inferencing

A writer may suggest an idea but not say it directly. Use your experience to make a conclusion about what the writer means. This is called making an inference. Use good sense when you make inferences. Base your inferences on details from the writer and on what you know.

## Key Vocabulary Words

**Business letter** A formal letter to a person or company

**Block style** The format of a letter in which all the parts begin at the left margin; paragraphs are not indented

**Modified block style** The format of a letter in which the return address, date, closing, signature, and typed name are near the center of the page; paragraphs are indented

**Memorandum** A formal business message with a special format; usually called a memo

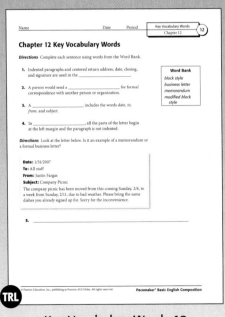

Key Vocabulary Words 12

# Writing a Business Letter

## Objectives

- To identify the eight parts of a business letter
- To write a business letter
- To use block style or modified block style

**Business letter**

A formal letter to a person or company

A **business letter** is a formal letter to a person or company. You may write a business letter to request information. You may also write a business letter to discuss a product or service or to apply for a job.

Here are the main differences between a personal letter and a business letter:

- The paper for writing a personal letter comes in many sizes, colors, and designs. The standard size for a business letter is 8½ x 11 inches. Use white or off-white paper for a business letter.

- You may write a personal letter by hand. You should write a business letter on a computer. The only part that is not typed is your signature.

- You can use both sides of the paper for a personal letter. However, most business letters are printed on only one side of the paper.

- A personal letter has five parts. A business letter has eight parts.

- A business letter uses formal language, not casual language. It does not sound like a personal letter.

*Large companies have a department that handles the mail.*

**Overview**  This lesson defines a business letter and outlines the format and styles one can use when writing professional correspondence.

### Objectives

- To identify the eight parts of a business letter
- To write a business letter
- To use block style or modified block style

**Student Pages**  289–294

**Teacher's Resource Library**

Activity  50

Modified Activity  50

Workbook Activity  50

Life Skills Connection  12

## Vocabulary

block style
business letter
modified block style

Write *block style* on the board and direct students to the example of this type of letter on page 291. Ask a volunteer to explain why they think this type of letter is called *block style*. Then tell students that the word *modified* means "slightly changed." Write *modified block style* on the board and direct the students to the example of this type of letter on page 292. Tell students to write down all the changes they notice between the two types of letters.

## Background Information

Sometimes, when you are addressing someone formally, it is acceptable to use an honorific title (such as *sir/madam*) in place of their full name. This is the case when you are writing a business letter to a company but do not know specifically whom you are addressing. In such a case, the letter may be addressed *Dear Sir or Madam*. (However, encourage students to always try their best to find the individual name of a person at the company.)

## 1  Warm-Up Activity

Ask students why it is not a good idea to use slang in a business letter. Explain the term *formal* as it relates to a business letter.

## 2  Teaching the Lesson

After they have read the text on page 289, ask students to summarize the rules for writing business letters. Then, list off a number of different scenarios for writing a letter, and have students respond if the situation calls for a business or personal letter.

## Practice A

Have students read the personal letter on page 271 to themselves. Have students think about what makes the letter seem different from the business letter on page 291.

### Practice A Answers

1. A heading is in a business letter but not in a personal letter. The heading shows the name and address of the sender. 2. An inside address is in a business letter but not in a personal letter. The inside address shows where the letter is being sent. 3. A typed name (and sometimes a title) appears only in a business letter.

### 3  Reinforce and Extend

#### GLOBAL CONNECTION

 Discuss with students the various means people now have to send messages and longer documents almost anywhere in the world. Students may mention networked computers and telecommunications satellites, faxes, and mailings that travel by land, sea, and air. Students who have received airmail letters from abroad may bring in the envelopes so that the group can look at the addresses and foreign stamps.

### Grammar Practice

In writing letters, it is always important to use correct spelling, punctuation, and grammar. However, while certain grammatical errors will be overlooked by friends and family, errors in English are unacceptable in business letters. Therefore, tell students that once they have composed their business letters, check diligently for errors of spelling, punctuation, and grammar. Then, ask them to have a friend or family member read the letter to make sure it is perfect.

### Reading Strategy: Inferencing

Students may infer that it is more formal than the personal letter.

**Reading Strategy:**
Inferencing

Look at the sample business letter on the next page. How is it different from a personal letter?

**NOTE**

A notation is a short note or abbreviation. *Optional* means not required. You do not have to include the optional notations in a business letter.

## The Parts of a Business Letter

Here are the eight parts of a business letter:

1.  heading with return address (sender's address)
2.  date
3.  inside address (receiver's address)
4.  salutation or greeting
5.  body
6.  closing
7.  handwritten signature
8.  typed name (and job title if appropriate)

Find these eight parts in the sample letter on page 291.

### Practice A

Look back at the personal letter on page 271. What three parts of a business letter are not in a personal letter? Write the three parts and describe the purpose of each one.

In a business letter, use a colon at the end of the salutation. Use a comma at the end of the closing. Sign your full legal name as your signature. You may use your middle initial.

▶ **EXAMPLE 1**

*Derek M. Anderson*
*Derek Mitchell Anderson*

Notice the optional notations at the bottom of the business letter on page 291. The initials *LH* are the initials of the sender, Lynda Hong. The initials *ck* show that an assistant prepared the letter (maybe someone named Cindy King). An enclosure is something that is sent along with the letter. The notation below the initials shows that Lynda Hong included a brochure with the letter.

| | |
|---|---|
| Heading | **National Sporting Goods**<br>1122 West Street, Chicago, IL 60600-2144 |
| Date | June 10, 2007 |
| Inside address | Mr. Walter Jones<br>Springfield High School<br>136 School Drive<br>Springfield, Oklahoma 73512 |
| Salutation | Dear Mr. Jones: |
| Body | We are delighted to send this letter to such a valued customer, Springfield High School.<br><br>We recently received a special shipment of top quality baseballs. As our attached brochure shows, we are offering this shipment to preferred customers at 25% off our usual price. However, you must act fast! This unusual offer is available only until June 15.<br><br>To take advantage of this special offer, call or write a letter making your request. Don't miss the opportunity to purchase these quality baseballs at such a savings! |
| Closing | Yours truly, |
| Signature | *Lynda Hong* |
| Typed name and title | Lynda Hong<br>Marketing Manager |
| Optional notations | LH:ck<br>Enclosure: Brochure |

**NOTE**

The heading of a business letter may include a company name. Some companies print special stationery with a heading that includes the company logo.

## Practice B

Use the sample letter to answer each question.

1. What is the name of Lynda Hong's company?
2. What punctuation mark follows the salutation?
3. What closing does Lynda Hong use in this letter?
4. What do the letters *LH:ck* mean?
5. What did Lynda Hong enclose with this letter?

*Writing for the Workplace*   Chapter 12   **291**

## Practice B

Have students recognize and point out some of the adjectives used in the business letter on page 291. Ask them what the purpose of adjectives might be in a business letter. Then tell them that sales letters, such as this one, make up a large portion of all business letters.

## Practice B Answers

**1.** Lynda Hong's company is National Sporting Goods. **2.** A colon follows the salutation. **3.** Lynda Hong uses the closing *Yours truly.* **4.** *LH* are the initials of the sender, Lynda Hong; *ck* are the initials of the assistant who prepared the letter. **5.** Lynda Hong enclosed a brochure.

## Practice C

Direct students to reread the block style business letter on page 291. Have them pay special attention to the differences in formatting between that letter and the modified block style letter on this page.

### Practice C Answers

1. He used the salutation *Dear Mr. Elliott.* 2. A colon is the punctuation mark that follows the salutation. 3. Derek uses the closing *Sincerely.* 4. The first way this style is different from block style is that the paragraphs are indented. A second way is that the heading, closing, signature, and typed name are aligned near the center of the page. 5. It is important to print or type your name under your signature because signatures are often unreadable by people who are unfamiliar with them.

**Block style**
The format of a letter in which all the parts begin at the left margin; paragraphs are not indented

**Modified block style**
The format of a letter in which the return address, date, closing, signature, and typed name are near the center of the page; paragraphs are indented

 **Brush Up on the Basics**

In the salutation of a business letter, use the title and last name of the person you are writing. At the end of the salutation, use a colon, not a comma. See Punctuation 23 in Appendix A.

## Business Letter Styles

You can use **block style** or **modified block style** for business letters. Block style has no indented paragraphs. All parts of the letter are lined up at the left margin. The letter on page 291 uses block style. Modified block style has indented paragraphs in the body, as shown below.

> 18 Silver Lane
> Springfield, OK 73510
> June 6, 2007
>
> Mr. Paul Elliott
> Western Industries
> One Western Plaza
> Centerville, Texas 79408
>
> Dear Mr. Elliott:
>
>     This letter is in response to your advertisement in the *Daily News.* I would like to apply for the position of ticket agent. I understand that this position is temporary.
>
>     For the past year, I have been employed at a gas station. My duties include selling parts and using a cash register. I believe I have the experience necessary to be a ticket agent.
>
>     I will call you on June 20. You may reach me at 555-7766 before then. I am available any Saturday for an interview.
>
>     Thank you for considering me for this position.
>
>                         Sincerely,
>
>                         *Derek Anderson*
>                         Derek Anderson

## Practice C

Read the sample letter in modified block style above. Then write the answer to each question.

1. What salutation did Derek use?
2. What punctuation mark follows the salutation?
3. What closing did Derek use?
4. Name two ways that the style of this letter is different from the one on page 291.
5. Why do you think a typed name follows the signature?

## Practice D

Choose one of the following prompts. Then write a business letter. If possible, use a computer to write and print it. Use either block style or modified block style. Include the eight parts of a business letter. Use the phone book to find the inside address. Use your own return address.

- Write a letter to a local museum. Ask for information about an exhibit. Include a reason for wanting this information.
- Write to a local radio or TV station. Express your opinion about a program. Include facts to back up your opinion.
- Write to a local company. Ask about summer employment. Include facts about your job experience, education, and personal qualities. Make the company want to hire you.

### GRAMMAR BUILDER

**Using Colons**

A colon is a punctuation mark. Use a colon in these places:

- in the heading in a memo
  *Date:*
- to introduce an idea or a list in a sentence
  *You will need these items: a magnet, a paper clip, and string.*
- after the salutation of a business letter
  *Dear Mr. Dozois:*
- between the hour and minutes when writing the time
  *1:40 PM*

Copy each item below. Add colons where they are needed.

1. Dear Sir or Madam
2. Practice begins at 430.
3. Buy these things at the store milk, bread, and bananas.

**Reading Strategy:**
Inferencing

Suppose you want to write a letter to ask for information. After reading this lesson, what can you infer about writing this type of letter?

*Writing for the Workplace*    *Chapter 12*    **293**

---

## Practice D

Go over the eight standard parts of a business letter with students again. Have volunteers participate in naming all eight parts.

### *Practice D Answers*

Letters will vary. Check for correct format, grammar, punctuation, and language.

### GRAMMAR BUILDER

Tell students that colons are an important tool in business letters. Have them scan the business letters from this lesson and find the colons. Students will learn about colon usage in memo headings in Lesson 12-3.

### *Grammar Builder Answers*

**1.** Dear Sir or Madam: **2.** Practice begins at 4:30. **3.** Buy these things at the store: milk, bread, and bananas.

### COMMON ERROR

Beginning writers often incorrectly use *and* and *but* to start sentences. Help students practice using these conjunctions to join two thoughts together. Teach them to begin sentences with their own separate thought.

### *Reading Strategy:* Inferencing

Students may infer that requesting information is one situation that calls for a business letter and not a personal letter.

### LIFE SKILLS CONNECTION

Divide the class into pairs after students have completed Life Skills Connection 12. Have partners exchange and read their business letters. After reading, have partners make recommendations on how the letters might be improved. Remind students to double-check format to make sure every part is included.

*Writing for the Workplace*    **293**

## Lesson 12-1 Review Answers

Ask students to give a reason for their choice. **1.** Yes **2.** No **3.** Yes **4.** No **5.** Yes **6.** Yes **7.** Yes **8.** No **9.** No **10.** Yes

### WRITE ABOUT IT

Tell students that a letter to the editor expresses a strong opinion. Then read one or two examples of letters to the editor from a recently published newspaper.

#### Write About It Answers

Letters should follow the correct format for business letters and contain a well-supported opinion.

## Six Traits of Writing Focus

| | | | |
|---|---|---|---|
| ✔ | Ideas | | Word Choice |
| ✔ | Organization | | Sentence Fluency |
| | Voice | | Conventions |

## Ideas

Stress to students that an important part of writing is forming and outlining their ideas. Encourage students to create an outline before writing, addressing all of the ideas they hope to cover.

Remind students that making an outline will also help them to organize their information clearly and smoothly.

Refer students to page WPH1 for further instruction on the Six Traits of Writing.

---

## LESSON 12-1

# REVIEW

Read the following salutations and closings. Which ones are appropriate for a business letter? Write *yes* or *no*.

1. Dear Mr. Levin:
2. Hi Harry,
3. Dear Manager:
4. Love,
5. Best regards,
6. To Whom It May Concern:
7. Cordially,
8. Hey, Mr. Jackson!
9. Take care,
10. Sincerely,

### WRITE ABOUT IT

**A Topic in the News**

Most newspapers publish letters to the editor. Editors usually receive more letters than they can publish. They will print letters that get their attention. Write a one-page business letter to the editor of a newspaper. Follow these instructions:

1. Choose a current news topic. Stick to this topic in your letter.
2. State your opinion and support it with details. If the topic is a problem, tell what you think should be done about it.
3. Check that your letter has all eight parts.
4. Revise your letter. Edit it carefully. Fix any mistakes.
5. Print your letter in ink or type it on a computer. Use block style or modified block style.
6. Address an envelope to the editor of your local newspaper. Mail your letter to the newspaper.

**Six Traits of Writing:**
*Ideas* message, details, and purpose

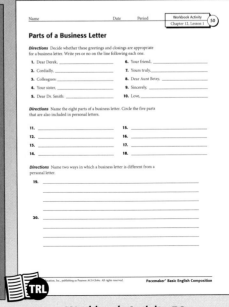

Activity 50, pages 1–2

Workbook Activity 50

# Addressing an Envelope

## Objectives

■ To write an address correctly

■ To address an envelope

### NOTE

The abbreviations for U.S. states are on page 405 in Appendix A. ZIP stands for Zone Improvement Plan. This code tells which post office is associated with a particular address.

When you send someone a letter, the envelope will be the first thing the person sees. When you address an envelope, write the complete address clearly and correctly.

## Writing an Address

An address has three standard lines, as shown in Example 1. An apartment or suite number goes at the end of the street address. You may spell out words like *Apartment, Avenue,* and *Street,* or use their standard abbreviations: *Apt., Ave.,* and *St.* Always use the proper abbreviation for a state, followed by the ZIP code. Use the complete ZIP+4 code if you know it.

▶ **EXAMPLE 1**

| | |
|---|---|
| Full Name | Luis Moreno |
| Street Address | 112 West Central Avenue, Apt. 3 |
| City, State, ZIP Code | Springfield, OK 73510 |

An envelope has both a return address and a mailing address. The return address is the sender's address. If an envelope cannot be delivered for some reason, the post office will return it to the sender.

Return address → Michelle Faber
1118 Starlight Lane
Dayton, OH 45432-3297

Mailing address → Ms. Joan Gillan
78 W. Taber Ave., Apt. 104
Anderson, IN 46011-1212

### Reading Strategy:
Inferencing

Look at the sample envelope. What can you infer about abbreviations in addresses?

Address your envelope clearly and correctly. Type or neatly print the address.

*Writing for the Workplace*  Chapter 12  **295**

---

**Overview** This lesson focuses on the proper way to address and mail an envelope.

### Objectives

■ To write an address correctly

■ To address an envelope

**Student Pages** 295–298

**Teacher's Resource Library**

**Activity** 51

**Modified Activity** 51

**Workbook Activity** 51

## Background Information

You may come across the abbreviation *c/o* on a piece of mail. The abbreviation stands for *care of* and is used to identify the person to whom the address normally belongs in cases where the intended recipient is someone else. The *c/o* line comes below the recipient's name and above the street address.

### 1  Warm-Up Activity

Explain the importance of penmanship when addressing an envelope. Explain that just the slightest error can send the letter many miles from its intended place. Have students copy the address on the envelope on page 295. Check to make sure that the students' writing is legible.

### 2  Teaching the Lesson

Tell each student to find a partner. Have them both address envelopes to one another. (If no envelopes are available, they can use a slip of paper). Be sure they correctly write both the address and the return address.

### Reading Strategy: Inferencing

Answers will vary. Students may infer that some abbreviations are acceptable in addresses.

---

### 3  Reinforce and Extend

#### GLOBAL CONNECTION

The ZIP code is the five-digit number code used to identify a post office in a certain area of the United States. The post office and package delivery companies use the ZIP code as their first identifier in delivering letters. There are no two identical ZIP codes in the country. Remind students to use the more specific nine-digit code in addresses whenever possible.

#### COMMON ERROR

Caution students to always use the complete street address, including the word or abbreviation for the type of street. In many larger cities, there may be a Lincoln Street, a Lincoln Avenue, a Lincoln Boulevard, etc. In order to avoid confusion and ensure quick delivery, remind the student to check the street designation.

## AT HOME

Have students bring in examples of envelopes addressed to their homes. They may examine elements such as postmarks, stamps, meter marks, and variations in the addresses.

## Practice A

Have students look at the sample envelope on page 295 to answer the questions.

### Practice A Answers

**1.** The complete return address is Michelle Faber, 1118 Starlight Lane, Dayton, OH, 45432-3297. **2.** The complete mailing address is Ms. Joan Gillan, 78 W. Taber Ave., Apt. 104, Anderson, IN 46011-1212. **3.** You usually write the name of the intended recipient on the first line of the address. **4.** On the second line of an address, you usually write the street address. **5.** On the third line of an address, you usually write the city, state, and ZIP code.

## Practice B

With all the possible variations in addresses, it is important to follow the proper order when writing them.

### Practice B Answers

**1.** The mistake is the name *Smith, Liz.* The name should be written *Liz Smith.* **2.** The mistake is that the ZIP code is listed before the city. The ZIP code should always be listed last. **3.** The second and third lines are mixed up in this address. **4.** The error is that Damon has no last name. **5.** The error is that there is no city listed before the state.

## Spelling Practice

Tell students that Americans borrowed many state names from other cultures, especially from Native Americans. *Illinois, South and North Dakota, Wyoming, Utah,* and other states are taken from Native American words. Have students make a list of state names they think are easy to misspell, and have them write each correctly three times.

 **NOTE**

Sometimes, the second line of an address is not a typical street address. Instead, it may have a post office box number (PO BOX 458), a rural route and box number (RR 5, BOX 10), or a highway contract route and box number (HC 4, BOX 45).

 **Brush Up on the Basics**

Abbreviate the state name in an envelope address. Use the U.S. Postal Service abbreviation. It gives each state two capital letters. For example, Texas is TX, and New York is NY. No period is needed. See Punctuation 4 in Appendix A.

### Practice A

Look at the sample envelope on page 295. Write the answer to each question.

1. What is the complete return address?
2. What is the complete mailing address?
3. What do you usually write on the first line of an address?
4. What do you usually write on the second line of an address?
5. What do you usually write on the third line of an address?

### Practice B

Read the following addresses. Find the mistake in each one. Rewrite each address correctly on your paper. Add any missing information.

1. Smith, Liz
   4398 First Avenue
   Aurora, CO 80014-7885

2. Miguel Garcia
   60 Harris St.
   01060-2224 Hampton, MA

3. Erik Gannon
   HARGATE, TN 37752-4008
   RR 2, BOX 407

4. Damon
   2931 East Amherst Drive
   Rosedale, MD 21240-3129

5. Ms. Alice Chan
   89 Main Street, Apt. 4
   California 92234-9641

**296** *Chapter 12   Writing for the Workplace*

## LEARNING STYLES

### Interpersonal/Group Learning

Have students work with a partner to find out at least one ZIP code for the city of each other's birth. After finding out the location, have each student research the possible ZIP codes using the Internet or material provided by the United States Postal Service. Once they have found the codes, have the students write all of the different numbers on the board.

## TEACHER ALERT

Point out to students that it is easy to confuse some state abbreviations. Arizona, Alabama, and Arkansas all contain similar letters and students may mix them up. Until they have mastered them, tell students to check the abbreviation before mailing an envelope.

Sometimes an address includes a company name. Then the address has four lines. The company name goes on its own line below the person's name.

Sometimes an address includes a person's job title. Add the title after the person's name on the first line. Use a comma. If you do not know the person's name, just use the job title.

## Practice C

Look at the two envelopes. Decide which one is addressed correctly. Write the letter of the correct envelope. Then describe the mistakes on the envelope that is wrong.

**Envelope A**

D. Diamond
1234 Archmore Rd.
Tucson, AZ 85727-2254

Editor
Fashion Flair
112 Center St.
Gainesville, FL 32602-2903

**Envelope B**

D. Diamond
1234 Archmore Road
Tucson 85727-2254

Fashion Flair
Della Lyons, Editor
Gainesville, FL 32602-2903
112 Center Street

**NOTE**

When you mail a payment, the envelope often has an address window. Before you seal the envelope, make sure the address shows through the window.

***Reading Strategy:***
Inferencing

How do you usually fold a business letter? How does your experience help you understand these directions?

### Preparing to Mail a Business Letter

A standard business envelope is 4⅛ x 9½ inches. Fold your letter in thirds before you insert it into an envelope. Follow these steps:

1. Place the letter face up on a desk.

2. Fold a little less than one third of the letter from the bottom toward the top.

3. Fold the top third down so the top edge is ¼ inch from the first fold.

4. Insert the second folded edge into the envelope first.

To complete the envelope, follow these steps:

1. Write or type the return address in the top left corner.

2. Write or type the mailing address in the center.

3. Put the correct postage stamp in the top right corner.

---

## Practice C

Offering a comparison helps students notice the differences between the correct and incorrect format.

### Practice C Answers

Envelope A is the correct envelope. Envelope B has quite a few problems. First, in the return address, the state is not included. Second, the mailing address lines are mixed up. The first line should be the person's name and title. The second line should be the company name. The third line should be the street address, and the last line should be the city, state, and ZIP code.

## ELL/ESL STRATEGY

**Language Objective:**
*To address and abbreviate correctly*

Students may have difficulty identifying all of the different street designations and abbreviations. Begin with the following: *Street (St.), Avenue (Ave.), Lane (Ln.), Court (Ct.), Boulevard (Blvd.), Way (Wy.), Route (Rte.), Circle (Cir.),* and *Drive (Dr.).* Encourage students to memorize the correct spelling and abbreviations.

***Reading Strategy:*** Inferencing

Students may say that there is a proper way to fold a letter. Folding a letter incorrectly may give others a bad impression.

## COMMON ERROR

It is not required to have a return address on an envelope in order to mail it. Therefore, many people only concern themselves with the mailing address. However, if there is any error or discrepancy whatsoever (people have moved, someone misreads your writing, you accidentally use the wrong ZIP code), the post office will have nowhere to return the letter. Additionally, many people who receive mail use the return address as a way to reply to the sender.

## LEARNING STYLES

**Logical/Mathematical**

Have students select a partner from somewhere not near their desk. Then divide the class into fourths. Give each quarter of the class a code: 001, 002, 003, and 004. Then, number students in every quarter; for example, 1–10 in code 001, 1–10 in 002, etc. Then tell students to address an envelope to their partner. The top line should be their name. The middle line should be their desk number, and the bottom line should be their class code. Collect all the envelopes and see if they can be delivered successfully. Explain that this is a similar way to how the post office delivers mail.

## IN THE COMMUNITY

Tell students that the United States Postal Service provides a list of abbreviations to use when writing addresses, as well as other postal information.

## Lesson 12-2 Review Answers

**1.** Derek Anderson, 18 Silver Lane, Springfield, OK 73510 **2.** Mr. Paul Elliot, Western Industries, One Western Plaza, Centerville, Texas 79408 **3.** 79408 **4.** It will return the envelope to the sender. **5.** Answers will vary. **6.** Envelope A is correct. Envelope B has the incorrect order for the mailing address. The street address with the apartment number should be on the second line. The city, state, and ZIP code should be on the third line.

---

> Derek Anderson
> 18 Silver Lane
> Springfield, OK 73510
>
> Mr. Paul Elliott
> Western Industries
> One Western Plaza
> Centerville, Texas 79408

Write the answer to each question.

**1.** What is the return address on the envelope above?

**2.** What is the mailing address on the envelope above?

**3.** What is the ZIP code for Western Industries on the envelope above?

**4.** Suppose the address for Western Industries is wrong. Where will the post office send this envelope?

**5.** Write your own address.

**6.** Look at the two envelopes below. Decide which one is addressed correctly. Write the letter of the correct envelope. Then describe the mistakes on the envelope that is wrong.

**Envelope A**

> Michelle Faber
> 1118 Starlight Lane
> Dayton, OH 45432-3297
>
> Ms. Joan Gillan
> 78 W. Taber Ave., Apt. 104
> Anderson, IN 46011-1212

**Envelope B**

> Michelle Faber
> 1118 Starlight Lane
> Dayton, OH 45432-3297
>
> Ms. Joan Gillan
> Anderson, IN 46011-1212
> Apt. 104
> 78 W. Taber Ave.

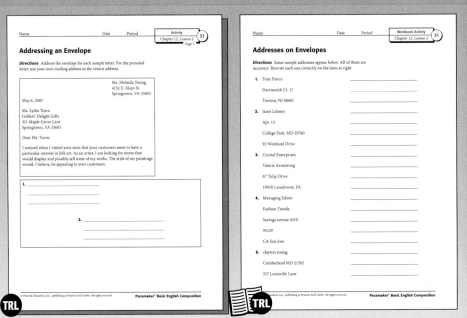

Activity 51, pages 1–2

Workbook Activity 51

# Writing a Business Memo

## Objectives
- To identify the parts of a memo
- To write a memo

**Memorandum**
A formal business message with a special format; usually called a memo

**NOTE**
A colon directs the reader's attention to the information that follows it.

*Reading Strategy:*
Inferencing

In Chapter 11, you read about personal messages. How are they different from business messages?

People often call a **memorandum** by its shorter name—memo. A memo is a formal message with a special format. Memos are used in business settings. Memos are usually sent to other people within a company or organization. A memo might be delivered to an employee, or it might be sent as an e-mail.

The form of a memo is different from a letter. Most memos use these words in the heading: *Date, To, From,* and *Subject.* A colon follows each word. There are no addresses in a memo. The sender does not sign a memo.

---

**MEMO**

**Date:** June 1, 2007
**To:** Ms. Hall
**From:** Ms. Lawson, Chairperson, Awards Committee
**Subject:** Awards Assembly

The school will have an Awards Assembly on Monday, June 11, at 2:00 PM. Because of lack of space in the gym, the committee decided that we will invite only the seniors.

Our next committee meeting is on June 5 at 3:30 PM in Room 216. We will discuss the program for the assembly.

---

### Practice A

Use the sample memo above to answer each question.

1. What words are used in the heading of a memo?
2. Who sent this memo?
3. What will happen on Monday, June 11, at 2:00 PM?
4. What did the committee decide?
5. There is no address in this memo. Why not?

## Practice A

Have students read the sample memo on page 299. Ask them to consider the similarities and differences between a memo and a business letter.

### Practice A Answers

**1.** *Date, To, From,* and *Subject* are the four words used in the heading of a memo. **2.** Ms. Lawson sent this memo. **3.** The school will hold an Awards Assembly on that date and time. **4.** The committee decided to invite only seniors. **5.** A memo is an internal letter, sent within a company or organization. Therefore, there is no need for an address.

---

## Lesson at a Glance

### Chapter 12 Lesson 3

**Overview** This lesson defines a memorandum and outlines the format and style one can use when writing short professional messages.

### Objectives
- To identify the parts of a memo
- To write a memo

**Student Pages** 299–305

**Teacher's Resource Library** (TRL)

Activity 52
Modified Activity 52
Workbook Activity 52
Writing on the Job 6
Building Research Skills 12

...............................................

## Vocabulary
**memorandum**

Write *memorandum* on the board and direct students to an example of this type of letter in their book.

...............................................

## Background Information

Stress that memos are not the proper format for personal correspondence. Memos are professional tools.

### 1 | Warm-Up Activity

List ideas that people at companies might need to communicate with one another about.

### 2 | Teaching the Lesson

After they have read the text on page 299, ask students to summarize the rules for writing memos. Then, list a number of different scenarios for business writing and have students decide if the situation calls for a business letter or a memo.

***Reading Strategy:*** Inferencing
Personal messages lack the formality and structure of business messages. While a personal message should still follow basic rules of writing and organization, the business message has a strict structure.

## Reading Strategy: Inferencing

A person would send a memo instead of a business letter if the recipients are within the company or organization.

## Practice B

Have students repeat the four words that should go on every memo: *Date, To, From,* and *Subject.* Explain why the omission of any of them could cause confusion.

## Practice B Answers

Students should follow the format as described. The memos will vary.

### COMMON ERROR

Explain that common computer abbreviations (*lol, wtg, brb*) are inappropriate in memos and should never be used. Remind students that spelling and grammar are important in all forms of business communication.

## Practice C

Before students complete this activity, ask a volunteer to read the note aloud.

## Practice C Answers

The memos will vary but should include the words *Date, To, From,* and *Subject* as well as the correct information from the note.

## 3 Reinforce and Extend

### LEARNING STYLES

**Body/Kinesthetic**

Pass out one of the three types of business messages (a letter in block style, a letter in modified block style, and a memorandum) to every member of the class. Have each student study their message. Then have them form groups by message type. Alternate going from group to group having students call out one of their message's characteristics.

Be specific when writing the subject of a memo. This will help readers understand its purpose.

### Practice B

Follow these directions to practice writing a memo.

1. Write *Memo* at the top of your paper.
2. List these words: *Date, To, From,* and *Subject.*
3. Put a colon (:) after each of these words.
4. Choose one of the following prompts.
   - Write a memo to a family member. Ask for something you need.
   - Write a memo to someone in your class. Ask to borrow their class notes.
5. Write your memo. Include the necessary information. Use today's date.

### Practice C

Read the following note. Rewrite it in memo form. Include all necessary information.

> March 7, 2007
>
> Dear Coach Jones,
>
> Several weeks ago you spoke to me about ordering 10 new baseball bats from Springfield Sporting Goods.
>
> Have these new bats arrived? Will 10 bats be enough for both the boys' and girls' teams?
>
> Please give me the bill for the bats when they arrive. I will see that it is paid promptly.
>
> Sincerely,
>
> Ms. Hall
> Prinicipal

### ELL/ESL STRATEGY

**Language Objective:**
*To write a memo*

Ask students for whom English is a second language to print on the chalkboard—in their primary language—the four words in a memo heading (*Date, To, From, Subject*). Then ask the whole class to use these words as an alternative way to complete Practice B on page 300.

## Practice D

Use the memo below to write the answer to each question.

1. What is missing from the heading of this memo?

2. Who sent this memo?

3. Who will receive this memo?

4. Where is the Art Club going on their field trip?

5. What is the purpose of this memo?

---

**MEMO**

**To:**    All teachers
**From:**  Mrs. Turner, Art Club Supervisor
**Subject:**

The Art Club will take a field trip to the Civic Center Art Museum on Monday, June 4. Students will meet at 9:00 AM in the art room and board the bus at 9:15 AM. Please excuse the club members from their classes that day.

I will send you a list of club members on Friday, June 1. Please give these students any assignments that they will need to make up.

---

## VOCABULARY BUILDER

**Deciding Between Commonly Confused Words**
Some words look or sound much the same. For example, is the last part of a meal the *desert* or the *dessert*? Would a boat use a *sale* or a *sail*? Make sure you choose the word you mean to use.
Write the word that completes each sentence below. Use a dictionary if you need help.

1. Everyone came to the meeting (except, accept) Jill.
2. Joe can eat more (then, than) anyone I know.
3. Which team will (lose, loose) the game?
4. (They're, Their, There) tickets were at the box office.

---

## Practice D

Have students read the memo on page 301 to themselves and then ask a volunteer to read it aloud.

### Practice D Answers

**1.** The date and the subject are missing in the memo. **2.** The memo was sent by Mrs. Turner. **3.** The memo is to all teachers. **4.** The Art Club is going to the Civic Center Art Museum. **5.** The purpose of the memo is to inform the other teachers about the upcoming field trip so that they may prepare make-up work for the students going.

## VOCABULARY BUILDER

Have a volunteer read each of the pairs of words in the sentences at the bottom of the feature. Listen closely to see if there is any difference in the pronunciation of the words.

### Vocabulary Builder Answers

**1.** except  **2.** than  **3.** lose  **4.** Their

## Writing Practice

Instruct students to write a fictitious memo to all the teachers at their school. Have the memo announce a play to be performed at the school auditorium. Tell them to include all of the important information (date of the performance, time, title, genre, how many showings). Remind students that this is not an advertisement, but a memo (informative, professional, and unbiased).

## Lesson 12-3 Review Answers

**1.** Both the date and the subject are missing from the memo. **2.** Answers will vary, but the subject should address the bat delivery and the bill. **3.** Coach Jones sent the memo. **4.** Ms. Hall should receive the memo. **5.** Coach Jones should not have signed his name because this is a memo. **6.** An address is not included because memos are normally internal documents or e-mails, not in need of a return address. **7.** The last sentence is grammatically incorrect. It may be written correctly as, "Since this is the first year for the girls' team, we needed these bats to complete our stock of new equipment." **8.** A bill is attached to the memo. **9.** Coach Jones ordered the bats for the girls' baseball team. **10.** Memos will vary.

Read the memo. Then write the answer to each question.

---

**MEMO**

**To:**   Ms. Hall
**From:** Coach Jones

I have attached to this memo the bill for the 10 new baseball bats. The boys' team has enough bats. These bats are for the girls' team. This year is the first year for the girls' team, we needed these bats to complete our stock of new equipment.

---

1. What information is missing from this memo?

2. Write a subject for the memo.

3. Who sent this memo?

4. Who will receive it?

5. Should Coach Jones have signed his name?

6. Why is an address not included?

7. Find the sentence mistake. Write the sentence correctly.

8. What is attached to the memo?

9. Who did Coach Jones order the bats for?

10. Rewrite the note below as a memo. Use today's date.

---

*Dear Coach Jones,*

*We have paid the bill for the new baseball bats from Springfield Sporting Goods. Thank you for ordering this equipment for the girls' team.*

*Sincerely,*
*Ms. Hall*

---

**302**   *Chapter 12   Writing for the Workplace*

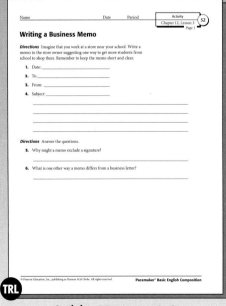

Activity 52, pages 1–2

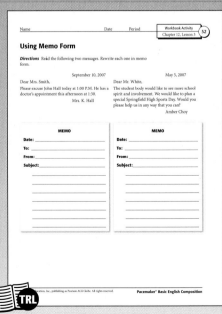

Workbook Activity 52

## Customer Service Representative

Jay Soledad works in a sporting goods store. His job is to handle customer complaints. He tells customers what can be done to fix the problem. Jay wants customers to feel good about doing business with the store. Read Jay's letter to a customer. Then answer the questions below.

### Score! Sports
1385 West Main St.
Westville, PA 00192

Bill Runel
2715 Maple St., Apt. 2A
Westville, PA 00192

Dear Mr. Runel:

We are sorry that the skateboard you purchased does not roll well. We stand behind our products and want you as a satisfied customer. You may bring your skateboard back for a full refund. If you wish, we can send it back to Zoom, Inc. for repair. Please bring your sales receipt and warranty card with the board.

Sincerely,

Jay Soledad

Jay Soledad
Customer Service

1. What problem does the letter address?

2. What does Jay suggest to Mr. Runel?

3. **CRITICAL THINKING** Why do you think Jay asks Mr. Runel to bring in the receipt and warranty card?

 ## LISTENING AND SPEAKING

Customer service workers may talk to customers on the phone or in a store. Here are some rules for settling customer complaints:

- Listen carefully to find out what the customer wants.
- Take notes and ask questions.
- State the complaint in your own words to be sure you understand it.

Think of a complaint you have had about a product. With a partner, role-model a dialogue about the complaint. Take turns being the customer and the customer service worker.

## WRITING ON THE JOB

Ask students to think about a time when they had to solve a problem or resolve a conflict. Have them imagine that they needed to write to someone with whom they must resolve an issue. Discuss why it would be important to write clearly and correctly. Have a volunteer read the introductory paragraph of Writing on the Job. Invite students to predict how Jay might respond to a customer who is complaining about a problem with a recent purchase. Then have them read the letter and answer the questions.

### *Writing on the Job Answers*

**1.** The skateboard that Bill Runel purchased does not roll well. **2.** Mr. Runel should bring the skateboard back. He should also bring his sales receipt and warranty. **3.** The receipt proves when and where he bought the skateboard. The warranty tells what the manufacturer will do to fix the problem.

### COMMON ERROR

 Students may be familiar with the common adage, "The customer is always right." However, impress upon students the fact that there is no excuse for a customer's offensive behavior, regardless of the mistake or problem. Remind students that it is always their responsibility to remain level-headed as a customer.

---

Writing on the Job 6

Ask students to think about jobs that require good questioning skills. Encourage them to brainstorm as many ideas as possible.

### Building Research Skills Answers

**1.** Think clearly and ask good questions. **2.** State the problem clearly. **3.** Facts are based on proof and are widely accepted. Using facts is logical. Opinions are based on emotion and personal belief. Using opinions may be illogical.

### Developing Inquiry Skills

Inquiry means asking questions and finding answers. Everyone needs to find answers. You may need an answer to a problem. You may need answers to questions about a topic. To find answers, you must be able to think clearly and ask good questions. The following steps will help you find the answers you need:

- State the problem or topic clearly.

- Write down your ideas and questions. For a problem, you might ask: What caused this problem? What are some different ways to solve it? For a topic, you might ask: Is the topic too broad to cover? What interests me about this topic?

- List all of your ideas. Decide which ones are reasonable and useful.

- Gather information from sources you can trust. As you read, focus your thinking with questions. Ask: Is this a fact or an opinion? What evidence supports this idea?

Write the answer to each question.

**1.** What two skills do you need to have to find answers?

**2.** To solve a problem, what is a good first step?

**3.** CRITICAL THINKING Why should you use facts, not opinions, to find answers?

### MEDIA

The media—newspapers, magazines, radio, TV, the Internet—is not always a good place to look for answers. Media messages may be one-sided or unfair. Think about the purpose of a TV program or a Web site. Is it trying to inform, entertain, or advertise? A news program gives facts. However, some news sources do not have the time or space to give all of the facts.

---

Name _____ Date _____ Period _____ | Building Research Skills | 12 | Chapter 12

**Developing Inquiry Skills**

Inquiry is the process of asking questions and finding out the answers.
Carl's Social Studies teacher told him to prepare a 2-page report on something that interested him about space. After thinking about it, he decided a summary of space travel would be an interesting topic that could fit into a 2-page report. Then he wrote down some questions about space travel: When did people first go into space? How far have people traveled in space? What is the future of space travel?
After thinking about the answers, Carl decided to use the library and the NASA Web site for most of his answers. There he found good facts and information for his report.

*Directions* Answer the questions

**1.** How did Carl decide on his topic?

**2.** Where did Carl go to gather reliable and useful sources?

**3.** CRITICAL THINKING Imagine your teacher told you to write a 2-page report on the environment. Like the example above, use the 4 steps on page 304 of your textbook to narrow your focus, ask questions, and think of reliable sources. Write how you would use these steps.

TRL

# SUMMARY

- Remember that a business letter is more formal than a personal letter.

- Use a computer to print a business letter. Use 8½- x 11-inch white paper.

- Include all eight parts in any business letter you write: heading with return address, date, inside address, salutation, body, closing, signature, and typed name.

- Use block style or modified block style for a business letter.

- Put a colon after the salutation of a business letter. Put a comma after the closing.

- Fold a business letter in thirds before putting it in the envelope.

- Address envelopes carefully.

- Write a complete address. Write the person's name on the first line. Write the street address on the second line. Write the city, state, and ZIP code on the third line.

- If you want to include a company or organization name in an address, write it on its own line below the person's name.

- If you want to include a person's job title in an address, write it after the name on the first line. Use a comma after the name.

- Write the return address in the top left corner of an envelope. Write the mailing address in the center. Put the postage in the top right corner.

- When you write a memo, include these words in the heading: *Date, To, From,* and *Subject.* Use a colon after each word, and follow this with the necessary information.

## GROUP ACTIVITY

Work in a small group to write a business letter. Choose a club or organization in your area that helps others. Write to ask how you can help the club or organization.

Be sure to use the correct format for your letter. In the body, write clear paragraphs with topic sentences. Revise and edit your letter.

## Chapter 12 Summary

Have volunteers read aloud each Summary item on page 305. Ask volunteers to explain the meaning of each item.

### ONLINE CONNECTION

The first Web site below brings you to the main page for the United States Postal Service. At this site you can find postal abbreviations, postage rates, and other information related to mailing items in the United States. The second site listed is an educational page that outlines the steps in writing a memo.

www.agsglobe.pmbec.com/page305a
www.agsglobe.pmbec.com/page305b

### GROUP ACTIVITY

Remind groups to begin by prewriting. In this case, have students do research on a few of the not-for-profit organizations in your town. Once they have found an organization that appeals to them, ask them to consider these questions: *Will your contribution make a difference? Is your help needed?* If they decide the organization is a good fit, have them begin to work on their letter.

## Chapter 12 Review

Use the Chapter Review to prepare students for tests and to reteach content from the chapter.

## Chapter 12 Mastery Test

The Teacher's Resource Library includes two forms of the Chapter 12 Mastery Test. Each test addresses the chapter Goals for Learning. An optional third page of additional critical-thinking items is included for each test. The difficulty level of the two forms is equivalent.

### Review Answers

Part A
1. business letter  2. memorandum  3. block style  4. modified block style

Part B
5. C  6. B  7. A

Part C
8. heading  9. body  10. signature
11. closing  12. inside address
13. salutation  14. typed name  15. date

---

**Word Bank**
block style
business letter
memorandum
modified block style

**Part A** Write the word or words from the Word Bank that complete each sentence.

1. A formal letter to a person or company is a _____.

2. A formal business message with a special format is a _____.

3. When you use _____, you begin all the parts of a letter at the left margin.

4. When you use _____, you indent the paragraphs in the body of a letter.

**Part B** Match each item in Column 1 with the place it belongs on an envelope in Column 2. Write the letter of your answer.

| Column 1 | Column 2 |
|---|---|
| 5. mailing address | **A** top left corner of envelope |
| 6. postage stamp | **B** top right corner of envelope |
| 7. return address | **C** center of envelope |

**Answer Bank**
body
closing
date
heading
inside address
salutation
signature
typed name

**Part C** Match each item with a business letter part from the Answer Bank. Write the name of the part.

8. the address of the sender and sometimes a company name

9. the main part of the letter

10. the handwritten name of the sender

11. "Yours truly," or "Sincerely,"

12. the name and address of the receiver

13. "Dear Ms. Moreno:" or "Dear Store Manager:"

14. the part below the signature

15. the month, day, and year

---

---

Name _____ Date _____ Period _____ | Mastery Test A / Chapter 12 / Page 1

**Chapter 12 Mastery Test A**

**Part A** Circle the correct answer.

1. Which of these is NOT one of the items on almost every memorandum?
   A to   B job title   C from   D subject

2. What punctuation follows the salutation in a business letter?
   A comma   B semicolon   C colon   D period

3. What goes in the upper right hand corner of an envelope?
   A date   B mailing address   C return address   D stamp

4. Which of the following would NOT be the subject of a memorandum?
   A Office Lunch   B The Presentation   C My Cat   D Today's Meeting

5. Which of these is an appropriate business letter closing?
   A Sincerely   B Tootles   C Later   D Peace

6. What is listed after the city and state in an address?
   A country   B continent   C ZIP code   D phone number

7. Which of these is a format used for writing business letters?
   A altered block   B block style   C square style   D modified square

8. A salutation in a letter is also known as what?
   A greeting   B closing   C ending   D address

**Part B** List the parts of a business letter.

9. _____   13. _____
10. _____   14. _____
11. _____   15. _____
12. _____   16. _____

**Part C** List the four things found on almost every memorandum.

17. _____   19. _____
18. _____   20. _____

© Pearson Education, Inc., publishing as Pearson AGS Globe. All rights reserved.   **Pacemaker® Basic English Composition**

---

Name _____ Date _____ Period _____ | Mastery Test A / Chapter 12 / Page 2

**Chapter 12 Mastery Test A,** continued

**Part D** Use the envelope to answer the questions or fill in the blanks below.

Jacob Minier
212 Clybourne Ave.
Illinois 60050

Darva Kowalski
Liberty Landscaping
San Antonio, Tx 50054
1210 Rosee St.

21. The _____ address is in the upper left hand corner.

22. The return address is missing the _____.

23. The _____ address is in the center of the envelope.

24–25. Name two things incorrect in the address of Darva Kowalski.

26. If Jacob Minier lived in apartment 2A, where would that be written?

27. The _____ goes in the upper right hand corner.

28. This envelope probably contains a _____ letter.

29. Why do you think the envelope contains that type of letter?

30. How should Jacob write the state in his return address?

© Pearson Education, Inc., publishing as Pearson AGS Globe. All rights reserved.   **Pacemaker® Basic English Composition**

---

Name _____ Date _____ Period _____ | Mastery Test A / Chapter 12 / Page 3

**Chapter 12 Mastery Test A,** continued

**Part E** Write your answer to each question. Use complete sentences. Support each answer with facts and examples from the textbook.

31. List three differences between a business letter and a memo.

32. List three differences between a business and a personal letter.

**Part F** Write a paragraph for each topic. Include a topic sentence, body, and conclusion in the paragraph. Support your answers with facts and examples from the textbook.

33. Imagine that your company is having an office party and that you are in charge of refreshments. You need to find out what most people prefer to eat and drink. What type of letter would best fit the circumstances? Explain.

34. Explain why you should always list a return address on an envelope.

© Pearson Education, Inc., publishing as Pearson AGS Globe. All rights reserved.   **Pacemaker® Basic English Composition**

**Part D** Rewrite each address correctly. Add any missing information. Use the state abbreviations on page 405.

16. Rom Leonhart,
    Apt A
    78 Kentmill Rd.
    Oakville, PA
    17539

17. GAIL COOPER
    1580 ETON WAY
    DELRAY BEACH
    33445 FLORIDA

18. Handy Pencil Company
    123 Broadway
    Sanford, GA 31402-2435
    Larry Frye
    Customer Service Rep.

19. Mr. Norman Li
    Box 800
    Maryland
    Annapolis, 21401

**Part E** Write the letter of the answer to each question.

20. What follows the salutation of a business letter?
    **A** a period   **B** a colon   **C** a comma   **D** a dash

21. What information is not part of an address?
    **A** ZIP code        **C** street name
    **B** phone number    **D** city name

22. Which of these could be a business salutation?
    **A** Enclosure: Photo   **C** Hi Amber!
    **B** Dear Mr. Elliot:    **D** Sincerely,

**Part F** Follow each set of directions.

23. Explain why a memo does not need an address.

24. Write your signature as if signing a business letter.

25. Write a short memo. Use the information in the note below. Use today's date.

> To all employees: I plan to choose a better phone system for our company by next fall. If you are interested in testing possible systems, please let me know this week. Ken Runion, Technology Manager

## Test Tip

When you write a test answer or essay, remember to check punctuation. Punctuation marks are like road signs. They help readers follow along.

---

## Review Answers

### Part D

16. Rom Leonhart
    78 Kentmill Rd., Apt A
    Oakville, PA 17539

17. Gail Cooper
    1580 Eton Way
    Delray Beach, FL 33445

18. Larry Frye, Customer Service Rep.
    Handy Pencil Company
    123 Broadway
    Sanford, GA 31402-2435

19. Mr. Norman Li
    Box 800
    Annapolis, MD 21401

### Part E

20. B  21. B  22. B

### Part F

23. A memo is an internal letter, sent within a company or organization. Therefore, there is no need for an address. 24. Signatures will vary but should include the student's full legal name. 25. Memos will vary. Look for a proper heading and inclusion of all relevant facts.

## WRITING PORTFOLIO

**Wrap-Up** Have students make a clean final copy of their revised and edited letters. You may want to collect the letters and read them anonymously to the class or have classmates share their letters in small groups. This project may be used as an alternative form of assessment for the chapter.

---

Chapter 12 Mastery Test B, pages 1–3

## PLANNING GUIDE

# Preparing to Write a Report

| | Student Pages | Student Lesson | | | Language Skills | | | | |
|---|---|---|---|---|---|---|---|---|---|
| | | Vocabulary | Practice Exercises | Lesson Review | Identification | Writing | Punctuation & Capitalization | Grammar & Usage | Listening, Speaking, & Viewing |
| **Lesson 13-1** Understanding the Parts of a Report | 311–315 | ✔ | ✔ | ✔ | ✔ | ✔ | ✔ | ✔ | ✔ |
| **Lesson 13-2** Choosing a Topic | 316–321 | ✔ | ✔ | ✔ | ✔ | ✔ | ✔ | ✔ | ✔ |
| **Lesson 13-3** Finding Information | 322–327 | ✔ | ✔ | ✔ | ✔ | ✔ | ✔ | ✔ | ✔ |
| **Lesson 13-4** Using Online Resources | 328–331 | ✔ | ✔ | ✔ | ✔ | ✔ | ✔ | ✔ | ✔ |
| **Lesson 13-5** Taking Notes | 332–337 | ✔ | ✔ | ✔ | ✔ | ✔ | ✔ | ✔ | ✔ |
| **Lesson 13-6** Creating an Outline | 338–345 | ✔ | ✔ | ✔ | ✔ | ✔ | ✔ | ✔ | ✔ |

## Chapter Activities

**Teacher's Resource Library**
Life Skills Connection 13: Library
    Research
Writing Tip 13: Planning Reports
English in Your Life 7: Writing a
    Résumé
Building Research Skills 13:
    Checking a Table of Contents
Key Vocabulary Words 13

## Assessment Options

**Student Text**
Chapter 13 Review

**Teacher's Resource Library**
Chapter 13 Mastery Tests A and B

**Teacher's Edition**
Chapter 13 Writing Portfolio

| | Student Text Features | | | | | | | | | Teaching Strategies | | | | | | | | | Learning Styles | | | | | Teacher's Resource Library | | | |
|---|---|---|---|---|---|---|---|---|---|---|---|---|---|---|---|---|---|---|---|---|---|---|---|---|---|---|---|
| | English in Your Life | Writing on the Job | Building Research Skills | Vocabulary Builder | Grammar Builder | Write About It | Group Activity | Reading Strategy | Six Traits | ELL/ESL Strategy | Background Information | Common Error | Life Skills Connection | Applications (Home, Career, Community, Global) | Online Connection | Teacher Alert | Speaking & Presenting Practice | Writing/Spelling/Grammar Practice | Auditory/Verbal | Body/Kinesthetic | Interpersonal/Group Learning | Logical/Mathematical | Visual/Spatial | Activities | Modified Activities | Workbook Activities | Self-Study Guide |
| | | | | | 315 | | | 313, 314 | | 312 | 311 | 314 | | 312 | | | | | | | | 312 | 315 | 53 | 53 | 53 | ✔ |
| | | | | 321 | | | | 316, 320 | | 318 | 316 | 319 | | 317, 318 | 317 | | | 321 | | | | | 317 | 54 | 54 | 54 | ✔ |
| | | | | | | | | 322, 326 | | 324 | 322 | 323 | 325 | | | | 325 | 325 | | 324 | 326 | | | 55 | 55 | 55 | ✔ |
| | | | | | | | | 329, 330 | | 330 | 328 | 329 | | | | | | 331 | | | | | | 56 | 56 | 56 | ✔ |
| | | | | | | | | 332, 333 | | 333 | 332 | 336 | | 334 | | 334 | | | 336 | | 335 | | | 57 | 57 | 57 | ✔ |
| | 343 | 344 | | | 342 | 345 | | 338, 341 | 342 | 340 | 338 | 340 | | | 345 | | | | | 341 | | | 339 | 58 | 58 | 58 | ✔ |

## Pronunciation Key

| | | | | | | | | | | | | | |
|---|---|---|---|---|---|---|---|---|---|---|---|---|---|
| a | hat | e | let | ī | ice | ô | order | ů | put | sh | she | | a in about |
| ā | age | ē | equal | o | hot | oi | oil | ü | rule | th | thin | ə { | e in taken |
| ä | far | ėr | term | ō | open | ou | out | ch | child | ᴛʜ | then | | i in pencil |
| â | care | i | it | ȯ | saw | u | cup | ng | long | zh | measure | | o in lemon |
| | | | | | | | | | | | | | u in circus |

## Modified Activities

The Teacher's Resource Library (TRL) contains a set of lower-level worksheets called Modified Activities. These worksheets cover the same content as the standard Activities but are written at a lower reading level.

## Skill Track

Use Skill Track for *Basic English Composition* to monitor student progress and meet the demands of adequate yearly progress (AYP). Make informed instructional decisions with individual student and class reports of lesson and chapter assessments. With immediate and ongoing feedback, students will also see what they have learned and where they need more reinforcement and practice.

## Chapter 13:
## Preparing to Write a Report
pages 308–347

## Lessons

**Skill Track for Basic English Composition**

**Teacher's Resource Library** **TRL**

Activities 53–58

Modified Activities 53–58

Workbook Activities 53–58

Life Skills Connection 13

Writing Tip 13

English in Your Life 7

Building Research Skills 13

Key Vocabulary Words 13

Chapter 13 Self-Study Guide

Chapter 13 Mastery Tests A and B

(Answer Keys for the Teacher's Resource Library begin on page 446 of the Teacher's Edition.)

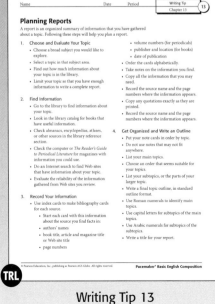

Writing Tip 13

Life Skills Connection 13

# Preparing to Write a Report

People have chores, or regular jobs at home, that they are expected to do. The person in the photo is taking the family dog for a walk. He probably does this every day after school. This job is important for the dog's health.

One job of a student is to write reports. Every year, you will probably be asked to write at least one. The work you put into a report is important. You gain valuable skills in the process. For example, you learn how to find sources of information and evaluate them. You practice summarizing details. You learn how to organize ideas in a logical way.

Chapter 13 will show you how to plan and write a report. It will explain how to choose a report topic, find information about it, take notes, and make an outline.

## GOALS FOR LEARNING

- To identify the three parts of a report
- To choose a report topic, and to make a list of keywords
- To find information in books, periodicals, and reference books
- To use online resources to find information, and to evaluate Internet information
- To take notes, to create bibliography cards, and to paraphrase
- To organize research information, and to create an outline

309

## Introducing the Chapter

Have students examine the photograph on page 308 and describe what it shows. Remind students that they have many different roles—as family members, friends, students, and sports team members, for example. Focus the discussion on their role as students and the school tasks they must perform in the classroom and at home. Direct the discussion toward report writing. Help students brainstorm a list of activities that they participate in as they prepare reports. Begin the discussion by noting that choosing a topic is one of the first steps. Encourage students to use the Goals for Learning as clues to the kinds of tasks involved in writing a report.

## Notes

Ask volunteers to read the notes that appear in the margins throughout the chapter. Then discuss them with the class.

## TEACHER'S RESOURCE

The AGS Globe Teaching Strategies in English Transparencies may be used with this chapter. The transparencies add an interactive dimension to expand and enhance the *Basic English Composition* program content.

## WRITING PORTFOLIO

Explain that students will develop and follow a plan for writing a report. Suggest that they design a step-by-step plan for completing a report. They can use the plan as they work on compiling information and preparing an outline for their written report throughout the chapter. Note that the first step in writing a report is choosing a topic. Have students work in groups to identify topics of interest to them and to choose one of the topics for their individual reports. This project may be used as an alternative form of assessment for the chapter.

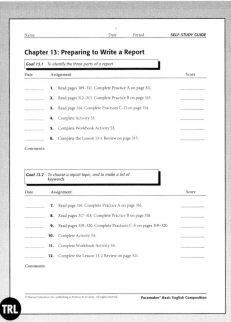

## Reading Strategy: Summarizing

Remind students that they summarize main ideas and details often. When they tell a friend about the lyrics of a new song, the plot of a show they saw on television, or the content of a news article, they are summarizing. Encourage students to summarize a familiar tale such as *The Three Little Pigs.* Ask: What and who is this story about? What happens in the story? (*Three little pigs build houses to protect themselves from the wolf.*)

### Key Vocabulary Words

| | |
|---|---|
| bibliography | periodical |
| browser | plagiarize |
| call number | report |
| catalog | research |
| index | search engine |
| keyword | subtopic |
| outline | table of contents |
| paraphrase | |

Read aloud the words to students and have them supply the definitions. Then use books, periodicals, and in-class computers to provide hands-on examples that illustrate the meanings of terms such as *table of contents, index, call number, periodical, keyword, search engine, browser,* and *bibliography.* Have groups of students organize the words into categories that might include book organization, computer searches, or report writing.

# Reading Strategy: Summarizing

When you summarize, you state the main idea and the most important details. Summarizing helps you understand and remember what you read. As you read this chapter, ask yourself questions like these:

- What is this chapter about?
- What is the main idea of this chapter?
- How is this idea broken into lessons?
- What details are most important in this chapter?

## Key Vocabulary Words

**Report** An organized summary of information about a topic; usually involving research

**Subtopic** A division or part of a larger topic

**Catalog** A list of items arranged in a special way

**Keyword** A word or phrase that you use to search for information about a topic

**Research** To find information about a topic

**Call number** A number that identifies a book and tells you where it is in a library

**Table of contents** A list of parts of a book and the page on which each part begins; usually at the beginning of a book

**Index** An alphabetical list of the topics and subtopics in a book with page numbers; usually at the end of a book

**Periodical** Any printed material that someone publishes on a regular basis

**Search engine** A computer program that searches the Internet for keywords and lists the places it finds them

**Browser** A computer program that allows you to use the information on Internet sites

**Bibliography** A list of sources that were used to write a report

**Paraphrase** To write someone else's ideas in your own words

**Plagiarize** To take credit for someone else's words

**Outline** A plan for writing a report that lists topics and subtopics in a certain order

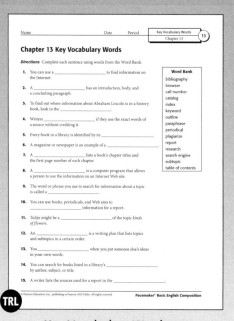

# Understanding the Parts of a Report

## Objectives

■ To identify the three parts of a report

■ To understand the purpose of each part of a report

**Report**

An organized summary of information about a topic; usually involving research

 **NOTE**

A short report is sometimes called an essay.

A **report** is an organized summary of information about a topic. For most reports, the writer needs to research the topic—to find the information. You build a report much like you build a paragraph. A paragraph is made of sentences, and a report is made of paragraphs.

The parts of a report are:

- the topic paragraph
- the body (paragraphs that give details)
- the summary paragraph

A report begins with a topic paragraph. This paragraph states the main idea of the report. It does the same job as a topic sentence in a paragraph. The body of a report is usually three or more paragraphs. It gives the details. The summary paragraph summarizes the report. It is like the summary or conclusion of a paragraph.

### Practice A

Complete each sentence by filling in the missing word. Write each word on your paper.

1. A report is a group of ___ about one topic.
2. The first part of a report is the ___.
3. Give details in the ___ of a report.
4. The last part of a report is the ___.
5. State the main idea of a report in the ___.

---

## Lesson at a Glance

### Chapter 13 Lesson 1

**Overview** This lesson focuses on the three major parts of a report—topic paragraph, body, and summary paragraph.

### Objectives

■ To identify the three parts of a report

■ To understand the purpose of each part of a report

**Student Pages** 311–315

**Teacher's Resource Library**

Activity 53

Modified Activity 53

Workbook Activity 53

## Vocabulary

**report**

Read the word *report* and its definition to students. Ask them to identify examples of reports. For example, they might identify a report they have written or a news report they have read or seen.

## Background Information

The main idea of a paragraph or report is the most important idea presented. The main idea and the topic are related. The topic is the subject of the report. The main idea expands on the topic, providing a focus for the report. It is the central thought about the topic.

---

## 2   Teaching the Lesson

As you analyze the parts of the sample report on page 312, make sure students identify the main idea in the topic paragraph, relevant details in the body, and the summary statement in the summary paragraph. Have students outline features of each part of a report as they read about writing that part.

### Practice A

On the board, write the name of each report part. List one or two words that tell about the part under its name. Then have students complete the activity.

### Practice A Answers

**1.** paragraphs **2.** topic paragraph **3.** body **4.** summary paragraph **5.** topic paragraph

## 1   Warm-Up Activity

Have students imagine that they are meeting each other for the first time. Ask them to introduce themselves to classmates and tell something about themselves. Relate the personal introduction to the introduction of a report. Explain that the introduction of a report gives its main idea.

## ELL/ESL STRATEGY

**Language Objective:**
*To identify main ideas*

Have students work with partners to identify the main idea in each paragraph of the sample report. Encourage students to label and number the parts of the report as they summarize the paragraphs. For example, they should label the main idea of the first paragraph as Topic Paragraph, the main idea of the second paragraph as Body Paragraph 1, the main idea of the third as Body Paragraph 2, and so on. They should label the final paragraph's main idea as Summary Paragraph. Once partners have completed the summarization activity, have them share their summaries with the class.

## IN THE COMMUNITY

Many communities, school districts, social service organizations, libraries, and park districts publish newsletters and reports that detail activities of the organizations and issues affecting them. Encourage students to acquire an organizational report or newsletter. Have them analyze an article to identify its parts and summarize its content.

Read the sample report below.

**Superstitions**

Topic paragraph

Some people will not walk under a ladder. Others worry if a black cat crosses their path. These people act this way because of superstitions. Superstitions are beliefs that no one can prove. However, many people believe that superstitions are true.

Body

Throughout the ages, there have been superstitions about salt. People once thought that salt had magic powers because it could keep things from decaying. The ancient Sumerians began the custom of throwing a pinch of salt over the left shoulder. They believed it would keep bad luck away. Several cultures considered spilled salt a sign of bad luck. Today, some people still toss a pinch of spilled salt over their left shoulder, just to be safe.

Even today, many people believe in signs of bad luck. Some feel they can control their future by avoiding such signs. Superstitious people never open umbrellas indoors because they think it will bring misfortune. They never step on cracks in the sidewalk. Most avoid the number 13 because they think that number brings bad luck. Some hotels do not have a room numbered 13—they go right from 12 to 14. Some buildings have no 13th floor. Even though these superstitions have no basis in fact, they certainly affect people's actions.

Just as there are signs of bad luck, so are there signs of good luck. Some people believe a four-leaf clover will bring good luck. Others think a horseshoe or a rabbit's foot is a sign of good fortune. People believe that picking up a pin or a penny means a bright tomorrow. Perhaps these good luck charms are popular because they make people feel better about the future.

Summary paragraph

As people become better educated, they believe less in superstitions. However, a large number of people will still toss salt over their left shoulder or go out of their way to avoid walking under a ladder. Many people cling to superstitions because they are a bit afraid that the beliefs might, indeed, be true.

## LEARNING STYLES

**Logical/Mathematical**
Do classmates and other students have superstitions? What are they? Suggest that small groups of students conduct a survey to find out what, if any, superstitions students have. Encourage students to prepare a questionnaire that asks questions such as these: Are you superstitious? What are your superstitions? Do you think finding a penny is good luck? Students should ask five to ten other students their questions. Have students compile their findings in a chart or graph and present them to the class.

## Writing the Topic Paragraph

The topic paragraph introduces the topic and main idea of your report. It may express your opinion about the topic. This paragraph helps the reader know what to expect from the rest of the report. The topic paragraph on page 312 states this opinion: "many people believe that superstitions are true."

### Practice B

Find the sentence in each paragraph that expresses the writer's opinion. Write the sentence on your paper.

1. The turkey is on the table. It is brown, crisp, and juicy. Smells of cinnamon and cranberries and sage dressing fill the air. The family gathers around the table. Thanksgiving is my favorite holiday.

2. Animals cannot talk. They cannot tell people what they are thinking. Their eyes, however, show feeling. They seem happy sometimes. At other times, they seem quite sad. There is no doubt in my mind. I believe that animals, just like people, have feelings.

3. Students go to Springfield High School every weekday for nine months of the year. They spend six hours of each day in Springfield's halls and classrooms. Because students spend so much time there, the school should be a better place. I think we could improve Springfield High School in several ways.

4. The sun was shining. Soccer fans filled the stands. The two best teams were facing each other on the field. It was going to be an exciting game.

5. Not long ago, most people believed a heavy machine could never stay up in the air. Today, airplanes fly across the country in a few hours. Two brothers, Wilbur and Orville Wright, made the dream of flight come true.

*Reading Strategy:*
Summarizing

What details on this page helped you understand what a topic paragraph is?

## Practice B

Review what opinions are. Ask students to differentiate fact and opinion. Make sure students understand that a fact is a piece of information that is known to be true and an opinion is a statement of someone's belief or viewpoint.

### *Practice B Answers*

**1.** Thanksgiving is my favorite holiday. **2.** I believe that animals, just like people, have feelings. **3.** I think we could improve Springfield High School in several ways. **4.** It was going to be an exciting game. **5.** Two brothers, Wilbur and Orville Wright, made the dream of flight come true.

### *Reading Strategy:* Summarizing

Students may say that the first paragraph on this page summarizes the purpose of a topic paragraph.

## Practice C

Have students work with partners to summarize each paragraph in the sample report. Remind them that a summary tells the main idea and the main details.

### Practice C Answers

Sample answers are given. **1.** Throughout the ages, there have been superstitions about salt. **2.** Even today, many people believe in signs of bad luck. **3.** Just as there are signs of bad luck, so are there signs of good luck.

## Practice D

Remind students that the main idea is the most important idea of a paragraph or report. Read each paragraph aloud. Discuss what the main idea or topic of the paragraph is. Then have students determine whether the concluding statement summarizes the main idea.

### Practice D Answers

**1.** no; The main idea is that student behavior must improve or some students may decide to attend school elsewhere. **2.** yes; The second sentence adds details that reinforce the writer's glad feeling about Thanksgiving.

### Reading Strategy: Summarizing

It is important to know that the body of a report provides supporting details for the report's main idea and that each paragraph in the body has its own main idea.

### COMMON ERROR

Students may confuse supporting details for the main idea as they read and write reports. Remind them that the main idea is the most important point that is made about a topic. Suggest that students use a word web to help them record details about a topic. They can use the details to help them identify the main idea.

---

**Reading Strategy:**
Summarizing

What is important to know about the body of a report?

## Writing the Body

After you write the topic paragraph, you develop the body of your report. The purpose of the body is to explain and support your main idea. The body includes details such as facts, examples, experiences, and reasons. Each paragraph in the body has its own main idea.

### Practice C

Number your paper from 1 to 3. Use the three body paragraphs in the sample report on page 312. Write one sentence to summarize the main idea of each paragraph.

### Writing the Summary Paragraph

The purpose of the last paragraph is to summarize the information in your report. Do not introduce a new idea in this paragraph. Restate the main idea of your report using different words. Bring the report to a strong and satisfying close for the reader.

### Practice D

The conclusion of each paragraph is in bold. Does it summarize the main idea? Write *yes* or *no* on your paper. Then explain your answer.

1. Indeed, the mood at Springfield High School must improve, or some students will stop going to class there. Students should make changes in their behavior before it is too late. **Next year, I will graduate and go on to college**.

2. I am glad that we celebrate the day the Pilgrims feasted at Plymouth Colony. **I always look forward to the sights, the smells, and the warm feelings of Thanksgiving**.

Write the answer to each question on your paper.

1. What is the purpose of a report?
2. What does a topic paragraph do?
3. What is the purpose of the body of a report?
4. What does the last paragraph do?
5. Why is it important to restate the main idea of the report at the end?

Write the word that completes each sentence.

6. A group of sentences about one topic is a ____.
7. A group of paragraphs about one topic is a ____.
8. In a report, the ____ paragraph states the main idea.
9. The ____ paragraph summarizes the report.
10. The ____ of a report contains the supporting details.

## GRAMMAR BUILDER

### Punctuating Adverb Clauses

An adverb clause works like an adverb. It answers questions about a verb, an adjective, or another adverb. An adverb clause may go at the beginning or the end of a sentence.

- An adverb clause at the beginning of a sentence is set off by a comma.
- An adverb clause at the end of a sentence is not set off by a comma.

Write each sentence. Underline the adverb clause. Add a comma if one is needed.

1. Adam plays soccer because he loves it.
2. If you have room I will ride with you.
3. When spring comes they will practice outdoors.

*Preparing to Write a Report* *Chapter 13* **315**

---

**Activity 53**

**Workbook Activity 53**

---

## Lesson 13-1 Review Answers

**1.** The purpose of a report is to summarize information about a topic. **2.** A topic paragraph presents the main idea of the report and often the opinion of the writer. **3.** The purpose of the body of the report is to provide details and examples. **4.** The last paragraph summarizes the main idea and the information presented. **5.** Restating the main idea at the end of a report brings closure to the report and reminds the reader of the main idea. **6.** paragraph **7.** report **8.** topic **9.** summary **10.** body

## LEARNING STYLES

### Visual/Spatial

Have pairs of students prepare a graphic organizer that identifies each part of a report and its main features and purpose. You might suggest that students create an outline or a chart that details the information. A chart might name the parts and have columns for purpose and features. Have the pairs present their graphics to the class. They may wish to provide copies for all students who can then use the graphics as a reference tool.

## GRAMMAR BUILDER

Some students may need additional help in recognizing adverb clauses. Point out that an adverb clause serves the same purpose as an adverb: it tells more about a verb, an adjective, or another adverb. The clause often can be moved to different positions within a sentence without a loss of meaning. (*I was not hungry until I smelled the bread. Until I smelled the bread, I was not hungry.*)

### Grammar Builder Answers

**1.** Adam plays soccer <u>because he loves it</u>.
**2.** <u>If you have room</u>, I will ride with you.
**3.** <u>When spring comes</u>, they will practice outdoors.

*Preparing to Write a Report* **315**

### Chapter 13 Lesson 2

**Overview** This lesson focuses on choosing and narrowing a topic for a report. It explains how to check out the topic to determine if it is too broad, too narrow, or appropriate for a report.

### Objectives

- To choose a topic for a report
- To narrow the topic of a report
- To make a list of keywords
- To use a catalog to find information about a topic

**Student Pages** 316–321

**Teacher's Resource Library**

Activity 54

Modified Activity 54

Workbook Activity 54

### Vocabulary

catalog         subtopic
keyword

Have students read the definition of each word. Briefly discuss the structure of the words *subtopic* and *keyword*. *Subtopic* is made up of the prefix *sub-* meaning "smaller part of" and the word *topic*. *Keyword* is a compound word made up of *key* meaning "important" and *word*. Then have students use all three words in a sentence.

### Background Information

Writing topics as well as topics of conversation often focus on popular culture. In the 1700s, Oliver Goldsmith reflected on the topics of conversation of polite society in his time. "They would talk of nothing but high life, and high-lived company, with other fashionable topics, such as pictures, taste, Shakespeare, and the musical glasses." Musical glasses were sets of glasses that were each tuned to specific notes and then played by rubbing or lightly hitting them. Goldsmith's observations reflected the culture of his time. Today popular culture focuses on very different topics.

---

### Objectives

- To choose a topic for a report
- To narrow the topic of a report
- To make a list of keywords
- To use a catalog to find information about a topic

**Reading Strategy:** Summarizing

What should you think about before you choose a topic?

---

# Choosing a Topic

The first step in writing a report is to choose a topic. Think of topics that interest you. You might start with a general subject, such as science, and list topics that fall within it. Look at the lists in Example 1.

▶ **EXAMPLE 1**

| Science | History | Music |
|---|---|---|
| energy sources | World War II | popular dances |
| the atom | early computers | the orchestra |
| earthquakes | sports | African music |

### Practice A

1. Choose one subject listed below. List five topics that are in that subject area. Then underline the topics that interest you most.
   - science
   - history
   - cultures
   - careers
   - geography
   - literature
   - math
   - transportation
   - music
   - art
   - technology
   - travel

2. Next, choose one of your underlined topics. Think about this carefully because this might be the topic for a report you will write. Write the topic.

3. Write 10 questions about the topic you chose. You will answer these questions in your report. For example, if you chose the history of baseball for your topic, you might write these questions:
   - Who invented the game of baseball?
   - When and where was it invented?
   - What were the first playing fields like?

---

### 1   Warm-Up Activity

Display a news, home, or sports magazine. Turn to its table of contents to identify an article. Then turn to the article. Have students help you identify the topic of the article from its title.

### 2   Teaching the Lesson

Ask: Why would a short report need a narrower topic than a longer report? *(Short reports cannot adequately develop details needed to explain broad topics.)* Ask students to name a topic for a paragraph, short report, or long report. List the topics on the board and help students brainstorm a list of keywords that they could use to search for information about the topics.

### Practice A

Read the bulleted list of twelve general subject areas with students. Briefly discuss topics that fall in each area. Tell students to choose the subject area of greatest interest to them. They may explore more than one subject area in their search for a report topic.

### *Practice A Answers*

Answers will vary for each of these questions but should show an understanding of topic and subtopic.

### *Reading Strategy:* Summarizing

Before choosing a topic, a report writer should think about his or her interests and the length of the report to be written.

**Subtopic**
A division or part of a larger topic

## The Length of Your Report

The directions for writing a report will tell you how long the report should be. The length of the report determines how broad or narrow your topic can be. Example 2 gives possible lengths for a paragraph, a short report, and a long report. Each has the same three parts.

▶ **EXAMPLE 2**

|              | Paragraph     | Short Report  | Long Report |
|--------------|---------------|---------------|-------------|
| Introduction | 1 sentence    | 1 paragraph   | 1 page      |
| Body         | 3–4 sentences | 3–4 paragraphs| 3–4 pages   |
| Summary      | 1 sentence    | 1 paragraph   | 1 page      |

## Narrowing Your Topic

Narrow your topic to fit the report length. The history of sports is a broad topic—too broad for a report. You could write a long book on that topic. Try to narrow your topic to one that you can handle in a report that is five or six pages.

Find **subtopics** within your topic. A subtopic is a division or part of a larger topic. You may need to find subtopics within your subtopics, too.

▶ **EXAMPLE 3**

| Topic      | the history of sports    |
|------------|--------------------------|
| Subtopics  | the history of baseball  |
|            | the history of soccer    |
|            | the history of track     |

*Amber loves dogs. She plans to write a report on popular dog breeds.*

### TEACHER ALERT

Lessons 13-2 through 13-6 take students through the process of preparing to write a report. Advise them to make a folder in which they can keep track of all their research. The first item to put in the folder is the list of possible topics.

### GLOBAL CONNECTION

Some subject areas such as literature, music, geography, art, and culture lend themselves to a global connection. Encourage students to identify topics with a global perspective. For example, for the subject area culture, they might list the *quinceanera* custom of Central and South American cultures as well as Mexico. For literature, students might consider comparing and contrasting Cinderella stories from around the world. For geography, students might look at the physical and human geography of specific countries. By writing reports on such topics, students can expand their understanding of the global community.

### LEARNING STYLES

**Visual/Spatial**

Help students make a display that visually compares the lengths of reports. Title the display "Length of Reports" and label each length modeled. For a paragraph, display a half sheet of white paper; for a short report, display two sheets of white paper; and for a long report, display six sheets of white paper.

The best topic for a report is neither too broad nor too narrow. For a topic that is too broad, you will find more information than you can handle for one report. For a topic that is too narrow, you will find little or no information at all. For a topic that is just right, you will find several books containing information about it.

▶ **EXAMPLE 4**

| Too Broad | the history of sports |
| Too Narrow | the history of the catcher's mitt |
| Just Right | the history of baseball |

**Practice B**

Identify the topic and subtopic in each pair. Write *topic* or *subtopic* next to each letter.

| Example: | **A** making earrings |
| | **B** making jewelry |

| Answer: | **A** subtopic |
| | **B** topic |

1. **A** growing vegetables
   **B** growing root vegetables

2. **A** computers from past to present
   **B** the first computers

3. **A** high schools in the United States
   **B** schools in the United States

4. **A** sunspots
   **B** the sun

5. **A** the history of Mexico
   **B** the Aztec Indians

## Practice B

Draw a square on the board and divide it into fourths. Explain that each smaller square is a part of the larger square. In the same way, a subtopic is related to a topic. It is a part of the bigger idea.

### Practice B Answers

**1.** A. topic B. subtopic **2.** A. topic B. subtopic **3.** A. subtopic B. topic **4.** A. subtopic B. topic **5.** A. topic B. subtopic

**Catalog**
A list of items arranged in a special way

## Checking Out Your Topic

One way to find out whether your topic is too broad or too narrow is to do a quick check at the library. Use the library **catalog** to look up your topic. A catalog is a list of items arranged in a special way. A library catalog lists every book, magazine, and recording in that library. In some libraries, the catalog is still on cards in drawers. Most public libraries also have their catalog on a computer.

### Practice C

Use a library catalog to look up each topic. Write the number of books that are available on the topic. Based on this information, decide if the topic is right for a report. Write one of these: *too broad, too narrow,* or *just right.*

1. computers
2. computers—history
3. video games
4. solar system
5. Venus—atmosphere

### Practice D

1. Look at the report topic you chose in Practice A on page 316. Use a library catalog to find out how much information is available on this topic. Decide if your topic is right for a report. Write *too broad, too narrow,* or *just right.*

2. Make a decision about your topic. Ask yourself these questions:
   - Am I interested in learning about this topic? (If not, choose another topic.)
   - Is this topic too broad? (If so, narrow it.)
   - Is this topic too narrow? (If so, make it broader.)

   Once you decide, write the name of your report topic.

Students often choose writing topics that are too broad or too narrow for the length of their papers. They then have difficulty developing the topic adequately. Help students identify the length of the report they are writing and choose a topic narrow or broad enough to be developed within that length.

## Practice C

The number of resources available for the topic is one criterion to consider when determining whether a topic is suitable for a report. Point out that if only one or two resources are available for a topic, the topic may be too narrow. If hundreds are available, it may be too broad.

### Practice C Answers

Responses will vary depending on the number of sources found. **1.** too broad **2.** too broad **3.** just right **4.** too broad **5.** just right

## Practice D

Students evaluate their chosen topic in this activity. First, they must determine whether the topic is too narrow or too broad. Then they must decide if they want to learn more about the topic. If they do, students should write the name of their report topic and place it in their folder.

### Practice D Answers

Responses will vary. You may want to plan an individual conference with each student.

## Practice E

Discuss keywords, explaining that students might begin with more general keywords and then focus in on narrower ones.

### Practice E Answers

Answers will vary. Sample answers are given. **1.** dog show, dog events, international dog shows, show dogs **2.** healthy breakfast, breakfast, cereal, fruit, nutrition, diet, nutritious foods **3.** video games, playing video games online, video game players, specific names of games or game players **4.** rock, pop, alternative, punk rock, opera, classical, folk, country, jazz **5.** presidents, Mount Vernon, American Revolution, American presidents

## Practice F

Remind students that librarians are available to provide help in accessing library catalogs. When doing a computerized catalog search for keywords, students should type their keywords into the subject category.

### Practice F Answers

Answers will vary.

### Reading Strategy: Summarizing

Details relating paper length to topics and the number of research resources available emphasize the importance of choosing a topic that is just right.

---

**Keyword**
A word or phrase that you use to search for information about a topic

## Making a List of Keywords

You have a list of questions that you want to answer in your report (from Practice A on page 316). You have checked in the library to be sure there is enough information to write a report. Now, you need to make a list of **keywords** for your topic. Keywords are the words that you use to search for information. You need keywords to search a library catalog or to search for Web sites on the Internet. A keyword can be a word or a phrase.

▶ **EXAMPLE 5**

| Topic | computers |
|---|---|
| Keywords | types of computers, personal computers, video games |

### Practice E

Write three or more keywords for each topic. Use what you already know about the topic to help you think of keywords. Try brainstorming. Spelling is important, so use a dictionary if you need one.

1. dog shows around the world
2. healthy breakfast foods
3. video games
4. types of music
5. George Washington

**Reading Strategy:**
Summarizing

Choosing the right topic is important. What details in the lesson helped you to see this?

### Practice F

Write a list of keywords about the topic you chose in Practice D. Try brainstorming. Check the spelling of your keywords in a dictionary. Use these keywords to search a library catalog or the Internet. The information you find may help you identify more or better keywords.

---

Answer each question by writing a complete sentence.

1. Why is it be hard to find information on some topics?

2. Why should you search in a library catalog before you choose a topic?

3. What is an example of a topic that is too broad? What is an example of a topic that is too narrow?

Each set contains one main topic and three subtopics. Write the main topic.

4. rock          opera        folk         types of music

5. vegetables    turnips      beans        carrots

6. poetry        literature   novels       short stories

7. poodles       dogs         collies      terriers

Write two subtopics for each topic.

8. languages     9. soccer     10. the solar system

---

## VOCABULARY BUILDER

### Using Library Books

A library has many types of books. It is helpful to know the names of these types.
- A *fiction book* is a story about imaginary people and events.
- A *nonfiction book* is about real people, things, or ideas.
- An *autobiography* is someone's life story written by that person.
- A *biography* is someone's life story written by another person.
- A *how-to book* tells you how to do something.
- A *reference book* has general facts and information about a topic. You will learn about reference books in the next lesson.

List the types of books you have read. Give an example of each.

---

*Preparing to Write a Report*   Chapter 13   **321**

---

*Preparing to Write a Report*   **321**

---

## Lesson 13-2 Review Answers

**1.** The topics might be too narrow or too current. **2.** You should search the catalog to find out what information is available. **3.** Answers will vary. A sample answer follows. The topic "computers" might be too broad. The topic "the first computer" might be too narrow. It depends on how long the report should be. **4.** types of music **5.** vegetables **6.** literature **7.** dogs Answers will vary for 8–10. Sample answers are given. **8.** languages—French, Spanish **9.** soccer—soccer fields, David Beckham **10.** the solar system—the sun, the planets

## VOCABULARY BUILDER

Point out to students that most libraries group their books into the types noted on page 321. If they are ever confused while looking for information, encourage them to ask a librarian to help. For the exercise, remind students that comic books or graphic novels should be considered fiction books.

### Vocabulary Builder Answers

Answers will vary. An example answer follows.
fiction—*The Red Badge of Courage*
bibliography—*George Washington*
how-to—*How to Draw Dragons*

## Spelling Practice

When using computerized library catalogs or Internet search engines to look up sources based on keywords, students must spell the keywords correctly to ensure that their search is valid. Remind them to use a dictionary to verify spellings if they are not sure of the correct spellings. Write the following keywords with their correct or incorrect spellings on the board.

1. nursary rymes (*nursery rhymes*)
2. farmers' market
3. biulding codes (*building*)
4. string instraments (*instruments*)
5. American Sign Lanquage (*Language*)

If a word is not spelled correctly, ask a volunteer to erase the word and write the correct word.

# Lesson at a Glance

## Chapter 13  Lesson 3

**Overview**  This lesson discusses finding information by using computer or card catalogs in libraries. It describes parts of books, different kinds of reference books, and periodicals as information resources.

## Objectives

- To use a call number to locate a book
- To use a table of contents or an index
- To identify important reference books
- To understand how periodicals are useful in research

**Student Pages**  322–327

**Teacher's Resource Library**

  Activity  55

  Modified Activity  55

  Workbook Activity  55

  Life Skills Connection  13

................................................

## Vocabulary

| | |
|---|---|
| call number | research |
| index | table of contents |
| periodical | |

After students have read the meanings for the terms, display a library book and periodical. Point out that both can be used to do research. Then ask students to identify the call number, table of contents, and index of the library book. Encourage them to name the periodical.

................................................

## Background Information

Many libraries organize their materials by the Dewey Decimal Classification. It is based on a system developed by Melvil Dewey in the late 1870s. The system classifies books into 10 main categories, which are divided into many subcategories. The classifications include generalities (000), philosophy and psychology (100), religion (200), social sciences (300), language (400), natural sciences and mathematics (500), technology and applied sciences (600), the arts (700), literature and rhetoric (800), and geography and history (900).

---

---

## LESSON 13-3  Finding Information

### Objectives

- To use a call number to locate a book
- To use a table of contents or an index
- To identify important reference books
- To understand how periodicals are useful in research

**Research**
To find information about a topic

**Call number**
A number that identifies a book and tells you where it is in a library

**Reading Strategy:** Summarizing

Which idea about searching a library catalog is most important to remember?

You have chosen a topic. Now you are ready to **research** your topic. To research means to find information about a topic. You will need to keep track of the books, magazines, and Web sites that you use. You will need to take notes as you investigate your topic. Where should you begin?

The library catalog is always the best place to begin. If your library has a computer catalog, you can search for information in several ways:

- Search by author. The catalog organizes author records alphabetically by last name (Doyle, Arthur Conan).
- Search by title. The catalog organizes title records alphabetically by the first important word. (*Hound of the Baskervilles, The*)
- Search by subject. For doing research, this search is probably most useful. The catalog organizes subject records alphabetically by the first important word of the topic. If your topic is a person, search by the last name first (Lincoln, Abraham).

Each book in the library has a unique **call number.** This number identifies the book and tells you where it is located in the library. Fiction books by the same author have similar call numbers. Nonfiction books on the same topic also have similar call numbers. The librarian uses these call numbers to group books together on the library shelves.

To search a computer catalog, follow the instructions that appear on the screen. When you select a specific book in your search, details about that book—including the call number—will appear on the screen.

---

---

## 1  Warm-Up Activity

Take students to the school library. Have them determine whether the school has a card catalog or a computer catalog or both. Ask the librarian to talk about the resources and organization of resources in the library.

## 2  Teaching the Lesson

Explain that writers use a variety of resources to compile research on their writing topic. Discuss the use of a library catalog. Ask students to identify the three ways that they can do a catalog search *(by author, title, or subject)*. Discuss the parts of books, using this book to identify features such as the table of contents.

**Reading Strategy:** Summarizing

Answers may vary. Sample answer: It is most important to remember that all books have call numbers and are organized by call numbers on the shelves.

## Practice A

Read the list of books. Write the titles of the books that would be on a shelf together.

- *The Grapes of Wrath* by John Steinbeck (fiction)
- *Chemistry's Everyday Uses* by Mary Ann Phelps (nonfiction)
- *Owning a Horse* by Dana Tran (nonfiction)
- *Kitchen Chemistry* by Chris Buckley (nonfiction)
- *The Red Pony* by John Steinbeck (fiction)
- *Caring for Ponies* by Theodore McKellips (nonfiction)

## Practice B

Study the computer catalog entry below. Write the answer to each question.

| | |
|---|---|
| AUTHOR: | Leonard, Grant |
| TITLE: | Motorcycle Classics / Grant Leonard. |
| PUBLISHED: | New York: Smithmark, 1992. |
| PAGING: | 80 p.: ill. |
| NOTES: | Includes index. |
| SUBJECTS: | Motorcycles |
| CALL NUMBER: | 629.227 / L581—Book—Available |

1. What is the last name of the author?
2. What is the title of this book?
3. Does this book have pictures in it? How do you know?
4. What is the copyright date of this book?
5. What is the call number?

**NOTE**

The abbreviation *ill.* in a catalog entry stands for "illustration." An illustration is a picture or diagram.

## Practice C

Read each situation. Decide what you would look up in a library catalog. Write *author*, *title*, or *subject* on your paper.

1. You are writing a report about Albert Einstein.
2. You would like to look at biology books by Jane B. Reese.
3. You are looking for books about global warming.
4. You are looking for a book about the history of music.
5. You would like to find a book about Chinese history called *The Long March*.

## Practice A

Have students write the name of each book listed with its information on a separate note card. They can then arrange the cards in different ways to determine which titles would be grouped together.

### Practice A Answers

1. *The Grapes of Wrath* and *The Red Pony*
2. *Chemistry's Everyday Uses* and *Kitchen Chemistry* 3. *Owning a Horse* and *Caring for Ponies*

## Practice B

Read the card aloud, pointing out the different information each line of the card gives. For example, the TITLE entry names the author as well as the title. Then have students answer the questions.

### Practice B Answers

1. Leonard 2. *Motorcycle Classics* 3. Yes, the abbreviation *ill.* in the PAGING entry means illustration. 4. 1992
5. 629.227/L581

### COMMON ERROR

Some students believe that a book's call number is the same in every library. However, every library develops its own call number based on its collection. For example, the catalog number for *Motorcycle Classics* by Grant Leonard might be 629.227/L581 at one library and 629.2275 Leo at another.

## Practice C

Discuss with students which catalog search is likely to give the most specific information. Help them conclude that a search by title is likely to yield only books with that title. Some titles may be used by more than one author, however. A search by author will provide only the books written by the named author. A search by subject will yield the largest number of resources by many different titles and authors.

### Practice C Answers

1. subject (author is a logical alternative answer) 2. author 3. subject 4. subject
5. title

## ELL/ESL Strategy

**Language Objective:**
*To identify the meaning of common catalog abbreviations*

Catalog entries include many different abbreviations. Some of these abbreviations will be unfamiliar to students learning English. Encourage students to keep a card file or notebook record of abbreviations they encounter as they view catalog entries. Students are likely to encounter these common abbreviations:

*ill.*  illustration
*col. ill.*  colored illustration
*p.*  page
© copyright
*ISBN*  International Standard Book Number

(Explain that every book has its own ISBN, which identifies it.)

## Practice D

Have volunteers read the sample table of contents and index on page 324 aloud. Briefly discuss their organizations. Discuss the index entry, pointing out the subentries and cross-reference.

### *Practice D Answers*

**1.** page 29 **2.** Chapter 3 **3.** page 32 **4.** Yes, Chapter 4 has information about motorcycles. **5.** Ships

## Learning Styles

### Body/Kinesthetic

Give each student a note card and a library book. Ask the student to use his or her book and note card to prepare a catalog card modeled after the one on page 323. Afterward collect and mix the cards and place the books on shelves. Give each student a card and ask each to find the correct book, matching it to its card.

---

**Table of contents**
A list of the parts of a book and the page on which each part begins; usually at the beginning of a book

**Index**
An alphabetical list of the topics and subtopics in a book with page numbers; usually at the back of a book

---

**Index**

Ocean liners, 25–29
  largest, 26, 28
  speeds of, 29
  *See also* Ships

---

**NOTE**

Look on page iii at the front of this textbook to see its table of contents.

---

## Finding Information Inside a Book

Suppose a library catalog has led you to a book that might be useful. You used the call number to find the book on the shelf. Now you need to look inside the book to see whether it contains the information you need.

A **table of contents** is in the front of many nonfiction books. It lists the parts of the book and the page on which each part begins. Below is part of a table of contents from a book about transportation.

---

### Contents

---

Many books also contain an **index.** The index is at the back of a book. It is an alphabetical list of all the topics and subtopics in the book with page numbers. The index entry at the left is from the same book about transportation.

### Practice D

Use the sample table of contents and index on this page. Write the answer to each question.

1. On which page would you find information about how fast ocean liners travel?

2. Which chapter of the book tells about submarines?

3. On which page does the chapter on submarines start?

4. If your research topic is *motorcycles*, would this book be useful to you? Why or why not?

5. What other topic could you look up in the index to find out about ocean transportation?

## Using Reference Books

A reference book is one that has facts and information about a topic. Most libraries have a reference section. These books are not loaned out, but are for use inside the library. Almanacs, encyclopedias, atlases, and biographical dictionaries are some well-known references. Many reference books are available online or on a CD-ROM.

- An almanac is published every year. Almanacs contain facts and records for current and past years. Major topics include sports, inventions, states and nations, and current issues. If you need information about the present or recent past, use an almanac.

- An encyclopedia can have one or many volumes. Encyclopedia articles cover a wide range of topics. Use an encyclopedia to get general information on your topic.

- An atlas is a book of maps. Atlases also contain facts about cities, states, countries, and world regions.

- A biographical dictionary contains information about famous people. Examples are *The International Who's Who* and *Who's Who in America*.

### Practice E

Read each question. Write the reference you could use to find the answer. Write *almanac*, *atlas*, *encyclopedia*, or *biographical dictionary*. There may be more than one correct answer.

1. Who is the mayor of El Paso, Texas?
2. What major highways cross Montana?
3. How many people visit the Grand Canyon each year?
4. Who was Albert Einstein?
5. What were the first computers like?

## LIFE SKILLS CONNECTION

Explain to students that they will use research skills throughout their lifetime. As adults, they may want to find out about career opportunities, the safety features of automobiles, or the availability of homes. They may even be required to do research as part of their jobs. Research skills will enable them to find and record the data they need. Pass out Life Skills Connection 13 and have students read the information provided. Explain that students should complete the worksheet as they explore the local or school library.

## Speaking and Presenting Practice

Have students work with partners to prepare a presentation that explains how to use a reference book such as an almanac, an atlas, or an encyclopedia to locate information on a topic. Students' presentations should identify when to use the particular resource, how to use its index, and how the resource is organized. Encourage students to use presentation tools such as posters or handouts.

## Practice E

Read the directions with students. Ask them to tell the kind of information that is found in each reference source. After students have completed the practice activity, discuss their choices.

### *Practice E Answers*

1. almanac  2. atlas  3. almanac
4. biographical dictionary, encyclopedia, almanac  5. encyclopedia

## Writing Practice

Have students choose one of the questions in Practice E, look up the information in the source they identified, and write an answer to the question.

**Reading Strategy:** Summarizing

Possible answer: Periodicals, such as newspapers, magazines, and journals, are printed regularly. They usually have more up-to-date information than books.

## Practice F

Be sure to remind students that they can always ask a librarian for help with card catalogs or computer catalogs. Also, some students will enjoy working on computers. Encourage these students to explore the catalogs. Then they may be able to help other students who are having difficulty.

## Practice F Answers

**1.** The name of the magazine is *Southern Living*. **2.** The article is four pages long. **3.** The article is in volume 30, number 11. **4.** The publication date is November 2006. **5.** Sample answer: It has a volume number and issue number, showing that the source is published on a regular basis.

---

**Periodical**

Any printed material that someone publishes on a regular basis

## Using Periodicals

As you research, look for information in **periodicals.** A periodical is any printed material published on a regular basis. A periodical might be published daily, weekly, or monthly. Newspapers, magazines, and journals are examples of periodicals. Periodicals usually have more up-to-date information than books. They are often available online.

To find articles from periodicals, search the library catalog. Most computer catalogs contain records for periodicals. Suppose you are researching the history of the Olympic Games. Here is a computer catalog entry that appears for the subject *Olympics*. It is an article from a magazine.

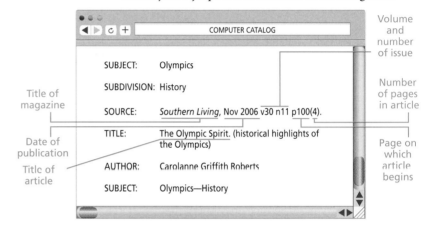

### Practice F

Study the catalog entry above. Then answer each question.

1. What is the name of the magazine?

**Reading Strategy:** Summarizing

How would you sum up this information about periodicals?

2. How long is the article "The Olympic Spirit"?
3. In what issue (volume and number) is the article?
4. What is the publication date of this article?
5. How can you tell that this publication is a periodical?

---

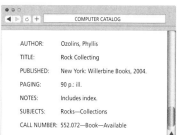

## LESSON 13-3 REVIEW

Answer each question about the catalog entry below.

| | |
|---|---|
| AUTHOR: | Ozolins, Phyllis |
| TITLE: | Rock Collecting |
| PUBLISHED: | New York: Willerbine Books, 2004. |
| PAGING: | 90 p.: ill. |
| NOTES: | Includes index. |
| SUBJECTS: | Rocks—Collections |
| CALL NUMBER: | 552.072—Book—Available |

1. What is the title of this book?

2. What is the subject of this book?

3. Who is the author?

4. What is the call number?

5. How many pages are in the book?

The table of contents and index entry below appear in the same book. Use them to answer each question.

6. On what page would you find information about weight machines?

7. Which chapter tells about stretching?

8. On what page does the chapter on stretching begin?

9. Would this book be useful to research walking as an exercise?

10. On what pages would you find information about free weights?

### Contents

Introduction ................................................. 1
Chapter 1. Aerobic Exercise ............................... 3
Chapter 2. Weight Training ............................. 20
Chapter 3. Walking and Running ...................... 32
Chapter 4. Stretching .................................... 43

### Index

Weights, 21–30
   free, 26, 28
   machines, 29
   *See also* Weight Training

*Preparing to Write a Report*    Chapter 13    **327**

---

*Lesson 13-3 Review Answers*

**1.** *Rock Collecting* **2.** rocks—collections
**3.** Phyllis Ozolins **4.** 552.072 **5.** 90
**6.** page 29 **7.** Chapter 4 **8.** page 43 **9.** yes
**10.** pages 26 and 28

### WRITING PORTFOLIO

**Checkpoint** Students can continue working on the Writing Portfolio project by identifying possible sources of information for their writing topic. Check students' progress and address any questions or concerns they may have.

---

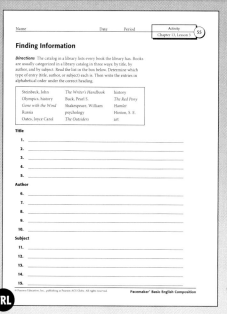

**Activity 55**

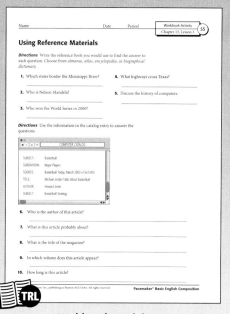

**Workbook Activity 55**

*Preparing to Write a Report*    **327**

### Chapter 13  Lesson 4

**Overview** This lesson explains what online resources are and how to use them.

### Objectives

- To use online resources to find information
- To complete an Internet search using a search engine
- To evaluate information you find on the Internet

**Student Pages** 328–331

**Teacher's Resource Library**

Activity 56

Modified Activity 56

Workbook Activity 56

### Vocabulary

browser          search engine

After defining the technical terms, relate them to words in common usage. For example, relate *browser* to browsing through the books in a bookstore or casually shopping in a clothing store. Relate *search engine* to physically looking for something. For example, if you misplace a backpack, you search, or look all around, for it. In much the same way, a search engine looks for information based on the keywords it is given.

### Background Information

Every Web site has a domain name. All domain names are structured in a similar way. They all have two or more parts separated by dots and end with a suffix that provides clues to the type of organization that operates the Web site. Following are a few of the common domain suffixes:

.com business organizations

.edu educational institutions including universities

.gov government agencies in the United States

.net networks such as Internet service providers

.org nonbusiness organizations

---

**LESSON**
## 13-4   Using Online Resources

### Objectives

- To use online resources to find information
- To complete an Internet search using a search engine
- To evaluate information you find on the Internet

**Browser**
A computer program that allows you to use the information on Internet sites

**Search engine**
A computer program that searches the Internet for keywords and lists the places it finds them

You can use online resources to find information for your report. You need a **browser** to use the information on a Web site. The top line of the browser has a place for you to type in the Web address. If you do not know the Web address, you can find it with a search engine.

A **search engine** will search the Internet for information related to your topic. A search engine is a computer program that searches the Internet for keywords and lists the places it finds them. It gives you a list of the Web sites that might have information about your topic.

Once you get a list of Web sites, review each description to see whether the site might contain information you need. Government and news sites may be very useful to you as you research your topic. Remember to pay attention to the dates on a Web site. Check to see when someone updated the site. Some sites might have old, useless information. Be sure to write down the Web address of each site.

---

### 1  Warm-Up Activity

Although many students have Internet access at home, others do not. Help students identify places where they can go to access the Internet, such as the school, library, or local office resource center.

### 2  Teaching the Lesson

Ask students to describe their experiences using a search engine to locate information. Discuss reasons why they may or may not have been successful. Ask students what they should look for when evaluating information on a Web site. (*Examples of what to look for include current information, factual information, identification of who put the information on the site, and other sources with the same information.*)

**Reading Strategy:**
Summarizing

In one or two sentences, summarize what this lesson is about.

**NOTE**

Spelling is very important when you use a search engine. If you do not spell a word correctly, you may not get the information you are looking for.

## Knowing What to Look Up

Before you start researching your topic, you need two things:

- a list of questions you want to answer in your report
- a list of keywords to use in your search

Suppose you are trying to answer this question: How did Valentine's Day begin? The keyword in that question is *Valentine's Day*. You could look up this phrase in a library catalog, an encyclopedia, or in the index of a book about holidays. In a search engine, you could type *Valentine's Day* or the question *How did Valentine's Day begin?* You might get as many as two or three million Web sites in your list. The search engine will list the top 10 sites first.

### Practice A

Read each question. Write the keyword or keywords that would help you find the answer.

1. What kinds of birds live in Hawaii?
2. What are the rules for the game of lacrosse?
3. What languages do people speak in the Philippines?
4. Are any lizards poisonous?
5. What plays did Lorraine Hansberry write?

### Practice B

Find a computer with a search engine. Type in each keyword. Then go to two or three of the Web sites that the search engine lists. Take some time to explore the available information.

1. hummingbirds
2. World Cup soccer
3. a current movie
4. your favorite TV program
5. William Shakespeare

*Preparing to Write a Report* Chapter 13 **329**

**3** **Reinforce and Extend**

### COMMON ERROR

Students often conclude that information found on Web sites and in books is always accurate. However, they may find opinions or inaccurate facts. Remind students that the facts they use to write a report should be accurate. Suggest that they fact-check their information by finding it in two or more sources. For example, ask them to find the height of the Eiffel Tower in two sources.

**Reading Strategy:** Summarizing

Possible answer: This lesson identifies how to do an Internet search and evaluate the information provided on the Internet.

## Practice A

Remind students that they used keywords to access information in library catalogs. The same keywords can be used to access Internet information. Once again, note that the more specific the keyword, the narrower the search results will be.

## Practice A Answers

Responses may vary. Sample answers follow. **1.** Hawaiian birds **2.** lacrosse rules, rules of lacrosse **3.** Philippine languages, languages of the Philippines **4.** lizards, poisonous lizards (Note: The only poisonous lizard known to the world is native to the desert southwest of the United States and Mexico. Its name is Gila Monster or Beaded Lizard.) **5.** Hansberry, Lorraine or Lorraine Hansberry. (Note: Her most famous play is *A Raisin in the Sun*.)

## Practice B

Encourage students who do not have computer access at home to use classroom or school computers. Ask students to record the name of the Web sites they visit.

## Practice B Answers

Responses will vary. Students should have time to explore and practice searching for information.

*Preparing to Write a Report* **329**

## Practice C

Tell students that sites ending in *.gov*, *.edu*, and *.org* may be more reliable than other sites. Suggest that they consult these sites first when looking for information.

### Practice C Answers

Responses will vary. Discuss the students' findings and conclusions with the class.

### *Reading Strategy:* Summarizing

Possible answer: When choosing Web sites for research, the student should evaluate whether the site is reliable and current.

---

### Recording Web Site Addresses

A list of sources may be required at the end of your report. You will learn more about this list, called a bibliography, in Chapter 14. When you make this list, you will need the complete Web address of each online source you used. When you take notes from a Web site, write down the complete address that appears in your search engine.

### Evaluating Information from the Internet

All Web sites are not the same. Some provide true information, while others contain opinions and rumors. Some Web sites are old and have out-of-date information. Before you use online information for a report, make sure it is good information. Follow these tips:

• Check that a reliable source operates the Web site. You can usually trust government and university sites. Their addresses end with *.gov* or *.edu.*

• Check that the information is current. You may need to look carefully for a copyright date. If there is no date, do not use the information.

• Find another Web site with the same information. You can usually find true information in many places.

• Find out who put the information on the Web site. Is the Web site really an advertisement?

• Think for yourself. Does the information sound true? Do not accept everything you read. Check it out first.

**NOTE**

Web site addresses that end with *.com* are doing business. They may be trying to sell or promote something.

**Reading Strategy:**
Summarizing

What is the most important idea to remember about choosing Web sites to use?

### Practice C

Use the search engine available with your browser. Look for Web sites about your topic. Go to at least five Web sites. Compare the information from each one. Write each Web site address on your paper. Write one or two pieces of information that each site offers about your topic. Use the tips above to decide which sites are reliable.

---

# REVIEW

Write the answer to each question on your paper.

1. What does a browser do?

2. What does a search engine do?

3. What is the name of the search engine that you use on your school computer?

4. What do you enter into a search engine to find Web sites?

5. Why should you check the date of the information on a Web site?

6. What is one way to know if the information on a Web site is true?

Write one keyword you might use to find information on each topic.

7. heart disease

8. Harvard University

9. the most popular movies of the year

10. a list of Grammy winners

## Lesson 13-4 Review Answers

**1.** A browser finds Web sites on the Internet if you enter the Web address. **2.** A search engine uses keywords to find Web sites with the information you are looking for. **3.** Answers will vary. **4.** a keyword **5.** It may be out of date. **6.** Sample answers: Check other Web sites. Use reliable sites such as those with addresses ending in *.gov* or *.edu*. **7.** heart **8.** Harvard **9.** movies **10.** Grammy

## Grammar Practice

Have students write complete sentences to answer questions 1–6 on the Lesson 13-4 Review. Then ask them to underline the subject of each clause or sentence and double underline the verb of each clause or sentence. Work through one example with students:

*A <u>browser</u> <u>finds</u> Web sites on the Internet if <u>you</u> <u>enter</u> the Web address.*

## WRITING PORTFOLIO

**Checkpoint** Have students add to their Writing Portfolio the list of Web sites accessed for Practice C on page 330. Check students' progress and address any questions or concerns they may have.

---

*Preparing to Write a Report*  Chapter 13  **331**

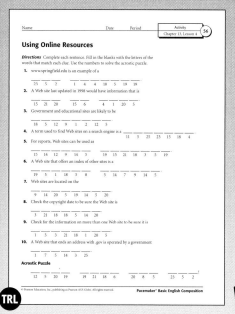

Activity 56

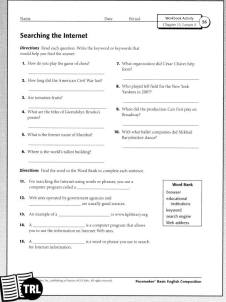

Workbook Activity 56

## Chapter 13  Lesson 5

**Overview**  This lesson focuses on taking notes from and paraphrasing research sources and recording bibliographic information from the sources.

### Objectives

- To take notes
- To paraphrase information
- To record information for a bibliography

**Student Pages**  332–337

**Teacher's Resource Library**

Activity  57

Modified Activity  57

Workbook Activity  57

### Vocabulary

bibliography  plagiarize
paraphrase

Have students look up each word in a dictionary and read its meaning. Provide an example of a bibliography entry and ask students to describe it. Then write the first sentence from the introductory paragraph on page 332 on the board. Tell students that if you used this sentence as it is written in a report, you would be plagiarizing unless you gave the textbook author credit for the sentence.

### Background Information

Some sources have two or more authors. Bibliography entries for these sources are tailored to accommodate the multiple authors. For books with two authors, the first author's name is written with the last name first and then the first name. A comma with the conjunction *and* separates the first author's name from that of the second author. The second name is written with the first name first. Books with more than two authors are handled in much the same way. However, one author's name could be cited and the term *et al.* (Latin for "and others") used in place of the other authors' names.

---

### Objectives

- To take notes
- To paraphrase information
- To record information for a bibliography

**Reading Strategy:** Summarizing

What is the main idea of the first paragraph on this page?

Before you can take notes, you must locate books, magazines, and Web sites that have information about your topic. Think about your report topic and the questions you hope to answer. Make a list of subtopics that you can start researching. Suppose Brandon is preparing a report on vegetable gardening. He has listed four possible subtopics to research:

▶ **EXAMPLE 1**

| Report Topic | growing vegetables |
|---|---|
| Subtopics | how to choose seeds |
| | how to prepare the soil |
| | when to plant each vegetable |
| | when to harvest each vegetable |

As Brandon does his research, he may change or add some subtopics. His list will help him take organized notes.

**Practice A**

Think about your own report topic. Write a list of subtopics to research.

*Find a quiet place to read and take notes.*

---

### 1 Warm-Up Activity

Display a number of books with bibliographies. Ask students to explain their organization. Be sure they note that the entries are arranged alphabetically by the author's last name.

### 2 Teaching the Lesson

Have students focus on the example entries, discussing how the entries for different types of sources—books, periodicals, and Web sites—are alike and different. Make sure students note the punctuation used within each entry. Help students locate the information they need to record on bibliography cards.

### Practice A

Students may want to consult a reference source to help them identify subtopics. Allow students to record their subtopics in a word web rather than a list.

### *Practice A Answers*

Responses will vary according to the topic the student selected. Check the list of subtopics before the student proceeds to the next activity.

### *Reading Strategy:* Summarizing

The main idea is to organize a list of research subtopics for which research information must be found.

**Bibliography**

A list of sources that were used to write a report

**Plagiarize**

To take credit for someone else's words

 **Brush Up on the Basics**

In a report, be sure that proper nouns are capitalized. See Capitalization 3–14 in Appendix A.

*Reading Strategy:*
Summarizing

How do the sample cards in this lesson help you understand the purpose of a bibliography card?

## Keeping Track of Your Sources

As you research various subtopics, you will find many different sources of information. Use index cards to keep track of the sources that seem helpful. Use a separate card for each source you think you will use. These cards will help you make a **bibliography.** A bibliography is a list of the sources you used to write your report. This list goes at the end of your report. Its purpose is to document the information in your report. Most likely, you are not an expert on the topic you write about. Therefore, you need to tell the reader where you got your information. You must always give credit for information and ideas that are not your own. Taking credit for someone else's writing or ideas is **plagiarizing.** Never plagiarize!

For a book, write the author's last name first on the card. Underline the book title. Write the place of publication, the publisher, and the date of publication.

Bartholomew, Mel. *Square Foot Gardening.*
North Adams, Massachusetts: Rodale Press.
2005.

### Practice B

Use the sample card above. Match each item in the first column with the correct information in the second column. Write the letter of your answer on your paper.

1. title                    A  Mel Bartholomew
2. author or editor         B  2005
3. publisher                C  Rodale Press
4. copyright                D  Square Foot Gardening
5. place of publication     E  North Adams, Massachusetts

*Preparing to Write a Report*   *Chapter 13*   **333**

## 3  Reinforce and Extend

### ELL/ESL STRATEGY

**Language Objective:**
*To discuss idioms*

Point out that two idioms are used in the first paragraph on page 333. Explain that an idiom is a phrase that has a meaning separate from the meaning of the individual words. Then write this sentence on the board: *Use index cards to keep track of the sources that seem helpful.* Underline the words "keep track of." Tell students that this idiom means "to follow the course of" or "to have a record of." Encourage students to use the idiom in sentences. If necessary, provide an example, such as "I use a calendar to keep track of my appointments."

Proceed in the same way with the idiom "give credit" in the sentence "You must always give credit for information and ideas that are not your own." The meaning of this idiom is "to recognize or make known the work of."

**Reading Strategy:** Summarizing

The sample cards show the kind of information a bibliography card should have and how that information should be arranged.

### Practice B

Write a sample bibliography card on the board and have students help you identify each part. Label the parts appropriately.

*Practice B Answers*

1. D  2. A  3. C  4. B  5. E

For a magazine article, write the author's last name first. Use quotation marks around the title of the article. Underline the name of the magazine. Include the volume number, date, and page numbers of the article.

> *Aziz, Martha. "Weeding and Watering,"*
> <u>*Gardening Today*</u> *10 (July 3, 2004).*

If you use an article from a Web site, write the author's last name first. Use quotation marks around the title of an article. Underline the name of a publication. Include the Web site. Include the volume number and publication date if available. Include the date that the site was last updated.

> *Ling, Marla. "Tips for City Gardeners."*
> *www.gardeners.org. 2006*

### Taking Notes

Once you have recorded the details about a source, you are ready to read it. When you find good information, stop and write it down. These are your notes. Use index cards to take notes. They are easy to put in order when you begin to write your report.

On each card, write the topic or subtopic that the notes will be about. Then write the notes. At the bottom, write where you found the information.

Look at Brandon's note card on the next page. Notice that he wrote a topic and subtopic at the top. At the bottom, he listed the source in a shortened form.

**Brush Up on the Basics**

If you use the exact words from a source, it must be a direct quotation in your report. Make sure you use quotation marks at the beginning and the end of a direct quotation. See Punctuation 16–18 in Appendix A.

**NOTE**

A synonym is a word that has the same meaning as another word. When paraphrasing information, you can use a thesaurus to find synonyms.

## Practice C

Use Brandon's note card below to answer each question.

1. What is the topic of this note card?
2. What is the subtopic?
3. What advice does the author give?
4. Who is the author?
5. On what page of the source did Brandon find this information?

---

*Choosing Seeds*

*Quality matters.*

*"Home gardeners will reduce the chance of disappointment if they choose high quality seeds." (p. 81)*

*It is important to read the information on the packages.*

*Jones, p. 81*

---

### Paraphrasing

As you take notes, use quotation marks around a writer's exact words. The other words in your notes should be your own. Instead of copying words and sentences, **paraphrase** the ideas you read about. When you paraphrase, you express someone else's ideas in your own words. In Example 2 on the next page, compare the direct quotation with the paraphrased notes.

## Practice C

Discuss the sample note card on page 335. Ask: Why are quotation marks placed around the first sentence? *(This sentence cites the exact words of the author.)* Why are quotation marks not used around the second sentence? *(This sentence paraphrases the author's information.)*

### Practice C Answers

**1.** Choosing seeds **2.** Quality matters **3.** Choose high quality seeds. Read the information on the packages. **4.** Jones **5.** page 81

### LEARNING STYLES

**Interpersonal/Group Learning**

Remind students that a paraphrase expresses the author's ideas in one's own words. Organize students into small groups. Assign each group a page of text from this book to paraphrase. Allow students to use dictionaries or thesauruses to help them in the task. Have students share the original copy and their paraphrase with the class.

## Practice D

Before students begin Practice D, point out that a paraphrase may be longer or shorter than the original document. Make sure students understand all the terms in the passage. They need to understand these terms so that they can paraphrase them.

### Practice D Answers

Responses will vary. Possible paraphrase is: According to Jones, it is important to order seeds early. Also, only order as many seeds as you need for one year. Seeds come in many varieties and are not likely to get a disease. It's possible that the seeds could last five years, but some only last one year.

## Practice E

Review the information in bibliography cards and note cards. Then have students begin taking notes for their topic.

### Practice E Answers

Responses will vary.

▶ **EXAMPLE 2**

**Quotation**   "By the late twentieth century, some population experts were warning of dangers. They pointed to evidence that planet Earth no longer had the agricultural and energy resources to support its enormous human population."

**Paraphrase**   Scientists of the late twentieth century were studying population changes. Some warned that there were too many people in the world. Because food and fuel were running out, many lives could be in danger.

### Practice D

The paragraph below is a direct quotation from a book. Paraphrase the information in this paragraph. Rearrange ideas. Use synonyms. Add or delete words.

"Order seeds well in advance of the planting season. Gardeners should order only the amount of seeds that they need for one growing season. Most seeds come in many varieties and can resist disease. Some seeds last for as long as five years, but others cannot be used after only one year."

### Practice E

Begin taking notes on your report topic. Follow these steps:

1. Find books, articles, and Web sites with information on your topic.

2. Prepare a bibliography card for each source you plan to use.

3. Take notes on index cards. Write a main topic or a subtopic at the top of each card. Put quotation marks around direct quotations. Paraphrase other information. Briefly identify the source.

**Card 1**

Chan, Maggie. *Interior Design*. Toronto: Colby Publishing, 2003.

**Card 2**

*Home Projects*. April 9, 2005. www.homeproj.com (June 5, 2005).

**Card 3**

Wilson, Kevin. "Using Decorative Fabrics." *Interiors 5* (April 10, 2007) 34–38.

**Card 4**

Decorating with Fabric
Fabrics can change the look of a room. "Fabrics such as velvet and silk will give a room a formal look. Denim and linen are more casual." (p. 36) Choose a fabric that will complement the decor.
Wilson, p. 36

Use the sample cards above to answer each question.

1. Which bibliography card is for a magazine article?

2. Which bibliography card is for a Web site?

3. Which bibliography card is for a book?

4. Who wrote the article "Using Decorative Fabrics"?

5. Why do the words *Decorating with Fabric* appear at the top of card 4?

6. What is the Home Projects Web site address?

7. Which of the sources has the most current information?

8. One card lists information found in the article by Kevin Wilson. On what page of the article was this information found?

9. Who is the author of the book *Interior Design*?

10. On what pages in the magazine is the article by Kevin Wilson?

*Lesson 13-5 Review Answers*
**1.** Card 3 **2.** Card 2 **3.** Card 1 **4.** Kevin Wilson **5.** It is a note card. That is the topic. **6.** www.homeproj.com **7.** the magazine, Card 3 **8.** page 36 **9.** Maggie Chan **10.** pages 34–38

## WRITING PORTFOLIO

**Checkpoint** Have students order and clip or band their bibliography cards alphabetically for easy reference. Check students' progress and address any questions or concerns they may have.

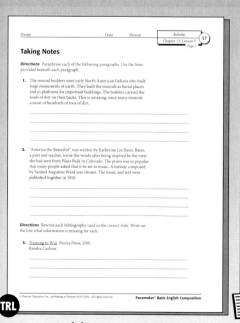

**Activity 57, pages 1–2**

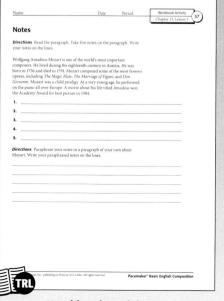

**Workbook Activity 57**

### Chapter 13  Lesson 6

**Overview**  This lesson focuses on the structure and development of writing outlines.

#### Objectives

- To sort note cards by topics and subtopics
- To organize information about a topic into a logical order
- To create an outline

#### Student Pages  338–345

#### Teacher's Resource Library **TRL**

Activity  58

Modified Activity  58

Workbook Activity  58

English in Your Life  7

Building Research Skills  13

## Vocabulary

#### outline

Have students examine the sample outline on page 341 and use it to write their own definition of the term. They can use the book's definition to check theirs.

## Background Information

In an outline, the entries for main topics are identified by Roman numerals. These numerals, used throughout Europe until the 1500s, have no place value. The numbers are written from left to right with the largest number written first. For example, 2,014 is written MMXIV.

| | | | |
|---|---|---|---|
| 1 | I | 9 | IX |
| 2 | II | 10 | X |
| 3 | III | 11 | XI |
| 4 | IV | 20 | XX |
| 5 | V | 50 | L |
| 6 | VI | 100 | C |
| 7 | VII | 500 | D |
| 8 | VIII | 1,000 | M |

---

# Creating an Outline

#### Objectives

- To sort note cards by topics and subtopics
- To organize information about a topic into a logical order
- To create an outline

**Reading Strategy:** Summarizing

Summarize the steps you would use to organize note cards.

When you have finished finding information, you will have many note cards. Before you can write your report, you need to organize your information and put it in order.

### Sorting Your Note Cards

Look at the topic or subtopic written at the top of each note card. Sort your cards. Put notes about the same topic or subtopic together.

If you have only one card on a topic, see whether it fits with one of the other topics. If you have a large pile of cards on one topic, you may need to separate them into subtopics.

Some of your notes may not fit anywhere. You do not have to use all of the information that you found when you researched your topic.

Brandon is writing a report about growing vegetables. He sorted his note cards into five groups, as shown in Example 1.

▶ **EXAMPLE 1**

Main Topics   planning the garden
choosing the seeds
harvesting
caring for the plants
preparing the soil

---

## 1  Warm-Up Activity

Write a set of ten index cards naming or showing vegetables and a set of ten cards for flowers. Mix the cards and ask students to organize them in some way. Talk about the different ways the cards could be organized. Alternatively, provide sets of objects, such as buttons, and have students organize them in several different ways.

**Reading Strategy:** Summarizing

Students should identify the main topics and subtopics and then sort the cards by those topics and subtopics.

## 2  Teaching the Lesson

Discuss the outline format, using the example on page 341. Make sure students understand that the topics and subtopics are ordered numerically and alphabetically. Main topics are identified by Roman numerals. Subtopics of the main topics are identified by capital letters. Subtopics of the capital letter entries are identified by Arabic numerals. As a class, develop an outline on the board by organizing an experience students have in common. For example, you might develop an outline for *A Typical School Day*. Main headings might include *Before School*, *The School Day*, and *After School*.

## Practice A

The bold word in each set is the main topic. Write each main topic. Next to it, write the subtopics that belong. Ignore any subtopics that do not relate to the main topic.

1. **furniture:** chair, table, window, sofa

2. **books:** magazine, dictionary, almanac, atlas

3. **clothes:** coat, hat, jewelry, shirt

4. **sports:** hockey, football, athlete, tennis

5. **musical instruments:** trumpet, band, clarinet, oboe

## Practice B

Look over the note cards you have been making for your report. Sort the cards by main topics. Write a list of your main topics in your report.

### Organizing the Information

Think about the main topics you have listed for your report. How will you present these topics in a logical order? There are many ways to organize the information. Choose the order that best fits your report topic. Study these possible arrangements:

- Chronological order—According to the time that the events happened

- Order of importance—From most important to least important (or from least important to most important)

- Order of size or cost—From largest to smallest, or from most expensive to least expensive

- Other orders—First, second, third; from easiest to hardest; from most popular to least popular; from nearest to farthest

## Practice A

Have students use their own words to tell the difference between a main topic and a subtopic.

## *Practice A Answers*

1. chair, table, sofa  2. dictionary, almanac, atlas  3. coat, hat, shirt  4. hockey, football, tennis  5. trumpet, clarinet, oboe

## Practice B

Have students gather and sort their note cards by main topic. Allow time for students to organize their cards. Then have them write a list of their main topics for their written report. Suggest that they use four to eight main topics.

## *Practice B Answers*

Responses will vary, but main topics should support the report topic.

---

**3  Reinforce and Extend**

### LEARNING STYLES

**Logical/Mathematical**
Have pairs of students develop a set of symbols or icons for the first three bulleted topic arrangements on page 339. Explain that each icon should be a visual representation of the type of organization. Afterward, invite the pairs to share their icons with the class. Choose a set of class icons and post them in the classroom to help students remember three ways to organize information.

# ELL/ESL STRATEGY

**Language Objective:**
*To identify and practice using an outline format*

Explain to students that an outline can be developed using words and phrases or complete sentences. Point out that the sample outline on page 341 uses words and phrases. Provide an example of how you might rewrite the first main topic in the sample outline on page 341. *(The first step is to plan the garden.)* Have English language learners work with partners to rewrite the rest of the outline entries in sentences. Then have students prepare a blank outline format. Ask them to use the format to outline this chapter. Suggest that they use the lesson titles as the main topics for the outline. They can discuss whether to add subtopics to the outline. Tell students that they can use their chapter outlines as useful study tools.

## COMMON ERROR

Students often list a single subtopic under a topic. Tell students that a topic is only divided if there are two or more subtopics.

## Practice C

Go over the directions with students. Tell them to use the listing of possible arrangements on page 339 as a reference.

### *Practice C Answers*

Answers may vary. Sample responses: **1.** chronological order—planning, choosing, preparing the soil, caring for the plants, harvesting **2.** least popular to most popular; organize by size of dog; organize by dog names in alphabetical order **3.** easiest way to most complicated; most effective to least effective; most common way to least common or vice versa **4.** most promising to least promising; least important to most important **5.** the five countries where soccer is most popular; the five reasons soccer is popular

Suppose Amber is writing a report on the history of computers. How should she arrange her information?

▶ **EXAMPLE 2**

| | |
|---|---|
| Report Topic | history of computers |
| Logical Order | chronological order, starting with the earliest computers and ending with the most recent computer technology |

### Practice C

Decide on an order for the information in each report. Suggest at least one way to arrange the information.

1. Brandon's report is about growing vegetables. His main topics are planning the garden, choosing the seeds, caring for the plants, harvesting, and preparing the soil.

2. Amber is investigating popular breeds of dogs in the United States. She has information about the five most popular breeds.

3. Sonia is investigating firefighting methods. She has facts on several ways to put out a fire.

4. Derek has researched four possible energy sources of the future.

5. Luis's report is about the popularity of soccer around the world.

### Practice D

Look over your list of main topics for your report. Decide on a logical order for your information. Describe this order and explain why you think it will work.

## Practice D

Remind students that they compiled the list of main topics for Practice B. Have them consult the list of possible arrangements on page 339 to help identify ways to organize their topics.

### *Practice D Answers*

Responses will vary. This is the ongoing chapter project that students are doing for their own report.

## Creating an Outline

An **outline** is a plan for writing a report. It lists topics and subtopics in a certain order. If you make an outline for your report, you will know what to write first, next, and last. A good outline makes writing a report easier.

Look at Brandon's outline below. He has chosen to use chronological order.

When you make an outline, use this format:

- List the main topics with Roman numerals (I, II, etc.).
- Indent the subtopics under each main topic. List these with capital letters (A, B, etc.).
- Indent the next level of subtopics even farther. List these with Arabic numerals (1, 2, etc.).

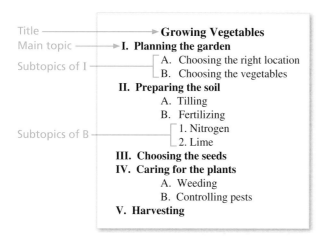

```
Title ─────────────▶ Growing Vegetables
Main topic ────────▶ I.  Planning the garden
Subtopics of I ─────    A.  Choosing the right location
                        B.  Choosing the vegetables
                    II. Preparing the soil
                        A.  Tilling
                        B.  Fertilizing
Subtopics of B ─────        1. Nitrogen
                            2. Lime
                   III. Choosing the seeds
                    IV. Caring for the plants
                        A.  Weeding
                        B.  Controlling pests
                     V. Harvesting
```

### Practice E

Look at the list of main topics for your report. Think about the order in which to present them. Add subtopics to your list. Write an outline for your report.

---

**Reading Strategy:** Summarizing

An outline is designed to provide a plan for writing by placing topics in a particular order.

### LEARNING STYLES

**Body/Kinesthetic**

Make an outline for a long encyclopedia article or textbook chapter. Cut apart the main topics and subtopics. Give one slip of paper to each student. Challenge students to read each other's headings and to arrange themselves across the front of the room to match the order of the original outline.

## Practice E

Read the instructions for Practice E along with the class. Encourage them to use Brandon's outline on page 341 as a guide if they have difficulty. Check their progress as they work. Address any questions or concerns.

## Practice E Answers

Outlines will vary but should show a logical arrangement of topics and subtopics as well as proper format.

## Lesson 13-6 Review Answers

**1.** Responses may vary. This activity requires some prior knowledge of the topics.

**List A:** Basic Car Care
I. Electrical system
  A. Battery
  B. Spark plugs
II. Cooling system
  A. Water pump
  B. Radiator
  C. Hoses
III. Engine lubrication
  A. Replacing the oil filter
  B. Changing the oil

**List B:** Jazz Music
I. Instruments used
  A. Trombone
  B. Trumpet
II. Important people
  A. Soloists
  B. Composers
III. Places to listen
  A. Concert halls
  B. Music clubs
  C. Radio

**2.** Responses may vary. Students should be able to explain their organization. Sample:

Olympic Games
I.  The importance of the Olympics
II.  How the games began
III.  Famous Olympic athletes
IV.  Summer games
V.  Winter games

### WRITE ABOUT IT

Students may want access to Internet, radio, or TV weather information or weather-related tools such as a thermometer, barometer, and hygrometer.

### Six Traits of Writing Focus

| | | | |
|---|---|---|---|
| | Ideas | | Word Choice |
| ✔ | Organization | ✔ | Sentence Fluency |
| | Voice | | Conventions |

### Organization

Have pairs of students exchange paragraphs. Have students suggest three ways the organization of their partner's paragraph could be improved. Then have the authors revise their work.

Remind students that smooth sentence fluency helps unite different parts of a paragraph. Tell students to consider adding transitional words and phrases.

Refer students to page WPH1 for descriptions of the Six Traits of Writing.

**342** *Chapter 13*

---

**List A:**
Basic Car Care

electrical system
water pump
engine lubrication
radiator
hoses
battery
replacing the oil filter
cooling system
changing the oil
spark plugs

**List B:**
Jazz Music

soloists
instruments used
trumpet
concert halls
important people
trombone
radio
music clubs
places to listen
composers

 **Six Traits of Writing:**
*Organization* order, ideas tied together

Follow each set of directions.

**1.** Read the two lists of topics and subtopics at the left. Choose either List A or List B. Rearrange the topics and subtopics into a logical order. Write an outline. Refer to the sample outline on page 341 as a guide.

**2.** Read the main topics below. They are for a report on the Olympic Games. Decide on a logical order to present these topics. Then list the topics in the order in which you would present them. Tell why you think your order is a good one.

**Report Title: Olympic Games**

**Main Topics:** summer games
        winter games
        famous Olympic athletes
        the importance of the Olympics
        how the games began

### WRITE ABOUT IT

**The Weather**
The weather affects your life in many ways. Much of what you do depends on temperature, wind, rain, or snow. Write a paragraph describing today's weather and its effect on you.
• Include some facts about the temperature, the precipitation, the cloud formation, the wind, or the humidity.
• Describe how the weather affected what you wore to school.
• Tell how it affected what you did today.
• Record how you feel about today's weather.
Include an interesting topic sentence and a conclusion. Give your paragraph a title. Then read your paragraph to another student.

---

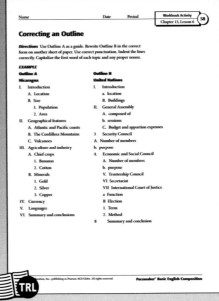

**Activity 58**

**Workbook Activity 58**

## Writing a Résumé

Joe Peterson wanted a job in sales. His town has four car dealerships. He wrote a résumé to tell about his skills and his past work. He tried to show all his good points. He made sure there were no mistakes in spelling or capitalization. Then he typed the résumé neatly. He took a copy of his résumé to the manager of each dealership. Read a section of Joe's résumé below. This section tells about his work experience. Then answer the questions.

### Experience

| | |
|---|---|
| 2004–2007 | Worked weekends at Bob's Auto Repair, 1919 W. Lincoln Highway<br>**Duties:** assist mechanics, change oil in cars |
| 2002–2004 | Worked in summer at Pete's Car Wash, 284 N. Fleet St.<br>**Duties:** wash and detail cars |

1. What does a résumé contain?

2. What is Joe's work experience?

3. **CRITICAL THINKING** How might Joe's past jobs help him get a job selling cars?

## SPEAKING AND LISTENING

When you are interviewed for a job, you can expect questions like these:
- What can you tell me about yourself?
- Why should I hire you?
- What qualities does it take to be a good _____?

Work with a partner. Choose an interesting job. Take turns interviewing each other for this job. Give clear, positive answers that show your good points.

Have students read the feature title and briefly discuss what a résumé is. Then ask students to read the feature silently and answer the questions.

### English in Your Life Answers

**1.** It tells the education, skills, and work experience of someone looking for a job. **2.** Joe worked three summers washing and detailing cars. Then he worked several years on weekends helping mechanics at an auto repair shop. **3.** His jobs have taught him a lot about cars.

---

TRL

English in Your Life 7

Display a variety of nonfiction books with tables of contents. Help students locate the table of contents in each book, pointing out that these pages follow the title and copyright pages and may also be preceded by a preface. Use the tables of contents to identify the different organizations of the books. Some books may have a unit and chapter organization whereas others may have only chapters. Ask questions to help students examine the tables of contents you display. For example, ask: Does this book have a unit and chapter organization? How many chapters are in this book? Does this book have an index? Discuss how the titles of the chapters provide clues to the chapter content. Ask questions such as What do you think Chapter 5 is about?

### Building Research Skills Answers

**1.** Chapter 3 **2.** It lists the titles of chapters in the book and the page on which each chapter begins. **3.** The table of contents shows the main ideas or topics covered. The index tells the page numbers where specific topics are discussed.

## Checking a Table of Contents

Suppose you find a book that looks helpful to your research. Turn first to the table of contents. This is a list in the front of the book. The table of contents lists the chapters of the book. It also lists the page on which each chapter begins. The chapter titles show the main ideas covered in the book.

Check whether any chapters in the book discuss your topic. Look at the sample table of contents below. For a report on hot air balloons, Chapter 2 would be helpful.

```
Table of Contents


Chapter 1
The Dream of Flight ..........4

Chapter 2
Hot Air Balloons and
    Gliders ...................21

Chapter 3
The First Airplane ..........53
```

If your topic is more specific, look in the index at the end of the book. It lists the topics discussed in the book in alphabetical order. It also gives the pages on which the topic is discussed.

Answer the following questions.

**1.** Look at the sample table of contents. Which chapter will help you if you need information about the earliest airplanes?

**2.** What information does a table of contents have?

**3.** **CRITICAL THINKING** How is a table of contents different from an index?

### TECHNOLOGY

A Web site will often have a menu on its home page, or main page. The menu is like an online table of contents. The menu lists the topics that the site covers. To go to a certain topic, click on that topic in the menu. Sometimes, whole textbooks are available online. Visit a Web site that interests you. Look at its menu and click on a topic. Write something new that you read there.

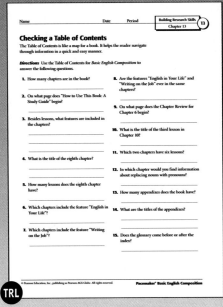

**Building Research Skills 13**

# SUMMARY

- Choose a report topic that interests you. List questions about your topic that you would like to answer.

- Choose a topic that matches the length of your report. The topic should not be too broad or too narrow.

- Check out your topic in a library catalog to make sure there is enough information available.

- Make a list of keywords. Use them to search for information in a library catalog or on the Internet.

- Use call numbers to find books on the library shelves. Use the table of contents and index of a book to find out if it contains the information you need.

- Use a variety of reference books, periodicals, and books. Use only reliable information from Web sites.

- Record information about your sources on index cards. You will use the cards later to prepare a bibliography.

- Write notes on index cards. Do not plagiarize. Either record direct quotations or rewrite information in your own words.

- Sort and organize your note cards. Choose a logical order for presenting the main topics.

- Make an outline showing the order of topics and subtopics. This will make writing the report easier.

- Include a topic paragraph, a body, and a summary paragraph in your report. In the topic paragraph, state the main idea and give your opinion.

## GROUP ACTIVITY

Work with a group to choose a report topic and find information. First, decide your purpose and audience. Then, decide on your topic. Next, brainstorm subtopic ideas.

Each member can do library or computer research on a subtopic. Take careful notes. Explain what you learned to your group. Then write an outline using your notes.

## Chapter 13 Summary

Have volunteers read aloud each Summary item on page 345. Ask volunteers to explain the meaning of each item.

### ONLINE CONNECTION

Students can find help for different aspects of report writing at the following Web sites:

www.agsglobepmbec.com/page345a
This Web site offers advice about researching and writing a school report.

www.agsglobepmbec.com/page345b
This Web site identifies what primary sources are and provides links to Web sites with major collections.

### GROUP ACTIVITY

Suggest that group members brainstorm a list of possible topics and choose a topic from the list. Groups may wish to divide tasks so that some students research Internet sources and others find information in books and periodicals. Students can compile their cards, sort them by topics, and refer to them when preparing outlines. Remind students about the structure and content of bibliography cards, note cards, and outlines.

# Chapter 13 Review

Use the Chapter Review to prepare students for tests and to reteach content from the chapter.

## Chapter 13 Mastery Test

The Teacher's Resource Library includes two forms of the Chapter 13 Mastery Test. Each test addresses the chapter Goals for Learning. An optional third page of additional critical-thinking items is included for each test. The difficulty level of the two forms is equivalent.

## *Review Answers*

### Part A

**1.** browser **2.** outline **3.** search engine **4.** report **5.** plagiarize **6.** subtopic **7.** table of contents **8.** paraphrase **9.** research **10.** call number **11.** index **12.** bibliography **13.** periodical **14.** keywords **15.** catalog

### Word Bank

bibliography
browser
call number
catalog
index
keywords
outline
paraphrase
periodical
plagiarize
report
research
search engine
subtopic
table of contents

**Part A** Find the word or words in the Word Bank that complete each sentence. Write your answer on your paper.

1. You need a _____ to connect to Web sites on the Internet.

2. An _____ is a plan for writing a report.

3. Use keywords and a _____ to find Web sites on the Internet.

4. A _____ is an organized summary of information about a topic.

5. Do not _____, or take credit for another person's ideas.

6. A _____ is a part of a larger topic.

7. A _____ lists the parts of a book and the page on which each part begins.

8. To _____ is to express someone else's ideas in your own words.

9. To _____ is to find information about a topic.

10. A _____ identifies a book and tells you where the book is located in the library.

11. The _____ of a book is an alphabetical list of all the topics and subtopics in the book.

12. A list of the sources a writer used to write a report is a _____.

13. Any printed material published on a regular basis is a _____.

14. Use _____ to help you search for information on a topic.

15. The library _____ is designed to help you locate books on a certain topic.

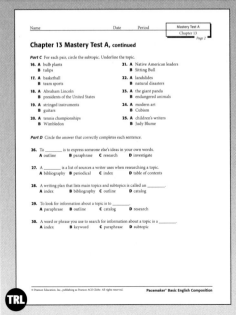

**Part B** Decide which of the topics below are included in this textbook, *Basic English Composition*. Use the table of contents and the index. Write *yes* if the topic is included. If the topic is not included, write *no*.

**16.** footnotes     **17.** clauses     **18.** outlines

**Part C** Paraphrase each direct quotation in one sentence.

**19.** "With a lifetime batting average of .317, Pittsburgh Pirates outfielder Roberto Clemente was an outstanding baseball player."

**20.** "The animal known as the big brown bat is actually only about 4 inches long."

**Part D** Write the letter of the answer to each question.

**21.** Which book would you find shelved near the nonfiction book *Mockingbirds and Other Songbirds* by Devon Jackson?
   **A** *To Kill a Mockingbird* by Harper Lee (fiction)
   **B** *How Birds Communicate* by Tina Rush (nonfiction)
   **C** *Song of Solomon* by Toni Morrison (fiction)
   **D** *Great Gospel Songs* by Bill Allan (nonfiction)

**22.** Which of the following is not a part of a report?
   **A** topic paragraph     **C** body
   **B** summary paragraph     **D** plagiarized sentences

**23.** Before you write a report, what do you need to have?
   **A** note cards     **C** bibliography cards
   **B** an outline     **D** all of the above

**Part E** Write the answer to each question.

**24.** Why do you need to write a bibliography card for each source you use?

**25.** Why do you need to evaluate Internet information?

**Test Tip**

When you answer an essay question, use transitional words and phrases. Transitions help you organize your ideas.

**WRITING PORTFOLIO**

**Wrap-Up** Have students review their note cards and outline. Ask them to consider these questions: Have you provided a good organization for writing a report? Do you need to add or delete subtopics from the outline? Have students make sure their note cards are organized and their outline is complete. They can then use these in writing a report in the next chapter. This project may be used as an alternative form of assessment for the chapter.

Chapter 13 Mastery Test B, pages 1–3

# Writing the Final Report

| | Student Pages | Vocabulary | Practice Exercises | Lesson Review | Identification | Writing | Punctuation & Capitalization | Grammar & Usage | Listening, Speaking, & Viewing | |
|---|---|---|---|---|---|---|---|---|---|---|
| | | **Student Lesson** | | | **Language Skills** | | | | | |
| **Lesson 14-1** Writing the First Draft | 351–355 | ✔ | ✔ | ✔ | ✔ | ✔ | ✔ | ✔ | ✔ | |
| **Lesson 14-2** Revising the Report | 356–359 | | ✔ | ✔ | ✔ | ✔ | ✔ | ✔ | ✔ | |
| **Lesson 14-3** Editing the Report | 360–363 | ✔ | ✔ | ✔ | ✔ | ✔ | ✔ | ✔ | ✔ | |
| **Lesson 14-4** Preparing a Bibliography | 364–367 | | ✔ | ✔ | ✔ | ✔ | ✔ | ✔ | ✔ | |
| **Lesson 14-5** Publishing the Final Report | 368–373 | ✔ | ✔ | ✔ | ✔ | ✔ | ✔ | ✔ | ✔ | |

## Chapter Activities

**Teacher's Resource Library**
Life Skills Connection 14: Writing a
   Short Report
Writing Tip 14: Using a Drafting
   Checklist
Writing on the Job 7: Bicycle
   Salesperson
Building Research Skills 14:
   Formatting a Document
Key Vocabulary Words 14

## Assessment Options

**Student Text**
Chapter 14 Review

**Teacher's Resource Library**
Chapter 14 Mastery Tests A and B
Chapters 1–14 Final Mastery Test

**Teacher's Edition**
Chapter 14 Writing Portfolio

| | Student Text Features | | | | | | | | | Teaching Strategies | | | | | | | | | Learning Styles | | | | | Teacher's Resource Library | | | |
|---|---|---|---|---|---|---|---|---|---|---|---|---|---|---|---|---|---|---|---|---|---|---|---|---|---|---|---|
| English in Your Life | Writing on the Job | Building Research Skills | Vocabulary Builder | Grammar Builder | Write About It | Group Activity | Reading Strategy | Six Traits | ELL/ESL Strategy | Background Information | Common Error | Life Skills Connection | Applications (Home, Career, Community, Global) | Online Connection | Teacher Alert | Speaking & Presenting Practice | Writing/Spelling/Grammar Practice | Auditory/Verbal | Body/Kinesthetic | Interpersonal/Group Learning | Logical/Mathematical | Visual/Spatial | Activities | Modified Activities | Workbook Activities | Self-Study Guide |
| | | | | 353 | | | 352, 354 | | 353 | 351 | 352 | | 353, 354 | | 352 | | | | | 352 | | 351 | 59 | 59 | 59 | ✔ |
| | | | | | | | 356, 357 | | 357 | 356 | 357, 358 | | | | | | 357, 359 | | | | | | 60 | 60 | 60 | ✔ |
| | | | | | | | 360, 361 | | 362 | 360 | 362 | | 361 | | | | 361, 363 | 363 | | | 361 | | 61 | 61 | 61 | ✔ |
| | | | 367 | | | | 364, 365 | | 366 | 364 | 365 | 365 | | | 364 | | 365 | | | | | | 62 | 62 | 62 | ✔ |
| 371 | 372 | | | | 370 | 373 | 369 | | 371 | 368 | 369 | | 370 | 373 | | 372 | 369 | | 369 | | | | 63 | 63 | 63 | ✔ |

## Pronunciation Key

| | | | | | | | |
|---|---|---|---|---|---|---|---|
| a | hat | e | let | ī | ice | ô | order | ù | put | sh | she |
| ā | age | ē | equal | o | hot | oi | oil | ü | rule | th | thin |
| ä | far | ėr | term | ō | open | ou | out | ch | child | ᵺ | then |
| â | care | i | it | ȯ | saw | u | cup | ng | long | zh | measure |

ə {
a in about
e in taken
i in pencil
o in lemon
u in circus
}

## Modified Activities

The Teacher's Resource Library (TRL) contains a set of lower-level worksheets called Modified Activities. These worksheets cover the same content as the standard Activities but are written at a lower reading level.

## Skill Track

Use Skill Track for *Basic English Composition* to monitor student progress and meet the demands of adequate yearly progress (AYP). Make informed instructional decisions with individual student and class reports of lesson and chapter assessments. With immediate and ongoing feedback, students will also see what they have learned and where they need more reinforcement and practice.

**Skill Track for
Basic English
Composition**

**Teacher's Resource Library** (TRL)

Activities 59–63

Modified Activities 59–63

Workbook Activities 59–63

Life Skills Connection  14

Writing Tip  14

Writing on the Job  7

Building Research Skills  14

Key Vocabulary Words  14

Chapter 14 Self-Study Guide

Chapter 14 Mastery Tests A and B

Chapters 1–14 Final Mastery Test

(Answer Keys for the Teacher's
Resource Library begin on page 446
of the Teacher's Edition.)

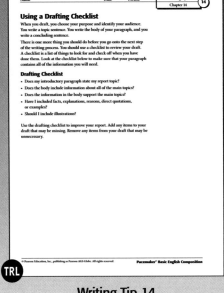

Writing Tip 14

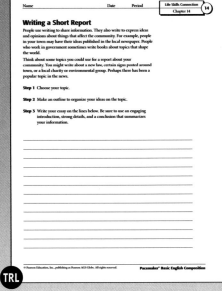

Life Skills Connection 14

# Writing the Final Report

**A**fter a long day, you need to rest and get ready for tomorrow. How can a calendar help you plan ahead? This photo shows a date when a final report is due. When you plan your time, you must remember tasks due tomorrow as well as tasks due much later.

Imagine you have a week left to write a final report. Do not wait until the last night to write it! Plan ahead. Make a schedule and give yourself the time to create a report you can be proud of.

Chapter 14 will give you the tools you need to revise, edit, and publish a report. It will also explain how to prepare a bibliography, which is a list of your sources.

## GOALS FOR LEARNING

- To write the first draft of a report
- To revise the content of a report
- To edit a report to fix mistakes in grammar, spelling, capitalization, punctuation, and word choice
- To prepare a bibliography
- To publish a final report

**349**

## Introducing the Chapter

Have students examine the photograph on page 348. Tell them to imagine this is their calendar and that they have circled the date. Have them imagine they have an important research report due on this date. Students may reason that they have plenty of time. Discuss with them the idea of a process. Point out that in this chapter they will learn the process of completing a final draft. Give them a deadline for their research reports and circle it on your calendar.

Review and discuss the Goals for Learning on page 349.

## Notes

Ask volunteers to read the notes that appear in the margins throughout the chapter. Then discuss them with the class.

## TEACHER'S RESOURCE

The AGS Globe Teaching Strategies in English Transparencies may be used with this chapter. The transparencies add an interactive dimension to expand and enhance the *Basic English Composition* program content.

## WRITING PORTFOLIO

Explain to students that they will use the five writing process steps to write a research report. They have already completed the prewriting step in Chapter 13. In this chapter, students will write a first draft, revise and edit the draft, prepare a bibliography, and publish the finished product. Express to students that they will work to complete this report while working through Chapter 14. These products can be used as an alternative form of assessment for the chapter.

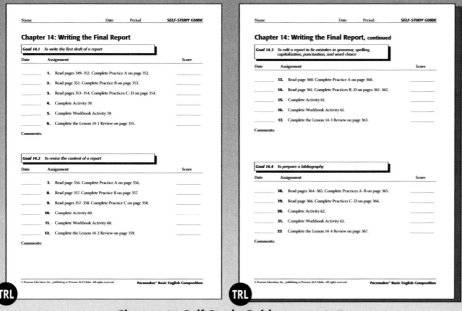

Chapter 14 Self-Study Guide, pages 1–3

## Reading Strategy:
## Text Structure

Explain to students how they can use the organizational structure of a text to better understand what they read. They can look to bold words, titles, or chapter headings to help remember the most important parts of a text. Use the checklist on page 350 to study the text structure of this chapter. How is the chapter organized? What are the key ideas?

.......................................................

## Key Vocabulary Words

draft                    publish
mechanics

Write *draft* and *mechanics* on the board. Have volunteers read the meanings of the terms aloud. Discuss with students the fact that these words have multiple meanings. Have them write a sentence for each meaning discussed. Then write *publish* on the board. Have a volunteer read the meaning aloud. Discuss with them what types of materials are published, both in and out of school. Direct them to write one or two sentences using the term.

.......................................................

# Reading Strategy: Text Structure

A textbook is organized to show what is important. Important ideas are often shown as titles or bold words. Examples give support to the main ideas. As you preview this chapter, notice how it is organized.

- Look at the chapter title, lesson titles, and Examples.
- Turn back a page to read the chapter's Goals for Learning.
- Ask yourself: How did the writer order the lessons in this chapter?
- Look at the parts of each lesson. Which parts are repeated in every lesson?
- Summarize the chapter by using its structure.

## Key Vocabulary Words

**Draft** An early version of writing; not the final version

**Mechanics** The spelling, capitalization, and punctuation of a written piece

**Publish** To share a written or visual message with others

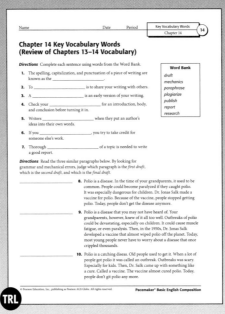

# Writing the First Draft

## Objectives

■ To write a topic paragraph

■ To use notes to write the body of a report

■ To use direct quotations in a report

■ To write a summary paragraph

**Draft**
An early version of writing; not the final version

*Brandon's report will explain how to stake tomato plants.*

Once you have finished your note cards and your outline, you are ready to write your report. The first version of your report is called the first **draft.** A draft is an early version of something you write. A draft is not the final version. To write your first draft, use the outline you created in Chapter 13. When you use an outline as a guide, the writing process is much easier.

### Writing the Topic Paragraph

Begin your report with a topic paragraph. This paragraph will tell your reader what the report is about.

Read Brandon's topic paragraph in Example 1. First he states his report topic: growing vegetables. Then he summarizes the main topics that his report will cover. The paragraph ends with an summary. Compare the sentences in this paragraph to Brandon's outline on page 341.

▶ **EXAMPLE 1**

You can successfully grow vegetables in your own backyard. Growing vegetables involves five steps. Begin by carefully planning the garden. Next, prepare the soil properly. Then choose the best seed. During the growing season, give the plants the necessary care. Finally, enjoy your harvest. Follow the detailed directions in this report to accomplish each of these steps. Harvest time will come much sooner than you think!

**Overview**  This lesson discusses the process of writing a first draft.

### Objectives

■ To write a topic paragraph

■ To use notes to write the body of a report

■ To use direct quotations in a report

■ To write a summary paragraph

**Student Pages**  351–355

**Teacher's Resource Library**

   Activity  59

   Modified Activity  59

   Workbook Activity  59

## Vocabulary

### draft

Write *draft* on the board. Have students read the meaning. Discuss with students that this word can be used as both a noun and a verb. Have them write a sentence using *draft* as a noun. You may wish to have them recite their sentences to compare. Then have them write a sentence using the term as a verb. Have them recite these as well.

## Background Information

Students would benefit from looking over their topic paragraph when completed. They want to be sure it is exciting and engaging. If it isn't exciting to them, then it probably won't engage the reader. Students should make sure they use varying sentence types and that their ideas flow well. Also, in a research report, students should not write about themselves or their opinions. Finally, first drafts should be shared. This is a way to get audience feedback before moving to the next writing step.

## 1  Warm-Up Activity

Before reading on, ask students what types of elements they think might be important to a first draft. Ask them why it might be important to make the first paragraph exciting.

## 2  Teaching the Lesson

After they have read the text on pages 351–354, ask students to summarize the elements of a first draft. Discuss direct quotations and make them aware of plagiarism. Answer any questions they have related to the lesson.

## 3  Reinforce and Extend

### LEARNING STYLES

#### Visual/Spatial

Read the first paragraph on page 351. Have students look at the outlines they created in Chapter 13. Encourage them to visualize how they will use the outline to complete each step of writing. In all steps of the writing process, students will benefit from using graphic organizers to visualize their reports.

## Practice A

Remind students that an outline helps students organize the major and minor points of their reports. Then have them use the given outline to complete the paragraph.

### Practice A Answers

Paragraphs will vary but should include one sentence about each of the four given topics.

### TEACHER ALERT

A well-written topic sentence also helps to make sure a topic is neither too narrow nor too broad. As a rule, students should consider whether their topic sentence can be developed in 3–5 detail sentences. If they cannot come up with that many relevant sentences, the topic is too narrow. If they cannot provide clear, precise information in one paragraph, the topic is too broad.

### Reading Strategy: Text Structure

Students may observe that the headings and bold words provide an overview of the lesson, similar to an outline. The features in the minor column add related details.

**Reading Strategy:**
Text Structure

Preview the lesson. Look at the headings, bold words, and features in the minor column.

Make your topic paragraph interesting so the reader wants to read more.

### Practice A

Write a topic paragraph for a report about fitness. Use the outline below. Write a sentence about each main topic.

Fitness

    I.   Eating the right foods

    II.  Exercising daily

    III. Getting proper rest

    IV. Having a good attitude

### Writing the Body Paragraphs

This is the largest part of your report. The body is organized into several paragraphs. These paragraphs present the details from your note cards. These details could be facts, examples, explanations, and reasons. To write the body of your report, follow your outline. Write paragraphs about each main topic and subtopic in your outline.

Write most of your report in your own words. Sometimes you will want to use the exact words of an author. When you were taking notes, you paraphrased information. You used quotation marks around words you copied exactly. You wrote the page where you found the quotation.

Study Brandon's paragraph in Example 2. Brandon included a direct quotation in this paragraph. The page number in parentheses tells where he found the quotation.

▶ **EXAMPLE 2**

> Choosing the best seeds for your garden is important. Scientists Robert Wiest and Augusta Low make this point: "Except in special cases, it pays for the gardener to buy seeds from reputable nurseries." (p. 24) They also tell gardeners to order seeds well ahead of planting time.

### LEARNING STYLES

**Interpersonal/Group Learning**

Create several introductory paragraphs with simple sentences and little vivid detail. Color code each paragraph, then write its sentences one by one onto note cards. Give each student one note card and have students sort themselves into groups by color. Then have them read each other's sentences and decide how to vary them to make them more engaging. When groups have rewritten their paragraphs to include their changes, read your original versions aloud. Then have students read their versions and discuss how they are improved.

Read Brandon's bibliography card and note card below. Write the answer to each question.

1. What is the source of the information on his note card?
2. Did he find this information in a book or a magazine?
3. Which sentence on his note card is a direct quotation?
4. From what page did he copy this direct quotation?
5. What is the main topic of Brandon's note card?

Wiest, Robert, and Augusta Low. "Backyard Vegetables." <u>Natural Homes Magazine</u> 3 (January 3, 2007) 24-28.

Preparing Soil
To have good soil you need organic matter, which is partly rotten plants. Gardeners should have a compost pile. "Some soils with naturally high fertility may need only nitrogen and compost." (p. 25) Add lime only if the soil needs it. Wiest and Low, p. 25

## GRAMMAR BUILDER

### Writing Compound Sentences
A compound sentence is two sentences that are joined with a conjunction. To write a compound sentence, use one of these conjunctions: *and, or, for, so, yet,* or *but.* Place a comma before the conjunction.

I look at the valley each day, and its beauty still amazes me. Join each pair of sentences. Use a conjunction that fits the meaning. Use a comma. Write the new compound sentence.
1. Yesterday it poured all day. Today the sun finally came out.
2. The canoes are loaded. We have had our breakfast.
3. This part of the river is deep. We will move slowly at first.

## GRAMMAR BUILDER

When students have completed the exercise, have them think of something they did that morning or the day before. Direct them to write a pair of compound sentences about something that happened during their day.

### Grammar Builder Answers
**1.** Yesterday it poured all day, but today the sun finally came out. **2.** The canoes are loaded, and we have had our breakfast. **3.** This part of the river is deep, so we will move slowly at first.

## Practice B
Have students reread the sample bibliography and note cards on page 353. Then have them answer the questions.

### Practice B Answers
**1.** Wiest, Robert, and Augusta Low **2.** magazine **3.** third sentence; it is in quotation marks **4.** page 25 **5.** preparing soil

## AT HOME

Using the sample bibliography and note cards on page 353, have students write their own bibliography and note cards. Students can choose any type of book they have in their home—fiction, nonfiction, cookbooks, how-to manuals, etc. They will write the bibliographical information on one card. On the second card, they will paraphrase one idea or section and make at least one citation.

## ELL/ESL STRATEGY

**Language Objective:** *To write questions as topic sentences*

English-learning students may have trouble with word order. They have learned that in English, the subject precedes the verb. However, in English questions, the subject often follows the verb or helping verb(s). Students will benefit by identifying the subject and verb in their sentences. Have students change the following sentences into questions:
*You know how to clean up your town.*
*You have had an exciting day.*
*You have a fear of small spaces.*

## Practice C

Discuss with students how a report might benefit from adding pictures or other visual devices. Direct them to create a list of illustrations they might add to enhance their own reports.

### Practice C Answers

Student lists will vary but should note illustrations that are appropriate for the topic.

## Practice D

Direct students to reread the outline given in Practice A. Have them look at the details they included in their paragraphs. Then have them brainstorm several ways they have learned to stay in shape. You might suggest students create a list to help write their summaries.

### Practice D Answers

Paragraphs will vary but should summarize information given in the original paragraph, as well as details they listed for staying in shape.

---

### IN THE COMMUNITY

 Have students obtain a copy of a local newspaper and examine the articles for citations. Point out the different ways newspaper articles will cite information from a source. Have students examine three articles and list cited information, source of the information, and whether the information was paraphrased or written as a direct quote.

---

### *Reading Strategy:* Text Structure

Students may state that the lesson is organized sequentially, or that it has a beginning, a middle, and an end.

---

---

*Reading Strategy:*
Text Structure

When you read, look for words such as *begin, now, then,* and *at the end.* What do they tell you about the way the lesson is organized?

Consider adding illustrations, or pictures, to the body of your report. They can make the information clearer and more interesting to the reader. For example, a chart that shows how to plant different kinds of vegetable seeds might be helpful in a report about growing vegetables.

### Practice C

Make a list of illustrations that you might include in your report. You may need to find additional information.

### Writing the Summary Paragraph

End your report with a summary paragraph. It repeats the main topics of your report. A summary paragraph does not have to be long. It brings the report to an end.

Brandon's summary paragraph is shown in Example 3. It sums up the main topics of his outline on page 341.

▶ **EXAMPLE 3**

Vegetables will grow even where there is limited space. If you want to see for yourself, just follow the steps given in this report. Start by making a plan, preparing the soil, and choosing the seeds. Caring for the plants can bring great satisfaction. Then you can have the enjoyment of picking ripe vegetables. You will enjoy many delicious meals!

### Practice D

Look back at the topic paragraph you wrote for Practice A on page 352. Reread the outline given in Practice A. Think about the information that might be in this report on fitness. Then write a summary paragraph that could end the report.

---

# REVIEW

Write the letter of the answer to each question.

1. What do you use as a guide when you write a report?
   **A** bibliography cards    **C** an outline
   **B** the report title      **D** your opinions

2. Which part of a report is usually the longest?
   **A** the main idea     **C** the summary paragraph
   **B** the body          **D** the topic paragraph

3. What is the last part of a report?
   **A** the main idea     **C** the summary paragraph
   **B** the body          **D** the topic paragraph

4. Why do you put quotation marks around a direct quotation?
   **A** to show that it is someone else's exact words
   **B** to show that you are paraphrasing
   **C** to show that it is information from a source
   **D** to show that the information may not be true

5. Follow the directions below to write a first draft of your report. Use your note cards and your outline.

   • Write a topic paragraph for your report.

   • Write the body of your report. Write strong paragraphs about each main topic and subtopic. Include details such as facts, examples, reasons, explanations, quotations, and illustrations. Use direct quotations (with page numbers) to emphasize important facts.

   • Write the last paragraph as a summary of the important points in your report.

---

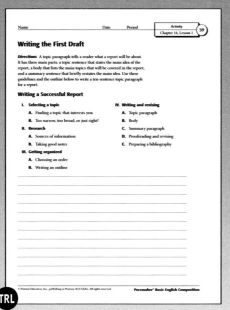

## Lesson at a Glance

### Chapter 14  Lesson 2

**Overview**  This lesson focuses on revising a first draft.

### Objectives

- To revise the organization of your report
- To revise the content of your report
- To revise to make your writing flow

**Student Pages**  356–359

**Teacher's Resource Library** ⓣⓡⓛ

Activity  60

Modified Activity  60

Workbook Activity  60

## Background Information

During the revision process, writers consider the content, organization, language, tone, and style of what they have written. Most writers can look at their work more objectively if they have set it aside for a time before reviewing it. If possible, give students at least one day between writing and revising reports.

### 1  Warm-Up Activity

Discuss with students why it is important to look over what they have written. What things do they need to look for? How can revising make their reports better?

### 2  Teaching the Lesson

After they have read pages 356–358, have them summarize the types of revisions they can make to improve their reports. Help them make a list of words that can help them transition from one idea to another.

**Reading Strategy:** Text Structure

Student lists will vary but may include revising for organization, content, and flow.

# Revising the Report

## Objectives

- To revise the organization of your report
- To revise the content of your report
- To revise to make your writing flow

**Reading Strategy:** Text Structure

As you read this lesson, make a list of the different ways to revise a report.

After you write your first draft, it is time to revise it. To revise means to make changes.

### Revising the Organization

First look at the organization of your report. Compare it to your outline. Are some parts of the report very long and others very short? Are some parts out of order? Perhaps you need to arrange some paragraphs differently. Perhaps you need to fix your outline.

### Practice A

Look at the outline below. Notice the three parts in bold. Two of the bold parts are in the wrong place. One bold part is not needed. Revise the outline. Write the new one on your paper.

Hummingbirds

  I.  Where to find hummingbirds
    A.  In summer
      **1.  Feeder nectar**
    B.  In winter
  II.  Types of hummingbirds
    A.  In North America
    **B.  In the western United States**
    C.  In Mexico and South America
  III.  How to attract hummingbirds
    A.  Garden flowers
      **1.  Location of feeders**
    B.  Feeders
      1.  Feeder types

## Practice A

Have students revise the outline on page 356, rewriting it on their own paper.

### Practice A Answers

Outlines will vary. A sample outline follows.

Hummingbirds

I.  Where to find hummingbirds
  A.  In summer
  B.  In winter
II.  Types of hummingbirds
  A.  In North America
  B.  In Mexico and South America
III.  How to attract hummingbirds
  A.  Garden flowers
  B.  Feeders
    1.  Feeder nectar
    2.  Feeder types
    3.  Location of feeders

### Revising the Content

Besides revising the organization, you need to revise the content—the information in the report. Ask yourself these questions:

- Did I say everything I wanted to say?
- Do my readers have the information they need to understand my topic?
- Have I written enough about the topic?
- Is there content that is missing?
- Is there extra content that is unnecessary or unrelated?

### Practice B

Read the draft of your report. Answer these questions.

1. Does your topic paragraph state the topic and introduce the report's main ideas?

2. Does the body include information about all of the main topics? Add missing details.

3. Do the details in the body support the main topics? Cross out sentences that do not add anything useful.

4. Have you included facts, explanations, reasons, direct quotations, or examples?

5. Does your report include an illustration? If not, can you add one?

### Adding Transitions and Sentence Variety

You have practiced using transitional words and phrases to connect sentences in a paragraph. Now, you need to use transitions to connect paragraphs. Read your report aloud and listen to the flow of the paragraphs. Add transitional words and phrases to help your reader move from one paragraph to the next.

Look at the sentence variety in your report. Can you move around words to create more interesting sentences? Can you combine short, related sentences into one longer sentence? Revise your sentences to add interest for your reader.

**Reading Strategy:**
Text Structure

After you read this lesson, look back at the list of objectives on page 356. Was each objective met?

*Writing the Final Report*    *Chapter 14*    **357**

### COMMON ERROR

Caution students against adding extra details and adjectives simply to create longer sentences. Rather than add variety, these wordy sentences become monotonous. Explain that they should always try to make their point in as few words as possible. Wordy paragraphs can only bore and confuse the reader.

### Practice B

Tell students to read over their reports and answer the questions. If you like, direct them to use complete sentences.

### *Practice B Answers*

Answers will vary.

### *Reading Strategy:* Text Structure

Students should name each objective and conclude that each was met.

### ELL/ESL STRATEGY

**Language Objective:**
*To understand transitional words*

Help the class compile a list of common transitional words on the board. Then ask students for whom English is a second language to write the words in their primary language. Ask a volunteer to begin a sentence. Encourage an ESL volunteer to step forward and add to the sentence an appropriate transitional word from the list on the board. Ask another volunteer to complete the sentence.

### Writing Practice

Make a set of cards, each for one transitional word. Distribute the cards to students. Direct students to write a sentence using their word. Shuffle the cards and repeat the exercise several times.

## Practice C

Have students read the sample and answer the questions on their paper. If you choose, direct them to write complete sentences.

### Practice C Answers

**1.** Then, On the other hand **2.** Answers will vary. **3.** Answers will vary.

### COMMON ERROR

Some transitions have a formal tone and may be used inappropriately in fiction and personal writing. Formal transitions are usually reserved for reports and nonfiction articles. Examples of formal transitions are *in conclusion, consequently, moreover, accordingly,* and *nevertheless.*

Use the three purple paragraphs below to practice revising.

1. Find the transitional words and phrases in the paragraphs. List them on your paper.

2. Look at the first words of the sentences. Can you move some of the words or phrases around to add variety? Find two sentences that you would change. Write the revised sentences on your paper.

3. Find two short sentences that you could combine with a conjunction. Write the new sentence on your paper.

Nearly everyone is excited to see a hummingbird sipping nectar from a flower. These tiny creatures arrive in late spring and stay until fall. All summer, they work daily to gather nectar, build nests, and raise their chicks. Then, they head across the Gulf of Mexico to winter in Central America.

You may be wondering what kind of hummingbirds you might see. The most common type is the ruby-throated hummingbird. There are dozens of other types, but they live mostly in tropical countries. The Rufus hummingbird is more common in the western part of the United States but occasionally lives in the east.

The best way to attract hummingbirds is to plant a garden with their favorite flowers. They love blossoms that are red and shaped like a tube. Two examples are columbine and Texas sage. They also like azaleas, honeysuckle, and morning glories. On the other hand, a feeder is also useful. Buy one that is red. Fill it with sugar water. Hang it in your garden. Hummingbirds will find it quickly.

Use your outline, note cards, and the first draft of your report to answer each question.

1. Does your topic paragraph state your report topic?

2. Is each main topic from the outline (I, II, III, etc.) mentioned in your topic paragraph? If not, revise that paragraph.

3. Did you write at least one paragraph about each main topic from the outline? If not, use your note cards and write the missing paragraph(s).

4. Does each paragraph have a topic sentence, supporting details, and a summary or conclusion? If not, revise any paragraphs that lack these parts.

5. Are there any sentences that do not relate to the topic? If so, cross these out.

6. Are your paragraphs connected with transitional words and phrases? Add more transitions if needed.

7. Does your report end with a summary paragraph? If not, write this paragraph.

8. Do you have any direct quotations in your report? If so, did you use quotation marks and identify the author? If not, rewrite your quotations correctly.

9. Reread your revised report. How does each paragraph sound? Check the checklist on page 134.

10. Exchange reports with another student. Read his or her report and make suggestions. Listen to your classmate's suggestions for your report. Make changes to your report as needed.

## Lesson 14-2 Review Answers
Answers will vary.

### WRITING PORTFOLIO

**Checkpoint** Students can continue working on their Writing Portfolio project. Check students' progress and address any questions or concerns they may have.

## Spelling Practice

Remind students that homophones are words that sound alike but have different spellings and meanings. Discuss some common homophones with students. List the following words on the board: *principle, principal; their, they're; plain, plane; past, passed; break, brake; piece, peace.* Have students write a sentence for each word. When students are finished, erase the board and write a sentence, leaving a blank where a homophone should be. Ask a volunteer to go to the board and write the proper word. Continue this exercise for all of the homophones.

**Activity 60**

**Workbook Activity 60**

## Chapter 14  Lesson 3

**Overview**  This lesson focuses on editing a report.

### Objectives

- To edit a report and make corrections
- To check the use of verb tense
- To fix mistakes in subject-verb agreement
- To fix mistakes in spelling, punctuation, and capitalization

**Student Pages**  360–363

**Teacher's Resource Library** (TRL)

Activity 61

Modified Activity 61

Workbook Activity 61

## Vocabulary

**mechanics**

Discuss the meaning of *mechanics* with students. Have students write three sentences using the word in this context.

## Background Information

It is common for a very young child to say a sentence such as *I runned fast* or *Grandma bringed me a present*. You may like to discuss with students why young children might make such mistakes in forming verbs. Students should see that the *-ed* ending is the regular way to form past tenses. You may choose to discuss how children learn the correct forms of irregular past tenses such as *ran* and *brought*.

### 1  Warm-Up Activity

Help students to think of people who create works of art and to understand the process of perfecting such works. Explain that writers also do this after finishing a first draft. By editing, a writer refines the text and corrects errors. Have students read the objectives on page 360, then predict ways they might improve their reports.

---

## LESSON 14-3  Editing the Report

### Objectives

- To edit a report and make corrections
- To check the use of verb tense
- To fix mistakes in subject-verb agreement
- To fix mistakes in spelling, punctuation, and capitalization

**NOTE**

If you need help identifying sentence fragments and run-on sentences, review Chapter 1.

**Reading Strategy:** Text Structure

What do the objectives of this lesson suggest about the process of editing?

At this stage in the writing process, you have already done most of the hard work. You have already revised your first draft. Now you are working with the second draft. You need to edit this draft. You learned how to edit in Chapter 5. To edit means to fix mistakes in grammar, spelling, capitalization, and punctuation. Choosing better words is also part of editing. As you edit, look for vague words and replace them with more specific ones.

Grammar is the correct use of sentence parts. Make sure your report has no sentence fragments or run-on sentences. Grammar includes using verbs correctly.

### Checking Verb Tense

Avoid shifting tenses within a report. Decide if your report will be written in the past tense or present tense. Then stick to that choice.

▶ **EXAMPLE 1**

Bands played at the wedding. The bride and groom chose them. Everyone enjoyed the music. (past tense)

Bands play at the wedding. The bride and groom choose them. Everyone enjoys the music. (present tense)

### Practice A

Find the verbs in the paragraph. List them on your paper. After each verb, write its tense: either *present* or *past*. Then choose one tense. Rewrite the paragraph using that tense only.

> The hummingbirds came to the feeders in April or May. All summer they feed on nectar. They stayed until October. Then they flew to Central America.

**360**  *Chapter 14  Writing the Final Report*

---

### 2  Teaching the Lesson

Stress to students that they are free to choose which verb tense they use. Then remind them that the tense should remain the same throughout the report. Show them how, in Example 1, the verb tense is constant.

**Reading Strategy:** Text Structure

Students may think they must be very careful and meticulous in the editing process.

## Practice A

Read the instructions with the students. Then have students read the sample paragraph and answer the questions on their paper. If you choose, have them switch tense—from past to present or from present to past—and rewrite the paragraph in that tense as well.

### Practice A Answers

came, past; feed, present; stayed, past; flew, past

Paragraphs may vary. A sample paragraph follows:

The hummingbirds come to the feeders in April or May. All summer they feed on nectar. They stay until October. Then they fly to Central America.

## Checking Subject-Verb Agreement

Review subject-verb agreement in Chapter 2. For each sentence in your report, make sure the subject and verb agree.

▶ **EXAMPLE 2**

One bird lands on the branch.
(singular subject, verb ends in -s)

Two birds land on the branch.
(plural subject, verb does not end in -s)

### Practice B

The four verbs in the paragraph below are in bold. Number your paper from 1 to 4. Find the subject of each bold verb. Write the subject and the verb on your paper. If the subject and verb agree, write *correct*. If they do not agree, write the correct verb form.

One hummingbird **feed** at a time. If a second one **comes** to the feeder, the first one **chase** it away. Hummingbirds **likes** to have the feeder to themselves.

## Fixing Mechanical Mistakes

Always check spelling, capitalization, and punctuation in anything you write. Mistakes in these areas are mistakes in **mechanics**. When you edit, correct these mistakes:

- misspelled words
- sentences that do not start with a capital letter
- proper nouns that do not start with a capital letter
- comma faults that create run-on sentences
- missing commas in a list of three or more items
- missing commas in compound and complex sentences
- missing or wrong end punctuation marks
- wrong use of apostrophes (Remember that contractions and possessive nouns have apostrophes.)

**Reading Strategy:**
Text Structure

How can this list help you remember what to watch for when you edit?

*Writing the Final Report*    *Chapter 14*    **361**

---

### CAREER CONNECTION

 Ask students why it would be extremely important to spell *personnel* correctly when applying for a job to a personnel department. Help students recognize that using correct spelling may not get them the job, but using incorrect spelling may prevent them from being considered.

**Reading Strategy:** Text Structure

Students may say they should check spelling, usage, and grammar closely. They may state the list helps them to check their reports word for word.

## Practice B

Read the instructions with the students. Then have students read the sample paragraph and answer the questions on their paper. If you choose, have them rewrite the entire paragraph using correct subject-verb agreement.

## Practice B Answers

**1.** hummingbird feed, feeds **2.** one comes, correct **3.** one chase, chases
**4.** Hummingbirds likes, like

## Writing Practice

Have students write a short paragraph with at least two errors per sentence. Paragraphs should include errors such as sentence fragments and run-ons as well as spelling, grammatical, and punctuation errors. When finished, have students trade paragraphs and edit each other's work.

### LEARNING STYLES

 **Logical/Mathematical**

Under the heading, "Editing Checklist," list the following items on the board: *spelling, punctuation, capitalization, subject-verb agreement, pronoun-antecedent agreement, tenses, plurals,* and *possessives*. Challenge the students to create a checklist of symbols to represent these items. Suggest that they draw one icon for each of the items. Encourage students to draw symbols that will bring to mind the items on the checklist.

# Practice C

Have students read the paragraph to find five mistakes. Have them rewrite the paragraph.

## Practice C Answers

The penguin is an unusual animal from the icy Antarctic. Some people say penguins look like little men wearing tuxedos. Penguins stand up on short legs. They walk with a waddle. Although they are birds, they can't fly. A bird called the albatross lives in the Antarctic too. Their strange walk and unusual appearance make penguins fun to watch.

## Practice D

Have students read the paragraph and list possible changes.

## Practice D Answers

Elm Street; spring; omit "Fall is my favorite season."; through the branches of the trees and hear; windows.; The sunlight; turns bright orange and makes the sky orange too.; beautiful; picture; book.

---

## COMMON ERROR

Students should be aware of the comma splice: the insertion of a comma between two clauses that could function as individual sentences. Students will often create this type of situation when learning to write compound sentences. Remind them to look carefully at their sentences during the revision and editing processes.

---

## ELL/ESL STRATEGY

**Language Objective:** *To properly use verbs and their tenses*

Ask students for whom English is a second language if their primary language has irregular verbs. If so, encourage them to give examples of these verbs. Have students print the present, past, and past participles of their chosen verbs on the board. Then ask them to say aloud three sentences in their language that illustrate the use of the irregular verbs.

---

### Brush Up on the Basics

Use a comma between the day and the year in a date. If the date does not end a sentence, add a comma after the year. *On April 28, 2007, the club had its first meeting.* See Punctuation 6 in Appendix A.

*A walk down Elm Street is refreshing.*

## Practice C

Read the paragraph below. Find five mistakes. Write the paragraph correctly on your paper.

   The penguin is an unusuel animal from the icy antarctic. Some people say penguins look like little men wearing tuxedos. Penguins stand up on short legs They walk with a waddle. Although they are birds they can't fly. A bird called the albatross lives in the Antarctic two. Their strange walk and unusual appearance make penguins fun to watch.

## Practice D

Read the paragraph below. Look for spelling mistakes, missing commas, capitalization mistakes, sentence fragments, and sentences that do not belong. List each change that you think is necessary.

   There is a new house on elm street. It is surrounded by beautiful trees. The trees are tall and have white flowers in the Spring. They look like they have been there for a hundred years. Fall is my favorite season. During the day, you can see the sun shining thrugh the brannches of the trees. And hear the birds chirping. The house has big windows the Sunlight comes in through the windows and makes the house very bright. At sundown, the sun turn bright orange And It makes the sky orange two. Just before it gets dark, you can see squirrels running across the branches. The beautful house on Elm Street is like a piture out of a book

Follow each set of directions.

1. Compare the two paragraphs below. The first one is a draft. The second one is the final copy. On your paper, list each change the writer made.

   The planet mars is more like earth than any other planet. Mars has polar caps that probably are of ice and snow. The caps get larger in the winter and slowly melt in the summer. Scientists thinks that Mars has an atmosphere. It is denser than Earth's atmosphere. The planet Venus has an atmosphere, too. During the day, the surface of Mars would be comfortably warm, but at night it became bitterly cold. There are no oceans! There is much less water on Mars than on Earth. Living beings exactly like humans could not live on Mars. However, some scientist believe there is plant life on the planet.

   The planet Mars is more like Earth than any other planet. Like Earth, Mars has polar caps that probably are made of ice and snow. Those caps get larger in the winter and slowly melt in the summer. Scientists think that Mars has an atmosphere. However, that atmosphere is denser than Earth's. During the day, the surface of Mars becomes comfortably warm, but at night it becomes bitterly cold. There are no oceans on Mars. In fact, there is much less water on Mars than on Earth. Although living beings exactly like humans could not live on Mars, some scientists believe there is plant life on the planet.

2. Edit your report carefully. Make corrections in grammar. Fix the mechanical mistakes. Choose more specific words. Use the checklist on page 138 as a guide.

---

*Writing the Final Report*    *Chapter 14*    **363**

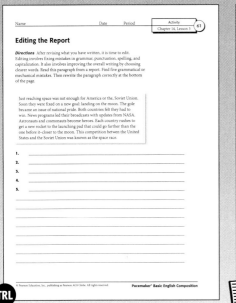

Activity 61          Workbook Activity 61

*Writing the Final Report*  **363**

---

## Lesson 14-3 Review Answers

**1.** Mars; Earth; Like Earth; made; Those; think; However, that atmosphere; remove "The planet Venus has an atmosphere, too."; becomes; becomes; There are no oceans on Mars; In fact; Although; Mars, some scientists  **2.** Answers will vary, but students should use the checklist on page 138 to edit their reports.

## Grammar Practice

Remind students that correcting fragmented and run-on sentences is part of the editing process. Write some fragmented and run-on sentences on the board. Ask volunteers to read one and tell whether it is a fragment or run-on. Then have them tell how to fix it. You may choose to have students write their own fragments and run-ons and give them to other students to correct.

### WRITING PORTFOLIO

**Checkpoint** Students can continue working on their Writing Portfolio project. Check their progress and address questions or concerns they may have.

### LEARNING STYLES

**Auditory/Verbal** Ask each student to create and write down a series of three related and run-on sentences. Then invite volunteers to stand before the class in pairs. Ask one member of the first pair to read aloud his or her run-on sentences without pausing for punctuation. Ask the other partner to step forward each time a point of punctuation is needed to divide the run-ons into sentences. Then have the partners switch roles. Continue until all the volunteers have read and added punctuation to their sentences.

## Chapter 14  Lesson 4

**Overview**  This lesson focuses on preparing a bibliography.

### Objectives
- To prepare a bibliography for a report
- To write titles correctly

**Student Pages** 364–367

**Teacher's Resource Library**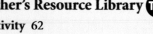

Activity 62

Modified Activity 62

Workbook Activity 62

Life Skills Connection 14

## Background Information

Bibliographies give credit to the authors of the works cited in research papers. They also direct readers to those sources when they want more information. Both print materials and the Internet should be used with caution. By the same token, writers need to make sure their bibliographies are accurate.

### 1  Warm-Up Activity

Show students a bibliography from a published work of nonfiction. Ask for their ideas about why bibliographies are included in such works. They may express their understanding that the author of the book is showing the thoroughness of the research, giving credit to other authors, and also helping readers who want to do more research on the subject.

### 2  Teaching the Lesson

Stress to students that bibliographies are written in a standard style. They should understand that "standard" means it is the universal style, or the style accepted as the rule. Go through the order and parts of a bibliography.

**Reading Strategy:** Text Structure

Students may notice the order within each entry as well as the alphabetical order of the entries.

---

## LESSON 14-4  Preparing a Bibliography

### Objectives
- To prepare a bibliography for a report
- To write titles correctly

**Reading Strategy:**
Text Structure

Use Example 1 as a guide to help you prepare a bibliography.

 **NOTE**
In a bibliography, the abbreviation *ed.* usually stands for editor. However, *ed.* can also stand for edition.

You are almost ready to publish the final copy of your report. Before you can do this, you need to prepare the bibliography. This goes at the end of your report. It is an alphabetical list of the sources you used.

Study the bibliography in Example 1. Notice the different formats for a book, an encyclopedia, a periodical, and a Web site.

▶ **EXAMPLE 1**

Allen, G., and M. K. Howard. *The History of Computers.* Chicago: Acme Books Co., 2003.

Brown, J. K., ed. *The Computer Encyclopedia.* New York: Computer Publications, Inc., 2000.

"Computer." *World Encyclopedia.* Vol. 3, 2002, 119–127.

"Computers of the Nineteenth Century." *Data World 8,* March 2005, 54–57.

Evan, Stacy. "Computers Yesterday and Today." *The Computer Journal 2,* August 2003. www.compjourn.com/evan.html (May 18, 2004).

When you researched your topic, you made bibliography cards to record details about each source. Use these cards to create your bibliography. Here are some important points to remember:

- Order your sources alphabetically by the author's last name. If there are two or more authors for a source, list it by whichever name is given first.
- If there is no author given, list the source by the first important word of the title. (Ignore these beginning words: *The, An,* and *A.*)

---

## TEACHER ALERT

Point out that it is important to be consistent in a bibliography, always using the same style and format for each entry. Make the additional point that the style of punctuation can vary from bibliography to bibliography. Emphasize that what is most important is that a bibliography have complete information (author, title, publisher, copyright date, pages).

**Reading Strategy:**
Text Structure

Some information is given as a bulleted list. What does this fact suggest about the information?

- For a book entry, include the author, title, place of publication, publisher, and date.

- For an article, give two titles: the article title and the title of the book, periodical, or Web site. Also include the author, date, page numbers, and any volume number.

- Indent the second line of each entry and any lines after that.

Your teacher may ask you to use a bibliography format that is slightly different than Example 1. Follow the format directions you are given.

### Practice A

Use the bibliography in Example 1. Write the answer to each question.

1. Why is the book *The History of Computers* listed before *The Computer Encyclopedia*?

2. What information comes first in each entry?

3. Who wrote the article on *The Computer Journal* Web site?

4. Which source has the most recent information?

5. Which entry is a periodical *not* found online?

### Practice B

Use the bibliography in Example 1. Write the answer to each question.

1. In book entries, what punctuation mark follows the place of publication?

2. On what pages would you find the article from *World Encyclopedia*?

3. What is the Web site address in the last entry?

4. When was the book by Allen and Howard published?

5. How do you list an entry if no author is given?

---

**Reading Strategy:** Text Structure

Students may state that each bullet is a main point or step in the process of writing a bibliography.

## Practice A

Have students use the bibliography in Example 1. If you choose, have them write answers in complete sentences.

### Practice A Answers

**1.** *Allen* comes before *Brown*. **2.** author's last name **3.** Stacy Evan **4.** "Computers of the Nineteenth Century" **5.** "Computers of the Nineteenth Century"

## Practice B

Have students use the bibliography in Example 1.

### Practice B Answers

**1.** colon **2.** pages 119–127 **3.** www. compjourn.com/evan.html **4.** 2003 **5.** by the first important word of the title

## 3 Reinforce and Extend

### LIFE SKILLS CONNECTION

Discuss with students some topics they can use for their reports. Stress that they should use the same format and writing skills they have already learned. Distribute Life Skills Connection 14 and have students complete it.

### COMMON ERROR

Punctuating bibliographies can be confusing. Students will commonly place a semicolon where a colon should be or use quotation marks around a title that should be italicized.

### Writing Practice

Have students pretend they are writing a bibliography for a report. Direct them to gather five books from home or from the library. They should use Example 1 and the guidelines from pages 364–365 to write a bibliography for the five books. Stress to students that they should follow all the rules for writing a bibliography.

## Practice C

Have students use the checklist on page 366 to rewrite the titles.

### Practice C Answers

1. "Tennis Tips from a Pro" 2. *Music to Live By* 3. "My Love Is True" 4. *The Hillsbury Post* 5. "Light Over the Hills"

## Practice D

Have students use Example 1 on page 364 to write the bibliography.

### Practice D Answers

The Auto Care Web site. www.autocare.org (December 13, 2002).

"Automobiles." *Universal Encyclopedia.* Vol. 1, 2006, 144–152.

Ramirez, Jane. "Fix It Yourself." *The Car Magazine,* Volume 7, March 2003, 67–72.

Richard, Blakeley. *Basic Car Care.* Seattle: Automotive Publications, 2005.

 **Brush Up on the Basics**

In a bibliography, use quotation marks around article titles and chapter titles. Use italics or an underline on other titles. See Punctuation 20 in Appendix A.

## Capitalizing and Punctuating Titles

Bibliographies and other kinds of writing contain titles. Follow these rules to capitalize and punctuate titles.

- Always capitalize the first word, the last word, and the main words in a title.
- The titles of books, magazines, newspapers, Web sites, plays, movies, and TV series should appear in italics. The titles of paintings and long musical works should also appear in italics. If you are writing by hand, underline these titles.
- Put quotation marks around the titles of short stories, articles, book chapters, poems, and songs.

### Practice C

Write each title correctly. The information in parentheses tells you the kind of title.

1. tennis tips from a pro (magazine article)
2. music to live by (book)
3. my love is true (song)
4. the hillsbury post (newspaper)
5. light over the hills (poem)

### Practice D

Use the information below to create a bibliography. Fix the order and format. Follow Example 1 on page 364.

Basic Car Care by Blakeley Richard. Automotive Publications published the book in Seattle in 2005.

"Fix It Yourself," an article by Jane Ramirez in The Car Magazine, Volume 7, March 2003, on pages 67–72.

"Automobiles," in Universal Encyclopedia, Volume 1, 2006, on pages 144–152. No author is given.

The Auto Care Web site updated on December 13, 2002. The Web site address is www.autocare.org.

Follow each set of directions.

1. Make a bibliography for your report. Follow the steps below.

   - Look through your stack of bibliography cards. Pull out any sources that you did not use to write your report.

   - Put your bibliography cards in alphabetical order according to the author's last name. If there is no author, use the first important word of the title of the article, book, or Web site.

   - Use the information on your cards to write an entry for each source. Follow the format shown in Example 1 on page 364.

2. Edit your bibliography. Correct any mistakes. Make a final copy to place at the end of your report.

---

## VOCABULARY BUILDER

**Understanding the Prefix *Biblio-***
What do these words have in common?

  bibliography    bibliology    bibliophile

They all contain the prefix *biblio-*, which comes from the Greek word meaning "book" or "books."

1. *Philo* means "love." Which word listed above means "a person who loves books"?

2. The ending *-logy* means "study of." Which word above means "the study of books"?

3. The ending *-graphy* means "a style of writing." Which word above means "a list of books"?

**Lesson 14-4 Review Answers**
**1.** Student bibliographies should follow the guidelines in the lesson. **2.** Edited bibliographies should have a correct style.

## VOCABULARY BUILDER

After students complete the activity, have them look through the dictionary for two or three other prefixes. Direct them to write a sentence using each prefix.

### *Vocabulary Builder Answers*

**1.** bibliophile **2.** bibliology **3.** bibliography

---

### Chapter 14  Lesson 5

**Overview**  This lesson focuses on publishing a final copy of a report.

### Objectives

- To prepare a title page for a report
- To publish a final report

**Student Pages**  368–373

**Teacher's Resource Library**

Activity  63

Modified Activity  63

Workbook Activity  63

Writing on the Job  7

Building Research Skills  14

---

## Vocabulary

**publish**

Discuss with students what types of things are published and how publishing is a way to share information. Raise a discussion about how *publish* is like *public, publicize,* and *publication.*

---

## Background Information

There are many ways students can enhance their final drafts to make them more appealing or to help the reader visualize the contents. Many students like to add photographs or illustrations to their final copies. Some students might like to submit their reports to a newspaper, magazine, or Web site that publishes student writing projects.

### 1  Warm-Up Activity

Make a sample report. Purposely omit the title page, author, and page numbers. Make sure all pages are out of order and give the sample to a student. Ask the student to put the report in proper order and tell what elements are missing.

---

**LESSON**
## 14-5  Publishing the Final Report

### Objectives
- To prepare a title page for a report
- To publish a final report

**Publish**
To share a written or visual message with others

Publishing is the last step of the writing process. To **publish** your writing means to share it with others. You can send or give your final copy to others, or you can make it available to them.

### Preparing the Final Report
Before you do this, your final report needs a title page or a cover sheet. This page should have the title of your report, your name, and the date. Your teacher may ask for other information on this page.

> **Popular Breeds of Dogs in the United States**
> Amber Choy
> June 1, 2007

**Practice A**

Make a title page for your report. Use the sample above as a guide.

### 2  Teaching the Lesson

Have students look over the guidelines on page 369. Use this and the sample report from the Warm-Up Activity to discuss the importance of the title page, student name, page numbers, and other elements of a report.

### Practice A

Read the instructions with the students. Then have students read the sample title page and create their own title pages.

### Practice A Answers

Title pages will vary, but all should follow the sample on page 368.

Put your report together in this order:

1. title page
2. report
3. bibliography
4. blank page at the end

You may prepare your final report in two ways. You may write the final copy by hand using ink. You may print the final copy with a computer. Here are some guidelines:

1. If you use a computer, double-space the report.
2. Use one side of the paper. Do not use the back side.
3. Number the pages at the bottom.
4. Put your name at the top of each page.
5. Center titles on the page.

Your teacher may give you other guidelines for preparing your report. For example, you may need to use a certain margin width or font size.

### Publishing Your Report

All of the work you have done on your report—from prewriting to editing—ends with publishing. Sharing your work is important. It is a chance to communicate your ideas with others. You can find out if other people like your work and if they agree with your ideas. Publishing is a way to give something to others. If it is a report, you are giving information. If it is a story, you are entertaining.

When you finish your report, turn in your final copy to your teacher. Pay attention to the due date so your final report is not late.

**NOTE**

One way to publish your writing is to present it as a speech to a group of people. See Appendix B for tips on giving a speech.

***Reading Strategy:***
Text Structure

What details are important to remember about publishing a report?

## 3 Reinforce and Extend

### COMMON ERROR

Students with less computer or word-processing experience may not understand automatic pagination or centering. Without assistance, these students can spend too much time trying to insert page numbers manually, often with poor results.

### LEARNING STYLES

**Body/Kinesthetic**

Students may benefit from separating their reports into many segments. Have them make copies of their reports and cut them into multiple parts. If reports are saved on a word-processing program, students can rearrange paragraphs. Have students put their papers in multiple arrangements. Then have them trade papers with other students and put the papers in proper order.

***Reading Strategy:*** Text Structure

Students may cite the order of report materials (title page, report, bibliography, blank page). Some may cite the formatting guidelines on page 369.

## Writing Practice

Gauge student interest in publishing their reports outside of the classroom. Have students consult a librarian or the Internet to find local and national publishers who accept student writing. Encourage students to prepare a copy of their reports for submission to a journal or Web site, following the publisher's guidelines for submissions.

## Lesson 14-5 Review Answers

**1.** title, name, date **2.** write by hand, use a computer **3.** no **4.** name at the top, page number at the bottom **5.** title page, report, bibliography, blank page

### WRITE ABOUT IT

Give a persuasive review of a movie, CD, or TV show, including both positive and negative points. As you talk, capture key words and phrases on a word web on the board. Be sure to include each element from the list on page 370. Then have students state whether they are interested in the reviewed product or not. Have them write their own persuasive reviews.

## Six Traits of Writing Focus

|   | Ideas | ✓ | Word Choice |
|---|-------|---|-------------|
|   | Organization |   | Sentence Fluency |
| ✓ | Voice |   | Conventions |

## Voice

Inform students that their writing voice should express their opinion even if it is not stated explicitly. Have students read their review to a partner. Ask the partner whether the opinion is positive or negative. If the partner cannot determine the opinion, the author should rewrite the review with a stronger voice.

Remind students that good word choice is a vital part of a writer's voice. In a descriptive paragraph, colorful adjectives are essential.

Refer students to page WPH1 for descriptions of the Six Traits of Writing.

### GLOBAL CONNECTION

Discuss some of the international issues that are currently in the news. Have students look over editorial and op-ed pages of newspapers to find opinion essays and letters on one of the issues. Together, identify the writer's position. Discuss the effectiveness of the written arguments.

---

# REVIEW

Write the answer to each question.

1. What information goes on a title page?

2. What are two ways to prepare the final copy of a report?

3. Should you use both sides of the paper?

4. What should go on the top and bottom of each page?

5. Write these report pieces in the correct order: *report, blank page, title page, bibliography*.

### WRITE ABOUT IT

**A Movie, Music CD, or TV Show**
Newspapers and magazines often have reviews of movies, music, and TV shows. A positive review can persuade a reader to see the movie, buy the music, or watch the show. A negative review can persuade a reader *not* to see or buy something. Write a short review of a movie, CD, or TV show. You can express either a positive or negative opinion. Try to persuade your reader to agree with you. Include the following:
- the title
- the author, director, or artist
- the main characters, actors, or musicians
- a summary of the plot or content
- what you like and do not like, and why
- your general opinion about the movie, CD, or TV show

Revise and edit your review. Make sure you have treated the title correctly. Then share your review with another student or send it to a local newspaper.

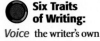

**Six Traits of Writing:**
*Voice* the writer's own language

---

Name _____ Date _____ Period _____   Activity
                                             Chapter 14, Lesson 5   **63**

**Publishing the Final Report**

*Directions* After writing, revising, and editing, it is time to publish your report. Publishing your writing means sharing it with others. Certain things must be prepared in order for the report to be ready for publication. First, you need a title page or cover sheet. Then, you must put your report together in this order: title page, report, bibliography, and a blank page at the end. Once you have done all this, it is time to share your writing.

Look at the examples of cover pages below. Each has a mistake. Correct the mistakes and rewrite the cover sheets.

1. **Trees of the West**
   April 20, 2007
   John Mitchell

2. **Baseball in the 1800s**
   My Report
   Alexis D'Argo
   January 31, 2007

3. Andrea Murphy
   March 15, 2007
   **Ancient Rome**

4. **Hibernation**
   Brenda Duckworth
   October 10, 2007

5. **The Transcontinental Railroad**
   Page 1
   Hunter Smith
   February 11, 2007

                                             **Pacemaker® Basic English Composition**

**Activity 63**

---

Name _____ Date _____ Period _____   Workbook Activity
                                             Chapter 14, Lesson 5   **63**

**Preparing to Publish**

Certain things must be prepared in order for your report to be ready for publication. You need a title page or cover sheet. Since this is the first thing anyone reading your report will see, it is important that it is done correctly.

*Directions* Use the information below to write a cover page for each report. Write a title based on the excerpt from the report.

1. On January 12, 2007, Mark Johnson writes: "Bats are one of nature's most fascinating creatures."

2. On May 29, 2007, Monty Griffin writes: "Prepare yourself to be amazed by the intriguing history of the circus!"

3. On March 1, 2007, Bobbi Sue Hanton writes: "Many people consider Alaska to be the last great American wilderness."

4. On April 18, 2007, Ben Cranshaw writes: "World War II could be called the most traumatic event of the 20th century."

5. On February 11, 2007, Anita Marquez writes: "Inventions aside, who were the Wright Brothers?"

                                             **Pacemaker® Basic English Composition**

**Workbook Activity 63**

## Bicycle Salesperson

Teresa Lopez has a job in a bicycle shop. She likes talking to customers. She finds out what they need. Then she points out the features of different bikes that fit the need. She shows why a certain bike is a good choice for them. Mr. Bali is buying a bike for his six-year-old son. Teresa made some notes about a child's bike she recommends. Read Teresa's notes. Then answer the questions below.

### Ace Flyer 300

Ace's IronGuard brakes stop the bike fast without slipping.

It has a paint finish protection, so it will not rust.

It comes with a 3-year guarantee. Ace will fix it free if something goes wrong.

It has the highest safety rating of all children's bikes.

1. What features make this the best bike in Teresa's opinion?

2. What is a guarantee? Why is this a selling point?

3. CRITICAL THINKING The most important reason comes last. Why might Teresa put the safety rating last?

### VIEWING AND LISTENING

TV advertisers use reasons, humor, and feelings to try to get you to buy something. The reasons do not always make sense. With a group, watch a TV ad carefully. Point out the sounds and sights that might make you want to buy the product. Then list the reasons it gives for buying the product. Talk about whether the reasons make sense.

*Writing the Final Report    Chapter 14*    **371**

---

# WRITING ON THE JOB

Have students read Teresa's notes and answer the questions. If you wish, have them use complete sentences. When they finish the exercise, hand out Writing on the Job 7 to students and have them complete it.

### *Writing on the Job Answers*

Wording of answers will vary. Sample answers are given. **1.** The bike is the best choice because it has good brakes, no-rust paint, a three-year guarantee, and the best safety rating of all children's bikes. **2.** A guarantee is a promise to fix the bike for free if something goes wrong. People will feel better buying the bike if they know they can have it fixed for free. **3.** Teresa knows the safety rating is the most important reason for Mr. Bali because he wants his son to be safe.

## ELL/ESL STRATEGY

**Language Objective:**
*To write a review of a foreign-language film*

Have students who are learning English watch a movie filmed in English. English-speaking students should watch a subtitled movie filmed in another language. Then have students write a review of the film. Reviews should include names of lead actors and the director, country of origin, year, length of film, and genre. Instruct students to discuss the parts they liked and disliked.

---

Writing on the Job 7

Have students read the feature and answer the questions. If you wish, direct them to use complete sentences.

### Building Research Skills Answers

**1.** You can add words, take them out, or move them from place to place. **2.** There should be white space around the margins and between typed lines. **3.** Software programs do not catch all the errors you can make in grammar and spelling.

## Speaking and Presenting Practice

Ask students to read Appendix B: Speaking Checklist, which begins on page 423. Allow them to use their reports or their reviews from page 370 to give a presentation. Time permitting, students should also be able to prepare a presentation on an entirely new subject. Stress that the presentation should be informational or persuasive. Suggest that students create note cards or an outline as a guide. They may also be encouraged to create and use simple visual aids. They may practice before a friend or family member or record their practice. Then have students share their presentations before the group.

## Formatting a Document

You can use a computer to write a report or create a presentation. With word-processing software, you can easily change your writing. You can add words or take them out. You can move words around. Word-processing software also allows you to do these things:

- Decide how much white space to leave—Give at least a 1-inch margin around the outside edge of the report. Double-space the text.

- Put facts into special formats—Create a table or chart to compare numbers or facts.

- Check spelling and grammar—The computer cannot catch all mistakes, but it catches many of them. Look at the screen of a spelling and grammar checker. When the checker finds a mistake, it gives suggestions for fixing it.

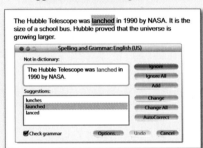

Write the answer to each question.

**1.** In what ways can you change a report using word-processing software?

**2.** Where should there be white space in a typed report?

**3.** CRITICAL THINKING Why do you need to edit your report even though the software checked it for grammar and spelling?

 **TECHNOLOGY**

Pictures, tables, and graphs add interest to a report. They also help readers understand important ideas. You can create simple tables and diagrams with most word processing software. You can also bring photos, diagrams, and other pictures into your report. They can be placed near the ideas they support or explain. For example, a report about volcanoes could show a diagram of the inside of a volcano. Does the word-processing software you use have a table formatting feature? If so, use it to make a simple table showing your class schedule.

### Formatting a Document

A computer is a key tool in the writing process. Word-processing programs allow you to alter and edit the words and format of your report after they have already been typed. You can use the software to adjust margins, create charts and tables, and check for spelling and grammatical errors. Understanding this technology is a key tool in helping you to produce the best possible report.

Use your experience with computer-writing programs to answer the questions below.

**1.** Explain the process, step-by-step, of running a spelling and grammar check on a document on your usual computer writing program.

**2.** Explain the process, step-by-step, of making a table on your usual computer writing program.

**3.** CRITICAL THINKING Think of two examples of mistakes in your writing that a computer spelling and grammar check would not catch. What does this show you?

**Building Research Skills 14**

# SUMMARY

- Use an outline to write the first draft of your report.

- Write a topic paragraph that states the report topic and gives the main ideas of the report.

- In the body of a report, provide details in organized paragraphs. Cover each main topic and subtopic on the outline. Use examples, facts, explanations, reasons, and direct quotations.

- End a report with a paragraph that summarizes the report.

- Carefully read and revise your first draft. Improve the organization and content. Add transitions between paragraphs. Use a variety of sentences.

- Edit your second draft carefully. Correct any mistakes in spelling, punctuation, and capitalization. Choose better words.

- Check the grammar of each sentence in a report. Make sure you use a consistent verb tense. Make sure each verb agrees with its subject.

- Prepare a bibliography that lists each source you used to write your report.

- Follow any special instructions about the format of your final report. Create a title page. Make a final copy of the report.

- Publish your final report by sharing it with others.

## GROUP ACTIVITY

In a small group, write a draft of a short report. Write about some part of your school. For example, you might choose its history, the library, or its students.

Trade drafts with another group. As you read their draft, make notes about how you would revise it. When your draft is returned, revise, edit, and publish the final report.

## Chapter 14 Summary

Have volunteers read aloud each Summary item on page 373. Ask volunteers to explain the meaning of each item.

## ONLINE CONNECTION

Some Web sites can assist in the report-writing process. They might offer standard guidelines, templates, and creative suggestions for writing research reports. The following sites may help:

www.agsglobepmbec.com/page373a

www.agsglobepmbec.com/page373b

## GROUP ACTIVITY

Discuss parts of the school that students might choose to write about. Perhaps they could walk around the school to get a better idea of its history. Remind groups to begin by prewriting and to follow the steps in the writing process.

## Chapter 14 Review

Use the Chapter Review to prepare students for tests and to reteach content from the chapter.

## Chapter 14 Mastery Test

The Teacher's Resource Library includes two forms of the Chapter 14 Mastery Test. Each test addresses the chapter Goals for Learning. An optional third page of additional critical-thinking items is included for each test. The difficulty level of the two forms is equivalent.

The Teacher's Resource Library includes the Final Mastery Test. This test is pictured on pages 444–445 of this Teacher's Edition. The Final Mastery Test assesses the major learning objectives of this text, with emphasis on Chapters 7–14.

### Review Answers

Part A
1. draft 2. publish 3. mechanics
Part B
4. C 5. A 6. A 7. C 8. B

---

**Word Bank**

draft
mechanics
publish

**Part A** Write the word from the Word Bank that completes each sentence.

1. A _____ is a version of your writing that is not final.

2. When you share your final version of writing, you _____ it.

3. When you edit the spelling, capitalization, and punctuation of your writing, you are editing the _____ of the piece.

**Part B** Write the letter of the answer to each question.

4. What do you use as a guide when you write a report?
   A bibliography cards   C an outline
   B the report title      D your opinions

5. Which word describes the last paragraph in a report?
   A summary    C details
   B outline     D introduction

6. Why should you put quotation marks around a direct quotation?
   A to show that you are using someone else's exact words
   B to show that you are paraphrasing
   C to show that your information is from a source
   D to show that you are using your own words

7. How do you order the sources in a bibliography?
   A by year                C by author's last name
   B by importance          D by type of source

8. How do you show a link between two sentences or paragraphs?
   A Change the verb tense.
   B Use a transitional word or phrase.
   C Change the speaker's point of view.
   D Use a run-on sentence.

---

**374**   *Chapter 14   Writing the Final Report*

---

### Chapter 14 Mastery Test A

Name _____ Date _____ Period _____   Mastery Test A / Chapter 14 / Page 1

**Part A** Match each phrase to the correct word. Write the letter of the correct answer on the line.

_____ 1. the part of a report that is always more than one paragraph
_____ 2. a guide for writing a report
_____ 3. another name for the topic paragraph
_____ 4. putting an author's information into your own words
_____ 5. they are put around an author's exact words
_____ 6. an early version of your report
_____ 7. when you complete a written message and share it with others
_____ 8. the list of sources used to write a report
_____ 9. the first page of a published report
_____ 10. it is put at the bottom of each page of a report

A bibliography
B body
C draft
D introduction
E outline
F page number
G paraphrasing
H publish
I quotation marks
J title page

**Part B** Each cover page has a mistake in grammar or spelling. Circle the mistake. Then, rewrite the cover page in the correct format on the lines below.

11. **The Water cycle** Ray Feller
    May 14, 2007
12. _____
13. Quinn Lake **Birth of a Glasher**
    June 3, 2007
14. _____

15. March 6, 2007! Mike Moffitt
    **Life in the Arctic**
16. _____

© Pearson Education, Inc., publishing as Pearson AGS Globe. All rights reserved.    **Pacemaker® Basic English Composition**

---

### Chapter 14 Mastery Test A, continued

Name _____ Date _____ Period _____   Mastery Test A / Chapter 14 / Page 2

**Part C** Look at the sentences below. If the sentence is correct, write correct on the line. If there is a mistake, write the correct word on the line.

17. Shakespeare's plays are timeless.   _____
18. Some plays are both funny and sad.   _____
19. *Twelfth Night* is an example of this.   _____
20. It tell a tale of loss and love.   _____
21. Feste, the clown, provide laughs.   _____
22. Duke Orsino loves Lady Olivia.   _____
23. Viola is disguises as Cesario.   _____
24. Olivia failed for Cesario.   _____
25. Mistaken identity creates problems.   _____

**Part D** Alphabetize these bibliography entries. Write a number from 1 to 5 in front of each item to show the correct alphabetic order.

_____ 26. Pruitt, B. E. "Drug Abuse Prevention Programs: Do They Work?" *NASSP Bulletin* (April 1993) 37–49.
_____ 27. "Alcohol and Youth." *Alcohol World* 15 (1991) 1.
_____ 28. Taylor, C. *The House That Crack Built.* San Francisco: Chronicle Books, 1991.
_____ 29. Hyde, M. *Know About Abuse.* New York: Walker & Company, 1992.
_____ 30. Collingwood, T.R., R. Reynolds, B. Jester, and D. Debord. "Enlisting Physical Education for the War on Drugs." *The Journal of Physical Education, Recreation, and Dance* 63 (February 1992) 25.

© Pearson Education, Inc., publishing as Pearson AGS Globe. All rights reserved.    **Pacemaker® Basic English Composition**

---

### Chapter 14 Mastery Test A, continued

Name _____ Date _____ Period _____   Mastery Test A / Chapter 14 / Page 3

**Part E** Write your answer to each question. Use complete sentences. Support each answer with facts and examples from the textbook.

31. Name two ways to make an introductory paragraph interesting to the reader.

32. What is the purpose of using quotations from a source in your report?

**Part F** Write a paragraph for each topic. Include a topic sentence, body, and conclusion in the paragraph.

33. Read the paragraph below. Find five mistakes. Write the paragraph correctly on your paper.
    Regular exercise keeps a person fit. People who exercise feels better and probably lives longer. Exercise helps people to maintain a healthy weight. and it stimulates the heart and lungs. Everyone should try to exercise every day

34. Explain what a writer does to revise and edit a report.

© Pearson Education, Inc., publishing as Pearson AGS Globe. All rights reserved.    **Pacemaker® Basic English Composition**

---

Chapter 14 Mastery Test A, pages 1–3

## Answer Bank

**A** pronoun and antecedent do not agree

**B** misspelled plural noun

**C** verb tense not consistent

**D** subject and verb do not agree

**E** run-on sentence with comma fault

**F** run-on sentence, but no comma fault

**G** sentence fragment

**H** wrong end punctuation

**I** missing apostrophe

### Test Tip

When you take a written test, show that you can use English well. Follow the rules of grammar, punctuation, and capitalization. Check your spelling.

**Part C** Each sentence contains a mistake. Find the type of mistake in the Answer Bank at the left. Write the letter of your answer. Use each answer once.

9. One hummingbird land on the feeder.

10. The childrens enjoyed watching the hummingbirds.

11. Yesterday they will feed the birds again.

12. Sonia had a new pen. She lost them at school yesterday.

13. Brandons report was very good.

14. Brandon wrote a report about vegetable gardening he turned it in today.

15. Are you interested in hummingbirds.

16. The hummingbirds and the feeders all summer.

17. The hummingbirds flew across the Gulf of Mexico, they spent the winter in Central America.

**Part D** Number your paper from 18 to 25. Find the mistakes in this paragraph. Write each sentence correctly.

i just read a book about the road to the white house this book begins by asking, "what makes a person want to be president" The book gives many reasons that peeple get into politics. For example, some wants to help others and make a difference. others the Feeling of power and the desire to be famous. People should remember that being the President is hard you may be famous, but you never have any time to yourself and so I recommend this book to anyone who want to be a Politician.

## Review Answers

### Part C

**9.** D **10.** B **11.** C **12.** A **13.** I **14.** F **15.** H **16.** G **17.** E

### Part D

**18.** I just read a book about the road to the White House. **19.** This book begins by asking, "What makes a person want to be president?" **20.** The book gives many reasons that people get into politics. **21.** For example, some want to help others and make a difference. **22.** Others like the feeling of power and have the desire to be famous. **23.** People should remember that being the president is hard. **24.** You may be famous, but you never have any time to yourself. **25.** I recommend this book to anyone who wants to be a politician.

## WRITING PORTFOLIO

**Wrap-Up** Have students make a clean final copy of their revised and edited reports. You may want to collect and read them anonymously to the class or have classmates share their reports in small groups. This project may be used as an alternative form of assessment for the chapter.

---

As you edit your writing, you may have questions. This appendix is designed to give you quick answers. It has four main parts: grammar, capitalization, punctuation, and spelling. Each part contains several numbered items. Each item summarizes a rule and shows examples.

## ▼ SENTENCES

**Grammar 1**  **Definition of a sentence**

A *sentence* is a group of words that expresses a complete thought. Every sentence must have a subject and a predicate. Every sentence begins with a capital letter and ends with a punctuation mark.

That loaf of bread just came out of the oven.

Is it too hot to eat?

It looks delicious!

**Grammar 2**  **Independent and dependent clauses**

A *clause* is a group of words with a subject and a verb. A sentence is an independent clause. An *independent clause* expresses a complete thought.

The election took place on the first Tuesday in November.

A *dependent clause* has a subject and a verb, but it does not express a complete thought.

Because it was snowing

**Grammar 3**  **Sentence fragments**

*Sentence fragments* are groups of words that do not express complete thoughts.

In the middle

Going to the soccer match

## Grammar 4 Run-on sentences

A *run-on sentence* has two or more ideas written as one sentence without correct punctuation or conjunctions.

| | |
|---|---|
| Run-on sentence | Amber and Sonia enjoy reading books they go to the library often. |
| Correct sentences | Amber and Sonia enjoy reading books. They go to the library often. |

## Grammar 5 Purposes of sentences

The four main reasons for writing a sentence are:
- to make a statement
- to ask a question
- to make a request or give a command
- to express emotion

A *declarative sentence* makes a statement. A declarative sentence ends with a period.

> A volcano in the Canary Islands is for sale.

An *interrogative sentence* asks a question. An interrogative sentence ends with a question mark.

> Who would want to buy a volcano?

An *imperative sentence* gives a command. An imperative sentence ends with a period or an exclamation point.

> Show me the list of buyers.

An *exclamatory sentence* expresses strong feelings. An exclamatory sentence ends with an exclamation point.

> They must be crazy!

## Grammar 6 Subjects and predicates in declarative sentences

Every sentence has two main parts, the subject and the predicate. The *subject* names the person, place, thing, or idea that the sentence is about. The *predicate* tells about the subject. The predicate always contains a verb.

In most declarative sentences, the subject comes before the predicate.

The sea captain        sailed across the ocean.
(subject)              (predicate)

### Grammar 7 Subjects and predicates in interrogative sentences

In most interrogative sentences, you separate the helping verb and the main verb to ask the question.

Did      the butler    lie about it?
(verb)   (subject)     (verb)

Are      we            going to the store today?
(verb)   (subject)     (verb)

### Grammar 8 Subjects and predicates in imperative sentences

Only the predicate of an imperative sentence is spoken or written. The subject of the sentence is understood. That subject is always *you*. When you make a request, it is polite to add the helping verb "please."

(You) Try some soup.

(You) Please tell me the answer.

### Grammar 9 Subjects and predicates in exclamatory sentences

Any kind of sentence can be exclamatory. These are sentences that express strong feeling.

How hungry I am! (statement)

Vote today! (command)

What are you doing! (question)

### Grammar 10 Compound subjects in sentences

A sentence with a compound subject has two or more subjects connected with a conjunction.

Jesse James and his brother Frank were famous outlaws in the Old West.

Cole, James, and Robert Younger were all members of the James gang.

## Grammar 11 Compound predicates in sentences

A sentence with a compound predicate has two or more verbs connected by a conjunction.

> The postal workers took in the tailless cat and named it Kojak.

> Kojak lives in the post office, catches mice, and plays with yarn.

## Grammar 12 Compound sentences

A *compound sentence* is made up of two sentences joined by a coordinating conjunction. A compound sentence has a subject and a predicate followed by another subject and another predicate.

> Howard told several jokes, but most of them were not funny.
> (subject)(verb)           (subject)      (verb)

## ▼ NOUNS

## Grammar 13 Definition of a noun

A *noun* is a word that names a person, a place, an idea, or a thing.

> That brave man crossed the ocean in a rowboat.

## Grammar 14 Singular and plural forms of nouns

Nouns can be singular or plural. The singular noun names one person, place, idea, or thing.

> Only one worker in that factory can name the secret ingredient.

The plural noun names more than one person, place, idea, or thing.

> Several workers in those two factories can name the secret ingredients.

## Grammar 15   Proper nouns and common nouns

A *common noun* is the name of any person, place, idea, or thing. Do not capitalize these words.

> The man stopped in the town and went to a museum.

A *proper noun* is the name of a particular person, place, idea, or thing. Capitalize the first letter of each important word in a proper noun.

> Max stopped in Chicago and went to the Art Institute.

## Grammar 16   Possessive nouns

A *possessive noun* shows ownership. Usually, a singular noun is made possessive by adding an apostrophe and -*s*.

> A piranha's teeth are as sharp as razors.

A plural noun that ends in  *s* is made possessive by adding only an apostrophe.

> The piranhas' teeth are as sharp as razors.

## Grammar 17   Nouns of direct address

A *noun of direct address* names the person you are speaking to. Separate a noun of direct address from the rest of the sentence with a comma.

> Where are you going, Sonia?

> I told you, Amber, that I have a rehearsal tonight.

## Grammar 18   Appositives

An *appositive* renames or identifies the noun that comes before it in a sentence. Separate an appositive from the rest of the sentence with commas.

> Luis, Sonia's cousin, moved to Ohio. (*Cousin* renames *Luis.*)

You can remove the appositive from the sentence and still have a complete thought.

> Luis moved to Ohio.

**Grammar 19**  **Definition of a verb**

A *verb* is a word that expresses action or being.

> The volcano erupted suddenly.  (action verb)

> The movie was exciting.  (state-of-being verb)

**Grammar 20**  **Infinitive verbs**

The *infinitive verb* is *to* plus the present tense.

> to be          to have          to run

**Grammar 21**  **Action verbs**

An *action verb* expresses physical or mental action.

> The committee members chose their favorite books.

> Each person had a favorite.

**Grammar 22**  **State-of-being verbs**

*State-of-being verbs* express a condition of the subject.

> The flag is on the roof of the building.

> The day seems cold.

**Grammar 23**  **Verb tenses**

Verbs express *tense*. Tense denotes time. There are three simple tenses and three perfect tenses:

| | |
|---|---|
| **Present** | Derek starts his job today. |
| **Past** | Derek started his job last week. |
| **Future** | Derek will start his job on Monday. |
| **Present Perfect** | Derek has started his job. |
| **Past Perfect** | Derek had started his job earlier. |
| **Future Perfect** | Derek will have started next Monday. |

To form the perfect tenses, use the helping verb *have* and the *past participle*. The past participle of a regular verb is the same as the past tense.

> He walked.    He has walked.

**Grammar 24**   **Forms of the verb *have***

The verb *have* can be an action verb.

> I have my homework today.

You also use *have* to form the perfect tenses.

> I have done my homework.

### Forms of *Have*

| Singular Subject | Plural Subject |
|---|---|
| (Brandon) has | (the boys) have |
| (I) have | (we) have |
| (you) have | (you) have |
| (he, she, it) has | (they) have |

**Grammar 25**   **Verb phrases**

A *verb phrase* includes a helping verb and a main verb. The main verb expresses action or state of being. The helping verb helps express time.

> The 13,000-pound bell had disappeared.

> Somebody must have stolen it.

**Grammar 26**   **Helping verbs**

The verbs before the main verb in a verb phrase are *helping verbs*. The most common helping verbs are forms of *be* (*is, are, am, was, were*), forms of *have* (*has, have, had*), and forms of *do* (*does, do, did*).

> That radio station is sponsoring a concert.

> The station has received 45,217 postcards.

**Grammar 27**   **Conditional helping verbs**

The conditional helping verbs are *should, shall, would, will, must, may, might, can,* and *could*.

Conditional verbs do not have an infinitive form. You would never say, "to may." They are used as helping verbs.

> Amber might get an A in English this semester.

## Grammar 28 Subject-verb agreement

Verbs have two forms in the present tense. The verb must agree with the subject in number (singular or plural). One present tense form of a verb agrees with singular subjects. This verb form ends with -s. Use the other form with plural subjects.

When a subject is singular, add -s or -es to the present tense of the verb.

> The snow falls gently. (*Snow* is a singular noun.)
>
> Sonia takes her violin to school. (*Sonia* is a singular noun.)

When a subject is plural, do not add -s or -es to the present tense of the verb.

> The students run. (*Students* is plural.)
>
> The dancers whirl around the stage. (*Dancers* is plural.)

## Grammar 29 Agreement of verbs with compound subjects

When the subject is compound, use the plural form of the verb.

> Amber and her brother clean the house on Saturdays.
>
> Sonia and Brandon enjoy music.

## Grammar 30 Present participle and the progressive tense of verbs

Form the present participle by adding -*ing* to the present tense.

> be—being        sing—singing        laugh—laughing

Use the helping verb *be* to form the progressive tenses.

| Present Progressive | Past Progressive |
| --- | --- |
| I am buying groceries. | I was buying groceries. |
| You are going today. | You were going yesterday. |
| He is doing his work. | He was doing his work. |
| They are eating now. | They were eating then. |

## Grammar 31    Forms of the verb *be*

*Be* is the most irregular verb. It has more forms than any other verb.

|  | Singular Subject | Plural Subject |
| --- | --- | --- |
| **Present Tense** | (Brandon) is | (the boys) are |
|  | (I) am | (we) are |
|  | (you) are | (you) are |
|  | (he, she, it) is | (they) are |
| **Past Tense** | (I) was | (we) were |
|  | (you) were | (you) were |
|  | (he, she, it) was | (they) were |

Marty is a gymnast.  (third-person singular subject)

Many people are his fans.  (third-person plural subject)

I am a pretty good gymnast, too.  (first-person singular subject)

Most verbs have one past tense form that tells about action or existence in the past. The verb *be* has two past tense forms: *was* and *were*. *Was* agrees with singular subjects. *Were* agrees with plural subjects.

The music was loud.  (singular subject)

Several neighbors were angry about it.  (plural subject)

## Grammar 32    Active and passive verbs

In a sentence, a verb can be *active* or *passive*. When the verb is active, the subject does the action. When the verb is passive, the action happens to the subject.

Amber found a rare coin.  (active)

The rare coin was found by Amber.  (passive)

Confusion happens when the writer does not name the person who did the action.

The coin was found.  (By whom?)

That horse is called a Palomino.  (By whom?)

**Grammar 33    Past tense of regular verbs**

The past tense of a regular verb ends in -d or -ed.

William Baxter invented an important part of the Morse code.

**Grammar 34    Irregular verbs**

When a verb does not form its past tense or past participle by adding -d or -ed, the verb is *irregular*.

Samuel Morse got all the credit.  (irregular past tense)

He has gotten all the credit.  (irregular past participle)

**Grammar 35    Irregular verbs: same past tense and past participle**

| Present | Past | Past Participle |
|---|---|---|
| bring(s) | brought | (has) brought |
| buy(s) | bought | (has) bought |
| catch(es) | caught | (has) caught |
| dig(s) | dug | (has) dug |
| feed(s) | fed | (has) fed |
| get(s) | got | (has) got (gotten) |
| hear(s) | heard | (has) heard |
| keep(s) | kept | (has) kept |
| lead(s) | led | (has) led |
| leave(s) | left | (has) left |
| lose(s) | lost | (has) lost |
| make(s) | made | (has) made |
| mean(s) | meant | (has) meant |
| send(s) | sent | (has) sent |
| sit(s) | sat | (has) sat |
| swing(s) | swung | (has) swung |
| teach(es) | taught | (has) taught |
| think(s) | thought | (has) thought |
| weep(s) | wept | (has) wept |
| win(s) | won | (has) won |

## Grammar 36  Irregular verbs: different past tense and past participle

| Present | Past | Past Participle |
|---|---|---|
| begin(s) | began | (has) begun |
| choose(s) | chose | (has) chosen |
| drive(s) | drove | (has) driven |
| fall(s) | fell | (has) fallen |
| fly (flies) | flew | (has) flown |
| forget(s) | forgot | (has) forgotten |
| give(s) | gave | (has) given |
| hide(s) | hid | (has) hidden |
| know(s) | knew | (has) known |
| ride(s) | rode | (has) ridden |
| ring(s) | rang | (has) rung |
| see(s) | saw | (has) seen |
| swim(s) | swam | (has) swum |
| take(s) | took | (has) taken |
| wear(s) | wore | (has) worn |
| write(s) | wrote | (has) written |

## Grammar 37  Irregular verbs: no change in form

| Present | Past | Past Participle |
|---|---|---|
| burst(s) | burst | (has) burst |
| cost(s) | cost | (has) cost |
| hit(s) | hit | (has) hit |
| put(s) | put | (has) put |
| read(s) | read | (has) read |
| set(s) | set | (has) set |

## Grammar 38  Irregular verbs: *do*, *eat*, and *go*

| Present | Past | Past Participle |
|---|---|---|
| do, does | did | (has) done |
| eat, eats | ate | (has) eaten |
| go, goes | went | (has) gone |

Grammar 39    Definition of a pronoun

A *pronoun* is a word that takes the place of a noun. The noun that the pronoun replaced is the *antecedent* of the pronoun.

> Roy Rogers became famous. He was a Western movie star. (The antecedent for *he* is *Roy Rogers*.)

A pronoun can replace a compound subject.

> Roy Rogers and Dale Evans often worked together. They made dozens of movies.
> (The antecedent for *they* is *Roy Rogers and Dale Evans*.)

Grammar 40    Personal pronouns

A personal pronoun takes the place of one or more nouns. These pronouns are *I, you, he, she, it, we, you,* and *they.*

> The entire family came to dinner. They enjoyed the meal very much. (*They* replaces *the entire family*.)

Grammar 41    Subject and object forms of personal pronouns

Each personal pronoun has a subject form and an object form. These forms are used in different ways in sentences.

|  | Subject | Object |
|---|---|---|
| **Singular** | | |
| First Person | I | me |
| Second Person | you | you |
| Third Person | he, she, it | him, her, it |
| **Plural** | | |
| First Person | we | us |
| Second Person | you | you |
| Third Person | they | them |

He read the wrong eye chart.

The army did not accept him.

**Grammar 42**  **Possessive pronouns**

A personal pronoun that shows ownership is a *possessive pronoun*. These pronouns do not use apostrophes.

These possessive pronouns are used before nouns in sentences: *my, your, his, her, its, our,* and *their*.

> Why are my gym shoes in your locker?

These possessive pronouns can stand alone in sentences: *mine, yours, his, hers, its, ours,* and *theirs*.

> Are these gym shoes mine, or are they yours?

**Grammar 43**  **Subject-verb agreement with personal pronouns**

The present tense verb form that agrees with singular nouns also agrees with the pronoun subjects *he, she,* and *it*.

> The woman shops in the mall. (singular subject)

> She shops in the mall. (A singular pronoun replaces a singular noun.)

The present tense verb that agrees with plural nouns also agrees with the pronoun subjects *I, you, we,* and *they*.

> The friends shop at the department store.

> I shop at the department store.

**Grammar 44**  **Indefinite pronouns**

*Indefinite pronouns* refer in a general way to people, places, things, and ideas. They can be singular or plural.

**Singular Indefinite Pronouns**

| | | | |
|---|---|---|---|
| anybody | either | neither | somebody |
| anyone | everybody | no one | someone |
| each | everyone | nobody | nothing |

> Everybody works. (singular pronoun and singular form of the present tense verb)

> Nobody is right about everything.

### Plural Indefinite Pronouns

| both | few | many | several |
|------|-----|------|---------|

Both need help.

Many need help.

### Singular or Plural Indefinite Pronouns

| all | any | most | none | some |
|-----|-----|------|------|------|

Most of the milk goes down easily.  (singular)

Most of the students go outside quickly.  (plural)

**Grammar 45**  **Subject-verb agreement with indefinite pronouns**

The present tense verb form that agrees with singular nouns also agrees with most indefinite pronouns.

Almost everyone remembers the Alamo.

No one knows exactly what happened there.

**Grammar 46**  **Reflexive pronouns**

A pronoun that refers back to a noun or pronoun in the same sentence is a *reflexive pronoun*. The reflexive pronouns are *myself, yourself, himself, herself, itself, ourselves, yourselves,* and *themselves.*

The witness had been talking to himself.

You should have bought yourself a ticket.

**Grammar 47**  **Demonstrative pronouns**

A word that points out one or more persons or things is a *demonstrative pronoun*. The demonstrative pronouns are *this, that, these,* and *those.*

These are my favorite shoes.

Nobody laughed at those.

### Grammar 48    Interrogative pronouns

*Interrogative pronouns* ask a question. These pronouns are *who, whom, whose, which,* and *what.*

> Who is your best friend?  (What person is your best friend?)
>
> What is that noise?  (What is the cause of that noise?)
>
> Which is that? Or which one is that?  (Of those two or more people or things, name one of them.)

### Grammar 49    Relative pronouns

*Relative pronouns* introduce clauses. *Who, whom, whose, which,* and *that* are relative pronouns.

> I don't know who is coming to the party.
>
> Derek said that he was coming to the party.
>
> Brandon asked which of their friends would be there.

### Grammar 50    *Who, whom,* and *whose*

*Who, whom,* and *whose* are interrogative pronouns. They can also be relative pronouns.

*Who* is the subject of a sentence or clause.

> Who was with Brandon?

*Whom* is an object.

> Derek did not know whom Brandon invited to the party.

*Whose* is a possessive form.

> Whose is that?

## ▼ Adjectives

**Grammar 51**   **Definition of an adjective**

An *adjective* is a word that describes or tells about a noun or pronoun. Adjectives tell *what kind*, *which one*, or *how many*.

> The exhausted players sat down.  (What kind of players?)
>
> The first assignment is due tomorrow. (Which assignment?)
>
> He bought several bags of groceries.  (How many bags?)
>
> The players were happy.  (How did they feel?)

**Grammar 52**   **Indefinite and definite articles**

*A*, *an*, and *the* are special kinds of adjectives. *A* and *an* are *indefinite articles*. Use *an* before a word that begins with a vowel or vowel sound. *The* is the definite article.

> A penguin cannot fly.
>
> They are looking for an honorable man.
>
> The apple tastes sweet. (a certain apple)

**Grammar 53**   **Predicate adjectives**

An adjective that comes after a linking verb and adds to the meaning of the subject is a *predicate adjective*.

> George Washington was tall.

**Grammar 54**   **Proper adjectives**

An adjective that is formed from a proper noun is a *proper adjective*. Each word in a proper adjective begins with a capital letter.

> The American dollar is worth less than the British pound.
>
> The new Spielberg film is great!

## Grammar 55 Comparative forms of adjectives

You can use an adjective to compare two or more people or things. When two people or things are compared, use the *comparative form* of an adjective. To make the comparative form, add *-er* to an adjective with one syllable. Use *more* or *less* before some adjectives with two syllables.

Tom is tall. (positive form)

Tom is taller than Mike. (comparative form)

Tom is amusing. (positive form)

Tom is more amusing than Mike. (comparative form)

## Grammar 56 Superlative forms of adjectives

When more than two people or things are compared, use the *superlative form*. Add *-est* to an adjective with one or more syllables. Use *most* or *least* before some adjectives with two syllables and all adjectives with more than two syllables.

Tom is funny. (positive form)

Tom is the funniest friend I have. (superlative form)

Tom is amusing. (positive form)

Tom is the most amusing friend I have. (superlative form)

## Grammar 57 *Good, better,* and *best*

The comparative and superlative forms of the adjective *good* are *better* and *best*.

Tom is a good friend. (positive form)

Tom is a better friend than Mike. (comparative form)

Tom is the best friend I have ever had. (superlative form)

**Grammar 58**    *Bad, worse,* and *worst*

The comparative and superlative forms of the adjective *bad* are *worse* and *worst*.

The weather was bad today.  (positive form)

The weather was worse today as compared to yesterday. (comparison form)

The weather was the worst I've ever seen.  (superlative form)

**Grammar 59**    Demonstrative adjectives

If the word *this, that, these,* or *those* is followed by a noun, the word is an adjective.

This house is mine.  (Which house?)

That car is Mr. Anderson's.  (Which car?)

These flowers are roses.  (Which flowers?)

Those shoes belong to Brandon.  (Which shoes?)

## ▼ ADVERBS

**Grammar 60**    Definition of an adverb

An *adverb* answers questions about a verb, an adjective, or another adverb. Adverbs usually tell *where, when, how,* or *how often.*

**Grammar 61**    Adverbs that answer questions about verbs

Adverbs answer the questions *how, when, how often,* or *where* something happened.

Sonia played her violin expertly.  (How did she play her violin?)

Amber arrived at school early.  (When did she arrive?)

Derek and Brandon practice soccer daily.  (How often?)

They prefer to eat lunch here.  (Where?)

Many adverbs that answer the question *how* end in *-ly.*

The actor accepted the prize proudly.

## Grammar 62  Adverbs that answer questions about adjectives and other adverbs

Some adverbs describe adjectives or other adverbs by telling how much or to what degree. They are called *adverbs of degree*. The most common adverbs of degree are *too*, *very*, *quite*, *extremely*, *really*, and *rather*.

> The house was very large.  (How large?)
>
> The temperature was too cold for swimming.  (How cold?)
>
> They were quite satisfied about the result.  (How satisfied?)

## Grammar 63  Comparative forms of adverbs

Adverbs can be used to compare the actions of two or more people or things. When only two people or things are compared, use the *comparative form* of an adverb. To make the comparative form, the word *more* or *less* is usually used before the adverb. Add *-er* to a few short adverbs.

> Derek runs fast.  (positive form)
>
> Derek runs faster than Brandon.  (comparative form)
>
> Sonia finished the test quickly.  (positive form)
>
> Sonia finished the test more quickly.  (comparative form)

## Grammar 64  Superlative forms of adverbs

When the actions of more than two people or things are compared, use the *superlative form*. To make the superlative form, the word *most* or *least* is usually used before the adverb. Add *-est* to a few short adverbs.

> Luis plays chess often. (positive form)
>
> Among the friends, Luis plays chess the most often. (superlative form)

## Grammar 65 — *Well, better,* and *best*

The comparative and superlative forms of the adverb *well* are *better* and *best*.

> That parrot behaved well. (positive form)
>
> The cat behaved better than your parrot. (comparative form)
>
> Of all the pets, the cat behaved the best. (superlative form)

## Grammar 66 — *Badly, worse,* and *worst*

The comparative and superlative forms of the adverb *badly* are *worse* and *worst*.

> The pet monkey behaved badly. (positive form)
>
> It behaved worse than your parrot. (comparative form)
>
> Of all the pets, the monkey behaved the worst. (superlative form)

## Grammar 67 — The adverb *not*

The adverb *not* changes the meaning of a word from positive to negative. Usually, you add a helping verb such as *do, would, could,* or *must* when you use *not*.

> The students handed in their homework.
>
> The students did not hand in their homework.

## Grammar 68 — Negative words

The adverb *not* is a negative word. Other common negative words are *no, never, no one, nobody, nothing, nowhere, hardly, barely,* and *scarcely*. Use only one negative word to make a sentence mean *no* or *not*.

| | |
|---|---|
| Correct | No one ever understands how I feel. |
| Wrong | No one never understands how I feel. |
| Correct | My friends never understand how I feel. |
| Wrong | None of my friends never understand me. |

## ▼ CONJUNCTIONS

**Grammar 69**  **Definition of a conjunction**

*Conjunctions* are words that connect two words, two parts of the sentence, or two sentences.

> The cardinals and the blue jays were fighting over the birdseed.

> They went to Arizona because they enjoy hot weather.

**Grammar 70**  **Coordinating conjunctions**

A word used to join two equal parts of a sentence is a *coordinating conjunction*. The most common coordinating conjunctions are *and*, *but*, and *or*.

> Many people drive across the country, but two men did it the hard way.

> Charles and James drove across the country and back again.

> They never stopped or took the car out of reverse gear.

**Grammar 71**  **Subordinate conjunctions**

A word used to begin an adverb clause is a *subordinate conjunction*. Common subordinate conjunctions are:

| | | | |
|---|---|---|---|
| after | before | though | when |
| although | if | unless | whenever |
| because | since | until | while |

**Grammar 72**  **Adverb clauses and complex sentences**

An *adverb clause* is a group of words that has a subject and a predicate but cannot stand alone as a sentence. An adverb clause functions like an adverb. It tells *when, where, how,* or *why*. It usually comes at the beginning or end of a sentence. A sentence formed from an adverb clause and a main clause is called a *complex sentence*.

> Whenever it is threatened, an opossum plays dead.

> It can be poked, picked up, and even rolled over while it remains completely rigid.

## Grammar 73  Correlative conjunctions

*Correlative conjunctions* work in pairs. They can connect words, phrases, or clauses.

> Either Derek or Brandon will call you later.
>
> Neither Amber nor Derek play the violin.
>
> Either Jorge will study, or he will not pass the test.

## ▼ INTERJECTIONS

## Grammar 74  Definition of an interjection

A word or phrase that expresses emotion is an *interjection*. A comma or an exclamation point separates an interjection from the rest of a sentence.

> Oh, now it makes sense.
>
> Wow! That is terrific news!

## ▼ PREPOSITIONS

## Grammar 75  Definition of a preposition

A word that shows the relationship of a noun or pronoun to some other word in a sentence is a *preposition*. The most common prepositions are listed below.

| | | | |
|---|---|---|---|
| about | before | during | over |
| above | behind | for | since |
| across | below | from | through |
| after | beneath | in | to |
| against | beside | into | under |
| along | between | like | until |
| among | beyond | of | up |
| around | by | off | upon |
| at | with | down | on |

## Grammar 76   Prepositional phrases

A preposition and a noun or pronoun form a *prepositional phrase*.

> Dr. David G. Jones set a new record for sit-ups.

> His family and friends were very proud of him.

Often, other words come between the preposition and the noun or pronoun. These words are also part of the prepositional phrase.

> He set a new record for consecutive straight-legged sit-ups.

## Grammar 77   Objects of prepositions

The noun or pronoun that follows a preposition is its *object*. A personal pronoun that is the object of a preposition should be in the object form. These are object-form pronouns: *me, you, him, her, it, us,* and *them.*

> The presents for Marie are on the table.

> The presents for her are on the table.

## Grammar 78   Prepositional phrases used as adjectives

You can use a prepositional phrase as an adjective. These prepositional phrases can describe a noun or pronoun in a sentence. They are directly behind the noun or pronoun they describe.

> The cafeteria at school sells soups of many flavors.

## Grammar 79   Prepositional phrases used as adverbs

You can use a prepositional phrase as an adverb. These prepositional phrases answer questions about a verb, an adjective, or another adverb in a sentence.

> The basketball team is playing at 8 PM.

**Grammar 80**   **Simple subjects**

The main noun or pronoun in the subject of a sentence is the *simple subject* of that sentence. The object of a preposition cannot be the simple subject of a sentence.

> A man from Ohio swam the entire length of the Mississippi River.  (The sentence is about a man.)

> A man swam the entire length of the Mississippi River. (You can remove the prepositional phrase and still have a complete sentence.)

**Grammar 81**   **Simple predicates**

The *simple predicate* of a sentence is the verb or verb phrase.

> Many people voted in the election.

> They could vote by absentee ballot.

**Grammar 82**   **Transitive and intransitive verbs**

A verb can be transitive or intransitive. A *transitive verb* sends the action to a direct object. An *intransitive verb* cannot have an object.

> **Transitive**   Luis mailed a letter to his aunt.

> **Intransitive**   They ran all the way home.

Some verbs can be transitive or intransitive.

> **Transitive**   Derek ran a good race.

> **Intransitive**   Derek ran very well.

In a dictionary, you may see the letters *v.t.* or *v.i.* beside a word that is a verb. These letters are abbreviations for "verb transitive" and "verb intransitive."

## Grammar 83　Direct objects

A noun or pronoun that tells who or what receives the action of a verb is the *direct object* of the verb. A personal pronoun that is a direct object should be in the object form. Object-form pronouns are *me, you, him, her, it, us,* and *them.*

> The postal carrier delivered the mail on time. (Delivered what?)

> We saw him through the window.　(Saw whom?)

## Grammar 84　Indirect objects

An *indirect object* is a noun or pronoun that tells *to whom, to what, for whom,* or *for what* something is done. An indirect object comes before a direct object and is not part of a prepositional phrase. An indirect object must be a noun or a pronoun. A personal pronoun that is an indirect object should be in the object form. Object-form pronouns are *me, you, him, her, it, us,* and *them.* A sentence with an indirect object always has a direct object.

> Amber gave Derek her telephone number.

> She gave him her telephone number.

## Grammar 85　Object complements

An *object complement* is a noun, pronoun, or adjective that renames or describes the direct object. Only a few verbs can have an object complement.

> She named her son Harry.　(*Son* is the direct object.)

> Gail makes me angry.　(*Me* is the direct object.)

## Grammar 86　Predicate nouns

A *predicate noun* is a noun or pronoun that follows a linking verb and renames the subject. If the predicate noun is a personal pronoun it should be in the subject form. The subject-form pronouns are *I, you, he, she, it, we,* and *they.*

> The best musician was Sonia.　(*Sonia* renames *musician.*)

> They became friends.　(*Friends* renames *they.*)

## ▼ CAPITALIZATION

**Capitalization 1**    **First word in a sentence**

Begin the first word of every sentence with a capital letter.

> Who won the writing contest?

> That man wrote a story about his first camping trip.

**Capitalization 2**    **Personal pronoun *I***

Write the pronoun *I* with a capital letter.

> At the last possible minute, I changed my mind.

**Capitalization 3**    **Names of people**

Begin each part of a person's name with a capital letter.

> Hernando Jones     Rosie Delancy     Sue Ellen Macmillan

Some parts of names have more than one capital letter. Other parts are not capitalized. Check the correct way to write each person's name. Look in a reference book or ask the person.

> JoAnne Baxter     Tony O'Hara     Jeannie McIntyre

**Capitalization 4**    **Initials in people's names**

Use a capital letter to write an initial that is part of a person's name.

> B. J. Gallardo     J. Kelly Hunt     John F. Kennedy

**Capitalization 5**    **Titles of people**

Begin the title before a person's name with a capital letter.

> Mr. Sam Yee        Captain Cook
>
> Dr. Watson         Governor Maxine Stewart

Do not use a capital letter if the title is not used before a person's name.

> Did you call the doctor?

> Who will be our state's next governor?

| Capitalization 6 | **Names of relatives** |
|---|---|
| | Capitalize names of relatives when they are part of the person's name. |

> Only Dad and Aunt Ellie understand it.
>
> She called her dad on the phone.

| Capitalization 7 | **Names of days and months** |
|---|---|
| | Begin the name of a day or a month with a capital letter. |

> Most people do not have to work on Saturday or on Sunday.
>
> At the equator, the hottest months are March and September.

| Capitalization 8 | **Names of holidays** |
|---|---|
| | Begin each important word in the name of a holiday with a capital letter. |

> They host a Fourth of July picnic and a Thanksgiving dinner.

| Capitalization 9 | **Names of streets and highways** |
|---|---|
| | Begin each word in the name of a street or highway with a capital letter. |

> Lombard Street is the most crooked road in America.

| Capitalization 10 | **Names of cities and towns** |
|---|---|
| | Begin each word in the name of a city or town with a capital letter. |

> In 2002, the Luis moved from Greenville to Springfield.

| Capitalization 11 | **Names of states, countries, and continents** |
|---|---|
| | Capitalize the name of a state, province, country, or continent. |

> The story was set in Nevada, but the film was shot in Mexico.

| Capitalization 12 | **Names of mountains and bodies of water** |
|---|---|
| | Capitalize names of mountains, rivers, lakes, and oceans. |

> The Mississippi River flows into the Gulf of Mexico.

| Capitalization 13 | **Abbreviations** |
|---|---|

If a word would begin with a capital letter, begin its abbreviation with a capital letter.

> On a scrap of paper, the patient wrote, "Wed.—Dr. Edwards."

| Capitalization 14 | **Titles of books, movies, plays, TV series** |
|---|---|

Use a capital letter to begin the first word, the last word, and every main word in the title of a work. The words *the*, *a*, and *an* do not begin with capital letters except at the beginning of a title. Coordinating conjunctions and prepositions also do not begin with capital letters.

> Pete was a character in the TV series *Friends for Life*.

| Capitalization 15 | **Proper adjectives** |
|---|---|

Begin a proper adjective with a capital letter. A proper adjective is an adjective that is formed from a proper noun. If the proper adjective is made with two or more nouns, capitalize each of them.

> That American author writes about English detectives.

> She loves Spanish movies.

| Capitalization 16 | **Direct quotations** |
|---|---|

Begin the first word in a direct quotation with a capital letter.

> Dr. Pavlik said, "What brings you in today?"

If the words that tell who is speaking appear in the middle of a quotation, do not begin the second part of the quotation with a capital letter.

> "What brings you," asked Dr. Pavlik, "into my office?"

| Capitalization 17 | **Greetings and closings in letters** |
|---|---|

Begin the first word in the greeting of a letter with a capital letter.

> Dear Mr. Lincoln:    Dear Uncle Abe,    Madam:

Begin the first word in the closing of a letter with a capital letter.

> Sincerely yours,    Very truly yours,    Love,

Punctuation 1    **End punctuation**

Use a period, a question mark, or an exclamation point at the end of every sentence. Do not use more than one of these marks at the end of a sentence.

Use a period at the end of a declarative sentence (a sentence that makes a statement).

> A hockey player must be able to skate backward at top speed.

Also use a period at the end of an imperative sentence (a sentence that gives a command).

> Keep your eye on the puck.

Use a question mark at the end of an interrogative sentence (a sentence that asks a question).

> Who is the goalie for their team?

Use an exclamation point at the end of an exclamatory sentence (a sentence that expresses strong feelings).

> That was a terrific save!

Punctuation 2    **Abbreviations**

Use a period at the end of each part of an abbreviation.

> J. T. Edwards

Most titles used before people's names are abbreviations. These abbreviations may be used in formal writing. (*Miss* is not an abbreviation and does not end with a period.)

> Dr. Blackwell    Mr. Bill Tilden

Most other abbreviations may be used in addresses, notes, and informal writing. Do not use them in formal writing.

> Lake Blvd.    Fifth Ave.    Mon., Dec. 24

## Punctuation 3  Organization names

Do not use periods in the abbreviations of names of agencies, organizations, or groups.

Tonight, station KMLT will air a program about the FBI.

## Punctuation 4  State abbreviations

Do not use periods after two-letter state abbreviations in addresses. This kind of abbreviation has two capital letters and no period.

Our address is 1887 West Third Street, Vista, CA 90048.

Use the following abbreviations in addresses.

### State Abbreviations

| | | | |
|---|---|---|---|
| Alabama | AL | Montana | MT |
| Alaska | AK | Nebraska | NE |
| Arizona | AZ | Nevada | NV |
| Arkansas | AR | New Hampshire | NH |
| California | CA | New Jersey | NJ |
| Colorado | CO | New Mexico | NM |
| Connecticut | CT | New York | NY |
| Delaware | DE | North Carolina | NC |
| District of Columbia | DC | North Dakota | ND |
| Florida | FL | Ohio | OH |
| Georgia | GA | Oklahoma | OK |
| Hawaii | HI | Oregon | OR |
| Idaho | ID | Pennsylvania | PA |
| Illinois | IL | Rhode Island | RI |
| Indiana | IN | South Carolina | SC |
| Iowa | IA | South Dakota | SD |
| Kansas | KS | Tennessee | TN |
| Kentucky | KY | Texas | TX |
| Louisiana | LA | Utah | UT |
| Maine | ME | Vermont | VT |
| Maryland | MD | Virginia | VA |
| Massachusetts | MA | Washington | WA |
| Michigan | MI | West Virginia | WV |
| Minnesota | MN | Wisconsin | WI |
| Mississippi | MS | Wyoming | WY |
| Missouri | MO | | |

## Punctuation 5   Initials

An initial is an abbreviation for a person's name. Use a period after an initial that is part of a person's name.

C. C. Pyle        Susan B. Anthony

## Punctuation 6   Commas in dates

Use a comma between the day and the year in a date. Do not use a comma in a date that has only the month and year. Do not use a comma in a date that has only the month and the day.

April 8, 1974, was an exciting day for Hank Aaron's fans.

Aaron hit his record-breaking home run on April 8, 1974.

April 8 is the anniversary of Aaron's famous home run.

He hit his final home run in July 1976.

## Punctuation 7   Commas in place names

Use a comma between the name of a city or town and the name of a state or country.

A large chocolate factory is in Hershey, Pennsylvania.

If the two names do not come at the end of a sentence, use another comma after the name of the state or country.

Hershey, Pennsylvania, is home to a large chocolate factory.

## Punctuation 8   Commas in compound sentences

Use a comma before the conjunction *and*, *but*, or *or* in a compound sentence.

Eighteen people tried, but no one succeeded.

| Punctuation 9 | **Commas in series** |
|---|---|

Use commas to separate the words or groups of words in a series. A *series* is three or more words or groups of words.

Place a comma after each item in a series except the final one. Place a comma between two or more adjectives before a noun. Do not use a comma between adjectives that work together as part of the same idea.

> That is a great Chinese restaurant.
>
> Amber visited Tokyo, Bangkok, and Hong Kong.
>
> Amber had an interesting, exciting trip.

| Punctuation 10 | **Commas after introductory phrases and clauses** |
|---|---|

Use a comma after an adverb phrase or clause at the beginning of a sentence.

> In the old dresser, Penny found the diamonds.
>
> In the old dresser lay the diamonds.

| Punctuation 11 | **Nouns of direct address** |
|---|---|

Use a comma before or after a noun of direct address.

> Fernando, that was a terrific pitch!
>
> That was a terrific pitch, Fernando!
>
> That, Fernando, was a terrific pitch!

| Punctuation 12 | **Appositives** |
|---|---|

Use a comma before an appositive at the end of a sentence. If an appositive appears in the middle of a sentence, use one comma before the appositive and another comma after it.

> Everyone voted for Shelley, our class president.
>
> Shelley, our class president, planned this event.

| Punctuation 13 | **Interjections** |
|---|---|

Use a comma or exclamation mark after an interjection.

> Well, we should probably think about it.
>
> Wow! That is a terrific idea!

| Punctuation 14 | Commas after greetings in personal letters |
|---|---|

Use a comma after the greeting in a personal letter.

> Dear Kay,     Dear Uncle Ted,

| Punctuation 15 | Commas after closings in letters |
|---|---|

Use a comma after the closing in a personal or business letter.

> Love,        Yours sincerely,

| Punctuation 16 | Quotation marks with direct quotations |
|---|---|

Use quotation marks at the beginning and the end of each part of a direct quotation.

> "Look!" cried Tina. "That cat is smiling!"

> "Of course," Tom joked, "it's a Cheshire cat."

| Punctuation 17 | Commas with direct quotations |
|---|---|

Usually, use a comma to separate the words of a direct quotation from the words that tell who is speaking.

> Jay asked, "Who won the game last night?"

> "The Tigers won it," said Linda, "in 14 innings."

| Punctuation 18 | End punctuation with direct quotations |
|---|---|

At the end of a direct quotation, use a period, a comma, a question mark, or an exclamation point before the closing quotation marks. If the direct quotation makes a statement or gives a command at the end of a sentence, use a period.

> Linda said, "The Tigers won last night's game."

If the direct quotation makes a statement or gives a command before the end of a sentence, use a comma.

> "The Tigers won last night's game," said Linda.

If the direct quotation asks a question, use a question mark.

> "Was it an exciting game?" asked Jay.

If the direct quotation expresses excitement, use an exclamation point.

> Linda yelled, "It was great!"

**Punctuation 19**  **Quotation marks with titles of works**

Use quotation marks around the title of a story, poem, song, essay, or chapter.

> "Have a Happy Day" is a fun song to sing.

If a period or a comma comes after the title, put the period or comma inside the closing quotation mark.

> A fun song to sing is "Have a Happy Day."

**Punctuation 20**  **Titles of works**

Put the title of a book, play, magazine, movie, TV series, or newspaper in italic type when you use a word-processing program.

> One of the best movies about baseball was *The Champion*.

Underline the title of a book, play, magazine, movie, TV series, or newspaper when you write it by hand.

> One of the best movies about baseball was The Champion.

## Punctuation 21    Apostrophes in contractions

A *contraction* is short form of a word or phrase. Use an apostrophe in place of the missing letter or letters in a contraction.

### Common Contractions

| | |
|---|---|
| aren't = are not | hasn't = has not |
| can't = cannot | haven't = have not |
| couldn't = could not | isn't = is not |
| didn't = did not | shouldn't = should not |
| doesn't = does not | weren't = were not |
| don't = do not | won't = will not |
| hadn't = had not | wouldn't = would not |
| I'd = I would, I had | we'll = we will |
| I'll = I will | we're = we are |
| I'm = I am | we've = we have |
| I've = I have | they'd = they would, they had |
| you'll = you will | they're = they are |
| you're = you are | they've = they have |
| you've = you have | that's = that is, that has |
| he's = he is, he has | what's = what is, what has |
| she's = she is, she has | who's = who is, who has |
| it's = it is, it has | there's = there is |
| let's = let us | here's = here is |

## Punctuation 22    Apostrophes in possessive nouns

Use an apostrophe and -*s* to write the possessive form of a singular noun.

> This cage belongs to one bird. It is the bird's cage.

Use only an apostrophe to write the possessive form of a plural noun that ends in -*s*.

> This is a club for boys. It is a boys' club.

Use an apostrophe and -*s* to write the possessive form of a plural noun that does not end in -*s*.

> This is a club for women. It is a women's club.

| Punctuation 23 | **Colons after greetings in business letters** |
|---|---|

Use a colon after the greeting in a business letter.

> Dear Mrs. Huan:          To Whom It May Concern:

| Punctuation 24 | **Colons in expressions of time** |
|---|---|

When you write time in numerals, use a colon between the hour and the minutes.

> 5:45 PM          9:00 AM

| Punctuation 25 | **Hyphens in numbers and fractions** |
|---|---|

Use a hyphen in a compound number from twenty-one to ninety-nine and in fractions.

> thirty-five          one-quarter     seven-eighths

| Punctuation 26 | **Hyphens in separated parts of words** |
|---|---|

Divide a word at the end of a line with a hyphen. Place the hyphen between syllables. A dictionary will show you exactly where you can divide a word.

> ap-ple          train-ing          punc-tu-a-tion

---

### ▼ WORDS THAT SOUND THE SAME

| Spelling 1 | *To*, *two*, and *too* |
|---|---|

to (prep.) Moving toward or showing a relationship

> The family went to Sacramento.

too (adv.) Very; also

> I ate too much. Did you eat a lot, too?

to (prep.) A word used before a verb to create an infinitive

> We like to dance and to sing.

two (adj.) A number

> Do you want two or three peaches?

**Spelling 2**   *Hear* and *here*

hear (vb.) To receive a sound through the ears

> I hear you loud and clear.

here (adv.) In this place

> We will meet here later.

**Spelling 3**   *Weak* and *week*

weak (adj.) Not strong

> Illness makes people feel weak.

week (n.) Seven days

> We went on a vacation for a week.

**Spelling 4**   *Piece* and *peace*

piece (n.) A part or section

> Take another piece of cake.

peace (n.) The absence of war; calm

> Can we have some peace and quiet, please?

**Spelling 5**   *Whether* and *weather*

whether (conj.) A word used to introduce two choices

> Whether the team wins or ties, it will make the playoffs.

weather (n.) The condition of the atmosphere at a certain time and place

> The weather changed from hot to cold.

**Spelling 6**   *Waist* and *waste*

waist (n.) Part of the body between the ribs and hips

> A belt fits around the waist.

waste (n.) Trash; (vb.) to use up carelessly

> That basket is for waste.

> Do not waste paper.

**Spelling 7**     *Brake* and *break*

brake (n.) Something that stops or slows motion; (v.t.) to stop or slow the motion

> The driver used the brake to slow down the bus.

break (v.i.) To separate into pieces; (n.) an interruption or pause

> Did that glass break while you were on a lunch break?

**Spelling 8**     *Past* and *passed*

past (adj.) Of a time gone by; (n.) times that have gone by

> We studied the past and learned about past events.

passed (v.t.) Past tense of pass

> The student passed the quiz yesterday.

**Spelling 9**     *Council* and *counsel*

council (n.) A group that meets to discuss issues or to govern

> The town council has six members.

counsel (n.) Advice; (v.t.) to give advice

> Ms. Allen is wise. She gives good counsel.

**Spelling 10**     *Through* and *threw*

through (adj.) Finished; (prep.) in and out of

> We will be through with our trip after we pass through this tunnel.

threw (v.t.) Past tense of throw

> Who threw the ball the last time?

**Spelling 11**  *Plain* and *plane*

plain (adj.) Clear and simple; not fancy

> The woman wore a plain blouse.

plane (n.) A flat surface

> The math students learned about lines that form a plane.

plane (n.) A shortened word for airplane

> The passengers boarded the plane.

plain (n.) A flat area of land

> Grass grew on the plain.

plane (n.) A woodworking tool for making a surface smooth and flat; (vb.) to use a tool to smooth a surface

> The carpenter used a plane to plane the shelf.

**Spelling 12**  *Principal* and *principle*

principal (adj.) First in importance; (n.) the head of a school

> What is the principal job of a school principal?

principle (n.) A basic truth; a rule

> The principle of freedom must be protected.

principal (n.) The amount of money on which interest is charged or paid

> Loan payments include interest and principal.

## ▼ WORDS THAT SOUND SIMILAR

**Spelling 13**  *Advice* and *advise*

advice (n.) Suggestions or information

> The teacher gave helpful advice.

advise (v.t.) To give suggestions or information

> What did the coach advise you to do?

**Spelling 14** *Than* and *then*

than (conj.) A word used in a comparison

Jon is taller than his father.

then (adv.) At that time; soon afterward

Then what happened?

**Spelling 15** *Quite* and *quiet*

quite (adv.) Completely; truly

I am not quite done reading.

quiet (adj.) Silent; making almost no noise

It is so quiet here!

**Spelling 16** *Personal* and *personnel*

personal (adj.) Private; having to do with a certain person

A diary is a personal form of writing.

personnel (n.) The employees of a business; (adj.) concerned with the employees of a business

A personnel manager was in charge of the workers.

**Spelling 17** *Affect* and *effect*

affect (v.t.) To influence someone or something

How does loud noise affect you?

effect (n.) Result; the influence of one thing on another

One effect of cold weather is frost.

**Spelling 18** *Were* and *where*

were (v.i.) Past tense of the verb be.

The children were in bed last night.

where (adv.) At or in what place.

Where did the children sleep?

## Spelling 19    *Loose* and *lose*

loose (adj.) Free; not tight

> Loose clothing is in style.

lose (v.t.) To misplace; to fail to win

> One team must lose the game.

## Spelling 20    *Choose* and *chose*

choose (v.t.) To pick out or select

> In a democracy, voters choose their leaders.

chose (v.t.) Past tense of choose; picked out or selected

> Last month the voters chose their leaders.

## Spelling 21    *Accept* and *except*

accept (vb.) To receive willingly

> I accept your explanation.

except (prep.) Other than; if not for the fact that; but

> Everyone was there except me.

### ▼ CONTRACTIONS AND POSSESSIVE PRONOUNS

## Spelling 22    *It's* and *its*

it's      A contraction of *it is*

> Whenever it's raining, the roof leaks.

its       A possessive pronoun used to show ownership

> Its windows need repair.

## Spelling 23    *You're* and *your*

you're   A contraction of *you are*

> If you're late for class, your teacher may be angry.

your     A possessive pronoun used to show ownership

> Your sweater is very pretty.

**Spelling 24**   *Who's* and *whose*

who's   A contraction of *who is* or *who has*

Who's that tall player?

whose   A possessive pronoun used to show ownership

No one knows whose team he is on.

---

▼ PLURAL NOUNS

**Spelling 25**   **Regular plural nouns**

Add *-s* to make most nouns plural.

| Singular | Plural |
|----------|--------|
| book | books |

**Spelling 26**   **Nouns that end in *-s, -z, -x, -sh,* or *-ch***

If a noun ends in *-s, -z, -x, -sh,* or *-ch,* then add *-es* to make it plural.

| Singular | Plural |
|----------|--------|
| guess | guesses |
| buzz | buzzes |
| ax | axes |
| leash | leashes |
| watch | watches |

**Spelling 27**   **Nouns that end in *-y***

Some nouns end with a vowel before the letter *y.* If there is a vowel before *y,* just add *-s* to make a plural noun. (The vowels are a, e, i, o, and u.)

| Singular | Plural |
|----------|--------|
| boy | boys |
| monkey | monkeys |

Some nouns end with a consonant before the *y.* Then you must change the *y* to *i* and add *-es* to make a plural noun.

| Singular | Plural |
|----------|--------|
| city | cities |
| story | stories |

### Spelling 28 Nouns that end in *-f* or *-fe*

Some singular nouns end with *-f* or *-fe*. Sometimes you just add *-s* to make a plural noun. At other times, you must change the *f* to *v* and add *-s* or *-es*. How can you tell what to do? Try pronouncing the plural noun carefully. Listen for the *f* or *v* sound.

| Singular | Plural |
|----------|--------|
| roof | roofs |
| belief | beliefs |
| leaf | leaves |
| wife | wives |

### Spelling 29 Nouns that end in *-o*

A few nouns end with *-o*. If there is a vowel before the *o*, just add *-s* to make a plural noun.

| Singular | Plural |
|----------|--------|
| radio | radios |
| stereo | stereos |

If a singular noun ends with a consonant before the letter *o*, you usually add *-es* to make it plural.

| Singular | Plural |
|----------|--------|
| hero | heroes |
| mosquito | mosquitoes |

With musical terms, just add *-s* to form the plural.

| Singular | Plural |
|----------|--------|
| piano | pianos |
| solo | solos |

### Spelling 30 *Child*, *man*, and *tooth*

Some plural nouns are irregular. An irregular plural noun does not form its plural by adding *-s* or *-es*.

| Singular | Plural |
|----------|--------|
| child | children |
| man | men |
| tooth | teeth |

**Spelling 31**    *Deer, sheep, and fish*

Sometimes the singular and plural forms of the noun are the same. The nouns *deer*, *sheep*, *moose*, *fish*, and *trout* are the same for both singular and plural subjects.

| Singular | Plural |
|----------|--------|
| one deer | several deer |
| one sheep | many sheep |

**Spelling 32**    Plurals of proper nouns

You may want to write the plural of a proper noun such as a family name. Add *-s* or *-es* to make a name plural.

> Ms. Choy and her family are the Choys.

> Eliza Chevez and her family are the Chevezes.

If a name ends with a consonant before the letter *y*, do not change the *y* to *i*.

> Sophie Stansky invited all the Stanskys to dinner.

> Kelly Takemura and Kelly Harte. are in our class; our class has two Kellys.

Do not use an apostrophe to make a plural. Use an apostrophe only to make a possessive.

**Singular Possessive Proper Nouns**

| James's cat | Kelly's pencil | Mr. Takemura's job |
|-------------|----------------|--------------------|

**Plural Possessive Proper Nouns**

| the Joneses' apartment | the Takemuras' dog |
|------------------------|--------------------|

**Spelling 33**    Plurals of letters and numbers

Do not use an apostrophe to make a plural. If, however, a plural letter would be confusing without an apostrophe, use one to make the letter plural. When making a plural with a number, do not use an apostrophe.

> Children learn their ABCs.

> The Vietnam War was fought in the 1960s.

**Spelling 34** ## Words with *ie* and *ei*

Words with *ie* or *ei* may confuse spellers. How can you tell which letter to put first? Memorizing this verse can help you.

Put *i* before *e*  (achieve, believe, thief)

Except after *c*  (receive, ceiling, deceit)

Or when sounded like *a*

As in *neighbor* and *weigh*.  (veil, sleigh, eight)

Unfortunately, some words do not follow the pattern in the verse. You can learn these exceptions. Look at each word, spell it aloud, and write it. The correct spellings will become familiar to you. Some exceptions:

| | | | |
|---|---|---|---|
| either | foreign | neither | leisure |
| height | caffeine | seize | science |
| weird | ancient | | |

**Spelling 35** ## Adding an ending to one-syllable words

Double the final consonant before adding an ending when the word has one syllable, ends in just one consonant, and has just one vowel before the final consonant. This is true for endings that begin with vowels: *-ing*, *-ed*, *-er*, *-est*, *-y*, and *-ist*.

### Words in Which the Final Consonant Is Doubled

hop + ed = hopped            shut + ing = shutting

big + er = bigger            wet + est = wettest

### Words in Which the Final Consonant Is Not Doubled

sweet + er = sweeter (Two vowels come before the final consonant.)

jump + ed = jumped (Two consonants come at the end.)

sad + ly = sadly    (The ending begins with a consonant.)

**Spelling 36**    **Adding an ending to two-syllable words**

Double the final consonant before adding an ending to a two-syllable word when the word ends in just one consonant, has only one vowel before the final consonant, and the second syllable is accented, or spoken with greater force, than the first syllable. This is true for endings that begin with vowels: *-ing, -ed, -er, -est, -y,* and *-ist.*

**Words in Which the Final Consonant Is Doubled**

begin + er = beginner

control + ed = controlled

forget + ing = forgetting

**Words in Which the Final Consonant Is Not Doubled**

| | |
|---|---|
| return + ed = returned | (The final syllable, *turn,* ends in two consonants.) |
| travel + er = traveler | (The final syllable, *el,* is not accented.) |
| repeat + ed = repeated | (Two vowels come before the final consonant.) |
| forget + ful = forgetful | (The ending begins with a consonant.) |

**Spelling 37**    **Adding an ending to words with a silent final *e***

When you add endings to words that have a silent final *e,* you may need to make a spelling change.

Keep the silent *e* before an ending that begins with a consonant.

safe + ly = safely

use + ful = useful

Drop the silent *e* before an ending that begins with a vowel.

take + ing = taking

noise + y = noisy

## Spelling 38    Spelling demons

Some words are misspelled more often than other words. The way to learn these spelling demons is to practice writing them correctly again and again. Here are 50 commonly misspelled words.

| | | |
|---|---|---|
| acquaint | experience | pleasant |
| across | false | privilege |
| athletic | February | realize |
| beautiful | film | recommend |
| benefit | finally | secretary |
| business | forty | separate |
| character | government | similar |
| clothes | grammar | since |
| committee | immediately | speech |
| decision | interesting | surprise |
| definite | knowledge | thorough |
| describe | library | together |
| description | minute | true |
| different | necessary | usually |
| disappear | ninety | Wednesday |
| disappoint | occasion | which |
| doctor | once | |

# Appendix B: Speaking Checklist

Speaking in front of an audience is one way to communicate. Common types of public speaking include speeches, presentations, debates, discussions, interviews, storytelling, and role playing. Use this checklist to help you plan a speech or presentation.

## Define Your Purpose and Audience

✔ If the speech is an assignment, read the instructions carefully. What will you be graded on? Will the speech be formal or informal? Will you stand in front of a podium? Can you interact with the audience?

✔ Decide on your purpose. Do you want to inform, entertain, persuade, explain, or describe something? Do you want to get the audience to act on an issue? Do you want to involve them in a discussion or debate?

✔ Identify your audience. Who are they?

✔ Think about what your audience already knows about the topic. Predict their questions, concerns, and opinions. What words are familiar to them? What may need explanation?

✔ Think about how your audience prefers to get information. Do they like visuals, audience participation, or lecture?

## Decide on Your Topic

✔ Choose a topic that is right for the purpose and assignment. Choose one that you know and enjoy, or choose one that you want to learn more about.

✔ Make sure the topic is important or interesting to the audience.

✔ Determine how long your speech should be. Is your topic narrow enough? Do you have enough time to share the details?

✔ Think about the kinds of details that will help you get across the main idea.

## Draft Your Speech

✔ Include an introduction, a body, and a conclusion.

✔ In the introduction, state your topic and purpose. Give your opinion.

✔ Establish yourself as an expert. Tell why you are the right person to give the speech based on your experiences.

✔ Get the attention of your audience so they want to listen. You might start your speech by asking a question, telling a story, describing something, giving a surprising fact, sharing a quotation, or making a memorable entrance.

- ✔ In the body of your speech, tell more about your main idea.

- ✔ Try to prevent misunderstandings.

- ✔ Include supporting details such as facts, explanations, reasons, examples, stories or experiences, and quotes from experts.

- ✔ Check the order of your supporting details. Do they build on each other? Is the order logical?

- ✔ If you are describing something, use figures of speech, specific words, and words that appeal to the senses.

- ✔ If you are telling a story, make sure it has a beginning, middle, and end.

- ✔ Repeat key phrases or words to help people remember your point. If something is important, say it twice.

- ✔ Use transitions such as, "This is so important it is worth repeating" or "As I said before, we must act now."

- ✔ In the conclusion, tie your speech together.

- ✔ If you asked a question in your introduction, answer it in the conclusion.

- ✔ If you outlined a problem in your introduction, offer a solution.

- ✔ If you told a story in your introduction, refer to that story again.

- ✔ You may want to ask your audience to get involved, to take action, or to find out more about your topic.

- ✔ Revise your speech. Add missing details. Make sure the details support the main idea. Make sure the body is organized in a logical way.

- ✔ Edit and proofread your script. Choose more specific words. Check your grammar.

## Select Audio/Visual Aids

- ✔ Decide if a visual aid would help your audience understand the main idea. Visual aids include posters, displays, objects, models, pictures or words on a screen or blackboard, and slide shows.

- ✔ Decide if handing out printed material, such as a list or diagram, would help the audience follow along.

- ✔ Decide if an audio recording or video clip would be helpful or interesting.

- ✔ Think about how the room is set up. Can the room be darkened for a slide show or video presentation? If the room is large, do you need a microphone or projector?

- ✔ Make sure the right technology and props are available. Do you need a projector, video or tape player, computer, overhead screen, display table, or easel? Do you need someone to hold something or turn on something?

- ✔ Make sure the audience will be able to clearly hear or see your audio/visual aids.

## Know Your Speech

✔ Every speaker is afraid of forgetting his or her speech. Choose one of the following ways to remember your speech.

✔ Hold a copy of the entire script. Highlight key phrases to keep you on track.

✔ Write an outline of your main points and supporting details. Use sentences. Write down anything that you want to say in a certain way.

✔ Write an outline using only key words. Choose words that will remind you what to say.

✔ Write key words, an outline, or your entire speech on note cards. Note cards are small and easy to hold. Number the cards in case they get out of order.

✔ Memorize your speech.

## Practice Your Speech

✔ Practice your speech several times so you are familiar with the words.

✔ If you plan to use a script, practice with it. Do not just read your script. Practice looking out at the audience.

✔ If you plan to use note cards or an outline, practice with them. Revise them as you practice.

✔ If you plan to use visual aids, practice with them. Decide when in the speech you will introduce them.

✔ If you plan to use some technology, be familiar with how it works.

✔ Practice sounding natural and confident. Practice looking comfortable and confident. Your voice and appearance are powerful parts of your speech.

✔ Decide what you will wear when you give your speech.

✔ Practice how you will move. Will you stand in one place? What gestures will reinforce your message?

## Give Your Speech

✔ Body language: Stand tall. Keep your feet shoulder-width apart. Do not cross your arms or bury your hands in your pockets. Do not rock back and forth. Use gestures to make a point. For example, hold up two fingers when you say, "My second point is . . ."

✔ Eye contact: Look at your audience. Spend a minute or two looking at each side of the audience. The audience will feel as if you are talking to them. Do not just look at your teacher, the front row, or one side.

✔ Voice strategies: Pronounce your words clearly. Do not speak too fast. Speak loud enough for everyone to hear. Change your volume, speed, or pitch to emphasize something. For example, you could say, "I have a secret. . . ." Then, you could lean toward the audience and speak in a loud, clear whisper.

# Appendix C: Listening Checklist

Listening is an important skill. You hear messages all the time—from other people and from the media. You are a listener at school, at home, at social events, at work, even in the car. You are a listener whenever you are part of a conversation or a discussion. It is important to understand and analyze the messages you hear. Use this checklist to become a better listener.

## Listen Actively

✔ Be prepared for listening. Complete any reading assignments that are due before a speech or presentation.

✔ Sit near the speaker and face the speaker directly.

✔ Sit up straight to show you are alert.

✔ Look at the speaker and nod to show you are listening.

✔ Focus on what the speaker is saying. Do not be distracted by others in the audience.

✔ Take short notes during the speech or presentation.

✔ After the speech, ask the speaker to explain unfamiliar words or confusing ideas.

## Be Appreciative and Thoughtful

✔ Relax and enjoy the listening experience.

✔ Think of the listening experience as an opportunity to learn.

✔ Respect the speaker and his or her opinions and ideas.

✔ Do not talk or make distracting gestures.

✔ Do not cross your arms. Open your arms to show you are open to receiving information.

✔ Try to understand the speaker's background, experiences, and feelings.

## Analyze the Message

✔ Predict what the speaker is going to say based on what you already know.

✔ Identify the main idea of the message.

✔ Determine the purpose of the message.

✔ Note details such as facts, examples, and personal experiences. Does each detail support the main idea?

✔ Determine if a supporting detail is a fact or an opinion. Watch for opinions that are not supported. Watch for unfair attacks on a person's character, lifestyle, or beliefs.

- ✔ Identify any details intended to trick or persuade. Watch for exaggerations of truth. Watch for cause-effect relationships that do not make sense.

- ✔ If there are audio/visual aids, do they contribute to the message? What effect do they have?

- ✔ After the speech, ask about any words or ideas you did not understand.

- ✔ Form your own conclusions about the message.

## Analyze the Speaker

- ✔ Analyze the speaker's experience and knowledge. Is he or she qualified to speak on the topic?

- ✔ Does the speaker seem prepared? Does the speaker appear confident?

- ✔ Analyze the speaker's body language. Is it appropriate?

- ✔ Consider the speaker's tone, volume, and word choices. What do they show?

## Take Notes

- ✔ Write down key ideas and phrases, not everything that is said. Abbreviate words.

- ✔ Summarize the main points of the message in your own words.

- ✔ Copy important visual aids, such as graphs, charts, and diagrams. Do not copy every detail.

- ✔ Use stars or underlining to highlight important information or main points.

- ✔ Use arrows to connect related information.

- ✔ Use lists, charts, bullets, or dividing lines to organize information.

- ✔ Circle anything that is confusing or needs to be explained. Ask about this later.

- ✔ Use the note-taking guidelines described on page xiii of this textbook.

*Appendix C* **427**

# Appendix D: Viewing Checklist

Visual messages are messages that you see. They may or may not contain words. Visual messages include artwork, posters, diagrams, videos, photos, slide shows, and ads. Use this checklist to help you analyze a visual message.

## Analyze Photos and Videos
✔ Identify the parts and features of the photo or video. What does it show?

✔ For videos, think about how movement is used to create the message. Is it fast or slow?

✔ Are written or spoken words part of the message? If so, how do the words affect what you see?

✔ Think about how the photo or video makes you feel. What mood is created? What are you reminded of?

## Analyze Artwork
✔ Notice how colors, shapes, lines, and textures are used. Do certain features seem important?

✔ Think about the artist's purpose. What message does the art express? Does it represent something? Does it show an opinion or a mood?

## Analyze Graphs, Charts, and Diagrams
✔ Graphs and charts are used to organize information. What information is shown? Is it clear?

✔ Graphs and charts often compare facts or numbers. What is being compared?

✔ Diagrams use shapes, lines, and arrows to show a main idea. What does the diagram show?

## Analyze the Overall Message
✔ Think about the main idea. What is the author/artist trying to say? Is he or she successful?

✔ Think about the purpose of the message. Is the author/artist trying to inform, persuade, or entertain?

✔ Look for facts and opinions. Is information presented fairly? Does the message express an opinion? Is exaggeration used?

✔ Think about how the parts of the message work together. Does each part support the main idea? Do any parts take away from the main idea?

✔ Sometimes a visual message is part of a presentation, display, or speech. How does the visual message tie into the whole presentation? Does it help the presenter make a point?

✔ What conclusion can you make after viewing this message?

✔ What will you remember most about this message?

# Appendix E: Reading Checklist

Good readers do not just read with their eyes. They read with their brains turned on. In other words, they are active readers. Good readers use strategies as they read to keep them on their toes. The following strategies will help you to check your understanding of what you read.

✔ **Summarizing** To summarize a text, stop often as you read. Notice these things: the topic, the main thing being said about the topic, important details that support the main idea. Try to sum up the author's message using your own words.

✔ **Questioning** Ask yourself questions about the text and read to answer them. Here are some useful questions to ask: Why did the author include this information? Is this like anything I have experienced? Am I learning what I hoped I would learn?

✔ **Predicting** As you read, think about what might come next. Add in what you already know about the topic. Predict what the text will say. Then, as you read, notice whether your prediction is right. If not, change your prediction.

✔ **Text Structure** Pay attention to how a text is organized. Find parts that stand out. They are probably the most important ideas or facts. Think about why the author organized ideas this way. Is the author showing a sequence of events? Is the author explaining a solution or the effect of something?

✔ **Visualizing** Picture what is happening in a text or what is being described. Make a movie out of it in your mind. If you can picture it clearly, then you know you understand it. Visualizing what you read will also help you remember it later.

✔ **Inferencing** The meaning of a text may not be stated. Instead, the author may give clues and hints. It is up to you to put them together with what you already know about the topic. Then you make an inference—you conclude what the author means.

✔ **Metacognition** Think about your thinking patterns as you read. Before reading a text, preview it. Think about what you can do to get the most out of it. Think about what you already know about the topic. Write down any questions you have. After you read, ask yourself: Did that make sense? If not, read it again.

# Glossary

## A

**Action verb** (ak′ shən vėrb)  A verb that tells what the subject of a sentence did, does, or will do (p. 41)

**Adjective** (aj′ ik tiv)  A word that describes a noun or pronoun (p. 72)

**Adverb** (ad′ vėrb)  A word that answers questions about a verb, an adjective, or another adverb; it tells when, how, how often, where, or to what degree (p. 74)

**Advertisement** (ad′ vər tīz′ mənt)  A message designed to attract the public's attention; also called an ad (p. 185)

**Advertiser** (ad′ vər tīz′ er)  A person who uses an advertisement to sell a product or service (p. 185)

**Alliteration** (ə lit′ ə ra′ shən)  Two or more words in the same sentence that begin with the same sound (p. 198)

**Anecdote** (an′ ik dōt)  A very short story about a funny or interesting event (p. 222)

**Antecedent** (an′ tə sēd′ nt)  The noun that a pronoun replaces (p. 63)

**Apostrophe (')** (ə pos′ trə fē)  A punctuation mark that you use to show a noun is possessive (p. 68)

**Audience** (ô′ dē əns)  The people who read your writing (p. 96)

## B

**Bibliography** (bib′ lē og′ rə fē)  A list of sources that were used to write a report (p. 333)

**Block style** (blōk stīl)  The format of a letter in which all the parts begin at the left margin; paragraphs are not indented (p. 292)

**Body** (bod′ ē)  The sentences in a paragraph that explain and support the main idea (p. 104)

**Brainstorm** (brān′ stôrm′)  To think freely about a topic and look for new, exciting ideas (p. 97)

**Browser** (brouz′ er)  A computer program that allows you to use the information on Internet sites (p. 328)

**Business letter** (biz′ nis let′ ər)  A formal letter to a person or company (p. 289)

## C

**Call number** (kôl num′ bər)  A number that identifies a book and tells you where it is in a library (p. 322)

**Catalog** (kat′ l ôg)  A list of items arranged in a special way (p. 319)

**Cause and effect** (kôz and ə fekt′)  Something that happens (effect) because of something else (cause) (p. 159)

**Character** (kar′ ik tər)  A person in a story (p. 222)

**Chronological order** (kron′ ə loj′ ə kəl ôr′dər)  An arrangement of events according to time, usually from the earliest event to the most recent event (p. 224)

**Comma fault** (kom′ ə fôlt)  The use of a comma instead of end punctuation to separate two sentences (p. 20)

**Comparative form** (kəm par′ ə tiv form)  The form of an adjective or adverb that you use to compare two people or things; formed by adding -er to the positive form or by adding the word *more* (p. 77)

**Compare** (kəm per′)  To point out how two things are alike or different (p. 154)

**Compound sentence** (kom′ pound sen′ təns) Two or more related ideas that are connected with a conjunction (p. 21)

**Conclusion** (kən klü′ zhən) A logical decision or opinion based on facts or evidence; the sentence at the end of a paragraph (p. 108)

**Conflict** (kon′ flikt) A problem or struggle at the center of a story (p. 258)

**Conjunction** (kən jungk′ shən) A word that connects related words or groups of words (p. 20)

**Connotation** (kon′ ə tā′ shən) An idea or feeling associated with a word (p. 204)

**Contrast** (kon′ trast) To point out how two things are different (p. 156)

## D

**Declarative sentence** (di klar′ə tiv sen′ təns) A sentence that states a fact (p. 6)

**Dependent clause** (di pen′ dənt klóz) A group of words with a subject and a predicate that does not express a complete thought (p. 51)

**Dialogue** (dī′ ə lôg) The words that people or story characters say to one another; conversation (p. 233)

**Direct quotation** (də rekt′ kwō tā′ shən) A quotation that reports someone's exact words; quotation marks are required (p. 238)

**Draft** (draft) An early version of writing; not the final version (p. 351)

## E

**Edit** (ed′ it) To correct mistakes in a piece of writing; to check spelling, punctuation, capitalization, grammar, and word choice (p. 135)

**E-mail** (ē′ māl′) An electronic message that you send from one computer to another (p. 278)

**Essay** (es′ ā) A short piece of writing about one topic (p. 253)

**Exaggeration** (eg zaj′ ə rā′ shən) An overstatement that says something is greater than it is (p. 208)

**Exclamatory sentence** (ek sklam′ ə tôr′ ē sen′ təns) A sentence that expresses strong feelings (p. 6)

## F

**Fact** (fakt) A piece of information that is known to be true (p. 176)

**Feminine** (fem′ ə nən) Relating to females (p. 64)

**Fiction** (fik′ shən) A piece of writing about imaginary people and events (p. 221)

**Figure of speech** (fig′ yər ov spēch) An expression that a writer uses for a particular purpose (p. 206)

## G

**Gender** (jen′ dər) Masculine or feminine (p. 64)

## I

**Imperative sentence** (im per′ ə tiv sen′ təns) A sentence that gives a command or makes a request (p. 6)

**Indefinite pronoun** (in def′ ə nit prō′ noun) A pronoun that refers to people, places, things, or ideas in a general way (p. 34)

**Indent** (in dent′) To start a sentence a certain distance from the left margin (p. 97)

| a | hat | e | let | ī | ice | ȯ | order | u̇ | put | sh | she | ə | a in about |
|---|-----|---|-----|---|-----|---|-------|----|-----|----|-----|---|------------|
| ā | age | ē | equal | o | hot | oi | oil | ü | rule | th | thin | | e in taken |
| ä | far | ėr | term | ō | open | ou | out | ch | child | ᴛʜ | then | | i in pencil |
| â | care | i | it | ȯ | saw | u | cup | ng | long | zh | measure | | o in lemon |
| | | | | | | | | | | | | | u in circus |

*Glossary* **431**

**Independent clause** (in´ di pen´ dənt klȯz) A group of words with a subject and a predicate that expresses a complete thought; a sentence (p. 51)

**Index** (in´ deks) An alphabetical list of the topics and subtopics in a book with page numbers; usually at the end of a book (p. 324)

**Indirect quotation** (in´ də rekt´ kwō tā´ shən) A quotation that reports what someone said without using the speaker's exact words; quotation marks are not used (p. 238)

**Internet service provider (ISP)** (in´ tər net´ sėr´ vis prə vīd´ er) A company that connects a computer to the Internet (p. 278)

**Interrogative sentence** (in´ tə rog´ ə tiv sen´ təns) A sentence that asks a question (p. 6)

**Irregular verb** (i reg´ yə lər vėrb) A verb that does not form its past and past participle by adding -ed or -d to the present tense (p. 36)

## K

**Keyword** (kē´ wėrd) A word or phrase that you use to search for information about a topic (p. 320)

## M

**Masculine** (mas´ kyə lin) Relating to males (p. 64)

**Mechanics** (mə kan´ iks) The spelling, capitalization, and punctuation of a written piece (p. 361)

**Memorandum** (mem´ ə ran´ dem) A formal business message with a special format; usually called a memo (p. 299)

**Message** (mes´ ij) Any communication; a message may be written, spoken, or shown visually (p. 274)

**Metaphor** (met´ ə fȯr) An expression that shows that two things are alike in some way (p. 206)

**Modified block style** (mod´ ə fīd blȯk stīl) The format of a letter in which the return address, date, closing, signature, and typed name are near the center of the page; paragraphs are indented (p. 292)

## N

**Nonfiction** (non´ fik´ shən) A piece of writing about real people and actual events (p. 221)

**Noun** (noun) A word that names a person, place, thing, or idea (p. 11)

**Novel** (nov´ əl) A long work of fiction (p. 221)

## O

**Opinion** (ə pin´ yən) The way a person thinks about something; a belief or viewpoint (p. 121)

**Outline** (out´ līn´) A plan for writing a report that lists topics and subtopics in a certain order (p. 340)

## P

**Paragraph** (par´ ə graf) A group of sentences about one idea (p. 97)

**Paraphrase** (par´ ə frāz) To write someone else's ideas in your own words (p. 335)

**Past participle** (past pär´ tə sip´ əl) The verb form that you use to form the perfect tenses (p. 36)

**Perfect tense** (pėr´ fikt tens) The present perfect, past perfect, or future perfect tense of a verb; a verb form that is made from a past participle and a form of *have* (p. 37)

**Periodical** (pir´ ē od´ ə kəl) Any printed material that someone publishes on a regular basis (p. 325)

**Personal letter** (pėr´ sə nəl let´ ər) An informal letter to a friend or relative (p. 271)

**Personal pronoun** (pėr´ sə nəl prō´ noun) A pronoun that refers to a person or a thing (p. 66)

**Personification** (pər son′ ə fə kā′ shən)  Giving human qualities to animals or objects (p. 207)

**Persuade** (pər swād′)  To convince someone to agree with an opinion, an idea, or a request; to change someone's opinion about something (p. 181)

**Phrase** (frāz)  Two or more words that work together (p. 13)

**Plagiarize** (plā′ jə riz′)  To take credit for someone else's words (p. 333)

**Plot** (plot)  The events in a story (p. 222)

**Plural** (plùr′ əl)  Referring to more than one person, place, thing, or idea (p. 31)

**Point of view** (point ov vyü)  The position of the storyteller in a story; either first-person or third-person point of view (p. 227)

**Positive form** (poz′ ə tiv form)  The form of an adjective or adverb that you use to describe one person or thing (p. 77)

**Possessive noun** (pə zes′ iv noun)  A word that shows ownership or a relationship between two things (p. 66)

**Postscript (P.S.)** (pōst′ script)  A short message at the end of a personal letter (p. 272)

**Predicate** (pred′ ə kit)  The part of a sentence that tells something about the subject; the predicate always contains a verb (p. 12)

**Preposition** (prep′ ə zish′ ən)  A word that shows a relationship between a noun or pronoun (its object) and other words in a sentence (p. 81)

**Prepositional phrase** (prep′ ə zish′ ə nəl frāz)  A group of words made up of a preposition and a noun or pronoun; it works like an adjective or an adverb in a sentence (p. 81)

**Prewriting** (prē rī′ting)  Preparing to write; the planning step of the writing process (p. 95)

**Pronoun** (prō′ noun)  A word that replaces a noun in a sentence (p. 11)

**Publish** (pub′ lish)  To share a written or visual message with others (p. 368)

**Q**

**Qualify** (kwol′ ə fī)  To make a statement less strong; to limit the meaning of a statement (p. 176)

**Quotation** (kwō tā′ shən)  Someone's exact spoken or written words; quotation marks are needed at the beginning and end of a quotation (p. 233)

**Quotation marks (" ")** (kwō tā′ shən märks)  The marks placed at the beginning and end of a direct quotation (p. 233)

**R**

**Regular verb** (reg′ yə lər verb)  A verb that forms its past tense and past participle by adding -ed or -d to the present tense (p. 36)

**Report** (ri pôrt′)  An organized summary of information about a topic; usually involving research (p. 311)

**Research** (ri serch′)  To find information about a topic (p. 322)

**Resolution** (rez′ ə lü′ shən)  A solution; an end to the conflict in a story (p. 259)

**Revise** (ri vīz′)  To change a piece of writing to make it better (p. 119)

**Rewrite** (rē rīt′)  To write again in a different way (p. 119)

**Run-on sentence** (run-on sen′ təns)  Two or more ideas written as one sentence without correct punctuation or a conjunction (p. 19)

**S**

**Screen name** (skren nam)  A name that you use as identification when sending and receiving e-mail (p. 278)

| | | | | | | | | | | |
|---|---|---|---|---|---|---|---|---|---|---|
| a | hat | e | let | ī | ice | ȯ | order | ù | put | sh | she |
| ā | age | ē | equal | o | hot | oi | oil | ü | rule | th | thin |
| ä | far | èr | term | ō | open | ou | out | ch | child | ŦH | then |
| â | care | i | it | ȯ | saw | u | cup | ng | long | zh | measure |

ə { a in about
e in taken
i in pencil
o in lemon
u in circus }

**Search engine** (sėrch en´ jən)  A computer program that searches the Internet for keywords and lists the places it finds them (p. 328)

**Sensory image** (sen´ sər ē im´ ij)  A word, phrase, or sentence that appeals to one or more senses (p. 197)

**Sentence** (sen´ təns)  A group of words that expresses a complete thought (p. 3)

**Sentence fragment** (sen´ təns frag´ mənt)  A group of words that does not express a complete thought; a part of a sentence (p. 15)

**Setting** (set´ ing)  The location and time of a story (p. 222)

**Short story** (shôrt stôr´ ē)  A short work of fiction (p. 221)

**Simile** (sim´ ə lē)  An expression using *like* or *as* that shows that two things are alike in a certain way (p. 206)

**Simple sentence** (sim´ pəl sen´ təns)  A sentence with one subject and one predicate (p. 11)

**Simple tense** (sim´ pəl tens)  The present, past, or future tense of a verb (p. 43)

**Singular** (sing´ gyə lər)  Referring to one person, place, thing, or idea (p. 31)

**Slogan** (slō´ gən)  A short phrase or sentence designed to catch the public's attention (p. 186)

**Solution** (sə lü´ shən)  An answer to a problem; a way of making a situation better (p. 162)

**State-of-being verb** (stāt-ov-bē´ ing vėrb)  A verb that tells about the condition of the subject of a sentence (p. 41)

**Style** (stīl)  A writer's individual way of using words (p. 210)

**Subject** (sub´ jikt)  The part of a sentence that names the person, place, thing, or idea that the sentence is about (p. 11)

**Subordinating conjunction** (sə bôrd´ n āt ing kən jungk´ shən)  A conjunction that joins a dependent clause to an independent clause (p. 51)

**Subtopic** (sub´ top´ ik)  A division or part of a larger topic (p. 317)

**Summary** (sum´ ər ē)  A sentence at the end of a paragraph that repeats the main idea using different words (p. 108)

**Superlative form** (sə pėr´ lə tiv form)  The form of an adjective or adverb that you use to compare three or more people or things; formed by adding -*est* to the positive form or by using the word *most* (p. 78)

**Synonym** (sin´ ə nim)  A word that has the same meaning as another word (p. 73)

**T**

**Table of contents** (tā´ bəl ov kən tents´)  A list of parts of a book and the page on which each part begins; usually at the beginning of a book (p. 324)

**Tense** (tens)  The time expressed by a verb (p. 13)

**Thesaurus** (thi sôr´ əs)  A book that lists words and their synonyms (p. 73)

**Topic sentence** (top´ ik sen´ təns)  A sentence that states the main idea of a paragraph; usually the first sentence of a paragraph (p. 100)

**Transition** (tran zish´ ən)  A change from one thing to another; often a change in time, place, situation, or thought (p. 127)

**V**

**Variety** (və rī´ ə tē)  A collection of things that are different or vary in some way (p. 123)

**Verb** (vėrb)  A word that expresses action or state of being; the main part of a predicate (p. 12)

**Verb phrase** (vėrb frāz)  A main verb and one or more helping verbs (p. 13)

**W**

**Writing prompt** (rī´ting prompt)  The directions for a writing assignment (p. 95)

# Index

## Acknowledgments

### Photo Credits

Cover, © TongRo Image Stock/Jupiter Images;
page WPH31, © Thomas M. Perkins/Shutterstock;
page 9, © Eri Morita/Getty Images; page 16, ©
Larry St. Pierre/Shutterstock; page 23, © Mandy
Godbehear/Shutterstock; page 28, © Fotolia;
page 38, © Punchstock; page 41, Isidora Milic/
Shutterstock; page 55, © Image 100/Jupiter Images;
page 60, © Robert Pernell/Shutterstock; page 74,
© Shutterstock; page 82, © Punchstock; page 87, ©
Corbis/Jupiter Images; page 90, © Enigma/Alamy;
page 98, © Jupiter Images; page 106, © Brian M.
Doty/Shutterstock; page 109, © Shutterstock; page
114, © Rob Bouwman/Shutterstock; page 129, ©
Super Stock; page 136, Jupiter Images; page 137, ©
Super Stock; page 142, © Robert Elias/Shutterstock;
page 154, © Jupiter Images; page 159, © Jupiter
Images; page 165, © BananaStock/SuperStock;
page 168, © Jupiter Images; page 180, © Ron
Chapple/Thinkstock/Alamy; page 185, © John
Lund/Jupiter Images; page 189, © Inspirestock/
Jupiter Images; page 192, © Jupiter Images; page
203, © Super Stock; page 208, © Corbis; page 211,
© Super Stock; page 216, © Alamy; page 225, ©
Photo Alto/Super Stock; page 235, © Punchstock;
page 239, © Peter Casolino/Alamy; page 244, © Yuri
Arcurs/Shutterstock; pages 250, 255, and 261, ©
Jupiter Images; pages 266 and 276, © Alamy; page
279, © Shutterstock; page 284, © Mikael Damkier/
Shutterstock; page 289, © Punchstock; page 299,
© Corbis; page 304, © C. Paquin/Shutterstock;
page 313, © Shutterstock; page 326, © Jupiter
Images; page 335, © Corbis; page 340, © Ana Maria
Marques/Alamy; page 343, © Anna Dzondzua/
Shutterstock; page 353, © Jupiter Images; page 363,
© Comstock Images

### Staff Credits

Melania Benzinger, Karen Blonigen, Nancy
Condon, Barbara Drewlo, Daren Hastings, Brian
Holl, Jan Jessup, Mariann Johanneck, Bev Johnson,
Mary Kaye Kuzma, Julie Maas, Daniel Milowski,
Carrie O'Connor, Deb Rogstad, Morgan Russell-
Dempsey, Julie Theisen, Peggy Vlahos, Charmaine
Whitman, Sue Will, Jen Willman

# Midterm Mastery Test

## Midterm Mastery Test Page 1

### Chapters 1–7 Midterm Mastery Test

**Part A** Match each term in column A with the correct definition or description in column B. Write the letter of the correct answer on the line.

| Column A | Column B |
|---|---|
| _____ 1. topic sentence | A the noun that a pronoun replaces |
| _____ 2. imperative sentence | B sentence that states the main idea of a paragraph |
| _____ 3. state-of-being verb | C a word that describes a noun |
| _____ 4. adjective | D a sentence that gives a command or makes a request |
| _____ 5. antecedent | E a verb that tells about the condition of the subject of a sentence |
| _____ 6. compare | F the time expressed by a verb |
| _____ 7. opinion | G a belief, attitude, or viewpoint about something |
| _____ 8. prewriting | H the planning or preparing stage of writing |
| _____ 9. tense | I to correct mistakes (spelling, grammar, and so on) in a piece of writing |
| _____ 10. edit | J to point out how two things are alike or different |

**Part B** Circle the answer that correctly completes each sentence.

**11.** A _____ is a group of words written as a sentence but lacking a subject or predicate.
A compound sentence  B simple sentence  C comma fault  D sentence fragment

**12.** Two or more ideas in one sentence without proper punctuation or conjunctions is a _____ sentence.
A complete  B run-on  C fragment  D compound

**13.** *Has* + the past participle of a verb forms the _____.
A clause  B verb phrase  C perfect tense  D simple tense

**14.** An _____ verb does not form its past tense by adding *-ed* or *-d* to its present tense form.
A irregular  B antecedent  C simple  D regular

**Pacemaker® Basic English Composition**

## Midterm Mastery Test Page 2

### Chapters 1–7 Midterm Mastery Test, continued

**15.** *Run* and *throw* are examples of _____ because they tell what someone is doing.
A action verbs  B verb phrases  C prepositions  D plurals

**16.** A _____ sentence restates the main idea of a paragraph in different words.
A topic  B conclusion  C summary  D detail

**17.** A writing _____ gives you directions for an assignment.
A paragraph  B body  C indent  D prompt

**18.** A _____ paragraph explains the steps in doing or making something.
A how-to  B comparison  C cause and effect  D problem/solution

**19.** A transition you would use in a cause-and-effect paragraph is _____.
A first  B next  C unlike  D because

**20.** A catchy, short phrase or sentence that keeps a product in your mind is _____.
A conclusion  B fact  C slogan  D topic sentence

**Part C** Read the paragraph. Then answer the questions below. Write your answers on the lines.

1. This paragraph is about why I should be able to decorate my own room. 2. For one thing, it is my space, it should reflect my personality. 3. Also, I spend a lot of ours there, so it should be pleasing to me. 4. Having the colors and things I chose around me would make me happy. 5. Most important, I taking pride in a room I decorated and keep it looking good. 6. Our Family and our home would be better off if you let me fix up my room.

**21.** Which sentence is the topic sentence? _____

**22.** List the transitions you find in the paragraph. _____

**23.** What is the purpose of this paragraph? _____

**24.** What is the purpose of Sentence 6? _____

**25.** What kindt of details does the writer use to support the topic sentence? _____

**26.** What error is found in Sentence 2? _____

**27.** What error is found in Sentence 3? _____

**28.** What error is found in Sentence 5? _____

**Pacemaker® Basic English Composition**

## Midterm Mastery Test Page 3

### Chapters 1–7 Midterm Mastery Test, continued

**29.** What error is found in Sentence 6? _____

**30.** Rewrite the first sentence to make it more interesting. _____

**Part D** Underline the word in parentheses that correctly completes each sentence.

**31.** Troy, Beth, and Chris all (enjoy, enjoys) cooking class.

**32.** Last week, Troy (has made, made) spaghetti.

**33.** Beth and Chris agreed (they, it) was delicious.

**34.** They complimented Troy on (him, his) cooking talent.

**35.** The three friends will prepare a Greek dinner for (their, us) final project.

**36.** Doesn't that sound (good, good?) I don't want to miss that day.

**37.** To me, Greek food is the (best, goodest) of all.

**38.** The olives are (tasty, tastier) than the cheese.

**39.** Beth wants to make Greek salad, (because, but) Chris doesn't like it.

**40.** Troy says they should make Italian food (after, because) everyone likes it.

**41.** (Next, Unlike) Troy, Beth thinks people should try new things.

**42.** Beth bought the food. (While, Then) they all prepared it.

**43.** (All, Many) teenagers love pizza.

**44.** (Usually, In my opinion) pepperoni pizza is the best kind.

**45.** Chris (has, have) tried anchovy pizza once.

**Pacemaker® Basic English Composition**

## Midterm Mastery Test Page 4

### Chapters 1–7 Midterm Mastery Test, continued

**Part E** Write your answer to each question. Use complete sentences. Support each answer with facts and examples from the textbook.

**46.** Underline the verb in the sentence below. Explain why it is a verb phrase.
Amber has helped Derek with his homework.

**47.** Read the topic sentence. Explain what kind of paragraph you expect to follow this sentence.
The computer of today is very different from the early computer.

**Part F** Write a paragraph for each topic. Include a topic sentence, body, and conclusion. Support your answers with facts and examples from the textbook.

**48.** Explain the parts of a paragraph and tell why each part is important.

**49.** Why do writers use adjectives, adverbs, and prepositional phrases?

**Pacemaker® Basic English Composition**

# Final Mastery Test

## Chapters 1–14 Final Mastery Test

**Part A** Match each term in column A with the correct definition or description in column B. Write the letter of the correct answer on the line.

| Column A | Column B |
|---|---|
| _____ **1.** topic sentence | **A** a verb that tells what the subject of a sentence did |
| _____ **2.** paraphrase | **B** a short message at the end of a personal letter |
| _____ **3.** declarative sentence | **C** sentence that states the main idea of a paragraph |
| _____ **4.** action verb | **D** to write someone else's ideas in your own words |
| _____ **5.** postscript (P.S.) | **E** a sentence that states a fact |
| _____ **6.** antecedent | **F** something that happens because of an earlier event |
| _____ **7.** call number | **G** the noun that a pronoun replaces |
| _____ **8.** cause and effect | **H** the first version of a written assignment |
| _____ **9.** conflict | **I** identifies a book and tells where it is in the library |
| _____ **10.** draft | **J** a problem or struggle at the center of a story |
| _____ **11.** business letter | **K** an idea or feeling associated with a word |
| _____ **12.** fact | **L** to correct mistakes (spelling, grammar, and so on) in a piece of writing |
| _____ **13.** edit | **M** the position of the storyteller in a story |
| _____ **14.** connotation | **N** a formal letter to a person or organization |
| _____ **15.** point of view | **O** a piece of information that is known to be true |

**Pacemaker® Basic English Composition**

**Final Mastery Test Page 1**

---

## Chapters 1–14 Final Mastery Test, continued

**Part B** Circle the answer that correctly completes each sentence.

**16.** Two clauses joined by a comma and the word *and* is a _____ sentence.
 **A** complete   **B** run-on   **C** fragment   **D** compound

**17.** *Has* + the past participle of a verb forms the _____.
 **A** clause   **B** verb phrase   **C** perfect tense   **D** simple tense

**18.** In the sentence *Terry ran home, ran* is an example of an _____ verb.
 **A** irregular   **B** antecedent   **C** simple   **D** regular

**19.** *He, they, she,* and *it* are all _____ pronouns.
 **A** personal   **B** possessive   **C** gender   **D** masculine

**20.** A _____ sentence ends a paragraph with an opinion or logical decision.
 **A** topic   **B** conclusion   **C** summary   **D** detail

**21.** To add to, delete from, or rewrite parts of your writing to improve it is to _____.
 **A** publish   **B** transition   **C** edit   **D** revise

**22.** A _____ paragraph looks at ways two things are alike and different.
 **A** how-to   **B** comparison   **C** cause and effect   **D** problem/solution

**23.** An opinion such as *Teens are bad drivers* should be _____ with the word *some*.
 **A** qualified   **B** disproved   **C** proved   **D** forgotten

**24.** Persuasive messages designed for the public are _____.
 **A** essays   **B** reports   **C** facts   **D** advertisements

**25.** A _____ uses *like* or *as* and shows how two things are alike.
 **A** description   **B** metaphor   **C** simile   **D** sensory image

**26.** The conversation between story characters is called _____.
 **A** dialogue   **B** fiction   **C** plot   **D** setting

**Pacemaker® Basic English Composition**

**Final Mastery Test Page 2**

---

## Chapters 1–14 Final Mastery Test, continued

**27.** When a test question asks you to identify or describe something, you should _____.
 **A** summarize its plot and setting   **C** list its steps
 **B** give its important characteristics   **D** circle the answer

**28.** A personal letter and a business letter both contain _____.
 **A** greeting and closing   **B** heading   **C** inside address   **D** typed name and title

**29.** The second line of the return address on an envelope contains the _____.
 **A** sender's name   **C** receiver's street address
 **B** sender's street address   **D** receiver's city, state, and ZIP code

**30.** The first paragraph of a report does the same job as the _____ of a paragraph.
 **A** conclusion   **B** body   **C** topic sentence   **D** subtopic

**Part C** Read the paragraph below to answer questions 31–35. On page 4, read the letter and answer questions 36–40. Then read the message and answer questions 41–45.

Luis and Jose argued about who would do the dishes. It's your turn, Jose insisted. Luis frowned and said, "But you said you would do dishes for five days if you lost the bet."

**31.** Who are the story characters and what is the setting? _____

_____

**32.** Is the point of view first person or third person? _____

**33.** Rewrite the second sentence to correct mistakes. _____

_____

**34.** What is the conflict in this story? _____

_____

**35.** Does this story use direct quotations or indirect quotations? _____

_____

**Pacemaker® Basic English Composition**

**Final Mastery Test Page 3**

---

## Chapters 1–14 Final Mastery Test, continued

Dear Judy
  Thank you for the senior picture and graduation announcement. You look so grown up! I am proud of you and look forward to attending your graduation ceremony.
Love

Aunt Cicely

**36.** Who sent this letter? _____

**37.** Which part of the letter has been left out? _____

**38.** Find two mistakes. Rewrite these parts correctly on the line. _____

_____

**39.** Explain where this part should be added: "P.S. Hello to your Mom and Dad." _____

_____

**40.** What is the purpose of the letter? _____

_____

July 12, 2008
To:      All staff
From:    Mario Prinza
Subject:  Sale of Mario's Restaurant
    With mixed feelings, I am reporting that I have sold my business to Lukio Stephanos. Thank you all for your good work over the years. The sale will take place in six months.

**41.** What kind of business message is this? _____

**42.** What should be added to line 1? _____

**43.** Who sent this message? _____

**44.** Who will receive the message? _____

**45.** What is the purpose of this message? _____

_____

**Pacemaker® Basic English Composition**

**Final Mastery Test Page 4**

# Final Mastery Test

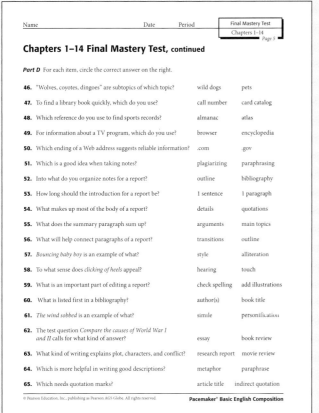

Final Mastery Test Page 5

Final Mastery Test Page 6

The lists below show how items from the Midterm and Final Mastery Tests correlate to the chapters in the student edition.

## Midterm Mastery Test

Chapter 1: 2, 9, 11, 12, 26, 29, 36

Chapter 2: 3, 13, 14, 15, 28, 31, 32, 45

Chapter 3: 4, 5, 33, 34, 35, 37, 38

Chapter 4: 1, 8, 16, 17, 21, 24

Chapter 5: 10, 22, 26, 27, 29, 30, 39, 40

Chapter 6: 6, 18, 19, 41, 42

Chapter 7: 7, 20, 22, 23, 25, 43, 44

### Critical-Thinking Items:

46. Chapter 2

47. Chapter 6

48. Chapter 4

49. Chapter 3

## Final Mastery Test

Chapter 1: 3, 16

Chapter 2: 4, 17, 18

Chapter 3: 6, 19

Chapter 4: 1, 20, 30, 56, 59

Chapter 5: 13, 21

Chapter 6: 8, 22

Chapter 7: 12, 23, 24

Chapter 8: 14, 25, 57, 58, 64

Chapter 9: 15, 26, 31, 32, 33, 35, 65

Chapter 10: 9, 27, 31, 34, 62, 63

Chapter 11: 5, 28, 36, 37, 38, 39, 40

Chapter 12: 11, 28, 29, 41, 42, 43, 44, 45

Chapter 13: 2, 7, 30, 46, 47, 48, 49, 50, 51, 52

Chapter 14: 10, 21, 53, 54, 55, 56, 59, 60, 61, 65

## Critical-Thinking Items:

66. Chapter 10

67. Chapter 8

68. Chapter 13

69. Chapters 8 and 10

## Activities

### Activity 1—Beginning and Ending a Sentence
**1.** Amber received her yearbook today. She wants her friends to autograph it. Together they look at the pictures and laugh. **2.** The seniors will graduate at the Capital Center. That is a huge building. Do you know where it is? **3.** Laura has a job at Pete's Grill. Amber will be a lifeguard. Both girls hope to go to junior college in the fall. **4.** Laura is looking forward to her summer vacation. She is going to see the Grand Canyon in June. Her parents and brother are going with her. **5.** Graduating is bittersweet. Everyone is looking forward to moving on to the next phase of their lives. Everyone is also sad to be leaving behind old friends. **6–10.** Sentences and word order may vary. Possible answers are shown. **6.** Immediately we got into heavy traffic. **7.** In the summer, everyone usually goes on vacation. **8.** Lately the weather has been hot and humid. **9.** The weather today is beautiful. **10.** Normally, I am a fan of cooler weather.

### Activity 2—Understanding the Purpose of a Sentence
**1.** D (!) **2.** A (.) **3.** C (. or !) **4.** B (?) **5.** A (.) **6.** C (.) **7.** A (.) **8.** A (.) **9.** C (.) **10.** A (.) **11.** B (?) **12.** A (.) **13.** A (.) **14.** D (!) **15.** C (.) **16.** A (.) **17.** B (?) **18.** D (!) **19.** C (.) **20.** A (.)

### Activity 3—Finding the Subject and Predicate
**1.** Daredevil Dave (rode) his motorcycle to the top of the ramp. **2.** The crowd (seemed) very far away. **3.** Dave (was) dizzy for a moment. **4.** (You) Do not (look) down. **5.** He (took) a deep breath. **6.** Dave (gunned) the motor. **7.** The motorcycle (flew) over 27 parked cars. **8.** (You) (Give) a cheer. **9.** Dave and his motorcycle (landed) safely. **10.** The crowd (breathed) a sigh of relief. **11.** prepared, past **12.** go, present **13.** watches, present **14.** scream, present **15.** will receive, future **16.** visited, past **17.** ate, past **18.** will regret, future **19.** manages, present **20.** made, past

### Activity 4—Correcting Sentence Fragments
**1.** sentence **2.** fragment **3.** sentence **4.** sentence **5.** fragment **6.** fragment **7.** fragment **8.** sentence **9.** fragment **10.** sentence **11–15.** Answers will vary. Possible answers are shown. **11.** He looked for a job downtown. **12.** The warm sun and cool breeze made us feel good. **13.** Ginny quickly did her homework. **14.** Did you hear about the accident last night? **15.** She forgot her book and needed to borrow mine.

### Activity 5—Correcting Run-On Sentences
**1.** Graduation will take place on June 4. What time is the ceremony? **2.** Students march into the gym. Then they sit in rows at the front. **3.** Friends and parents sit in the bleachers. They are thrilled and happy. **4.** Mayor Smith will give a talk to the graduates. He is well liked. **5–10.** Sentence corrections will vary. Possible answers are shown. **5.** comma fault—A yearbook editor makes a yearbook. The job has many responsibilities. **6.** compound sentence **7.** comma fault—Pages are checked for mistakes. Are you good at proofreading? **8.** compound sentence **9.** comma fault—Here is my yearbook. Please sign it for me. **10.** comma fault—How many pictures of you are in the yearbook? There are twelve of me.

### Activity 6—Making the Subject and Verb Agree
**1–10.** The given words should be circled. **1.** wants **2.** need **3.** say **4.** learns **5.** bring **6.** has **7.** carries **8.** are **9.** hate **10.** are **11.** plural, see **12.** plural, click **13.** plural, walk **14.** plural, cause **15.** singular, is **16.** plural, take **17.** singular, goes **18.** singular, makes **19.** singular, excites **20.** plural, give

### Activity 7—Using Irregular Verbs
**1.** got **2.** made **3.** swung **4.** teach **5.** took **6.** won **7.** know **8.** driven **9.** eaten **10.** begins **11.** gone **12.** go **13.** had **14.** began **15.** ate **16.** drove **17.** saw **18.** seen **19.** will begin **20.** begun

### Activity 8—Using Verbs and Verb Phrases
**1.** could eat **2.** brought **3.** will share **4.** has **5.** told **6.** may have been **7.** began **8.** had given **9.** is being given **10.** should do **11.** has been planning, present perfect **12.** are, present **13.** will use, future **14.** listens, present **15.** have taken, present perfect **16.** asked, past **17.** make, present **18.** has become, present perfect **19.** will get, future **20.** looked, past

### Activity 9—Using Conjunctions to Combine Ideas
**1.** or **2.** and **3.** and **4.** but **5.** nor **6.** so **7.** yet **8.** or **9.** so **10.** but **11.** Tom has a good memory, but he still forgot his sister's birthday. **12.** Do you want to go skiing, or would you rather stay inside? **13.** In her garden, Mary grows peas, squash, tomatoes, and cucumbers. **14.** Andrea buys many books and DVDs, so she has run out of room on her bookshelves. **15.** She will either buy new shelves or give away some books.

### Activity 10—Using Other Kinds of Conjunctions
**1–5.** Sentences may vary. Possible sentences are shown. **1.** After David stayed up all night, he fell asleep in class. **2.** Until you called Laura, she had not received the news. **3.** As Miki was telling the story, Don was acting it out. **4.** Because the class was canceled, we are going to the park. **5.** We took a lot of pictures when we were at the family reunion. **6.** Because the sun was shining in her eyes, Stacy could not read the sign. **7.** Although they arrived late, they did not miss any of the movie. **8.** After my brothers have hiked all day, they like to relax around a campfire. **9.** She spun gracefully as she danced across the stage. **10.** Whenever Tom visits us, we always have a good time. **11.** Malik cannot come over unless your room is cleaned up. **12.** If Alex cannot be friendly to the guests, he should stay in the kitchen. **13.** Jess and Lila can leave when Rob gets here. **14.** Before Nate was hired, the work had been piling up. **15.** While her grandmother was in the hospital, Betsy was very anxious.

### Activity 11—Replacing Nouns with Pronouns
**1.** his, Derek **2.** it, car **3.** her, Laura **4.** his, Brandon **5.** she, teacher **6.** their, Amber and Sara **7.** I, Eliza **8.** them, houses **9.** it, dog **10.** they, boys **11.** A motorcycle is noisy, and it goes too fast. **12.** Walkers use the trail often for their exercise. **13.** Sela is jogging on the trail in her new shoes. **14.** Park workers mow or spray the weekds. **15.** The trail is there for all who want to enjoy it.

### Activity 12—Using Plural and Possessive Nouns
**1.** bus's, buses, buses' **2.** city's, cities, cities' **3.** woman's, women, women's **4.** bike's, bikes, bikes' **5.** wolf's, wolves, wolves' **6.** child's, children, children's **7.** pony's, ponies, ponies' **8.** leaf's, leaves, leaves' **9.** dress's, dresses, dresses' **10.** goose's, geese, geese' **11.** country's, countries, countries' **12.** box's, boxes, boxes' **13.** week's, weeks, weeks' **14.** tree's, trees, trees' **15.** idea's, ideas, ideas'

## Activity 13—Adding Adjectives and Adverbs

**1–5.** Answers will vary. Sample answers are given. **1.** The younger children fed the tame ducks at the pond. **2.** The wet, heavy snow fell quietly all night. **3.** Lynn and Melody will perform a French song next. **4.** Please bring a chocolate sheet cake to the supper. **5.** She was only slightly tired from the previous day's chores. **6.** eagerly, how **7.** Today, when **8.** up, where **9.** especially, to what degree **10.** Hastily, how

## Activity 14—Comparing with Adjectives and Adverbs

**1.** more exciting **2.** most frequently **3.** juiciest **4.** sweet **5.** less lively **6.** faster **7.** loudly **8.** largest **9.** funniest **10.** more politely **11.** I felt better today, but I am still sick. **12.** My effort could not have been worse. **13.** This game is more exciting than last week's. **14.** The store is least busy on Mondays. **15.** Moira did a better job than Keira.

## Activity 15—Adding Prepositional Phrases

**1.** The (puppy) in this cage is the one I want. **2.** Will you choose the (shirt) with tropical flowers or the (shirt) with blue stripes? **3.** Cara read a (poem) by Langston Hughes. **4.** He keeps a (journal) of his travels. **5.** The (table) in the corner would look better here. **6.** The questions on page 75 are difficult. **7.** The main (character) in this TV show is very funny. **8.** Leslie's (cousins) from Mexico are arriving today. **9.** Did you read the (letter) from Ron? **10.** The (gloves) in the top drawer are my best ones. **11.** Maria (spilled) coffee on her white shirt. **12.** Passengers (should put) their bags in the overhead bins. **13.** My family always (goes) to Florida. **14.** At the concert, Maurine and Steve (performed) a duet. **15.** Laura rushed, so she (left) her keys at home. **16.** The scissors (were shared) by everyone. **17.** In the morning, we (will discuss) the changes. **18.** The city council (will meet) again on June 15. **19.** (Look) at this beautiful landscape! **20.** (Will) the thief (return) for the money?

## Activity 16—Planning to Write a Paragraph

**1–4.** Answers will vary. Sample answers are given. **1.** I will write about the importance of eating healthy foods. **2.** My purpose is to explain how diet helps you be healthy. **3.** I will include reasons, facts, and examples. **4.** reason 1, fact or example; reason 2, fact or example; reason 3, fact or example **5.** topic sentence **6.** body/detail **7.** body/detail **8.** body/detail **9.** body/detail **10.** summary/conclusion

## Activity 17—Writing a Topic Sentence

**1.** B **2.** A **3.** B **4.** A **5.** B **6–10.** Answers will vary. Sample answers are given. **6.** The hottest fashions this year are sure to be too expensive and ridiculous for me. **7.** Soccer has helped me get in shape this year. **8.** There is an art to reading a newspaper. **9.** Sunburn is public enemy number 1 as far as your skin is concerned. **10.** The time to start thinking about your career is today.

## Activity 18—Writing Supporting Details

Answers will vary. A sample answer is given.
Skiing is an expensive sport, so find out in advance what it will cost you to ski at your chosen ski resort. Skiing takes both coordination and balance, so be prepared to take a lesson or two and then practice before heading out on the advanced slopes. Keep in mind that staying out in the cold for a long time can lead to hypothermia. Be sure you are dressed warmly for the cold. Enjoy your day of skiing, and then relax in the comfortable ski lodge.

## Activity 19—Writing a Summary or Conclusion

**1.** B, conclusion **2.** A, summary **3.** B, summary **4.** B, summary **5.** A, conclusion

## Activity 20—Writing an Interesting Topic Sentence

**1–10.** Answers will vary. Possible answers are given. **1.** My sixteenth birthday party turned out to be special—a special disaster! **2.** My automatic homework pal will make your life easy. **3.** Susan is the biggest shopaholic I know. **4.** Do you know how Valentine's Day got started? **5.** You have to be a little crazy to play rugby. **6.** There is an evil plot going on in my house—and it features vegetables! **7.** What could be better in summer than a week on a houseboat? **8.** A letter from my Uncle Paul is an EVENT. **9.** The best New Year's Eve celebrations take place at home. **10.** Could you find an hour a day to exercise?

## Activity 21—Using Sentence Variety

**1–5.** Answers will vary. Sample answers are given. **1.** Luckily, the assignment is rather easy. **2.** With a heavy heart, Tom showed his mother his report card. **3.** Fortunately, we will be able to attend your party. **4.** Stealthily, the lioness hunts her prey. **5.** Eventually, this project will be completed.
Paragraphs will vary. A sample answer is given.
The snowshoe hare is good at keeping out of sight. In winter, it has a white coat that blends in with the snow. In warmer months, it has a reddish-brown coat that matches the dry leaves and dirt. Hares try to stay hidden, so they live where shrubs provide thick cover. What is more, they feed at night or in early morning, when light is low. Few people ever get to see a snowshoe hare in the wild.

## Activity 22—Adding Transitions

Answers will vary. Sample answers are given. **1.** A dog is a faithful companion. Also, it provides endless entertainment. **2.** There has been no rain for a month. As a result, my flowers have wilted. **3.** For hours we waited. At last the door opened. **4.** I'm going to feed the cat. First, I'm going to wash my hands. **5.** A computer can help you put your finances in order. For example, you can use a computer to create a budget plan.

## Activity 23—Revising a Paragraph

Answers will vary. Sample sentences are given. **1.** While they seem alike, moths and butterflies are actually different in a number of ways. **2–4.** Moths have fat bodies and dull colors, while butterflies have thinner bodies and are colorful. **5–6.** In addition, butterflies have knobs on the ends of their antennae, but moths do not. **7–8.** Butterflies fly in the day; in contrast, moths fly after sundown. **9.** (This sentence is crossed out.) **10–11.** Unlike moths, which rest with their wings spread out flat, butterflies rest with wings pressed together overhead.
**12–15.** Answers will vary. Sample answers are given. **12.** We left because the concert was awful. **13.** The dinner will be a good fundraiser because many people will buy tickets. **14.** Adventure movies are exciting! **15.** We will rent a DVD on Saturday night.

## Activity 24—Editing Your Paragraph

**1.** I (seen) a really great movie last Saturday nite. **2.** (They) was called *The creature from beyond*. **3.** the cretur had terrific makeup and was horrifiing. **4.** people in the theater (was) on the edge of (they) seats when the creature attackted the supermarket. **5.** (It) isn't anything like a horrer film to get (you) heart going!
Paragraph should read: I saw a really great movie last Saturday night. It was called *The Creature from Beyond*. The creature had terrific makeup and was horrifying. People in the theater were on the edge of their seats when the creature attacked the supermarket. There is nothing like a horror film to get your heart going!

## Activity 25—Explaining How to Do Something

2, 5, 3, 1, 4

Paragraphs will vary. A sample answer is given.

It is quick and easy to locate information about a topic online. First, go to a search engine on the Internet. Then type a search term for the topic you are interested in. Next, click on the "go" or "search" button to begin your search. The search engine will give you a list of descriptions of Web sites about your topic. Read these descriptions and choose a site that looks useful. Finally, go to the site and get the information you need.

## Activity 26—Giving Information

Answers will vary. Sample answers are given.

If you want to be healthy and feel good, you must get physical exercise. For one thing, exercise works your muscles and heart. This keeps them in shape. In addition, exercise releases chemicals that make you feel cheerful and positive. If you want to lose weight, exercise will burn off calories. Get moving for your health!

**1.** Physical exercise is important for everyone. **2.** Exercise keeps you in shape, it makes you feel good, and it helps you lose weight. **3.** Get moving for health! It supports my details. **4.** The main idea is clear and supported by details. I could improve my paragraph with more information about how exercise gets your muscles in shape. **5.** "Get Your Shape in Shape"

## Activity 27—Comparing and Contrasting

**1–4.** Underline *like, By contrast, Both, On the other hand.* **5–7.** Both dogs have long hair, weigh more than 100 pounds, and were bred to do specific jobs. **8–10.** They are different in coloration, land of origin, and type of work they do. **11–15.** Items listed will vary, but should all represent members of the same category. Sentences will vary but should compare specific examples of the chosen category.

## Activity 28—Showing Cause and Effect

**1.** B **2.** A **3.** A **4.** B **5.** A **6–10.** Answers may vary in wording. Sample answers are given. **6.** The dog had rolled in the mud, so we gave it a bath. **7.** Because the market had a great sale on produce, we bought many fresh vegetables. **8.** Since the world is very large and changing all the time, many people do not know about its countries. **9.** We watch TV and read newspapers every day. As a result, we learn about places we may never visit. **10.** Because my family came to this country from Greece, I chose to write a report on Greece.

## Activity 29—Explaining a Solution to a Problem

Answers will vary. Sample solutions and details are given. **1.** Stop spending money on snacks and drinks at school. **2.** Stop carrying so much cash on hand. **3.** Ask for an increase in allowance in exchange for doing more at home. **4.** Join one or two clubs. **5.** Observe people and give sincere compliments. **6.** Make an effort to start conversations at lunch. **7.** I will join clubs that are interesting to me, so I will be enthusiastic. **8.** I will meet people there with whom I will have something in common. **9.** Students have more opportunities to talk and interact in clubs than in class. **10.** Since clubs meet after school, I will probably start sharing rides with people in the club.

## Activity 30—Stating an Opinion

**1.** Bill Murray is our funniest comedian. **2.** He has been an entertainer for more than thirty years. **3.** Murray got his start in Chicago. **4.** His two best films are *Stripes* and *Groundhog Day* **5.** Nobody can make us laugh like Bill Murray.

Opinions will vary. Sample opinions are given. **6.** Snowy days are a perfect time to stay indoors. **7.** Reading books makes your mind sharper. **8.** Most daytime TV is not worth watching. **9.** Everyone should recycle all the resources they can. **10.** My homework load is too heavy. **11.** My morning schedule is too hectic. **12.** A new car smells funny. **13.** The new "layered look" is flattering for girls. **14.** Babysitting is the best way for teens to make money. **15.** Everyone must get a high school degree to succeed.

## Activity 31—Separating Facts from Opinions

Student supplied qualifiers will vary. Sample qualifiers are given. **1.** in my opinion **2.** Circle *seem to be* **3.** Circle *Sometimes* **4.** Most people **5.** Circle *might be* **6.** opinion **7.** fact **8.** opinion **9.** opinion **10.** fact **11.** fact **12.** opinion **13.** fact **14.** opinion **15.** fact

## Activity 32—Supporting Your Opinion

Circle details 2, 3, 4, 7, 8

Paragraphs will vary. A sample paragraph is given.

Still Valley needs a neighborhood park. As you have probably noticed, children have to play ball in the street. There is no reason for this, when there are several acres of land in our neighborhood for sale at a good price. Studies have shown that communities with parks have fewer children who get in trouble. What is more, neighbors of all ages would enjoy the flowers and open space of a park. Let's speak up at the next town council meeting to get the park we need.

## Activity 33—Writing an Advertisement

**1.** The slogan sells a brand of greeting cards. **2.** The slogan does not contain facts. **3.** The word *love* appeals to emotions. **4.** Answers will vary. A sample answer is given. Readers might add the words *and show how much you care.* **5.** Sending one of these greeting cards through the mail is a good way to show your love for someone.

Slogans will vary but should be catchy and memorable.

## Activity 34—Choosing Words That Appeal to the Senses

**1.** touch **2.** taste **3.** smell **4.** hearing **5.** sight **6.** touch **7.** taste **8.** hearing **9.** smell **10.** sight **11.** The light breeze lulled me to sleep like a lullaby. **12.** With a roar, the saw ripped raggedly through the board. **13.** The tiny shrew's shrill cry made me shrink away. **14.** The peas popped out of their pod and plopped in a bowl. **15.** The fragile fawn lay hidden in the farmer's field.

## Activity 35—Choosing Specific Words

**1.** pens **2.** German Shepherd **3.** lime **4.** handshake **5.** tulip **6.** hamster **7.** compositions **8.** Daily News **9.** pancakes **10.** lunch **11.** envelope **12.** giggle **13.** sail **14.** Palomino **15.** staple **16.** bake **17.** waltz **18.** rock and roll **19.** shout **20.** wristwatch **21–25.** Answers will vary. Sample answers are given. **21.** We drove to Texas for vacation. **22.** Some friends came with us. **23.** The scenery was inspiring. **24.** We saw several cities. **25.** I thought the trip was extraordinary.

## Activity 36—Using Figures of Speech

**1.** metaphor **2.** simile **3.** personification **4.** simile **5.** simile **6.** metaphor **7.** simile **8.** metaphor **9.** personification **10.** metaphor **11–15.** Answers will vary. Sample answers are given. **11.** That piece of pie is so tiny you need a magnifying glass to find it. **12.** I drank so much water that I floated away. **13.** Megan was so angry that her glare melted the snow. **14.** That player is so tough that bricks break when they get near him. **15.** Zach is so stubborn that a hundred mules won't get him to budge.

## Activity 37—Developing a Writing Style

**1.** three **2.** Two are similes; one is personification. **3.** Students may list any two of the following: catfish, whale, boat, skin, scars, fins, body, mouth, whiskers, situation, house fire. **4.** Students may list any two of the following: twisted, thrashed, gulped, twitched **5.** sight. **6.** Students may choose either of the following sentences: Its <u>slippery</u>, dark <u>skin</u> was <u>striped</u> with <u>scars</u>. But the <u>fish's</u> situation was about as <u>funny</u> as a house <u>fire</u>. **7.** The first and last sentences are 12 words; sentences 2–5 are 8, 8, 6, and 8. More sentences are short. **8.** The writer used mostly short sentences to make the fish's struggle stand out. **9.** These words make the struggle vivid and show the fish is an old warrior. **10.** Sentences will vary. A sample sentence is given. The writer's style is colorful and concerned.

## Activity 38—Telling a Story

Answers will vary in wording. **1.** The story is about a cat hunting a bird. **2.** The characters are a sparrow and an orange cat. **3.** It takes place in a yard in winter. **4.** A sparrow is on the ground eating. **5.** A cat sees it and sneaks up on it. **6.** A person makes a noise and calls to the cat. **7.** The bird flies away. **8.** The cat goes in to eat. **9.** fiction **10.** The sparrow returned to the seeds with a watchful eye.

## Activity 39—Putting Events in Order

2, 4, 1, 3, 5      6, 10, 8, 7, 9      Stories may vary in wording. A reasonable version is given.

The Walt family adopted an adorable little puppy in 2003. They named him Oskar. As he grew up, Oskar showed a real talent for playing Frisbee. Allan Walt thought Oskar's leaps into the air were fantastic. One spring day in 2007, Allan and Oskar were playing Frisbee in the park. Allan threw the disc farther and farther so people could see how talented Oskar was. When the Frisbee flew into the woods, Oskar chased it and did not return.

Allan called and searched for Oskar for a long time but did not find him. He returned home sad and upset. The family agreed they would put up posters tomorrow. That night as the family watched TV, they heard a scratching at the door. A very dirty Oskar bounded into the house wagging his tail.

"Where have you been?" demanded Allan sternly, but he was hugging the muddy dog. Now Oskar and Allan play Frisbee in the yard. In the park, Oskar is on a leash!

## Activity 40—Deciding on Point of View

**1.** first person **2.** third person **3.** third person **4.** first person **5.** third person **6.** third person **7.** first person **8.** third person **9.** third person **10.** first person **11–15.** Answers will vary. Sample answers are given. **11.** Sherry fixed herself a bowl of cereal and fruit. **12.** I have blueberries in my oatmeal. **13.** I enjoy eating it every day of the week. **14.** Elmer doesn't know why, but he doesn't like oatmeal. **15.** I usually buy myself a bagel.

## Activity 41—Using Verb Tense Correctly

Words in parentheses should be written above the crossed out words.
He ~~reads~~ (read) card after card. None of the cards ~~seems~~ (seemed) exactly right for Sarah.
**1.** B **2.** A **3.** A **4.** B **5.** A **6.** B **7.** A **8.** B **9.** A **10.** B

## Activity 42—Writing Dialogue

**1.** "A man downtown just ran over himself," said Anne. **2.** "Oh no!" exclaimed Rita. "How did he do that?" **3.** "The man asked me to run across the street and mail a letter for him," explained Anne. **4.** "I could not do it," Anne continued, "because I was already late." **5.** "What happened then?" Rita asked eagerly. **6.** "He ran over himself, of course,"

giggled Anne. **7.** Rita rolled her eyes and said, "That is a real groaner." **8.** "Well, you laughed, didn't you?" replied Anne. **9.** Rita responded, "I owe you one." **10.** "Good," said Anne. "I love a good joke."

## Activity 43—Using Direct and Indirect Quotations

**1.** direct **2.** indirect **3.** indirect **4.** direct **5.** direct **6.** indirect **7.** direct **8.** direct **9.** indirect **10.** direct **11.** Jordan said, "No life has been found on other planets." **12.** Tim asked, "Do you think that means there is life only on Earth, Jordan?" **13.** Jordan replied, "There could be life somewhere in the universe." **14.** He explained, "We have explored very little of the universe." **15.** He went on, "There could be another planet like Earth somewhere."

## Activity 44—Answering Test Questions

Sentences will vary. Make sure student answers identify each item correctly. Possible sentences are given. **1.** Theodore Roosevelt was the twenty-sixth president of the United States. **2.** A trilogy is a literary or dramatic work such as a play or novel written in three parts. **3.** An oboe is a double-reed woodwind musical instrument. **4.** Melton is a thick, warm wool cloth. **5.** A riot is a conflict involving two or more groups of people. **6.** Joseph Stalin was the premier of the Soviet Union during the 1940s and part of the 1950s. **7.** NASA, which stands for National Aeronautics and Space Administration, is the space agency of the United States. **8.** Formerly a British crown colony, Hong Kong is a major city on the southeastern coast of China. **9.** A vegan is a vegetarian who does not eat eggs, cheese, milk, or other non-meat animal products. **10.** A haberdasher is a retailer that specializes in men's clothing.

## Activity 45—Writing an Essay

Notes will vary. Check student notes to make sure student understands the concepts of notes as a prewriting activity. Also check notes for quantity (10 notes).

## Activity 46—Writing a Report About a Book, Movie, or TV Show

Reports will vary. Check the report for size (15 sentences). Check also to make sure student understands the basic structure of the report using the pointers and includes all the parts. Make sure final draft reflects the student's effort to revise the report to add variety and clarity.

## Activity 47—Writing a Personal Letter

February 4, 2007
Dear Kelli,

How are you doing at college? Do you enjoy living in a dorm? Tell me about your roommate.

I'm staying busy these days. I'm working hard on getting good grades and staying caught up on my assignments. I'm also trying out for a part in a musical.

I can't wait to see you next month. Write to me when you have some time.

As always,

*Maria Gomez*

**1.** Date **2.** Salutation **3.** Body **4.** Closing **5.** Signature

## Activity 48—Writing a Message

1. **To:** Rick Bailey
2. **Date:** April 4, 2007    **Time:** 2:26 p.m.
3. **While you were out**
4. **Mr./Ms.** Bailey
5. **Phone No.**

☑ TELEPHONED  ☐ WAS IN TO SEE YOU  ☐ WANTS TO SEE YOU
☐ PLEASE CALL  ☐ WILL CALL BACK  ☐ RETURNED YOUR CALL  ☐ URGENT

**Message:** Your dentist appointment is canceled. Your mother will pick you up after school to take you to work. Ms. Johnson

## Activity 49—Writing an E-Mail Message

E-mail messages will vary. Make sure the student has included complete e-mail addresses (including screen name, ISP, and suffix) for both the sender and the recipient.
**1.** D **2.** C **3.** B **4.** E **5.** A

## Activity 50—Writing a Business Letter

Numbers in parentheses indicate sequence. From top to bottom, the boxes are: closing (**6**), date (**2**), writer's name and title (**8**), handwritten signature (**7**), body (**5**), heading or return address (**1**), inside address (**3**), salutation (**4**).
**9.** modified block style **10.** Paragraphs in modified block style are indented, instead of flush left.

## Activity 51—Addressing an Envelope

**1.** Ms. Lydia Turin
311 Maple Grove Lane
Springtown, VA

**2.** Ms. Melinda Young
Golfers' Delight Gifts
4132 E. Main St.
Springtown, VA 33603

Return address should be student's mailing address. Make sure the student uses the correct format for the return address.

**3.** Student's address
_____
_____

**4.** Mr. Scott Jones
1212 Leahy St.
Pierson, CA 90063

**5.** Including a return address protects the letter from getting lost, if the mailing address is incorrect. If the mailing address is incorrect, the post office can return the letter.

## Activity 52—Writing a Business Memo

**1–4., 7–10.** Memos will vary. Make sure the student's memo includes all of the necessary information: date, sender's name, recipient's name, subject, and message. For the first memo, make sure the student has presented his or her idea clearly. For the second memo, make sure all of the important details from the notice are included in the message.
**5.** Answer will vary. A sample answer is given. Memos are not as formal, and the sender is already identified in the "From" line.

**6.** Answer will vary. A sample answer is given. Memos are usually only one or two short paragraphs long. In contrast, the length and quantity of paragraphs in a business letter can vary.

## Activity 53—Understanding the Parts of a Report

4: body paragraph; 2–3: body paragraph; 1: topic paragraph; 5: summary paragraph; 2–3: body paragraph; African elephants and Indian elephants are different species of elephants with differing sizes and features.

## Activity 54—Choosing a Topic

Answers will vary. Possible answers are given. **1.** *Alice in Wonderland, The Secret Garden, The Wizard of Oz* **2.** luge, speed skating, curling **3.** Orpheus, Athena, gorgon **4.** ballet, tap, salsa **5.** hockey, football, baseball **6.** Electoral College, campaigns, primaries **7.** brakes, transmission, tires **8.** cameras, making prints, lighting **9.** NASA, Neil Armstrong, Voyager II **10.** warm-up, strength training, aerobics

## Activity 55—Finding Information

**Title: 1.** *Gone with the Wind* **2.** *Hamlet* **3.** *The Outsiders* **4.** *The Red Pony* **5.** *The Writer's Handbook* **Author: 6.** Buck, Pearl S. **7.** Hinton, S. E. **8.** Oates, Joyce Carol **9.** Shakespeare, William **10.** Steinbeck, John **Subject: 11.** art **12.** history **13.** Olympics, history **14.** psychology **15.** Russia

## Activity 56—Using Online Resources

**1.** Web address **2.** out of date **3.** reliable **4.** keyword **5.** online sources **6.** search engine **7.** internet **8.** current **9.** accurate **10.** agency **Acrostic Puzzle:** Let's surf the Web!

## Activity 57— Taking Notes

**1–2.** Paraphrases will vary. Make sure the student includes all of the important information from the paragraph.
**3.** Carlson, Kendra. Training to Win.
   Peoria Press, 2001.
   Missing information: city of publication
**4.** "Setting Realistic Training Goals."
   Sports M.D. August 25, 2004.
   www.sportsmd.net/traingoals.htm
   Missing information: author's name, date of last Web site update
**5.** Wilkins, A.B. Spring Training!
   Chicago: 2004.
   Missing information: publisher

## Activity 58—Creating an Outline

Outlines will vary. Possible outlines are given.
**Sports Around the World**
**I.** Individual Sports
   **A.** Track and field
   **B.** Tennis
   **C.** Swimming
   **D.** Gymnastics
   **E.** Skiing
   **F.** Cycling
**II.** Team Sports
   **A.** Soccer
   **B.** Basketball
   **C.** Baseball
   **D.** Volleyball
   **E.** Ice hockey
   **F.** Football

**Balanced Nutrition from the Four Food Groups**

I. Starches
- **A.** Rice
- **B.** Pasta
- **C.** Whole wheat bread

II. Fruits and Vegetables
- **A.** Grapes
- **B.** Banana
- **C.** Carrots
- **D.** Lettuce

III. Dairy Products
- **A.** Milk
- **B.** Cheese
- **C.** Yogurt

IV. Proteins
- **A.** Chicken
- **B.** Fish

## Activity 59—Writing the First Draft

Paragraphs will vary. Make sure the student includes all four of the main topics—selecting a topic, research, getting organized, and writing and revising—in his or her topic paragraph.

## Activity 60—Revising the Report

**1.** *Mission to Mars?* should go under *IV. The future of space flight.*
**2.** *1. Cable TV uses satellites* should be deleted **3.** *A. People once believed the moon was made of cheese* should be deleted. **4.** *1. Tragedies of the space race* should go under *B. Space race.* **5.** *1. My trip to the Kennedy Space Center* should be deleted.

## Activity 61—Editing the Report

Five mistakes are as follows: **1.** *the, Soviet Union.* Delete the comma.
**2.** *The gole* should be spelled *goal.* **3.** *Astronauts and cosmonauts become heroes* should be *became heroes.* **4.** *Each country rushes* should be *rushed.*
**5.** *This competition betwen the United States* should be *between.*

## Activity 62—Preparing a Bibliography

Make sure student has indented all lines after the first one for each entry.

1. Flanagan, Patrick. <u>Ireland: The People and Places of the Emerald Isle</u>. Boston: Shamrock Book Co., 2000.
2. Collins, Shawn. <u>The History of Northern Ireland</u>. San Francisco: Acme Press, 1998.
3. Clendennin, Moira. "The Greening of Belfast." <u>UK Today</u> 24, June 12, 2001, 25–28.
4. Lenox, Liza. "Fast Facts About Modern Irish History." January 8, 2003. www.eire.uk/fastfacts.htm (March 13, 2003).
5. "Northern Ireland." <u>World Encyclopedia</u>. Vol. 14, 2002, 521–525.
6. Reece, Susanna, ed. <u>War and Peace in Ireland: Essays on the History of Northern Ireland</u>. Chicago: Greenwood Publications, 1998.
7. Franken, Leslie, and Michael Lorie. <u>Legends and Legacies of Modern Ireland</u>. New York: Sampson Publishing Company, 1998.
8. Dugan, Stephen. "Doves over Dublin." <u>World Watch Journal</u> 12, March 15, 2000, 38–41.
9. Jung, Norman. "Understanding the Irish." <u>Ireland</u> 4, June 2003, 18–20.
10. Fremont, Jessica. "Passion, Pride, and Prejudice in Northern Ireland." September 21, 2003. www.irelandweb.edu (February 8, 2004).

## Activity 63—Publishing the Final Report

**1.** The name should come above the date. **2.** *Hibearnation* is spelled incorrectly. It should be *hibernation.* **3.** *My Report* should be deleted.
**4.** *Page 1* should be deleted. **5.** The title, *Ancient Rome,* should be on the top line.

# Modified Activities

## Modified Activity 1—Beginning and Ending a Sentence

**1.** Amber got her yearbook today. She wants her friends to sign it. They look at the pictures and laugh. **2.** Laura has a job at Pete's Grill. Amber will work at the pool. Both girls will go to junior college in the fall. **3.** Laura is excited about her vacation. She is going to the Grand Canyon. Her parents and brother are going too. **4.** Graduating can be happy and sad. Everyone is looking forward to moving on. Everyone is also sad to be leaving old friends. **5–8.** Sentences and word order may vary. Possible answers are shown. **5.** Suddenly I saw a huge black cloud. **6.** They ran down the hill carefully. **7.** Today the weather is beautiful. **8.** We finally finished our work.

## Modified Activity 2—Understanding the Purpose of a Sentence

**1.** D—(!) **2.** A—(.) **3.** C—(. or !) **4.** B—(?) **5.** A—(.) **6.** C—(.) **7.** B—(?) **8.** A—(.) **9.** D—(!) **10.** C—(.) **11.** A—(.) **12.** D—(!) **13.** C—(.) **14.** A—(.) **15.** B—(?) **16.** D—(!)

## Modified Activity 3—Finding the Subject and Predicate

**1.** Dave (rides) a big motorcycle. **2.** He (wins) many races. **3.** A Sunday race (brings) a big crowd. **4.** I (smell) motor oil. **5.** A good stunt (gives) everyone a thrill. **6.** The motorcycle (flew) over 27 parked cars. **7.** (You) (Give) a cheer. **8.** Everyone (had) a good time. **9.** slid, past **10.** go, present **11.** watches, present **12.** scream, present **13.** will get, future **14.** went, past **15.** ate, past **16.** will be, future

## Modified Activity 4—Correcting Sentence Fragments

**1.** sentence **2.** fragment **3.** sentence **4.** fragment **5.** fragment **6.** sentence **7.** fragment **8.** sentence **9–12.** Answers will vary. Possible answers are shown. **9.** He looked for a job downtown. **10.** The warm sun and cool breeze made us feel good. **11.** I heard about the accident last night. **12.** She forgot her book.

## Modified Activity 5—Correcting Run-On Sentences

**1.** Graduation is on June 4. What time will it be held? **2.** Students march into the hall. Then they sit at the front. **3.** Their families watch them. They are thrilled and happy. **4–8.** Sentence corrections will vary. Possible answers are shown. **4.** comma fault—A yearbook editor makes a yearbook. The job has many parts. **5.** compound sentence **6.** comma fault—Pages are checked for mistakes. Can you find spelling mistakes? **7.** compound sentence **8.** comma fault—Here is my yearbook. Please sign it for me.

## Modified Activity 6—Making the Subject and Verb Agree

**1.** have **2.** want **3.** learns **4.** carries **5.** has **6.** are **7.** hate **8.** are **9.** plural, walk **10.** plural, cause **11.** singular, is **12.** plural, take **13.** singular, watches **14.** plural, see **15.** singular, makes **16.** singular, excites

## Modified Activity 7—Using Irregular Verbs

**1.** got **2.** made **3.** teach **4.** won **5.** knew **6.** eaten **7.** drove **8.** begins **9.** go **10.** had **11.** began **12.** ate **13.** drove **14.** seen **15.** begun **16.** took

## Modified Activity 8—Using Verbs and Verb Phrases

**1.** could eat **2.** has brought **3.** will share **4.** has **5.** told **6.** began **7.** is being given **8.** should do **9.** has called—present perfect **10.** made—past **11.** will use—future **12.** had listened—past perfect **13.** will have taken—future perfect **14.** make—present **15.** has become—present perfect **16.** will get—future

## Modified Activity 9—Using Conjunctions to Combine Ideas

**1.** or **2.** and **3.** but **4.** nor **5.** so **6.** yet **7.** so **8.** and **9.** Tom loves his sister, but he still forgot her birthday. **10.** Would you like water or iced tea? **11.** Mary grows peas, squash, and tomatoes in her garden. **12.** Amy and Ron own many books, so their shelves are crowded.

## Modified Activity 10—Using Other Kinds of Conjunctions

**1–5.** Sentences may vary. Possible sentences are shown. **1.** After David was up all night, he fell asleep in class. **2.** Until you called Laura, she had not heard the news. **3.** While Miki was telling the story, Don was acting it out. **4.** We took many pictures when we were at the family reunion. **5.** I run every day because I need exercise. **6.** Because the sun was shining, I felt cheerful. **7.** Although we arrived late, we did not miss any of the movie. **8.** She spun gracefully as she danced across the stage. **9.** Ray cannot come over unless you clean your room. **10.** If Alex feels ill, he should go to bed. **11.** You can leave when Nate gets here. **12.** Before Rob was hired, the work had been piling up.

## Modified Activity 11—Replacing Nouns with Pronouns

**1.** his, Brandon **2.** it, car **3.** her, Laura **4.** his, Derek **5.** she, teacher **6.** their, Amber and Sara **7.** I, Eliza **8.** it, dog **9.** A motorcycle is noisy, and it goes too fast. **10.** Dana is jogging on the trail in her new shoes. **11.** The trail is there for all who want to enjoy it. **12.** Zeke rides his bike on the trail.

## Modified Activity 12—Using Plural and Possessive Nouns

**1.** country's, countries, countries' **2.** week's, weeks, weeks' **3.** woman's, women, women's **4.** bike's, bikes, bikes' **5.** wolf's, wolves, wolves' **6.** child's, children, children's **7.** pony's, ponies, ponies' **8.** leaf's, leaves, leaves' **9.** dress's, dresses, dresses' **10.** goose's, geese, geese's **11.** bus's, buses, buses' **12.** city's, cities, cities'

## Modified Activity 13—Adding Adjectives and Adverbs

**1–5.** Answers will vary. Sample answers are given. **1.** Carrie's little dog jumps and plays continuously. **2.** Please bring the fruit salad to the dining table. **3.** The preschool children fed the hungry ducks at the pond. **4.** Chad finally took a well-deserved trip to England. **5.** This illustrated article describes the recent events. **6.** Today, when **7.** very, to what degree **8.** usually, how often

## Modified Activity 14—Comparing with Adjectives and Adverbs

**1.** largest **2.** politely **3.** more gracefully **4.** more exciting **5.** sweeter **6.** loudest **7.** faster **8.** more lively **9.** I felt better today, but I am still sick. **10.** My day could not have gone worse. **11.** The store is least busy on Mondays. **12.** You did a better job than Ben.

## Modified Activity 15—Adding Prepositional Phrases

**1.** The (man) in the green car is my father. **2.** The main (character) in this TV show is very funny. **3.** His (cousins) from Mexico are visiting today. **4.** Did Ron send a (letter) about his plans? **5.** The (table) in the hall would look better here. **6.** He keeps a (journal) of his travels. **7.** Cara read a poem by Maya Angelou. **8.** The (questions) on page 75 are hard. **9.** Maria (spilled) coffee on her white shirt. **10.** I (must have left) my keys at home. **11.** In the morning, we (will discuss) the changes. **12.** Please (store) your bags in the closet. **13.** We always (eat) fish on Fridays. **14.** I (am going) to the store now. **15.** I (will buy) chips for you. **16.** The kittens (rubbed) against my legs.

## Modified Activity 16—Planning to Write a Paragraph

**1–3.** Answers will vary. Sample answers are given. **1.** why you should eat healthy foods **2.** to explain how food helps you be healthy **3.** reasons, facts, and examples **4.** topic sentence **5.** body/detail **6.** body/detail **7.** body/detail **8.** summary/conclusion

## Modified Activity 17—Writing a Topic Sentence

**1–7.** Answers will vary. Sample answers are given. **1.** Dancing is very <u>good exercise</u>. **2.** I always <u>get nervous</u> before a big test. **3.** The sections of a newspaper are in a <u>logical order</u>. **4.** Sunburn is not only painful, <u>it is dangerous</u>! **5.** Getting a job last summer turned out to be <u>a lot of work</u>. **6.** My goldfish Ranger is <u>quite a character</u>. **7.** Our soccer <u>fields need some help</u>. **8.** Taking the bus is a good way to <u>conserve fossil fuel</u>. **9.** B **10.** A **11.** B **12.** B

## Modified Activity 18—Writing Supporting Details

Answers will vary. A sample answer is given.
Weather conditions can affect your skiing experience. Be sure to dress warmly for the cold. If your skin gets too cold, you can harm yourself. Don't push yourself too hard—recognize when it's time to rest and warm up.

## Modified Activity 19—Writing a Summary or Conclusion

**1.** B **2.** A **3.** B **4.** B

## Modified Activity 20—Writing an Interesting Topic Sentence

**1–8.** Answers will vary. Sample answers are given. **1.** Skipping breakfast is a sure-fire way to turn yourself into a zombie! **2.** A well-planned winter vacation can prevent cabin fever. **3.** My dad will do almost anything to get out of shopping. **4.** Are you looking for a better Valentine's Day gift than candy or flowers? **5.** If you want to learn about yourself, play a sport. **6.** Our dog Butter is no watchdog, but he is the world's best sport. **7.** I could not get along without my sneakers. **8.** When I got a letter from Lia, I didn't know whether to laugh or cry.

## Modified Activity 21—Using Sentence Variety

**1–4.** Answers will vary. Sample answers are given. **1.** On Sundays, her mother always makes French toast. **2.** In the jungle, the lion hunts for food. **3.** Dreamily, Annie and Daniel walked down the wooded path. **4.** By Friday, this project will be completed.
Answers will vary. A sample answer is given.
A frog begins as an egg floating in the water. Soon the eggs hatch into tadpoles, which also swim in the water. At first, the tadpoles look something like little fish with tails. Gradually, the tadpoles grow legs and lungs. Then they have become young frogs.

## Modified Activity 22—Adding Transitions

**1–4.** Answers will vary. Sample answers are given. **1.** I skipped breakfast. As a result, I ran out of energy at 10. **2.** We waited nervously for the tow truck. At last it rolled into sight. **3.** Salads can be loaded with calories. For example, salad dressing often contains a lot of fat and sugar. **4.** Jan picked up the cake for the party. Meanwhile, we blew up balloons and made streamers.

## Modified Activity 23—Revising a Paragraph

**1–8.** Answers will vary. A sample answer is given.
**1.** Can you tell a moth from a butterfly? **2–4.** Moths are fatter and have dull colors, while butterflies have thinner bodies and more colorful wings. **5–6.** Also, moths have plain feelers, but butterflies have feelers with round ends. **7–8.** Finally, moths rest with their wings flat, and butterflies rest with their wings pressed together above their bodies.
**9–10.** Answers will vary somewhat. Sample answers are given.
**9.** Adventure movies are exciting. **10.** This Saturday we will rent a movie.

## Modified Activity 24—Editing Your Paragraph

**1.** Do you like <u>horrer</u> movies? **2.** If you do, you (was) sure to love *The haunted house*. **3.** It (be) full of <u>scairy</u> <u>gosts</u> and <u>wierd</u> noises. **4.** (me) (spending) the <u>hole</u> movie sitting on the edge of my seat.
Paragraph should read: Do you like horror movies? If you do, you are sure to love *The Haunted House*. It is full of scary ghosts and weird noises. The characters cannot get out of the house. I spent the whole movie sitting on the edge of my seat.

## Modified Activity 25—Explaining How to Do Something

2, 3, 1, 4
Paragraphs will vary. A sample paragraph is given.
Improving your nutrition can be a simple process. Start by asking your school nurse about healthier foods. Next, buy healthy snacks you will enjoy eating. Finally, commit to eating healthy snacks by cutting out junk food. You will soon feel the benefits of healthy snacking.

## Modified Activity 26—Giving Information

Paragraphs will vary. A sample paragraph is given.
My favorite sport is track for several reasons. It gets me outside in the fresh air. I love to run and jump. Best of all, I am good at it and can win events. Track is the most fun for me.
**1.** My favorite sport is track. **2.** It is done outside, it lets me run and jump, and I am good at it. **3.** Track is the most fun for me. Yes. **4.** I could make the topic sentence more interesting, and I could add more detail about why I like running and jumping. **5.** Why I Love Track

## Modified Activity 27—Comparing and Contrasting

**1–4.** At least four of these transitions should be underlined: *both, Both, However, While, On the other hand* **5–6.** Students may list any two of the following: both have long hair, weigh more than 100 pounds, and do specific jobs. **7–8.** Students may list any two of the following: they are different colors, come from different countries, and do different jobs. **9–12.** Items listed will vary but should all represent members of the same category.
Sentences will vary but should compare two of the items listed in 9–12 by showing how they are alike or different.

## Modified Activity 28—Showing Cause and Effect

**1.** A **2.** B **3.** A **4.** B
**5–8.** Sentences will vary in wording. Sample answers are given.
**5.** Because my family came from Greece, I wrote a report on Greece.
**6.** Since the market had a great sale on fruits and vegetables, we bought many fresh vegetables. **7.** My dad replaced junk food with fruits and vegetables. As a result, he has lost 20 pounds. **8.** We gave the dog a bath because it had rolled in the mud.

## Modified Activity 29—Explaining a Solution to a Problem

Answers will vary. Sample answers are given. **1.** Notice things about people and give them compliments. **2.** Help people when they need help. **3.** Join a club after school. **4.** This solution will work because it will let me talk and do things with others. **5.** A club is fun and people are easier to talk to there. **6.** A club is active and people do things as a group. **7.** The things people in a club do together make bonds between them. **8.** You feel friendlier towards people when you get to know them.

## Modified Activity 30—Stating an Opinion

1. (Eddie Murphy is a very funny man.) 2. He has been making people laugh for over twenty years. 3. Murphy started as a standup comic. 4. (His best movie is *Beverly Hills Cop.*) 5. (Nobody can make us laugh like Eddie Murphy.) Opinions will vary. Sample opinions are given. 6. Making your bed makes the whole room seem nicer. 7. Romantic movies are ridiculous. 8. Most daytime TV shows are awful. 9. Reading books is not as much fun as watching movies. 10. My homework is boring. 11. New clothes make you feel good about yourself. 12. Babysitting is very hard work.

## Modified Activity 31—Separating Facts from Opinions

1–5. The following words and phrases should be circled. 1. In my opinion 2. Sometimes 3. seem to be 4. In some situations 5. might be 6. opinion 7. fact 8. fact 9. opinion 10. opinion 11. opinion 12. fact

## Modified Activity 32—Supporting Your Opinion

Listed details should be circled. 2. Children have to play ball in the street. 3. There is no park on this side of town. 4. Studies show that kids with no place to play get in trouble. 7. There is enough land for sale at a good price. 8. Both young and old could enjoy the beauty of a park. Paragraphs will vary. A sample paragraph is given.
Still Valley needs a neighborhood park. There is no park at all on this side of town, and our children suffer because of this. I see them playing in the street every day because it is too far to go across town. This is dangerous. Also, studies show that kids with no place to play get in trouble. Let's demand a park for the good of our kids.

## Modified Activity 33—Writing an Advertisement

1. The slogan sells greeting cards. 2. The slogan does not use facts. 3. The word love appeals to emotions. 4. Sending one of these cards is a good way to show your love for someone.
Slogans and ads will vary. A sample answer is given.
"Lightweights, the cards that are good for you!"

## Modified Activity 34—Choosing Words That Appeal to the Senses

1. smell 2. taste 3. touch 4. hearing 5. sight 6. touch 7. taste 8. hearing 9. The peas popped out of their pod. 10. Slow waves washed over the warm sand. 11. The cheesecake was light, lemony, and luscious. 12. A tiger roared and ripped at its cage.

## Modified Activity 35—Choosing Specific Words

1. library 2. dog 3. lime 4. Tampa 5. rose 6. shout 7. music 8. *Daily News* 9. pancakes 10. lunch 11. waltz 12. giggle 13. sail 14. cow 15. peek 16. bake 17–20. Answers will vary. Sample answers are given. 17. We flew to Texas for vacation. 18. Some friends came with us. 19. The scenery was spectacular. 20. We saw several historic sites.

## Modified Activity 36—Using Figures of Speech

1. The water is as clear as crystal.—simile 2. Juan is the apple of her eye.—metaphor 3. The wind moaned in the trees.—personification 4. The tulips bowed to the rain.—personification 5. He eats like a pig.—simile 6. She is a crab when she is tired.—metaphor 7. Laura is a puzzle to me sometimes.—metaphor 8. That job is a dream come true.—metaphor 9. Amanda is as sweet as pie.—simile 10–12. Answers will vary. Sample answers are given. 10. That piece of pie is so small that it would leave an ant hungry. 11. I was so hot that I melted my shoes. 12. Megan was so happy that she floated away.

## Modified Activity 37—Developing a Writing Style

1. Students may list any two of the following three figures of speech: as big as a whale, old-man whiskers, as funny as a house fire. 2. Students may list any two of the following: catfish, whale, boat, skin, scars, fins, body, mouth, whiskers, problem, house fire. 3. Students may list any two of the following: twisted, flopped, sucked, waved. 4. sight 5. Students may list fins, fat, flopped or fish's, funny, fire. 6. Short sentences make the fish's struggle stand out. 7. The words show the fish is a fighter but is suffering. 8. The writer's style is caring but colorful.

## Modified Activity 38—Telling a Story

1. a cat hunting a bird 2. a bird and an orange cat 3. a snowy yard 4. A bird sits in the snow eating seeds. 5. A cat sees it and sneaks toward it. 6. A door opens and a person calls the cat. 7. The bird flies off. 8. The cat goes inside.

## Modified Activity 39—Putting Events in Order

3, 1, 2, 4  5, 7, 6, 8
Stories will vary somewhat in wording. A sample story is given.
In 2003, the Walt family adopted a puppy named Oskar. Oskar loved playing with Allan as he grew up. One day in 2007, Oskar and Allan Walt were playing in the park. Allan would throw a stick and Oskar would chase it. One throw went by the woods. Oskar saw a squirrel. He chased it into the woods and did not return.
"Here, Oskar!" called Allan. Allan looked everywhere for Oskar but did not find him. Finally, he had to go home alone, but he was sad and upset. Later that night, something scratched on the door. There was Oskar! He ran into the house wagging his tail. "Welcome home, boy!" Allan laughed.

## Modified Activity 40—Deciding on Point of View

1. first person 2. third person 3. third person 4. first person 5. third person 6. third person 7. first person 8. third person 9–12. Answers will vary. Sample answers are given. 9. Kaylie ate a breakfast bar his morning. 10. I have berries in my cereal. 11. I eat it every day of the week. 12. Dan does not like cereal.

## Modified Activity 41—Using Verb Tense Correctly

1. B 2. A 3. B 4. B 5. A 6. A 7. A 8. The words in parentheses should be written above the crossed out words:
After they ~~try~~ (tried) another cookie, Ben suggested watching a DVD. Maria ~~brings~~ (brought) the cookies with them. ... Maria ~~says~~ (said), "I'll help you!"

## Modified Activity 42—Writing Dialogue

1. "Did you hear about the thief who stole a calendar?" asked Anne. 2. "No," said Rita. "What happened to him?" 3. "He got twelve months," laughed Anne. 4. "I can't believe I fell for that," said Rita. 5. Anne asked, "Do you know why we never run out of math teachers?" 6. Rita said, "No, but I'll bet you will tell me." 7. "Because they always multiply," said Anne. 8. "I like that joke," said Rita.

## Modified Activity 43—Using Direct and Indirect Quotations

1. ("You must be kidding," said Tim.) 2. Jordan said that he had been outside last night. 3. He said that the sky was clear. 4. ("But what did you see?" questioned Tim.) 5. ("I saw a bright light in the sky," Jordan said.) 6. Tim asked whether the light moved or was still. 7. ("It stayed still for a minute. Then it zoomed away," said Jordan.) 8. Tim said that most UFO reports can be explained. 9–12. Answers may vary. Sample answers are given. 9. Jordan said, "No life has been found on other planets." 10. Tim asked, "Jordan, do you think there is life only on Earth?" 11. Jordan said, "There could be life somewhere in space."

**12.** He added, "We have not traveled very far into space."

## Modified Activity 44—Answering Test Questions

Sentences will vary. Make sure student answers identify each item correctly. Possible sentences are given. **1.** Formerly a British crown colony, Hong Kong is a major city on the southeastern coast of China. **2.** Frida Kahlo is a Mexican artist best known for her colorful, and often surreal, paintings. **3.** Theodore Roosevelt was the twenty-sixth president of the United States. **4.** A trilogy is a literary or dramatic work such as a play or novel written in three parts. **5.** NASA, which stands for National Aeronautics and Space Administration, is the space agency of the United States. **6.** The oboe is a reed instrument known for its haunting and unusual tone. **7.** Chicken pox is a virus that causes fever and itchy red sores on the skin. **8.** A vegan is a vegetarian who does eat not eggs, cheese, milk, or other non-meat animal products.

## Modified Activity 45—Writing an Essay

Notes will vary. Check student notes to make sure student understands the concept of notes as a prewriting activity. Also check the quantity of notes (8 notes).

## Modified Activity 46—Writing a Report About a Book, Movie, or TV Show

Reports will vary. Check the report to make sure student understands the basic structure of the report using the pointers and includes all the parts. Also check the size of the report (12 sentences).

## Modified Activity 47—Writing a Personal Letter

February 4, 2007
Dear Aunt Sue,

Thank you very much for the new photo album. Did Mom tell you I am taking a photography class at the community center? The album will be a perfect place to display my work.

We all enjoyed the homemade jam you sent, too. Your recipe has always been my favorite.

I am looking forward to seeing you in June.

As always,
*Andy Lewis*

**1.** Date **2.** Salutation **3.** Body **4.** Closing

## Modified Activity 48—Writing a Message

Messages will vary. Make sure student answer reflects all of the information that is given in the scenario described. A possible message is given.

**1.** **To:** Mom
**2.** **Date:** April 4, 2007      **Time:** 2:26 p.m.
**While you were out**
**3.** **Mr./Ms.** Liza
**of:** Book Nook
**Phone No.**
**4.** ☑ TELEPHONED ☐ WAS IN TO SEE YOU ☐ WANTS TO SEE YOU
☑ PLEASE CALL ☐ WILL CALL BACK      ☐ RETURNED YOUR CALL ☐ URGENT
**5.** **Message:** The book you ordered last week has come in. You can pick it up at the front counter. Rick

## Modified Activity 49—Writing an E-Mail Message

E-mail messages will vary. Make sure the student has included complete e-mail addresses (including screen name, ISP, and suffix) for both the sender and the recipient.
**1.** B **2.** D **3.** A **4.** C

## Modified Activity 50—Writing a Business Letter

Numbers in parentheses indicate sequence. From top to bottom, the boxes are: closing (**6**), date (**2**), writer's name and title (**8**), handwritten signature (**7**), body (**5**), heading or return address (**1**), inside address (**3**), salutation (**4**).

## Modified Activity 51—Addressing an Envelope

Return address should be student's mailing address. Make sure the student uses the correct format for the return address.

**1.** Student's address
_____
_____
      **2.** Mr. Scott Jones
      1212 Leahy St.
      Pierson, CA 90063

**3.** Answers will vary. A sample answer is given. Including a return address protects the letter from getting lost, if the mailing address is incorrect. If the mailing address in incorrect, the Post Office can return the letter. **4.** No; it needs a stamp.

## Modified Activity 52—Writing a Business Memo

**1–8.** Memos will vary. Make sure the student's memo includes all of the necessary information: date, sender's name, recipient's name, subject, and message. For the first memo, make sure the student has presented his or her idea clearly. For the second memo, make sure all of the important details from the notice are included in the message.

## Modified Activity 53—Understanding the Parts of a Report

2–3, body paragraph; 2–3, body paragraph; 4, summary paragraph; 1, topic paragraph; These elephants are different species with differing sizes and features.

## Modified Activity 54—Choosing a Topic

Answers will vary. Possible answers are given. **1.** brakes, transmission, tires **2.** cameras, making prints, lighting **3.** NASA, Neil Armstrong, Voyager II **4.** luge, speed skating, curling **5.** hockey, football, baseball **6.** John F. Kennedy, Abraham Lincoln, Franklin D. Roosevelt **7.** salsa, tango, ballet **8.** Hercules, Arachne, Medusa

## Modified Activity 55—Finding Information

**Title: 1.** *Gone with the Wind* **2.** *The Outsiders* **3.** *The Red Pony* **4.** *The Writer's Handbook* **Author: 5.** Hinton, S. E. **6.** Shakespeare, William **7.** Steinbeck, John **8.** Tolkien, J.R.R **Subject: 9.** Olympics, history **10.** psychology **11.** rivers, Amazon **12.** Russia

## Modified Activity 56—Using Online Resources

**1.** keyword **2.** online sources **3.** Web address **4.** out of date **5.** search engine **6.** internet **7.** reliable **8.** current
**Acrostic Puzzle:** Let's surf the Web!

*Teacher's Resource Library Answer Key*   **455**

## Modified Activity 57—Taking Notes

**1.** Paraphrases will vary. Make sure the student includes all of the important information from the paragraph.

**2.**     Carlson, Kendra. <u>Training to Win</u>.
     New York: Peoria Press, 2001.

**3.**     Kovac, Nayda. "Training
     Goals." <u>Sports M.D.</u> August 25, 2004.
     www.sportsmd.net

**4.**     Wilkins, A.B. <u>Spring Training!</u>
     Chicago: Play Ball Press, 2004.

## Modified Activity 58—Creating an Outline

The Four Food Groups: Rice, subtopic; Dairy Products, main; Fruits and Vegetables, main; Cheese, subtopic; Carrots, subtopic; Grapes, subtopic; Pasta, subtopic; Proteins, main; Yogurt, subtopic; Starches, main; Nuts, subtopic; Fish, subtopic.

**Sports:** Track and Field, subtopic; Soccer, subtopic; Basketball, subtopic; Baseball, subtopic; Individual Sports, main; Team Sports, main; Swimming, subtopic; Gymnastics, subtopic; Skiing, subtopic; Volleyball, subtopic; Football, subtopic; Cycling, subtopic.

Outlines will vary. Possible outlines are given.

### The Four Food Groups

**I.** Starches

    **A.** Rice

    **B.** Pasta

**II.** Fruits and Vegetables

    **A.** Grapes

    **B.** Carrots

**III.** Dairy Products

    **A.** Cheese

    **B.** Yogurt

**IV.** Proteins

    **A.** Fish

    **B.** Nuts

### Sports Around the World

**I.** Individual Sports

    **A.** Track and field

    **B.** Swimming

    **C.** Gymnastics

    **D.** Skiing

    **E.** Cycling

**II.** Team Sports

    **A.** Soccer

    **B.** Basketball

    **C.** Baseball

    **D.** Volleyball

    **E.** Football

## Modified Activity 59—Writing the First Draft

Paragraphs will vary. Make sure the student includes all four of the main topics in his or her topic paragraph. Also check for correct length (8 sentences).

## Modified Activity 60—Revising the Report

**1.** *Cable TV uses satellites* should be deleted. **2.** *A. People once believed the moon was made of cheese* should be deleted. **3.** *1. Tragedies of the space race* should go under *B. Space race.* **4.** *1. My trip to the Kennedy Space Center* should be deleted.

## Modified Activity 61—Editing the Report

Four mistakes are as follows: **1.** *the, Soviet Union.* Delete the comma. **2.** *The gole* should be spelled goal. **3.** *Astronauts become heroes* should be *became heroes.* **4.** There should be a period at the end of *…that could go farther than the one before it.*

## Modified Activity 62—Preparing a Bibliography

Make sure student has indented all lines after the first one for each entry.

  **1.** Lenox, Liza. "Fast Facts About Modern Irish History." January 8, 2003. www.eire.uk/fastfacts.htm (March 13, 2003).

  **2.** "Northern Ireland." <u>World Encyclopedia</u>. Vol. 14, 2002, 521–525.

  **3.** Jung, Norman. "Understanding the Irish." <u>Ireland</u> 4, June 2003, 18–20.

  **4.** Franken, Leslie, and Michael Lorie. <u>Legends and Legacies of Modern Ireland</u>. New York: Sampson Publishing Company, 1998.

  **5.** Reece, Susanna, ed. <u>War and Peace in Ireland: Essays on the History of Northern Ireland</u>. Chicago: Greenwood Publications, 1998.

## Modified Activity 63—Publishing the Final Report

**1.** The name should come above the date. **2.** *Hibearnation* is spelled incorrectly. It should be *hibernation.* **3.** The title, *Ancient Rome,* should be on the top line. **4.** *Page 1* should be deleted.

# Workbook Activities

## Workbook Activity 1—How a Sentence Begins and Ends

**1.** In the spring we planted a garden. We planted green peppers and squash first. Later we planted tomatoes. **2.** My grandmother sent me a CD for my birthday. I wrote a letter to thank her. She was pleased. **3.** My friends and I started a singing group. We practice five times a month. I think we need more practice. **4.** Today it rained. The streets were flooded. We could not get our car out of the garage. **5.** There was an announcement in the newspaper about an upcoming concert. Tickets go on sale next week. I would love to go to that concert. **6.** Yesterday my sister went to the bank. She wanted to deposit her paycheck. She also wanted to get some quarters for the machines at the laundry. **7.** I saw an announcement on the bulletin board. The coach is having tryouts for the soccer team. Should my friend and I go? **8.** Every year the garden club has a sale. The club members offer many different kinds of plants. They tell customers all about the plants. **9.** What two things must a writer do? First a writer must think of an idea to write about. He or she also must decide how to write about the idea. **10.** My new digital camera takes amazing pictures. I love photography. I would like to take a class to learn more about it.

## Workbook Activity 2—What Is the Purpose of a Sentence?

**1.** statement—(.) **2.** question—(?) **3.** question—(?) **4.** statement—(.) **5.** statement—(.) **6.** statement—(.) **7.** statement—(.) **8.** command—(.) **9.** question—(?) **10.** statement—(.) **11.** statement—(.) **12.** statement—(.) **13.** question—(?) **14.** command—(.) **15.** question—(?) **16.** question—(?) **17.** statement—(.) **18.** command—(.) **19.** question—(?) **20.** command—(.)

## Workbook Activity 3—Look for the Subject and Predicate

**1.** <u>Dad</u> <u>plans to lose weight</u>. **2.** Many <u>people</u> <u>diet in January</u>. **3.** <u>(You)</u> <u>Drink at least eight glasses of water a day</u>. **4.** <u>Fruits</u> and <u>vegetables</u> <u>give us many vitamins and minerals</u>. **5.** <u>Fats</u> and <u>oils</u> <u>should be eaten moderately</u>. **6.** <u>Whole grains</u> <u>provide fiber</u>. **7.** Most <u>dieters</u> <u>do not stick to a strict diet</u>. **8.** <u>They</u> <u>get too hungry</u>. **9.** <u>(You)</u> <u>Eat plenty of good, nutritious food</u>. **10.** An exercise <u>program</u> <u>also takes off pounds</u>. **11–20.** Underlined words are given. **11.** kept—B **12.** messed—B **13.** tracked—B **14.** looks—A **15.** lasts—A **16.** will make—C **17.** will exercise—C **18.** runs—A **19.** ran—B **20.** will run—C

## Workbook Activity 4—Sentence Fragments

**1.** fragment, predicate **2.** fragment, subject **3.** fragment, subject **4.** fragment, predicate **5.** fragment, subject **6.** sentence **7.** fragment, predicate **8.** fragment, subject **9.** sentence **10.** fragment, predicate **11–15.** Sentences will vary. Possible sentences are shown. **11.** The highest diving board looms against the sky. **12.** A very small boy stood at the edge of the board. **13.** His mother looked up at the boy with concern. **14.** Everyone watched to see what would happen. **15.** The confident boy jumped into the water.

## Workbook Activity 5—Run-On Sentences

**1.** The baseball game begins at 7:30 p.m. **2.** Pick me up at 6:30. **3.** I don't want to be late. **4.** The Wolves are playing the Cougars. **5.** The Wolves have won six games. **6.** The Cougars have won four. **7.** The batter hit the ball hard. **8.** The left fielder ran back. **9.** The ball went over the fence. **10.** It was a home run. **11.** The crowd cheered wildly. **12.** People love to see home runs. **13.** The batter jogged around the bases. **14.** He waved to the crowd. **15.** His teammates met him at home plate.

## Workbook Activity 6—Subject and Verb Agreement

**1.** singular, throws **2.** plural, are **3.** singular, makes **4.** singular, has **5.** plural, love **6.** plural, dance **7.** singular, gets **8.** singular, knows **9.** singular, comes **10.** plural, go **11.** enjoy **12.** knows **13.** bakes **14.** likes **15.** jumps **16.** call **17.** stay **18.** clap **19.** plans **20.** wants

## Workbook Activity 7—Irregular Verbs and Verb Tenses

**1.** took, past **2.** won, past **3.** did, past **4.** have eaten, present perfect **5.** go, present **6.** had seen, past perfect **7.** will drive, future **8.** will have begun, future perfect **9.** have seen, present perfect **10.** has taught, present perfect **11.** have, present **12.** had taken **13.** will have taught **14.** has gone **15.** have known

## Workbook Activity 8—Verbs and Verb Phrases

**1.** <u>will</u> arrive **2.** <u>has</u> visited **3.** <u>is</u> watching **4.** stopped **5.** <u>had</u> bought **6.** <u>should have</u> noticed **7.** <u>will</u> start **8.** <u>has</u> asked **9.** ran **10.** <u>can</u> be **11–15.** Sentences may vary. Possible sentences are shown. **11.** I tiptoed up the front steps, but the squeaky door gave me away. **12.** My parents always worry when I am late. **13.** correct **14.** That way they will know that I am all right. **15.** correct

## Workbook Activity 9—Conjunctions Help Combine Ideas

**1.** Derek was bored, tired, and hungry. **2.** He shoved his books into his locker, slammed the door, and ran to the exit. **3.** Amber likes shopping, dancing, and cooking. **4.** June has a deep laugh, but Grace has a high, shrill laugh. **5.** Hou sings very well, and he could win the talent contest. **6.** Will you have toast <u>or</u> pancakes with your eggs? **7.** I love breakfast, <u>but</u> I usually rush through it. **8.** I always have people to see, places to go, <u>and</u> things to do. **9.** We should relax <u>and</u> look around us, <u>but</u> we never have time. **10.** We should <u>either</u> do less <u>or</u> sleep more. **11.** <u>Not only</u> kids <u>but also</u> their parents are stressed out. **12.** Some of us are taking yoga, <u>and</u> that relaxes us. **13.** Grandpa <u>and</u> Grandma walk <u>or</u> dance for exercise. **14.** He tried to teach me the foxtrot, <u>but</u> I was too clumsy. **15.** Take time to relax, <u>or</u> you will not be happy.

## Workbook Activity 10—Other Kinds of Conjunctions

**1.** I go to the flower show <u>whenever</u> it comes to town. **2.** <u>While you are at camp</u>, you will learn outdoor skills. **3.** <u>Because he loves the great outdoors</u>, Brian enjoys camp. **4.** <u>When it snows</u>, we can build a snowman. **5.** Venus attended design school <u>so that she could make her own clothes</u>. **6.** You will find it <u>if you look harder</u>. **7.** <u>Until we find the key</u>, we aren't going anywhere. **8.** <u>Since he started dance class</u>, Al has lost ten pounds. **9.** I will set the table <u>while you finish making dinner</u>. **10.** <u>Although she loves lasagna</u>, Mom doesn't make it herself. **11–15.** Sentences may vary. Possible sentences are shown. **11.** After the storm was over, we went outside. **12.** When dinner is ready, we can eat. **13.** Cathy got new sneakers because her old ones had worn out. **14.** If you do my chores for a week, I will tutor you in math. **15.** Although I love dogs, I am allergic to them.

## Workbook Activity 11—Using the Right Pronoun

**1.** They **2.** her **3.** his **4.** it **5.** She **6.** he **7.** him **8.** it **9.** them **10.** they **11.** She, subject **12.** them, object **13.** they, subject **14.** He, subject **15.** him and me, object

## Workbook Activity 12—Plurals and Possessives

**1.** singular, video's **2.** singular, wife's **3.** plural, people's **4.** plural, men's **5.** singular, toothbrush's **6.** plural, suitcases' **7.** singular, fox's **8.** plural, coaches' **9.** plural, feet's **10.** plural, radios' **11.** the wolf's howl **12.** the calves' pen **13.** Amber's dog Lucky **14.** the children's room **15.** the Smiths' vacation **16.** a book's cover **17.** the cities' parks **18.** the people's choice **19.** the family's car **20.** two cats' food

## Workbook Activity 13—Using Adjectives and Adverbs for Better Sentences

**1–5.** Sentences will vary. Sample sentences are given. **1.** I like vanilla ice cream with hot fudge sauce on it. **2.** Derek drives cautiously in bad weather. **3.** The new girl asked Derek to go to the early movie. **4.** The untrained sprinter was winded after a short run. **5.** The history exam lasted two hours and was extremely difficult. **6.** The children's library has numerous books that are useful for research. **7.** Our favorite dinner at Al's Beef is the grilled fish. **8.** The flowers for were lovely and fresh. **9.** On a hot day, we often go to the local beach. **10.** The evening ended abruptly after he accidentally spilled his drink. **11.** A terrified cat meowed pitifully from the treetop. **12.** A yellow cab sped by and splashed me thoroughly with dirty water. **13.** Unexpected gifts are always welcome. **14.** Isaac was happily surprised by the late announcement. **15.** A mature horse is generally relaxed on the trail.

## Workbook Activity 14—Using Adjectives and Adverbs to Compare

**1.** better **2.** more filling **3.** least **4.** worse **5.** tallest **6.** slower **7–10.** Sentences will vary. Sample sentences are given. **7.** The third option is the wisest choice. **8.** Raw fruits and vegetables are better for you than cooked ones. **9.** Of all the appetizers, I liked the chipotle shrimp most. **10.** Lee got out his wallet more quickly than Jeff did.

## Workbook Activity 15—Identifying Prepositional Phrases

**1.** under the table, adverb **2.** with us, adverb **3.** in the mail, adverb **4.** with fresh fruit, adjective **5.** at 10 a.m., adverb **6.** to the library, adverb **7.** from my dad, adjective **8.** behind the radiator, adverb **9.** on the Civil War, adjective **10.** between the cities, adjective **11.** against the war, adjective **12.** during the move, adverb **13.** for the party, adjective **14.** with chocolate icing, adjective **15.** around thirty people, adverb

## Workbook Activity 16—Understanding Writing Prompts and Paragraph Prompts

**1.** purpose: to compare life in two different times; audience: teacher; topic: life in 1800 and today; key words: essay, compare, 1800, today **2.** purpose: to describe a writing style; audience: teacher and classmates; topic: works of Edgar Allan Poe; key words: paragraph, describe, stories, Poe

Sentences in Part B should be ordered **3.** 2 **4.** 5 **5.** 3 **6.** 1 **7.** 4

## Workbook Activity 17—Identifying Good Topic Sentences

**1.** A **2.** B **3.** B **4.** A **5.** B **6.** B **7.** B **8.** A **9.** A **10.** A

## Workbook Activity 18—Staying on the Topic

**1.** A **2.** D **3.** E **4.** B **5.** C **6.** F **7.** Juan had homework to do. **8.** Mexico is not involved in space exploration. **9.** Reading is an enjoyable hobby. **10.** Everyone will enjoy the cake.

## Workbook Activity 19—Choosing Strong Summaries and Conclusions

**1.** B **2.** B **3.** A **4.** A **5.** B.

## Workbook Activity 20—Writing Strong Topic Sentences

**1–8.** Answers will vary. Sample answers are given. **1.** If you want to make it to the major leagues of baseball, start working now! **2.** Novels that explore character are better than a seat at the theater. **3.** I spent last weekend time traveling in the attic. **4.** Fresh spices and herbs set gourmet food apart from ho-hum food. **5.** To get your dream job, stop dreaming and start building your skills. **6.** When you swim, that boring list of rules might just save your life. **7.** A sunset is like a trip to an art gallery, a symphony, and a spa all rolled into one. **8.** What do you and a mosquito have in common?

## Workbook Activity 21—Creating Interesting Sentences

**1–10.** Answers will vary. Sample answers are given. **1.** In the summer, we seldom watch TV. **2.** Usually, we are too busy with outdoor activities. **3.** In this area, the weather is always sunny and warm. **4.** Lately, we have not had much rain in our town. **5.** Suddenly, I heard thunder rumbling in the background. **6.** Immediately, everyone was sure that we would have rain. **7.** Slowly, we opened the door and looked outside. **8.** After a few minutes, the thunder stopped. **9.** At that moment, the sky was clear as far as we could see. **10.** Someday soon we will get rain.

## Workbook Activity 22—Adding Transitional Words and Phrases

**1–5.** Answers will vary. Sample answers are given. **1.** Derek walked onto the tennis court. At last he was ready to serve. First he tossed the ball into the air. Then he hit it hard. This time he really wanted to win the match. **2.** For a while, Amber watched the waves coming in. Then she looked around anxiously for her parents. Finally she saw them and held their hands. The ocean just looked too rough today. **3.** Computers do many things to help us. For example, they keep banking records. Furthermore, they solve difficult math problems. In addition, they even control traffic lights in big cities. **4.** Brandon studied the pitcher carefully. Soon it would be his turn to bat. A solid hit would bring in the winning run. At last he stepped up to the plate. His eyes followed the ball until it met his bat. As a result, he had helped win the game. **5.** Eliza wanted to make cookies for the bake sale. First, she turned on the oven and gathered ingredients. Next, she mixed the ingredients in a large bowl with a wooden spoon. Then, she spooned the cookie dough onto a baking sheet, and popped it into the oven to bake.

## Workbook Activity 23—Improving Paragraph Drafts

**1.** My little brother, on the other hand, is a slob. **2–15.** Added sentences will vary. Sample sentences are given. **2.** My bed is always smoothly pulled up and arranged with throw pillows. **3.** My books, papers, and supplies are arranged on shelves and in drawers. **4.** She enjoys singing. **5.** When a friend is sick, Carrie is there with soup or a get well note. **6.** If you have a problem to work out, she listens quietly while you talk. **7.** It is not pleasant to have enemies. **8.** Make an effort to remember the names and likes of people you have met. **9.** Talk in a friendly and relaxed way, and show interest in others. **10.** You should not look at the sun directly. **11.** Many stars arranged in constellations may be seen on a clear night. **12.** Planets such as Venus are easily visible, too. **13.** A thesaurus lists synonyms and antonyms for many words. **14.** The dictionary also provides parts of speech and different forms of words. **15.** Most interesting of all, it gives a shorthand history of the word.

## Workbook Activity 24—Correcting Mistakes in Writing

**1.** Some citizens treat our city too carelessly. **2.** Many people, for example, still drop litter in the streets. **3.** Others pollute the air by burning trash. **4.** Some citizens even leave broken appliances in vacant lots. **5.** Others let their dogs roam and do not clean up after them. **6.** A few irresponsible people even damage buildings. **7.** For example, they draw and write on them. **8.** They may even break windows. **9.** A clean city gives us something to be proud of. **10.** How beautiful our city would be if people only took care of it!

## Workbook Activity 25—Writing a How-To Paragraph

Answers will vary. Sample answers are given. **1.** The paragraph tells you how to buy your first automobile. **2.** The first step in shopping for an automobile is to find out your budget—both cash and loan money. **3.** Underline these words: *first step, Now, When, All of these steps.* **4.** Students should list three of the following: get your finances in order, look at cars in your price range, list what is important to you in a car, test drive a favorite and have a mechanic check it out. **5.** The last sentence is a summary. It repeats *decision* and points back to "all of these steps."

## Workbook Activity 26—Explaining What Something Means

Answers will vary in wording. Sample answers are given. **1.** The paragraph defines a *convertible.* **2.** The dictionary defines convertible as "a car with a top that can be removed or lowered." **3.** A convertible makes us feel adventurous and glamorous. It has an image of being sporty and fast. It lets you enjoy a beautiful day. **4.** The convertible's appeal is related to how we imagine ourselves in it. **5.** The paragraph ends with a summary.

## Workbook Activity 27—Understanding How Two Things Are Alike and Different

**1.** cow **2.** writer **3.** automobile **4.** riverbed **5.** neck **6–10.** Sentences will vary but should include the four related words from the analogies in 1–5. Sample answers are given. **6.** Both a colt and a calf, which are the babies of a horse and a cow, can walk within minutes of birth. **7.** A writer can't do without a pen any more than a carpenter can work without a saw. **8.** Unlike the driver of a car, the pilot of an airplane moves along an invisible route. **9.** Like the blood that flows in your veins, the water that flows through a riverbed keeps the land alive. **10.** The hand and the head are marvelous tools, but they require the help of the wrist and the neck to function.

## Workbook Activity 28—Understanding When One Event Causes Another

**1.** reasonable **2.** not reasonable **3.** reasonable **4.** reasonable **5.** reasonable **6–10.** Answers will vary. Sample answers are given. **6.** People are recycling more items. They are buying items that have less packaging. **7.** More people are wearing seat belts. Fewer people are drinking and driving. **8.** The high price of gas has made people drive less. People are more worried about the safety of traveling. **9.** The price of computers has become reasonable. People feel that a computer is important to their lives. **10.** Traffic was getting snarled because so many people were waiting to turn into the mall. Several accidents happened at this entrance.

## Workbook Activity 29—Identifying Problems and Solutions

Answers will vary in wording. Sample answers are given. **1.** The writer wants to make the varsity basketball team and get playing time. **2.** The solution is to improve skills and show the coach that the writer is good enough. **3.** The writer will practice free throws and dribbling daily, play pickup games on weekends, and play on a park district team. **4.** The paragraph ends with a conclusion. **5.** "By working hard, I am sure to improve enough to make the starting squad."

## Workbook Activity 30—Learning About Opinions

Wording of answers will vary. Sample answers are given. **1.** Fast food is fattening and bad for your health. **2.** It has a lot of fat and sugar in it. **3.** Americans eat too much of it. **4.** Being fat can cause diseases. **5.** I disagree with the writer because fast food restaurants also sell healthy things such as salad, fruit, and juice. **6.** Rainforests are needed and should not be cut down. **7.** Erosion will ruin the soil. **8.** Animals lose their homes. **9.** We lose an important source of oxygen. **10.** I agree with the writer because we have already seen areas turn into deserts and the atmosphere become too warm.

## Workbook Activity 31—Is That a Fact?

**1.** opinion **2.** fact **3.** opinion **4.** opinion **5.** fact **6.** opinion **7.** opinion **8.** fact **9.** opinion **10.** fact **11–15.** Answers may vary in wording. Reasonable answers are given. **11.** It will probably be cold on the field. **12.** Sometimes parents do not understand their teens. **13.** In my opinion, plasma TVs are the best TVs. **14.** Music may soothe the soul. **15.** Lack of sleep makes many people grouchy.

## Workbook Activity 32—Persuading with Facts and Opinions

Sentences and paragraphs will vary. Sample answers are given. **1.** If the government tries to ban transfat, they have gone too far. **2.** People have the right to choose the foods they will eat. **3.** Choosing unhealthy foods from time to time should not be against the law. **4.** Laws are meant to protect us from harm by others, not poor choices. **5.** The government wouldn't tell you what kind of clothes to wear, so it should not tell you what kinds of foods you have to eat.

By trying to ban transfat, the government has stuck its nose too far into our personal lives. Does anyone doubt that they have the right to choose the foods they will eat? Of course not! It isn't against the law to drink alcohol, so not all unhealthy things get banned. Our laws should protect us from real harm, not the bad judgment of eating a doughnut. If we let the government tell us what foods we can eat, will we next let them tell us what kind of clothes to wear?

## Workbook Activity 33—Ads That Convince

Answers and ads will vary. Sample answers are given. **1.** The purpose of my ad will be to convince students to pick up litter and stop throwing trash on the grounds. **2.** Trash makes us look trashy. A clean image will help build school pride. The class with the cleanest section of the school grounds will win a pizza party. **3.** I could use before and after pictures, showing how crummy a place looks with trash all around and how good it looks when it is cleaned up. **4.** "Show your class. Pitch in!" **5.** I want students to remember that keeping the school clean shows they have class. Advertisements will vary, but should make the student's point in an appealing way.

## Workbook Activity 34—Writing with Sense Appeal

Answers will vary. Sample answers are given. **1.** In the distance we could hear a band playing. **2.** The snake's scales felt cool and smooth. **3.** The milk shake tasted creamy and sweet. **4.** The lizard with the blue head zipped up the wall. **5.** A loaf of bread baking smelled yeasty and spicy. **6.** bumble bees buzzing around buds **7.** swimming in swift waters swept by wind **8.** a lush, luxurious limousine **9.** the maddening mystery of magic **10.** a jar of jelly gleaming like a jewel

## Workbook Activity 35—Being Exact in Descriptions

**1–5.** Answers will vary. Sample answers are given. **1.** The radio blared out the startling news. **2.** A weather-beaten cowboy galloped into town. **3.** In the hallway, students gossiped between classes. **4.** Exhausted soldiers returned to the camp. **5.** We saw newborn squirrels sleeping in a nest. **6.** career, scientist, biologist **7.** container, bag, backpack **8.** wildlife, deer, buck **9.** musician, singer, soprano **10.** place, building, post office

## Workbook Activity 36—Describing by Comparing

**1.** B **2.** D **3.** A **4.** C **5.** B **6–10.** Answers will vary. Sample answers are given. **6.** That Ferris wheel is so big that you could touch the moon if you ride it. **7.** To the king, the princess is a crown jewel. **8.** The sun and moon battled for the sky. **9.** Victor spends money like it was water. **10.** The music was so loud it took all the curl out of my hair.

## Workbook Activity 37—Writing Choices for Style

Paragraphs will vary. A sample paragraph is given.

Joe and Mandy thought that Miss Iris, who lived in the <u>old house</u> on the hill, was a witch. Her long white hair streamed loose around her head (like seaweed.) She waved her cane at them and muttered something they could not hear. Then she <u>went</u> into the crooked little house. Fearful but curious, they watched and wondered if there were ghosts inside, too. Answers will vary. Sample answers based on the sample paragraph are given. **1.** witch, streamed, muttered **2.** mysterious dark cottage, disappeared **3.** four long; one short **4.** (Words are circled in paragraph.) **5.** The paragraph is about a mysterious old woman whom kids watch.

## Workbook Activity 38—Story Time

Stories will vary but must include one or more characters, a clear time and place, and a series of events in chronological order.

## Workbook Activity 39—What Happened Next?

Words to be underlined: in 1829, In 1876, Over the next ten years, When, in 1886, in 1909 Story event summaries will vary in wording. Sample wording is given. **1.** Geronimo was born in 1829 in the Southwest. **2.** In 1876, the Apaches were forced onto a reservation. **3.** Geronimo and others ran away many times and were hard to find. **4.** He finally surrendered in 1886. **5.** Geronimo died in Oklahoma in 1909.

## Workbook Activity 40—Who Is the Storyteller?

I was very hungry. I went to my locker to get my lunch, but it was not there. I wondered what had happened to it. I thought about my morning. Then I remembered that I had left my lunch on the counter at home. I borrowed some money from my friend Drew to buy lunch.

## Workbook Activity 41—When Did It Happen?

Adam had a job interview at Ben's Bookstore. He introduced himself to the store manager, Ms. Lorenzo. They talked about his work experience. Adam told about his job at the library. Ms. Lorenzo thanked Adam. She said that she would call him soon. As he left, Adam felt good about the interview. The next day, he received a call. Ms. Lorenzo asked him to start work that weekend. Adam was happy to have the job.

## Workbook Activity 42—Creating Dialogue

"Did you see that?" asked Derek.

"I sure did," said Sonia, "and I could not believe my eyes."

Derek continued, "Why would anyone wear his glasses hanging from just one ear?"

"Maybe he started to take them off," said Sonia, "and forgot halfway."

"Or maybe," laughed Derek, "that is how he keeps from losing his glasses."

## Workbook Activity 43—Knowing When to Use Quotation Marks

Some answers may vary slightly in wording. Sample answers are given. **1.** Mr. Womack asked, "Did anyone lose a pair of gloves?" **2.** Sam replied, "The gloves are Megan's." **3.** My sister said, "You can borrow my sweater." **4.** Mom asked, "Did you clean the bathroom?" **5.** I said, "No, but I will do it after school." **6.** Mrs. Davis reminded us, "Your unit test will be Friday." **7.** Van asked, "Do you want to study with me on Wednesday?" **8.** Bree said, "I forgot to buy pencils and paper." **9.** I said, "You can borrow paper from me today." **10.** Lynn said, "Bree is forgetful."

## Workbook Activity 44—Writing a Short Answer to a Test Question

Answers will vary. Make sure student answers are written as complete sentences. Possible answers are given. **1.** Benjamin Franklin invented the Franklin stove and bifocal lenses. **2.** Yellowstone National Park lies mainly within Wyoming but spreads into Idaho and Montana as well. **3.** Edgar Allan Poe was an American writer best known for his macabre stories and poems. **4.** The first permanent English colonial settlement in America was at Jamestown, Virginia. **5.** The planet closest to the sun is Mercury. **6.** The capital of the United States is Washington, D.C. **7.** Christopher Columbus was an explorer for Spain. **8.** The Pulitzer Prize is an award for excellence in various forms of writing published in the United States. **9.** George Washington was the first president of the United States. **10.** The Japanese bombed Pearl Harbor on December 7, 1941.

## Workbook Activity 45—Planning an Essay Answer

Answers and student essays will vary.

## Workbook Activity 46—Writing a Report

Reports will vary. Student reports should include title, author, setting, characters, plot, and opinion of the book, movie, or TV show.

## Workbook Activity 47—Create a Personal Letter

Personal letters will vary. Make sure the letter includes all five parts of a personal letter: date, salutation, body, closing, and signature.

## Workbook Activity 48—Take a Message

**1.** time, date, information needed by person who will receive the message **2.** time, date **3.** time, date, name of the person who wrote the message **4.** time, date, name of the person who wrote the message **5.** time, date, information needed by the person who will receive the message

## Workbook Activity 49—Understanding Electronic Mail (E-Mail) Messages

**1.** Derek Anderson **2.** Brandon Tucker **3.** BrandonTucker@Springfield.edu **4.** Springfield.edu **5.** Call after track practice.

## Workbook Activity 50—Parts of a Business Letter

**1.** no **2.** yes **3.** yes **4.** no **5.** yes **6.** no **7.** yes **8.** no **9.** yes **10.** no **11–18.** Students should circle date, salutation (greeting), body, closing, and signature among their answers. **11.** heading or return address **12.** date **13.** inside address **14.** salutation (greeting) **15.** body **16.** closing **17.** handwritten signature **18.** typed name and title **19–20.** Answers will vary. Possible answers are given. Business letters are typed rather than written by hand. Business letters include heading, inside address, and typed name and title.

## Workbook Activity 51—Addresses on Envelopes

**1.**  Tony Pierce
    17 Dartmouth Ct.
    Trenton, NJ 08601

**2.**  Janet Lahney
    92 Westland Drive, Apt. 13
    College Park, MD 20740

**3.**  Valerie Armstrong
    Crystal Enterprises
    67 Tulip Drive
    Lansdowne, PA 19050

**4.**  Managing Editor
    Fashion Trends
    4210 Sartoga Ave.
    San Jose, CA 95129

**5.** Clayton Young
517 Louisville Lane
Cumberland, MD 21502

## Workbook Activity 52—Using Memo Form

```
                    MEMO
Date:        (Today's date)
To:          Mrs. Smith
From:        Mrs. K. Hall
Subject:     John Hall

Please excuse John today at 1:00 P.M. He has
a doctor's appointment this afternoon at
1:30.
```

```
                    MEMO
Date:        (Today's date)
To:          Mr. White
From:        Amber Choy
Subject:  Springfield High Sports Day
The student body would like to see more
school spirit and involvement. We would
like to plan a special Springfield High Sports
Day. Would you please help us in any way
that you can?
```

## Workbook Activity 53—Expressing Opinion in a Report

**1.** This is one of the most important and well-written documents in American history. **2.** Chameleons are among the best-known and most interesting lizards. **3.** Victoria Falls is an amazing sight. Yet, the biggest and most wonderful natural attraction of all is Africa's wildlife. (Students may also list the first sentence: Africa is a land of natural wonders that attract tourists.) **4.** All are a great way to meet friends with the same interests. **5.** It is hard to believe that anyone would be willing to endure such severe conditions. (Students may also list this sentence: It is a cold and unwelcoming world.)

## Workbook Activity 54—Topic Selection

**1.** A narrow; B broad **2.** A narrow; B broad **3.** A broad; B narrow **4.** A narrow; B broad **5.** A broad; B narrow **6.** A broad; B narrow **7.** A narrow; B broad **8.** A broad; B narrow **9.** A narrow; B broad **10.** A broad; B narrow

## Workbook Activity 55—Using Reference Materials

**1.** atlas **2.** biographical dictionary, encyclopedia **3.** almanac **4.** atlas **5.** encyclopedia **6.** Howard Jones **7.** Michael Jordan's insights into basketball strategy **8.** *Basketball Today* **9.** 13 **10.** one page

## Workbook Activity 56—Searching the Internet

**1.** how to play chess **2.** American Civil War **3.** tomatoes **4.** Gwendolyn Brooks's poems **5.** Mumbai **6.** world's tallest building **7.** César Chávez **8.** 2007 New York Yankees **9.** *Cats,* the play **10.** Mikhail Baryshnikov **11.** search engine **12.** educational institutions **13.** Web address **14.** browser **15.** keyword

## Workbook Activity 57—Notes

Notes and paraphrase will vary. Make sure the student has included all important information from the paragraph.

## Workbook Activity 58—Correcting an Outline

**United Nations**
**I.** Introduction
    **A.** Location
    **B.** Buildings
**II.** General Assembly
    **A.** Composed of
    **B.** Sessions
    **C.** Budget and apportion expenses
**III.** Security Council
    **A.** Number of members
    **B.** Purpose
**IV.** Economic and Social Council
    **A.** Number of members
    **B.** Purpose
**V.** Trusteeship Council
**VI.** Secretariat
**VII.** International Court of Justice
    **A.** Function
    **B.** Election
        **1.** Term
        **2.** Method
**VIII.** Summary and Conclusion

## Workbook Activity 59—Organizing Topics to Write a Report

**A Typical Home Office**
**I.** Office furniture
    **A.** Desk
    **B.** Work table
    **C.** Chair
    **D.** Bookshelves
**II.** Types of equipment
    **A.** Telephone
    **B.** Computer
        **1.** Modem
        **2.** Printer
**III.** Supplies
    **A.** Paper
    **B.** Pens and pencils
    **C.** Stapler
    **D.** Tape

## Workbook Activity 60—Adding Transitions

Answers will vary. Examples are given **1.** Just twelve years later, in 1969, man walked on the moon. **2.** However, riding on top of a rocket was dangerous. **3.** Finally, splashdown was when the capsule landed in the ocean. **4.** Unfortunately, shuttles have also given us tragedy. **5.** However, this is not something that could happen tomorrow.

## Workbook Activity 61—Subject-Verb Agreement

**1.** one astronaut fit **2.** correct **3.** has not traveled into space **4.** correct **5.** astronauts can live **6.** Neil Armstrong walked **7.** Many astronauts hope **8.** correct **9.** They cheer loudly **10.** returned to space

## Workbook Activity 62—Creating a Bibliography

**1.** Garner, Jim. <u>Using a Video Camera</u>. Chicago: Crown Books, 2001. **2.** Knott, George. <u>You Can Be a Sports Announcer</u>. New York: The New Publishers, Inc., 2003. **3.** Oringel, Bob. <u>Editing for Fun and Profit</u>. Bowie, Md.: Bowie Community Television, 2002. **4.** Romero, Christine. "You Can Edit." <u>Editor's Journal</u>, Vol. 4, April 2003, 6–8. **5.** "Video Editing." <u>Television Encyclopedia</u>. Vol. 11, 2004, 300–305.

## Workbook Activity 63—Preparing to Publish

**1.** The title should come above the name and be in bold. The author's name should not be hold. **2.** *Werld* is spelled incorrectly. It should be *World*. **3.** Delete the unnecessary line, *Prepare yourself to be amazed!* **4.** *Page 1* should be deleted. **5.** The title, **Alaska,** should be on the top line.

# Key Vocabulary Words

### Key Vocabulary Words 1

**1.** sentence **2.** subject **3.** predicate **4.** noun **5.** pronoun **6.** verb **7.** verb phrase **8.** phrase **9.** tense **10.** declarative sentence **11.** interrogative sentence **12.** imperative sentence **13.** exclamatory sentence **14.** simple sentence **15.** sentence fragment **16.** run-on sentence **17.** comma fault **18.** compound sentence **19.** conjunction

### Key Vocabulary Words 2

**1.** action verbs **2.** state-of-being verbs **3.** subordinating conjunctions **4.** indefinite pronouns **5.** past participles **6.** simple tense **7.** perfect tense **8.** perfect tense **9.** simple tense **10.** simple tense **11.** An independent clause expresses a complete thought and is the same as a sentence. A dependent clause does not express a complete thought. **12.** A word is singular if it refers to one person, place, thing, or idea. A word is plural if it refers to more than one person, place, thing, or idea. **13.** A regular verb forms the past tense and past participle forms by adding *-ed* or *-d* to the present tense. An irregular verb has past tense and past participle forms that do not do this.

### Key Vocabulary Words 3

**1.** B **2.** F **3.** C **4.** G **5.** A **6.** E **7.** H **8.** D **9.** thesaurus **10.** synonym **11.** personal pronoun **12.** preposition **13.** positive form **14.** superlative form **15.** possessive noun **16.** prepositional phrase

### Key Vocabulary Words 4

**1.** C **2.** C **3.** A **4.** B **5.** B **6.** A **7.** B **8.** D **9.** C **10.** D

### Key Vocabulary Words 5

**1.** revise **2.** point of view **3.** edit **4.** rewrite **5.** variety **6.** transition **7.** revise **8.** edit **9.** edit **10.** revise

### Key Vocabulary Words 6

**1.** topic sentence **2.** cause-and-effect **3.** body **4.** solution **5.** transition **6.** contrast **7.** summary **8.** compare **9.** revise **10.** conclusion

### Key Vocabulary Words 7

**1.** D **2.** F **3.** I **4.** E **5.** J **6.** G **7.** B **8.** H **9.** A **10.** C **11.** fact **12.** persuade **13.** advertisement **14.** opinion **15.** slogan

### Key Vocabulary Words 8

**1.** style **2.** figure of speech **3.** Alliteration **4.** sensory images **5.** connotation **6.** exaggeration **7.** personification **8.** metaphor **9.** simile **10.** C **11.** B **12.** D **13.** E **14.** A

### Key Vocabulary Words 9

**1.** nonfiction **2.** fiction **3.** short story **4.** novel **5.** plot **6.** character **7.** setting **8.** chronological order **9.** point of view **10.** anecdote **11.** quotation **12.** indirect quotation **13.** dialogue **14.** quotation marks **15.** direct quotations

### Key Vocabulary Words 10

**1.** fiction **2.** nonfiction **3.** essay **4.** dialogue **5.** conflict **6.** plot **7.** character **8.** setting **9.** resolution **10.** anecdote

### Key Vocabulary Words 11

**1.** resolution **2.** conflict **3.** Internet service provider **4.** screen name **5.** postscript **6.** e-mail **7.** personal letter **8.** essay **9.** message **10.** character

### Key Vocabulary Words 12

**1.** modified block style **2.** business letter **3.** memorandum **4.** block style **5.** memorandum

Key Vocabulary Words 13
**1.** search engine **2.** report **3.** index **4.** plagiarize **5.** call number
**6.** periodical **7.** table of contents **8.** browser **9.** keyword **10.** research
**11.** subtopic **12.** outline **13.** paraphrase **14.** catalog **15.** bibliography

Key Vocabulary Words 14
**1.** mechanics **2.** publish **3.** draft **4.** report **5.** paraphrase **6.** plagiarize
**7.** research **8.** second draft **9.** final draft **10.** first draft

# English in Your Life

### English in Your Life 1—Writing a Letter of Thanks
**1.** I got my algebra test back today. I got a B on it! **2.** Thank you for making me study and practice. **3.** First, he ran two sentences together without putting a period at the end of one sentence and a capital at the beginning of the next sentence. Then he wrote a phrase that belonged with the previous sentence as though it were a sentence on its own.

### English in Your Life 2—Explaining How to Do Something
**1.** A. dinner, B. salad, C. right, D. soup, E. tip/top **2.** knife, teaspoon, soup spoon **3.** Answers will vary. A sample answer is given. The words I added gave the directions more detail, which makes them clearer. Providing specifics about the items and their placement makes the directions easier to follow.

### English in Your Life 3—Writing to Solve a Problem
Answers will vary. Reasonable answers are given. **1.** At last, Now, Then **2.** Is there anyone with carpentry experience who could help me this Saturday at 9? Please call me at 890-3318 if you can help at that time. **3.** They show time order and connect short, choppy sentences into a smooth, longer sentence. They make the ideas easier to follow.

### English in Your Life 4—Writing a Cover Letter
Answers will vary. Reasonable answers are given. **1.** He will already know what libraries are like and what jobs to expect to do. **2.** Transportation to and from work can be a problem for many young people. **3.** I think Ms. Coover will like Jim's love of books because it shows he will enjoy the work. Satisfied workers are usually motivated.

### English in Your Life 5—Telling a Story
**1.** Abby believes that Gail made fun of her and purposely didn't help her. **2.** Abby spread a rumor about Gail and Sam. Answers will vary. A sample answer is given. **3.** Gail should apologize for laughing at Abby and explain why she did not help her. Abby should apologize for her lie and tell others the truth.

### English in Your Life 6—Writing an Invitation
**1.** Lunch is in the faculty dining room on April 18, at noon. **2.** Club members will serve German food and perform German music and dances. **3.** The club needs to know how many people will attend so they know how much food to make.

### English in Your Life 7—Writing a Résumé
Answers will vary depending on students' individual experiences. At a minimum, a student should list name and contact information, school, and a reference.

# Writing on the Job

### Writing on the Job 1—Sports Writer
**1.** saves; playing; will be **2.** Goalie Lynn Roman saved the day by stopping six shots on goal by the Stingers. The Stingers played (OR were playing) without their star forward Camie Sinjay, who sprained her ankle in the opening minutes. This break was (OR would be) just enough for the Jets, who won the contest 3–2. **3.** Answers will vary but should include a logical reason for the correction.

### Writing on the Job 2—Office Assistant
**1.** B **2.** A **3.** The purpose of paragraph 1 is to thank the client and to inform them that future offers will be sent.

### Writing on the Job 3—Hospital Kitchen Helper
**1–3.** Answers will vary. Sample answers are given. **1.** Owen is explaining a problem with the hospital kitchen dishwasher and his solution to that problem. **2.** The problem with the dishwasher is that it isn't heating the water enough to kill bacteria. To solve the problem, Owen has called a repairman to fix the machine. **3.** Proper sanitation is needed to protect people from infection. If the dishwasher doesn't kill bacteria, hospital patients could become even sicker!

### Writing on the Job 4—Pet Store Worker
**1.** Students may list *frisky, curious,* or *social.* **2.** Students may list *burrow, gnaw, shred,* or *scoop.* **3.** Answers will vary. A sample answer is given. People always want to pick up gerbils and play with them. Ellen wants to make sure the gerbils are safely handled.

### Writing on the Job 5—Children's Librarian
**1.** Joe Montana; the author probably likes football and picked a football hero to write about. **2.** Joe Montana was a quarterback. As a quarterback he would be one of the players that would help the team win the four Super Bowl games. **3.** Using *hero* and *legend* would make someone want to read about a great football player. The questions would be used to get you interested in the book.

### Writing on the Job 6—Customer Service Representative
Answers will vary. Reasonable answers are given. **1.** The letter's purpose is to make sure that a customer is satisfied with her product. **2.** awesomely **3.** In the process of the letter, James also reminded Ms. Harris that Office Central could fill her other needs, such as printer cartridges and furniture. James is hoping that Ms. Harris being a happy customer will make her a return customer.

### Writing on the Job 7—Bicycle Salesperson
**1.** The Mercurion mentions aerodynamic design because it is a racing bicycle. Cyclists interested in this bike would be interested in speed, which is affected by aerodynamic design. **2.** yes, she mentions the warranty for both bikes. She might do this because she feels it is an important feature on any bike and is worthy of mention. **3.** Answers will vary. However, make students expound on basic ideas. For example, if they say they want a bike for city cycling, check that they are quite specific, i.e., they want reliable breaks or a basket for errands.

# Building Research Skills

## Building Research Skills 1—Using an Encyclopedia
**1.** Volumes 3 and 6 **2.** It would be in the first half of Volume 3. **3.** She could look up her key words in the Index. It would list the volumes and page numbers where these key words are discussed.

## Building Research Skills 2—Narrowing a Topic
**1.** teaching dogs to heel **2.** traits of the border collie **3.** Answers will vary. A sample answer is shown. Dear Roger, This topic is too broad. You could write a long book about it. You will not have room to talk about all the details you should.

## Building Research Skills 3—Using a Dictionary
**1.** 4, the second **2.** the second meaning **3.** The plural form can be either *aquariums* or *aquaria.*

## Building Research Skills 4—Blending Ideas in Your Writing
**1.** The following notes are circled: a crystal form of carbon; usually clear; cut surfaces are facets; hardest material in nature; shine with great brilliance when faceted; form deep in the earth; very great pressure and high temperatures **2–3.** Answers will vary. Sample answers are given. **2.** This paragraph discusses the formation and some physical attributes of diamonds. **3.** The circled notes all contain information on how a diamond is formed and processed. Some physical attributes are also discussed. The focus is on the physical and scientific aspects of diamonds, instead of their cosmetic value.

## Building Research Skills 5—Using a Library's Online Catalog
**1.** subject **2.** biography; Carl Sandburg: A Pictorial Biography by Joseph Haas **3.** Answers will vary. A sample answer is given. The biography has pictures Anne might copy to illustrate her report. It will have a lot of detailed information about Sandburg's life. If she wants to write a short report, an encyclopedia might be better.

## Building Research Skills 6—Using Your Own Words
**1.** Underlined words and phrases should include: *All spiders, spin, strong, fiber, silk, webs, walls, burrows, egg sacs, wrap, prey* **2.** "line the walls of their burrows" **3.** A drawing could help remind the note-taker of the specific place that produces spider's silk—the abdomen.

## Building Research Skills 7—Using Periodicals
**1.** Hawaiian worms and mangrove forests **2.** 71 **3.** As it is located in the Science and Medicine section, I think that "Mending Broken Hearts" is about the treatment of heart disease. It could be about new surgical options or advances in heart medicine. Either way, the article's location and title strongly suggest that the fight against heart disease is the topic.

## Building Research Skills 8—Using Graphs and Tables
**1.** 17 million more cats **2.** 39% **3.** Answers will vary. A sample answer is given. There are more pet owners with two or more cats than with two or more dogs. This might be because dogs require more space for exercise and have to be taken outside by owners several times a day.

## Building Research Skills 9—Reading a Newspaper
**1.** Sections B and C contain sports news and information about leisure time and travel (Community Digest, Entertainment, and Travel). **2.** Section A contains local, state, national, and world news, a list of police reports, and writers' opinions about news. **3.** The editorial page is at the end of section A, after news stories. It contains columns and letters to the editor about issues in the news. Reporting facts is the paper's most important job. Opinions need to be separated and clearly marked.

## Building Research Skills 10—Judging Information Sources
**1.** encyclopedia **2.** glossary **3.** magazine **4.** newspaper **5.** dictionary **6.** online

## Building Research Skills 11—Using a Phone Book
**1.** HWY stands for Highway. **2.** No, the businesses have different area codes. **3.** Answers will vary. A sample answer is given. You could look up the address in the phone book. Then, using the address, you could find the street on a map.

## Building Research Skills 12—Developing Inquiry Skills
**1.** Carl found his topic by thinking about the broader subject proposed by his teacher. He thought of something interesting that would fit the length of the report. **2.** Carl used the library and the NASA Web site. **3.** Answers will vary. A sample answer is given. The topic is global warming. Questions: When did scientists first begin to notice global warming? Are we sure global warming is real and not just odd weather patterns? What does global warming mean for weather in the future? Sources: the library and a reputable meteorological Web site.

## Building Research Skills 13—Checking a Table of Contents
**1.** 14 **2.** viii **3.** Reading Strategy, lesson reviews, Grammar Builder, Vocabulary Builder, Write About It, English in Your Life, Writing on the Job, Building Research Skills, Chapter Summary, Chapter Review **4.** Writing to Describe **5.** 4 lessons **6.** 1, 3, 5, 7, 9, 11, 13 **7.** 2, 4, 6, 8, 10, 12, 14 **8.** No **9.** 168 **10.** "Writing a Book Report or Movie Review" **11.** Chapters 9 and 13 **12.** Chapter 3 **13.** 4 **14.** Handbook on Editing, Speaking Checklist, Listening Checklist, and Viewing Checklist **15.** before

## Building Research Skills 14—Formatting a Document
**1.** Answers will vary. However, if the student is using Microsoft Word, they would access Tools, then the Spelling and Grammar subtopic. **2.** Answers will vary. However, if the student is using Microsoft Word, they could access Table, then the Insert subtopic, followed by the specific parameters for the table columns. **3.** Answers will vary. An incorrect use of punctuation might not be caught, i.e., a period used instead of a question mark. Additionally, a misspelling that happens to be another word, *an* instead of *and*, would not be picked up by the computer. This proves the importance of a human proofread in order to catch all possible mistakes.

## Life Skills Connection

Completed activities will vary for each student. Life Skills Connection activities are real-life activities that students complete outside the classroom. These activities give students the opportunity to practice the concepts taught in Pacemaker® *Basic English Composition*. Check completed activities to see that students followed directions, completed each step, filled in all charts and blanks, provided reasonable answers to questions, wrote legibly, and used appropriate terms and proper grammar.

## Writing Tips

The Writing Tip sheets are meant to be quick references for students as they write assignments, essays, and reports. The sheets can be used while students practice English composition and when they write for other classes. The sheets can help students to proof and check their work. Have copies of the sheets available to students whenever needed.

## Self-Study Guides

Self-Study Guides outline suggested sections from the text and workbook. These assignment guides provide flexibility for individualized instruction or independent study.

## Preparing for Writing Tests

### Test 1—Writing Prompts

**1.** Purpose: to persuade     Format: letter
**2.** Purpose: to describe     Format: paragraphs
**3.** Purpose: to inform     Format: list
**4.** Purpose: to entertain     Format: paragraphs
**5.** Purpose: to persuade     Format: letter

### Test 2—Organizing Your Writing
Information in organizers will vary.

### Test 3—Proofreading for Errors

**1.** Jason and Rico were trying to **decide** what to **do** on a Saturday afternoon. **2.** Earth is the **third** planet from the **sun**. **3.** Do you **know** where they have hung **their** poster? **4.** Abraham Lincoln **delivered** the **Gettysburg** Address at the dedication of the cemetery in Gettysburg, Pennsylvania. **5.** Anita and Terry **live** in the **same** apartment building.

### Test 4—Writing Test Practice
Essays and answers will vary.

## Mastery Tests

See page 474 for the Scoring Rubric for Short-Response Items in Part E and Essay Items in Part F of the Mastery Tests. The rubric can be used for the items in Part E and Part F of the Chapter Mastery Tests, Midterm Mastery Test, and Final Mastery Test.

### Chapter 1 Mastery Test A
**Part A**
**1.** A **2.** A **3.** B **4.** C **5.** A
**Part B**
**6.** command—(.) **7.** question—(?) **8.** statement—(.) **9.** strong emotion—(!) **10.** command—(.) **11.** statement—(.) **12.** question—(?) **13.** statement—(.) **14.** command—(.) **15.** question—(?)
**Part C**
**16.** complete sentence **17.** complete sentence **18.** run-on **19.** fragment **20.** complete sentence **21.** fragment **22.** fragment **23.** run-on **24.** fragment **25.** complete sentence
**Part D**
Answers will vary. Possible answers are shown. **26.** The weather was dry. The lawn needed to be watered often. **27.** Juan bought a computer, and then he found better software. **28.** What time does the basketball game start? I want to go. **29.** Almanacs are books of facts. Do you need to know the capital of Botswana? You can find the answer in an almanac. **30.** Canada is a huge country. It stretches 3,326 miles from east to west. The United States is on its southern border.
**Part E**
**31.** A writer shows a reader when a complete idea ends with a period, a question mark, or an exclamation mark. **32.** Run-on sentences push two or more ideas together, making it hard to understand where one idea ends and another begins.
**Part F**
**33.** The writer has joined two sentences as though they were one. To fix the mistake, she should add a period after *sunny*. This signals the end of the first idea. Then she should capitalize the t in *tomorrow*. This shows a new idea is beginning. **34.** A verb is the main word in the predicate. The predicate is all the words in a sentence that tell about the subject. It may tell what the subject did: *went to the store, danced the hula*. Or it may tell what the subject is: *was unhappy, are on the hall table*. The verb is the word within this word group that tells the action or state of being: *went, danced, was, are*.

### Chapter 1 Mastery Test B
**Part A**
**1.** question mark **2.** sentence fragment **3.** conjunction **4.** tense **5.** run-on
**Part B**
**6.** C **7.** B **8.** A **9.** D **10.** C **11.** A **12.** B **13.** A **14.** C **15.** B
**Part C**
**16.** fragment **17.** fragment **18.** fragment **19.** sentence **20.** fragment **21.** sentence **22.** sentence **23.** fragment **24.** run-on **25.** run-on
**Part D**
Sentences will vary. Possible answers are shown. **26.** The storm came suddenly. The branches twisted in the wind. **27.** When are you coming over? I'll turn on the porch light. **28.** Once my brother and I found twenty dollars. It was lying on the sidewalk. **29.** Dictionaries give many kinds of information about a word. Did you know they contain word histories? **30.** China has the world's largest population. Over 3 billion people live there. Imagine how big the cities are!

## Part E

**31.** A group of words is a sentence if it expresses a complete idea and contains both a subject and a predicate. **32.** A command that is spoken with great excitement or emotion could also be an exclamation.

## Part F

**33.** The writer ran together two sentences as though they were one. The mistake can be fixed by separating them into two sentences. This means putting a period after *desserts* and capitalizing the *C* in *chocolate*. It can also be fixed by making a compound sentence. To do this, you would add a comma and the word *and* after *desserts*. **34.** In a compound sentence, the job of a conjunction is to join two ideas and show the relationship between them. For example, you could join two sentences with a comma and *and* if they are very similar. *And* adds them together. Two other sentences might give opposite ideas. They could be joined by the conjunction *but*.

## Chapter 2 Mastery Test A

### Part A

**1.** lasts **2.** take **3.** dream **4.** falls **5.** watch **6.** feels **7.** goes **8.** are **9.** get **10.** rings, disappears

### Part B

**11.** A **12.** C **13.** B **14.** D **15.** B

### Part C

**16.** (has) gone **17.** (will) return **18.** (will have) bought **19.** (should) wash **20.** (can) slice **21.** (did) put **22.** (must be) finished **23.** (might) cut **24.** (has) peeled **25.** (will) be

### Part D

Some answers may vary. Sample answers are shown. **26.** Today there was lightning and thunder. **27.** Mom likes dancing, but Dad refuses to dance at all. **28.** You may write either a poem or a short story. **29.** While she was waiting for the bus, Amber read her book. **30.** Moises moved his coat so that Chantal could have a seat.

### Part E

Answers will vary. Possible answers are shown. **31.** An irregular verb does not form the past or past participle forms by adding *-ed* or *-d*. **32.** When an action verb (go) is combined with a helping verb or verbs (will), it becomes a verb phrase (will go).

### Part F

Answers will vary. Possible answers are shown. **33.** Perfect tenses show the order of events in the past, present, and future. Sometimes you need to explain what happened before something else happened in the past. For example, *The store had closed ten minutes before we got there.* The past perfect tense tells what happened before the second past event. **34.** The clauses are related, but only the second one can stand alone as a sentence. *Until you apologize* is not a complete thought. It makes me wonder, "Until you apologize, what will happen?" When you join it with *I will be upset about your comment*, you understand the whole idea.

## Chapter 2 Mastery Test B

### Part A

**1.** singular, lasts **2.** plural, take **3.** plural, dream **4.** singular, falls **5.** plural, watch **6.** singular, is **7.** singular, goes **8.** plural, are **9.** plural, get **10.** singular, rings; singular, disappears

### Part B

**11.** painted **12.** saw **13.** taken **14.** eaten **15.** swung **16.** sleep **17.** done **18.** taught **19.** drove **20.** seen

### Part C

**21.** A **22.** B **23.** D **24.** A **25.** C

## Part D

Some sentences may vary. Possible answers are shown. **26.** correct **27.** Cantaloupe, honeydew, and casaba are melons. **28.** My legs are sunburned, so I keep them covered. **29.** correct **30.** Moises moved his coat so that Chantal could sit down.

## Part E

Answers will vary. Possible answers are shown. **31.** A verb phrase contains a main verb and one or more helping verbs before it. **32.** The words *and*, *but*, and *or* are used to join related words, phrases, or sentences.

## Part F

Answers will vary. Possible answers are shown. **33.** The sentences are too short, and they repeat many of the same words. They sound choppy and elementary. By using one subject and joining the three verbs, you can make a good sentence: *The cat hissed, scratched me, and hid under the couch.* **34.** The past and past participle forms of a verb show past action. Most verbs form the past tense by adding *-ed* or *-d* to the present tense form. The past participle form is the same but always occurs with a form of *has*. Some verbs are irregular. They have other spellings or even other words used for the past and past participle forms.

## Chapter 3 Mastery Test A

### Part A

**1.** comparative **2.** antecedent **3.** possessive **4.** adverb, adverb **5.** apostrophe **6.** adjective **7.** preposition **8.** superlative **9.** synonym **10.** gender

### Part B

**11.** brightest **12.** younger **13.** most gifted **14.** more amazing **15.** friendlier (or more friendly)

### Part C

**16.** B **17.** C **18.** D **19.** B **20.** B

### Part D

**21.** prepositional phrase **22.** adjective **23.** adverb **24.** adverb **25.** adjective **26.** prepositional phrase **27.** adjective **28.** adjective **29.** prepositional phrase **30.** adverb

### Part E

Answers will vary. Possible answers are shown. **31.** *Badder* is not a word; the comparative form of *bad* is *worse*. **32.** The pronoun it is singular and has no gender.

### Part F

Answers will vary. Possible answers are shown. **33.** Possessive nouns are created by adding an apostrophe and *-s* to singular nouns or an apostrophe alone to regular plural nouns. The noun names a person, place, or thing, such as *Mary*, *home*, and *book*. The possessive form shows that the person, place, or thing owns something: *Mary's coat, a home's style, and a book's cover.* **34.** Adverbs, adjectives, and prepositional phrases make writing specific and interesting. They describe nouns and verbs to help writers show exactly what they mean. For example, *The boy ran* gives only a general impression of someone doing something. *The thin boy in ragged clothes ran away with the new shoes* is much more specific and interesting.

## Chapter 3 Mastery Test B

### Part A

**1.** D **2.** A **3.** A **4.** A **5.** B

### Part B

**6.** Amber sometimes calls Derek after doing her homework. **7.** Derek asked Amber what she thought about watching a DVD on Friday. **8.** Amber said, "Eliza and Brandon want to join us." **9.** Amber asked Derek to call their friends about Friday. **10.** The little dog ran after a rabbit and lost its way.

**Part C**

Answers will vary. Sample answers are given. **11.** to Washington
**12.** delicious **13.** very **14.** yesterday **15.** wonderful **16.** with blue stones
**17.** reckless **18.** Fifteen **19.** Last month **20.** loudly

**Part D**

**21.** brightest **22.** younger **23.** most gifted **24.** greater **25.** friendlier
**26.** shorter **27.** funnier **28.** most beautiful **29.** less **30.** less

**Part E**

Answers will vary. Sample answers are given. **31.** When you compare two things, you add *-er* to a one-syllable adjective. You do not add *more* at the same time. **32.** The pronoun *she* is feminine and singular.

**Part F**

Answers will vary. Possible answers are shown. **33.** Adverbs tell when, where, how, how often, and to what degree an action occurred. For example, the adverbs *yesterday*, *there*, *rarely*, and *quickly* could tell more about the verb *went*. Adverbs can tell more about an adjective or another adverb, too. For example, *extremely* could tell how quickly or how small. **34.** Pronouns replace nouns and let us avoid repeating the same words over and over. *Ben shined Ben's shoes and brushed Ben's hair carefully. Ben was going on a date.* These sentences sound silly because they repeat the noun Ben. Pronouns that refer to *Ben* can make these sentences better: *Ben shined his shoes and brushed his hair carefully. He was going on a date.*

## Chapter 4 Mastery Test A

**Part A**

**1.** C **2.** G **3.** D **4.** J **5.** F **6.** E **7.** A **8.** B **9.** G **10.** I

**Part B**

**11–20.** Bathing a dog is easy if you follow the steps in my method. First, gather shampoo, a sponge, a bucket or shower head, and a brush. Next, wet the dog all over with warm water. Apply shampoo and rub it in, using your fingers to scrub. Wash the dog's face with a sponge dipped in water. Rinse the dog with water, using a bucket or shower head. Rub the dog dry with towels. Let the dog shake off the excess water. Comb the dog when its coat is dry. At the end, you are left with a clean, happy dog!

**Part C**

**21.** C **22.** A **23.** D **24.** B **25.** A

**Part D**

**26.** 1 **27.** 1 or 5 **28.** 2 **29.** 5 **30.** 1

**Part E**

**31.** A paragraph needs a topic sentence to explain the main idea. **32.** A summary sentence or a conclusion ties the details together and brings the paragraph to a close.

**Part F**

**33–34.** Answers will vary. Sample answers are given. **33.** The paragraph is about the unusual winter in Alaska. The details describe how people work, study, and live in darkness. The concluding sentence is about a new topic—Alaska's summer. Instead, the paragraph should end with a sentence about Alaska's weird winter. **34.** A paragraph is a group of sentences that tell about one main idea. Most of the time, it begins with a topic sentence that states the main idea. Then the writer gives details to support or expand on that main idea. These details should all be relevant and in a logical order. Finally, the writer concludes the paragraph by restating the main idea in different words or by drawing a logical conclusion from the details.

## Chapter 4 Mastery Test B

**Part A**

**1.** B **2.** B **3.** C **4.** B **5.** B

**Part B**

**6.** 3 **7.** 7 **8.** 6 **9.** 2 **10.** 10 **11.** 4 **12.** 8 **13.** 5 **14.** 9 **15.** 1

**Part C**

Answers for 19 may vary. Sample answers for this item are given.
**16.** sentence 1 **17.** sentences 1 and 6 **18.** sentence 6 **19.** The English language has been greatly influenced by other languages. **20.** sentence 1

**Part D**

**21–22.** (The snake dance of the Hopi people of Arizona is special.) Hopi dancers carry live rattlesnakes in their mouths as they dance. They know how to handle the snakes, so they are rarely bitten. Watching a snake dance is a thrilling experience. **23–24.** (To take proper care of a horse, you need to buy all the right equipment.) First, you need tools to groom the horse. Then, you should get a halter and lead rope for catching and leading your horse. Don't forget about hay, grain, and vitamins. Of course, to ride you need tack, including a saddle and saddle blanket. Horse owners have empty wallets and happy horses! **25.** Answers will vary. A sample answer is given. The Basics of Horse Care

**Part E**

**31–32.** Answers will vary. Sample answers are given. **31.** Taking an Alaskan cruise has always been a dream of mine. **32.** In the body of a paragraph, the writer develops the main idea with sentences that support and explain it.

**Part F**

**33–34.** Answers will vary. Sample answers are given. **33.** The paragraph is about the shyness of the writer's dog. The body gives examples of the dog's shy behavior. The final sentence should make some comment summing up this topic. A sentence about the owner's cat is on another topic completely. **34.** A paragraph may end with a summary statement or a conclusion. A summary statement restates the main idea, but it uses different wording than the topic sentence. A conclusion gives a decision or opinion the writer has made based on the details. The conclusion must be logical. Either a summary or a conclusion gives a feeling of completeness to the paragraph.

## Chapter 5 Mastery Test A

**Part A**

**1–10.** Answers will vary. Sample answers are given. **1–2.** The cat had been sleeping on a window sill when it rolled and fell off. **3–4.** Because an awning broke its fall, it landed safely on the ground. **5–6.** Although this story is amazing, there have been more dramatic survivals. **7–8.** A dog lost on a family vacation amazingly found its way home. **9–10.** The family is not sure how it survived the 500-mile, 3-month-long trip.

**Part B**

**11–15.** Answers will vary. Sample answers are given. **11.** My grandfather doesn't say much, but he has a heart of gold. **12.** I once lost 10 pounds in a week, but being sick is a tough way to do it. **13.** If my dream comes true, one day my name will include the title "Dr". **14.** Would you be a fascinating millionaire or a boring one? **15.** Are your collections turning you into a real pack-rat?

**Part C**

**16–20.** Answers may vary. Sample answers are given. **16.** For example, **17.** Then **18.** First, **19.** As a result **20.** However,

**Part D**

**21.** A **22.** G **23.** capitalization **24.** It **25.** D and E **26.** tumble **27.** Answers may vary. A sample answer is given: In addition, **28.** Hot, capital letter **29.** their, there **30.** Answers will vary. A sample answer is given. A trip to Yellowstone National Park is a colorful and exciting experience.

**31–32.** Answers will vary. Sample answers are given. **31.** To make a topic sentence interesting, ask a question or express a clear point of view. **32.** Transitional words and phrases connect sentences smoothly and help you follow the ideas.

**Part F**

**33–34.** Answers will vary. Sample answers are given. **33.** The topic sentence is boring, obvious, and full of unnecessary words. I would rewrite it to say, "To me, video games are a great way to relax and gain skill." This sentence tells specifically why I like video games. Readers can picture and understand the benefits of playing the games. **34.** To edit a paragraph, a writer fixes any mistakes in the writing. He or she checks for misspelled words, missing or wrong punctuation, and errors in capitalization. The writer also fixes any mistakes in grammar or usage. Editing makes a paragraph easy to understand because it gets rid of distracting errors.

## Chapter 5 Mastery Test B

**Part A**

**1–10.** Answers will vary. Sample answers are given. **1.** Nervously, **2.** In one sweaty palm, **3.** At last **4.** For a minute **5.** Quickly **6.** Still **7.** The truth is **8.** Eventually **9.** Just in time **10.** Immediately

**Part B**

**11.** B **12.** A **13.** B **14.** B **15.** B

**Part C**

**16.** for example **17.** then **18.** first **19.** as a result **20.** however

**Part D**

**21–30.** Answers will vary. Sample answers are given. **21–22.** Yellowstone National Park is famous for its stunning geological features. **23–24.** Geysers shoot steam and hot water high into the air. **25–26.** Hot springs with bright colored minerals simmer and steam. **27–28.** Mudpots bubble and boil while steam vents hiss. **29.** Waterfalls tumble down cliffs and mountain slopes. **30.** Yellowstone's unusual geology truly sets it apart.

**Part E**

**31–32.** Answers will vary. Sample answers are given. **31.** A question grabs readers' attention by making them curious. **32.** Transitions connect the ideas in sentences smoothly and logically.

**Part F**

**33–34.** Answers will vary. Sample answers are given. **33.** The topic sentence contains unnecessary words. You do not need to tell readers what you are going to do. Just do it. I would write, "Few men led a more colorful and exciting life than Wild Bill Hickok." This introduces the topic. It also makes readers wonder what Hickok did that was so exciting. **34.** A writer makes changes in a draft to improve it. This is called revising. One way to revise is to take out details that are off the topic. Another is to add more details to develop the main idea. Revision may also involve putting ideas in different order and changing wording to make it more specific and vivid.

## Chapter 6 Mastery Test A

**Part A**

**1.** compare **2.** inform **3.** show how to do something **4.** explain a solution to a problem **5.** show how to do something **6.** contrast **7.** show cause and effect **8.** show cause and effect **9.** inform **10.** explain a solution to a problem

**Part B**

**11.** Unlike **12.** because **13.** while **14.** Similarly **15.** Next **16.** First **17.** Finally **18.** despite **19.** instead **20.** In addition

**Part C**

Sentences will vary. Sample sentences are given. **21.** Both football and soccer involve kicking a ball and moving it to a goal to score. **22.** A horse is large and covered with hair, while a lizard is small and covered with scales. **23.** Both pizza and spaghetti have a tangy, Italian tomato sauce on them. **24.** Ants and honeybees are both insects with six legs. **25.** Laptop computers are lighter and easier to transport than desktop computers.

**Part D**

**26.** B **27.** D **28.** A **29.** A **30.** A

**Part E**

Answers will vary. Sample answers are given. **31.** The best joke tellers have a style all their own. **32.** One of the main reasons for war is the desire for power.

**Part F**

Paragraphs will vary. Sample paragraphs are given. **33.** A thesaurus is your ticket to better writing. It provides lists of synonyms to help you avoid boring repetition of key words. It also provides antonyms to help you set up interesting contrasts. Finally, a thesaurus lists related words that can help you expand your topic. With a thesaurus, you will never be at a loss for words. **34.** The little blonde girl in my old yearbook isn't much like me at sixteen. For one thing, of course, I am much taller. My hair is darker now, and I wear it short instead of in a ponytail. Most important, I am much more confident than that shy girl. Inside, I still feel I am the same dreamer I always was.

## Chapter 6 Mastery Test B

**Part A**

**1.** B **2.** D **3.** A **4.** A **5.** C **6.** D **7.** D **8.** A **9.** C **10.** C

**Part B**

**11.** C **12.** A **13.** B **14.** E **15.** D

**Part C**

Sentences will vary. Sample sentences are given. **16.** Both fishing and hunting are outdoor activities that can feed a family. **17.** Unlike a dog, a cat gives itself a bath. **18.** Hamburgers usually do not have preservatives in them, but hot dogs rely on these chemicals to keep them from going bad. **19.** Vegetable gardens are usually planted in straight rows, but flower gardens are often planted in clusters. **20.** Songs and poems both involve rhythmic words and phrases.

**Part D**

**21.** D **22.** A **23.** F **24.** B **25.** G **26.** E **27.** C **28.** I **29.** J **30.** H

**Part E**

Sentences will vary. Sample sentences are given. **31.** Traveling by train and by bus is no longer as common as it once was. **32.** Even if it is good-natured, teasing is often embarrassing to the person being teased.

**Part F**

Paragraphs will vary. Sample paragraphs are given. **33.** On an essay test, you often need to write an informative paragraph to answer a question. Your topic sentence will be a rewording of the question as a statement, plus addition of a main idea. Use the question to decide how to develop your supporting details. For example, a *why* question calls for reasons or an explanation. A *what* question usually calls for facts. Don't forget to end your paragraph with a summary or a conclusion. **34.** Our school baseball uniforms are nicer than our track uniforms. The baseball uniforms are new and sharp looking, while the track uniforms are old and ratty looking. The track team is dressed in faded black, while the baseball team is dressed in crisp white with black pinstripes. Baseball uniforms are much more expensive than track uniforms. With new uniforms, our school track team would win with pride.

Chapter 7 Mastery Test A

**Part A**

**1.** D **2.** A **3.** C **4.** D **5.** A

**Part B**

**6.** fact **7.** opinion **8.** fact **9.** opinion **10.** fact **11.** opinion **12.** opinion **13.** opinion **14.** fact **15.** opinion

**Part C**

Check marks beside **16.**, **17.**, **19.**, **21.**, **22.**, **23.**

**Part D**

Answers will vary. Sample answers are given. **26.** The Lifeline 2000 . . . give your social life a healthy heartbeat. **27.** A new you in just three weeks with the Step 'n Glide. **28.** young people **29.** people who want to get in shape **30.** Ads will vary. A sample ad is given. Ready to trade those extra pounds for extra muscles and an extra-ordinary heart? Try the new Step 'n Glide—and glide your way to health! Studies show that 80% of Step 'n Glide owners lose weight. So, step aside, extra pounds! Glide away, puny muscles! And say hello to a new you—in just 3 weeks—with the Step 'n Glide.

**Part E**

Answers will vary. Sample answers are given. **31.** An opinion is not a true statement because it cannot be proven true or false. **32.** To persuade readers that your opinion is right, you need to give reasons.

**Part F**

Paragraphs will vary. Sample paragraphs are given. **33.** Opinions are easy to identify. An opinion expresses someone's personal feeling. Opinions often contain a word such as *best, favorite, always, good, worst,* or *unimportant*. If a statement cannot be proven true or false, it is an opinion rather than a fact. Statements of opinion may be qualified, showing they are not always true, as in *Many teenagers drive fast*. **34.** A slogan is a short, catchy phrase or sentence that sticks in your mind. Advertisers often think up slogans to sell their products because people will remember them. For example, advertisers might use the slogan "A Lotion as Wet as the Ocean" as an instant way to make people think of Sea Mist Lotion. A slogan makes you think of something the advertiser wants you to remember about the product, such as how much moisture the lotion contains.

Chapter 7 Mastery Test B

**Part A**

**1.** advertisement **2.** slogan **3.** opinion **4.** fact **5.** qualify **6.** persuade **7.** reasons **8.** advertiser **9.** always **10.** benefits

**Part B**

**11.** fact **12.** opinion **13.** fact **14.** opinion **15.** opinion

**Part C**

**16.** an opinion **17.** a qualifier **18.** slogan **19.** persuade **20.** 3

**Part D**

Answers will vary. Sample answers are given. **21.** Cell phones are the greatest invention of the century. **22.** Dating is a special form of torture. **23.** Purple is a terrible color to paint a house. **24.** Homework is only useful when it is creative. **25.** Reality TV is totally fascinating to me. **26.** Show your family you love them with hot, delicious Five-Grain Fiesta. **27.** Jacket-of-All-Trades: a multi-function coat for any occasion. **28.** Keep a leaner, greener profile with the Green Machine. **29.** An electric car would save you money on gas. **30.** You would feel good about doing your part to reduce global warming.

**Part E**

Answers will vary. Sample answers are given. **31.** You should use qualifiers like *usually* to show that a statement is not always true, as in *Usually October is a cool month*. **32.** A statement is a fact if you can

show proof that it is true, for example by looking in an encyclopedia or observing something.

**Part F**

Paragraphs will vary. Sample paragraphs are given. **33.** Advertisers have several ways of getting us to buy their products. First, they may tell us how the product will help us. Second, they may tell us how we will be harmed if we do not have the product. Last, they may tell us why their product is better than another one. No matter what, advertisers want to make their product seem desirable to us. **34.** There are many times when you want to convince someone to agree with you. You might want to persuade a parent to let you do something. You might need to convince a boss to give you a raise. Or you might want to get voters to support your candidate. Persuasive writing shows you know how to back up your opinion or suggestion with convincing facts, reasons, and details.

Chapter 8 Mastery Test A

**Part A**

**1.** C **2.** A **3.** B **4.** D **5.** A

**Part B**

**6.** exaggeration **7.** simile **8.** metaphor **9.** personification **10.** alliteration

**Part C**

**11.** hearing **12.** sight **13.** smell **14.** taste **15.** touch **16.** taste **17.** hearing **18.** sight **19.** smell **20.** touch

**Part D**

**21.** supermarket **22.** bake **23.** dances **24.** trout **25.** county **26.** thermometer **27.** howled **28.** nonfiction **29.** mansion **30.** drives

**Part E**

Answers will vary. Sample answers are given. **31.** The words you choose, the variety of your sentences, and your choice of subject help create your writing style. **32.** Specific words provide exact details so the reader can picture your subject better.

**Part F**

Paragraphs will vary. Sample paragraphs are given. **33.** Metaphors and similes are two ways of making comparisons in writing. Both are figures of speech using words in a way that gives them unusual meanings. Metaphors compare two things directly: *He is a teddy bear*. On the other hand, similes compare two things indirectly, using *like* or *as*: *His hand is like a claw*. **34.** Sensory images draw the senses into written work. The five senses bring us details about the world. When writing involves the senses, we use our experience to imagine how things look, sound, smell, taste, and feel. Our mental image of the subject is more vivid and complete.

Chapter 8 Mastery Test B

**Part A**

**1.** connotation **2.** sensory image **3.** alliteration **4.** personification **5.** simile

**Part B**

**6.** C **7.** B **8.** A **9.** D **10.** B

**Part C**

**11.** salesman **12.** lion **13.** hamburger **14.** city council **15.** moth **16.** hammer **17.** whispering **18.** magazines **19.** pickup truck **20.** fly

**Part D**

**21.** alliteration **22.** personification **23.** exaggeration **24.** simile **25.** metaphor **26.** personification **27.** simile **28.** alliteration **29.** exaggeration **30.** metaphor

**Part E**

Answers will vary. Sample answers are given. **31.** Alliteration is used to create interesting patterns of sound by repeating the beginning sounds of words. **32.** Figures of speech add imagination and originality to writing with unusual comparisons.

**Part F**

Paragraphs will vary. Sample paragraphs are given. **33.** I hope to develop a clear, interesting style of writing by using words carefully. First, I will try to use specific words and sensory images to make details clear and easy to picture. Then I will create figures of speech using as exaggeration and metaphors that make readers think and imagine. Last, I will write sentences that are different lengths and kinds to give my writing a smooth rhythm. Before long, I will be writing a best-seller! **34.** A paragraph of description includes supporting details that paint a clear picture. Unlike a paragraph of persuasion, which uses reasons, facts, and examples, a description includes vivid images. A description appeals to the five senses to create striking mental pictures for readers. A persuasive paragraph puts reasons in order of importance, but a description moves logically from feature to feature.

## Chapter 9 Mastery Test A

**Part A**

**1.** dialogue **2.** fiction **3.** setting **4.** novel **5.** quotation marks **6.** plot **7.** direct quotation, quotation **8.** anecdote **9.** nonfiction **10.** point of view

**Part B**

**11.** in chronological order **12.** They wandered and grew weak. **13.** A dog rescues the explorers. **14.** third person **15.** the last sentence

**Part C**

Sentences may use either past tense or present tense but not both in the same sentence. These answers use past tense throughout. **16.** I cleaned out the stalls and polished my tack. **17.** I worked at the stables every weekend. **18.** My horse was an Appaloosa, and it stayed in a corral. **19.** I wanted to win a contest, so I practiced often. **20.** When it was raining, I would ride indoors.

**Part D**

**21.** "Can I take the car to practice?" Pat asked. **22.** Pat asked if she could take the car to practice. **23.** "Yes, you may," Mom said, "but be careful." **24.** Mom said that Pat could but she should be careful. **25.** "It is supposed to rain," she added. **26.** Mom said that it was supposed to rain. **27.** "Thanks," said Pat. "I should be home by 7." **28.** Pat thanked her mom and said that she should be home by 7. **29.** "Goodbye," called Mom. "Have fun." **30.** Pat's mom told her goodbye and to have fun.

**Part E**

Answers will vary. Sample answers are given. **31.** A writer makes the order of events in a story clear by using chronological order. **32.** Direct quotations give someone's exact words. Indirect quotations report what someone said without using exact words.

**Part F**

Paragraphs will vary. Sample paragraphs are given. **33.** In first-person point of view, a character tells the story and uses *I, me, my, myself*. For example, if I wrote about my life, I would write, "I was born in Georgia." In third-person point of view, the storyteller is not a character in the story. Instead, he or she describes what each character says and does: *He offered her a ride. She refused.* Because readers get "inside the story" with a first-person narrator, these stories can feel more exciting and immediate. **34.** Though a story is only one paragraph long, it still has three parts and three elements. The three parts are beginning, middle, and end; the three elements are plot, character, and setting. The story begins with a sentence that introduces the characters, setting, and situation. Its detail sentences report plot events and character reactions in order. Its concluding sentence tells the outcome and resolves the plot.

## Chapter 9 Mastery Test B

**Part A**

**1.** dialogue **2.** fiction **3.** setting **4.** novel **5.** quotation marks **6.** plot **7.** direct quotation **8.** anecdote **9.** nonfiction **10.** point of view

**Part B**

**11.** in chronological order **12.** Ben fell into the water. **13.** The boys hold onto the boat until they are rescued. **14.** third person **15.** Sentence 4 uses present tense (dives, drags) instead of past tense (dove, dragged).

**Part C**

**16.** verb tense **17.** quotation marks **18.** other punctuation **19.** point of view **20.** point of view **21.** quotation marks **22.** other punctuation **23.** verb tense **24.** point of view **25.** quotation marks

**Part D**

**26–30.** Answers may vary. Sample answers are given. **26.** Pat asked, "May I take the car to practice?" **27.** Mom said, "Yes, you can, but be careful." **28.** "I heard that it is going to rain," she added. **29.** "I should be home by 7," Pat said. **30.** "Goodbye, Pat," called Mom. "Have fun."

**Part E**

**31.** In a story, use quotation marks around the exact words spoken by each character. **32.** Stories are mostly written in chronological order to make it easy to follow the events.

**Part F**

Answers will vary. Sample answers are given. **33.** In my autobiography I would use first-person point of view. Since I am the storyteller, I have to use the pronouns *I, me, my, myself,* and *mine*. I describe things the way I saw them or the way they happened to me. If someone else told my life story, he or she would use third-person and the book would be a biography. **34.** The setting of a story lets readers know where and when the story is taking place. This is important information because it affects the characters and the events. For example, if the setting is on a distant tropical island in 1870, the characters are less likely to be rescued than they would in 1970. Their survival will depend on what food, water, and shelter they can find. The mood of the story will be affected by the wild beauty and danger that surround them.

## Chapter 10 Mastery Test A

**Part A**

Sentences will vary. Possible sentences are given. **1.** The Mojave Desert is in California. **2.** Jane Addams was awarded the Noble Peace Prize. **3.** Every four years presidential elections are held in the United States. **4.** A cyclops is a mythological giant with one eye. **5.** The Caspian Sea is the world's largest lake.

**Part B**

Sentences will vary. Sample sentences are given. **6.** This book is about the world's largest volcano. **7.** Popular winter sports include skating, skiing, and sledding. **8.** Mount Elbert is one of the highest mountains in Colorado. **9.** People send cards or gifts for Valentine's Day on February 14th. **10.** Millard Fillmore was thirteenth president of the United States.

**Part C**

**11.** C **12.** B **13.** A **14.** C **15.** B

**Part D**

**16.** C **17.** H **18.** A **19.** G **20.** B **21.** E **22.** I **23.** J **24.** D **25.** F

**Part E**

Answers will vary. Sample answers are given. **26.** Global warming is causing an increase in the Earth's temperature, which is effecting the environment. **27.** Adams School is located at 425 Adams Street in Adams, Ohio.

**Part F**

Answers will vary. **28.** The paragraph may include the facts listed. **29.** The paragraph should include a topic sentence, details about the topic, and a conclusion or summary.

## Chapter 10 Mastery Test B

**Part A**

**1.** D **2.** B **3.** C **4.** D **5.** C

**Part B**

Sentences will vary. Possible sentences are given. **6.** Greenland is the world's largest island. **7.** The Mississippi River ends in the Gulf of Mexico. **8.** The Aztecs founded Mexico City. **9.** The collie is a breed of longhaired dog. **10.** The first library was established about 4,000 years ago.

**Part C**

Sentences will vary. Sample sentences are given. **11.** Skyscraper fans will love this book. **12.** Popular summer activities include swimming and sun tanning. **13.** Denali is one of Alaska's most beautiful peaks. **14.** Dolphins are warm-blooded animals that live in the ocean. **15.** George Washington was the first president of the United States.

**Part D**

**16.** I **17.** B **18.** A **19.** C **20.** F **21.** D **22.** E **23.** G **24.** J **25.** H

**Part E**

Answers will vary. Sample answers are given. **26.** Antarctica is a large continent that is located around the South Pole. **27.** Tennis is my favorite sport.

**Part F**

Answers will vary. **28.** The paragraph may include the facts listed. **29.** The paragraph should include a topic sentence, details about the topic, and a conclusion or summary.

## Chapter 11 Mastery Test A

**Part A**

**1.** Ms. Hughes **2.** JasonMorris@Springfield.edu **3.** HeatherHughes@YoungWriters.com **4.** Contest Rules **5.** HeatherHughes **6.** school **7.** to ask about a poetry contest **8.** Sincerely, **9.** JasonMorris **10.** YoungWriters

**Part B**

**11.** date **12.** signature **13.** body **14.** salutation **15.** comma

**Part C**

**16.** D **17.** B **18.** B **19.** B **20.** A

**Part D**

**21.** postscript **22.** screen name **23.** service **24.** comma **25.** signature **26.** e-mail **27.** date **28.** ISP **29.** body **30.** message

**Part E**

Answers will vary. Sample answers follow. **31.** E-mail is like a personal letter because it has a salutation/closing/body. **32.** A personal letter is different from e-mail because you don't write the date on e-mail. Also, letters are written on paper. E-mails are written on a computer.

**Part F**

Messages will vary. Sample message follows.

**33.**

| To: Mom | |
|---|---|
| **Date:** April 4, 2007 | **Time:** 2:45 p.m., Tuesday |
| **While you were out** | |
| **Mr./Ms.** Mrs. Monroe | |
| **Message:** Mom, Mrs. Monroe called. She was wondering if you want to meet for coffee at Ziggy's Café on Saturday, at 11:00 a.m. Call her back before 7:30 to confirm. Love, Jenny | |

**34.** Letters will vary, but should include the five elements of a personal letter.

## Chapter 11 Mastery Test B

**Part A**

**1.** Mr. James **2.** MiaKane@Springfield.edu **3.** JerryJames@YoungArtists.com **4.** YoungArtists **5.** Art Exhibition **6.** Springfield **7.** to ask about the art exhibition **8.** Sincerely **9.** educational **10.** JerryJames

**Part B**

**11.** time **12.** date **13.** who called **14.** important details **15.** your name

**Part C**

**16.** ISP **17.** E-mail **18.** message **19.** screen name **20.** caller's name

**Part D**

**21.** E **22.** A **23.** H **24.** G **25.** J **26.** D **27.** C **28.** F **29.** B **30.** I

**Part E**

Answers will vary. Sample answers follow. **31.** A personal letter is different from e-mail because you don't write the date on e-mail. Also, letters are written on paper. E-mails are written on a computer. **32.** E-mail is like a personal letter because it has a salutation/closing/body.

**Part F**

**33.** Letters will vary, but should include the five elements of a personal letter.

**34.** E-mails will vary. Sample e-mail is given.

TO: TimJacobs@Springfield.edu

FROM: JennyWebb@Springfield.edu

SUBJECT: Monster Movie Marathon?

Tim,

If you're not busy tonight, meet me at the Walnut Street Cinema at 7:15. They are having a monster movie marathon. Kris and I would love for you to come!

Jenny

## Chapter 12 Mastery Test A

**Part A**

**1.** B. **2.** C. **3.** D. **4.** C. **5.** A. **6.** C. **7.** B. **8.** A.

**Part B**

**9–15.** Answers can be in any order. A sample order is given. **9.** Heading **10.** Date **11.** Inside address **12.** Salutation **13.** Body **14.** Closing **15.** Signature **16.** Typed name and title

**Part C**

**17–20.** Answers can be in any order. A sample order is given. **17.** To **18.** From **19.** Date **20.** Subject

**Part D**

**21.** return **22.** the city or town **23.** mailing **24.** Tx should be TX **25.** The street address should be above the city, state, and ZIP code. **26.** After the street address **27.** The stamp goes in the upper right hand corner of the envelope. **28.** business letter **29.** It is being mailed to a business. **30.** The state should be abbreviated to IL.

**Part E**

**31.** A business letter is sent in the mail, but a memo may be posted or sent electronically. A business letter includes a hand-written signature. A memo does not include addresses. **32.** A personal letter is casual, not formal. The language of a business letter is professional. You do not need a header in a personal letter. You are also not required to include a typed name and title under you signature.

**Part F**

Answers will vary. Sample answers follow. **33.** Since the letter would be going around just inside the company, it would be quickest and easiest to use a memorandum. **34.** The return address is important if the letter's mailing address was written incorrectly or if the person receiving the letter wants to use the return address in order to mail a response.

## Chapter 12 Mastery Test B

**Part A**

**1–4.** Answers can be in any order. A sample order is given. **1.** To **2.** From **3.** Date **4.** Subject

**Part B**

**5.** 5 **6.** 8 **7.** 2 **8.** 4 **9.** 1 **10.** 6 **11.** 7 **12.** 3

**Part C**

**13.** C **14.** A **15.** F **16.** D **17.** H **18.** G **19.** E **20.** B

**Part D**

**21.** upper right hand side **22.** center **23.** ZIP code **24.** street address **25.** state abbreviation **26.** upper left hand side **27.** end **28.** personal **29.** business **30.** abbreviated

**Part E**

Answers will vary. Sample answers are given. **31.** A business letter has a header. A business letter has a typed inside address. A business letter uses professional language in the body. **32.** While they are both intended for a professional setting, memos are shorter than business letters. A memo is not sent through the mail. Memos and business letters can contain the same type of information, or be sent to the same people.

**Part F**

Answers will vary. Sample answers are given.
**33.** Since the letter would be going around just inside the company, it would be quickest and easiest to use a memorandum. **34.** A business letter will set a more professional tone than e-mail. The potential employer would be more likely to see you as a serious candidate for the job. If you introduced yourself through e-mail, you may be viewed as someone with only casual interested in the job.

## Chapter 13 Mastery Test A

**Part A**

**1.** E **2.** D **3.** A **4.** B **5.** C

**Part B**

**6.** encyclopedia **7.** almanac **8.** atlas **9.** almanac **10.** biographical dictionary **11.** encyclopedia **12.** atlas **13.** encyclopedia **14.** biographical dictionary **15.** almanac

**Part C**

**16.** bulb plants, (tulips) **17.** (basketball) team sports **18.** (Abraham Lincoln) Presidents of the United States **19.** stringed instruments, (guitars) **20.** tennis championships, (Wimbledon) **21.** Native American leaders, (Sitting Bull) **22.** (landslides) natural disasters **23.** (the giant panda,) endangered animals **24.** modern art, (Cubism) **25.** children's writers, (Judy Blume)

**Part D**

**26.** B **27.** A **28.** C **29.** D **30.** B

**Part E**

Answers will vary. Sample answers are given. **31.** The history of soccer is a broad topic that cannot be adequately discussed in just two pages. **32.** Writing an outline can help structure a report. Without an outline, a report is more likely to be disorganized and rambling. Working from an outline can help a writer to stay on topic.

**Part F**

Paragraphs will vary. Sample paragraphs are given. **33.** By writing the topic or subtopic at the top of a note card, you can readily see the topic discussed on the card. This will make it easier to organize the cards by topic and subtopic. In turn, this makes preparing the outline easier. Labeling the note cards simplifies the organizing and outlining of the research information. **34.** I would organize a report about the Beatles chronologically. This would allow me to talk about their early struggling years first. Then I can talk about their growing popularity in England and around the world, as I show how their music evolved. This organization would show their growth as musicians and songwriters over time.

## Chapter 13 Mastery Test B

**Part A**

**1.** D **2.** B **3.** A **4.** C **5.** C

**Part B**

**6.** A topic B subtopic **7.** A subtopic B topic **8.** A topic B subtopic **9.** A topic B subtopic **10.** A subtopic B topic

**Part C**

**11.** bibliography **12.** outline **13.** research **14.** introductory paragraph **15.** periodicals **16.** paraphrase **17.** keyword **18.** call numbers **19.** browser **20.** plagiarize

**Part D**

Answers will vary. The order of topics and subtopics will vary, and should be checked for correct grouping. A sample grouping is given. **21.** (I) A **22.** (II) A **23.** (II) B **24.** I **25.** (IIA) 1 **26.** II **27.** (II) C **28.** (I) B **29.** (IIA) 2 **30.** T

**Part E**

**31.** Answers will vary. A sample answer is given. You can avoid plagiarism by taking thorough, well-documented notes. If you fail to document your source on a note card, you may forget that you are directly quoting the source. As a result, you may assume that the note is paraphrased, and use it directly in your report. Good note-taking can prevent this. **32.** Answers will vary. A sample answer is given. The history of cars is a broad topic that cannot be adequately discussed in just two pages.

**Part F**

Paragraphs will vary. Sample paragraphs are given. **33.** I would organize a report about my favorite comic book chronologically. This would allow me to talk about how the plots and characters changed over time. This organization would show the differing story lines and the changes in style and character growth. **34.** If you write your bibliography first, you can keep your notes organized by source. This will help you to correctly and consistently label the sources on your note cards.

Chapter 14 Mastery Test A

**Part A**

**1.** B **2.** E **3.** D **4.** G **5.** I **6.** C **7.** H **8.** A **9.** J **10.** F

**Part B**

**11.** The lower case c is circled.

**12.**   The Water Cycle
        Ray Feller
        May 14, 2007

**13.** *Glasher* is circled.

**14.**   Birth of a Glacier
        Quinn Lake
        June 3, 2007

**15.** The exclamation point is circled.

**16.**   Life in the Arctic
        Mike Moffitt
        March 6, 2007

**Part C**

**16.** correct **18.** correct **19.** is **20.** tells **21.** provides **22.** correct **23.** disguised **24.** falls **25.** correct

**Part D**

**26.** 4 **27.** 1 **28.** 5 **29.** 3 **30.** 2

**Part E**

Answers will vary. Possible answers are given. **31.** Begin sentences with "you." Use a lively topic sentence. **32.** Using quotations from a source adds both sentence variety and a reliable, academic tone to your report.

**Part F**

Answers may vary. Sample answers are given. **33.** Regular exercise keeps a person fit. People who exercise feel better and probably live longer. Exercise helps people to maintain a healthy weight, and it stimulates the heart and lungs. Everyone should try to exercise every day. **34.** When revising, writers add details and remove unnecessary information. They add transitional words and make sure they have used varied sentence types.

Chapter 14 Mastery Test B

**Part A**

**1.** page number **2.** draft **3.** publish **4.** bibliography **5.** title page **6.** outline **7.** introduction **8.** paraphrasing **9.** quotation marks **10.** body

**Part B**

**11.** *may* is circled. **12.** The space between *28* and *2007* is circled (there should be a comma in this space). **13.** *Goverment* is circled. **14–16.** Answers will vary. Sample answers are given.

**14.**   **The Rise of Augustus Caesar**
        Eliot Dupree
        May 13, 2007

**15.**   **The Gladiatorial Games**
        Anton Edwards
        October 28, 2007

**16.**   **Roman Government**
        Natalie Evans
        January 5, 2007

**Part C**

**17.** are **18.** Some **19.** is **20.** tells **21.** Olivia **22.** disguised **23.** falls **24.** Mistaken **25.** creates

**Part D**

**26.** 5 **27.** 4 **28.** 1 **29.** 3 **30.** 2

**Part E**

Answers will vary. Possible answers are given. **31.** You must document your sources to prove that they are reliable and that you did not plagiarize. A bibliography is necessary for documenting sources. **32.** Begin sentences with "you." Use a lively concluding sentence.

**Part F**

Answers may vary. Sample answers are given. **33.** Do you have a particular talent? You can use your talent to help others. Put on a piano recital at a retirement center. Help paint a colorful mural in a hospital's children's wing. Feed the hungry with kind words and warm food at a soup kitchen. By sharing your gifts with others, you will receive gifts in return. **34.** Writing multiple drafts of a report gives the author the chance to create the best work possible. Through reworking a report, the author can weed out any errors and improve the language until they are satisfied.

Chapters 1–7 Midterm Mastery Test

**Part A**

**1.** B **2.** D **3.** E **4.** C **5.** A **6.** J **7.** G **8.** H **9.** F **10.** I

**Part B**

**11.** D **12.** B **13.** C **14.** A **15.** A **16.** C **17.** D **18.** A **19.** D **20.** C

**Part C**

**21.** Sentence 1 **22.** For one thing, Also, Most important **23.** to persuade parents to let the writer decorate his or her own room **24.** to end the paragraph with a logical conclusion **25.** reasons or arguments why the parents should agree **26.** Sentence 2 is a run-on sentence. Add so after the second comma. **27.** *Ours* should be spelled *hours*. **28.** *Taking* should be *would take*. **29.** Family should not be capitalized. **30.** Sentences will vary. A sample sentence is given. It is only fair for you to let me decorate my own room.

**Part D**

**31.** enjoy **32.** made **33.** it **34.** his **35.** their **36.** good? **37.** best **38.** tastier **39.** but **40.** because **41.** Unlike **42.** Then **43.** Many **44.** In my opinion **45.** has

**Part E**

Answers will vary. Sample answers are given. **46.** *Has helped* is a verb phrase because it combines a helping verb (*has*) and an action verb (*helped*). **47.** I would expect this topic sentence to begin a paragraph of comparison, describing several differences between early and current computers.

**Part F**

Paragraphs will vary. Sample paragraphs are given. **48.** The topic sentence, detail sentences, and concluding sentence of a paragraph work together with one purpose. First, the topic sentence expresses a main idea. Then supporting detail sentences provide facts, details, reasons, or examples that back up that main idea. A final sentence either gives a logical conclusion or restates the main idea. Every part of the paragraph has helped readers understand one idea better. **49.** Adjectives, adverbs, and prepositional phrases add detail and exactness to the idea expressed in a sentence. A sentence can be just two words, such as *Alice smiled*. Some adjectives help readers picture Alice: *tired, sweaty*. An adverb lets readers know how she smiled: *triumphantly*. A prepositional phrase could tell readers where this action happened: *from the winner's circle*. *Tired, sweaty Alice smiled triumphantly from the winner's circle* creates a vivid picture, thanks to adjectives, adverbs, and prepositional phrases.

**Part A**

**1.** C **2.** D **3.** E **4.** A **5.** B **6.** G **7.** I **8.** F **9.** J **10.** H **11.** N **12.** O **13.** L **14.** K **15.** M

**Part B**

**16.** D **17.** C **18.** A **19.** A **20.** B **21.** D **22.** B **23.** A **24.** D **25.** C **26.** A **27.** B **28.** A **29.** B **30.** C

**Part C**

**31.** The story is about Luis and Jose, at home in the kitchen. **32.** The point of view is third person. **33.** "It's your turn," Jose insisted. **34.** The boys argue over who will do the dishes. **35.** The story uses direct quotations. **36.** Aunt Cicely sent the letter. **37.** The date has been left out. **38.** Dear Judy, / Love, **39.** The postscript should be added after the signature. **40.** The purpose is to thank Judy and let her know her aunt will attend graduation. **41.** This is a memo (or memorandum). **42.** *Date:* should be added to line 1. **43.** Mario Prinza sent the message. **44.** Workers at Mario's Restaurant will receive the message. **45.** The purpose is to notify workers of the sale of the restaurant.

**Part D**

**46.** wild dogs **47.** call number **48.** almanac **49.** browser **50.** .gov **51.** paraphrasing **52.** outline **53.** 1 paragraph **54.** details **55.** main topics **56.** transitions **57.** alliteration **58.** hearing **59.** check spelling **60.** author(s) **61.** personification **62.** essay **63.** movie review **64.** metaphor **65.** article title

**Part E**

Answers will vary. Sample answers are given. **66.** The answer should be changed to a complete sentence by adding "A tadpole is" to the fragment and placing a period at the end. **67.** "Mysteries" is the most specific category because it names one kind of novel.

**Part F**

Paragraphs will vary. Sample paragraphs are given. **68.** The Roman numerals and capital letters represent part of an outline. An outline helps writers organize notes. The first main idea of the report would go beside the I. The second main idea would go beside the II. Details that support the first main idea would be written beside A and B. After the outline is prepared, the writer can use it to write a draft of a report. **69.** Your skeleton is a complicated system with many jobs. The skeletal system is made up of 200 bones and their connecting points, or joints. Its jobs include giving the body a shape, supporting muscles, allowing for movement, and protecting body parts. For example, bones protect your brain, heart, and lungs. Without your skeleton, you could not survive.

Scoring Rubric for Short-Response Items in Part E of the Mastery Tests

2 points—The student demonstrates a solid understanding of the content by providing:
- a complete set of accurate facts that support the answer
- a clearly stated answer to the question

1 point—The student demonstrates a partial understanding of the content by providing *one* of the following:
- a complete set of accurate facts that support the answer
- a clearly stated answer to the question

0 points—The student fails to demonstrate an understanding of the content by doing *one* of the following:
- includes no facts or incorrect facts, and fails to provide a clearly stated answer
- provides no answer at all

Scoring Rubric for Essay Items in Part F of the Mastery Tests

3 points—The student demonstrates a solid understanding of the content by providing:
- a complete set of accurate facts that support the answer
- a clearly stated answer to the essay's primary question
- a standard essay response (topic sentence, body, conclusion)

2 points—The student demonstrates a good understanding of the content by providing *two* of the following:
- a complete set of accurate facts that support the answer
- a clearly stated answer to the essay's primary question
- a standard essay response (topic sentence, body, conclusion)

1 point—The student demonstrates a partial understanding of the content by providing *one* of the following:
- a complete set of accurate facts that support the answer
- a clearly stated answer to the essay's primary question
- a standard essay response (topic sentence, body, conclusion)

0 points—The student fails to demonstrate an understanding of the content by doing *one* of the following:
- includes no facts or incorrect facts, fails to answer the essay's primary question, and fails to include a standard essay response (topic sentence, body, conclusion)
- provides no answer at all